Portrait of America

Portrait of America

Volume 1 from the Cliff Dwellers to
the End of Reconstruction

SECOND EDITION

Stephen B. Oates
UNIVERSITY OF MASSACHUSETTS, AMHERST

HOUGHTON MIFFLIN COMPANY
BOSTON
Dallas
Geneva, Illinois
Hopewell, New Jersey
Palo Alto
London

For Greg and Stephanie with my love

Printed in the U.S.A.
Library of Congress Catalog Card Number: 77-77432
ISBN: 0-395-25372-1

Contents

The second edition of this anthology, like the first, is dedicated to the proposition that historical writing can be literature. In compiling selections for it, I chose writings distinguished as much for their literary merit—for the human drama they chronicle, the enigmas they capture, and the truths they imply—as for their analytical explanations. I deliberately sought biographical portraits, dramatic narratives, and artful essays by some of our best literary craftsmen. These writings portray the American past as a story of real people who actually lived, who struggled, enjoyed triumphs, and suffered failures and heartbreaks just like people in our own time. Thus *Portrait of America* is an attempt to capture the living past. It is, in the words of Aldous Huxley, an effort "to render, in literary terms, the quality of immediate experience."

The anthology is intended for use largely in college survey courses. It could be utilized as a supplement to a textbook or to a list of paperback readings. Or, for instructors who provide their classes with detailed, comprehensive lectures and who find a textbook redundant and a paperback list too expensive, *Portrait of America* could serve as the basic reading. There is much in the way of thought-provoking material gathered here: essays replete with ideas, narratives and biographies which capture real-life situations, and eyewitness accounts of slavery and the race issue in antebellum America that provide a gripping sense of immediacy. Furthermore, as I chose secondary materials, I tried not to compromise modern historical interpretations just to get a provocative selection. For example, I chose the works of David Donald and Kenneth M. Stampp because their accounts of Reconstruction are both imaginatively pre-

sented *and* modern in their approach. Generally, this is the guideline I followed in compiling and revising the entire volume, although my first criterion was always that selections must be artfully composed and suffused with human insight. My feeling is that, since college survey audiences are not professional ones, they might enjoy reading history if it were presented in exciting and palatable form. I hope *Portrait of America* presents history that way. The introductions to the selections are an effort to tie them all together so that they might stand more or less as connected episodes.

As I set about revising the anthology, I strove to present as balanced a coverage as possible, alternating essays with biographical portraits and dramatic narratives, within the traditional "periods" that historians have used to order the American past. Thus, the second edition provides generally equal space to all the significant eras in the American narrative, from the time of the ancient Pueblos, the European discovery of America, and the colonial beginnings down through the cataclysm of Civil War and the ordeal of Reconstruction. Still, as in the first edition, the unifying element in the present volume is its emphasis on artful and humanistic historical writing.

In compiling this book, I drew on the expertise of several congenial and interested colleagues. I want to extend my appreciation to Professor Charles C. Alexander of Ohio University and Professors Hugh F. Bell, Jack Tager, and Leonard L. Richards of the University of Massachusetts, Amherst, for their helpful professional counsel, and to Mr. Douglas E. Herman and his fellow teaching assistants at Ohio University who furnished me with a rigorous and illumi-

nating critique. Very useful reviews were provided by Professors Gerald S. Henig, California State University at Hayward; James B. Lane, Indiana University; and James F. Cook, Floyd Junior College. All three have been extremely helpful and I wish to thank them for their advice and encouragement.

S.B.O.

I The Edge of Change

1

Like Figures in a Dream: The Pueblo Indians

Paul Horgan

Alaska and spreading out across North, Central, and South America. In time the Indians of North and South America claimed more than 400 major tribal groups, whose cultures ranged from primitive hunters in wind-swept Utah to highly advanced civilizations like that of the Pueblos. *Portrait of America* begins appropriately with an examination of those long-ago people and their complex and unique society. In the following narrative, distinguished alike for its human compassion and lyrical style, Paul Horgan captures the spirit and life of the Pueblos, as they resided in their cliff cities and then abandoned them one by one, never to return.

If one follows the highway west from Durango, Colorado, one soon passes by Mesa Verde National Park, situated in the southwestern corner of the state. Here, in the rugged mountains and mesas, a community of Pueblo Indians once resided in remarkable stone dwellings, some nestled in caves along a steep canyon wall.

Today, one can still see scores of prehistoric Pueblo ruins at Mesa Verde, from the subterranean lodges of the seventh and eighth centuries to the cliff dwellings themselves, carved out of the mountains and canyons between the ninth and thirteenth centuries. The most striking of these ruins is the Cliff Palace, composed of scores of multistoried apartments located under overhanging cliffs.

Mesa Verde was not the only place in the Southwest inhabited by the ancient Pueblos. There were additional cities in the mountains of northern New Mexico and northeastern Arizona. Some of the Pueblo ruins in Arizona are so breathtaking— like fairy-tale cities etched in the rock of the cliffs —that one finds it hard to believe that real people actually lived there.

The Pueblos were among the original Americans —those Indian people who migrated from northeast Asia about 15,000 to 25,000 years ago, crossing the Bering Strait between what is now Siberia and

The Ancients

There was no record but memory and it became tradition and then legend and then religion. So long ago that they did not know themselves how long, their ancestors, the ancient people, moved. They went with the weather. Seasons, generations, centuries went by as each brought discovery of places farther toward the morning, across vacant Asia. They were guided that way by the lie of mountains, whose vast trough lay northeastward and southwestward. There was toil enough for people in taking their generations through valleys, without crossing the spines of mountains. But valleys end at the sea, and finally the people saw it too. The Asian continent ended, except for an isthmus of land or ice that remained above the waters. They crossed it, not in a day, or a year perhaps; perhaps it took lifetimes to find and keep what the bridge led to. But lost memory has no time, only action; and they came to North America, bringing their

animals, their blind history, their implements and the human future of two continents. Once again they encountered mountains which became their immovable guides. The entire vast new land lay on an axis of north and south, and its greatest mountains did also. Having entered at the north, the people must move southward, between the sea and the mountains.

Movement, however laborious, slow and lost in dangers it may have been, was the very nature of their lives. Through age after age it took them down the continent, across another isthmus, and into the great continent to the south, until the antipodean ice fields were joined by the disorderly but urgent line of mankind. Movement was what kept them alive, for they lived by hunting animals that followed the seasons.

They knew how to twist vegetable fibres until they had string. They could bend a branch until it made a bow by which a string could be tautly stretched. With bow, then, and arrow, they brought down game. There was another weapon, a throwing stick, with which to kill. Fish in the streams were taken with the harpoon. Its points, and those of arrows, were chipped from stone; often from glittering, sharp volcanic glass. Birds and fish were snared with nets. These measures travelled easily. They were light, efficient, and imaginative.

There were others called alive in their consequence. To make fire, the ancient people set a wooden drill into a socket in a small wooden hearth, and rotated the drill with their palms. Smoke came. They blew upon it. Coals glowed and under breath burst into flame. It was possible to cook. They heated stones and in vessels of wood or bark, even of animal hide dried and toughened, cooked the booty of the hunt. When it was time again to move, valuable leftovers could be carried in baskets invented and woven as baggage. With them travelled, or crouched to eat, a clever, fond and valiant friend whose ancestors too had made the timeless migration. He was the dog.

Throughout ages of lost memory the people possessed the new continents and found great regions within which to rove, above and below the equator, as loosely scattered groups. Vast localisms determined their ways—whether they pursued animals on plains, or hunted for berries in mountains, or clung to the unvarying climate of warm zones in one luxuriant wilderness after another. It took a mystery of the vegetable world to unfold for them in slow discovery a new way of life. There was a seed which could be eaten. It could be planted. It could be watered and made to grow at the hunter's will. It could multiply. It could be carried far and planted elsewhere. Wherever it took root it afforded food. It made a place where the people could stay season after season. It kept the hunters home, and their women and children and dogs, relieved of their wandering in search of life itself. Up from the warm zones of the earth it travelled from tribe to tribe, until most of the people who lived in the huge valleys and basins of the cordilleras knew how to use it, and using it, gradually discovered the arts of living together. Their histories were changed by it. The laws of its growth created their dwellings, their sense of property and brought them their gods, and its crushed seed became their most habitual and sacred offering in prayer. It was maize, or Indian corn.

In becoming farmers the ancient people looked for the most suitable places in which to remain. Corn needed water. Water flowed down the mountains making streams. In the grand valleys were many isolated mountain fragments standing separate whose heights were secure against animal and human dangers. When people could stay where they chose to stay there was time, there was imagination, to improve their conditions of life. A surplus of corn required some place in which to store it, safe against waste and thieving little animals. Dry caves in rocky cliffs seemed made by nature for the purpose. But food was wealth and people protected it in the caves by hauling

stones, making enclosures which they sealed with clay which dried solid. The wall of a bin protecting food could be extended to make walls which gave shelter. Boldly beautiful rooms were made in the cliffs, some of masonry, some carved with obsidian knives out of rich soft yellow tufa itself. Arising independently, some at the same time, some at other times, and almost all on the western slopes of the continental divide in the American Southwest, many such cliff cities of the high plateaus were settled and developed by hunters who learned how to become farmers. After thousands of years of migration across continents in search of the always moving forms of live food, it took only a few hundred years of settled agriculture for the ancient people to discover how to satisfy their prime hunger, and find time and ways in which to recognize other hungers and give form to their satisfaction, socially, morally and spiritually. And though in their slowly developed mastery of how to grow corn they needed not only the seed but also water, they established their plateau cities not by the banks of the three or four great rivers that rose in the mountain system that had pointed the path for their ancestors, but on mesas and in valleys touched by little streams, some of them not even perennial in their flow.

Nor did all of the ancient people find the secret of maize. Some who found eastern gateways in the mountains spread themselves out on the great plains where for long succeeding centuries they continued to rove as hunters, governed by solstice and the growing seasons of animal feed. In time the wanderers heard of the plateau cities and their riches stored against hunger and the hardships of travel. Raids resulted, and battle, devastations and triumphant thefts, leaving upon the withdrawal of the nomads new tasks of rebuilding and revival according to the customs of the farmers who long ago had given up the bare rewards of the chase for hard but dependable and peaceful cultivation of the land.

If there was little regular communication between the scattered cliff cities of southwestern Colorado, northeastern Arizona, and northern New Mexico, and if there were local differences between their ways, still they solved common mysteries in much the same fashion and in their several responses to the waiting secrets of earth, sky and mind, they made much the same fabric of life for people together.

The Cliffs

The fields were either on the mesa top above the cliff cities or on the canyon floor below. At sunup the men went to cultivate their crops. Corn was planted a foot deep, and earth was kept piled up about the stalks, to give them extra growing strength and moisture. Every means was used to capture water. Planting was done where flood waters of the usually dry stream beds came seasonally. But there were long summers without rain. The winter snows filtered into porous sandstone until they met hard rock and found outlets in trickles down canyon walls. The people scooped basins out of the rock to collect such precious flow, from which they carried water by hand to the growing stalks. The mesa tops were gashed at the edges by sloping draws which fell away to the valley floor, like the spaces between spread fingers. Between the great stone fingers the people built small stone dams to catch storm waters running off the plateau. Occasionally springs came to the surface in the veined rock of the cliffs and were held sacred.

Seeds were planted and crops cultivated with a stick about a yard long which could poke holes in the earth or turn it over. The prevailing crop was red corn, and others were pumpkin, beans and cotton. Wild sunflowers yielded their seeds which were eaten. When the crop was harvested it became the charge of the women, who were ready to receive it and store it in baskets which they wove to hold about

two bushels. Flat stone lids were fashioned to seal the baskets, which went into granaries built by the men. Part of the seed was ground between suitably shaped stones, and part was kept for planting. If meal was the staff of life, it was varied by meat from wild game including the deer, the fox, the bear, the mountain sheep and the rabbit.

As they lived through the centuries learning how to work and build together, the ancient people made steady and continuous progress in all ways. If their first permanent houses had only one room with a connecting underground ceremonial chamber and storeroom, they increasingly reflected the drawing together of individuals into community life in a constantly elaborated form of the dwelling. The rooms came together, reinforcing one another with the use of common walls, and so did families. The rooms rose one upon another until terraced houses three and four stories high were built. The masonry was expert and beautiful, laid in a variety of styles. The builders were inventive. They thought of pillars, balconies, and interior shafts for ventilation. They made round towers and square towers. And they placed their great house-cities with an awesome sense of location, whether on the crown of a mesa or in the wind-made architectural shell of a long arching cave in the cliffside. The work was prodigious. In one typical community house fifty million pieces of stone were quarried, carried and laid in its walls. Forests were far away; yet thousands of wooden beams, poles and joins were cut from timber and hauled to their use in the house. From the immediate earth untold tons of mortar were mixed and applied—and all this by the small population of a single group dwelling.

The rooms averaged eight by ten feet in size, with ceilings reaching from four feet to eight. There were no windows. Doors were narrow and low, with high sills. The roof was made of long heavy poles laid over the walls, and thatched with small sticks or twigs, finally covered with mud plaster in a thick layer. The floor was of hard clay washed with animal blood and made smooth, in a shiny black. Walls were polished with burnt gypsum. Along their base was a painted band of yellow ochre, taken as raw mineral from the softly decaying faces of the cliffs where great stripes of the dusty gold color were revealed by the wearing of wind and water. Round chambers of great size and majesty were built underground for religious and ceremonial use. Many cities had a dozen or more such rooms, each dedicated to the use of a separate religious cult or fraternity. One had a vault with a covering of timber which resounded like a great drum when priests danced upon it.

In the ceremonial kivas men kept their ritual accessories and the tools of their crafts. They made tools out of bones—deer, rabbit, bird, and of deerhorn and mountain sheep horn. Their knives and hunting points and grinding tools and scraping tools for dressing skins and gravers for carving and incising and axes and chisels for cutting and shaping wood and mauls for breaking rock were made out of stone.

Baskets were woven for light, mobile use at first, when the people kept moving, and as they found ways to settle in their cities they continued to use baskets for cooking, storage and hauling. But more durable and more widely useful vessels could be made out of clay; and so the women developed in connection with domestic arts the craft of pottery. Their early attempts imitated the construction of basketry, with long clay ropes coiled into enclosing form which was not smoothed over on the surface. But for greater comeliness and better protection against leakage and breakage the surfaces of pots were eventually made smooth and fired with glazes. Natural mineral pigments gave each locality its characteristic pottery style—now red clay, again ochre, white gypsum, iron-black.

In warm weather the people lived naked; in cold they wore fur-cloth and feather-cloth robes and leggings, and dressed skins. Thread was made from yucca fibre. Both men and

women wore ornaments created out of beads—stone, shell, bone. Feather tassels, bright with color, hung from garments. Small pieces of chipped or cut turquoise were put together in mosaic for pendants and bracelets. Fashion had its power, modifying out of sheer taste rather than utility various details of dress. The sandal fringe of one period was missing from the next.

For hundreds of years this busy life with all its ingenuities, its practices whose origins lacking written record were lost among the dead ancestors, its growing body of worship of all creation, its personal and collective sorrows, its private and communal joys, rose and flourished with the affirmative power of living prophecy. Were they being readied to imagine a greatness beyond themselves in the future? Already they had found for the material face of life a grace and beauty whose evidence would endure like the mountain stuff out of which they had made it. The people grew their nourishment on plateaus that reached toward the sun. They put about themselves like garments the enfolding substances of cliffs. They looked out in daylight upon breathtaking views of intercourse between sky and ground, where light and shadow and color and distance in their acts of change made in every moment new aspects of the familiar natural world. Amidst the impassive elegance of mountains, valleys and deserts they fulfilled their needs with intimacy and modesty in their use of natural things. With no communication through time but the living voice, for they had no records but their own refuse, the power of their hooded thoughts brought them a long way from the straggle out of Asia tens of centuries before to the flowering civilization of the cliffs, the plateaus and the canyons.

And at just the long moment in their story when all material evidence seemed to promise life more significant than that which they had so laboriously made so beautiful, mysteriously, in city after city among the plateaus, they left it never to return.

To the River

Their departures were orderly. Not all occurred at the very same instant, but all took place late in the thirteenth century and early in the fourteenth, and all gave evidence of having been agreed upon. Their houses were left standing. Their rooms were neat and emptied of possessions needed for travel and new life elsewhere. But for occasional bits of corn and stalk and tassel the food bins were bare. The dead were left in peaceful burial according to regular custom. Few personal objects—clothing, jewelry, ceremonial effects—were left behind. Fires died in their proper places. There was no sign of the applied torch. Sudden natural calamity—earthquake, flood, lightning-set holocaust—played no part. The cities, one by one, at the point of their highest development, were left to time and the amber preservative of dry sunlit air.

Again the people left no record, and carried none with them, written, or even pictorial, to explain these abandonments. Perhaps for a few generations memory told the story, until gradually it was lost in the recesses of time. The only records which can be consulted are those of the natural world. They have been much invoked and disputed by experts.

The trees have testified. By counting the rings of annual growth in the cross section of a trunk, a system of dating has been devised. By comparing the thickness and thinness of the successive rings, periods of relative wetness or dryness have been tabulated. According to such information the century of the migrations from the plateaus coincided with a period of increasing dryness, until crops could no longer be watered, and the people were faced with living on the seed corn and finally starvation. A search for new watered lands was the only recourse.

Erosion has been blamed. Too much timber was cut for building use. Bared forest lands permitted too rapid runoff of storm-water. Gul-

lies were lengthened until their waters became ungovernable for flood-farming. Old fields had to be abandoned and new ones begun farther from the houses and from water sources.

But erosion presupposes flow of water, and the drought theory contradicts the erosion theory. And though some scientists say that the entire region during its whole period of occupation by people has been slowly growing drier, they say further that the rate of desiccation would not in itself account for these migrations. And one of the greatest of the communities—in Chaco Canyon—was abandoned a century before the tree-ring evidence of the great drought. On top of this, lately, the whole responsibility of the tree-ring theory has been shaken by comparison of ancient rings formed when there were no written records with more recent rings which when checked against modern meteorological records show no consistent correlation with thickness and thinness of the rings in wet and dry periods as scientifically recorded. The drought theory holds no firm answer.

In the canyon of the Rito de los Frijoles the river is an ever-flowing stream. Yet the cliff dwellings there and the houses of the canyon floor were abandoned just like communities near streams which were intermittent and for the most part dry. Lack of water was not a motive for the silencing of the Rito.

The mystery has been attacked in other ways.

Did the soft rock of the cliff dwellings disintegrate too fast and force the people to move? But the rooms are still intact today.

Were there epidemics of other disease? Burials reveal no evidence of unusual numbers of deaths in any one period.

Was the prevailing diet of corn meal—hard and coarse, and especially when old as hard as gravel—the cause of disease? Recovered skulls show teeth ground down to the bone as a result of chewing the tough meal. Tooth decay led to abscesses, lodged poisons, rheumatism, arthritis and diet deficiencies. Did the people go to look in new places for other foods? But wherever they resettled, corn remained their staple food, and does today.

Did nomadic enemies cut off water supplies and drive the people from their towns? There would have been battles, and if defeated, the city dwellers would have left their homes in disarrayed flight. There was no evidence to indicate siege and defeat.

Did the pattern of community life become so complex as the towns grew that political quarrels between clans and religious fraternities broke apart the order of existence and made communal life impossible and migration imperative? If so, then why did not one or more clans survive dissension and continue in possession of the houses? But no one was left behind. And when the people found their new homesites, they recreated the same social pattern they had expressed in the cliff cities, in some instances building even larger cities with greater populations and more group divisions.

All efforts to explain the mystery on the basis of physical or material motives come to nothing. What is left? Where might the explanation lie? The people left beautiful cities and looked for new places to live. Consulting the favor of the natural world, many of them came at last through the barrier mountains to the river, the big river, P'osoge, or the big water, Ha^{n}n^{y}ap'akwa, or just the river, Tšina, where they found scattered settlements of people raising corn and living in primitive pit-houses. Life was already blessed there. The new settlers joined the old. The Pueblos of the Rio Grande were founded. What drove the people from the silent cities they had left behind them might well have been something they carried within themselves; something with more power over their acts than heat or cold, rain or dust, sickness or war or dissension. If they had reason to believe that their gods had abandoned them where they lived, the people would have had to go and find them again, in order to live

at peace with the world of nature. As everything had its abiding spirit, not only things that grew, but inanimate things, and places, so with the loss of that spirit would be lost blessing, protection, safety. In fear and trembling the people would have had to abandon a place, no matter how splendid, from which the ruling deity had withdrawn. Any event, natural or imaginary, which would withdraw the gods of a place would make it accursed, and dangerous to life; and no matter how great hitherto it may have become, it would be abandoned.

They told stories through the centuries of such a motive for migration from various places. What was believed true of one place could be so of another.

In cliff towns of the Pajarito Plateau west of the river the people said that A-wan-yu lived among them, their deity. He was the plumed snake, creature of both air and land. A time came when they lost favor with him. He abandoned them, retired to the sky, and became the major galaxy of stars which reached across the central heavens as the Milky Way. Without him the people were at a loss. They gathered their life and its objects and, leaving their rooms in modest order, went away to build new cities on the river.

At the greatest of cliff cities (Mesa Verde) the people began to build a temple to the sun. It sat upon a crown of the mesa between valley and sky. Using the skin-colored stone of the place, they quarried and shaped their blocks and raised their walls in expert masonry. The temple contained many rooms. The largest was a round one in the center. Little junipers whose shape echoed the pull of the wind grew all about the temple. Close to its doors the mesa's cliffs swept away to the valley floor far below. It was a noble site facing the rising sun. To reach it with stone and timber took prodigious work. The work went slowly. The walls rose carefully to the same successive heights day by day or year by year. But they were never finished. Before they could be, all human life

departed from the mesa, with its fields on top, its farms below in the valley, and its magnificent community houses high up in the faces of the cliffs. What if before the sun temple could be completed there was no god to receive in it? The people could only leave what they had partially done, with all of its walls unfinished at the same height, and go away.

Long later, in another ancient town, east of the river, the people kept a great black snake in the kiva, who had power over their life. They fed him the fruits of the hunt—deer, antelope, rabbit, bison, birds. From him they received all they needed to eat and to wear— corn, squash, berries, fruit of the yucca and cactus; shoes, leggings, shirts of soft deerskin. One night at midnight he left them. In the morning they found that he was gone. He left his track and they followed it. It took them down a dry river of white stones and clay (Galisteo Creek) which at last entered into the big river (Rio Grande), where the track was lost in the ever-flowing water. They returned to their town and discussed their trouble. "The snake has gone. What are we going to have of those things which he gave us? He has gone away. Now we also must be going away," they said. They worked together at the sorrowful job of taking up their things, and went down the dry river to the big river, where they found another town already living. There they took up their lives again amidst the gods of that place.

Fear of their gods may well have sent the cliff people from the mesas to the river. Bringing their high culture from the plateaus, the people wedded it to the primitive human ways they found along the Rio Grande, and once again with the approval of the gods made for themselves a settled life, sure of land, water, and corn, and of what explained fear and what creation.

.   .   .

Cliff Palace at Mesa Verde. As Horgan states, the cliff dwellers were inventive people: they built terraced houses three and four stories high. "They thought of pillars, balconies, and interior shafts for ventilation. They made round towers and square towers. And they placed their great house-cities with an awesome sense of location, whether on the crown of a mesa or in the wind-made architectural shell of a long arching cave in the cliffside." (Courtesy of The National Park Service, United States Department of the Interior.)

Community

It was an organized life whose ruling ideas were order, moderation, unanimity. All ways were prescribed, all limits set, and all people by weight of an irresistible power took part in the town life. Examples of such controls elsewhere suggested that they must come from a ruler, a presiding head of state whose decrees could only be obeyed, on pain of despotic gesture. But the Pueblo people had no ruler; no despot. The irresistible power which ordered their communal life was the combined and voluntary power of the people—all the people, in each town, giving continuity to inherited ways by common agreement.

Everybody, together, in a pueblo, owned all

the land, all the religious edifices and ritual objects. Assignment of use was made by a council of elders. Heads of families were granted the use of portions of land, which could be reallotted every year, according to change in families through marriage or death. Religious properties were assigned to proper organizations.

Crops grown by families upon their assigned plots belonged to them alone. Families owned objects which they made for their own use. Families were given permanent possession of rooms in the pueblo for as long as the family existed and could build additional space as needed. When a family died out its apartments were abandoned and went into ruins.

Since property was entirely for use, and not for sale or trade within the pueblo, everybody lived upon the same scale. Their rooms were alike. Their holdings in food, clothing, furniture, were about the same. Living closely together, they interfered very little with their immediate neighbors, though within the family there was no privacy and no desire for any. Outbursts of feeling, emotion, violence, were bad form, and so was indulgence in authority for its own sake, instead of for the propriety it was meant to preserve. Nobody was supposed to stand out from everyone else in any connection but that which had to do with official duties. Everyone understood that certain work —official or religious—had to be done by someone who was given, by common consent, the authority to do it. But nobody was supposed to propose himself for the job, or go out after it. If he was chosen for it, a man with real reluctance but equally real obedience to the wishes of his associates accepted it and did his serious best while in office. If anybody in such a position showed the wrong attitude, or indeed, if anyone at all transgressed against the accepted way of things, he was shown his error in the ridicule he received from other people. He did not like to be laughed at in the town, or made sport of by the clowns in the dances, and he would mend his ways if he had gone too far

out of line. There was no excuse for him to feel differently from anybody else, and to behave accordingly. As there was a proper way to perform all acts, everyone not only understood ritual but performed it. United in gesture, the pueblo had a strong sense of its own identity. Everyone agreed how things were and had to be and should be. Understanding so, there could be few disappointments in life, and few complete bafflements.

Certain towns had thin, narrow, long stones which rang with a clear song when struck. They were hung by deerskin thongs to the end, outdoors, of a roof beam. The singing stones could be heard in the town and the near-by fields. To summon men for meetings, the stones were struck. Meetings were held often, for the town had many organizations, each with particular work to do.

In some towns, all people were divided into two cults—the Summer, or Squash, People; and the Winter, or Turquoise, People. Other towns knew four seasons of the year, and organized accordingly. All towns had secret societies with particular social duties, all religious in form. At the head of the pueblo, as guardian of all spiritual lives, was the cacique. He served for life. He had many duties, for no important act was ever done without ritual, and it was he who blessed and approved all ceremonies. In his own life he invoked holiness with fasting and prayer. That he might be free entirely for his sacred offices he was relieved of all other work. His house was built for him. Other people planted for him and cultivated his crops and made his harvests. In his shrines he kept fetishes which had to be fed with rabbit meat. Men went on special hunts to bring him rabbits, and the sacred food was prepared by his appointed helper, who cooked the rabbits, and also kept his house for him, making fires, sweeping the packed earthen floor, and ministering to his needs.

The cacique made important appointments to the priesthood. Two of these were the war priests, named for the twin boy-gods Masewi

and Oyoyowi. They held office for a year. Part of their duty was to observe the cacique in the performance of his duties, and to admonish him if he was negligent. Each year he appointed ten assistants to the war priests. His influence was great, his position among the people that of the fountainhead of all spiritual belief and practice. He was both father and mother to them, a living analogue of the source of their lives. Upon his death his successor was chosen by the war priests from his own secret society.

The cult was a medium through which the people could formally take part in the religious life of the pueblo. Everyone belonged to one or another of the cults in the town. Membership was hereditary, except that a girl who married entered the cult of her husband. If she was widowed she could choose between remaining in the cult of her husband or returning to that of her father. The cult had a head who was in charge of all its activities. The most sacred of objects were the masks used in the kachina dances—those great group prayers in which the gods of rain were believed by women and children to be actually present in the dance. These masks, and the costumes that went with them, and the miniature carved figures representing the godly kachinas, were kept by the cult leader as his own personal duty. He alone could mix the turquoise green paint used in decorating the masks. Not everyone could have masks. Only married men of mature experience could have them. With the mask came powers—the wearer turned into someone else. His real person was hidden not only from the spectator but delivered from himself. Behind the mask he was the godlike being which the people saw. He escaped into a new and sacred dignity, leaving behind him the weak man of every day to whom he must return when he doffed his mask again but surely with some lingering joy and a new strength.

The cult had its ceremonial home in the large chamber of the kiva, sacred to its own members. It was usually circular, sometimes underground, generally above ground. Here was the very house of power and ritual. It was entered through a hatch in the roof, by a tall ladder which leaned down to the floor. A small altar stood in the room, sometimes against the wall, sometimes free. Before it was a small round hole. This was called by the same name as the original place where the people came up into the world—Shipapu. A shaft built into the wall brought air to the altar, and with it could come and go the spirits addressed in prayer. Smoke from fires built before the altar was carried out through the entrance hatch in the roof by the spirits of the kachinas. On another plane of experience and discovery, the air descending through the shaft made the fire draw, and set up circulation which drew smoke to the roof and out into the air through the hatchway. At about the height of a kneeling man, a deep shelf or seat ran around the wall of the interior. The wall was sometimes painted with sacred images and symbols of weather, animals, birds, plants, and human actions, all with ritual purposes. ,

The whole kiva itself was a powerful symbol. It was like a small butte with a flat top, a land form often seen. In its interior it gave passageway to the two worlds—the earth-world above, through the hatch to natural life of land, creatures and sky; and the nether-world below, through the portal of the world's womb from which all had come so long ago. Both worlds were made to join in the kiva. Here the holy pigments were prepared, and the costumes for the dances. Inherited rituals were studied and learned here. Sacred objects remained in the kiva when not in use out of doors. Fetishes were fed there. Boys were initiated there into knowledge and power of which they had known only animal intimations. There dancers painted and dressed for their outdoor ceremonials, and when readied came in a crowding line up the ladder through the hatch, over the roof and down to the ground. To perpetuate the kiva in filling vacant

kiva offices, there the members met in conclave. There in the significant number of four times—invocation of the whole world through its four quarters—ceremonies were prepared during four days of vomiting and other purifications.

Each kiva group was dedicated to the ceremonial work of one of the seasons. Since ritual and its texts were elaborate, and long, and transmitted only by memory with no written records, and since every phase of community life was accompanied by its ceremonial observance, no one cult could learn and execute the liturgy for all occasions. Yet certain events, like the great corn dance, called upon two or more cults to perform in the plaza, alternately throughout the day-long invocation of the spirits of fertility and growth, when one group would dance while the other waited to take its place, with all joining at the end.

So the religious life of the people was formalized in groups that separately represented neither the whole town nor a single clan but drew symmetrically upon the population until all were included, empowered in the same terms, and actors of the same myths. Religion was not a thing apart from daily life. It *was* daily life, a formalization, an imitation of nature, an imagined control of the elements, and of what was obscure in the spirit of men and women.

In addition to the major divisions of the kiva groups, which cut boldly through the whole company of the town for organized religious acts, there were smaller groups with specialized missions whose members were not chosen along the lines of kiva organization. These were the secret societies. Each had its unique purpose. There was one in charge of war. Another appointed all holders of major non-religious offices. Another comprised the koshare, the clowns of the dances who served also as the disciplinarians, through censure or ridicule, of individuals who offended against the unspoken but powerful sense of restraint

and decorum that governed behavior. Several others were curing societies, and together constituted the medicine cult. And another embraced the hunters of the town. All selected and initiated their own members throughout the generations.

.   .   .

Thus comfort through organized observances.

The whole year had its cycle of them.

All winter the river ran shallow and lazy from the faraway north, and deep against the sky of the whole valley the snow was locked on the peaks by cold air. The fields by the pueblo were dry and the irrigation ditches which ran to them from the river were overgrown with the dry golden stalks, the pink brush, of the past year's weeds. In March* it was time to clean the ditches and then with prayer, dancing and prayer sticks, open the ditches to bring the river water in upon the spring plantings. The masked gods came from the otherworld to attend. They were seen right there in their masks among the dancers.

In April with four days of preparations the assembled kiva groups of the pueblo held a dance for the blessing of corn, which would come to summer harvest. Water, rain, were the greatest of blessings, and all was asked in their name, and in their image, gesture, and sound. The curing societies during this month went into retreat for purification and for prayer, again invoking rain, upon whose coming the lives of plant and person and animal alike depended. They retreated to their houses which they called, during the retreat, Shipapu, the same as the place of origin, through which everyone had come up. The retreat over, dances followed, again with the gods in their masks,

* For convenience I have used modern calendric names, which of course were not accessible to the Pueblo Indians of the Rio Grande in the period before recorded history.

who also had spent the same time in retreat at the real Shipapu. Well into the summer, retreats and emergence ceremonies continued.

In early summer the ceremony was held by the curing societies to pull the sun to the south, where his hot light would make long days and help things to grow.

In full summer they danced again for corn. Sometimes they started out in clear day, with all the kiva groups in fullest magnificence under a spotless blue sky which gave back heat like stone near fire. Rain could never come from such a sky. But all day they pounded the prayer into the ground and showered the sound of falling drops of rain from the air to the earth while the heat grew and grew and the shadows of the houses stood like triangles painted on pottery in black paint; and presently they might see without giving any sign what loomed in the north and the west against the ringing blue—dazzling white thunderheads marching slowly and powerfully over the sky toward this town, these fields and seeds. The blessings were vast and visible; and late in the day as the prayer still beat its way into the ground, the light might change, and the clouds meet over all, and brown color of the bodies and the town and the earth all alike would turn dark like the river as rain came and fell upon them and answered them and the sparkling green shoots of the corn in the fields. Sometimes it rained so hard and long that the earth ran and the gullies deepened, and new cracks appeared leading to them, and rocks rolled scouring new ways to the river, and the river rose and flowed fast carrying unaccustomed things sideways in the queer sailing current of flood.

In September as the border of summer and winter was reached the Summer People and the Winter People both held dances. Autumn brought hunting dances too, and some of them were given later in wintertime. In November came the feast of the dead, when all the ancestors came back to the pueblo to visit for a day

and a night. It was a blessed occasion and a happy one. And before long it was time to urge the four curing societies to watch the sun, and call it back to the north before it went too far southward.

In midwinter the kiva groups chose their officers for the next year, and held dances to honor them, to bless them and to make them know the right ways. The curing societies now frequently in the winter held general cures for everyone. People could come to the curing ceremonies with their ailments and have them included with the other ills against which the doctors gave battle. They purged everyone, the whole town, of evil spirits. Again they cried out and struck blows against the witches, while all heard the encounters, and were reassured.

In February the koshare danced, the clowns, the critics, who hazed the people, sometimes to laughter, sometimes to shame, the spirit of irony and perversity thus accounted for and made useful.

And it was by then observed that the sun was safely on his way north again, and there was a ceremony to confirm this and give thanks.

Then the winter's weeds stood thick again in the ditches, and the path of life from the river to the fields had to be readied. Once again it was time to burn the weeds away, clean the ditches, let the river in, and set the plantings of another year.

It was an organized life based upon the desire for peace. The Pueblos rarely went to war unless they had to resist attack. The war society with its chief captains Masewi and Oyoyowi maintained the magic necessary to use in times of crisis from without the town. The war society was also a medium for the forgiveness of killing. Its members—all men—were those who had brought upon themselves the danger of having killed someone. This danger was the same whether the killing was accidental, murderous, or in sanctioned conflict. If there was blood upon a man he had to join the

war society to wipe it out. He then became a defender of his people. He was confirmed with ceremony. After his initiation he went—like all boys and men after initiations and dances—to the river to bathe his body and his thoughts.

As for thoughts, when grave matters were in the air, requiring the judgment of the cacique and his council, these leaders fasted. They did penance the better to make wise decisions. Their fasting was known about. At home they abstained. In the kiva they abstained. They spoke to no one of what lay heavily upon their thoughts, but their concern was plain to all. Soon there was wonder, and gossip, worry; something was brewing; what would it be; was there anywhere to turn but once again to blind Nature?

But at last the council would speak to them. At evening, the town crier went to his rooftop. Perhaps the sky was yellow behind him and the house fires sent their smokes upward in unwavering lines of pale blue above the earth's band of twilight. The murmur of talk was like the sound of the river beyond its groves. Facing four ways in succession, the crier told four times what the council had decided and what it wanted of the people. On their roofs, or by their walls, or in their fields, the people heard him, and gave no kind of response; but they all heard and in proper order and time did what was asked of them.

.   .   .

On the Edge of Change

So the Pueblo people agreed without exception in their worship, their work, their designs for making things in the largest to the smallest forms, their views of property, the education of their children, the healing of their sick, and their view of death.

A clear and simple and within its limits a satisfactory plan of living together was understood by everybody, and complied with. But tragically it lacked the seed of fullest humanity. Mankind's unique and unpredictable gift was not encouraged to burgeon in Pueblo society. Individuality, the release of the separate personality, the growth of the single soul in sudden, inexplicable flowering of talent or leadership or genius, were absent. In harmony with all nature but individual human nature, the people retained together a powerful and enduring form of life at the expense of a higher consciousness—that of the individual free to unlock in himself all the imprisoned secrets of his own history and that of his whole kind, and by individual acts of discovery, growth and ability, to open opportunities that would follow upon his knowledge for all who might partake of them. It was costly, that loss of the individual to the group. The essential genius of humanity, with all its risks, and yet too with its dazzling fulfillments, was buried deep in the sleeping souls of the Indians by the Rio Grande.

They solved with restraint and beauty the problem of modest physical union with their mighty surroundings.

But only to their gods did they allow the adventure, the brilliance, the gift of astonishment that came with individuality. Those mythic heroes, those animal personifications ranged sky and earth and underworld performing prodigies, releasing dreams for the dreamers, perhaps beckoning inscrutably toward some future in which the people too might find freedom before death to be individuals in nature instead of units among units in a perfected animal society whose loftiest expression of the human properties of mind and soul was an invisible tyranny of fear that bent them in endless propitiation before inanimate matter.

The deep alien sadness of such a life was borne with dignity. They lived like figures in a dream, waiting to be awakened. Possibly if

left to their own time and development, they would have awakened by themselves to discover another and greater environment than the physical one to which they were already accommodated with economy and tenacity. The inner environment of the conscience, the responsible and endlessly replenished human soul, the recognition of God within mankind above a multitude of gods without—these might have come as their own discoveries to those people who already had climbed far from forgotten antiquity.

But men of another order were making ready to come to the river as ministers of enlightenment and shock and the strongest necessity of their epoch.

2

The Lord Admiral

Paul Horgan

states, Portugal sought an ocean route to Asia's fortunes; in the fifteenth century, her hardy navigators, pioneers of nautical astronomy, sailed around the African Cape and opened a sea route to India. Meanwhile Columbus dreamed of a Western route across the Atlantic—which was not unfeasible since intelligent Europeans in the fifteenth century knew the world was round. Finally, he persuaded the King and Queen of Spain to commission him Lord Admiral of the Ocean Sea and to provide money, men, and ships for his voyage. He would sail under the flag of Spain.

In the following chronicle, Paul Horgan writes about Columbus and his celebrated voyage with such drama and such a sense of immediacy that one can almost feel the ocean spray on the deck of the *Santa Maria,* as it and its tiny sister ships sailed westward with the sun, heading toward an unexpected destiny.

The "men of another order" Horgan mentioned in the first narrative were Spanish conquistadors, who in the sixteenth century brought the flags of Old World Christendom to North and South America, thereby initiating centuries of conflict between white and red peoples that led to the near extermination of the first Americans.

The story of the white man's coming begins in the fifteenth century, when the European world was slowly spinning its way out of the Middle Ages, slowly becoming aware of the treasures—and mysteries—of distant Asia. There were many who dreamed of the fabled Orient, but none more passionately than a visionary Genoese sailor named Christopher Columbus, who was certain that he could reach the Orient westward across largely uncharted Atlantic waters. Whatever nation financed his project, Columbus contended, would enjoy the shortest route to the riches of Japan and India—silks, gems, tapestries, and highly prized spices. Since the Crusades, Europeans had bought these luxuries from Italian merchants, who got them from Arab traders in the Holy Lands. But in the thirteenth and fourteenth centuries, travelers like Marco Polo reported that Asia was the source of the succulent goods the Italians brought out of the Near East. After the rise of Europe's nation

The Light

Was that a light? Standing on the sterncastle he looked again through the darkness of ten o'clock at night. The ship was in considerable movement, for it had been a rough day—the roughest, he noted, of any they had met during the whole voyage. To see a distant light one should be still. He saw it again, but it was "so obscured," he said, that he could not be sure he was seeing the first sign of land. He called to Pero Gutierrez, who had left his post as butler of the King's dais in Castile to come on the voyage.

"There seems to be a light," said the Lord Admiral, indicating where. "Watch for it."

He called also to Rodrigo Sánchez of Segovia, the King's accountant whose duty it was to keep books on all wealth that might be found—gold, jewels, spices—to insure that the

---

Crown would receive its royal fifth share. The Lord Admiral told him to watch, too, for the light. Sánchez came to look.

"There!"

Gutierrez saw it, and so again did the Lord Admiral. It showed once or twice. It was like the light of a small wax candle which was raised and lowered. From where he stood Sánchez could not see it, and said so.

What was it? They thought it might be a torch in the hands of fishermen who raised and lowered it in their work. When it vanished in the darkness so suddenly, they thought perhaps that it was a light being carried from one house to another. Nobody knew. Word of it went through the ship. It had shown so briefly that few were sure it was a sign of land.

They had been at sea for just under five weeks. Only the Lord Admiral knew exactly how far they had come. The sailors were doubtful. But his own confidence was so great that even before sailing from the Canary Islands he had given orders to all ship commanders that there would be no night sailing after passing a point seven hundred leagues (or something over two thousand miles) from those islands.

Now he changed his orders. After sunset, when the sailors gathered together in each ship, as in every nightfall, to chant the prayer to the Queen of Heaven, after which they went to their cramped quarters to sleep, the Lord Admiral signalled that the course was changed from west south west to west. There might be danger of running aground in this, and he warned all to keep a sharp lookout. But there was also hope, for by running straight westward they might sooner see land, and he changed his orders to meet what all longed for. They ran before the wind at twelve miles an hour. The full-blown sails of the three caravels looked like the cheeks of the winds made visible on old maps. To the man who should first see land, said the Lord Admiral, he would immediately give a silk doublet, over and beyond the reward promised by the King and Queen— a grant of ten thousand maravedis a year for life, or about a third of a seaman's pay.

Few slept that night, watching for land and daylight.

The Lord Admiral

They said of him, Christopher Columbus, born in Genoa, and now in the service of King Ferdinand and Queen Isabella of Castile and Aragon, that he "was affable . . . though with a certain gravity," and that he was "a skilled man, eloquent and a good Latin scholar, and very glorious in his affairs," and that he was "a learned man of great experience" who did not waste his time in manual or mechanical tasks, which would hardly suit "the grandeur and immortality of the wonderful deeds he was to perform."

He stood taller than the average and was sturdily made. His eyes were lively in his ruddy and freckled face. His hair was "very red." He wore a hat with a wide brim turned up like a bowl. Over a doublet with full sleeves and knee breeches he put a cloth-of-Segovia poncho which hung down fore and aft and was open at the sides for his arms. His straight sword with a basket hilt was slung by straps from his girdle. He could be "graceful when he wished, irate when he was crossed." One purpose ruled him, and he pressed forward with it in all works of preparation, persuasion and deed. It was his wish to discover what was unknown about the world.

"To this my wish," he wrote, "I found Our Lord"—he was a deeply religious man—"most propitious, and to this end I received from Him a spirit of intelligence. In seamanship He made me abundant, of astrology"—by which he meant astronomy—"He gave me enough, as well as geometry and arithmetic, and of ingenuity in mind and hands to draw this sphere and on it cities, rivers and mountains, islands

and harbours, everything in its right place. In this time I have seen and studied all writings, cosmography, histories, chronicles and philosophy and other arts.''

He read the Greek, Egyptian, Roman and French geographers, and he gathered travellers' tales wherever he could from mariners who had sailed farther than he. He had a copy of the first Latin edition of the travels of Marco Polo, and pondering it, he marked its margins with his comments. From the idea of the table-top world of the Middle Ages, the advanced cartographers of his day were coming to see the world as a sphere, and the Lord Admiral understood and agreed with them. The pleasures of theory were important, but if a man was given to action as well as thought, they led straight to testing in the world. A most pressing concern of his time was to find a direct sea route to India. The Lord Admiral Columbus like others was concerned with it, but his solution of the problem was like nobody else's. It began in his mind, as an intellectual concept.

At the end of his book, Marco Polo wrote, two centuries before Columbus, "I believe it was God's will that we should return, so that men might know the things that are in the world." On Marco Polo's testimony, India, China and Japan were vast and rich beyond measure. Gold, silver, and jewels were the familiar items of value. The king of Malabar wore so many gems and pearls that they were worth more than a great city. Another chronicler, writing to Columbus, declared that the royal palaces of the east were immense, one river alone had two hundred palatial cities with marble bridges along its banks, and the palaces of Japan were covered with solid gold. Beyond these, spices abounded in the east, and were needed in quantity by Europeans to make palatable the meat they ate which was often spoiled in slow transfer from slaughterhouse to table. Well: in a single "very noble port called Zaiton . . . every year they load and unload a hundred

large ships laden with pepper, besides many other ships loaded with other spices." For Columbus, his view of the shape of the world must hold the secret of how to find a direct sea route to the Indies which would make useless the overland animal caravans of the Polo family and all who had gone eastward after them.

As early as June, 1474, Paolo the physician of Florence was writing to Columbus, "I perceive your noble and grand desire to go to the places where the spices grow." Thinking of where the Portuguese had gone by sea, far south along the coast of Africa, Columbus asked himself why, if men could sail so far south, they might not be able to sail to the west, far enough to find land. If they could, must not such land be India? He had read in Seneca's treatise on the elements, winds, earthquakes and comets, the statement, written in about 63 A.D., that "A ship may sail in a few days with a fair wind from the coast of Spain to that of India." There was no proof of this so far, but the idea was not so new as to seem absurd. Columbus knew of men before his time who swore they had seen land west of the Canary Islands, and once in Madeira, an "unknown pilot" who lay dying told him how his ship had been driven by storm to an island far westward in the Atlantic sea. Moreover, there had once been cast up on the shores of Ireland a corpse whose features were clearly oriental which must have come across the Atlantic from Cathay.

Rumor seized upon all evidence, however small, and to many men brought only idle wondering. But as for others, a son of Christopher Columbus said long afterward, "from small matters some draw substance for great deeds." For Columbus believed "that since all the water and land in the world formed a sphere, it would be possible to go around it from East to West until men stood feet to feet, one against the other, at opposite ends of the earth."

He spent the better part of two decades bringing his theory to the test. The hardest part

of this task was to find the backing for it which he could not supply himself.

He first approached King João of Portugal, and "offered to discover the Indies." So grand a confidence carried with it certain conditions. Columbus required honors, titles and riches in return. The King put him off, meanwhile sending in secret a ship of his own to carry out Columbus's plan and take the Indies for himself. Such royal treachery deserved its end: the King's mariner returned with nothing to show but his own incompetence and happy ridicule for the vision of Columbus. Portugal held out nothing but sorrow for Columbus. Now widowed, he left Lisbon secretly, in 1484, taking along his son Diego, and proceeded to Spain where he started all over again to lift his great plan to the attention of princes, appealing to King Ferdinand and Queen Isabella.

Columbus was a son of his time, the dawning Renaissance, when the spirit of discovery in all of man's arts and sciences was breaking across the European world. But the new spirit was not fostered everywhere in a spontaneous recognition of its power for growth. Seven years passed without action by Ferdinand and Isabella upon the plan of Columbus. While he waited for them to act, he made overtures to Henry VII of England and Charles VIII of France—but these came to nothing. But finally, when the King and Queen had completed the old Spanish design of expelling the Moors from Spain, and establishing unity for the Spanish kingdoms and peoples, they acted at last to approve the expedition to India. After early objections, they agreed to the personal conditions of Columbus, by which he became a nobleman with the address of *Don*, and Lord Admiral of the Ocean Sea, and viceroy and governor forever of all the islands and continents which he would discover. They agreed further that these powers would descend to his heirs forever, and that he should retain a tenth of all the wealth he should find, and that he should receive all the salaries of his separate

positions as admiral, viceroy and governor, and that he should himself appoint or remove all officers of his own government in India, and that those other officers appointed by the Crown to represent the royal interests should be chosen from lists prepared by him.

He knew the art of dealing with princes. Having told them what he would do, he assured the King and Queen that it was what they themselves ordered him to do.

"Your Highnesses," he wrote, "took thought to send me, Christopher Columbus, to the said parts of India, to see those princes and peoples and lands and the character of them and of all else, and the manner which should be used to bring about their conversion to our holy faith, and ordained that I should not go by land to the eastward, by which way it was the custom to go, but by way of the west, by which down to this day"—a day shortly before he was to sail—"we do not know certainly that any one has passed . . ."

He promised to keep a journal, day and night, of the whole expedition. Now royally commissioned, he went rapidly ahead with his preparations. Included in his equipment were letters from his King and Queen addressed to the Grand Khan of China, who ruled all lesser kings of the orient.

The Voyage

The fleet made ready in the harbor of Palos, where for weeks men and supplies were brought together. The Lord Admiral had three ships. All needed caulking, and he watched the caulkers at work while the ships were careened in the shipyards. He thought they did a poor job, and they knew it. To avoid having to do their work over, they ran away. To his regret, now and later, he had to accept the ships as they were.

On Thursday night, August second, 1492, the commander and all his men went to the

church of St. George in Palos. There they confessed their sins and received Holy Communion. The unknown lay ahead and it would be well to meet it in a state which would render danger less terrible. Long before daybreak, the Lord Admiral went on board his flagship. Half an hour before sunrise, he gave the order to up anchors, and in the grey light of sky and water, to a salute from the shore battery of lombards, he sailed "with very many supplies and with many a seaman, on the third day of August, of the same year, on a Friday." Setting his course for the Canary Island possessions of Spain, he said he felt it "very fitting that I should forget sleep and give much attention to navigation, because it should be so. And these things will be a great labour."

The armored Spaniard wore a visored helmet, with a neckpiece, called a casque. The admiral's ships—caravels—looked like casques floated upside down in the water, higher at stern than at bow, and with masts higher than their lengths. *Santa Maria*, the flagship, was rated at a hundred tons' burden. She was fifty feet long, eighteen feet wide, and carried stone ballast, like the fleet's other vessels. *Pinta* was smaller, at fifty tons, and *Niña* still smaller, at forty. They carried three masts, with immense square sails on the mainmasts.

With him in the flagship the Lord Admiral carried 39 officers and men. In *Pinta*, Martín Alonso Pinzón commanding, there were twenty-six, and in *Niña*, under Vicente Yañez Pinzón, twenty-two. Each ship bore a pilot, a navigator who was also first officer, and a surgeon. Most of the seamen came from Palos, and the officers were sons of leading families there. Three sailors were criminals released from life-imprisonment to serve out their sentences in the dangers of the expedition. Four foreigners were in the roster—a Venetian, a Portuguese, and two Genoese, one of whom was the Lord Admiral. Among the men was one who spoke Arabic. He was expected to be helpful in conducting conversations with the Chinese and Japanese. The men were paid in gold—seven dollars a month for seamen, fourteen for officers, and four dollars sixty cents for cabin boys, or gromets.

In their small sugar-loaf hats, their slashed doublets of Segovia cloth or leather, their spikes of dagger and sword, their ballooning knee breeches and rough-skin leather boots or shoes, they were hardy and simple, for the most part. Their sun-ripened faces with sharp dark eyes showed to the world various tempers and characters, but in one matter they were all of one mind. This was their faith in God and the proper expression of it through their religion. No other expression of all life could possibly be accepted. They took their belief with them as the most natural of possessions. They were prepared to bestow it upon others as the greatest of all gifts, and if it might not be wanted, then they would offer it again with sword and torch—not for cruelty, as they saw it, but in ultimate mercy. For the rest, after much they had heard, they were prepared to become rich, if they lived, and if the Lord Admiral's lands were as he said they were.

Though not all were content. Beating southward for the Fortunate Isles, as Ptolemy called the Canaries, Cristóbal Quintero, who owned *Pinta*, and Gómez Rascón were "exasperated at the voyage," as the Lord Admiral said. He had noticed before sailing from Palos how they had been "inclined to oppose and pick holes" in the enterprise. On Monday, August sixth, three days out, the rudder of *Pinta* jumped from its gear. At some risk, it was repaired. The Lord Admiral must conclude that Quintero and Rascón were responsible for the breakdowns. *Pinta* continued to steer badly. She shipped water. He might replace her with another caravel when he reached The Grand Canary.

But when he reached the Canaries he undertook full repairs of *Pinta*, and he had *Niña's* rigging changed from lateen to square sails, whose greater area would take more wind. He

remained there from August ninth until September sixth. While the refittings proceeded, he listened to vehement reports by "many honourable Spaniards" of the Islands who swore that each year on their voyages they saw land to the west of the Canaries. All evidence in support of this theory was important to the Lord Admiral. Preparing to sail again, he took into the ships new stocks of water, meat and wood. Sailing, he ordered a new course—west: no qualifying directions of north or south: but due west, in full accord with the plans he had worked out for so many years through books, maps, and the testimony of other mariners. In the latitude of the Canary Islands, the prevailing winds blew to the westward. The Lord Admiral proposed to go with them.

Others would prevent him, if they could.

On the first day out of Gomera a caravel from the island of Hierro signalled him with a warning. Three Portuguese caravels were beating about the westward course "to take him," under orders of King João. The Lord Admiral concluded that this menace could be traced to "the envy which the King felt because he had gone to Castile." Despite a continued calm the fleet passed safely by the interceptors. At three o'clock in the morning on September eighth the calm broke with winds from the northwest, and shipping great seas across the bows, making slow progress, the fleet bore to the west again. On the following day the Lord Admiral recorded an advance of fifteen leagues.

Thinking of how long the voyage might have to be, and of how time and the unknown could work on men at sea, he resolved to log fewer leagues than he made each day. So, actually sailing farther than they knew, the crews might come to land sooner than they could properly expect.

In his log he kept record of both great and small events. At night, on September fifteenth, there was a mystery. "They saw fall from the sky a marvellous branch of fire into the sea at a distance of four or five leagues from them."

In the next day, the "air was soft and refreshing . . . the sea smooth as a river." The Admiral said that the only thing missing was "the singing of the nightingale." The wind held steady to the west for many days, and the crewmen feared that "no winds ever blew to carry them back to Spain." And then they encountered a head wind. If this slowed their progress it was also a blessing, as the Lord Admiral saw, for the men were "much excited" with relief to know that a homeward wind could yet be had.

Soon after, the sea was smooth enough so that many sailors went swimming. They saw schools of gilded fish. At sunset in the same day, a great hope broke forth from *Pinta*. From her masthead she threw out a standard, and from one of her gunports she fired a lombard. Captain Martín Alonso Pinzón mounted the sterncastle of *Pinta* and "in great delight called the Admiral, asking for a reward from him because he had sighted land"—the ten thousand maravedi life income promised by the sovereigns. At sunrise and sunset, by order of the fleet commander, all ships closed upon the flagship, when with mist clearing, all could see farther.

Hearing this report of land, the Lord Admiral kneeled down and gave thanks to God. In *Pinta* all prayed with their captain the *Gloria in excelsis Deo*. The crew of *Niña* went up the rigging to look, and all declared that they saw land to the southwest. The Lord Admiral agreed that he saw it twenty-five leagues away and changed his course to approach it. All night long and into the next afternoon they sailed in a smooth sea—"like a river" with "breezes sweet and very soft" and the men swam again, but there was no land. What they had seen was a cloudbank. They resumed the course due west. A chart was sent back and forth between the flagship and *Pinta* on a rope. To mark the passing time, a sand glass was turned over every half hour day and night.

The greatest ship of the fleet was no larger than a small house. Three dozen men filled her

completely. Her bow was round and blunt and it buried itself in every wave. She rocked like a bowl. Her heavy canvas pushed her down into the water as well as forward. In the trough of a moderately heavy sea even her high sterncastle would be lost to sight, with only the misted sails showing above. Sailors knew the emptiness of the ocean, where through low clouds the light closed and opened so swiftly. After a bright instant of sunlight which lifted the spirits, how quickly hope could die when the clouds closed again over the watery wilderness. In the spin of wind across wave the men knew a lost sameness. When somebody was bewildered or directionless, he would say in a common expression that he was "all at sea." Not knowing where they were going, the sailors of this fleet held the ocean doubly empty in their minds and unchanging, with the little casquelike ships cockling and leaning over their own bows against ridge after ridge of waves, on and on, it must seem forever, and all the same.

What abided with them in their land longing were the power and vigilance of the Lord Admiral. "Christopher Columbus," said an early Churchman in a famous *History of the Indies*, "in the arts of navigation exceeded without any doubt all others who lived in his day." The sailors in his ships who knew his seamanship called him "divine," and the days passed straining to the westward, while all watched for signs of land.

On Thursday October fourth a gromet on the flagship saw forty birds together skimming the waves often catching water with their webbed feet. They were petrels. He found a small stone out of the ballast and threw it at the birds and hit one. Two boobies flew by. A frigate bird came to the rigging, and they saw a white bird "like a gull." The wind freshened during the night, and they made eleven miles an hour, and in the day they advanced fifty-seven leagues, but for his men the Lord Admiral recorded forty-five. Many more petrels appeared above the calm smooth sea, and many flying fish sailed into the ship. There was mystery in a bird far out at sea, and an even greater one in fish that went like birds in short arcs of flight.

At sunrise two days later, as the ships were closed together for sighting exercise in the lifting mist, *Niña*, small and swift under her great canvas, sent up her standard to the peak and fired a lombard, declaring land. Again the fleet pounded through a day to nightfall without coming to any shore, though the Lord Admiral believed that they might "sleep on land" that night, for a great flock of birds came over the ships from the north, flying southwest, as if to find land, or perhaps he thought, to fly "from the winter which was about to come to the lands whence they came." He remembered that "most of the islands which the Portuguese have held had been discovered through birds," and since these birds flew southwestward, he ordered a change in course to the same direction, to be tried for two days.

Monday, October eighth, the following day, brought another suggestion of land—breezes fragrant with scent wafting over a calm sea. Drifting vegetation "seemed to be very fresh." Many land birds were about. A night later the darkness over the ships was alive, and "all night they heard birds passing." If they were near land, still they saw none, and "here the men could bear no more," but the Lord Admiral spoke to them, encouraged them, and added flatly that complaints were to no avail, since no matter what, "he was going to the Indies and must pursue his course, until with the help of Our Lord, he found them."

That he must find them he was sure by all means—his philosophy, the charts he had studied and extended, the currents of the winds, the kinds of fish he had seen, the flights of birds, the drifts of branches in the sea, the perfume of land on the air, the objects worked

by men which only today, October eleventh, Thursday, he had seen in the tumbling of the roughest sea of the voyage. The mystery awaiting its answer then gave him the vision of the light which must only come from a shore.

As the gromet turned over the half-hour glass at midnight, the fleet rode forward under a moon just past full. Jupiter was rising in the east, behind the ships. They sailed in close formation. Every man awake was a lookout in the strong moonlight. *Pinta*, lighter than *Santa Maria*, stood out ahead of her. At two o'clock the wind carried a long cry from the forecastle of *Pinta*. Rodrigo de Triana, who came from a suburb of Seville, cried,

"*Tierra! Tierra!*"

They looked. Six miles to the west, as the Lord Admiral reckoned it, lay a long shore on the moonlit horizon. The man who cried out "Land! Land!" was the first Spaniard to see the new world. Thirty-three years later he lost his life to it, in another expedition.

The Lord Admiral ordered all sail taken in, except mainsails, and all the rest of the night, the ships "kept jogging" back and forth in sight of land, waiting for the daybreak of Friday, October twelfth, 1492, when safely they could come to shore.

New World

At dawn they saw a coral island about thirteen miles long. They sailed toward it. Ruffled combers proclaimed the presence of reefs all along her seaward side, and indeed, on her leeward side for all her shore except for one and three quarter miles. Through that gap in the breakers the Lord Admiral took his fleet into a shallow bay and anchored in five fathoms of green water facing the broad curve of coral sand. The island was six miles wide. It lay in the twenty-fourth parallel of latitude and the meridian of 74° 30' west of Greenwich. What

was it named? Whatever its name, the Lord Admiral named it San Salvador. It lay "in one line from east to west" in the latitude of the island of Hierro in the Canaries.

On the sands they "immediately saw naked people." Lowering a boat, and taking with him from the other ships his two captains, and Rodrigo de Escobedo, the secretary of the fleet, and Rodrigo Sánchez de Segovia, the King's accountant, and some armed sailors, the Lord Admiral crossed the lagoon and touched ashore. He carried the royal standard and the others carried the banners of the Green Cross which was the fleet's flag, bearing in addition to the cross the crowned monograms of the King and Queen. When they landed they saw bright green forests and little streams of water and many kinds of fruit.

Awaited by the island people who gathered in growing numbers, the Lord Admiral, addressing the witnesses from the ships, took possession of the new land for his sovereigns according to the prescribed legal process, with its pronouncements of the crown, its prayers, and its tenure across time.

The island people watched.

They were naked as when they were born. How beautiful they were, "with very handsome bodies and very good faces." They were as gentle, generous and trusting as they were beautiful. They bore no arms, and not knowing what a sword was they curiously clutched a Spanish blade and cut themselves. Some bore old wounds, and explained that these were given by invading people from other islands. The Lord Admiral decided that the invaders were mainlanders who came to take these people as slaves. They said their island was called Guanahaní. Some of the people were painted in various colors, including black. How intelligent they were! He believed they understood all that was said to them. They would make excellent servants, and surely they would readily become Christians. They indicated

Christopher Columbus, as depicted by Italian painter Sebastiano del Piombo. Tall and sturdy, with red hair and freckled face, Columbus could be "graceful when he wished, irate when crossed." (Courtesy of The Metropolitan Museum of Art, gift of J. Pierpont Morgan, 1900.)

clearly how they believed that the Lord Admiral and his men had come from Heaven.

He bestowed gifts on them—little bells of copper or brass such as men at home tied to the feet of falcons the better to trace the flight of these gaming birds, and those little cones of metal which bound the ends of laces or thongs, and little caps of red cloth, and little necklets of blue beads. With exquisite civility the islanders accepted these as treasures. Such lovable people

should be known at home, and the Lord Admiral proposed to bring home six of them who could meet the King and Queen and learn Spanish. As for animals, he saw none, except for parrots.

Later in the day, when the staff had returned to the ships' boats, the islanders swam out to see them alongside, and took delight in the strangeness they saw, and so did the crewmen. On Saturday, the next day, they saw from shipboard how more people came through the trees to the beach and then how they came to the ships in canoes made from long treetrunks. The Lord Admiral could not help remarking on their comeliness again. They all had fine, broad brows, and large, lovely eyes. They had handsome straight legs and no fat. If a canoe turned over, the paddlers went with it, swam neatly alongside it and righted it and then bailed it out with gourds. Now they brought things to give in trade—"balls of spun cotton and parrots and spears and other trifles" and among these the Lord Admiral looked closely for gold.

All he saw was a small golden ornament worn in the nose by some of the islanders— Indians, as the men must call them, since this was the first land of India which they had reached, just as the Lord Admiral had said they would. Now he asked where the gold came from, and the Indians indicated that they came from an island to the southward, where the king had much of it, and large utensils made of it. He asked them to take him there, but they would not. He thought of Japan, the great island which he must find next. The Indians said there was land also to the north, but it was from there that attackers came. The Lord Admiral resolved to go to the southwest, "to seek the gold and precious stones."

The visitors stayed on board all day. How easy they were to get along with. They gave all they had for the smallest trifle—a broken dish or glass cup. Some dived off the ship and swam

to shore with these treasures fearing to lose them if they could give nothing in return. Their gentleness continued to amaze. How easily they could all be captured and returned to Spain; or fifty armed soldiers could control them in their own island where they could be "forced to do whatever may be wished." At nightfall they returned to shore in their canoes, leaving the Lord Admiral to consider his next move. But he knew: "I wish to go and see if I can find the island of Japan."

He spent Sunday the fourteenth coasting along the island of San Salvador in the ships' boats. He saw Indian villages from which on seeing him the people came forth "calling us and giving thanks to God." They brought him food. Later he landed and found a splendid piece of high ground where a fort could be built. He saw the most beautiful stands of trees that he had ever seen. Then, and in many later days, he recorded the loveliness of the new lands, which never ceased to enchant him. Every new place was lovelier than the last— "the singing of little birds is such that it seems that a man could never wish to leave this place; the flocks of parrots darken the sun . . . it is a marvel. There are, moreover, trees of a thousand types, all with their various fruits and all scented, so that it is a wonder." He saw good harbors and many rivers and fine mountains and great serpents and more than once he would come upon dogs that could not bark. Above all, throughout his journal, he celebrated the people of this first island and all others. He told the King and Queen to "believe that in all the world there cannot be a people better or more gentle." Full of love and without greed, they loved "their neighbors as themselves." They had the softest voices and they always smiled. They touched the Spaniards and kissed their hands and feet "wondering at them." Their generosity was as sweet as that of children, giving whatever they had for any scrap without noticing how little they received,

and with significance the Lord Admiral reported to his employers that the Indians would do the same "with spices and gold, if they had any."

He could stay there forever, but he had set himself a limit of two days at San Salvador. Japan beckoned. If by chance he should miss that great island, the Lord Admiral, knowing well his fifteenth century maps, felt sure of coming instead to China. Early on Sunday afternoon, October fourteenth, keeping on board seven of the islanders as specimens for the sovereigns, and opening with every thrust before the wind a great new world for all centuries to come, the fleet set sail for Japan.

Columbus returned to America three times and explored the Ocean Sea north and west of San Salvador. But he never found Japan—proof of all his theories, goal of all his dreams. Still, he remained undaunted. If he had not found the Orient, then he had discovered a New Paradise on Earth where European man might experience a true renaissance of the soul. He wrote from America in 1500: "God made me the messenger of the new heaven and the new earth of which He spoke in the Apocalypse by St. John, after having spoken of it by the mouth of Isaiah; and He showed me the spot where to find it." In 1506 Columbus died, convinced to the end that he had discovered an "earthly paradise" in America.

3

Passage to America: 1630

Marion L. Starkey

The discovery of America had a profound impact on the Old World: not only did the opening of this enormous new frontier stimulate the European imagination (as reflected in both artistic and scientific expression), but it also brought about a clash of imperial energies as Spain, Portugal, and France all vied with one another in staking out claims to the New World. While Portugal received Brazil (thanks to a Papal edict in 1493), Spain claimed the rest of South and Central America and sent out explorers to look for gold and silver there. After Balboa crossed the Isthmus of Panama, Hernando Cortés conquered Mexico and the Aztecs' splendorous cities. Other gold-hungry conquistadors explored the sunless woods of Florida and the humid brush country of South Texas; the brutish Pizarro marched across Peru, sadistically liquidating the civilized Incas and confiscating their magnificent treasuries; and Francisco Vásquez de Coronado, striking in his gilded armor, set out to find the fabled seven cities of gold in the American Southwest. Coronado discovered no cities of gold, but his expedition did make contact with the Pueblo Indians along the Rio Grande, roamed the wind-swept country between the Grand Canyon and the Southern Rockies, and explored the moon-like plains of what is now eastern New Mexico,

the Texas Panhandle, and southwestern Kansas. By the 1550s, powerful Spain had a virtual monopoly of the New World, with a sprawling colonial empire which comprised most of South America, Central America, Mexico, the Caribbean Islands, Florida, and the American southwest from Texas to California.

Meanwhile, French explorers searched eastern Canada for the "Northwest Passage," a legendary waterway that was supposed to connect the Atlantic and Pacific oceans and that, under French control, would give them access to the luxuries of Asia. Unable to find such a passage, France was content to establish a fur-trading empire in Canada, her explorers, traders, and missionaries advancing west to the Great Lakes and then southward down the Mississippi to New Orleans.

England, however, was slow to join the race for colonies, although John Cabot's voyage to North America in 1497 had given England a claim to the New World. Finally, under Queen Elizabeth the English challenged Spain's rule of the oceans and her domination of the New World: adventurous "sea dogs" under John Hawkins raided Spanish commerce on both the Atlantic and Pacific oceans; and in 1588, in a dramatic sea battle, the English navy defeated the Spanish Armada and gave England virtually undisputed control of the seas. Thanks to the persuasive arguments of Sir Walter Raleigh, Sir Humphrey Gilbert, and Richard Hakluyt, all champions of colonization, England at last began to build a New World empire. After an abortive attempt to found a colony on Roanoke Island, North Carolina, Queen Elizabeth and her successor James I authorized private corporations called joint stock companies to establish Jamestown, Plymouth, and Massachusetts Bay colonies. As the number of colonies increased, a great migration began to English North America, some people going there for religious reasons, others to obtain land and to make more money than was possible back on the "tight little isle."

Modern textbooks, in delineating the imperial struggle on the part of England, France, and Spain for control of the New World, often neglect the people themselves who endured the hardships of the Atlantic passage to begin new lives on the American frontier. In the following narrative, Marion L. Starkey recounts one such passage in

27

1630, when John Winthrop and his Puritan followers crossed "a cruel Atlantic" to found the Massachusetts Bay colony.

On April 12, 1630, the flagship *Arbella*, followed by her three consorts, passed Land's End and plunged her bow into the boiling Atlantic. It was the Sabbath, and the passengers should have gathered to hear the Reverend Mr. George Phillips commemorate the occasion in sermon and prayer. But the minister lay ignominiously ill in his cabin, and so in their quarters, cabins for the gentry, 'tween decks or gun room for the simple, lay most of his flock.

Only three days earlier this miserable company had faced mortal peril with stout hearts. Eight sail had been seen aft, coming as if from Dunkirk where the Spaniards were, and though outnumbered, the little convoy, the *Arbella*, *Ambrose*, *Jewel*, and *Talbot*, had readied for battle. Women and children were hustled out of the way, such "bed matter" as might take fire cast overboard. The longboats were lowered, and the men, armed with muskets, took posts behind the colored screens of "waist cloths."

One shot was fired, "a ball of wild fire," which the captain fastened to an arrow and sent into the water. It burned there a long time, and the people watched, as if it were a sign, and held themselves steadfast. In the hold the children did not weep and the women did not panic. They trusted in the Lord, and old England lay to the starboard. Would the enemy dare give battle within sight of Portland?

It did not, for this was not the enemy. Most were fishing craft, peaceably bound for Canada and the Grand Banks off Newfoundland. "Our fear and danger were turned into mirth and

entertainment," observed Governor John Winthrop on the *Arbella*. The musket shot was used to salute each ship as it passed; the children scrambled back to deck to cheer and wave.

But the same women and children, the same men, who had braced themselves to meet the enemy with fortitude, did nothing of the sort when they met the Atlantic. It came at them head on in the teeth of a gale, and there was no arming against a sea of such troubles. They could not hold their footing on a deck that dipped away or rose to smite them; there was no point of rest for the eyes now that the last rock of Scilly was under a horizon where mountains skipped like young lambs. On deck the very livestock bellowed its dismay, and in their cabins, in their bunks and hammocks, the people heaved and moaned.

Now they knew themselves irrevocably committed to the unknown. They were voyaging into outer space, and though they could claim no priority in this venture, so many having gone before, they were none the less entering a way of life as remote from their imagination as if they were voyaging to another planet.

They had been on their way since March, hovering off the coast of England, tarrying here for supplies, here for a favorable wind. For those in authority, like John Winthrop and Captain Peter Milborne of the *Arbella*, those who had to concern themselves with provision and water, the delay had been onerous. For others it had been good to have England beside them so long. There had been no sudden break with the known and loved; merciful providence had been weaning them by degrees. Sometimes Lady Arbella and her gentlewomen had visited ashore. There had been sport for the children at Cowes when an ox and wethers had been fetched aboard, the beasts lowing and bleating as they were heaved to deck.

But these easy, reassuring days were now forever gone. They had done with England, which with all its iniquities had been a green

and pleasant land. Now they remembered that the bravest accounts of life in the Americas had been punctuated with death. Women big with child recalled that the first English child born on American soil, little Virginia Dare, had been lost with all her colony, leaving not a trace behind. Other settlers had survived only after starving times, corn planted on graves so that the enemy red men could not number the dead; they had heard of felons offered a choice between America and the gallows who gratefully chose the gallows.

For death they could prepare themselves, and prayerfully in England they had done so. But the humiliation of this particular misery had been outside their reckoning. So on the wild Sabbath when the convoy entered the Atlantic, even Mr. Phillips lay in his cabin and had no heart, or rather no stomach, to lift up his flock with exhortation.

2

Shortly after midday on Monday, Governor Winthrop went to his cabin for a look at his two young sons. Stephen was twelve, and Adam had just observed his tenth birthday aboard. "Our boys are well and cheerful and have no mind for home," he had written to his wife, who had remained behind. "They lie both with me and sleep as soundly in a rug (for we use no sheets here) as they ever did in Groton." But that had been written from Cowes, two weeks ago. There was no health in them now and no cheer; Adam could not control a puppy-like whimper when he saw his father.

"Up with you," said Winthrop. "I need you on deck."

The lads stared at him glassy-eyed. What he asked seemed no less than what Abraham had asked of Isaac; but though this was a kind father, he was firm, and feebly they obeyed. The deck still lurched, but less heavily, and once they were out of the cabin they were in

the sun. The waves rushed to meet the dipping bowsprit, but under a blue sky they looked sportive, like dolphins. Adam retched once more; then he felt better and looked to his father for orders.

"Fetch your playmates. Tell them the governor wants them."

Grim to enter the stuffy quarters 'tween decks with their smell of sick and of the necessary tubs, but gratifying to use the imperative and invoke "my father, the governor." At this command the children straggled up to deck and dumbly looked to the revered figure for orders. They were unexpected; he was calling them not to pray but to sport; they were to have a tug of war.

A rope had been rigged, under Winthrop's direction, from steerage to mainmast, and as the young people came he told them to lay hold of it, some on one side, some on the other. Some children stared blankly, asking leave to die in peace, but a governor is obeyed. They pulled on the rope, rather after the manner of women easing their labor pains. They pulled halfheartedly at first, then with a will as those on the other side yanked it away. The sun shone warm on their backs and dispelled the chill that had struck to the marrow. Presently they shouted as gaily as if they were home on the village green, and their mothers, hearing mirth, ventured out, and as the governor put it, "They soon grew well and merry."

The crew looked on with various feelings. There were among them profane fellows irritated to be in the service of a "praying company" like these Puritans, and inclined to sneer. But the sport was in the spirit of the merry England of the late Elizabeth, and more of them relished it than not. Some seamen undertook to teach the children and the young men some of their "harmless exercise." "Some would play the wags with them," the governor remarked, but did not interfere since it "did our people much good."

Thomas Dudley, Winthrop's second in com-

mand, looked on without comment. Already he suspected that of which he would soon have much to say, that the governor was given to "lenity." They were here embarked on a venture of high moral emprise; if they were to hark back for health's sake to idle merriment, surely there should have been seemly preliminaries of admonition and prayer.

Winthrop had not forgotten prayer. Later in the afternoon, when he heard two bells struck, he remembered that this was Monday and drew apart to his cabin to commune with God and his wife. "Monday and Friday at five of the clock at night, we shall meet in spirit till we meet in person," he had written his Margaret. She was remaining in their Groton home with the younger children until she could give birth. She was his third wife, and he loved her as dearly as he had loved them all: the first for whom he had at seventeen interrupted his studies at Cambridge; the second whose holy dying soon after childbirth he had recorded with pious awe in his journal. "I will only take thee now and my sweet children in mine arms and kiss and embrace you, and so leave you with God," he had written her.

There would be times, as he would confess from America, when under the pressure of business he would let the hour of sanctified rendezvous go by unremarked, but this first day on the Atlantic was not one of them. He came out of his cabin restored and refreshed and joined the society that he had known so long at Tattershall.

3

On the flagship the gentlefolk were already old acquaintance, and not from the voyage alone. Most were of the company who at Tattershall, seat of the Earl of Lincoln, had for months been planning this adventure. It was to be the firmest planting that America had yet seen—eight vessels were to follow this convoy—and

the practical details had been multitudinous. Not the least had been convincing Winthrop, already a settled man well along in his forties, and so an elder statesman in this young company, that he should lead it.

With him was the earl's young sister, lovely Lady Arbella, who recently and proudly had taken the prosaic name of Mrs. Isaac Johnson. None addressed her thus. She would be Lady Arbella to the last, and in her honor the old name of the flagship, *Eagle*, had been painted out and hers substituted. As for her husband, no one considered him prosaic. As ardent in his devotions as her ladyship, he had dedicated much of his substantial fortune to make this migration possible.

There were two of Lincoln's former stewards, Thomas Dudley and Simon Bradstreet. With the latter was his impressionable young wife Anne, who at eighteen was an old married lady. In her two years of happy marriage to an adored husband, the union had not yet been blessed with children, and this was a grief to the girl. Sometimes she consoled herself by writing verses, but not just now; there was too much motion on the *Arbella*, too little privacy. It was the governor who recorded the odyssey of the voyage in prose in his journal.

Not of the Tattershall elect, and unmarked by them except perhaps as a boisterous tomboy engaging in the tug of war, was the ten-year-old who later became Anne Pollard. She may not have been on the *Arbella*, but if not she was close by on the *Jewel* or the *Ambrose*; she had to be, for Anne was to lay undisputed claim to being the first settler of Boston. First, by virtue of a flying leap from the bow of a longboat; undisputed, because she was to survive Lady Arbella, John Winthrop, Simon and Anne Bradstreet, and everyone else who might say her nay.

She was to live beyond the turn of the century, past her own century mark, and celebrate this feat by doing on her best lace-edged cap and bib to sit for her portrait to a limner. She

was toothless by that time (the early Americans' teeth were not their most durable part) but her deep-set eyes were alert, and doubtless the obscure sign painter who took his name from her (Pollard Limner) listened as he painted, to the story that had delighted her children, grandchildren, great grandchildren, and the generations of publicans who visited her tavern in Boston, which she had first known as a place of swamps and hollows, covered with blueberry bushes.

But there were uncounted leagues to travel before Boston could be thought of. One gale was past; there would be others, and not gales only but full storms. Sometimes the little fleet was driven back farther than the distance it could gain in a day's sailing, and the other ships which had been left behind came near. The voyage was long, but it was prosperous. On the *Arbella* there were no deaths. After the first gale most passengers found their sea legs. Once, a maidservant feeling the motion took "hot waters" for her stomach's sake, overdid it, and fell seriously ill. But she recovered. Mr. Phillips came out to catechize the children and preach his Sabbath sermons; and though the deck dipped and soared, and congregation and divine alike received an aspergation of spindrift, the folk stood steadfast from "firstly to tenthly."

For most of his life, like his father Adam before him, John Winthrop had kept a journal. In it he now recorded the wonders of the great Atlantic, which he observed as eagerly as his young sons. Once a whale came straight at them and "would not shun us, so we passed within a stone's cast as he lay spouting up water." Even when there was no land within two hundred leagues there were fowl, flying and swimming. At night Winthrop remarked the steady declining of the North Star and that the moon, especially when new, was smaller than the moons of England. By day he discovered that in these southerly latitudes the sun "did not give so much heat as in England."

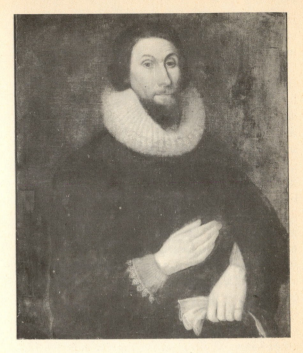

John Winthrop, first governor of Massachusetts Bay colony. A prosperous gentleman with a university degree, Winthrop was sober, stubborn, and deeply religious—traits which came to epitomize the Puritan character. Still, Winthrop was not a cold man. He had three different wives and loved and cherished them all. (Courtesy, American Antiquarian Society.)

Nor was the journey devoid of human encounters. It was, after all, more than a century since the new world had swum like a new planet into Europe's ken, and many nations were launching expeditions to probe its contours and to fish the fecund banks off the northern shores. Often the *Arbella* hailed such fellow travelers and spoke them in passing, or tried to. Sometimes a small craft plying lonely shunned them, taking them for the Spanish, who, since the Pope had awarded them all the Americas, the bulge of Brazil excepted, were not disposed to extend the right hand of fellowship to trespassers.

Apart from such wayfarers there were the other members of the convoy. Sometimes they lost each other for a day or two, but so far as wind and wave permitted they kept within sight of each other's sails, each taking its turn to carry a light in the mizzenmast after sundown. On a "still calm" in fair weather there was visiting between ships. Once the *Arbella* sent her skiff to the *Jewel* for a hogshead of meal "because we could not come by our own," and the skiff returned with not only the neighborly loan but the *Jewel's* master and John Revel, part owner of the *Arbella*. So a feast was prepared, and Captain Lowe on the *Ambrose* was signaled to come share it. There were several such dinner parties, the officers dining in the roundhouse, the ladies apart in the great cabin. When the officers returned to their own ships, the *Arbella* fired a salute of three shots.

One shot was fired (and the sails dipped) for other cause. A woman on the *Arbella* was in travail, and the nearest midwife was far ahead on the *Jewel*. At the signal the *Jewel* trimmed her sails and stayed. When they were within speaking distance, the midwife hiked up her skirts and got down the swaying Jacob's ladder of one ship and up again to the next, where she safely delivered the child. (Child and midwife were nameless; the governor did not anticipate posterity's greed for exact information.)

He had much to do beside watch whales and feast with visiting captains. If the captain was in charge of the ship and crew, he was in charge of the landsmen, and when there was division between them he had to intervene. Not long after the first gale the captain conducted the governor to the gun room to see for himself what a mess the men quartered there had made of the place. "It was so beastly and noysome with their victuals and beastliness and would endanger the health of the ship." The governor retired for prayer and then gave orders: fatigue detail for the landsmen. Four would clean for the first three days, another

four for the second, and so in rotation so long as they remained on the ship.

Once it was a passenger who complained of abuse from a petty officer, and the captain had the latter hung up by his hands with a weight about his neck. Distressed by such severity, the governor persuaded the captain to lenience. But he himself ordered similar punishment for a servant he caught cheating a child. The servant had sold the child a threepenny box for the promise of three biscuits a day. At the time he was caught he had received forty biscuits and had sold most of them to other servants. This was capital enterprise on a small scale, but the governor was no student of the theory that Puritanism and capitalism went hand in hand. He had a basket of stones hung about the servant's neck and stood him with his hands tied up to a bar for two hours.

4

The ocean was a foretaste of eternity. It was as if the ocean had no end; it became a way of life. Yet even the Atlantic was finite. By early June they were off the Grand Banks, that rendezvous of fishermen from Europe over. Lines were cast from deck and cod jigged up, "very great fish," some one and a half feet long, and this was God's mercy, for aside from their weariness of eating salt fish, the supply was running out.

It was eerie going on the Banks. The fog lay so thick on the water that the ships lost each other, yet overhead the sun shone bright. The captain had soundings taken, and finding them shallow, fitted the *Arbella* to another mainsail lest she be driven on the shoals. On dark nights he would not risk retiring to his cabin.

On Tuesday June 8, overpowering the rank odors of the ship, they caught the scent of land, "so pleasant a sweet air as did much refresh us, and there came a smell offshore like

the smell of a garden." Before them the horizon steadied at last; land was in sight, the hills about Penobscot Bay.

It was only a four days' sail down the coast to their provisional destination, Salem, or Naumkeag as it was still called, and there they had a holiday. Some were set ashore at Cape Ann, where the children scrambled about picking strawberries. Lady Arbella and the other gentlefolk enjoyed the hospitality of John Endicott, governor in these parts until Winthrop came, and in his sturdy frame house supped on venison pastry and good beer.

Their troubles were over. Their troubles were just beginning. Even Endicott's house (which he had commandeered from its builder, Roger Conant, and floated down from Beverly for his own use) was no Tattershall. The common sort there still lived in makeshifts; some had made dugouts in the banks, shoring up the dirt walls with timber and covering the ground with reeds; some lived in still ruder arrangements of poles, brushwood, sailcloths, and skins.

Their plantings were nondescript. They were hungry, and living in expectation of this "supply" of provisions already nearly exhausted during the long voyage. There had been many deaths, among them Francis Higginson, whose lyric accounts of the new land had impelled many to follow.

Little Anne Bradstreet looked on this sorry way of life and clung to her husband while her heart sank within her. The Lady Arbella held herself valiantly and made no complaint. But for her the journey had been hard; before the summer was over she would be dead. "She stopped at New England on her way to Heaven," as Cotton Mather would put it; her stricken husband would survive her only a month.

Not all the ships of this "great migration," nearly a dozen of them, had made so prosperous a voyage as the flagship. On the *Talbot*

an infection had come aboard while she hovered off England, and fourteen had died of it. Governor Winthrop's son Henry, a scapegrace but beloved, was not one of these, but the day after the *Talbot* came in he drowned in an attempt to swim a creek. Heavily the governor turned to the task of finding a place for the "sitting down" of all these people and a means of building and planting before winter should close in on them.

5

This passage to America in 1630 was far from the first; on its scale, and better provided than most, it was not even characteristic. No two voyages, even of ships traveling in company, were alike. Nevertheless the *Arbella* may stand as a symbol of the thousand and one migrations to America in the seventeenth century.

The migrants had been coming to Virginia since 1607 (or 1587 if you count the lost Colony of Roanoke). A little group of English exiles had been settled out Cape Cod way for a decade. The Dutch had posts on the Hudson and Connecticut. A group of settlers already in Newfoundland, unhappy at the long winters, were looking down the coast to Chesapeake Bay. In Sweden the great Gustavus Adolphus was listening to estimates of fortunes to be made on the Delaware. Presently Swedes and Finns would be planting along the river; Germans were to follow, Huguenots, Portuguese Jews.

The migrants came not from Europe only. Already Africa had sent a handful of settlers to Virginia. In England's Sugar Islands, including Barbados, founded while the concept of Massachusetts was evolving, planters would find their lands too narrow and look to the southern coast.

The migrants came as they had come on the

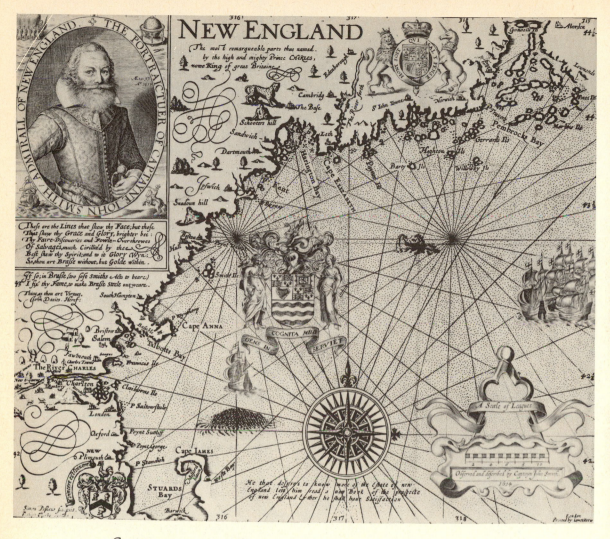

Contemporary map of the coast of Plymouth and Massachusetts Bay colonies. The map originally appeared in John Smith's Advertisements for the unexperienced planters of New England, *published in 1631 in London. (By permission of The Harvard College Library.)*

Arbella, and for few was it a pleasure cruise. Some voyages would be swift, counted in weeks, some would stretch over long months. On some ships quarters would be kept sweet with washings of vinegar and the burning of herbs, and the provisions would be wholesome and ample. On others passengers endured filth and sickened on rancid rations. Some would come without the loss of a passenger; some would become plague ships. Children would be born on other ships, some to early death, some to live to hale old age.

And ahead of all lay the brutal task of breaking ground and building shelter.

II Births and Rebirths

4

The Beginnings

Carl N. Degler

Americans lived for some 169 years under British rule. To place the colonial era in chronological perspective, that is how many years elapsed between Jefferson's rise to power in 1800 and the first moon landing in 1969. As Carl Degler observes, the first one hundred years of colonial life were extremely significant in terms of what Americans would think and do for generations afterwards. Synthesizing from an impressive array of modern writings and adding fresh and provocative insights of his own, Degler explores the crucial themes of seventeenth-century America, with an eye to those developments which helped make the United States what it is today. The result is a moving portrait of those early-day colonists, whose experiences speak to us across the decades.

In more ways than is often recognized, the one hundred years after the death of Elizabeth I in 1603 comprise the first century of the modern world. A number of developments peculiar to modern European thought cluster within these years: the true beginnings of modern science in the work of Galileo and Newton, Harvey and Boyle; the first expression of modern democratic ideas by the Levelers and in the Army Debates of the English Civil Wars; the decisive break in a millennium of religious dominance with the end of the wars of religion and the acceptance of the principle of religious tolerance; the achievement of lasting constitutional and representative government in England with the Glorious Revolution of 1688. It was also the time of the first permanent settlement of English colonists.

For America, its origin in this first century of the modern era was filled with meaning. In the New World, the future was still fluid. Europe's ways, both the new and the old, could be planted in America free of the choking weeds of outmoded habits. America would be a testing ground, but it would be difficult to predict what would happen. Some of the European ways would wither; some would strike root; still others would change and adapt to the new environment. For a good part of the century this plasticity was characteristic. But then, by the end of the century, the mold had hardened. In a number of ways what Americans would be for generations to come was settled in the course of those first hundred years.

1. Capitalism Came in the First Ships

To men coming from the "tight little isle" the vast land of America, though untamed and dense with forest, was remarkably like the old, both in the flora that covered it and in the crops that it would yield. Although in a region like New England settlers would soon discover the soil to be thin and unfertile compared with that of the more southern colonies, it was not a desert, and from the beginning a well-organ-

From pp. 1–36 in *Out of Our Past: The Forces That Shaped Modern America*, revised edition, by Carl N. Degler. Copyright © 1959, 1970 by Carl N. Degler. Reprinted by permission of Harper & Row, Publishers, Inc.

ized group like the Massachusetts Bay people were able to wring a comfortable, if not opulent, living from the lean and rocky soil. The Chesapeake colonies had better soil and, as it turned out, a climate conducive to the production of a staple of world-wide appeal—the infamous weed, tobacco.

A land endowed with such promise could not fail to attract a continuous stream of men and women from the shops and farms of Europe. For centuries the problem in Europe had been that of securing enough land for the people, but in the New World the elements in the equation were reversed. "I hear . . . that servants would be more advantageous to you than any commodity," wrote a Londoner to a Virginian in 1648. For over three centuries, through wars and revolutions, through economic disaster and plague, the underlying, insistent theme of American history was the peopling of a continent.

Though the pervasive influence which Frederick Jackson Turner attributed to the frontier in the shaping of the American character can be overestimated, the possibility of exaggeration should not hide the undeniable fact that in early America, and through most of the nineteenth century, too, land was available to an extent that could appear only fabulous to land-starved Europeans. From the outset, as a result, the American who worked with his hands had an advantage over his European counterpart. For persistent as employers and rulers in America might be in holding to Old World conceptions of the proper subordination of labor, such ideas were always being undercut by the fact that labor was scarcer than land.

The imagination of men was stretched by the availability of land in America. Though land was not free for the taking, it was nearly so. In seventeenth-century New England there were very few landless people, and in the Chesapeake colonies it was not unusual for an indentured servant, upon the completion of his term, to be granted a piece of land. Thus,

thanks to the bounty of America, it was possible for an Englishman of the most constricted economic horizon to make successive jumps from servant to freeman, from freeman to freeholder, and, perhaps in a little more time, to wealthy speculator in lands farther west. Not all men were successful in America, to be sure, but, as the emigration literature reveals, enough were to encourage most men in the new land to strive hard for wealth and success.

In America the availability of land rendered precarious, if not untenable, those European institutions which were dependent upon scarcity of land. Efforts to establish feudal or manorial reproductions in the New World came to nothing. The Dutch, for example, tried to set up an ambitious system of patroons, or great landowners, whose broad acres along the Hudson were intended to be worked by tenants. In keeping with the manorial practices common in Europe, the patroon was to dispense justice and administer in his own right the government of his little kingdom. But contrary to the popular tradition that sees these patroonships carrying over into the period of English rule after 1664, only two of the Dutch grants outlasted New Netherland, and of them, only one was in existence ten years later. Under English rule only Rensselaer retained his original grant; all the others returned or forfeited them to the Dutch West Indies Company. It is significant that the other land-granting policy of the Dutch, that of individual small holdings, was much more successful.

At the beginning, Lord Baltimore's attempt to erect manors in Maryland and to create a feudal aristocracy enjoyed more success than that of the Dutch. Some sixty manors were established in the province during the seventeenth century, the lords of which constituted a kind of new Catholic aristocracy. On at least one of these manors, that of St. Clement, manorial courts-leet (for tenants) and baron (for freeholders) were actually held, private justice

being dispensed by the lord. But here too the experiment of transplanting European social ways to the free and open lands of America was to prove futile. Slavery and the plantation were much more efficient ways for utilizing land than the outmoded manor; moreover, tenants were restive in the face of free lands to the west.

The failure in New York and Maryland to reconstitute the manors of Europe did not prevent the founders of the Carolinas from making one more attempt. In the Fundamental Constitutions of 1669 provisions were included for "leet-men" who would not be able "to go off from the land of their particular lord" without permission. Moreover, it was decreed that "all children of leet-men shall be leet-men, and so to all generations." Atop this lowest stratum of hereditary tenants was erected a quasi-feudal hierarchy of caciques and landgraves, capped by a palatine. It seems hardly necessary to add that this design, so carefully worked out in Europe, was implemented in America only to the extent of conferring titles upon the ersatz nobility; the leetmen, so far as the records show, never materialized. Indeed, the Fundamental Constitutions caused much friction between the settlers and the proprietors. Even though the hereditary nature of leetmen was discarded in 1698, the popular assembly never accepted the revised Constitutions. By the opening years of the eighteenth century, the baronies which had been taken up ceased to exist, having become simply estates or farms, none of which enjoyed the anticipated array of tenants.

Thus in those areas where an attempt was made to perpetuate the social system of Europe, it was frustrated almost from the beginning. Quite early in the colonial period, great disparities of wealth appeared in the agricultural South, as elsewhere, but this was stratification resting initially and finally upon wealth, not upon honorific or hereditary conceptions derived from Europe. As such, the upper class in America was one into which others might move when they had acquired the requisite wealth. And so long as wealth accumulation was open to all, the class structure would be correspondingly flexible.

In New England there was no experimentation with feudal or manorial trappings at all. The early history of that region is a deliberate repudiation of European social as well as religious practices. As early as 1623, for example, William Bradford wrote that communal property arrangements had failed in Plymouth and that as a consequence the governing officials divided the land on an individual basis. Individual ownership of land, so typical of American land tenure ever since, was thus symbolically begun. The larger colony of Massachusetts Bay, in its first codification of laws, the Body of Liberties of 1641, made explicit its departure from feudal and manorial incidents upon landholding. "All our lands and heritages shall be free from all fines and licenses upon Alienations, and from all hariotts, wardships, Liveries, Primerseisins, yeare day and wast, Escheates and forfeitures. . . ."

The failure of America to inherit a feudal aristocracy carried implications for the future which transcended the mere matter of land tenure. The very character of the society was affected. As we have seen already, it meant that wealth, rather than family or tradition, would be the primary determinant of social stratification. Furthermore, the absence of a feudal past in America has meant that there are no classes which have a vested interest in the social forms of an earlier age. American society, as a consequence, has never split into perpetually warring camps of reactionaries and radicals in the way, for example, French society has been riven ever since the Great Revolution. Moreover, without a feudal past America offers only the thinnest of soils into which a conservatism of the European variety can sink its roots. Almost all Americans, regardless of class, have shared a common ideology of

Lockean or Whig liberalism. The so-called conservatives of the American past have been only more cautious liberals. There has been in America no widely held tradition analogous to the conservatism of Edmund Burke. Burke's considerable doubts about the hopefulness of progress, the efficacy of reason, and the value of revolution have found few sympathetic ears in America. Only some ante-bellum Southerners like Thomas Dew and George Fitzhugh showed any signs of a Burkean conservative outlook. And those murmurings were killed off with the end of slavery. The conservativism of a Senator Barry Goldwater today is really only a species of nineteenth-century liberalism, as his emphasis upon laissez faire and individualism makes clear.

There are economic as well as political consequences which flow from the fact that America was born free of the medieval tradition of aristocracy. These are seen in purest form if we contrast the attitudes of French and American businessmen of today. (It is not so true of Englishmen because participation in trade never carried the taint it did in France.) Recruitment into management has often been hampered in France, John Sawyer has shown, because of the tradition of family enterprises. Businesses, as a result, were confined to a limited group of potential entrepreneurs and managers, "much like hereditary fiefs." Instead of being able to draw upon the population at large for the best men available, French business enterprises have often been handicapped by adherence to a feudal-like familism. Moreover, a feudally derived aristocratic disdain for trade and business still permeates French thought. As a consequence, the French businessman, unlike the American, is beset by a nagging feeling that success in business carries little prestige, and is perhaps a sign of unfashionable materialism. Hence he does not drive to expand his business or to make a lot of money; he is satisfied with a comfortable, gentlemanly living. As Sawyer concluded, "the French businessman has *himself* been unable to slough off the anti-capitalist sentiment in his social inheritance." Devoid of such an inheritance, America was also free of such inhibitory attitudes; from the beginning, to paraphrase a President of the United States, the main business of America has been business.

In place of medieval and aristocratic notions about the degrading nature of trade and business, seventeenth-century Englishmen brought to America two forms of that bourgeois spirit which Max Weber has called the Protestant ethic: Puritanism and Quakerism. It is possible to overemphasize the extent to which Puritanism departed from medieval conceptions of a just price, prohibitions on interest, and so forth, for such restrictions on unfettered capitalism also formed a part of Puritan economic practice in Massachusetts. But the general loosening of economic restraints which Puritanism unquestionably condoned, and its strong accent on work and wealth accumulation, bestowed religious sanction upon business enterprise. The backward-looking and forward-looking economic attitudes of Puritanism are both apparent in a Massachusetts statute of 1633. The first part of the law, in keeping with medieval practices, prescribed the proper wages for bricklayers, wheelwrights, and other skilled craftsmen, while the second part of the statute ordered "that noe person, hawseholder or other, shall spend his time idely or unprofflably, under paine of such punishment as the Court shall thinke meet to inflicte. . . ." The close connection the Puritans saw between godliness and worldly success is implied in a story told by Governor Winthrop in his *History*. The story concerns one Mansfield who arrived in Massachusetts poor but "godly." With the help of a local rich man, "this Mansfield grew suddenly rich, and then lost his godliness, and his wealth soon after."

The calling or occupation of a Christian was an important conception in Puritan thought; it also serves as an illuminating instance of the

tight linkage between religion and economics. To the Puritan, a Christian's work was a part of his offering to God. "As soon as ever a man begins to look toward God and the way of his Grace," the Reverend John Cotton taught, "he will not rest til he find out some warrantable calling and employment." No matter what the calling, "though it be but of a day laborer," yet he will make of it what he can, for "God would not have a man receive five talents and gain but two; He would have his best gifts improved to the best advantage." To work hard is to please God. As Cotton Mather, the grandson of Cotton, said at the end of the century, "Would a man *Rise* by his Business? I say, then let him Rise to his Business. . . . Let your *Business* ingross the most of your time."

Important, but often overlooked in the Puritan conception of the calling, was the idea of social obligation. For a calling to be "warrantable," John Cotton emphasized, a Christian "would see that his calling should tend to public good." Moreover, he continued, "we live by faith in our vocations, in that faith, in serving God, serves man, and in serving man, serves God." Cotton Mather at the end of the century put it even more succinctly. One should have a calling "so he may Glorify God by doing Good for *Others*, and getting of *Good* for himself." It was this cementing of social conscience to thoroughgoing individualism which saved Puritanism from degenerating into a mere defense of economic exploitation.

If the earliest New England divines, like John Cotton, had some doubts about the trader because—as the medieval schoolmen had contended—he bought cheap and sold dear, later Puritans easily accepted the new economic order. Cotton Mather, in good Calvinist fashion, argued that there "is every sort of law, except the Popish, to justify a regulated *usury*. 'Tis justified by the law of necessity and utility; humane society, as now circumstanced, would sink, if all *usury* were impracticable." By the end of the century the bulging warehouses, the numerous ships in Boston Harbor, and the well-appointed mansions of the merchants bore ample testimony to the compatibility of Puritanism and wealth-getting.

Widely recognized as the dominance of Puritan economic ideals may be in New England, it is less often acknowledged that the thriving commercial center of Philadelphia owed much of its drive to a similar ethic among the Quakers. It was William Penn, not John Winthrop, who advised his children to "cast up your income and live on half; if you can, one third; reserving the rest for casualties, charities portions." Simple living, as the bewigged Cotton Mather reminds us, was more a trait of Quakers in the seventeenth and eighteenth century than of Puritans. Indeed, so concerned were the Friends over the vices of ostentation and vanity that they would not permit portraits to be painted of themselves. The only concessions to the ego were black silhouettes. "Be plain in clothes, furniture and food, but clean," William Penn told his children, "and the coarser the better; the rest is folly and a snare." Furthermore, he counseled, diligence "is the Way to Wealth: *the diligent Hand makes Rich. . . . Frugality* is a Virtue too, and not of little Use in Life, the better Way to be Rich, for it has less Toil and Temptation."

As early as the seventeenth century, "the legend of the Quaker as Businessman" was widely accepted. This view, which was very close to the truth, pictured the Friends as shrewd, canny traders, "singularly industrious, sparing no Labour or Pains to increase their Wealth," as one seventeenth-century observer put it. Much like the Puritans, the Quakers were eminently successful in the counting-house, preaching and practicing that doctrine of the calling which united religion and bourgeois economic virtues in happy and fruitful marriage.

As New Englanders fanned out into the upper Middle West in the late eighteenth and early nineteenth centuries, the seed of Puritan-

At left, Puritan women in Sunday dress. As Degler points out, Puritan dress was not drab and severe, but was rather "in the English Renaissance style." Puritan ladies like those above wore masks to protect their faces from the sun and wind, and wore chicken skin gloves in bed to keep their hands white. (Reproduced from Hollar, Ornatus Muliebris Anglicanus, *1640.) At right, Southern planters in the colonial period ordered their Sunday clothes from London. If they were Anglicans (that is, members of the Church of England), they looked like the sartorial figure above. (Reproduced from Pugh,* London, *vol. IV, 1807.)*

ism, now stripped of its theological skin, was planted across America. Furthermore, if one recognizes that the doctrine of the calling was Calvinist before it was Puritan, then the numbers of people imbibing that economic precept with their religious milk swells to impressive proportions. At the time of the Revolution, Ralph Barton Perry has calculated, one out of every two white Americans was a Calvinist of some persuasion.

Though no longer clothed in theological vestments, the virtue of work and wealth has remained with Americans. As Max Weber pointed out, the advice of Franklin's Poor Richard is but the Puritan ethic shorn of its theology; in Franklin the Puritan has become the Yankee. No longer anxious about unearthly salvation, but keenly concerned about a good bargain, the American still carries the telltale brand of Puritanism.

2. Were the Puritans "Puritanical"?

To most Americans—and to most Europeans, for that matter—the core of the Puritan social heritage has been summed up in Macaulay's well-known witticism that the Puritans prohibited bearbaiting not because of torture to the bear, but because of the pleasure it afforded the spectators. And as late as 1925, H. L. Mencken defined Puritanism as "the haunting fear that someone, somewhere, may be happy." Before this chapter is out, much will be said about the somber and even grim nature of the Puritan view of life, but quips like those of Macaulay and Mencken distort rather than illumine the essential character of the Puritans. Simply because the word "Puritan" has become encrusted with a good many barnacles, it is worth while to try to scrape them off if we wish to gain an understanding of the Puritan heritage. Though this process is essentially a negative one, sometimes it is clarifying to set forth what an influence is *not* as well as what it is.

Fundamental to any appreciation of the Puritan mind on matters of pleasure must be the recognition that the typical, godly Puritan was a worker in the world. Puritanism, like Protestantism in general, resolutely and definitely rejected the ascetic and monastic ideals of medieval Catholicism. Pleasures of the body were not to be eschewed by the Puritan, for, as Calvin reasoned, God "intended to provide not only for our necessity, but likewise for our pleasure and delight." It is obvious, he wrote in his famous *Institutes*, that "the Lord have endowed flowers with such beauty . . . with such sweetness of smell" in order to impress our senses; therefore, to enjoy them is not contrary to God's intentions. "In a word," he concluded, "hath He not made many things worthy of our estimation independent of any necessary use?"

It was against excess of enjoyment that the Puritans cautioned and legislated. "The wine is

from God," Increase Mather warned, "but the Drunkard is from the Devil." The Cambridge Platform of the Church of 1680 prohibited games of cards or dice because of the amount of time they consumed and the encouragement they offered to idleness, but the ministers of Boston in 1699 found no difficulty in condoning public lotteries. They were like a public tax, the ministers said, since they took only what the "government might have demanded, with a more *general imposition* . . . and it employes for the welfare of the publick, all that is raised by the *lottery*." Though Cotton Mather at the end of the century condemned mixed dancing, he did not object to dancing as such; and his grandfather, John Cotton, at the beginning saw little to object to in dancing between the sexes so long as it did not become lascivious. It was this same John Cotton, incidentally, who successfully contended against Roger Williams' argument that women should wear veils in church.

In matters of dress, it is true that the Massachusetts colony endeavored to restrict the wearing of "some new and immodest fashions" that were coming in from England, but often these efforts were frustrated by the pillars of the church themselves. Winthrop reported in his *History*, for example, that though the General Court instructed the elders of the various churches to reduce the ostentation in dress by "urging it upon the consciences of their people," little change was effected, "for divers of the elders' wives, etc., were in some measure partners in this general disorder."

We also know now that Puritan dress—not that made "historical" by Saint-Gaudens' celebrated statue—was the opposite of severe, being rather in the English Renaissance style. Most restrictions on dress that were imposed were for purposes of class differentiation rather than for ascetic reasons. Thus long hair was acceptable on an upper-class Puritan like Cromwell or Winthrop, but on the head of a person of lower social status it was a sign of

vanity. In 1651 the legislature of Massachusetts called attention to that "excess in Apparell" which has "crept in upon us, and especially amongst people of mean condition, to the dishonor of God, the scandall of our profession, the consumption of Estates, and altogether unsuitable to our poverty." The law declared "our utter detestation and dislike, that men or women of mean condition, should take upon them the garb of Gentlemen, by wearing Gold or Silver Lace, or Buttons, or Points at their knees, or to walk in great Boots; or Women of the same rank to wear Silk or Tiffany hoods, or Scarfes, which tho allowable to persons of greater Estates, or more liberal education, is intolerable in people of low condition." By implication, this law affords a clear description of what the well-dressed Puritan of good estate would wear.

If the Puritans are to be saved from the canard of severity of dress, it is also worth while to soften the charge that they were opposed to music and art. It is perfectly true that the Puritans insisted that organs be removed from the churches and that in England some church organs were smashed by zealots. But it was not music or organs as such which they opposed, only music in the meetinghouse. Well-known American and English Puritans, like Samuel Sewell, John Milton, and Cromwell, were sincere lovers of music. Moreover, it should be remembered that it was under Puritan rule that opera was introduced into England—and without protest, either. The first English dramatic production entirely in music —*The Siege of Rhodes*—was presented in 1656, four years before the Restoration. Just before the end of Puritan rule, John Evelyn noted in his diary that he went "to see a new opera, after the Italian way, in recitative music and scenes. . . ." Furthermore, as Percy Scholes points out, in all the voluminous contemporary literature attacking the Puritans for every conceivable narrow-mindedness, none asserts that they opposed music, so long as it was performed outside the church.

The weight of the evidence is much the same in the realm of art. Though King Charles' art collection was dispersed by the incoming Commonwealth, it is significant that Cromwell and other Puritans bought several of the items. We also know that the Protector's garden at Hampton Court was beautified by nude statues. Furthermore, it is now possible to say that the Puritan closing of the theaters was as much a matter of objection to their degenerate lewdness by the 1640's as an objection to the drama as such. As far as American Puritans are concerned, it is not possible to say very much about their interest in art since there was so little in the seventeenth century. At least it can be said that the Puritans, unlike the Quakers, had no objection to portrait painting.

Some modern writers have professed to find in Puritanism, particularly the New England brand, evidence of sexual repression and inhibition. Though it would certainly be false to suggest that the Puritans did not subscribe to the canon of simple chastity, it is equally erroneous to think that their sexual lives were crabbed or that sex was abhorrent to them. Marriage to the Puritan was something more than an alternative to "burning," as the Pauline doctrine of the Catholic Church would have it. Marriage was enjoined upon the righteous Christian; celibacy was not a sign of merit. With unconcealed disapprobation, John Cotton told a recently married couple the story of a pair "who immediately upon marriage, without ever approaching the *Nuptial* Bed," agreed to live apart from the rest of the world, "and afterwards from one another, too. . . ." But, Cotton advised, such behavior was "no other than an effort of blind zeal, for they are the dictates of a blind mind they follow therein and not of the Holy Spirit which saith, *It is not good that man should be alone.*" Cotton set himself against not only Catholic asceticism but also the view that women were the "unclean vessel," the tempters of men. Women,

rather than being "a necessary Evil are a necessary Good," he wrote. "Without them there is no comfortable Living for Man. . . ."

Because, as another divine said, "the Use of the Marriage Bed" is "founded in man's Nature" the realistic Puritans required that married men unaccompanied by wives should leave the colony or bring their wives over forthwith. The Puritan settlements encouraged marriages satisfactory to the participants by permitting divorces for those whose spouses were impotent, too long absent, or cruel. Indeed, the divorce laws of New England were the easiest in Christendom at a time when the eloquence of a Milton was unable to loosen the bonds of matrimony in England.

Samuel Eliot Morison in his history of Harvard has collected a number of examples of the healthy interest of Puritan boys in the opposite sex. Commonplace books, for example, indicate that Herrick's poem beginning "Gather ye rosebuds while ye may" and amorous lines from Shakespeare, as well as more erotic and even scatological verse, were esteemed by young Puritan men. For a gentleman to present his affianced with a pair of garters, one letter of a Harvard graduate tells us, was considered neither immoral nor improper.

It is also difficult to reconcile the usual view of the stuffiness of Puritans with the literally hundreds of confessions to premarital sexual relations in the extant church records. It should be understood, moreover, that these confessions were made by the saints or saints-to-be, not by the unregenerate. That the common practice of the congregation was to accept such sinners into church membership without further punishment is in itself revealing. The civil law, it is true, punished such transgressions when detected among the regenerate or among the nonchurch members, but this was also true of contemporary non-Puritan Virginia. "It will be seen," writes historian Philip A. Bruce regarding Virginia, "from the various instances given relating to the profanation of Sunday, drunkenness, swearing, defamation, and sexual immorality, that, not only were the grand juries and vestries extremely vigilant in reporting these offences, but the courts were equally prompt in inflicting punishment; and that the penalty ranged from a heavy fine to a shameful exposure in the stocks . . . and from such an exposure to a very severe flogging at the county whipping post." In short, strict moral surveillance by the public authorities was a seventeenth-century rather than a Puritan attitude.

Relations between the sexes in Puritan society were often much more loving and tender than the mythmakers would have us believe. Since it was the Puritan view that marriage was eminently desirable in the sight of God and man, it is not difficult to find evidence of deep and abiding love between a husband and wife. John Cotton, it is true, sometimes used the Biblical phrase "comfortable yoke mate" in addressing his wife, but other Puritan husbands come closer to our romantic conventions. Certainly John Winthrop's letters to his beloved Margaret indicate the depth of attachment of which the good Puritan was capable. "My good wife . . . My sweet wife," he called her. Anticipating his return home, he writes, "So . . . we shall now enjoy each other again, as we desire. . . . It is now bed time; but I must lie alone; therefore I make less haste. Yet I must kiss my sweet wife; and so, with my blessing to our children . . . I commend thee to the grace and blessing of the lord, and rest. . . ."

Anne Bradstreet wrote a number of poems devoted to her love for her husband in which the sentiments and figures are distinctly romantic.

To my Dear and loving Husband
I prize thy love more than whole Mines of
    gold
Or all the riches that the East doth hold.
My love is such that Rivers cannot quench,
Nor aught but love from thee give recom-
    pense.

In another poem her spouse is apostrophized as

> My head, my heart, mine Eyes, my life, nay
>   more
> My joy, my Magazine of earthly store

and she asks:

> If two be one, as surely thou and I,
> How stayest thou there, whilst I at Ipswich
>   lye?

Addressing John as "my most sweet Husband," Margaret Winthrop perhaps epitomized the Puritan marital ideal when she wrote, "I have many reasons to make me love thee, whereof I will name two: First, because thou lovest God and, secondly, because thou lovest me. If these two were wanting," she added, "all the rest would be eclipsed."

It would be a mistake, however, to try to make these serious, dedicated men and women into rakes of the Renaissance. They were sober if human folk, deeply concerned about their ultimate salvation and intent upon living up to God's commands as they understood them, despite their acknowledgment of complete depravity and unworthiness. "God sent you not into this world as a Play-House, but a Work-house," one minister told his congregation. To the Puritan this was a world drenched in evil, and, because it truly is, they were essentially realistic in their judgments. Because the Puritan expected nothing, Perry Miller has remarked, a disillusioned one was almost impossible to find. This is probably an exaggeration, for they were also human beings; when the Commonwealth fell, it was a Puritan, after all, who said, "God has spit in our faces." But Professor Miller's generalization has much truth in it. Only a man convinced of the inevitable and eternal character of evil could fight it so hard and so unceasingly.

The Puritan at his best, Ralph Barton Perry has said, was a "moral athlete." More than most men, the Puritan strove with himself and with his fellow man to attain a moral standard higher than was rightfully to be expected of so depraved a creature. Hence the diaries and autobiographies of Puritans are filled with the most torturous probing of the soul and inward seeking. Convinced of the utter desirability of salvation on the one hand, and equally cognizant of the total depravity of man's nature on the other, the Puritan was caught in an impossible dilemma which permitted him no rest short of the grave. Yet with such a spring coiled within him, the Puritan drove himself and his society to tremendous heights of achievement both material and spiritual.

Such intense concern for the actualization of the will of God had a less pleasant side to it, also. If the belief that "I am my brother's keeper" is the breeding ground of heightened social conscience and expresses itself in the reform movements so indigenous to Boston and its environs, it also could and did lead to self-righteousness, intolerance and narrow-mindedness, as exemplified in another product of Boston: Anthony Comstock. But this fruit of the loins of Puritanism is less typical of the earthy seventeenth-century New Englander than H. L. Mencken would have us think. The Sabbatarian, antiliquor, and antisex attitudes usually attributed to the Puritans are a nineteenth-century addition to the much more moderate and essentially wholesome view of life's evils held by the early settlers of New England.

To realize how different Puritans could be, one needs only to contrast Roger Williams and his unwearying opponent John Cotton. But despite the range of differences among Puritans, they all were linked by at least one characteristic. That was their belief in themselves, in their morality and in their mission to the world. For this reason, Puritanism was intellectual and social dynamite in the seventeenth century; its power disrupted churches, defied tyrants, overthrew governments, and beheaded kings.

The Reformation laid an awesome burden on the souls of those who broke with the Roman

Church. Proclaiming the priesthood of all believers, Protestantism made each man's relationship to God his own terrifying responsibility. No one else could save him; therefore no one must presume to try. More concerned about his salvation than about any mundane matter, the Puritan was compelled, for the sake of his immortal soul, to be a fearless individualist.

It was the force of this conviction which produced the Great Migration of 1630–40 and made Massachusetts a flourishing colony in the span of a decade. It was also, ironically, the force which impelled Roger Williams to threaten the very legal and social foundations of the Puritan Commonwealth in Massachusetts because he thought the oligarchy wrong and himself right. And so it would always be. For try as the rulers of Massachusetts might to make men conform to their dogma, their own rebellious example always stood as a guide to those who felt the truth was being denied. Such individualism, we would call it today, was flesh and bone of the religion which the Puritans passed on. Though the theocracy soon withered and died, its harsh voice softened down to the balmy breath of Unitarianism, the belief in self and the dogged resistance to suppression or untruth which Puritanism taught never died. Insofar as Americans today can be said to be individualistic, it is to the Puritan heritage that we must look for one of the principal sources.

In his ceaseless striving for signs of salvation and knowledge of God's intentions for man, the Puritan placed great reliance upon the human intellect, even though for him, as for all Christians, faith was the bedrock of his belief. "Faith doth not relinquish or cast out reason," wrote the American Puritan Samuel Willard, "for there is nothing in Religion contrary to it, tho' there are many things that do transcend and must captivate it." Richard Baxter, the English Puritan, insisted that "the *most Religious*, are the *most* truly, and *nobly rational*." Religion and reason were complementary to the Puritan, not antithetical as they were to many evangelical sects of the time.

Always the mere emotion of religion was to be controlled by reason. Because of this, the university-trained Puritan clergy prided themselves on the lucidity and rationality of their sermons. Almost rigorously their sermons followed the logical sequence of "doctrine," "reasons," and "uses." Conscientiously they shunned the meandering and rhetorical flourishes so beloved by Laudian preachers like John Donne, and in the process facilitated the taking of notes by their eager listeners. One of the unforgivable crimes of Mistress Anne Hutchinson was her assertion that one could "feel" one's salvation, that one was "filled with God" after conversion, that it was unnecessary, in order to be saved, to be learned in the Bible or in the Puritan writers. It was not that the Puritans were cold to the Word—far from it. A saint was required to testify to an intense religious experience—almost by definition emotional in character—before he could attain full membership in the Church. But it was always important to the Puritans that mere emotion—whether it be the anarchistic activities of the Anabaptists or the quaking of the Friends—should not be mistaken for righteousness or proper religious conduct. Here, as in so many things, the Puritans attempted to walk the middle path—in this instance, between the excessive legalism and formalism of the Catholics and Episcopalians and the flaming, intuitive evangelism of the Baptists and Quakers.

Convinced of reason's great worth, it was natural that the Puritans should also value education. "Ignorance is the mother (not of Devotion but) of Heresy," one Puritan divine declared. And a remarkably well-educated ministry testified to the Puritan belief that learning and scholarship were necessary for a proper understanding of the Word of God. More than a hundred graduates of Cambridge and Oxford Universities settled in New England before 1640, most of them ministers. At

the same date not five men in all of Virginia could lay claim to such an educational background. Since Cambridge University, situated on the edge of Puritan East Anglia, supplied most of the graduates in America, it was natural that Newtown, the site of New England's own college, would soon be renamed in honor of the Alma Mater. "After God had carried us safe to New-England," said a well-known tract, some of its words were immortalized in metal in Harvard Yard, "one of the next things we longed and looked after, was to advance learning, and perpetuate it to posterity; dreading to leave an illiterate ministry to the churches, when the present ministers shall lie in the dust." "The College," founded in 1636, soon to be named Harvard, was destined to remain the only institution of higher learning in America during almost all the years of the seventeenth century. Though it attracted students from as far away as Virginia, it remained, as it began, the fountainhead of Puritan learning in the New World.

Doubt as one may Samuel Eliot Morison's claims for the secular origins of Harvard, his evidence of the typically Renaissance secular education which was available at the Puritan college in New England is both impressive and convincing. The Latin and Greek secular writers of antiquity dominated the curriculum, for this was a liberal arts training such as the leaders had received at Cambridge in England. To the Puritans the education of ministers could be nothing less than the best learning of the day. So important did education at Harvard seem to the New Haven colony in 1644 that the legislature ordered each town to appoint two men to be responsible for the collection of contributions from each family for "the mayntenaunce of scolars at Cambridge. . . ."

If there was to be a college, preparatory schools had to be provided for the training of those who were expected to enter the university. Furthermore, in a society dedicated to the reading of the Bible, elementary education was indispensable. "It being one chief project of that old deluder Satan to keep men from the knowledge of the Scriptures" began the first school laws of Massachusetts (1647) and Connecticut (1650). But the Puritans supported education for secular as well as religious reasons. The Massachusetts Code of 1648, for instance, required children to be taught to read inasmuch "as the good education of children is of singular behoof and benefit to any Commonwealth."

The early New England school laws provided that each town of fifty families or more was to hire a teacher for the instruction of its young; towns of one hundred families or more were also directed to provide grammar schools, "the master thereof being able to instruct youths so far as they may be fitted for the University." Though parents were not obliged to send their children to these schools, if they did not they were required to teach their children to read. From the evidence of court cases and the high level of literacy in seventeenth-century New England, it would appear that these first attempts at public-supported and public-controlled education were both enforced and fruitful.

No other colony in the seventeenth century imposed such a high educational standard upon its simple farming people as the Puritans did. It is true, of course, that Old England in this period could boast of grammar schools, some of which were free. But primary schools were almost nonexistent there, and toward the end of the seventeenth century the free schools in England became increasingly tuition schools. Moreover, it was not until well into the nineteenth century that the English government did anything to support schools. Primary and secondary education in England, in contrast with the New England example, was a private or church affair.

Unlike the Puritans, the Quakers exhibited little impulse toward popular education in the seventeenth and early eighteenth centuries. Be-

cause of their accent on the Inner Light and the doctrine of universal salvation, the religious motivation of the Puritans for learning was wanting. Furthermore, the Quakers did not look to education, as such, with the same reverence as the Puritans. William Penn, for example, advised his children that "reading many books is but a taking off the mind too much from meditation." No Puritan would have said that.

Virginia in the seventeenth century, it should be said, was also interested in education. Several times in the course of the century, plans were well advanced for establishing a university in the colony. Free schools also existed in Virginia during the seventeenth century, though the lack of village communities made them inaccessible for any great numbers of children. But, in contrast with New England, there were no publicly supported schools in Virginia; the funds for the field schools of Virginia, like those for free schools in contemporary England, came from private or ecclesiastical endowment. Nor was Virginia able to bring its several plans for a college into reality until William and Mary was founded at the very end of the century.

Though the line which runs from the early New England schools to the distinctly American system of free public schools today is not always progressively upward or uniformly clear, the connection is undeniable. The Puritan innovation of public support and control on a local level was the American prototype of a proper system of popular education.

American higher education in particular owes much to religion, for out of the various churches' concern for their faiths sprang a number of colleges, after the example of the Puritans' founding of Harvard. At the time of the Revolution, there were eight colleges besides Harvard in the English colonies, of which all but one were founded under the auspices of a church. William and Mary (1693) and King's College, later Columbia (1754), were the work of the Episcopalians; Yale (1701) and Dartmouth (1769) were set up by orthodox Congregationalists dissatisfied with Harvard; the College of New Jersey, later Princeton (1747), was founded by the Presbyterians; Queens College, later Rutgers (1766), by the Dutch Reformed Church; the College of Rhode Island, later Brown (1764), by the Baptists. Only the Academy of Philadelphia, later the University of Pennsylvania (1749), was secular in origin.

The overwhelming importance of the churches in the expansion of American higher education during the colonial period set a pattern which continued well into the nineteenth century and to a limited extent is still followed. Well-known colleges like Oberlin, Wesleyan, Haverford, Wittenberg, Moravian, Muhlenberg, and Notre Dame were all founded by churches in the years before the Civil War. By providing a large number of colleges (recall that England did not enjoy a third university until the nineteenth century), the religious impulses and diversity of the American people very early encouraged that peculiarly American faith in the efficacy and desirability of education for all.

When dwelling on the seminal qualities of the seventeenth century, it is tempting to locate the source of the later American doctrine of the separation of Church and State and religious freedom in the writings of Roger Williams and in the practices of provinces like New York, Maryland and Pennsylvania. Actually, however, such a line of development is illusory. At the time of the Revolution all the colonies, including Rhode Island, imposed restrictions and disabilities upon some sects, thus practicing at best only a limited form of toleration, not freedom of religion—much less separation of Church and State. Moreover, Roger Williams' cogent and prophetic arguments in behalf of religious freedom were forgotten in the eighteenth century; they could not exert any influence on those who finally worked out the doctrine of religious freedom enshrined in the

national Constitution. In any case, it would have been exceedingly difficult for Williams to have spoken to Jefferson and the other Virginians who fought for religious freedom. To Williams the Puritan, the great justification for freedom of religion was the preservation of the purity of the Church; to the deistic Virginians, the important goal was the removal of a religious threat to the purity and freedom of the State.

3. Rights of Englishmen

For one who cherishes American political institutions, the manner in which representative government began in the seventeenth century might well make him shudder as well as wonder. The process was largely "accidental," arbitrary and hardly to be anticipated from the nature of things. This is especially true of Virginia, where the whole precedent of self-government in America was first worked out. When in 1619 the Virginia Company suggested that the colonists "might have a hande in the governinge of themselves," there was, as Charles Andrews has pointed out, "no sufficient reason, legal or other, why a popular assembly should be set up in Virginia." It was all that casual.

The precarious existence of this first representative assembly in America was emphasized in 1624, when the Crown, for various reasons, revoked the Company's charter, the King declaring that "the Government of the Colonies of Virginia shall immediately depend upon Our Selfe." Thus was terminated the legal authority for an assembly. Three times between 1625 and 1629 the planters held "conventions" for specific purposes, but these were neither regular nor legitimate assemblies. Beginning in 1630, however, and each year thereafter, without any encouragement from the Crown, the Virginians held an Assembly and presumed to legislate. Interestingly enough, in the light of the later Revolution, among their earliest laws was a prohibition upon the Governor and the Council—both of whom were appointed by the Crown—to "lay any taxes or impositions, upon the colony, theire land or commodities, otherwise then [sic] by the authoritie of the Grand Assembly." The legal authority for the Assembly, however, was still in doubt, for the King had not assented to its existence, and no one disputed his final and complete authority. Then in 1637 the royal instructions to the Governor contained a call for an Assembly, but the failure to provide for annual sessions indicated that the Crown was still undecided on the matter. Finally, the Governor's instructions in 1639 made it clear that the King had responded favorably to the colony's persistent requests for a continuing representative assembly.

The importance of this decision as a precedent can hardly be exaggerated. Virginia was the first English settlement to fall under the direct control of the Crown, and its forms of government could not fail to influence, if not determine, those of subsequent royal colonies —and, it should be remembered, in time all but four of the thirteen colonies would be royal.

The evolution of Massachusetts' government was somewhat different; the fact that the charter was brought with the settlers insured that events in America would be the determining factors. The narrow limits of the charter, which was intended for the running of a corporation, not a community, came under attack in the first year, when over a hundred settlers applied for the rights of freemen. At that point the decision was made to open the coveted rank to "such as are members of some of the churches within the lymitts of" the colony. This broadening of the franchise signalized the transformation of the corporation into a true commonwealth, composed of citizens with rights and duties. In practice, confining citizenship to church members was not as restrictive as might at first be supposed, for this was, after all, a Puritan venture. There were towns like Roxbury in 1638—

40, for example, which consisted of sixty-nine householders, of whom fifty-nine were church members and voters.

For the first four years Massachusetts was governed by the magistrates, who, in turn, were elected by the whole body of freemen; there being no representative assembly, the magistrates made the laws. It is more than coincidental, however, that at about the same time the Virginia Assembly was putting itself on record as opposing taxation by the executive, a similar remonstrance was afoot in Massachusetts. Early in 1632, Winthrop tells us, a group of ministers and elders of Watertown "delivered their opinion, that it was not safe to pay moneys" levied upon the people by the Governor and the assistants, "for fear of bringing themselves and posterity into bondage." The coincidence, of course, is not accidental, for it simply underscores the common English origins of the two widely separated colonies. For centuries Englishmen had jealously guarded their right to levy their taxes locally; they continued to do so in the New World. Moreover, in the first part of the seventeenth century the issue of taxation and representative government was before the eyes of the whole nation as King and Parliament carried on their struggle for supremacy. It was to be expected that history and current events would both be reflected in the two English colonies in America.

As the number of settlers in Massachusetts increased, thereby rendering it more and more difficult for all freemen to meet together, it became necessary either to abandon the meeting of freemen, a step which men like Governor Winthrop apparently urged, or else to elect deputies or proxies who would act for the general body of freemen. At the insistence of the freemen, the latter method was accepted at the same time that it was agreed that taxes would be levied only by the legislature. Thus, in May, 1634, the first representative assembly met in Boston, with each town sending three deputies. It was understood that they "shall

have full power and voice of all and said freemen," except for the election of the magistrates.

The history of constitutional development in both Massachusetts and Virginia makes it quite apparent that the ordinary man's dogged insistence upon self-government in America was perhaps the most important single factor in the establishment of the representative government we esteem today. Even an opponent of popular government, John Winthrop, expressed grudging admiration for the people's ingenious if illogical pursuit of their own governance. Noting their appeal to the patent or charter in a recent dispute with the magistrates, Winthrop wryly commented that it "may be observed how strictly the people would seem to stick to their patent, where they think it makes for their advantage, but are content to decline it, where it will not warrant such liberties as they have taken up without warrant from thence."

If representative government can be said to have triumphed in the seventeenth century, it can also be said that the idea of democracy, defined as government by the consent of all the governed, was born in that century. The line to the present, however, is more tenuous, the traces fainter; not until the nineteenth century was democracy in full flower. But the beginnings of the democratic idea are already to be found in the Puritans' conception of the covenant. The idea of an agreement between the ruler and the ruled as the basis for government was very well understood in seventeenth-century Protestant America, not only because of the contemporary theological use of it, but because the extensive and close reading of the Bible among all classes made the idea common coin. The covenants with Adam, with Noah, and with Abraham were well-known Biblical agreements between God and men. Only by the agreement of all concerned, read the Cambridge Church Platform of 1648, could "we see . . . how members can have Church-power over one another mutually." It was natural that this

religious or Biblical example should be extended to civil affairs, especially in a new land where the usual sanctions for government were wanting. Thomas Hooker of Connecticut fame, for example, applied the covenant idea directly to government when he wrote, "there must of necessity be a mutual agreement . . . before, by any rule of God," men "have any right or power, or can exercise either, each toward the other."

Since the Church, according to Puritan thought, could be brought into existence only by the action of the whole membership, and the minister was called and ordained by the congregation, it was hardly to be expected that the state would long remain outside such popular participation. It was this germ of democracy which never ceased to ferment within the hard shell of Puritan government. In a very real sense, Puritanism, with its doctrines of individualism and the covenant, contained the seeds of its own destruction as an authoritarian government.

"Nothing is more striking to a European traveler in the United States than the absence of what we term the government, or the administration," wrote Alexis de Tocqueville after his tour of the United States in the 1830's. "Written laws exist in America, and one sees the daily execution of them; but although everything moves regularly, the mover can nowhere be discovered." The reason for this, Tocqueville concluded, was the great importance and strength of local government in America. Over a century later local self-rule still means much to Americans, as the appeals to its principles by modern conservatives and opponents of centralized government make evident.

It is not to be doubted that the strength of local government in America derives from the English heritage of the first settlers. Immigrants brought with them a long experience in local self-rule in the shires and towns of old England. But the distribution of the two primary forms of local government in the United States—the town of New England and the county of Virginia—is largely the result of geography and the motivations of the people who settled in the two sections of English America. When the Puritans landed in Massachusetts, they laid out their settlements in a form that best secured the object of their coming—that is, the practice of their religion. Instead of the spreading out over the land in individual farms—a procedure which would have hampered church attendance and hindered control over the religious and moral life of the people—the seventeenth-century settlements took the shape of compact villages, with the farming land stretching around the periphery. Though such a nucleated village was similar to those in England and on the Continent, the fact that settlers in Virginia evolved a much different scheme of settlement makes it clear that religious and social aims, not the European inheritance, were the controlling factors.

The Englishmen who settled in Virginia, once the dangers of Indian attacks and starvation had been surmounted, spread themselves out on individual farms, forsaking the village settlement so familiar to many of them in England. (It is true that in the western part of England, especially in Devon, whence some settlers came to Virginia, separate farmsteads were well known, but even there the nucleated village was common.) The settlers in Virginia quickly found that large plantations situated along the great rivers of the tidewater were best suited to the growing of tobacco. These widely separated plantations became so typical of the colony that by the end of the century Virginian historian Robert Beverley was regretting they had ever gotten started. "This Liberty of taking up Land and the Ambition each Man had of being Lord of a vast, tho' unimproved Territory, together with the Advantage of many Rivers, which afforded a commodious Road for shipping at every Man's Door, has made the Country fall into . . . an unhappy Settlement

and course of Trade." As a result, he continued, "to this Day they have not any one place of Cohabitation among them, that may reasonably bear the Name of a Town."

The forms of local government adopted in both Virginia and New England reflected the configuration of the settlements. With population spread thin by the centrifugal forces of geography and economy, the county, with its sheriffs, justices of the peace, and county court, all inherited from England, became the Virginian, and by extension, the southern form of local government. In New England, geographical forces were largely neutral—there were no navigable rivers to encourage the spreading out of population—while religion acted as a powerful cohesive force. Though as early as 1650 a Connecticut law spoke of the "great abuse of buying and purchasing home lots and laying them together, by means, whereof great depopulations are like to follow," the village or town, clustering around the all-important meetinghouse, was the typical New England form of local government, with town meeting and selectmen.

Since the church was self-governing in New England, it was to be anticipated that the town meeting, which was in some seventeenth-century towns indistinguishable in membership from the church, should be also. Indeed, it might be said with justice that the town meeting, so peculiar to New England and so remarkable to Tocqueville, was the natural offspring of the religion and geography of New England. In practice the town meeting was one of the most democratic features of seventeenth-century life. All residents of the Massachusetts town, whether they were church members or not, could speak at meeting, though before 1647 only "saints" could vote. After that date and at the instance of the freemen, it was provided that all male residents over twenty-three could vote, be elected to town offices, and serve on juries, regardless of church membership. Recent investigations make it clear that all

through the Puritan era most men in Massachusetts could participate in town government if they wished to. The New England town was truly a training ground for responsible and democratic government.

From what has been said up to now regarding the political institutions of the seventeenth-century colonists, it is apparent that they were formative for modern Americans. But the adaptation of English political ways to America, especially the representative assembly, exercised a further influence upon the course of American history. The very rhetoric and framework within which the revolutionary crisis of 1765–76 was carried out stemmed from the political forms which Americans had evolved in the wilderness. Indeed, without this particular development of representative assembly, local government, and political freedom, the Revolution, if it took place at all, would have had different goals and different slogans. For this reason, if for no other, this haphazard, often accidental, transfer of English political ways to America is suffused with a significance which origins otherwise rarely enjoy.

4. Black Men in a White Men's Country

As the germ of the Revolution is to be detected in the political history of the seventeenth century, so the genesis of the Civil War is implicit in its social history. In late August, 1619, said John Rolfe, a Dutch ship dropped off "twenty Negars" at Jamestown. But, contrary to popular history, the American race problem did not begin then. It would be another half century before slavery, as it was to be known later, was clearly established in America. As late as 1671 the Governor of Virginia estimated that Negroes made up less than 5 per cent of the population.

For most of the seventeenth century, Virginia society consisted largely of small, independent, landowning farmers; slave plantations

as they would be known in the eighteenth century were not only few in number but their owners were relatively insignificant politically and socially.

Not until the opening years of the eighteenth century were land-holding yeomanry and indentured servants displaced to any appreciable degree by Negro slaves. Whereas in 1671, 5 per cent of the population was Negro, in 1715 the figure was up to 24 per cent, and by 1756 Negro slaves accounted for over 40 per cent of the population. (By 1724, Negro slaves outnumbered whites more than two to one in South Carolina.) As slavery grew in importance, so did the great planter; by the end of the seventeenth century, the landed squire with his scores of slaves had superseded the sturdy yeoman in the political and social affairs of Virginia. The causes for this sharp shift in class power in the province do not concern us here. The reason for discussing it at all is in order to make clear that for most of the century neither the institution of slavery nor the Negro was an important part of the life of Virginians.

Yet it must be said that slavery and racial discrimination began in the seventeenth century. Over a century ago, that most perspicacious student of America, Alexis de Tocqueville, pointed to slavery as the origin of the American prejudice toward the black man. Contrary to the situation in antiquity, he remarked, "among the moderns the abstract and transient fact of slavery is fatally united with the physical and permanent fact of color." Furthermore, he added, in the North "slavery recedes, but the prejudice to which it has given birth is immovable." More modern historians have also stressed this causal connection between the institution of slavery and the color prejudice of Americans. And it is patent to anyone conversant with the nature of American slavery, especially as it functioned in the nineteenth century, that the impress of bondage upon the character and future of the black man in this country has been deep and enduring.

But if one examines the early history of slavery in the English colonies and the reaction of Englishmen toward black men, it becomes evident that the assumption that slavery is responsible for the low social status of Negroes is open to question. For one thing, the institution of slavery as it was to be delineated in law by the end of the seventeenth century, apparently did not prevail when the first Negroes came to Jamestown. Or at least it did not appear in the statute books of Virginia until 1660. Indeed, it is this late appearance of the status of slavery in law that has led some historians to argue that prior to the 1660's Negroes enjoyed a status equal to that of white indentured servants. To historians of that persuasion slavery was the force that dragged down the Negro to social inferiority and discrimination. Unfortunately for this view, the recent scholarship of Winthrop Jordan concludes that the exact status of Negroes during the first decades in America cannot be known for certain, given the available sources. One reason that the status cannot be surely known is that there is some cause to believe that Negroes were discriminated against long before the institution of slavery appeared in the law. In short, if one is seeking to uncover the roots of racial prejudice and discrimination against the Negro in America, the soundest procedure would be to abandon the idea that slavery was the causal factor. In place of it, one ought to work on the assumption that discrimination preceded slavery and by so doing helped to reinforce it. Under this assumption American race prejudice originated in the discriminatory social atmosphere of the early seventeenth century, long before slavery was written into law. When slavery did appear in the statutes, it could not help but be shaped by the folk bias within which it grew. Thus legal slavery in the English colonies reinforced and helped to perpetuate the discrimination against the black man that had prevailed from the beginning of settlement.

Simply because the Negro differed from the Englishman in a number of ways, it was unlikely that men of the seventeenth century would accord the black man an equal status with Englishmen. Even Irishmen, who were white, Christian, and European, were held to be literally "beyond the Pale," and some were even referred to as "slaves." The African, after all, was a heathen at a time when "Christian" was a title of import. Moreover, he was black and culturally different. As one sixteenth-century English observer of Africans phrased it, "although the people were blacke and naked, yet they were civill." In Shakespeare's play, Brabantio's horror at his daughter's elopement with the black Othello reflects the seventeenth-century Englishman's consciousness of the Negro's differences. "Damned as thou art, thou hast enchanted her," exclaims the outraged father, ignoring the fact of Othello's Christianity. Only in a bewitched state, he argues, would his daughter shun "the wealthy curled darlings of our nation . . . to incur a general mock" and leave her family in order to seek "the sooty bosom of such a thing as thou." Desdemona herself admitted that she perceived the Moor's "visage in his mind"—an acknowledgment that his difference in countenance would have been a serious obstacle to a love less profound than hers. In *Titus Andronicus* Tamora is reviled by Bassianus for loving the Moor Aaron. "Believe me, queen, your swarth Cimerian doth make your honour of his body's hue, spotted, detested and abominable." Why, he asks her, are you wandering in the forest "with a barbarous Moor"?

But a feeling that Englishmen and Negroes were different did not depend upon vague impressions gained from chance or occasional contact with black men or Moors in England. The fact that Negroes arrived in English America as the cargo of the international slave trade unquestionably fostered a sense of superiority among Englishmen. If the noble and commanding Othello could be stigmatized as a "thing," how much more likely it was that degrading terms be applied to those wretches newly spilled out of the slave ships! It was to be anticipated that from the beginning a special inferior position would be assigned black men.

Such, indeed, was the fact even though the Virginia and Maryland records in the years between 1620 and 1660 rarely refer to "slaves" but speak mainly of "Negroes." The failure to use the term slave should not blind us to the real possibility that the status for which it stood was already in being. The legal definition of the inferior status which Englishmen in America—both in New England and in the Chesapeake colonies—were building for Negroes was imprecise in those early years. But that an inferior status was in the process of being worked out seems undoubted. Moreover, the treatment accorded another dark-skinned heathen people, the Indians, offers further evidence that enslavement was early the lot reserved for Negroes. Indian slavery was practiced in all the English settlements almost from the beginning; rarely were any distinctions made between Indians and Negroes when discriminatory legislation was enacted. But let us now turn to the beginnings of slavery in the English colonies.

The colonies of Virginia and New England had ample opportunity to learn of discriminatory practices against Negroes from island settlements of Englishmen like Bermuda and New Providence in the Caribbean. As early as the 1620's and 1630's these colonies provided a discriminatory or outright slave status for Negroes. In 1623, for example, the Assembly of Bermuda passed an act restraining "the insolencies of the Negroes," limiting the black man's freedom of movement and participation in trade, and denying him the right to bear arms. The Puritan venture of New Providence Island in the western Caribbean was notorious for its pirating of Negro slaves from the Spanish colonies in order to sell them or use them on its plantations. By the 1640's, according to

the contemporary historian Richard Ligon, Barbados, another Caribbean English settlement, was using Negroes as outright slaves.

There is evidence as early as the 1630's and 1640's that Virginia and Maryland were singling out Negroes for discriminatory treatment as compared with white indentured servants. One Hugh Davis in Virginia in 1630 was "soundly whipped before an assembly of Negroes and others for abusing himself to the dishonor of God and the shame of Christians, by defiling his body in lying with a Negro." An act passed in Maryland in 1639 enumerated the rights of "all Christian inhabitants (slaves excepted)." The slaves referred to could have been only Indians or Negroes since all white servants were Christians. Negroes were specifically denied the right to bear arms in Virginia in 1640 and in Maryland in 1648, though no such prohibition was put upon white servants; indeed, in statutes that prohibited Negroes from being armed, masters were directed to arm the white servants.

It is significant that though both Maryland and Virginia passed statutes to fix limits to the terms for indentured servitude for those who came without written contracts, Negroes were never included in such protective provisions. The first of such statutes were enacted in 1639 in Maryland and in 1643 in Virginia. Three times before 1660—in 1643, 1644, and 1658—the Virginia Assembly included Negro and Indian women among the "tithables," though white women were never included in such a category. The discrimination was a recognition of the fact that Negro and Indian women worked in the fields, whereas white women, servants or no, usually did not.

Two cases for the punishment of runaway servants in Virginia throw some light on the status of Negroes by 1640. The first case concerned three runaways, of whom two were white men and the third a Negro. All three were given thirty lashes, and the white men had the terms owed their masters extended a year, at the completion of which they were to work for the colony for three more years. The other, "being a Negro named *John Punch* shall serve his said master or his assigns for the time of his natural Life here or elsewhere." It is obvious that the Negro's punishment was the most severe and that his penalty, in effect, was reduction to slavery, though it is also clear that up until his sentencing he must have had the status of a servant.

The second case, also of 1640, suggests that by that date some Negroes were already slaves. This one also involved six white men and a Negro who had plotted to run away. The punishments meted out varied, but Christopher Miller, "a dutchman (a prince agent in the business)," was given the harshest treatment of all: thirty stripes, burned with an "R" on the cheek, a shackle on his leg for a year "and longer if said master shall see cause," and seven years of service for the colony upon completion of his time due his master. The only other one of the plotters to receive the stripes, the shackle, and the burning of the "R" was the Negro Emanuel, but, significantly, he did not receive any sentence of work for the colony. Apparently he was already serving his master for a lifetime—i.e., he was a slave.

From a proceeding before the House of Burgesses in 1666 it appears that as early as 1644 that body was being called upon to determine who was a slave. In 1666 the records of the House report that in 1644 the Assembly "adjudged" a certain mulatto "no slave" even though he had been bought "as a Slave for Ever." No reasons are given as to why he was freed, but we do know that his master was surprised, for he petitioned for recompense. The Assembly refused the request, however, contending that it was not a public obligation to relieve those buyers who made poor purchases. In any case, it is clear that even this Negro served a term the length of which—twenty-one years—was unheard of for a "Christian servant."

In early seventeenth-century inventories of estates there are two distinctions which appear in the reckoning of the value of servants and Negroes. Uniformly, the Negroes are more valuable, even as children, than any white servant. Secondly, the naming of a servant is usually followed by the number of years yet remaining to his service; for the Negroes no such notation appears. Thus, in an inventory in Virginia in 1643, a twenty-two-year-old white servant, with eight years still to serve, was valued at 1,000 pounds of tobacco, while a "Negro boy" was rated at 3,000 pounds; a white boy with seven years to serve was listed as worth 700 pounds. An eight-year-old Negro girl was calculated to be worth 2,000 pounds. On another inventory in 1655, two good men servants with four years to serve were rated at 1,300 pounds of tobacco, and a woman servant with only two years to go was valued at 800 pounds. But two Negro boys, who had no limit set to their terms, were evaluated at 4,100 pounds apiece, and a Negro girl was said to be worth 5,500 pounds.

Such wide differences in the valuation of Negro and white "servants" strongly suggest, as does the failure to indicate term of service for Negroes, that the latter were slaves. Beyond a question, there was some service which these blacks were rendering which enhanced their value—a service, moreover, which was not or could not be exacted from the whites. Furthermore, a Maryland deed of 1649 suggests slave status not only of lifetime term but also of inheritance. Three Negroes "and all their issue both male and female" were deeded.

More positive evidence of true slavery is afforded by the court records of the 1640's and 1650's. In 1646, for example, a Negro woman and a Negro boy were sold to Stephen Charlton to be of use to him and "his heyers etc. for ever." A Negro girl was sold in 1652 to one H. Armsteadinger "and his heyers . . . forever with all her increase both male and female."

One investigator, Susie Ames, describes the case of two Negroes brought into the eastern shore of Virginia in 1635. Over twenty years later, in 1656, the widow of the master was bequeathing the child of one of the original Negroes and the other Negro and her children. This was more than mere servitude—the term was longer than twenty years and apparently the status was inheritable.

It is true that, concurrently with these examples of onerous service or actual slavery exacted from Negroes, some black men did gain their freedom. But such instances do not deny the existence of discrimination or slave status; they simply testify to the unsteady evolution of a status for the Negro. Indeed, the tangential manner in which recognition of Negro slavery first appeared in the Virginia statutes strengthens the supposition that the practice long preceded the law. In 1660, in a statute dealing with punishments for runaway servants, only casual reference was made to "those Negroes who are incapable of makeing satisfaction by addition of time." Apparently, everyone at the time knew what was meant by the circumlocution.

But as legal questions of status arose from time to time, clarification of the Negroes' position had to be written into law. Thus in 1662 Virginia declared that the status of offspring would follow that of the mother in the event of a white man getting a Negro with child. When Maryland in 1664 prescribed service for Negroes *durante vita* and included hereditary status through the *father*, it also prohibited unions between the races. The preamble of the statute offers a clue as to the motives behind this separation of the races. Prohibition of intermarriage is necessary because "divers free born *English* women, forgetful of their free condition, and to the disgrace of our nation, do intermarry with Negro slaves," from which fact questions of status of issue have arisen. Therefore, the law was enacted in order to pre-

vent harm to masters and "for deterring such free-born women from such shameful matches. . . ." Interestingly enough, the South Carolinian slave code of 1712 justified special legislation for Negroes on grounds of cultural difference. "The Negroes and other slaves brought unto the people of this province . . . are of barbarous, wild, savage natures, and such as renders them wholly unqualified to be governed by the laws, customs, and practices of this province. . . ."

Regardless of the reasoning behind the singling out of Negroes, as early as 1669 the law in Virginia implicitly viewed Negroes as property. An act of that year assured masters that they would not be held responsible for the accidental death of a slave as a result of punishment because it should be presumed that no man would "destroy his owne estate." But it still would be a long while before the legal status of slave property would be finally settled. In 1705, for example, Virginia law declared slaves to be real estate, though with many exceptions. Similarly, in South Carolina slaves were first denominated real estate in 1690 and then chattels in 1740. By 1750, the law in the southern colonies settled on chattels as the proper designation of slave property.

The important point is not the evolution of the legal status of the slave, but the fact that discriminatory legislation regarding the Negro long preceded any legal definition of slavery. Equally important, in view of the commonly held view that numbers of Negroes determined the inferior status imposed upon the black, is the evidence of discrimination long before numbers were large. In 1680 Virginia enacted a series of regulations which were very close to the later slave codes in restricting the movement of Negroes, prohibiting their bearing arms, and providing capital punishment for those who ran away or offered resistance to whites. Yet it would be another twenty years before the Negroes would make up even a fifth of the total population of Virginia. In short, long before slavery was an important part of the labor system of the South, the Negroes had been fitted into a special and inferior status.

The same process whereby the white man's sense of difference regarding the Negro shaped the status of the black man can be traced in the northern colonies. Englishmen there, like their countrymen in the southern colonies, inherited no legal basis for slavery; yet a slave status and an inferior position for the black man developed in New England, even though there the economic need for black labor was considerably less than in the South.

So few Negroes were imported into New England during the seventeenth century that references to their status are scattered, but those pieces of evidence which are available suggest that from the earliest years an especially low status, if not slavery itself, was reserved for the Negro. One source of 1639, for example, tells of a Negro woman being held as a slave on Noddles Island in Boston Harbor. Her master sought to mate her with another Negro, but, the chronicler reported, she kicked her prospective lover out of bed, saying that such behavior was "beyond her slavery." It is also well known that the first Massachusetts legal code, the Body of Liberties of 1641, permitted enslavement of those who are "sold to us," which would apply to Negroes brought by the slave ships.

Nor was the use of Negroes as slaves unknown or undesirable to the Puritans. One correspondent of John Winthrop in 1645, for instance, talked of the desirability of war against the Indians, so that captives might be taken who could be exchanged "for Moores [Negroes], which will be more gayneful pilladge for us then [sic] wee conceive, for I doe not see how wee can thrive untill wee get into a stock of slaves sufficient to doe all our business, for our children's children will hardly see this great Continent filled with people. . . ."

Moreover, he went on, "servants" will not stay but "for verie great wages. And I suppose you know verie well how we shall maynteyne 20 Moores cheaper than one English servant." The following year the United Colonies (Massachusetts, Plymouth, New Haven, and Connecticut colonies) decreed, in order to save prison costs, that contumacious Indians would be delivered up to those they had injured or "be shipped out and exchanged for Negroes" as the case might justify. That enslavement of Negroes was well known in New England by the early 1650's is evident from the preamble of a Rhode Island statue of 1652. It was said that it "is a common course practised amongst Englishmen to buy Negers, to that end they may have them for service or slaves forever. . . ."

Though the number of Negroes in New England was exceedingly small, the colonies of that region followed the same path as the southern provinces in denying arms to the blacks in their midst. In 1652, Massachusetts had provided that Indians and Negroes should train in the militia the same as whites. But this ruling apparently caused friction, for in 1656 the earlier law was countermanded by the words "henceforth no Negroes or Indians, although servants of the English, shalbe armed or permitted to trayne." Connecticut in 1660 also excluded Indians and "Negar servants" from the militia and "Watch and Ward," although as late as 1680 it was officially reported to London that there were no more than thirty "slaves" in the colony.

Edward Randolph as commissioner of the Crown reported in 1676 that there were a few indentured servants in Massachusetts, "and not above two hundred slaves in the colony," by which he meant Negroes, for he said they "were brought from Guinea and Madagascar." Yet not until 1698 did the phrase "Negro slave" appear in the Massachusetts statutes. Practice was preceding law in New England just as it had in the South. In 1690, discrimination against the few Negroes in Connecticut

reached the point where all Negroes were forbidden to be found outside the town bounds without "a ticket or a pass" from either master or the authorities, the restriction applying equally to free Negroes and slaves. Furthermore, it was provided that ferrymen would be fined if they permitted Negroes without passes to use their ferries. And though as early as 1680 official reports to London were distinguishing between slaves and servants, statute law barely defined the institution of slavery. In 1704, for example, the Governor gave it as his opinion that all children born of "Negro bondwomen are themselves in like condition, i.e. born in servitude," but he admitted that no law had so provided. Legislation, he said, was "needless, because of the constant practice by which they are held as such. . . ." In 1703, Massachusetts provided that "molatto and Negro slaves" could be set free only if security was given that they would not be a charge on the community, and two years later a prohibition against sexual relations between Negroes and whites was enacted. In 1717, Negroes were barred from holding land in Connecticut.

Thus, like the southern colonists, the New Englanders enacted into law, in the absence of any prior English law of slavery, their recognition of Negroes as different in race, religion, and culture. It should be especially noted that in many instances discriminations were made against all Negroes, whether slave or free—a fact which reinforces the argument that the discrimination preceded slavery and was not simply a consequence. Unquestionably, the coincidence of slavery with discrimination fastened still more firmly the stigma of inferiority upon the Negro, but slavery must be absolved of starting the cycle.

Once the sense of difference between the two peoples was embodied in law, the logic of the law widened the differences. All through the early eighteenth century, judges and legislatures in all the colonies elaborated the law along the discriminatory lines laid down from

the beginning. In this, of course, especially in the South, they had the added incentive of perpetuating and securing a labor system which had become indispensable to the economy. As a consequence, the cleavage between the races was deepened and hardened.

In time the correspondence between the black man and slavery would be so perfect that it would be difficult to realize that the Negro was not always and everywhere in a degraded status. Thus began in the seventeenth century the Negro's life in America. With it commenced a moral problem for all Americans which still besets us in the middle of the twentieth century. Though started casually, thoughtlessly, and without any preconceived goal, the web became so interwoven, so complex, so tightly meshed, that John C. Calhoun could say, in 1850, slavery "has grown with our growth, and strengthened with our strength. . . ."

5

The Witches of Salem Village

Kai T. Erikson

As Degler observed in his discussion of slavery, seventeenth-century America had its unseemly sides. Among the worst were the witch panics that rocked Puritan Massachusetts in the 1680s and early 1690s. Just why these occurred has been hotly debated for generations. Brooks Adams, writing in the 1880s, blamed them on clerical "bigots" like Increase and Cotton Mather, who, Brooks said, fanned the excitement to restore their declining religious power. On the other hand, Chadwick Hansen has recently argued that witchcraft "did exist and was widely practiced in seventeenth-century New England, as it was in Europe at the time," and that some people were so terrified of these witches that they suffered "hysterical symptoms" and occasionally even died. Thus the "mass hysteria" that swept Massachusetts Bay in the early 1690s must be understood in the clinical sense of the term; the hysteria arose because of a genuine "popular fear" of actual witchcraft.

Other writers, however, contend that the witch hysteria was merely symptomatic of the time, an age when people were plagued with superstitions and monstrous fears—fears of Satan and God, fears of the Unknown—which spawned religious persecutions and witch hunts on both sides of the Atlantic. Still other historians maintain that the witch panics must be placed in the context of Puritan society in Massachusetts Bay, a society undergoing severe religious and cultural change. By the 1680s, the Puritan movement had lost much of its zeal and sense of mission; the church itself had become exclusive and hereditary; Puritan youth had become disenchanted and alienated from the world of their parents, and scores of other people had become increasingly preoccupied with material pleasures and comforts. The result was that many anxious leaders and citizens began to see satanic "conspiracies" at work to erode the cherished institutions of their already shaky society. Out of this spiral of fear and insecurity came the witch scare in Boston in the 1680s and the far more terrible outbreak at Salem Village in 1692, one which shook Massachusetts Bay to its foundations.

On the other hand, the witch panic that began at Salem Village may have had entirely local origins. Paul Boyer and Stephen Nissenbaum, for example, now argue that local factionalism produced the witchcraft accusations which terrorized that unhappy village.

At any rate, those who read Erikson's account will want to draw their own conclusions about the causes of the witchcraft accusations at Salem and the mass hysteria which followed. For these, too, like the developments Degler described in the previous chapter, have implications for our own time.

The witchcraft hysteria that began in Salem Village (a town some miles away from Salem itself) is probably the best known episode of Massachusetts history and has been described in a number of careful works. . . .

Between the end of the Quaker persecutions in 1665 and the beginning of the Salem witchcraft outbreak in 1692, the colony had experienced some very trying days. To begin with,

From pp. 137–159 in Kai T. Erikson, *Wayward Puritans: A Study in the Sociology of Deviance*. Copyright © 1966 by John Wiley & Sons, Inc. Reprinted by permission.

the political outlines of the commonwealth had been subject to sudden, often violent, shifts, and the people of the colony were quite uncertain about their own future. The King's decrees during the Quaker troubles had provoked only minor changes in the actual structure of the Puritan state, but they had introduced a note of apprehension and alarm which did not disappear for thirty years; and no sooner had Charles warned the Massachusetts authorities of his new interest in their affairs than he dispatched four commissioners to the Bay to look after his remote dominions and make sure that his occasional orders were being enforced. From that moment, New England feared the worst. The sermons of the period were full of dreadful prophecies about the future of the Bay, and as New England moved through the 1670's and 1680's, the catalogue of political calamities grew steadily longer and more serious. In 1670, for example, a series of harsh arguments occurred between groups of magistrates and clergymen, threatening the alliance which had been the very cornerstone of the New England Way. In 1675 a brutal and costly war broke out with a confederacy of Indian tribes led by a wily chief called King Philip. In 1676 Charles II began to review the claims of other persons to lands within the jurisdiction of Massachusetts, and it became increasingly clear that the old charter might be revoked altogether. In 1679 Charles specifically ordered Massachusetts to permit the establishment of an Anglican church in Boston, and in 1684 the people of the Bay had become so pessimistic about the fate of the colony that several towns simply neglected to send Deputies to the General Court. The sense of impending doom reached its peak in 1686. To begin with, the charter which had given the colony its only legal protection for over half a century was vacated by a stroke of the royal pen, and in addition the King sent a Royal Governor to represent his interests in the Bay who was both an Anglican and a man actively hostile to the

larger goals of New England. For the moment, it looked as if the holy experiment was over: not only had the settlers lost title to the very land they were standing on, but they ran the very real risk of witnessing the final collapse of the congregational churches they had built at so great a cost.

The settlers were eventually rescued from the catastrophes of 1686, but their margin of escape had been extremely narrow and highly tentative. In 1689 news began to filter into the Bay that William of Orange had landed in England to challenge the House of Stuart, and hopes ran high throughout the colony; but before the people of the Bay knew the outcome of this contest in England, a Boston mob suddenly rose in protest and placed the Royal Governor in chains. Luckily for Massachusetts, William's forces were successful in England and the Boston insurrection was seen as little more than a premature celebration in honor of the new King. Yet for all the furor, little had changed. At the time of the witchcraft hysteria, agents of Massachusetts were at work in London trying to convince William to restore the old charter, or at least to issue a new one giving Massachusetts all the advantages it had enjoyed in the past, but everyone knew that the colony would never again operate under the same autonomy. As the people of the Bay waited to hear about the future of their settlement, then, their anxiety was understandably high.

Throughout this period of political crisis, an even darker cloud was threatening the colony, and this had to do with the fact that a good deal of angry dissension was spreading among the saints themselves. In a colony that depended on a high degree of harmony and group feeling, the courts were picking their way through a maze of land disputes and personal feuds, a complicated tangle of litigations and suits. Moreover, the earnest attempts at unanimity that had characterized the politics of Winthrop's era were now replaced by some-

thing closely resembling open party bickering. When John Josselyn visited Boston in 1668, for instance, he observed that the people were "savagely factious" in their relations with one another and acted more out of jealousy and greed than any sense of religious purpose.[1] And the sermons of the day chose even stronger language to describe the decline in morality which seemed to darken the prospects of New England. The spirit of brotherhood which the original settlers had counted on so heavily had lately diffused into an atmosphere of commercial competition, political contention, and personal bad feeling.

Thus the political architecture which had been fashioned so carefully by the first generation and the spiritual consensus which had been defended so energetically by the second were both disappearing. At the time of the Salem witchcraft mania, most of the familiar landmarks of the New England Way had become blurred by changes in the historical climate, like signposts obscured in a storm, and the people of the Bay no longer knew how to assess what the past had amounted to or what the future promised. Massachusetts had become, in Alan Heimert's words, "a society no longer able to judge itself with any certainty."[2]

In 1670, the House of Deputies took note of the confusion and fear which was beginning to spread over the country and prepared a brief inventory of the troubles facing the Bay:

Declension from the primitive foundation work, innovation in doctrine and worship, opinion and practice, an invasion of the rights, liberties and privileges of churches, an usurpation of a lordly and prelatical power over God's heritage, a subversion of the gospel order, and all this with a dan-

gerous tendency to the utter devastation of these churches, turning the pleasant gardens of Christ into a wilderness, and the inevitable and total extirpation of the principles and pillars of the congregational way; these are the leaven, the corrupting gangrene, the infecting spreading plague, the provoking image of jealousy set up before the Lord, the accursed thing which hath provoked divine wrath, and doth further threaten destruction.[3]

The tone of this resolution gives us an excellent index to the mood of the time. For the next twenty years, New England turned more and more to the notion that the settlers must expect God to turn upon them in wrath because the colony had lost its original fervor and sense of mission. The motif introduced in this resolution runs like a recurrent theme through the thinking of the period: the settlers who had carved a commonwealth out of the wilderness and had planted "the pleasant gardens of Christ" in its place were about to return to the wilderness. But there is an important shift of imagery here, for the wilderness they had once mastered was one of thick underbrush and wild animals, dangerous seasons and marauding Indians, while the wilderness which awaited them contained an entirely different sort of peril. "The Wilderness thro' which we are passing to the Promised Land," Cotton Mather wrote in a volume describing the state of New England at the time of the witchcraft difficulties, "is all over fill'd with Fiery flying serpents. . . . All our way to Heaven, lies by the Dens of Lions, and the Mounts of Leopards; there are incredible Droves of Devils in our way."[4] We will return

---

[1] John Josselyn, "An Account of Two Voyages to New-England," *Collections of the Massachusetts Historical Society*, Vol. III, Third Series, p. 331.
[2] Alan Heimert, "Puritanism, The Wilderness and The Frontier," *New England Quarterly*, XXVI (1953), p. 381.

[3] Hutchinson, *History*, I, p. 232. The page number here was taken from a later edition of Hutchinson's work than the one cited in other footnotes in the present study. See the Lawrence S. Mayo edition (Cambridge, Mass.: Harvard University Press, 1936).
[4] Cotton Mather, "Wonders of the Invisible World," Boston and London, 1693, found in Samuel G. Drake, editor, *The Witchcraft Delusion in New England* (Roxbury, Mass.: W. Elliot Woodward, 1866), pp. 80–81.

to discussion of this wilderness theme at the conclusion of the chapter, but for the moment it is important to note that Massachusetts had lost much of its concern for institutions and policies and had begun to seek some vision of its future by looking into a ghostly, invisible world.

It was while the people of the colony were preoccupied with these matters that the witches decided to strike.

1

No one really knows how the witchcraft hysteria began, but it originated in the home of the Reverend Samuel Parris, minister of the local church. In early 1692, several girls from the neighborhood began to spend their afternoons in the Parris' kitchen with a slave named Tituba, and it was not long before a mysterious sorority of girls, aged between nine and twenty, became regular visitors to the parsonage. We can only speculate what was going on behind the kitchen door, but we know that Tituba had been brought to Massachusetts from Barbados and enjoyed a reputation in the neighborhood for her skills in the magic arts. As the girls grew closer together, a remarkable change seemed to come over them: perhaps it is not true, as someone later reported, that they went out into the forest to celebrate their own version of a black mass, but it is apparent that they began to live in a state of high tension and shared secrets with one another which were hardly becoming to quiet Puritan maidens.

Before the end of winter, the two youngest girls in the group succumbed to the shrill pitch of their amusements and began to exhibit a most unusual malady. They would scream unaccountably, fall into grotesque convulsions, and sometimes scamper along on their hands and knees making noises like the barking of a dog. No sooner had word gone around about this extraordinary affliction than it began to

spread like a contagious disease. All over the community young girls were groveling on the ground in a panic of fear and excitement, and while some of the less credulous townspeople were tempted to reach for their belts in the hopes of strapping a little modesty into them, the rest could only stand by in helpless horror as the girls suffered their torments.

The town's one physician did what he could to stem the epidemic, but he soon exhausted his meagre store of remedies and was forced to conclude that the problem lay outside the province of medicine. The Devil had come to Salem Village, he announced; the girls were bewitched. At this disturbing news, ministers from many of the neighboring parishes came to consult with their colleague and offer what advice they might. Among the first to arrive was a thoughtful clergyman named Deodat Lawson, and he had been in town no more than a few hours when he happened upon a frightening exhibition of the devil's handiwork. "In the beginning of the evening," he later recounted of his first day in the village,

> I went to give Mr. Parris a visit. When I was there, his kinswoman, Abigail Williams, (about 12 years of age,) had a grievous fit; she was at first hurried with violence to and fro in the room, (though Mrs. Ingersoll endeavored to hold her,) sometimes making as if she would fly, stretching up her arms as high as she could, and crying "whish, whish, whish!" several times. . . . After that, she run to the fire, and began to throw fire brands about the house; and run against the back, as if she would run up the chimney, and, as they said, she had attempted to go into the fire in other fits.[5]

Faced by such clear-cut evidence, the ministers quickly agreed that Satan's new challenge

[5] Deodat Lawson, "A Brief and True Narrative of Witchcraft at Salem Village," 1692, in *Narratives of the Witchcraft Cases, 1648–1706*, edited by George Lincoln Burr (New York: Scribner's, 1914), p. 154.

would have to be met with vigorous action, and this meant that the afflicted girls would have to identify the witches who were harassing them.

It is hard to guess what the girls were experiencing during those early days of the commotion. They attracted attention everywhere they went and exercised a degree of power over the adult community which would have been exhilarating under the sanest of circumstances. But whatever else was going on in those young minds, the thought seems to have gradually occurred to the girls that they were indeed bewitched, and after they had been coaxed over and over again to name their tormentors, they finally singled out three women in the village and accused them of witchcraft.

Three better candidates could not have been found if all the gossips in New England had met to make the nominations. The first, understandably, was Tituba herself, a woman who had grown up among the rich colors and imaginative legends of Barbados and who was probably acquainted with some form of voodoo. The second, Sarah Good, was a proper hag of a witch if Salem Village had ever seen one. With a pipe clenched in her leathery face she wandered around the countryside neglecting her children and begging from others, and on more than one occasion the old crone had been overheard muttering threats against her neighbors when she was in an unusually sour humor. Sarah Osburne, the third suspect, had a higher social standing than either of her alleged accomplices, but she had been involved in a local scandal a year or two earlier when a man moved into her house some months before becoming her husband.

A preliminary hearing was set at once to decide whether the three accused women should be held for trial. The girls were ushered to the front row of the meeting house, where they took full advantage of the space afforded them by rolling around in apparent agony whenever some personal fancy (or the invisible agents of the devil) provoked them to it. It was a remark-able show. Strange creatures flew about the room pecking at the girls or taunting them from the rafters, and it was immediately obvious to everyone that the women on trial were responsible for all the disorder and suffering. When Sarah Good and Sarah Osburne were called to the stand and asked why they sent these spectres to torment the girls, they were too appalled to say much in their defense. But when Tituba took the stand she had a ready answer. A lifetime spent in bondage is poor training for standing up before a bench of magistrates, and anyway Tituba was an excitable woman who had breathed the warmer winds of the Caribbean and knew things about magic her crusty old judges would never learn. Whatever the reason, Tituba gave her audience one of the most exuberant confessions ever recorded in a New England courtroom. She spoke of the creatures who inhabit the invisible world, the dark rituals which bind them together in the service of Satan; and before she had ended her astonishing recital she had convinced everyone in Salem Village that the problem was far worse than they had dared imagine. For Tituba not only implicated Sarah Good and Sarah Osburne in her own confession but announced that many other people in the colony were engaged in the devil's conspiracy against the Bay.

So the hearing that was supposed to bring a speedy end to the affair only stirred up a hidden hornet's nest, and now the girls were urged to identify other suspects and locate new sources of trouble. Already the girls had become more than unfortunate victims: in the eyes of the community they were diviners, prophets, oracles, mediums, for only they could see the terrible spectres swarming over the countryside and tell what persons had sent them on their evil errands. As they became caught up in the enthusiasm of their new work, then, the girls began to reach into every corner of the community in a search for likely suspects. Martha Corey was an upstanding woman in the village whose main mistake was to snort incredulously

at the girls' behavior. Dorcas Good, five years old, was a daughter of the accused Sarah. Rebecca Nurse was a saintly old woman who had been bedridden at the time of the earlier hearings. Mary Esty and Sarah Cloyce were Rebecca's younger sisters, themselves accused when they rose in energetic defense of the older woman. And so it went—John Proctor, Giles Corey, Abigail Hobbs, Bridgit Bishop, Sarah Wild, Susanna Martin, Dorcas Hoar, the Reverend George Burroughs: as winter turned into spring the list of suspects grew to enormous length and the Salem jail was choked with people awaiting trial. We know nothing about conditions of life in prison, but it is easy to imagine the tensions which must have echoed within those grey walls. Some of the prisoners had cried out against their relatives and friends in a desperate effort to divert attention from themselves, others were witless persons with scarcely a clue as to what had happened to them, and a few (very few, as it turned out) were accepting their lot with quiet dignity. If we imagine Sarah Good sitting next to Rebecca Nurse and lighting her rancid pipe or Tituba sharing views on supernatural phenomena with the Reverend George Burroughs, we may have a rough picture of life in those crowded quarters.

By this time the hysteria had spread well beyond the confines of Salem Village, and as it grew in scope so did the appetites of the young girls. They now began to accuse persons they had never seen from places they had never visited (in the course of which some absurd mistakes were made),[6] yet their word was so little questioned that it was ordinarily warrant enough to put respected people in chains.

From as far away as Charlestown, Nathaniel Cary heard that his wife had been accused of witchcraft and immediately traveled with her to Salem "to see if the afflicted did know her." The two of them sat through an entire day of hearings, after which Cary reported:

> I observed that the afflicted were two girls of about ten years old, and about two or three others, of about eighteen. . . . The prisoners were called in one by one, and as they came in were cried out of. . . . The prisoner was placed about seven or eight feet from the Justices, and the accusers between the Justices and them; the prisoner was ordered to stand right before the Justices, with an officer appointed to hold each hand, lest they should therewith afflict them, and the prisoner's eyes must be constantly on the Justices; for if they looked on the afflicted, they would either fall into their fits, or cry out of being hurt by them. . . . Then the Justices said to the accusers, "which of you will go and touch the prisoner at the bar?" Then the most courageous would adventure, but before they had made three steps would ordinarily fall down as in a fit. The Justices ordered that they should be taken up and carried to the prisoner, that she might touch them; and as soon as they were touched by the accused, the Justices would say "they are well," before I could discern any alteration. . . . Thus far I was only as a spectator, my wife also was there part of the time, but no notice taken of her by the afflicted, except once or twice they came to her and asked her name.

After this sorry performance the Carys retired to the local inn for dinner, but no sooner had they taken seats than a group of afflicted girls burst into the room and "began to tumble about like swine" at Mrs. Cary's feet, accusing her of being the cause of their miseries. Remarkably, the magistrates happened to be sitting in the adjoining room—"waiting for this," Cary later decided—and an impromptu hearing took place on the spot.

[6] John Alden later reported in his account of the affair that the girls pointed their fingers at the wrong man when they first accused him of witchcraft and only realized their mistake when an obliging passer-by corrected them. See Robert Calef, "More Wonders of the Invisible World," Boston, 1701, in Burr, *Narratives*, p. 353.

Being brought before the Justices, her chief accusers were two girls. My wife declared to the Justices that she never had any knowledge of them before that day; she was forced to stand with her arms stretched out. I did request that I might hold one of her hands, but it was denied me; then she desired me to wipe the tears from her eyes, and the sweat from her face, which I did; then she desired she might lean herself on me, saying she should faint. Justice Hathorne replied, she had strength enough to torment those persons, and she should have strength enough to stand. I speaking something against their cruel proceedings, they commanded me to be silent, or else I should be turned out of the room. An Indian . . . was also brought in to be one of her accusers: being come in, he now (when before the Justices) fell down and tumbled about like a hog, but said nothing. The Justices asked the girls, "who afflicted the Indian?", they answered "she" (meaning my wife). . . . The Justices ordered her to touch him, in order of his cure . . . but the Indian took hold of her in a barbarous manner; then his hand was taken off, and her hand put on his, and the cure was quickly wrought. . . . Then her mittimus was writ.[7]

For another example of how the hearings were going, we might listen for a moment to the examination of Mrs. John Proctor. This record was taken down by the Reverend Samuel Parris himself, and the notes in parentheses are his. Ann Putnam and Abigail Williams were two of the most energetic of the young accusers.

Justice: Ann Putnam, doth this woman hurt you?
Putnam: Yes, sir, a good many times. (Then the accused looked upon them and they fell into fits.)

Justice: She does not bring the book to you, does she?[8]
Putnam: Yes, sir, often, and saith she hath made her maid set her hand to it.
Justice: Abigail Williams, does this woman hurt you?
Williams: Yes, sir, often.
Justice: Does she bring the book to you?
Williams: Yes.
Justice: What would she have you do with it?
Williams: To write in it and I shall be well.
Putnam to Mrs. Proctor: Did you not tell me that your maid had written?
Mrs. Proctor: Dear child, it is not so. There is another judgment, dear child. (Then Abigail and Ann had fits. By and by they cried out, "look you, there is Goody Proctor upon the beam." By and by both of them cried out of Goodman Proctor himself, and said he was a wizard. Immediately, many, if not all of the bewitched, had grievous fits.)
Justice: Ann Putnam, who hurt you?
Putnam: Goodman Proctor and his wife too. (Some of the afflicted cried, "there is Proctor going to take up Mrs. Pope's feet —and her feet were immediately taken up.)
Justice: What do you say Goodman Proctor to these things?
Proctor: I know not. I am innocent.
Williams: There is Goodman Proctor going to Mrs. Pope (and immediately said Pope fell into a fit).
Justice: You see, the Devil will deceive you. The children could see what you was going to do before the woman was hurt. I would advise you to repentance, for the devil is bringing you out.[9]

[7] Reproduced in Calef, "More Wonders," in Burr, *Narratives*, pp. 350–352.

[8] The "book" refers to the Devil's registry. The girls were presumably being tormented because they refused to sign the book and ally themselves with Satan.
[9] Hutchinson, *History*, II, pp. 27–28.

This was the kind of evidence the magistrates were collecting in readiness for the trials; and it was none too soon, for the prisons were crowded with suspects. In June the newly arrived Governor of the Bay, Sir William Phips, appointed a special court of Oyer and Terminer to hear the growing number of witchcraft cases pending, and the new bench went immediately to work. Before the month was over, six women had been hanged from the gallows in Salem. And still the accused poured in.

As the court settled down to business, however, a note of uncertainty began to flicker across the minds of several thoughtful persons in the colony. To begin with, the net of accusation was beginning to spread out in wider arcs, reaching not only across the surface of the country but up the social ladder as well, so that a number of influential people were now among those in the overflowing prisons. Nathaniel Cary was an important citizen of Charlestown, and other men of equal rank (including the almost legendary Captain John Alden) were being caught up in the widening circle of panic and fear. Slowly but surely, a faint glimmer of skepticism was introduced into the situation; and while it was not to assert a modifying influence on the behavior of the court for some time to come, this new voice had become a part of the turbulent New England climate of 1692.

Meantime, the girls continued to exercise their extraordinary powers. Between sessions of the court, they were invited to visit the town of Andover and help the local inhabitants flush out whatever witches might still remain at large among them. Handicapped as they were by not knowing anyone in town, the girls nonetheless managed to identify more than fifty witches in the space of a few hours. Forty warrants were signed on the spot, and the arrest total only stopped at that number because the local Justice of the Peace simply laid down his pen and refused to go on with the frightening charade any longer—at which point, predictably, he became a suspect himself.

Yet the judges worked hard to keep pace with their young representatives in the field. In early August five persons went to the gallows in Salem. A month later fifteen more were tried and condemned, of which eight were hung promptly and the others spared because they were presumably ready to confess their sins and turn state's evidence. Nineteen people had been executed, seven more condemned, and one pressed to death under a pile of rocks for standing mute at his trial. At least two more persons had died in prison, bringing the number of deaths to twenty-two. And in all that time, not one suspect brought before the court had been acquitted.

At the end of this strenuous period of justice, the whole witchcraft mania began to fade. For one thing, the people of the Bay had been shocked into a mood of sober reflection by the deaths of so many persons. For another, the afflicted girls had obviously not learned very much from their experience in Andover and were beginning to display an ambition which far exceeded their credit. It was bad enough that they should accuse the likes of John Alden and Nathaniel Cary, but when they brought up the name of Samuel Willard, who doubled as pastor of Boston's First Church and President of Harvard College, the magistrates flatly told them they were mistaken. Not long afterwards, a brazen finger was pointed directly at the executive mansion in Boston, where Lady Phips awaited her husband's return from an expedition to Canada, and one tradition even has it that Cotton Mather's mother was eventually accused.[10]

This was enough to stretch even a Puritan's boundless credulity. One by one the leading men of the Bay began to reconsider the whole question and ask aloud whether the evidence accepted in witchcraft hearings was really suited to the emergency at hand. It was obvious that people were being condemned on the testi-

[10] Burr, *Narratives*, p. 377.

mony of a few excited girls, and responsible minds in the community were troubled by the thought that the girls' excitement may have been poorly diagnosed in the first place. Suppose the girls were directly possessed by the devil and not touched by intermediate witches? Suppose they were simply out of their wits altogether? Suppose, in fact, they were lying? In any of these events the rules of evidence used in court would have to be reviewed—and quickly.

Deciding what kinds of evidence were admissible in witchcraft cases was a thorny business at best. When the court of Oyer and Terminer had first met, a few ground rules had been established to govern the unusual situation which did not entirely conform to ordinary Puritan standards of trial procedure. In the first place, the scriptural rule that two eye-witnesses were necessary for conviction in capital cases was modified to read that any two witnesses were sufficient even if they were testifying about different events—on the interesting ground that witchcraft was a "habitual" crime. That is, if one witness testified that he had seen Susanna Martin bewitch a horse in 1660 and another testified that she had broken un-invited into his dreams twenty years later, then both were witnesses to the same general offense. More important, however, the court accepted as an operating principle the old idea that Satan could not assume the shape of an innocent person, which meant in effect that any spectres floating into view which resembled one of the defendants must be acting under his direct instruction. If an afflicted young girl "saw" John Proctor's image crouched on the window sill with a wicked expression on his face, for example, there could be no question that Proctor himself had placed it there, for the devil could not borrow that disguise without the permission of its owner. During an early hearing, one of the defendants had been asked: "How comes your appearance to hurt these [girls]?" "How do I know," she had answered

testily, "He that appeared in the shape of Samuel, a glorified saint, may appear in anyone's shape."[11] Now this was no idle retort, for every man who read his Bible knew that the Witch of Endor had once caused the image of Samuel to appear before Saul, and this scriptural evidence that the devil might indeed be able to impersonate an innocent person proved a difficult matter for the court to handle. Had the defendant been able to win her point, the whole machinery of the court might have fallen in pieces at the magistrates' feet; for if the dreadful spectres haunting the girls were no more than free-lance apparitions sent out by the devil, then the court would have no prosecution case at all.

All in all, five separate kinds of evidence had been admitted by the court during its first round of hearings. First were trials by test, of which repeating the Lord's Prayer, a feat presumed impossible for witches to perform, and curing fits by touch were the most often used. Second was the testimony of persons who attributed their own misfortunes to the sorcery of a neighbor on trial. Third were physical marks like warts, moles, scars, or any other imperfection through which the devil might have sucked his gruesome quota of blood. Fourth was spectral evidence, of the sort just noted; and fifth were the confessions of the accused themselves.

Now it was completely obvious to the men who began to review the court's proceedings that the first three types of evidence were quite inconclusive. After all, anyone might make a mistake reciting the Lord's Prayer, particularly if the floor was covered with screaming, convulsive girls, and it did not make much sense to execute a person because he had spiteful neighbors or a mark upon his body. By those standards, half the people in Massachusetts might qualify for the gallows. This left spectral

11 Cotton Mather, "Wonders of the Invisible World," in Drake, *The Witchcraft Delusion*, p. 176.

evidence and confessions. As for the latter, the court could hardly maintain that any real attention had been given to that form of evidence, since none of the executed witches had confessed and none of the many confessors had been executed. Far from establishing guilt, a well-phrased and tearfully delivered confession was clearly the best guarantee against hanging. So the case lay with spectral evidence, and legal opinion in the Bay was slowly leaning toward the theory that this form of evidence, too, was worthless.

In October, Governor Phips took note of the growing doubts by dismissing the special court of Oyer and Terminer and releasing several suspects from prison. The tide had begun to turn, but still there were 150 persons in custody and some 200 others who had been accused.

In December, finally, Phips appointed a new session of the Superior Court of Judicature to try the remaining suspects, and this time the magistrates were agreed that spectral evidence would be admitted only in marginal cases. Fifty-two persons were brought to trial during the next month, and of these, forty-nine were immediately acquitted. Three others were condemned ("two of which," a contemporary observer noted, "were the most senseless and ignorant creatures that could be found"),[12] and in addition death warrants were signed for five persons who had been condemned earlier. Governor Phips responded to these carefully reasoned judgments by signing reprieves for all eight of the defendants anyway, and at this, the court began to empty the jails as fast as it could hear cases. Finally Phips ended the costly procedure by discharging every prisoner in the colony and issuing a general pardon to all persons still under suspicion.

The witchcraft hysteria had been completely checked within a year of the day it first appeared in Salem Village.

12 Calef, "More Wonders," in Burr, *Narratives*, p. 382.

2

Historically, there is nothing unique in the fact that Massachusetts Bay should have put people on trial for witchcraft. As the historian Kittredge has pointed out, the whole story should be seen "not as an abnormal outbreak of fanaticism, not as an isolated tragedy, but as a mere incident, a brief and transitory episode in the biography of a terrible, but perfectly natural, superstition."[13]

The idea of witchcraft, of course, is as old as history; but the concept of a malevolent witch who makes a compact with Satan and rejects God did not appear in Europe until the middle of the fourteenth century and does not seem to have made a serious impression on England until well into the sixteenth. The most comprehensive study of English witchcraft, for example, opens with the year 1558, the first year of Elizabeth's reign, and gives only passing attention to events occurring before that date.[14]

In many ways, witchcraft was brought into England on the same current of change that introduced the Protestant Reformation, and it continued to draw nourishment from the intermittent religious quarrels which broke out during the next century and a half. Perhaps no other form of crime in history has been a better index to social disruption and change, for outbreaks of witchcraft mania have generally taken place in societies which are experiencing a shift of religious focus—societies, we would say, confronting a relocation of boundaries. Throughout the Elizabethan and early Stuart periods, at any rate, while England was trying to establish a national church and to anchor it in the middle of the violent tides which were sweeping over the rest of Europe, increasing

13 George L. Kittredge, *Witchcraft in Old and New England* (New York: Russell E. Russell, 1956), p. 329.
14 Wallace Notestein, *History of Witchcraft in England* (Washington, D.C.: The American Historical Society, 1911).

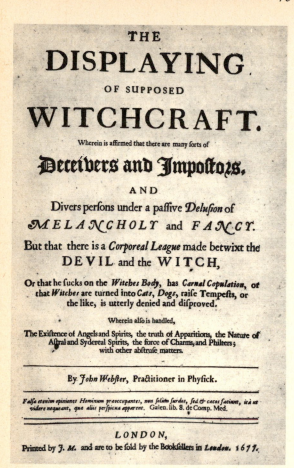

THE
DISPLAYING
OF SUPPOSED
WITCHCRAFT.

Wherein is affirmed that there are many sorts of

Deceivers and Impostors,

AND

Divers persons under a passive *Delusion* of
MELANCHOLY and *FANCY*.

But that there is a *Corporeal League* made betwixt the
DEVIL and the WITCH,

Or that he sucks on the *Witches Body*, has *Carnal Copulation*, or
that *Witches* are turned into *Cats, Dogs*, raise *Tempests*, or
the like, is utterly denied and disproved.

Wherein also is handled,

The Existence of Angels and Spirits, the truth of Apparitions, the Nature of
Astral and Sydereal Spirits, the force of Charms, and Philters;
with other abstruse matters.

By *John Webster*, Practitioner in Physick.

*False etenim opiniones Hominum praeoccupantes, non solùm surdos, sed & caecos faciunt, ità ut
videre nequeant, quae aliis perspicua apparent.* Galen. lib. 8. de Comp. Med.

LONDON,
Printed by *J. M.* and are to be sold by the Booksellers in *London.* 1677.

Title page of the most famous attack against witch-craft published in seventeenth-century England. Books like Webster's were circulated in colonial America, too. (Courtesy of The Pennsylvania State University Libraries.)

attention was devoted to the subject. Elizabeth herself introduced legislation to clarify the laws dealing with witchcraft, and James I, before becoming King of England, wrote a textbook on demonology which became a standard reference for years to come.

But it was during the Civil Wars in England that the witchcraft hysteria struck with full force. Many hundreds, probably thousands of witches were burned or hung between the time the Civil Wars began and Oliver Cromwell emerged as the strong man of the Common-wealth, and no sooner had the mania subsided in England than it broke out all over again in Scotland during the first days of the Restoration. Every important crisis during those years seemed to be punctuated by a rash of witchcraft cases. England did not record its last execution for witchcraft until 1712, but the urgent witch hunts of the Civil War period were never repeated.

With this background in mind, we should not be surprised that New England, too, should experience a moment of panic; but it is rather curious that this moment should have arrived so late in the century.

During the troubled years in England when countless witches were burned at the stake or hung from the gallows, Massachusetts Bay showed but mild concern over the whole matter. In 1647 a witch was executed in Connecticut, and one year later another woman met the same fate in Massachusetts.[15] In 1651 the General Court took note of the witchcraft crisis in England and published an almost laconic order that "a day of humiliation" be observed throughout the Bay,[16] but beyond this, the waves of excitement which were sweeping over the mother country seemed not to reach across the Atlantic at all. There was no shortage of accusations, to be sure, no shortage of the kind of gossip which in other days would send good men and women to their lonely grave, but the magistrates of the colony did not act as if a state of emergency was at hand and thus did not declare a crime wave to be in motion. In 1672, for example, a curious man named John Broadstreet was presented to the Essex County Court for "having familiarity with the devil," yet when he admitted the charge the court was so little impressed that he was fined for telling

---

[15] Winthrop, *Journal*, II, pp. 323, 344–345. Altogether, five or possibly six persons were executed for witch-craft in New England prior to the outbreak of 1692.
[16] *Massachusetts Records*, IVa, pp. 52–53.

a lie.[17] And in 1674, when Christopher Brown came before the same court to testify that he had been dealing with Satan, the magistrates flatly dismissed him on the grounds that his confession seemed "inconsistent with truth."[18]

So New England remained relatively calm during the worst of the troubles in England, yet suddenly erupted into a terrible violence long after England lay exhausted from its earlier exertions.

In many important respects, 1692 marked the end of the Puritan experiment in Massachusetts, not only because the original charter had been revoked or because a Royal Governor had been chosen by the King or even because the old political order had collapsed in a tired heap. The Puritan experiment ended in 1692, rather, because the sense of mission which had sustained it from the beginning no longer existed in any recognizable form, and thus the people of the Bay were left with few stable points of reference to help them remember who they were. When they looked back on their own history, the settlers had to conclude that the trajectory of the past pointed in quite a different direction than the one they now found themselves taking: they were no longer participants in a great adventure, no longer residents of a "city upon a hill," no longer members of that special revolutionary elite who were destined to bend the course of history according to God's own word. They were only themselves, living alone in a remote corner of the world, and this seemed a modest end for a crusade which had begun with such high expectations.

In the first place, as we have seen, the people of the colony had always pictured themselves as actors in an international movement, yet by the end of the century they had lost many of their most meaningful contacts with the rest of the world. The Puritan movement in England had scattered into a number of separate sects, each of which had been gradually absorbed into the freer climate of a new regime, and elsewhere in Europe the Protestant Reformation had lost much of its momentum without achieving half the goals set for it. And as a result, the colonists had lost touch with the background against which they had learned to assess their own stature and to survey their own place in the world.

In the second place, the original settlers had measured their achievements on a yardstick which no longer seemed to have the same sharp relevance. New England had been built by people who believed that God personally supervised every flicker of life on earth according to a plan beyond human comprehension, and in undertaking the expedition to America they were placing themselves entirely in God's hands. These were men whose doctrine prepared them to accept defeat gracefully, whose sense of piety depended upon an occasional moment of failure, hardship, even tragedy. Yet by the end of the century, the Puritan planters could look around them and count an impressive number of accomplishments. Here was no record of erratic providence; here was a record of solid human enterprise, and with this realization, as Daniel Boorstin suggests, the settlers moved from a "sense of mystery" to a "consciousness of mastery,"[19] from a helpless reliance on fate to a firm confidence in their own abilities. This shift helped clear the way for the appearance of the shrewd, practical, self-reliant Yankee as a figure in American history, but in the meantime it left the third generation of settlers with no clear definition of the status they held as the chosen children of God.

In the third place, Massachusetts had been founded as a lonely pocket of civilization in the

---

[17] Essex County Records, I, p. 265.
[18] Essex County Records, V, pp. 426–427.

[19] Daniel Boorstin, *The Genius of American Politics* (Chicago: University of Chicago Press, 1953).

midst of a howling wilderness, and as we have seen, this idea remained one of the most important themes of Puritan imagery long after the underbrush had been cut away and the wild animals killed. The settlers had lost sight of their local frontiers, not only in the sense that colonization had spread beyond the Berkshires into what is now upper state New York, but also in the sense that the wilderness which had held the community together by pressing in on it from all sides was disappearing. The original settlers had landed in a wilderness full of "wild beasts and wilder men"; yet sixty years later, sitting many miles from the nearest frontier in the prosperous seaboard town of Boston, Cotton Mather and other survivors of the old order still imagined that they were living in a wilderness—a territory they had explored as thoroughly as any frontiersmen. But the character of this wilderness was unlike anything the first settlers had ever seen, for its dense forests had become a jungle of mythical beasts and its skies were thick with flying spirits. In a sense, the Puritan community had helped mark its location in space by keeping close watch on the wilderness surrounding it on all sides; and now that the visible traces of that wilderness had receded out of sight, the settlers invented a new one by finding the shapes of the forest in the middle of the community itself.[20]

And as the wilderness took on this new character, it seemed that even the Devil had given up his more familiar disguises. He no longer lurked in the underbrush, for most of it had been cut away; he no longer assumed the shape of hostile Indians, for most of them had retreated inland for the moment; he no longer sent waves of heretics to trouble the Bay, for most of them lived quietly under the protection of toleration; he no longer appeared in the armies of the Counter-Reformation, for the old battlefields were still and too far away to excite the imagination. But his presence was felt everywhere, and when the colonists began to look for his new hiding places they found him crouched in the very heart of the Puritan colony. Quite literally, the people of the Bay began to see ghosts, and soon the boundaries of the New England Way closed in on a space full of demons and incubi, spectres and evil spirits, as the settlers tried to find a new sense of their own identity among the landmarks of a strange, invisible world. Cotton Mather, who knew every disguise in the Devil's wardrobe, offered a frightening catalogue of the Devil's attempts to destroy New England.

> I believe, there never was a poor Plantation, more pursued by the wrath of the Devil, than our poor New-England. . . . It was a rousing alarm to the Devil, when a great Company of English Protestants and Puritans, came to erect Evangelical Churches, in a corner of the world, where he had reign'd without control for many ages; and it is a vexing Eye-sore to the Devil, that our Lord Christ should be known, and own'd and preached in this howling wilderness. Wherefore he has left no Stone unturned, that so he might undermine his Plantation, and force us out of our Country.
>
> First, the Indian Powawes, used all their Sorceries to molest the first Planters here; but God said unto them, Touch them not! Then, Seducing spirits came to root in this Vineyard, but God so rated them off, that they have not prevail'd much farther than the edges of our Land. After this, we have had a continual blast upon some of our principal Grain, annually diminishing a vast part of our ordinary Food. Herewithal, wasting Sicknesses, especially Burning and Mortal Agues, have Shot the Arrows of Death in at our Windows. Next, we have had many Adversaries of our own Language, who have been perpetually assaying to deprive us of those English Liberties, in the encourage-

---

[20] See, again, the very interesting paper "Puritanism, The Wilderness and the Frontier" by Heimert.

ment whereof these Territories have been settled. As if this had not been enough; the Tawnies among whom we came have watered our Soil with the Blood of many Hundreds of Inhabitants. . . . Besides all which, now at last the Devils are (if I may so speak) in Person come down upon us with such a Wrath, as is justly much, and will quickly be more, the Astonishment of the World.[21]

And this last adventure of the Devil has a quality all its own.

Wherefore the Devil is now making one Attempt more upon us; an Attempt more Difficult, more Surprising, more snarl'd with unintelligible Circumstances than any that we have hitherto Encountered. . . . An Army of Devils is horribly broke in upon the place which is the center, and after a sort, the First-born of our English Settlements: and the Houses of the Good People there are fill'd with the doleful shrieks of their Children and Servants, Tormented by Invisible Hands, with Tortures altogether preternatural.[22]

The witchcraft hysteria occupied but a brief moment in the history of the Bay. The first actors to take part in it were a group of excited girls and a few of the less savory figures who drifted around the edges of the community, but the speed with which the other people of the Bay gathered to witness the encounter and accept an active role in it, not to mention the quality of the other persons who were eventually drawn into this vortex of activity, serves as an index to the gravity of the issues involved. For a few years, at least, the settlers of Massachusetts were alone in the world, bewildered by the loss of their old destiny but not yet aware of their new one, and during this fateful interval they tried to discover some image of themselves by listening to a chorus of voices which whispered to them from the depths of an invisible wilderness.

[21] Cotton Mather, "Wonders of the Invisible World," in Drake, *The Witchcraft Delusion*, pp. 94–95.

[22] Ibid., pp. 16–17.

6

Meet Dr. Franklin

Richard B. Morris

Benjamin Franklin, who called himself "the printer of Philadelphia," was one of the most remarkable human beings Colonial America ever produced. He not only personified the frugality, hard work, restlessness, and occasional irreverence of Colonial Americans, but came to symbolize their growing sense of nationality as well. In his long lifetime, he tried his hand at virtually every trade and profession young America had to offer—among other things, he was a farmer, a printer, a scientist, an author, a philosopher, a statesman, a diplomat, and a connoisseur of women. In the latter capacity, he composed an article on the cultivation of a mistress and became a legendary womanizer. According to one anecdote, he sired so many children that a colleague was moved to quip that it was not Washington but Benjamin Franklin who was "the real father of our country." Franklin would have appreciated the anecdote, for he had a consummate sense of humor. But above all, he had an unflagging love for liberty and the natural rights of man.

Still, Franklin was a complex and often contradictory man. As Richard B. Morris demonstrates in his lively and candid portrait, Franklin went through identity crises like anyone else, indulged in literary pranks, and had ambivalent attitudes about women. Though he abhorred violence, he was a devious individual who rebelled against convention and authority and in time became a leading American revolutionary. At the same time, Franklin regarded himself as truly a citizen of the world who hoped one day "that not only the Love of Liberty, but a thorough Knowledge of the Rights of Man, may pervade all the Nations of the Earth, so that a Philosopher may set his Foot anywhere on its Surface, and say, 'This is my Country.' "

Deceptively simple and disarmingly candid, but in reality a man of enormous complexity, [Benjamin] Franklin wore many masks, and from his own time to this day each beholder has chosen the mask that suited his fancy. To D. H. Lawrence, Franklin typified the hypocritical and bankrupt morality of the do-gooder American, with his stress upon an old-fashioned Puritan ethic that glorified work, frugality, and temperance—in short, a "snuff-coloured little man!" of whom "the immortal soul part was a sort of cheap insurance policy." Lawrence resented being shoved into "a barbed-wire paddock" and made to "grow potatoes or Chicagoes." Revealing in this castigation much about himself and little insight into Franklin, Lawrence could not end his diatribe against the most cosmopolitan of all Americans without hurling a barbed shaft at "clever America" lying "on her muck-heaps of gold." F. Scott Fitzgerald quickly fired off a broadside of his own. In *The Great Gatsby*, that literary darling of the Jazz Age indicted *Poor Richard* as midwife to a generation of bootleggers.

If Lawrence and Fitzgerald were put off by Franklin's commonsense materialism which verged on crassness or if Max Weber saw Franklin as embodying all that was despicable in both the American character and the capital-

From pp. 6–30 in *Seven Who Shaped Our Destiny* by Richard B. Morris. Copyright © 1973 by Richard B. Morris. By permission of Harper & Row, Publishers.

ist system, if they and other critics considered him as little more than a methodical shopkeeper, they signally failed to understand him. They failed to perceive how Franklin's materialism was transmuted into benevolent and humanitarian ends, how that shopkeeper's mind was enkindled by a ranging imagination that set no bounds to his intellectual interests and that continually fed an extraordinarily inventive and creative spark. They failed to explain how the popularizer of an American code of hard work, frugality, and moral restraint had no conscientious scruples about enjoying high living, a liberal sexual code for himself, and bawdy humor. They failed to explain how so prudent and methodical a man could have got caught up in a revolution in no small part of his own making.

Franklin would have been the first to concede that he had in his autobiography created a character gratifying to his own vanity. "Most people dislike vanity in others, whatever share they have of it themselves," he observed, "but I give it fair quarter where I meet it." Begun in 1771, when the author had completed a half-dozen careers and stood on the threshold of his most dramatic role, his autobiography constitutes the most dazzling success story of American history. The penniless waif who arrived in Philadelphia disheveled and friendless, walking up Market Street munching a great puffy roll, had by grit and ability propelled himself to the top. Not only did the young printer's apprentice manage the speedy acquisition of a fortune, but he went on to achieve distinction in many different fields, and greatness in a few of them. In an age when the mastery of more than one discipline was possible, Franklin surpassed all his contemporaries as a well-rounded citizen of the world. Endowed with a physique so strong that as a young man he could carry a large form of type in each hand, "when others carried but one in both hands," a superb athlete and a proficient swimmer, Franklin proved to be a talented printer, an enterprising newspaper editor and publisher, a tireless promoter of cultural institutes, America's first great scientist whose volume on electricity turned out to be the most influential book to come out of America in the eighteenth century, and second to none as a statesman. Eldest of the Founding Fathers by a whole generation, he was in some respects the most radical, the most devious, and the most complicated.

From the available evidence, mainly provided by the subject himself, Franklin underwent two separate identity crises, when, as modern-day psychoanalysts suggest, the subject struggles for a new self and a new conception of his place in the world. In adolescence Franklin experienced a psychological crisis of the kind that Erik Erikson has so perceptively attributed to personages as disparate as Martin Luther and Mahatma Gandhi. Again, Franklin, the middle-aged man seeking a new image of himself, seems the prototype of Jung's classic case. As regards the first crisis, Franklin's autobiography reveals a sixteen-year-old rebelling against sibling rivalry and the authority of his household, using a variety of devices to maintain his individuality and sense of self-importance.

Born in Boston in 1706, the tenth son of Josiah and Abiah Folger Franklin, and the youngest son of the youngest son for five generations, Franklin could very easily have developed an inferiority complex as one of the youngest of thirteen children sitting around his father's table at one time. Everything about the home reduced Franklin's stature in his own eyes. When his father tried to make a tallow chandler and soap boiler out of him, he made it clear that his father's trade was not to his liking. His father then apprenticed the twelve-year-old lad to his brother James, who had started a Boston newspaper, the *New England Courant*, in 1721. For the next few years Benjamin was involved in one or another kind of rebellion.

Take the matter of food. Benjamin, an omnivorous reader, devoured a book recommending a vegetarian diet. Since his brother James boarded both himself and his apprentices at an-

other establishment, Franklin's refusal to eat meat or fish proved an embarrassment to his elder brother and a nuisance to the housekeeper. Franklin, to save arguments which he abhorred, worked out a deal with his brother, who agreed to remit to him half the money he paid out for him for board if he would board himself. Concentrating on a frugal meatless diet, which he dispatched quickly, Franklin, eating by himself, had more time to continue his studies. While eating one of his hastily prepared meals he first feasted on Locke's treatise *On Human Understanding*.

A trivial episode, indeed, but this piece of self-flagellation forecast a lifelong pattern of pervasive traits. Benjamin Franklin did not like to hurt anyone, even nonhuman creatures. He avoided hostilities. Rather than insisting upon getting the menu he preferred, he withdrew from the table of battle and arranged to feed himself. This noncombative nature, masking a steely determination, explains much of Franklin's relation with others thereafter. Even his abandonment of the faddish vegetarian diet provides insights into the evolving Franklin with his pride in rational decision. On his voyage from Boston to Philadelphia, he tells us, his ship became becalmed off Block Island, where the crew spent their idle moments catching cod. When the fish were opened, he saw that smaller fish came out of the stomachs of the larger cod. "Then, thought I," he confessed in his autobiography, "If you eat one another, I don't see why we mayn't eat you." With that, he proceeded to enjoy a hearty codfish repast and to return at once to a normal flesh-eating diet. With a flash of self-revelation, he comments, "So convenient a thing it is to be a *reasonable creature*, since it enables one to find or make a reason for everything one has a mind to do."

Franklin's rebellion against authority and convention soon assumed a more meaningful dimension. When, in 1722, his brother James was jailed for a month for printing critical remarks in his newspaper about the authorities, the sixteen-year-old apprentice pounced on the chance to achieve something on his own. He published the paper for his brother, running his own name on the masthead to circumvent the government. Continually quarreling with his overbearing brother, Franklin determined to quit his job, leave his family and Boston, and establish himself by his own efforts unaided. The youthful rebel set forth on his well-publicized journey to Philadelphia, arriving in that bustling town in October, 1723, when he was little more than seventeen years of age.

To carve out a niche for himself in the printing trade, Franklin had to keep a checkrein on his rebellious disposition. For weeks he bore without ill temper the badgering of his master Keimer. When the blow-up came, Franklin, rather than stay and quarrel, packed up and lit out. Once more he was on his own. "Of all things I hate altercation," he wrote years later to one of his fellow commissioners in Paris with whom he was continually at odds. He would write sharp retorts and then not mail the letters. An operator or negotiator *par excellence*, Franklin revealed in his youthful rebellion against family and employers the defensive techniques he so skillfully utilized to avoid combat. Yet there was little about Franklin's behavior which we associate with neurotics. He was a happy extrovert, who enjoyed the company of women, and was gregarious and self-assured, a striking contrast to Isaac Newton, a tortured introvert who remained a bachelor all his life. Suffice to say that Franklin never suffered the kind of nervous breakdown that Newton experienced at the height of his powers, and as a result his effectiveness remained undiminished until a very advanced age.

If Franklin early showed an inclination to back away from a quarrel, to avoid a head-on collision, if his modesty and candor concealed a comprehension of his own importance and a persistent deviousness, such traits may go far to explain the curious satisfaction he took in perpetrating hoaxes on an unsuspecting and gullible

Benjamin Franklin. Witty, self-confident, and extremely intelligent, Benjamin Franklin succeeded in everything he tried, from publishing a Philadelphia newspaper and Poor Richard's Almanac *to wooing the ladies of Paris. (Courtesy of The Historical Pictures Service—Chicago.)*

public. The clandestine side of Franklin, a manifestation of his unwillingness to engage in direct confrontation, hugely benefited by his sense of humor and satirical talents. An inveterate literary prankster from his precocious teens until his death, Franklin perpetrated one literary hoax after another. In 1730, when he became the sole owner of a printing shop and proprietor of the *Pennsylvania Gazette*, which his quondam boss Keimer had launched a few years earlier, Franklin's paper reported a witch trial at Mount Holly, New Jersey, for which there is no authority in fact.

Franklin's greatest hoax was probably written in 1746 and perpetrated the following year, when the story ran in London's *General Adver-*

tiser. Quickly it was reprinted throughout England, Scotland, and Ireland, and in turn picked up by the Boston and New York papers. This was his report of a speech of Polly Baker before a Massachusetts court, in defense of an alleged prosecution for the fifth time for having a bastard child. "Can it be crime (in the nature of things I mean) to add to the number of the King's subjects, in a new country that really wants people?" she pleaded. "I own it, I should think it as praiseworthy, rather than a punishable action." Denying that she had ever turned down a marriage proposal, and asserting that she was betrayed by the man who first made her such an offer, she compared her role with that of the great number of bachelors in the new country who had "never sincerely and honourably courted a woman in their lives" and insisted that, far from sinning, she had obeyed the "great command of Nature, and of Nature's God, *Encrease and Multiply*." Her compassionate judges remitted her punishment, and, according to this account, one of them married her the very next day.

How so obviously concocted a morality tale as that one could have gained such wide credence seems incredible on its face. Yet the French sage, the Abbé Raynal, picked it up for his *Histoire Philosophique et Politique*, published in 1770. Some seven years later, while visiting Franklin at Passy, Raynal was to be disabused. "When I was young and printed a newspaper," Franklin confessed, "it sometimes happened, when I was short of material to fill my sheet, that I amused myself by making up stories, and that of Polly Baker is one of the number."

When some years later Franklin's severe critic John Adams listed Polly Baker's speech as one of Franklin's many "outrages to morality and decorum," he was censoring not only Franklin's liberal sexual code but the latter's inability to throw off bad habits in old age. Franklin's penchant for pseudonymous writing was one side of his devious nature and evidenced his desire to avoid direct confrontation. He continued in later life

to write a prodigious number of letters under assumed names which appeared in the American, English, and French press, some still undetected. His sly "Edict by the King of Prussia," appearing in an English newspaper in 1773, was a parody, in which Frederick the Great threatened reprisals against England for failing to emancipate the colonists from Germany that originally settled the island. As commissioner in Paris Franklin reputably wrote a vitriolic hoax, *The Sale of the Hessians,* in which a Count de Schaumbergh expressed delight that 1,605 of his Hessians had been killed in America, 150 more than Lord North had reported to him. This was a windfall, since he was entitled to a sum of money for every fatality suffered by the mercenaries he had sold to George III. In the midst of delicate negotiations with the British to end the war of the American Revolution the irrepressible Franklin fabricated a hoax about the scalping of Americans by Indians in the pay of the British, and then printed it in the guise of a *Supplement to the Boston Independent Chronicle.* Gruesome propaganda indeed, but Franklin justified his deception to the censorious Adams by remarking that he believed the number of persons actually scalped "in this murdering war by the Indians to exceed what is mentioned in invoice."

The image of himself Franklin chose to leave us in his unfinished autobiography was of a man on the make, who insincerely exploited popular morality to keep his printing presses running. Yet he himself, perhaps tongue in cheek, would have said that the morality of *Poor Richard* was foreshadowed by the plan of conduct Franklin had put down on paper on a return voyage in 1726 to Philadelphia from London, where he had spent almost two years in an effort to be able to buy equipment to set himself up as a printer. Later in life Franklin praised the plan as "the more remarkable, as being formed when I was so young, and yet being pretty faithfully adhered to quite through to old Age." The plan stressed the practice of extreme frugality until he had paid his debts, as well as truthfulness, industry, and the avoidance of speaking ill of others.

Franklin, the sixteen-year-old apprentice, absorbed the literary styles of his brother James and other New England satirists running their pieces in the *Courant,* and he clearly used the *Spectator* as his literary model. He produced the Silence Dogood letters, thirteen in a row, until, he admitted, "my small fund of sense for such performances was pretty well exhausted." Until then even his own brother was not aware of the identity of the author. Typical was No. 6, which criticized pride in apparel, singling out such outlandish fashions as hoop petticoats, "monstrous topsy-turvy *Mortar-Pieces* . . . neither fit for the Church, the Hall, or the Kitchen," and looming more "like Engines of War for bombarding the Town, than Ornaments of the Fair Sex."

If the Dogood letters satisfied Franklin's itch for authorship, *Poor Richard* brought him fame and fortune. Lacking originality, drawing upon a wide range of proverbs and aphorisms, notably found in a half-dozen contemporary English anthologies, Franklin skillfully selected, edited, and simplified. For example, James Howell's *Lexicon Tetraglotton* (London, 1660), says: "The greatest talkers are the least doers." *Poor Richard* in 1733 made it: "Great talkers, little doers." Or Thomas Fuller's *Gnomolonia* (London, 1732): "The way to be safe is never to be secure"; this becomes in *Poor Richard,* 1748: "He that's secure is not safe." Ever so often one of the aphorisms seem to reflect Franklin's own views. Thus, *Poor Richard* in 1747 counseled: "Strive to be the *greatest* Man in your Country, and you may be disappointed; Strive to be the *best,* and you may succeed: He may well win the race that runs by himself." Again, two years later, *Poor Richard* extols Martin Luther for being "remarkably *temperate* in meat and drink," perhaps a throwback to Franklin's own adolescent dietary obsessions, with an added comment, *"There was never any* industrious *man who was not a* temperate *man."* To the first American pragmatist what was moral was what worked and what worked was moral.

If there was any priggish streak in the literary Franklin it was abundantly redeemed by his bawdy sense of humor and his taste for earthy language. Thus, to *Poor Richard*, foretelling the weather by astrology was "as easy as pissing abed." "He that lives upon Hope dies farting." The bawdy note of reportage guaranteed a good circulation for Franklin's *Gazette:* Thus in 1731:

We are credibly inform'd, that the young Woman who not long since petitioned the Governor, and the Assembly to be divorced from her Husband, and at times, industriously solicited most of the Magistrates on that Account, has at last concluded to cohabit with him again. It is said the Report of the Physicians (who in Form examined his *Abilities*, and allowed him to be in every respect *sufficient*) gave her but small Satisfaction; Whether any Experiments *more satisfactory* have been try'd, we cannot say; but it seems she now declares it as her Opinion, That *George is as good as de best.*

Franklin's ambivalent views of women indubitably reflected his own personal relations with the other sex. In his younger days he took sex hungrily, secretly, and without love. One of his women—just which one nobody knows for sure—bore him a son in 1730 or 1731. It was rumored that the child's mother was a maidservant of Franklin's named Barbara, an accusation first printed in 1764 by a political foe of Franklin's, reputedly Hugh Williamson. Whether it was this sudden responsibility or just the boredom of sowing his wild oats, Franklin came to realize that "a single man resembles the odd half of a pair of scissors." Having unsuccessfully sought a match with a woman who would bring him money, Franklin turned his thoughts back to Deborah Read, the girl he had first courted in Philadelphia and then jilted. Rebounding from that humiliation, Deborah married a potter named Rogers who quickly deserted her. Then she did not even bother to have the marriage annulled, relying instead on the rumor that her

husband had left behind him a wife in England. Franklin, so he tells us in his autobiography, conveniently overlooked "these difficulties," and "took her to wife, September 1st, 1730." The illegitimate child, William, whether born before or after Franklin's common-law marriage to Deborah, became part of the household, a convenient arrangement for Franklin while a constant reminder to Deborah of her spouse's less than romantic feelings about her. Soon there arose between Deborah and William a coldness bordering on hostility.

The married Franklin's literary allusions to women could be both amicable and patronizing; he could treat them as equals but show downright hostility at times. He portrayed the widow Silence Dogood as frugal, industrious, prosaic, and earthy, but somehow retaining her femininity. Such inferiority as women appeared to have must be attributed to their inferior education. While believing in the moral equality of the sexes, Franklin did not encourage women to enter unconventional fields of activity. He stuffed his *Almanack* with female stereotypes, perhaps charging off his own grievances to the sex in general. He frequently jabbed at "domineering women," with Richard Saunders the prototype of all henpecked husbands and Bridget, his "shrewish, clacking" wife. Scolding, gossipy women and talkative old maids are frequent targets of Franklin's jibes. A woman's role in life, he tells us, is to be a wife and have babies, but a man has a more versatile role and therefore commands a higher value.

Franklin's bagatelles "On Perfumes" and "On Marriages," frequently if furtively printed, kept under wraps for years by the Department of State, attained a clandestine fame, but few in the nineteenth century dared to print either. With the sexual revolution of the twentieth century and the penchant for scatological vocabulary, Franklin's letter on marriage and mistresses attained respectability and wide circulation. In essence, Franklin, in a letter dated June 25, 1745, commended marriage as the state in which

a man was "most likely to find solid Happiness." However, those wishing to avoid matrimony without forgoing sex were advised to choose "*old Women to young ones.*" Among the virtues of older women he listed their more agreeable conversation, their continued amiability to counteract the "Diminution of Beauty," the absence of a "hazard of Children," their greater prudence and discretion in conducting extramarital affairs, and the superiority of techniques of older women. "As in the dark all Cats are grey, the Pleasure of corporal Enjoyment with an old Woman is at least equal, and frequently superior, every Knack being by Practice capable of Improvement." Furthermore, who could doubt the advantages of making an old woman "*happy*" against debauching a virgin and contributing to her ruin. Finally, old women are "*so grateful!!*"

How much this advice reflected Franklin's own marriage of convenience remains for speculation. *Poor Richard* is constantly chiding cuckolds and scolding wives, and suggesting that marital infidelity is the course of things. "Let thy maidservant be faithful, strong, and homely." "She that paints her Face, thinks of her Tail." "Three things are men most liable to be cheated in, a Horse, a Wig, and a Wife." Or consider poor Lubin lying on his deathbed, both he and his wife despairing, he fearing death, she, "that he may live." Or the metaphor of women as books and men the readers. "Are Women Books? says Hodge, then would mine were an *Almanack*, to change her every Year."

Enough examples, perhaps, have been chosen to show that Franklin's early view of women was based on a combination of gross and illicit sexual experiences and a less than satisfying marriage with a wife neither glamorous nor intellectually compatible.

Abruptly, at the age of forty-two, Franklin retired from active participation in his printing business. He explained the action quite simply: "I flattered myself that, by the sufficient tho' moderate fortune I had acquir'd, I had secured leisure during the rest of my life for philosophical studies and amusements." These words masked the middle-age identity crisis that he was now undergoing. Seeking to project himself on a larger stage, he did not completely cut his ties to a less glamorous past, including a wife who was a social liability, but conveniently eluded it. Now he could lay aside the tools of his trade and the garments of a petit bourgeois and enter the circles of gentility. Gone were the days he would sup on an anchovy, a slice of bread and butter, and a half-pint of ale shared with a companion. His long bouts with the gout in later life attest to his penchant for high living, for Madeira, champagne, Parmesan cheese, and other continental delicacies. Sage, philanthropist, statesman, he became, as one critic has remarked, "an intellectual transvestite," affecting a personality switch that was virtually completed before he left on his first mission (second trip) to England in 1757. Not that Franklin was a purely parochial figure at the time of his retirement from business. Already he had shown that passion for improvement which was to mark his entire career. Already he had achieved some local reputation in public office, notably in the Pennsylvania Assembly. Already he had displayed his inventive techniques, most notably his invention of the Pennsylvania fireplace, and had begun his inquiries into the natural sciences.

Now, on retirement from private affairs, he stood on the threshold of fame. In the subsequent decade he plunged into his scientific investigations and into provincial politics with equal zest. Dispatched to England in 1757 to present the case of the Pennsylvania Assembly against the proprietor, he spent five of the happiest years of his life residing at the Craven Street residence of Mrs. Margaret Stevenson. Mrs. Stevenson, and especially her daughter Mary, provided for him a pleasant and stimulating home away from home. Reluctantly he returned to Philadelphia at the end of his five-year stay, so enraptured of England that he even

contemplated settling there, "provided we can persuade the good Woman to cross the Seas." Once more, in 1764, he was sent abroad, where he stayed to participate in all the agitation associated with the Grenville revenue measures. Snugly content in the Stevenson ménage, Franklin corresponded perfunctorily with his wife back in Philadelphia. Knowing that Deborah was unwilling to risk a sea voyage to join him in London, Franklin did not insist. And although he wrote his wife affectionate letters and sent her gifts, he never saw her again. She died of a stroke in December, 1774, without benefit of Franklin's presence.

It was in France after the American Revolution had broken out that Franklin achieved more completely that new identity which was the quest of his later years. There the mellow septuagenarian, diplomat, and peacemaker carried out a game with the ladies of the salon, playing a part, ironic, detached but romantic, enjoying an *amitié amoureuse* with his impressionable and neurotic neighbor, Mme. Brillon in Passy, flirting in Paris with the romantically minded Comtesse d'Houdetot, and then in the rustic retreat of Auteuil falling in love with the widow of Helvétius, whom he was prepared to marry had she been so inclined. In the unreal world of the salon Franklin relished the role of "papa." Still he avoided combat or confrontation even in his flirtation. Where he scented rejection, he turned witty, ironic, and verbally sexual.

He found time, while engaged in the weighty affairs of peacemaking during the summer of '82, to draw up a treaty of "eternal peace, friendship, and love" between himself and Madame Brillon. Like a good draftsman, Franklin was careful to preserve his freedom of action, in this case toward other females, while at the same time insisting on his right to behave without inhibitions toward his amiable neighbor. Some months before he had written her:

I often pass before your house. It appears desolate to me. Formerly I broke the Com-

mandment by coveting it along with my neighbor's wife. Now I do not covet it any more, so I am less a sinner. But as to his wife I always find these Commandments inconvenient and I am sorry that they were ever made. If in your travels you happen to see the Holy Father, ask him to repeal them, as things given only to the Jews and too uncomfortable for good Christians.

Franklin met Mme. Brillon in 1777, and found her a beautiful woman in her early thirties, an accomplished musician, married to a rich and tolerant man, twenty-four years her senior. To Mme. Brillon Franklin was a father figure, while to Franklin she combined the qualities of daughter and mistress. Part tease, part prude, Mme. Brillon once remarked: "Do you know, my dear papa, that people have criticized the sweet habit I have taken of sitting on your lap, and your habit of soliciting from me what I always refuse?" In turn, Franklin reminded her of a game of chess he had played in her bathroom while she soaked in the tub.

If Franklin was perhaps most passionately fond of Brillon, other ladies of the salon set managed to catch his eye, among them the pockmarked, cross-eyed Comtesse d'Houdetot, who made up in sex appeal what she lacked in looks. Unlike Rousseau, who cherished for the Comtesse an unrequited passion, which he widely publicized in his posthumous *La Nouvelle Héloise*, Franklin's relations with her never seemed to border on close intimacy. Contrariwise, Franklin carried on a long flirtation with the widowed Mme. Helvétius. Abigail Adams, John's straitlaced wife, was shocked at the open intimacies between the pair. Franklin complained that since he had given Madame "so many of his days," she appeared "very ungrateful in not giving him one of her nights." Whether in desperation or because he really felt the need to rebuild some kind of family life, he proposed to her. When she turned him down, he wrote a bagatelle, recounting a conversation with

Madame's husband in the Elysian Fields, as well as his own encounter with his deceased wife Deborah. He then dashed into print with the piece, an odd thing to do if he were deadly serious about the proposal. As Sainte-Beuve remarked of this episode, Franklin never allowed himself to be carried away by feeling, whether in his youth or in old age, whether in love or in religion. His romantic posture was almost ritualistic. He almost seemed relieved at the chance to convert an emotional rebuff into a literary exercise.

Franklin's casual attitude toward sexual morality was shared by his son and grandson. Himself illegitimate, William, who sought to efface the cloud over his origin by becoming an arrant social climber and most respectable Tory, also sired an illegitimate son, William Temple Franklin, whose mother remains as much a mystery as William's own. Temple, engaged at Franklin's behest by the American peace commissioners as secretary in Paris, had an affair with Blanchette Caillot, a married woman by whom he had a child and whom he abandoned on his return to America.

If Temple was a playboy, that charge could never fairly be leveled at his grandfather. The Old Doctor, an irrepressible activist and do-gooder, embodied in his own career that blend of practicality and idealism which has characterized Americans ever since. Convinced from early youth of the values of self-improvement and self-education, Franklin on his return to Philadelphia from his first trip to England organized the Junto, a society half debating, half social, attesting both to the sponsor's belief in the potentialities of continued adult education and to his craving for intellectual companionship not provided in his own home. Then came the subscription library, still flourishing in Philadelphia. Franklin's plans for an academy, drawn up in 1743, reached fruition a decade later, and were a positive outgrowth of his conviction that an English rather than a classical education was more suitable to modern man and

that most colleges stuffed the heads of students with irrelevant book knowledge. Then, too, the Pennsylvania Hospital project drew upon his seemingly inexhaustible fund of energy, hospitalization being defended by him as more economical than home care. So did his organization of a local fire company, and his program for a tax-supported permanent watch, and for lighting, paving, sweeping, draining, and deicing the streets of Philadelphia. Convinced of the virtues of thrift and industry, Franklin could be expected to take a dim view of poor relief, and questioned "whether the laws peculiar to England which compel the rich to maintain the poor have not given the latter a dependence that very much lessens the care of providing against the wants of old age." Truly, this revolutionary, if he returned to us today, might well be aghast at the largess of the modern welfare state with its indifference to the work ethos.

Franklin evolved what he called his "moral algebra" to explain his code of ethics, a system which clearly anticipated Jeremy Bentham. In a letter to Joseph Priestley written in 1772 he outlined his method of marshaling all the considerations pro and con for a contemplated decision, setting them down in parallel columns, and then pausing for a few days before entering "short hints" for or against the measure. Subtracting liability from assets, one would come up with a moral or political credit or debit. Franklin never narrowed down the springs of human conduct to pain and pleasure, as did Bentham, but assumed a more complex set of motives. Franklin's moral algebra stemmed in part from his bookkeeping mentality, in part from his desire to reduce life to an orderly system.

That the oldest of American Revolutionaries should be committed to controlled, orderly change takes on larger significance when one seeks explanations as to why the American Revolution did not pursue the violent, even chaotic, course of the French. Nowhere is this better illustrated than in Franklin's evolving view about the Negro and slavery, in neither of

which subjects did he show any active interest until well after middle life (after due allowance for the fact that as printer he published a few antislavery tracts in his earlier years). By shrewd calculation he demonstrated that the labor of a slave in America was dearer than that of an iron or wool worker in England. Embodying these calculations in what turned out to be a seminal paper on American demography, written when he was forty-five, Franklin did not let himself get actively drawn into the Negro question for another twenty years, and then he agreed to serve as a trustee for an English fund to convert Negroes. As a Deist he could hardly have been passionately aroused by the prospect of saving souls, but may have consented to serve because of the degree of respectable public exposure involved. Earlier, in 1764, he was prepared to concede that some Negroes had "a strong sense of justice and honour," but it was not until 1772, when he was sixty-six years old, that he became aroused about the slave trade, that "detestable commerce." By the next year he was on record sympathizing with the movement to abolish slavery, and in 1787 he became president of the Pennsylvania Abolition Society, the oldest society of its kind in the world. He soon proposed a program for the education of free blacks in trades and other employment to avoid "poverty, idleness, and many vicious habits."

Franklin's last public act before his death was the signing of a memorial to Congress from his own Abolition Society asking for justice for the blacks and an end in the "traffic in the persons of our fellowmen." When Southern congressmen denounced the measure he sent to the press one of the last writings to come from his pen, a fictional account of an observation by an official of Algiers in 1687 denying a petition of an extremist sect opposing the enslaving of Christians. Accordingly, the divan resolved, in Franklin's tongue-in-cheek reporting, " 'The doctrine that plundering and enslaving the Christians is unjust, is, at best, problematical; but that it is the interest of this state to continue the practice,

is clear: therefore let the petition be rejected.' "

A man of the Enlightenment, Franklin had faith in the power and beneficence of science. In moments snatched from public affairs during the latter 1740's and early 1750's—moments when public alarms interrupted his research at the most creative instant—he plunged into scientific experimentation. While his lightning kite and rod quickly made him an international celebrity, Franklin was no mere dilettante gadgeteer. His conception of electricity as a flow with negative and positive forces opened the door to further theoretical development in the field of electromagnetism. His pamphlet on electricity, published originally in 1751, went through ten editions, including revisions, in four languages before the American Revolution. Honors from British scientists were heaped upon him, and when he arrived in England in 1757 and again in 1764, and in France in 1776, he came each time with an enlarged international reputation as a scientist whom Chatham compared in Parliament to "our Boyle" and "our Newton."

Pathbreaking as Franklin's work on electricity proved to be, his range of scientific interest extended far beyond theoretical physics. He pioneered in locating the Gulf Stream, in discovering that northeast storms come from the southwest, in making measurements of heat absorption with regard to color, and in investigating the conductivity of different substances with regard to heat. A variety of inventions attested to his utilitarian bent—the Franklin stove, the lightning rod, the flexible metal catheter, bifocal glasses, the glass harmonica, the smokeless chimney. Indefatigable in his expenditure of his spare time on useful ends, he made observations on the nature of communication between insects, contributed importantly to our knowledge of the causes of the common cold, advocated scientific ventilation, and even tried electric shock treatment to treat palsy on a number of occasions.

To the last Franklin stoutly defended scientific experimentation which promised no immediate

practical consequences. Watching the first balloon ascension in Paris, he parried the question, "What good is it?" with a characteristic retort, "What good is a newborn baby?"

Committed as he was to discovering truth through scientific inquiry, Franklin could be expected to be impatient with formal theology. While not denigrating faith, he regretted that it had not been "more productive of Good Works than I have generally seen it." He suggested that, Chinese style, laymen leave praying to the men who were paid to pray for them. At the age of twenty-two he articulated a simple creed, positing a deistic Christian God, with infinite power which He would abstain from wielding in arbitrary fashion. His deistic views remained unchanged when, a month before his death, Ezra Stiles asked him his opinion of the divinity of Jesus. Confessing doubts, Franklin refused to dogmatize or to busy himself with the problem at so late a date, since, he remarked, "I expect soon an opportunity of knowing the truth with less trouble."

Unlike the philosophes who spread toleration but were intolerant of Roman Catholicism, Franklin tolerated and even encouraged any and all sects. He contributed to the support of various Protestant churches and the Jewish synagogue in Philadelphia, and, exploiting his friendship with the papal nuncio in Paris, he had his friend John Carroll made the first bishop of the Catholic Church in the new United States. He declared himself ready to welcome a Muslim preacher sent by the grand mufti in Constantinople, but that exotic spectacle was spared Protestant America of his day.

Although he fancied the garb of a Quaker, a subtle form of reverse ostentation that ill-accorded with his preachments about humility, Franklin was no pacifist. During King George's War he urged the need of preparedness upon his city and province, praising "that *Zeal* for the *Publick Good,* that *military Prowess, and* that *undaunted Spirit,*" which in past ages had distinguished the British nation. Like most of the Founding Fathers he could boast a military experience regardless of its brevity, and in Franklin's case it lasted some six weeks. Following Braddock's disastrous defeat in December, 1755, Franklin as a civilian committeeman marched into the interior at the head of an armed force, directing an improvised relief program for the frontier refugees who had crowded into Bethlehem and seeing about the fortifying of the Lehigh gap. Back in Philadelphia he organized a defense force known as the "Associators," of which he was elected colonel. As in his other projects, he entered into these military arrangements with gusto, all to the annoyance of the proprietor, who regarded Franklin as a dangerous political rival and who regularly vetoed all tax bills which included military levies on the proprietary estate of the Penn family.

Once again, almost a decade later, he took command of a military force—this time to face down a frontier band known as the Paxton Boys who in 1764 set out on a lawless march to Philadelphia to confront the government with a demand for protection against the Indians. Franklin issued a blazing pamphlet denouncing the Paxton Boys for their attacks on peaceful Indians and organized and led a force to Germantown, where he confronted the remonstrants and issued a firm warning. The Paxton Boys veered off, and order was finally restored. "For about forty-eight hours," Franklin remarked, "I was a very great man, as I had been once some years before in a time of public danger."

Franklin's brief exposure as a military figure, combined with his leadership of the antiproprietary party, and his general prominence and popularity had by now made him anathema to proprietor and conservatives alike. Standing out against the Establishment, Franklin was heartened by the enemies he had made. A thorough democrat, Franklin had little use for proprietary privileges or a titled aristocracy. In his Silence Dogood letters written as far back as 1723 he had pointed out that "Adam was never called

Master Adam; we never read of Noah *Esquire*, Lot *Knight* and *Baronet*, nor the *Right Honourable* Abraham Viscount Mesopotamia, Baron of Carian; no, no, they were plain Men." Again, *Poor Richard* engaged in an amusing genealogical computation to prove that over the centuries it was impossible to preserve blood free of mixtures, and "that the Pretension of such Purity of Blood in ancient Families is a mere Joke." With perhaps pardonable inconsistency Franklin took the trouble to trace his own family back to stout English gentry, but his basic antiaristocratic convictions stood the test of time. When, in the post-Revolutionary years, the patrician-sounding Society of the Cincinnati was founded in America, Franklin in France scoffed at the Cincinnati as "hereditary knights" and egged on Mirabeau to publish an indictment of the Order which set off an international clamor against its hereditary character.

For courts and lawyers, defenders of property and the status quo, Franklin reserved some of his most vitriolic humor. His *Gazette* consistently held up to ridicule the snobbery of using law French in the courts, excessive legal fees and court costs, and the prolixity and perils of litigation. For the lawyers who "can, with Ease, Twist Words and Meanings as you please," *Poor Richard* shows no tolerance. Predictably, Franklin took the side of the debtor against the creditor, the paper-money man against the hard-currency man.

Franklin's support of paper money did not hurt him in the least. As a matter of fact, the Assembly gave him the printing contract in 1731 for the £40,000 in bills of credit that it authorized that year. This incident could be multiplied many times. Franklin ever had an eye for the main chance. Whether as a poor printer, a rising politician, or an established statesman-scientist, he was regarded by unfriendly critics as a man on the make of dubious integrity. One of the improvements Franklin introduced as deputy postmaster general of the colonies was to make the carrying of newspapers a source of revenue and to compel his riders to take all the papers that were offered. On its face a revenue producer and a safeguard against monopoly, the ruling could hardly damage Franklin, publisher or partner of seven or eight newspapers, a chain stretching from New York to Antigua, and even including a German-language paper in Pennsylvania.

Accumulating a tidy capital, Franklin invested in Philadelphia town lots, and then, as the speculative bug bit him, plunged into Nova Scotian and western land ventures. His secretive nature seemed ideally suited to such investments, in which he followed a rule he laid down in 1753: "Great designs should not be made publick till they are ripe for execution, lest obstacles are thrown in the way." The climax of Franklin's land speculations came in 1769 when he joined forces with Samuel Wharton to advance in England the interests of the Grand Ohio Company, which was more British than colonial in composition. This grand alliance of speculators and big-time politicians succeeded in winning from the Privy Council on July 1, 1772, a favorable recommendation supporting their fantastic dream of a colony called Vandalia, to be fitted together from the pieces of the present-day states of Pennsylvania, Maryland, West Virginia, and Kentucky. There Franklin's love of order would replace that frontier anarchy which he abhorred.

Standing on the brink of a stunning success, the Vandalia speculators were now put in jeopardy by Franklin's rash indiscretion in turning over to his radical friends in Massachusetts some embarrassing letters of Governor Thomas Hutchinson which had been given to him in confidence. Indignant at Franklin's disloyalty, the Crown officers refused to complete the papers confirming the grant to the Grand Ohio Company. With his usual deviousness, Franklin, in concert with the banker Thomas Walpole, publicly resigned from the company. In reality Walpole and Franklin had a private understanding by which the latter would retain his two

shares out of the total of seventy-two shares of stock in the company. As late as April 11, 1775, Franklin, Walpole and others signed a power of attorney authorizing William Trent to act on their behalf with respect to the grant, hardly necessary if Franklin was indeed out of the picture. In the summer of 1778 Franklin had a change of heart and decided to get back his original letter of resignation. When Walpole complied, Franklin added thereto a memorandum asserting: "I am still to be considered as an Associate, and was called upon for my Payments as before. My right to two shares, or two Parts of 72, in that Purchase still continues . . . and I hope, that when the Trouble of America is over, my Posterity may reap the Benefits of them." Franklin's posterity, it should be pointed out, stood a much better chance were England to retain the Old Northwest and the Crown validate the Grand Ohio claim than were title thereto to pass to the new United States, whose claim to that region Franklin would be expected by Congress to press at the peacemaking. Such an impropriety on Franklin's part was compounded by his casual attitude about his carrying on a correspondence with a British subject in wartime while officially an American commissioner to France.

Franklin's critics denounced his penchant for nepotism, his padding the postmastership payroll with his relatives, the pressure he exercised on his fellow peace commissioners to have the unqualified Temple Franklin appointed as secretary to the Commission, and his willingness to have his grandnephew Jonathan Williams set up as a shipping agent at Nantes. Franklin's conduct of his office in France continued to supply grounds for ugly charges. What is significant is not that Franklin was guilty as charged but rather that the suspicion of conflict of interest would not die down despite his own disclaimer. At best, Franklin in France was untidy and careless in running his office. What can be said about a statesman whose entourage numbered a secretary who was a spy in British pay, a maître d'hôtel who was a thief, and a grandson who was a playboy! Only a genius could surmount these irregularities and achieve a stunning triumph. And Franklin had genius.

Because of Franklin's prominence in the Revolutionary movement it is often forgotten that in the generation prior to the final break with England he was America's most notable imperial statesman, and that the zigzag course he was to pursue owed more to events than to logic. As early as 1751 he had proposed an intercolonial union to be established by voluntary action on the part of the colonies. Three years later, at Albany, where he presented his grand design of continental union, he included therein a provision for having the plan imposed by parliamentary authority. A thorough realist, Franklin by now saw no hope of achieving union through voluntary action of the colonies, and, significantly, every delegate to the Albany Congress save five voted in favor of that provision. Twenty years later a number of these very same men, chief of them Franklin himself, were to deny Parliament's authority either to tax or to legislate for the colonies.

Franklin's Plan of Union conferred executive power, including the veto, upon a royally appointed president general, as well as the power to make war and peace and Indian treaties with the advice and consent of the grand council. That body was to be chosen triennially by the assemblies of the colonies in numbers proportionate to the taxes paid into the general treasury. Conferring the power of election upon the assemblies rather than the more aristocratic and prerogative-minded governor's councils constituted a notable democratic innovation, as was his proposal for a central treasury for the united colonies and a union treasury for each colony.

Each intensely jealous of its own prerogatives, the colonial assemblies proved cool to the plan while the Privy Council was frigid. As Franklin remarked years later, "the Crown dis-

approved it as having too much weight in the democratic part of the constitution, and every assembly as having allowed too much to the prerogative; so it was totally rejected." In short, the thinking of the men who met at Albany in 1754 was too bold for that day. In evolving his Plan of Union Franklin had shown himself to be an imperial-minded thinker who placed the unity and effective administration of the English-speaking world above the rights and rivalries of the separate parts. Had Franklin's Plan of Union been put in operation it would very likely have obviated the necessity for any Parliamentary enactment of taxes for the military defense and administration of the colonies.

If Britain did not come up with a plan of union of her own soon enough to save her own empire, the Americans did not forget that momentous failure of statesmanship. Franklin's plan constituted the basic core of that federal system that came into effect with the First Continental Congress and, as proposed in modified form by Franklin in 1775, provided a scheme of confederation pointing toward national sovereignty. While the Articles of Confederation drew upon notions embodied in the Albany Plan, such as investing the federal government with authority over the West, it rejected Franklin's proposal to make representation in Congress proportional to population, a notion which found recognition in the federal Constitution. Writing in 1789, Franklin was justified in his retrospective judgment about his Albany Plan of Union. His was a reasonable speculation that had his plan been adopted "the different parts of the empire might still have remained in peace and union."

Franklin's pride in the Empire survived his letdown in 1754. In April, 1761, he issued his famous Canada pamphlet, "The Interest of Great Britain," wherein he argued the case for a plan which would secure for Great Britain Canada and the trans-Appalachian West rather than the French West Indian islands, arguments

upon which Lord Shelburne drew heavily in supporting the Preliminary Articles of Peace of 1762 that his sponsor Lord Bute had negotiated with France.

For Franklin, 1765 may be considered the critical year of his political career. Thereafter he abandoned his role as imperial statesman and moved steadily on a course toward revolution. Some would make Franklin out as a conspirator motivated by personal pique, and while one must concede that Franklin's reticence and deviousness endowed him with the ideal temperament for conspiracy and that his public humiliation at the hands of Crown officials provided him with all the motivation that most men would need, one must remember that, above all, Franklin was an empiricist. If one course would not work, he would try another. Thus, Franklin as agent for Pennsylvania's Assembly in London not only approved the Stamp Act in advance, but proposed many of the stamp collectors to the British government. To John Hughes, one of his unfortunate nominees who secured the unhappy job for his own province, Franklin counseled "coolness and steadiness," adding

> . . . a firm Loyalty to the Crown and faithful Adherence to the Government of this Nation, which it is the Safety as well as Honour of the Colonies to be connected with, will always be the wisest Course for you and I to take, whatever may be the Madness of the Populace or their blind Leaders, who can only bring themselves and Country into Trouble and draw on greater Burthens by Acts of rebellious Tendency.

But Franklin was a fast learner. If the violence and virtual unanimity of the opposition in the colonies to the Stamp Act took him by surprise, Franklin quickly adjusted to the new realities. In an examination before the House of Commons in February, 1766, he made clear the depth of American opposition to the new tax, warned

that the colonies would refuse to pay any future internal levy, and intimated that "in time" the colonists might move to the more radical position that Parliament had no right to levy external taxes upon them either. Henceforth Franklin was the colonists' leading advocate abroad of their rights to self-government, a position grounded not only on his own eminence but on his agency of the four colonies of Pennsylvania, New Jersey, Massachusetts, and Georgia. If he now counseled peaceful protest, it was because he felt that violent confrontations would give the British government a pretext for increasing the military forces and placing the colonies under even more serious repression. A permissive parent even by today's lax standards, Franklin drew an interesting analogy between governing a family and governing an empire. In one of his last nostalgic invocations of imperial greatness, Franklin wrote:

> Those men make a mighty Noise about the importance of keeping up our Authority over the Colonies. They govern and regulate too much. Like some unthinking Parents, who are every Moment exerting their Authority, in obliging their Children to make Bows, and interrupting the Course of their innocent Amusements, attending constantly to their own Prerogative, but forgetting Tenderness due to their Offspring. The true Act of governing the Colonies lies in a Nut-Shell. It is only letting them alone.

A hostile contemporary, the Tory Peter Oliver, denounced Franklin as "the *instar omnium* of Rebellion" and the man who "set this whole Kingdom in a flame." This is a grotesque distortion of Franklin's role. While he was now on record opposing the whole Grenville-Townshend-North program as impractical and unrealistic, the fact is that his influence in government circles declined as his reputation in radical Whig intellectual circles and in the American colonies burgeoned. It must be remembered that, almost down to the outbreak

of hostilities, he still clung to his post of absentee deputy postmaster general of the colonies, with all the perquisites thereto attached. All that dramatically changed in the years 1773–74, a final turning point in Franklin's political career.

Franklin had got his hands on a series of indiscreet letters written by Thomas Hutchinson and Andrew Oliver, the governor and lieutenant governor of Massachusetts Bay respectively, and addressed to Thomas Whately, a member of the Grenville and North ministries. The letters, which urged that the liberties of the province be restricted, were given to Franklin to show him that false advice from America went far toward explaining the obnoxious acts of the British government. Tongue in cheek, Franklin sent the letters on to Thomas Cushing, speaker of the Massachusetts House of Representatives, with an injunction that they were not to be copied or published but merely shown in the original to individuals in the province. But in June, 1773, the irrepressible Samuel Adams read the letters before a secret session of the House and later had the letters copied and printed.

The publication of the Hutchinson-Oliver letters, ostensibly against Franklin's wishes, caused an international scandal which for the moment did Franklin's reputation no good. Summoned before the Privy Council, he was excoriated by Solicitor General Alexander Wedderburn. The only way Franklin could have obtained the letters, Wedderburn charged, was by stealing them from the person who stole them, and, according to one account, he added, "I hope, my lords, you will mark and brand the man" who "has forfeited all the respect of societies and of men." Henceforth, he concluded, "Men will watch him with a jealous eye; they will hide their papers from him, and lock up their escritoires. He will henceforth esteem it a libel to be called a man of letters; *homo trium literarum!*" Of course, everyone in the audience knew Latin and recognized the three-lettered word Wedderburn referred to as "fur," or thief.

Discounting Wedderburn's animosity, the solicitor general may have accurately captured the mental frame of mind of Franklin at this time when he remarked that "Dr. Franklin's mind may have been so possessed with the idea of a Great American Republic, that he may easily slide into the language of the minister of a foreign independent state," who, "just before the breaking out of war . . . may bribe a villain to steal or betray any state papers." There was one punishment the Crown could inflict upon its stalwart antagonist, and that was to strip him of his office as deputy postmaster general. That was done at once. Imperturbable as was his wont, Franklin remained silent throughout the entire castigation, but inwardly he seethed at both the humiliation and the monetary loss which the job, along with his now collapsed Vandalia scheme, would cost him. He never forgot the scorching rebuke. He himself had once revealingly remarked that he "never forgave contempt." "Costs me nothing to be civil to inferiors; a good deal to be submissive to superiors." it is reported that on the occasion of the signing of the treaty of alliance with France he donned the suit of figured blue velvet that he had worn on that less triumphal occasion and, according to an unsubstantiated legend, wore it again at the signing of the Preliminary Peace Treaty by which Great Britain recognized the independence of the United States.

Believing he could help best by aiding Pitt in his fruitless efforts at conciliation, Franklin stayed on in England for another year. On March 20, 1775, he sailed for America, convinced that England had lost her colonies forever. On May 6, 1775, the day following his return to Philadelphia, he was chosen a member of the Second Continental Congress. There he would rekindle old associations and meet for the first time some of the younger patriots who were to lead the nation along the path to independence.

An apocryphal story is told of Franklin's journey from Nantes to Paris, to which he was to be dispatched by Congress. At one of the inns in which he stayed, he was informed that the Tory-minded Gibbon, the first volume of whose *History* had been published in the spring of that year, was also stopping. Franklin sent his compliments, requesting the pleasure of spending the evening with the historian. In answer he received a card stating that notwithstanding Gibbon's regard for the character of Dr. Franklin as a man and a philosopher, he could not reconcile it with his duty to his king to have any conversation with a rebellious subject. In reply Franklin wrote a note declaring that "though Mr. Gibbon's principles had compelled him to withhold the pleasure of his conversation, Dr. Franklin had still such respect for the character of Mr. Gibbon, as a gentleman and a historian, that when, in the course of his writing a history of the *decline and fall* of empires, the *decline and fall* of the British Empire should come to be his subject, as he expects it soon would, Dr. Franklin would be happy to furnish him with ample materials which were in his possession."

III "When in the Course
of Human Events…"

7

A New Kind of Revolution

Carl N. Degler

The first American revolution, as Clinton Rossiter put it, occurred long before Thomas Jefferson wrote the Declaration of Independence. The first revolution was a social or cultural one, as American colonists over the decades developed their own customs and institutions, until they came to have a sense of common nationality. Carl Degler describes this awakening of American nationality and goes on to explain, through an imaginative use of metaphor, how the final break with England was indeed a new kind of revolution.

Americans Have New Rights

"It is . . . to England that we owe this elevated rank we possess," remarked Crèvecoeur, "these noble appellations of freemen, freeholders, citizens; yes it is to that wise people we owe our freedom. Had we been planted by some great monarchy, we should have been mean slaves of some distant monarch." It was for sound historical reasons that during the Revo-

lutionary crisis the colonials stoutly asserted their claims to the "rights of Englishmen." Yet despite the English substance at the core of colonial political forms, the colonists departed in a number of ways from the example of the mother country. Frequently these deviations were merely novel twists given to English institutions; sometimes they were new institutions called into being by the new conditions in America. But whatever the nature of the changes, by the middle of the eighteenth century the forsaking of English practices was in evidence and the American constitutional system of the future was visible.

A common political vocabulary can certainly serve to bind together a colony and a mother country. But when the meaning behind the words is different, then the stage is set for misunderstanding, recrimination, and conflict. During the 1850's the North and the South found themselves in this dangerous position; the colonists and the English in the years immediately preceding the American Revolution also fell into this predicament. Steeped as they were in the English political language, the colonials spoke in what they thought was the common intellectual coin of the Empire, neglecting to observe that the American experience had given the words a content quite different from that accepted by the Englishmen with whom they debated. That Americans and Britons were saying different things when they employed the same words did not become apparent until after 1765, but the actual differences in political and constitutional practices of the two peoples were there long before the Stamp Act.

It is true, of course, as Crèvecoeur implied, that in many respects the political institutions

of England were reproduced in close detail in the colonies. By the middle of the eighteenth century, for instance, all of the mainland colonies except four were headed by a Royal Governor, appointed by the King and therefore bearing a relation to the people of the colony similar to that of the King to the British people. Moreover, each of the thirteen colonies enjoyed a representative assembly, which was consciously modeled, in powers and practices, after the British Parliament. The resemblance to the English example was carried still further in the division of the colonial assemblies into upper and lower houses in emulation of the House of Commons and the House of Lords. In both England and the colonies, furthermore, the suffrage was exercised only by property holders; in all the colonies, as in England, it was an axiom, as an act of South Carolina put it in 1716, that "none but such persons who have an interest in this Province shall be capable to elect or be elected."

Though in the letter the English and colonial constitutions were similar, in the spirit they were moving in different directions. For example, English constitutional development from the earliest years of the seventeenth century had been sometimes drifting, sometimes driving, but always moving in pursuit of the absolute power of Parliament. The most unmistakable sign of this tendency was the assertion that the King was under the law, as exemplified in the Petition of Right in 1628, the judgment and execution of Charles I in 1649, and finally the *de facto* deposition of James II in 1689. Together with this resolute denial of the divine right of kings went the assertion that Parliament was unlimited in its power; that it could change even the Constitution by its ordinary acts of legislation, just as it had created the Constitution by its past acts. By the eighteenth century, as today, the British accepted the idea that the representatives of the people were omnipotent; that, as the aphorism has it, "Parliament can do anything

except change a man into a woman and a woman into a man."

The colonials did not look upon the English Parliament with such fond eyes, nor—equally important for the future—did they concede that their own assemblies possessed such wide powers. There were good historical reasons for this. Though to the English the word "Constitution" meant nothing more nor less than the whole body of law and custom from the beginning of the kingdom, to the colonials it meant a written document, enumerating specific powers. This distinction in meaning is to be traced to the fact that the foundations of government in the various colonies were written charters granted by the Crown. These express authorizations to govern were tangible, definite things. Over the years the colonials had often repaired to the timeless phrases and sonorous periods in their charters to justify themselves in the struggle against rapacious Governors or tyrannical officials of the Crown. More than a century of government under *written* constitutions convinced the colonists of the necessity for and efficacy of protecting their liberties against government encroachment by explicitly defining all governmental powers in a document.

Even before the Stamp Act was passed, James Otis of Massachusetts articulated the striking difference between the colonial and British conceptions of Parliamentary power and the nature of constitutions. "To say the Parliament is absolute and arbitrary is a contradiction," he asserted. Parliament cannot alter the supreme law of the nation because "the Constitution is fixed; and . . . the supreme legislative . . . cannot overlap the Bounds of it without destroying its own foundation." Here, long before the Revolution, was a succinct expression of what was to become the cardinal principle of American constitutionalism, clearly setting it off from the English in both practice and theory.

It is worth emphasizing that it was English

practice which was moving away from colonial. Earlier in the seventeenth century, in the minds of jurists like Sir Edward Coke, Otis's arguments would have carried much weight, but now the mutability of the Constitution was widely accepted in England. The colonials in the middle of the eighteenth century, as we shall have occasion to notice during the Revolutionary crisis, were following the old-fashioned and more conservative line.

There was another way in which English and colonial constitutional developments were drifting apart. The intimate relation between the executive and Parliament, so characteristic of English and continental democracies today, was already taking shape in the middle of the eighteenth century. The executive was the cabinet of ministers, who were drawn from the Parliament itself; as a result there was no separation of powers, the executive and legislative branches being merely different manifestations of the same body. This development, however, did not take place in America. The existence, for one thing, of a royally appointed Governor made such a development impossible; he could not be readily supplanted by a cabinet or ministerial council. Moreover, by having written constitutions or charters, the colonies were limited to the forms provided in earlier days. Under such circumstances it is not surprising that the colonial leaders entirely overlooked what was happening in England. From their distance they remained convinced that the King—like their own Royal Governors—was the real executive. Thus, because of the peculiarly American experience, the colonists were committed to a conception of government quite at variance with the English.

An important corollary to the English doctrine of parliamentary absolutism was the assumption that the colonies were subject to the legislative power of that body. For most of the seventeenth century the doctrine was no more than an assumption, and so the colonies did not feel it. This was partly because parlia-

mentary supremacy was achieved late in the century—in 1689—and partly because the British government, embroiled in successive wars with Holland and France, did not seek to test its authority with the colonies.

This practice of "salutary neglect," as Burke named it, provided a long period during which the colonies developed self-reliance and their own ideas of government. The representative assembly in each of the provinces was widely viewed as the focus of government, peculiarly American, and constitutionally competent for all internal legislative purposes. The sole political tie of any consequence between the colonies and England was through the Royal Governor, and in four of the thirteen provinces there was not even this connection. It was to be expected, therefore, that the colonies should grow to think of their little assemblies as bearing the same relation to the Crown as the Parliament of Great Britain. Such a conception of colonial equality with England, however, ran counter not only to the strong current of parliamentary absolutism we have already noticed; it also flew in the face of a growing movement to centralize the government of the Empire in London.

There is irony in the growing divergence between England and the colonies regarding the power of representative assemblies. No institution introduced into the New World was probably more English than the representative assembly; yet it was this very political form, transformed by the American experience, which, more than anything else, served to bring about a break between the colonies and the Mother of Parliaments.

With the franchise, as with the parliamentary power, the colonists took a typically English institution and remade it into a wedge which drove the two peoples apart. Though both England and the colonies based the franchise on property holding, in the mother country this practice produced a small electorate. In America, however, the same require-

ment resulted in a quite different effect. Since property was widely distributed, even the use of property qualifications identical with those in England resulted in the colonies in a large electorate, occasionally even approaching universal manhood suffrage. The studies of Robert Brown in the history of colonial Massachusetts, for example, have made it clear that in both provincial and town elections well over a majority of men—perhaps 80 per cent—could vote. When Thomas Hutchinson was defeated in Boston in 1749 he said of the 200 votes he received: "they were the principal inhabitants, but you know we are governed not by weight but by numbers." At another time Hutchinson remarked with obvious distaste: "The town of Boston is an absolute democracy. . . ." Even allowing for some exaggeration on the part of a defeated politician, these statements of a contemporary indicate that large numbers of men could vote in colonial Massachusetts.

Though some of the other colonies probably could not boast as wide a franchise as Massachusetts or other New England provinces, the franchise in the eighteenth century in all the colonies was considerably wider than is often supposed. Richard McCormick, for example, has shown that in New Jersey the property qualifications were quite easy for the great majority of the adult males to meet. Indeed, he has uncovered instances where the regulations at the polls were so lax that women, boys, and even Negroes voted. Milton Klein has shown that in New York as many as 55 per cent of the adult white males actually voted, suggesting that the eligible actually reached proportions close to 100 per cent. In Pennsylvania, Albert McKinley has estimated, at least one half of the males in a farming area outside Philadelphia could vote, though the figure would be lower in the city itself. Robert and Katherine Brown have found a wide participation in elections in Virginia, often taken as an aristocratically inclined province in the colonial

period and after. In a general survey of the colonial suffrage, Chilton Williamson has found that in virtually all areas, where figures are available, the proportion of adult white males who could vote was at least 50 per cent. In some places, as we have seen, it reached 75 per cent. Furthermore, unlike Virginians and other colonists, South Carolina voters also enjoyed the democratic device of the secret ballot. In short, the forms of political democracy were already beginning to appear in the colonial period.

.   .   .

Related to both the political and constitutional innovations of the colonials was their defense of freedom of the press against the arbitrary power of government. The trial of John Peter Zenger in New York in 1735 is justly considered a landmark in the history of freedom. Under the English and colonial law of that time, the sole responsibility of a jury in a trial for seditious libel was to determine whether the accused had in fact written the alleged libel. Whether the material was in fact libelous was left up to the judge to decide. Since, in Zenger's case, Judge De Lancey was a creature of the Governor against whom the alleged libel was directed, the results of the trial seemed a foregone conclusion. This high probability was further enhanced when Zenger and his attorneys announced that they conceded Zenger's responsibility for writing and printing the article in question.

The drama and long-range significance of the case, however, turns upon the action of Andrew Hamilton, who assumed the leadership of the defense. Contending that the truth of Zenger's charges was the crux of the case, Hamilton argued that a press, unfettered by official control, was indispensable in a society claiming to be free. Truth, he said, was a legitimate, nay, a necessary defense in a libel suit. Almost casually he conceded Zenger's authorship of the

offending piece. But then he turned to the jury and, in a masterful presentation, urged upon the jurors a new course. Disregarding the law and appealing to their love of liberty, Hamilton challenged the jurors to decide the larger question of whether the charges Zenger levied against the Governor were true or not. If they were, Hamilton advised, then the jury should acquit the printer. Despite its sure knowledge that it was affronting a powerful and partisan judge, the jury nobly matched Hamilton's boldness and found Zenger not guilty.

It is true that censorship of the press, particularly by the assemblies, and even trial for libel in which truth was not accepted as a defense, occurred after the Zenger case. But there were no more trials for seditious libel in New York for the rest of the colonial period. Moreover, the trial and its outcome produced repercussions in England. Radicals and Whigs, won over by the brilliant colonial innovation in behalf of a free press, began a campaign in support of American liberty which was to reach its full power at the time of the Revolution in the voices of Burke, Fox, John Wilkes, Dr. Price, and Colonel Barré.

The principle inherent in the Zenger decision was not quickly implemented in America, as Leonard Levy has pointed out. It was not until 1798, during the Jeffersonians' powerful attacks upon the theory of the Sedition Act that the modern view of freedom of the press was worked out. Heretofore, all sides to the question, including the Jeffersonians themselves, had accepted the idea that a government had a right to suppress statements critical of its officials. The new view, going beyond that set forth in Zenger, asserted that if a society was to be considered free it could not suppress criticism under the old rubrics of "seditious libel" or "a licentious press." In fact, the crime of seditious libel, *i.e.,* bringing government into disrepute by attacking its officials, was abandoned. The concept that truth was a defense in a libel suit—the central principle in the Zenger

case—was established in New York law in the case of Henry Coswell in 1804 through the joint efforts of Alexander Hamilton and James Kent. The doctrine was reinforced by legislative act in 1805 and inserted, for good measure, in the state constitutions of 1821 and 1846. It was not until 1791, however, with Fox's Act, that English juries were granted the right to determine whether the writing in question was libelous or not, and it was not until 1843 that truth was accepted as a defense in a libel suit under English law.

"All of Us Americans"

In the course of the Zenger trial Andrew Hamilton had chided the attorney general for his constant citing of English precedent. "What strange doctrine is it to press everything for law here which is so in England," the clever Philadelphian exclaimed. Hamilton knew full well that the law of England prevailed in the colonies, but he was playing upon the colonials' growing pride of country.

In the years after 1740 the colonials became increasingly conscious of themselves as Americans. To be sure, there were very few outright demands for independence. It would take a good number of years, during which a consciousness of kind was only dawning, before the idea of independence would be thought of, much less advocated. Nevertheless, for two decades or more before the Revolutionary crisis of the late 1760's, Americans were expressing the feeling that they were different from Europeans, that they had a destiny of their own.

Ironically enough, the most obvious manifestations of this budding sense of Americanism appear in the course of the wars with France in the 1740's and 1750's, when colonials fought side by side with the English. During most of the century-long struggle against France in the seventeenth and eighteenth centuries, Britain had not demanded that the

American colonies contribute anything more than the defense of their home areas and perhaps an occasional foray into adjacent French-held Canada. But beginning with the so-called War of Jenkins' Ear in 1739, which was first waged against Spain and then (as King George's War) against France, Britain stepped up her expectations of colonial military support. In 1741 the home government succeeded in goading the colonials to assist in the mounting of an offensive against Cartagena, the great port of the Spanish Main.

In part because the enterprise was a colossal fiasco, but largely because American and European soldiers were thrown together under novel circumstances, the differences between Americans and Europeans were sharply illuminated for both sides. Admiral Vernon, the British commander of the expedition, for example, consistently referred to the colonials as "Americans." The colonials, in turn, referred to their supposed blood brothers, the English, as "Europeans." The words, of course, had been used before, but never so generally or consistently as at this time. The failure of the Cartagena expedition added its bit to the splitting apart of the two national groups. The Americans came away convinced that the English were callous and cruel in their treatment of colonials, and the English soldiery and officers were disgusted with what they stigmatized as the cowardice and ineffectiveness of the colonial soldier.

When the New Englanders under Sir William Pepperell succeeded in capturing the French fortress at Louisbourg in the St. Lawrence in 1745, the colonials' incipient pride of country burst forth. To some it seemed to prove, as one bit of doggerel put it, that in valor

> . . . the British Breed
> In Western Climes their Grandsires far
>   exceed
> and that New England Schemes the Old
>   Surpass,

> As much as Gold does tinkling Brass;
> And that a Pepp'rell's and a Warren's Name,
> May vie with Marlb'rough and a Blake for
>   Fame.

With the fall of Quebec in 1759, there was loosed a flood of prophecies that the star of American destiny was in the ascendant. "A new world has arisen," exulted the *New American Magazine,* "and will exceed the old!" It is noteworthy, considering its nationalistic name, that the magazine was then in its first year of publication. One scholar, Richard Merritt, in examining the colonial press of the mid-eighteenth century, found a remarkable increase in the early 1760's in references to "America" and "Americans" at the same time that there was a falling off in references to the connection with England. He finds, in short, a rise in American self-awareness prior to the catalyst of the Stamp Act crisis in 1765.

Meanwhile a developing American nationality was evident—perhaps less spectacularly, but nonetheless profoundly—in other ways. Under the influences of distance and the new environment, the mother tongue of the colonists was undergoing change. New words from the Dutch and Indian languages, for example, were constantly being added to the speech of the English in America; words like "boss," "stoop," "cruller," "crib," "scow," and "spook" came from the Dutch. The Indian names were all over the land, and they made America exotic for Englishmen as they still do for Europeans.

Americans also made up words, some of which reflected the new environment. "Back country" and "backwoods" were designed to describe the novelty of the frontier. Bullfrog, canvasback, lightning bug, razorback, groundhog, potato bug, peanut, and eggplant are similar colonial name tags for new natural phenomena.

Familiar English words sometimes assumed new meanings in America. "Lumber" in eigh-

teenth-century England meant unused furniture, but in the colonies it was applied to the raw wood—and so it has remained. "Pie" in England, to this day, means a meat pie, but in the colonies that was a "potpie"; "pie" was reserved for fruit pastry. Dry goods in England included all nonliquids, like corn or wheat; the colonials, however, changed the meaning to textiles only. The same alteration took place with the word "rock," which in England denoted a large mass; in America as early as 1712 it was being applied to a stone of any size. "Pond" was an English word meaning an artificial pool, but in unkempt America it came to mean any small lake. Certain words obviously attached to the English environment were lost in America, where their referents did not exist: fen, heath, moor, wold, bracken, and downs. It is not to be wondered, therefore, that in 1756 lexicographer Samuel Johnson was talking of an American dialect.

The burgeoning sense of Americanism was reflected also in the colonials' image of themselves. When Eliza Pinckney of South Carolina was presented at King George's Court in 1750, she insisted upon being introduced as an "American." That same year an advertisement in a Boston paper advertised beer as "American" and urged that Bostonians should "no longer be beholden to Foreigners for a Credible [sic] Liquor, which may be as successfully manufactured in this country." It is not the self-interest which is important here, but the fact that the advertiser obviously felt he could gain by making an appeal to a sense of American pride among his potential customers. This feeling among Americans that they were different from Europeans was put forth explicitly by a Carolinian in 1762. Speaking about the question of sending young colonials to England for their education, he said it would be most surprising if a British education should suit Americans, "because the Genius of our People, their Way of Life, their circumstances in Point of Fortunes, and Customs, and Manners and

Humours of the Country, difference us in so many important Respects from Europeans. . . ." Such an education could not be expected to fit Americans, he went on, any more "than an Almanac, calculated for the Latitude of London, would that of Williamsburg."

As relations between the colonies and the mother country worsened after 1765, expressions of Americanism became more explicit and sometimes belligerent. Colonial students at Edinburgh University before 1765 commonly designated themselves as from the various provinces, but at the time of the Stamp Act, Samuel Bard wrote, he and several others began to style themselves "Americans" and the precedent was followed by many in subsequent years. About the same time Ezra Stiles of New Haven drew up a plan for an "American Academy of Science," which was designed, he said, "for the Honor of American Literature, contemned by Europeans." He stipulated that only native-born Americans should be members. And at the Stamp Act Congress, Christopher Gadsden of South Carolina urged the gathered colonial leaders to take cognizance of their common nationality. "There ought to be no New England man, no New Yorker, known on the Continent," he advised, "but all of us Americans. . . ."

The magic of the moment and the atmosphere in the new country were so potent that John Morgan, newly arrived at Philadelphia from London in 1765, declared, only a year later, "I consider myself at once as a Briton and an American." Such an ambivalent attitude must have been common among colonials in the early stage of the crisis between the colonies and the mother country. But regardless of Morgan's own ambiguous feelings, his work in helping to establish the new medical school at Philadelphia was hailed by Benjamin Rush as an aid to the growing self-consciousness of the people of America. Pointedly calling Britain an alien land, Rush wrote Morgan that no longer would the colonial student have to tear "himself from

every tender engagement" and brave the dangers of the sea "in pursuit of knowledge in a foreign country."

One of the most curious but very clear manifestations of a growing American awareness of differences between the peoples of the Old and New Worlds was the widespread belief that English society was morally inferior, even decadent, when compared with the social character of the colonies. As early as 1735 Lewis Morris, visiting England, wrote in his diary that he and his party "wish'd ourselves in our own Country, far from the deceits of a court." London appeared to Ebenezer Hazard as at once a wonderful "little World" and a "Sink of Sin." In 1767, English social conditions appeared shocking to William S. Johnson, who found the extremes of wealth and misery "equally amazing on the one hand and disgusting on the other." Benjamin Rush wrote from Edinburgh in 1767 that "every native of Philadelphia should be sent abroad for a few years if it was only to teach him to prize his native country above all places in the world."

Standing out against the decadence of England in the minds of colonials and of some Englishmen was the example of America as the hope of the world. In 1771, John Penn, who was certainly no radical, wrote that he considered Great Britain "as an Old Man, who has received several strokes of the Palsy, and tottering upon the brink of the Grave, whereas America was growing daily toward perfection." In 1745 a writer in the *Gentleman's Magazine* drew the lesson from the American success at the seige of Louisbourg that the colonials were truly in the classical tradition so dear to the men of the eighteenth century. He saw the colonists in "the great image of the ancient Romans leaving the plow for the field of battles, and retiring after their conquests to the plow again." For many Englishmen, America seemed to be utopia in actuality. But it was the Americans who above all were convinced of the moral superiority of their society. Colonials returned from Europe overflowing with tales of the iniquities they had witnessed in London or commenting on the manifest corruption of British politics. As early as 1748, Josiah Quincy was saying he was fearful that the venality of English political life would ruin the country. The self-righteousness of Americans toward Britain in the 1750's and 1760's reminds one of nothing so much as an adolescent's indignant strictures against his parent's timeworn but now suddenly recognized foibles. The American people were coming of age.

Along with adolescent carping, assertions of moral superiority, and self-righteousness in the years before 1765, there were also a few strong hints that independence was coming. The war against the French in Canada prompted some Americans to anticipate separation from England. Peter Kalm, for example, traveling through the colonies in 1748, was told that after the French were expelled from the western borders of the colonies, independence would come in a matter of thirty to fifty years. Once the "Gallicks" are removed, John Adams thought in 1755, the colonies would be able to go it alone. "The only way to keep us from setting up for ourselves," he wrote, "is to disunite us."

In 1760 and after, when the British government was wrestling with the question of whether or not the French should be expelled completely from the North American continent, there was much speculation as to the effect such expulsion would have upon the restive colonies. Though the canny Franklin blandly assured Parliament that the removal of the French would bind the colonies still closer to Britain, less suspect parties, like Comptroller Weare, pointed out that never before in history had an industrious and favored people like the Americans hesitated to break away from their mother country when they had the power to do so. It is highly likely, he added, "that a thousand leagues distance from eye and strength of government" would suggest just

that *"to a people accustomed to more than British liberty."* Also of this opinion was a correspondent of the *Gentleman's Magazine* in 1760. "If the people of our colonies find no check from Canada, they will extend themselves, almost without bounds into the inland parts. . . . What the consequences will be," he added ominously and prophetically, "to have a numerous, hardy, independent people possessed of a strong country, communicating little, or not at all with England, I leave to your own reflections."

There was more behind the thought of independence than the removal of the French threat. There was the coming to climax of the whole history of a geographically separate and different people in America. English traveler Andrew Burnaby noticed it in 1759 when he pointed out that the growing cities of the coast were already turning their citizens into "great republicans" and that the farm dwellers too had "fallen into the same errors in their ideas of independency."

In a vague cultural sense, the colonies were ready for the parting of the ways with Britain. What still remained was something which would cleanly and definitely cut the political ties connecting the two peoples. The occasion would come after 1763 when Britain sought to find a new basis for its relations with the continental colonies, for then the differences between the two peoples would be translated into political terms.

.   .   .

A New Kind of Revolution

Though the colonists had long been drifting away from their allegiance to the mother country, the chain of events which led to the Revolutionary crisis was set in motion by external factors. The shattering victory of the Anglo-American forces over the French in the Great War for the Empire (1754–63), as Lawrence Gipson has rechristened the French and Indian War, suddenly revealed how wide the gulf between colonists and mother country had become. The very fact that the feared French were once and for all expelled from the colonial backdoor meant that another cohesive, if negative, force was gone. At least one friend of Britain, looking back from the fateful days of 1776, thought that "had Canada remained in the hands of the French, the colonies would have remained dutiful subjects. Their fears for themselves in that case," he reasoned, "would have supplied the place of the pretended affection for this nation. . . ." What actual effect the removal of the French produced upon the thinking of the colonists is hard to weigh, but there can be little doubt that the Great War for the Empire opened a new era in the relations between the colonies and the mother country.

Great Britain emerged from the war as the supreme power in European affairs: her armies had swept the once-vaunted French authority from two continents; her navy now indisputably commanded the seven seas. A symbol of this new power was that Britain's ambassadors now outranked those of France and Spain in the protocol of Europe's courts. But the cost and continuing responsibilities of that victory were staggering for the little island kingdom. Before the war the annual expenditures for troops in America and the British West Indies amounted to £110,000; now three times that sum was needed to protect the western frontier, suppress Indian revolts and maintain order. Furthermore, the signing of the peace found Britain saddled with a debt of £130 million, the annual charges of which ran to another £4 million. Faced with such obligations, the British government was compelled to reassess its old ways of running an empire, particularly in regard to the raising of new revenues.

Before the war, the administration and cost of the Empire were primarily, if not completely,

a British affair. Imperial defense on the high seas was in the hands of the Royal Navy, and though the colonies were called upon from time to time to assist in the war with France, the bulk of the fighting was sustained by British troops. In return, the colonies had acquiesced in the regulation of their trade through a series of so-called Navigation Acts, which were enacted and enforced by the British authority; no revenues, however, except those collected as import or export duties, were taken from the colonies by Britain.

Under the pressure of the new responsibilities, the British authorities began to cast about for a new theory and practice of imperial administration into which the colonies might be fitted as actively contributing members. Prior to the war the government had been willing to protect the West Indian sugar interests at the expense of the rest of the Empire. But now, in the interest of increased revenue, the old protective duty, which was much too high to bring any return, was cut in half, thus permitting French molasses to compete with British West Indian in the English and colonial markets. In 1766, this molasses duty, in a further effort to increase revenue, was cut to two thirds of what it had been before the war. In short, the need for imperial revenues, not private interests, was now dictating legislation. The Stamp Act of 1765 and the Townshend duties of two years later were similar efforts to spread the financial burdens of the Empire among the beneficiaries of the British triumph over the French.

It seemed only simple justice to London officialdom that the colonies should share in the costs as well as the benefits to be derived from the defeat of the ancient enemy. At no time, it should be noticed, were the colonies asked to contribute more than a portion of the price of their own frontier defense. The stamp duty, for instance, was envisioned as returning no more than a third of the total military expenditures in America; the remainder would be borne by the home government. And because the colonists had difficulty scraping together the specie with which to pay such duties, the British government agreed to spend all the revenue obtained from the stamp tax in the colonies in order to avoid depleting the scanty colonial money supply. Nor were Americans heavily taxed; it was well known that their fiscal burden was unique in its lightness. In 1775 Lord North told the House of Commons that the per capita tax payments of Britons were fifty times those of the Americans. It was not injustice or the economic incidence of the taxes which prompted the colonial protests; it was rather the novelty of the British demands.

The new imperial policies of the British government caught the Americans off guard. Reveling in the victory over the French, the colonists confidently expected a return to the lax, uninterested administration of the prewar years and especially to their old freedom from any obligation to support the imperial defenses. Therefore, when the first of the new measures, the Sugar Act of 1764, became law, the Americans protested, but on a variety of grounds and without sufficient unity to command respect. By the time of the Stamp Act in the following year, however, the colonists were ready.

The essential colonial defense, from which the colonies never deviated, was a denial that the British Parliament had any right in law or custom to lay taxes upon the colonies for revenue purposes. Such taxes, the colonials insisted, could only be levied by the colonial legislatures. Actually, this expression of the colonial constitutional position was as novel as the imperial policy. Never before had there been an occasion for such an assertion simply because England had heretofore confined her colonial legislation to the regulation of trade. It is true that the Pennsylvania Charter of 1681 specifically reserved to the British Parliament the right to tax the colony; but since Parliament had never used this power, the colonists had a case when they said the new British taxes were historically unknown and therefore un-

constitutional. The details of this controversy, in which merit is by no means the exclusive possession of either side, do not concern us here. The important fact is not whether the Americans or the British were right in their respective readings of imperial constitutional history, but that the colonials believed they were right and acted accordingly. Regardless of the constitutional niceties involved, it is patent that the English had waited too long to assert their authority. Too many Americans had grown accustomed to their untrammeled political life to submit now to new English controls. In brief, the colonists suddenly realized that they were no longer wards of Britain, but a separate people, capable of forging their own destiny.

This conviction runs all through the polemics of the Revolutionary crisis. For underlying the constitutional verbiage which Englishmen and Americans exchanged were two quite different assumptions about the nature of the British Empire and the character of the American people. Whereas Englishmen saw America as a part of an Empire in which all elements were subordinate to Britain, the Americans, drawing upon their actual history, saw only a loose confederation of peoples in which there were Britons and Americans, neither one of whom could presume to dictate to the other. The colonials, in effect, now felt themselves Americans, not displaced, subordinate Englishmen. Jefferson suggested this to the King himself when he wrote in his *Summary View of the Rights of British America:* "You are surrounded by British counsellors. . . . You have no minister for American affairs, because you have none taken from us." Furthermore, even after 1776 many a Loyalist exiled in Britain found the English annoying and strange—evidence of the fact that residence in America had worked its influence even upon those loyal to the Crown. "It piques my pride, I must confess," wrote one expatriated Loyalist, "to hear us called 'our colonies, our plantations,' in such

terms and with such airs as if our property and persons were absolutely theirs, like the 'villains' in their cottages in the old feudal system."

The imperial view so confidently advanced by Grenville and others of the British administration came too late; the Americans were not interested in making a more efficient Empire to be manipulated from Whitehall. Because of this basic conflict in assumptions, American demands continued to leapfrog ahead of British concessions right up to the Carlisle Peace Mission in the midst of the Revolutionary War. Even ministerial assurances in 1769 that there would be no further imperially imposed taxes failed to divert the colonial drive toward equality with Britain. The child was truly asserting himself, and, as so often happens, the parent was reluctant to strike him down.

Measured against the age of Hitler and Stalin, the British overlords of the eighteenth century appear remarkably benign in their dealings with the colonies in the years after 1763. For it is a fact that the colonies were in revolt against a potential tyrant, not an actual one. Much more fearsome in the eyes of the politically sensitive colonials was the direction in which the British measures tended rather than the explicit content of the acts. As Bernard Bailyn has pointed out after a survey of some 400 tracts of the Revolutionary era, Americans were convinced that a conspiracy was afoot in Britain to deprive them of their liberties, though historians can find little basis for such political paranoia. But that such fear was a source of revolutionary fervor, Bailyn has no doubt. Furthermore, Englishmen could never bring themselves to enforce, with all the power at their command, what they believed was the true nature of the Empire, that is, the subordinate position of the colonies. More than once General Thomas Gage, commanding the British troops in America, reported that his forces were too scattered to preserve proper order and government in the colonies. "I am

concerned to find in your Lordship's letters," he wrote from New York in 1768, "that irresolution still prevails in our Councils; it is time to come to some determination about the disposition of the troops in this Country."

Part of this irresolution was born of British confusion as to what should be the government's purpose, as the hasty repeals of the stamp and Townshend duties testify on the one hand, and the remarkably inept Tea Act reveals on the other. Part of it stemmed from the fact that within their own house, so to speak, were Americans: at times Lord Chatham himself, at all times Edmund Burke, Colonel Isaac Barré, John Wilkes, and Dr. Price, who insisted that Americans possessed the rights of Englishmen. "The seditious spirit of the colonies," George Grenville wryly complained on the floor of Commons in 1776, "owes its birth to the factions in this House."

Divided as to aims and devoid of strong leadership, the British permitted the much more united colonists, who were blessed with superb and daring leadership, to seize and hold the initiative. Not until the very end—after the destruction of the tea at Boston Harbor in 1773—did the patience of the British ministry run dry. By then, however, the years of acrimony, suspicion, and growing awareness of the differences between the two peoples had done their work, and the harsh coercive measures taken against Massachusetts only provoked counterviolence from all the colonies. Lexington and Concord, Bunker Hill and Independence Hall, were then not far behind.

By implication, the interpretation of the coming of the Revolution given here greatly subordinates the role of economic factors. Since the economic restrictions imposed upon the colonies have traditionally played a large role in most discussions of the causes of the Revolution, they deserve some comment here. Those who advance an economic explanation for the Revolution argue that the series of economic measures enacted by Britain in the century before 1750 actually operated to confine, if not stifle, the colonial economy. Therefore, it is said, the colonies revolted against Britain in an effort to break through these artificial and externally imposed limits. On the surface and from the assumptions of twentieth-century economic life, the mercantilistic system appears severe and crippling and worthy of strong colonial opposition. But before such speculative conclusions can be accepted, they deserve to be checked against the facts.

Several historians have sought to measure quantitatively the restrictive effects of English mercantilism upon the colonial economy. Their conclusions, it can be said at the outset, are generally in the negative. For example, take the three major British limitations on colonial manufactures. On the statute books the Iron Act of 1750 appears to halt the erection of additional slitting mills in the colonies, but the fact is that many were set up after that date, regardless of the act's prohibitions, and to such an extent that by 1776 there were probably more such mills in America than in England. Nor, Lawrence Harper tells us, did the Woolens Act of 1699, designed to prevent colonial competition with a major English industry, actually inhibit American endeavors in the field, since few Americans cared to engage in the industry. True, Harper concluded that the colonial beaver-hat industry suffered from the restrictions of the Hat Act of 1732, but, as he adds, that branch of economic activity could hardly be considered an important segment of the economy. And those are the three major British efforts to "stifle" American manufacturing.

Nor can the restrictions on the settlement of the West be viewed, as some historians have asserted, as a significant motive for the Revolution. For one thing, movement into the West was never absolutely halted, and as early as 1764 the Proclamation Line of the previous year was being moved westward to permit settlement beyond the mountains. Furthermore, as Thomas Abernathy has shown, the

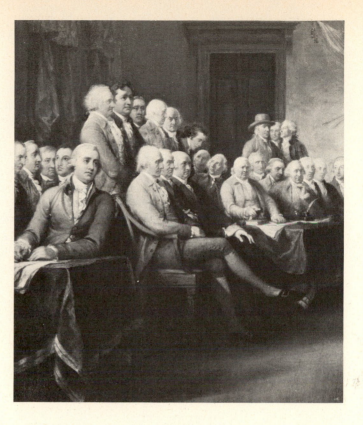

Virginia gentry—often cited as heavily involved in western land speculation and therefore concerned with restrictions on the West—were not vitally interested in the matter economically, though the religious and political implications of the later Quebec Act, for example, did arouse them. All in all, it would appear that the western land question may have been an irritating factor, but, in view of the changing and indecisive English policy, hardly a revolution-making force.

Perhaps the most that can be said quantitatively about the burden of the whole navigation or mercantilist system in which England encased the colonies is that the regulations con-cerning the routing of trade added between $2.6 million and $7 million to the cost of doing business in the colonies. Over against this, however, must be placed the fact that the system did not seem a burden to the colonies. Very few objections to the navigation system appear in the voluminous literature of the crisis. In fact, so acceptable did it appear to that jealous American, Benjamin Franklin, that in 1774 he suggested to Lord Chatham that all the basic Navigation Laws be re-enacted by the colonial legislatures as an earnest [declaration] of colonial loyalty. Furthermore, in October of that year, the first Continental Congress publicly declared the colonies willing to "cheerfully

On July 2, 1776, as this painting shows, a committee consisting of Thomas Jefferson, Benjamin Franklin, Robert Livingston, Roger Sherman, and John Adams submitted a draft of the Declaration of Independence to the Second Continental Congress. Jefferson (second from the right) is laying the document before John Hancock. Franklin stands to Jefferson's left, Livingston, Sherman, and Adams to his right. (Oil painting by John Trumbull, copyright Yale University Art Gallery.)

consent to the operation of such acts of the British Parliament, as are bona fide, restrained to the regulation of our external commerce, for the purpose of securing the commercial advantages of the whole empire to the mother country, and the commercial benefits of its respective members. . . ." In short, the navigation system was acceptable. Certainly laws the repressive nature of which no one was disturbed about can hardly be accepted as the grounds for a revolution.

No better economic argument can be made for taxation as a cause for the Revolution. Despite the tradition of oppressive taxation which the myth of the Revolution has spawned,

the actual tax burden of the colonies was much heavier in the seventeenth century than in the years immediately before the conflict. On a per capita basis, taxes were five times greater in 1698 than they were in 1773. The lightness of the British taxes in the pre-Revolutionary period is also shown by the fact that the duty on molasses in 1766 was only a penny a gallon, or less than the duty the federal government imposed in 1791. As Lord North pointed out in 1775, taxation of the Americans was neither excessive nor oppressive.

From the unconvincing character of the economic explanations for the coming of the Revolution, it would appear, therefore, that

the underlying force impelling the break was the growing national self-consciousness of the Americans. "The Revolution was effected before the war commenced," John Adams remarked years afterward. "The Revolution was in the minds and hearts of the people. . . ." The origins of the "principles and feelings" which made the Revolution, Adams thought, "ought to be traced back . . . and sought in the history of the country from the first plantations in America." For a century and a half the Americans had been growing up and now they had finally come of age. Precisely because the Revolution was the breaking away of a young people from a parent, the substance of the Revolution was political. The argument concerned the question of parental authority, because that is the precise point at which tension appears as the child approaches maturity and seeks to assert his independence. Unfortunately for Britain, but like so many modern parents, the mother country had long before conveniently provided the best arguments in favor of freedom. And the colonists had learned the arguments well. For this reason, the rhetoric of the Revolutionary argument was in the language of the British political and constitutional tradition.

As children enjoying a long history of freedom from interference from their parent, the Americans might well have continued in their loose relationship, even in maturity, for they were conservative as well as precocious. History, however, decreed otherwise. Britain's triumph in the Great War for the Empire put a new strain on the family relationship, and so intense was the pressure that Americans could not fail to see, as the argument increased in acrimony, that they were no longer members of the English family, but rather a new people, with their own separate destiny. Some Americans saw it earlier than others; a good many saw it by 1776. John Penn, while in England in 1773, was struck by the English ignorance "with respect to *our* part of the world (for

I consider myself more American than English). . . ." To South Carolinian Henry Laurens, the Boston Port Act hit at "the liberty of all Americans," not just at that of the people of Massachusetts. Once they were convinced of their essential difference as a people and that British obduracy would not melt, Americans could not accept the old familiar arrangements. Anything less than their independence as a people was unacceptable; it would take Englishmen another generation to realize that the disagreement was as deep as that.

At no time during the ten-year crisis, however, were most Americans spoiling for a rupture with England merely for the sake of a break. Indeed, no one can run through the constitutional arguments of that day without being struck with the reluctance—almost misgivings—with which Americans reached the conclusion of independence. After attending the Continental Congress in 1774, Washington, for example, was "well satisfied that" independence was not "desired by any thinking man in all North America." And, as late as July 6, 1775—over two months after the embattled farmers made their stand at the "rude bridge"—Congress denied any "designs of separation from Great Britain and establishing independent states."

This was no heedless, impetuous overthrow of an oppressor; rather it was a slowly germinating determination on the part of Americans to counter and thwart a change in their hitherto established and accepted ways of governing. Except for the long-deferred assertion of independence, the whole corpus of Revolutionary rhetoric—and nothing lends itself more to radicalism than words—was conservative, expressive of the wish to retain the old ways. The demands made upon Britain were actually pleas for a return to the old relationship: repeal the Stamp Act, the Townshend Acts, the Mutiny Acts; restore trial by jury as abrogated by the expanded admiralty courts; remove the restrictions recently placed upon western migration.

One needs only to run through that famous list of grievances in the Declaration of Independence to be forcefully reminded that what these revolutionaries wanted was nothing but the *status quo ante bellum.*

"We have taken up arms," the Continental Congress carefully explained in July, 1775, two months after Lexington, "in defense of the freedom that is our birth-right, and which we ever enjoyed til the late violation of it. . . ." These men had been satisfied with their existence, they were not disgruntled agitators or frustrated politicians; they were a strange new breed—contented revolutionaries.

8

1777:
Year of Decision

Howard J. Peckham

Certainly the American Revolution was full of men on both sides who were distinguished for heroism and courage against adversity. But this is only half the story. Throughout the Revolution, English and Americans alike were plagued with internal division, incompetence, and outright duplicity. The Americans, for their part, were hardly united about fighting for independence. Only a minority actively supported the rebellion. Many people opposed it; and many others could not have cared less about the whole thing. Some colonists happily traded with both armies; others were devout loyalists when British troops were in the vicinity, only to become eloquent rebels when the Continental Army passed by. While the Americans may have had the best general in George Washington, colonial volunteers often fought without regard for rules, discipline, or orders, charging forward with all the organization of stampeding cattle. And cattle would have been immeasurably easier to drill. Baron von Steuben, the Prussian drillmaster, became so exasperated with the sloppiness and indifference of colonial troops that he once screamed at them in French: "Viens, Walker, mon ami, mon bon ami! Sacré! Goddam de gaucheries of dese badauts! Je ne puis plus. I can curse dem no more!" Then, as if lack of discipline were not bad enough, many volunteers set out for home after battles, thinking that the war was over or claiming that crops had to be harvested. During the eight years of war, an estimated 400,000 men fought in the colonial army; yet the turnover was so rapid that at no single time did Washington have more than 18,000 troops in the field. At the same time, he was beset with chronic shortages of money, guns, and supplies—and with feuding generals, too, a few of whom plotted in the infamous Conway cabal to oust him from command.

The British also had problems. The "colonial war" was extremely unpopular back home, with many of England's leading politicians—and some of her generals as well—advocating colonial independence. Moreover, British troops (including German mercenaries) suffered from supply shortages, low morale, and inept leadership. General Thomas Gage was perhaps the best British commander in North America, but the government summoned him home after Breed's Hill and replaced him with corpulent William Howe, who was more interested in wine and women than in fighting a war. In fact, as Howard J. Peckham demonstrates in his graceful account of the crucial campaigns in 1777, British leadership from the strategists in London to many of the officers in the field was remarkably inept. Thanks to British errors, Americans won a decisive victory in 1777—one that largely determined the outcome of the war.

Convinced at last that the American revolt might become a major war, Parliament determined to bring it to a speedy end by providing the massive force that Gage had advised at the outset. An army of fifty-five thousand was authorized for America, but recruiting pro-

From pp. 38–39, 58–80 in *The War for Independence* by Howard J. Peckham. © 1958 by The University of Chicago. Reprinted by permission of The University of Chicago Press.

ceeded so slowly that several German princes were appealed to for mercenaries. English subsidies to European armies were nothing new, and these princes were relatives or friends of George III's Hanoverian family. Altogether thirty thousand German troops were hired at varying fees paid to their rulers, seventeen thousand of them from Hesse-Cassel. In consequence, all of them were dubbed "Hessians" in America, a term spit out in contempt. British and German troops destined for America in 1776 amounted to forty-two thousand, an ample number if properly deployed and led. Yet this powerful blade was not to be wielded lustily.

In England the American Revolution was a political issue. The King and his friends, chiefly Tories, had sought to ease the financial burden left by the Seven Years' War by getting money from the colonies. For a dozen years they had tried various tax measures without success and produced only revolt. The parliamentary minority, largely Whig, had supported many of the American protests and arguments as opposition policy. Their aim was not to deny the supremacy of Parliament over the colonies but to embarrass and reduce the political power of the King. If George III wished to continue exercising the power he loved, then he must defeat the American colonies. First, he had to do it promptly, before his old enemies, France and Spain, should be tempted to make matters worse for him. Second, he must do it cheaply. War cost money and added to the national debt, while armed occupation of defeated colonies would require more funds than could be extracted from them by taxation. Therefore the object of victory was not bitterness, which would ruin the King too, but colonial reconciliation to the idea of sharing the cost of empire. It was to be a limited war.

Concentrating on the army rather than the navy as the primary instrument of victory, Britain decided to divide the colonies and expose the weakness of the separated regions.

The commanders were empowered to accept submission before launching their invasion; if that failed, they were to give battle, demonstrate their military superiority, then offer an armistice again at some favorable moment. Even the stubborn Americans would soon see the foolishness of persisting in their own ruination when it was so unnecessary. . . .

. . .

The British campaign of 1777 was to complete and extend the strategy envisioned the year before. Of course, it was to be the final campaign.

The fabric was tailored in London by that incompetent apprentice, Lord Germain. His first pattern was drawn by General Howe [commander of all British forces south of Canada], who roused himself sufficiently to propose marching ten thousand men into Pennsylvania to seize the rebel capital, rout the Congress, and arm the loyalists. He would leave two thousand men in garrison at Newport, Rhode Island, four thousand in New York City, and three thousand on the lower Hudson, partly to "facilitate in some degree the approach of the army from Canada," which Howe expected to reach Albany in September. The total of nineteen thousand troops committed did not include the loyalists in arms (whom the British called provincials). Germain indorsed this plan, although what was to be gained by seizing Philadelphia if Washington's army remained intact defied answer, as the inconclusiveness of capturing New York had already demonstrated.

A different cut to the garment was advocated by Burgoyne, who returned to England again at the end of 1776. He proposed to succeed where Carleton had failed by a descent from Canada over two routes: via Lake Champlain, and from the west via Lake Ontario and the Mohawk River; the two routes were to converge on Albany. On reaching that town he

would arrange with Howe for the control of the Hudson River so as to cut off New England and to enable Howe "to act with his whole force to the southward." Germain liked this pattern, too, and the three thousand men Howe was leaving for cooperative use seemed ample. Burgoyne, of course, was named to command the northern army; Carleton, whom Germain disliked, was knighted and left to his civil duties as governor. Howe was informed of Burgoyne's plan.

The fundamental weakness of Burgoyne's scheme, however, was the same as Howe's: its success would not end the war. Cutting the communication between New England and the other colonies was not fatal; New England would not be taken out of the war unless its coast were blockaded too, and only then after a long passage of time.

Just as Germain began to sew up his cloth, he received a revised pattern from Howe. On counting his men again, the general had decided to leave twenty-four hundred at Newport, forty-seven hundred in New York plus three thousand provincials to serve defensively around the city, and to take eleven thousand to Philadelphia *by sea*. Germain should have gulped at this realignment, for the three thousand regulars who were to push up the Hudson at Burgoyne's call were not in the picture. Howe cannot be excused for this omission merely because he wrote to Carleton that neither he nor Burgoyne should count on aid from him. Moreover, in approaching Philadelphia by water Howe would establish no overland communication with New York. Why he made these new decisions never has been determined. As for Germain, he may have thought the very fact that Howe would keep Washington engaged in Pennsylvania would serve Burgoyne adequately by clearing his path. So he approved this altered plan, too, expressing only the hope that Howe would be victorious in time to assist Burgoyne up the Hudson. Having committed himself to a strategy of double envelopment, Germain was responsible for co-ordinating the two expeditions so as to avoid simultaneous commitment in two widely separated theaters.

Germain, the King, Howe, Burgoyne—all of them may be excused for failing to anticipate one fatal development: no one could have believed then that a *second* American army, *larger* than Washington's, would be raised in the vicinity of Albany and thrown against Burgoyne. But none of them is to be forgiven for making plans to end the war that overlooked the absolute necessity of drawing Washington into battle and destroying his army.

Burgoyne's Invasion

About four thousand British and three thousand German troops were assembled in Canada in June, 1777, for Burgoyne's trek, a total of seven thousand or more, plus, it is reported, two thousand women! He had able subordinates in Major General William Phillips, a veteran artilleryman, in Brigadier General Simon Fraser, and in Major General Baron Friedrich Adolph von Riedesel of Brunswick, a warmhearted cavalryman, thirty-nine years old, whose wife and children traveled the wilderness with him. Carleton assisted by calling in militia and Indians, but neither group responded with any enthusiasm after the past year's experience. Only about two hundred and fifty French-Canadians and American loyalists enrolled, and some fourteen hundred Indians showed up for the bloodletting. Commanding one band of warriors was Governor Carleton's nephew Christopher, a man with an Indian as well as a white wife, who dressed like a savage, painted his face, and wore a ring in his nose.

Burgoyne dispatched Colonel Barry St. Leger with seven hundred regulars and loyalists, plus almost a thousand of the braves under the educated Mohawk, Joseph Brant, up the St. Lawrence to Lake Ontario. The general himself

concentrated his main force at Fort St. John's on the Richelieu River (almost due east of Montreal) and embarked on June 15. Entering Lake Champlain, the army was rowed without resistance up the long lake in gunboats and Canadian boats called bateaux developed in the fur trade. They made a pretty picture on the water: dozens of large and small craft, colorful uniforms, sunlight flashing on musket barrels and wet paddles, bands playing. The flotilla approached Fort Ticonderoga on June 30. Burgoyne was fortunate to find the defending Americans crippled by quarreling commanders.

Schuyler, who had hardly distinguished himself in 1776, was, as might be expected of a second-rate, stubborn man, unwilling to resign his command of the Northern Department. New England militia especially objected to the wealthy landowner of New York. Congress ordered Gates back to lead the field army that was being raised, but he refused to serve under Schuyler. Major General Arthur St. Clair, a former British officer who had been with Washington at Trenton, was accordingly sent up and put in charge of Ticonderoga, now much strengthened by the young Polish engineer, Colonel Thaddeus Kosciuszko. This fort was expected to hold up the British by withstanding a siege for weeks. Yet St. Clair had only two thousand Continentals and three hundred artillerymen to man the stone fort, its outworks, and Mount Independence, across the narrows on the Vermont shore. Nine hundred militia were due daily. Behind Ticonderoga and to the southwest was a higher eminence, Mount Defiance, wild, heavily wooded, and unfortified.

Burgoyne split his advance forces, and Phillips, swinging west around Fort Ticonderoga, spotted Mount Defiance. "Where a goat can go, a man can go," he declared, "and where a man can go he can drag a gun." His engineers cut a path and hauled cannon up the slope on July 3 and 4, and Phillips pointed

them down on Ticonderoga. St. Clair took the hint and evacuated the fort the next night, leaving immense stores and a hundred cannon. His troops crossed a bridge of boats to Mount Independence, picked up the troops there, and swung southward in a wide arc. Fraser and Riedesel gave chase, defeated a rear guard at Hubbardton (Vermont), and harried St. Clair all the way down to Fort Edward on the Hudson, a dilapidated old stockade halfway between Ticonderoga and Albany. Burgoyne overran Ticonderoga, established himself at Skenesborough, twenty-three miles above Fort Edward, and then took a rest for three weeks.

Washington was alarmed by this rapid advance and detached Major Generals Benedict Arnold and Benjamin Lincoln north with reinforcements. Lincoln was a Massachusetts farmer and politician of forty-four, heavily built, and a good steady soldier. Congress was disgusted with both St. Clair and Schuyler. It acted to remove the latter and ordered Gates up to assume full command. In the interim granted by Burgoyne, Schuyler moved up troops from Albany until he had forty-five hundred men. He set them to work felling trees in a tangled matting along the way that the British had to proceed. Great boulders were rolled down the hillsides into the creek crossings. New England militia began pouring in as word of Gates's coming spread; although he was from Virginia, they trusted him more than Schuyler.

The fatal delay of the British was owing to Burgoyne's insistence on advancing in force—infantry, forty-two cannon, wagons (including thirty carts with his own baggage and liquor), and women—all of which meant cutting a road through woods and over streams. He was oblivious to the need for haste. Besides, he was living in a loyalist's fine house and had found a pretty mistress in his entourage. Finally on July 24 he pushed forward fourteen miles to abandoned Fort Anne.

His Indians ranged out ahead on both sides.

Near Fort Edward they came upon the cabin of a loyalist widow, Mrs. McNeil, a cousin of General Fraser. Visiting her was Jane McCrea, sister of a rebel but in love with a loyalist and former neighbor who was returning with Burgoyne's expedition. Reputedly beautiful, she at least was possessed of distinctively long hair, sometimes said to have been blonde. The Indians roughly seized both women and started in two parties back to the British camp. Mrs. McNeil arrived first and berated her cousin for this savage treatment. When the other party arrived, it escorted only Jane's unmistakable scalp. On the way the Indians had quarreled over their prize and killed, stripped, and mutilated her. Burgoyne demanded that her murderer be delivered up and sentenced him to death. A Canadian officer interceded and warned that the Indians would desert if the sentence was carried out. Burgoyne faltered and released the warrior, thereby incurring the sharp edge of this propaganda weapon. The story of the massacre and Burgoyne's condoning it spread rapidly through New York and New England. More and more militiamen turned their feet toward Albany. Even the New York loyalists wondered how safe they were from Burgoyne's undiscriminating savages. The killing of Jane McCrea, one of those vivid and magnified incidents of a campaign, passed into folklore and folk song, and the incrimination has blackened Burgoyne's name to this day.

The British finally reached Fort Edward on July 29. Schuyler had withdrawn down the Hudson twenty-five miles to Stillwater, where Kosciuszko laid out a defensive position to intrench. Burgoyne paused again, and here early in August he heard news both reassuring and ominous: St. Leger was approaching Fort Stanwix, one hundred miles west, but Howe was belatedly leaving New York headed south, blithely ignorant of any obligation to move up the Hudson unless Washington did. However, Burgoyne was not worried about himself.

Hearing of rebel supplies and horses gath-ered at Bennington, forty miles to the southeast, he dispatched Colonel Friedrich Baum on August 11 with 550 men to seize them. The German marched straight to his doom, for in the town there happened to be gathered 1,500 New Hampshire militia under Brigadier General John Stark, who had held the rail fence at Breed's Hill. Three days out Baum sighted militia in front of him and sent back for reinforcements. On August 16 Stark spread out his men to surround Baum. The latter saw these shirt-sleeved men on his flanks and assumed they must be loyalists coming to join him. He soon learned otherwise when Stark began his frontal attack.

"There they are!" he cried. "We'll beat them before night, or Molly Stark will be a widow."

Surrounded, Baum's men fought stubbornly but hopelessly; only nine of them escaped. In the afternoon 640 reinforcements under Colonel Heinrich von Breymann came near. Stark rounded up his men and moved forward to pitch into a second battle that soon saw Breymann fleeing west again. The battle of Bennington cost Burgoyne over two hundred killed and seven hundred prisoners, and staggered him. Stark lost thirty killed and forty wounded.

While Burgoyne rested at Fort Edward, Colonel St. Leger was in trouble. At Fort Oswego, New York, which he reached in mid-July, he was joined by over a hundred New York loyalists under Sir John Johnson, son of the late Sir William Johnson, long-time Crown superintendent of Indian affairs. The enmity between loyalists and patriots in upper and western New York was especially bitter, because the loyalists included royal officials who were able to turn the Iroquois, whom they had long supervised, against the frontier rebels. Political disagreement had rapidly degenerated into civil warfare with its attendant burning, plundering, and murder of neighbor against neighbor.

St. Leger's enlarged task force struck out eastward to attack old Fort Stanwix, now renamed Fort Schuyler (Rome, N.Y.). The garri-

son there amounted to seven hundred and fifty, but the commandant, Colonel Peter Gansevoort, daily expected a reinforcement of eight hundred under General Nicholas Herkimer, local landholder and son of a German immigrant. Informed of this coming reinforcement, Joseph Brant laid an ambush for Herkimer in a ravine near Oriskany. The Americans marched blindly into the trap on August 6 and then proceeded with bloody stubbornness to fight their way out. Losing an appalling 50 per cent of their men, they finally routed the Indians but gave up trying to reach the fort.

St. Leger laid siege to Fort Schuyler. Gansevoort got two men out during a night storm to seek help. They sped all the way to General Schuyler's headquarters, where Benedict Arnold offered to lead a relief column. He picked up a thousand volunteers eager to fight under him and hurried westward through the woods. In an effort to scare off St. Leger's Indian allies, Arnold sent on ahead a subnormal Dutchman who was well known to many of the Iroquois and acknowledged by them to be "touched" only by the Great Spirit. They regarded him with awe because of his dim-wittedness. The Dutchman was instructed to report that an American force as numerous as the leaves on the trees was marching on Fort Schuyler. His undoubted story cooled the war fever of the braves, especially after their taste of resistance at Oriskany. Helping themselves to British liquor and clothing, they melted away into the forest. The loyalists, of no mind on second thought to face their infuriated neighbors, followed them. St. Leger's expedition was suddenly skeletonized to a remnant of regulars. He had no choice but to give up the siege on August 22 and withdraw to Oswego. This channel of Burgoyne's surge was dammed.

Gates now arrived at Stillwater and took over command. The American position had much improved in the past few weeks. Washington sent him Colonel Daniel Morgan's new corps of riflemen, and militia continued to march in. As soon as Arnold returned from his western triumph, Gates moved him six miles north to some higher ground called Bemis Heights, which Kosciuszko fortified. They were in no hurry to have Burgoyne advance, and he gave them plenty of time. It was September 13 before he had collected supplies for thirty days and was ready to get his heavy caravan in motion again. It took him five days to come in sight of Bemis Heights and mount an attack. He ordered three columns out the next morning under Riedesel, Fraser, and himself. Riedesel was to keep close to the river while Fraser and Burgoyne came together on the American left on the farm of one Isaac Freeman.

Watching the approach, Gates was content to wait in the fortifications. Impatient Arnold wanted to go out and meet the enemy in the woods of Freeman's farm, abandoning the advantage of the protected position. At length Gates let Arnold take Morgan's riflemen and Dearborn's New Hampshire regiment (three veterans together of the march to Quebec) and burst out against Fraser. Arnold got into some difficulty, sent back for more regiments, and then sliced between Fraser and Burgoyne. The latter stood firm, but Arnold thought he could roll over Fraser. Gates refused his second plea for reinforcements, and at nightfall Arnold withdrew, fuming. Although the British remained on the battleground, they had lost nearly 600 men. Arnold's action had cost 320 Americans, 65 of them killed. Gates had been saved from an attack he might not have withstood and afterward had missed an opportunity to achieve a decisive victory. He did not mention Arnold in reporting the engagement, and the latter resented it in hot words. He asked to leave the area and was deprived of his command for insubordination. Fellow officers persuaded him not to resign, and he hung around in a long sulk, drawing to him the friends of Schuyler who resented Gates's ascendancy.

Lincoln then organized a strike far behind Burgoyne at Ticonderoga itself. His columns occupied Skenesboro, carried Mount Defiance

and Mount Independence, but could not take the stout old stone fort. They took three hundred prisoners, released one hundred captured Americans, and generally gave Burgoyne the jitters. After the battle of September 19, his advance stalled again for two weeks, time he could not afford to lose because of the limited rations he carried. Gambler that he was, he decided to wait on the next word from General Clinton, who had sent him a message that he was about to strike up the Hudson from New York City.

Howe Moves to Pennsylvania

Sir William Howe's seaborne invasion was way off schedule. He pulled his last troops out of New Jersey early in July and put them on board transports. He left a garrison of seventy-two hundred in New York under Clinton, newly returned from England with a knighthood to mollify his smoldering resentment over the published version of the naval attack on Charleston. Howe finally sailed down the coast on July 23.

Storms and calms made a short voyage disagreeably long, and he finally landed at the head of Chesapeake Bay, fifty miles southwest of Philadelphia, on August 25. At sea he had received a further letter from Germain expressing the foolish hope that Howe's campaign would be finished in time to cooperate with Burgoyne's army! His fourteen thousand weary troops marched north and east to Brandywine Creek. They hardly endeared themselves to the rich countryside. Two of his men were hanged and five whipped for plundering. Howe's secretary noted that the "Hessians are more infamous and cruel than any. It is a misfortune we ever had such a dirty, cowardly set of contemptible miscreants."

Washington had marched his eleven thousand men from Morristown down to Philadelphia as soon as he could determine where Howe's transports were headed. He came up to the British in Delaware not far from their debarkation point and moved north in a parallel line with them to the Brandywine. Nathanael Greene wrote to his wife of this new theater of war:

Here are some of the most distressing scenes imaginable—the inhabitants generally desert their houses, furniture moving, cattle driving, and women and children travelling off on foot—the country all resounds with the cries of the people—the enemy plunders most amazingly.

The likeliest place for crossing the Brandywine was Chad's Ford, and here Washington put several brigades under Greene behind earthworks. Pennsylvania militia guarded his left, and Sullivan and Stirling commanded the right. The line was not unlike that on Long Island, outside Brooklyn, and Washington did not intend to let the enemy march around his flank as it had a year ago. This was the second pitched battle for him.

On September 11 Howe moved to cross the creek. Lieutenant General Baron Wilhelm von Knyphausen, the sixty-one-year-old commander of the Hessians, appeared at the ford late in the morning as if to engage Greene. Washington was sure this was not the main attack and soon heard that another body of the enemy had moved north. He sent a warning to Sullivan, but, seeing no one, that general concluded the information must be wrong. Howe was repeating his Long Island tactic, however, and he had started Cornwallis north at daybreak. His lordship marched so far that he crossed the Brandywine far beyond the American right. In fact when he turned back it took him until four o'clock in the afternoon to make contact. Then with five thousand troops, Cornwallis overwhelmed the deceived Sullivan. Greene staved off defeat only by an extraordinary reversal of the Virginia Continentals. He pulled them out of line, marched four miles

through broken country in fifty minutes, and held Cornwallis at bay while the whole American army pulled back under cover of darkness to Chester. Howe suffered ninety killed and almost five hundred wounded, but Washington is believed to have lost three hundred killed, probably six hundred wounded, and four hundred prisoners. The Americans had been outgeneraled, but Washington defended Sullivan when Congress tried to break him.

All organization shattered, the men flowed in the direction of Chester, companies, regiments, and brigades fragmented and intermingled. How far they might have marched is uncertain. But on the east side of Chester Creek stood a French youth of nineteen who, with a small guard, brought the retreat to a halt. He was a volunteer without rank and wore a hasty bandage around one leg. His name was long and noble, but the men knew him simply as "Lafayette."

Only Greene's division came up unbroken, and Washington with it. Then began the sorting out of the men and the restoring of units. It was a curious sort of withdrawal, without panic. Captain Enoch Anderson wrote that he heard no despairing remarks. "We had our solacing words already for each other—'Come, boys, we shall do better another time.'"

In the next week the American army retreated to the Schuylkill River on the edge of Philadelphia, swung north, and darted west to make an attack that was drowned out in torrential rains that soaked their powder. Brigadier General Anthony Wayne was left near Paoli, where he had lived as a boy, with fifteen hundred men to threaten Howe's left. He lay hidden in a wood and thought his presence was unknown, but loyalists carried the news to the British. On the night of September 20 one of Howe's subordinates, Lord Grey, led a bayonet attack on Wayne, inflicting two hundred to three hundred casualties and taking seventy-one prisoners. Howe then advanced to a position between Washington and the

Quaker city, and Congress was warned to flee. It adjourned to York, and Howe entered the capital on September 26.

Washington was not through yet. Reinforcements came to him that restored his army to more than eleven thousand. He returned toward Germantown, north of Philadelphia, where Howe had stationed without intrenchments his main force of less than nine thousand. Their line extended about three miles east from the Schuylkill. Washington's troops were stretched out for seven miles west to east. But there were four roads running southward, converging gradually as they entered or passed Germantown. Washington planned to march his men down those four roads on the night of October 3 so that they would hit the British at dawn simultaneously on both flanks and at two places frontally. The four columns were to be led by Sullivan, Greene, John Armstrong, and William Smallwood. The directions on how to keep to the main roads were sketchy at best. Coordination is difficult to achieve at night and no maneuver for half-trained troops. This kind of wide-jawed pincer movement had ancient precedents, but in those maneuvers the outside lines were made up of the strongest forces. Washington put his heaviest strength in the two center columns.

A drop in temperature raised a heavy fog late at night. Nevertheless, the attack began well with surprise. Sullivan hit first and rolled the enemy back. Some delay occurred when the British held a stone house like a fortress, and Washington finally left a detachment to contain the place while the column pressed on. Meanwhile, Greene was delayed half an hour by a bewildered guide. While he was hurrying into action, his right wing under Adam Stephen, who had been drinking, mistook Sullivan's left in the fog for the enemy and opened fire on Wayne's men. Discovery of this bloody error broke up both divisions. Yet when Greene's main ramming force struck, he broke the British line, smashed into town, and en-

gaged in bloody house-to-house fighting. Victory was in sight, but there was no pressure on the British flanks. Armstrong had been too easily turned back, and Smallwood had not arrived.

Cornwallis came running out of Philadelphia with reinforcements; Grant drove some troops between Sullivan and Greene. The sound of firing on all sides, plus the fog, seems to have confused the Americans and, as Washington reported, "when every thing gave the most flattering hopes of victory, the troops began suddenly to retreat." It was a heartbreaking outcome. Even Howe's dog got confused in the mist and followed the retreating Americans. Washington returned him under a flag of truce.

All the American generals were disappointed and angered by the turn of events at Germantown, principally because they were puzzled by it. Wayne was caustic: "We ran from Victory." While Howe suffered 100 killed and 420 wounded, Washington counted 152 killed, 521 wounded, and 400 captured. Stephen was court-martialed for his blunder and dismissed from the service. Washington was criticized in Congress, his performance soon contrasted with Gates's at Saratoga.

Saratoga

With the exciting prospect of Clinton stabbing the Americans in the back, Burgoyne deluded himself and gambled away sixteen precious days in idleness against his dwindling provisions. Clinton did make a thrust up the river (Howe's parting suggestion), but he was as cautious as Burgoyne was reckless. Delaying until he received reinforcements from England, he seized Forts Montgomery and Clinton from Putnam's command and reached West Point on October 8. The messengers between Clinton and Burgoyne were frequently captured. Burgoyne could not learn exactly where Clinton was or how fast he was moving. On his part,

Clinton was disconcerted to hear from Burgoyne's last messenger, October 5, that the distressed commander was soliciting *orders* from Clinton, a deft shifting of responsibility for the outcome of a dubious operation. Clinton quickly eluded this yoke and returned to New York City. His subordinate, Major General John Vaughan, pushed northward and burned Kingston on October 15. He was only forty-five miles below Albany, but time had run out.

Gradually Burgoyne realized that time was all in Gates's favor. Besides his casualties, he had lost other soldiers by desertion and almost all his Indians. Already he was outnumbered: fifty-two hundred to the Americans' seven thousand, plus twenty-five hundred militia that had recently moved up behind him. The strain from nightly harassment and from summer clothing in the cold fall was telling on his men; yet he had to put them on half-rations on October 3. He called a council of war to which he proposed an all-out attack on Gates's left by a wide sweep through the woods. The realistic Riedesel recommended retreat until the army was within reach of Lake Champlain, where it could embark if necessary or advance again when Clinton reached Albany. Fraser agreed with him; Phillips said nothing. Burgoyne declared that retreat was disgraceful but finally consented to modify his offensive move. On October 7 he put sixteen hundred and fifty of his troops in motion with ten cannon to strike at the American left. It was an uncertain, even pointless reconnaissance in force. At least there was no lack of command, for the four generals accompanied this detachment. The column proceeded slowly less than a mile beyond their intrenchments and then drew up in a long line on open ground.

As soon as Gates learned of the approach he accepted the enticing invitation to attack, for a woods at either end of Burgoyne's line provided cover for flank advances safe from cannon. "Order on Morgan to begin the game," he said. Hard-bitten, easy moving Dan Morgan

led his rifle corps around through the woods to fire on Burgoyne's right. Enoch Poor's brigade was to strike his left. When these two were in position, Ebenezer Learned's brigade would take on the center. Gates stayed at his headquarters throughout the battle, which was proper if not inspiring. Hearing the musket fire, Arnold could not stand inaction. He forgot his pique, leaped on his horse, and galloped out of camp. Gates sent an aide in pursuit to order him back.

Suddenly Arnold appeared at the head of Learned's Connecticut troops waving his sword and shouting, a dynamic personality of tremendous military reputation and popularity. He was the spark that ignited the American attack. The men cheered and surged against Burgoyne's Germans. Poor had already chewed up the grenadiers on the British left, and Morgan's riflemen were knocking over the light infantry on the right. Fraser was mortally wounded. Burgoyne ordered a retreat to the fortified lines. This withdrawal, however, did not break off the battle. Arnold scooped up all the loose troops he could find and pressed a further attack. The Americans were also immensely heartened by the arrival of three thousand Albany militia.

Burgoyne's foolishness had released a swarm of hornets. He needed luck now to save his army. His disorganized detachment did not get back into the redoubts they normally held. Arnold was on their heels, a fighting fool leading a charmed life, once galloping down between the two lines of fire to reach a party of Morgan's riflemen. These he led boldly against the first redoubt, held by Colonel von Breymann and his surviving Germans. Frantic and tyrannical, the Brunswicker beat his men to make them hold on, until one of them turned and shot him dead. Then they gave up the redoubt, but their last volley killed Arnold's horse and broke the general's leg, the same one wounded at Quebec. The way was open, however, to carry Burgoyne's whole position. Gates committed no more men to the attack and was not in a position to see the advantage given him. When Arnold lay on the ground, immobile at last, Gates's aide reached him with orders to return to camp. The fire went out of the American attack and night descended. Thus ended the second battle of Freeman's Farm, or of Bemis Heights as it is also known. Gates suffered only 150 casualties in the late afternoon drubbing given the enemy. He did give Arnold much credit in his report, and Burgoyne gave him all.

The captured redoubt was held, and next day Burgoyne knew he must move. In the harvests of Freeman's Farm he had lost not only two good officers but nearly one thousand men. He ordered a retreat, leaving five hundred sick and wounded behind. Heavy clouds opened and rain poured down. After three days of intermittent slogging through mud, the weary troops reached Saratoga (Schuylerville, N.Y.), only seven miles to the north. Attracted by the comforts of the Schuyler mansion, Burgoyne ordered a halt. American militia lay ahead of him and across the river, too. With the British lion wounded and at bay, Gates's army swelled in the next ten days to seventeen thousand hunters ready for the kill.

Completely surrounded and dispirited, Burgoyne asked Gates for terms on October 13. The latter required unconditional surrender, when he should have demanded that Burgoyne propose terms which he would modify or accept. As a result, haggling went on for four days, and when Burgoyne boasted that he had "succeeded to dictate every term" he was correct. He did not so much capitulate as reach an agreement, or convention, by which he gave up not his men but their arms; the men were to march to a port, embark for England, and not serve again in North America. The terms were generous to a fault, for Burgoyne's men would simply release other British troops for service in America, as Washington pointed out to Congress. So the "convention army" was kept

British General John Burgoyne, surrendering to the Americans at Saratoga. Burgoyne haggled with them for four days before they came to terms (which were "generous to a fault"): Burgoyne would take his men back to England and would never serve again in North America. ("The Surrender of General Burgoyne" painted by John Trumbull. Courtesy of Yale University Art Gallery.)

near Boston throughout the winter, then marched to Virginia for safer keeping, and never sent home. One result was that hundreds deserted to begin a new and better life on the frontier.

Before Congress is condemned for breaching an agreement that ought not to have been made, the reader should know that Howe promptly sent secret word to Burgoyne that once he got his men on transports the Germans might return to England, but the three thousand British troops should be brought around

to New York for reassignment! In consequence of this order, Burgoyne and his men sought every opportunity to provoke their American guards into some illegal act that he could use later to justify his planned violation of the convention.

An actor to the last, Burgoyne seemed to enjoy playing his role of defeated general and "guest" of Gates. "The fortune of war has made me your prisoner," he announced when he met Gates. Schuyler came up for the ceremony and Burgoyne was embarrassed to con-

fess he had burned the former's house. He got off a letter to Clinton that began with a dramatic flourish:

> After two very sharp actions, infinite fatigue, disappointment of intelligence from you, & a thousand other untoward circumstances, I was compelled to fall back to Saratoga.

And for three pages a play-by-play account of the proceedings was narrated. At length he admitted surrender and then struck a pose of martyred valor:

> I have had some narrow personal escapes, having been shot through my hat & waistcoat, & my horse hit, in the last action. If my reputation suffers among the respectable part of my profession, I shall think those escapes unfortunate.

It did and they were. He made his exit from the military stage unmourned, unhonored, and unsung. His very own blunders and ill-judgments had rung down the curtain.

Philadelphia

Howe was not safely ensconced in Philadelphia yet. He had to rely on ships for supplies, and the Americans still held the lower Delaware—held it with two forts, floating batteries, and *chevaux-de-frise* (sharpened stakes held on the bottom in iron sockets and pointed upward at an angle so as to puncture ship hulls). Howe pulled his men out of Germantown and called for help from his brother, the admiral. A joint attack on Fort Mercer, at Red Bank, New Jersey, cost Colonel von Donop his life along with more than three hundred casualties and two ships, without success. Colonel Christopher Greene, who had marched with Arnold to Quebec, was the stubborn defender, commanding only four hundred men.

That same day, October 22, Howe was writing a long letter to Lord Germain. He had heard of Burgoyne's retreat, but he discounted rebel rumors of his surrender. Anticipating criticism, he expressed surprise to hear that Burgoyne had "expected a co-operating army at Albany." Bluntly confessing that there was "no prospect of terminating the war to the advantage of Great Britain" in the present campaign, Howe expatiated on plans for the next, making impossible demands: ten thousand men for New England, fifteen thousand for the South, garrisons to hold New York and Philadelphia, etc. Then he abruptly changed his tone.

> From the little attention, my Lord, given to my Recommendations since the commencement of my command, I am led to hope I may be relieved from this very painful Service, wherein I have not the good fortune to enjoy the necessary confidence and Support of my Superiors.

Howe knew he had failed, both as a peacemaker and as a conqueror, and he was going to get his resignation in before news of Burgoyne's surrender should reach London.

Next the British turned their attention to Fort Mifflin on Mud Island, Pennsylvania, and, with naval guns mounted on shore, shelled it for five days. The surviving half of the small garrison escaped to Colonel Greene in Fort Mercer. So Cornwallis led two thousand troops against the stronghold in a second assault on November 10. Greene at last abandoned the fort and got away safely, having "sold" his position at an exorbitant price.

Howe was now secure in the rebel capital. With its forty thousand population, Philadelphia was also the largest city in America—indeed, it was larger than any city in England except London. Therefore its capture seemed like an important victory. But what had Howe won? Washington's army stood intact at the

north portal when it should have been destroyed. Indeed, the benefit of his holding Washington away from Burgoyne had been negated by the rise of a second army at Stillwater. The total number of Americans under arms was temporarily larger than it ever had been, and units from Gates's command were now joining Washington.

The loyalists alleged to populate southeastern Pennsylvania failed to appear after the plundering marches of the British and Germans. Some of the people tried to be neutral, but many of them were pacifistic Quakers, of no use to the invader beyond serving as suppliers. And all of this year's effort had wound up by costing a British army at Saratoga. Any hope once held of cutting off supplies to Washington's army disappeared. Small wonder that Howe settled down in the city with his mistress and his gambling cronies for an agreeable winter until his resignation should be accepted.

Neither Howe nor Washington was aware that the character of the war was changing that winter. The miscarriage of British plans for the campaign of 1777 meant far more than the failure of the biggest offensive the colonial office had put together; it signaled the impossibility of ever trying it again under circumstances so favorable, because the first failure encouraged France and her friends to intervene openly on the side of the Americans. A colonial rebellion was merging into a world war.

9

These United Colonies

Edmund S. Morgan

The fighting continued until Cornwallis surrendered his British army at Yorktown in 1781. But it would take another two years before British and American negotiators could work out a peace treaty acceptable to both sides. In the meantime, Americans had set about creating the political machinery necessary to sustain an independent nation. The Second Continental Congress, called in 1775, continued as an emergency, all-purpose central government until 1781, when the Articles of Confederation were finally ratified and a new one-house Congress elected. Americans also perfected their state governments, in order to preserve the rights and practices they had enjoyed as British subjects. Edmund S. Morgan, one of our finest literary historians, recounts the political developments during the Revolution and shows that while significant changes occurred, there was no radical reconstruction of American society at this time.

When the world was told on July 4, 1776, that "these United Colonies are, and of right ought to be Free and Independent States," not even the members of the Continental Congress knew precisely what they had done. The ties that formerly bound them to Great Britain were cut. What was left? "Nothing," said a few, who saw themselves in the "state of nature." If they were right, then everything would have to be rebuilt from the ground up: territorial boundaries, schools, business companies, law courts, churches, towns—all would be reduced to nothing; all would have to be reconstructed.

Most Americans thought nothing so drastic was needed. In a few years they would look on in mingled admiration and horror while the people of France reduced themselves to such a state of nature, but among themselves there was little urge to rebuild society. Though they had committed themselves to the principle of human equality, most of them applied it only in equating themselves with Englishmen and did not stop to examine whatever inequities might exist in their relations with each other. The important thing was not to reform society but to keep government subordinate to it. There was no reason, they thought, why a government which had got out of hand might not be replaced by a proper one without destroying the social fabric for which government should form a protective coating. One could simply peel off the old government and put on the new.

John Locke himself, the great authority on the subject, had never claimed that the dissolution of government would throw a people back into the state of nature. He in fact emphasized that society came into existence before government and could survive a change of government, as English society had done in 1688. If England could do it in 1688, America could in 1776.

From pp. 88–100 in *Birth of the Republic* by Edmund S. Morgan. © 1956 by The University of Chicago. Reprinted by permission of The University of Chicago Press.

Since these ideas prevailed among the majority, the change from British to American government was made with very little fuss. After Lexington the royal governors fled back to England without waiting for the Declaration of Independence. Provincial congresses, in most cases almost indistinguishable from the old assemblies, assumed provisional control of their respective areas. The Continental Congress in May, 1776, advised the people to set up regular governments on their own authority, and by July 4 they had already begun to do so.

In constructing these new governments the ex-colonists did not forget the century and a half during which they had lived in contentment under British rule. They still possessed an admiration for the British constitution that was only slightly tarnished by their recent experiences. Until their final repudiation of the King they had insisted that they were contending only for what the constitution required. They still believed that it was they who stayed true to it while King and Parliament betrayed it. The fact nevertheless remained that it had been betrayed: for all its excellence it had not been proof against tyranny. The problem was to design a government containing all the virtues of the British constitution but with added safeguards to prevent the kind of deterioration they had just witnessed.

There were actually two kinds of government to build, central and local. They began discussing the central one, as we shall see, even before independence but were unable to finish it for several years. In forming the local state governments they were more successful: ten were completed by the end of 1776 and the rest by 1780. They were not perfect, but they did furnish greater protection to human liberty than could be found in any other part of the world at the time.

The most striking thing about these state governments is that they all had their wings clipped by written constitutions in which their powers were strictly limited and defined. In Rhode Island and Connecticut the old colonial charters continued to serve this purpose, but in each of the other states a special document was drafted. The British constitution was unwritten, and in the recent dispute each side had pelted the other with historical precedents. Though the colonists gave as good as they got in this fracas, they had had enough of it and were now unanimous in feeling that their new governments should have something more than tradition to limit and guide them.

A written constitution, then, was their first line of defense against tyranny, and it generally contained a bill of rights defining certain liberties of the people which government must not invade under any pretext: general warrants and standing armies were forbidden; freedom of the press, the right to petition, trial by jury, habeas corpus, and other procedures that came to be known as "due process of law" were guaranteed.

In their haste to get a properly limited government in operation most states allowed their provincial congresses to assume the task of drafting a constitution and putting it into effect. The people of Massachusetts seem to have been the first to see the danger of this procedure. When their provisional legislature handed them a constitution in 1778, they refused the gift, not merely because they did not like it, but also because they had decided that the people should endow the government with a constitution and not vice versa. If, they reasoned, a government can make its own constitution, the government can change it and thus fall into tyranny. Accordingly a special convention was held in 1780 and a constitution established by the people acting independently of government. Other Americans, equally concerned with the dangers of usurpation, saw at once the desirability of the Massachusetts procedure. Though by this time it was too late for most states to use it, the new method was shortly followed in creating a government for the United States.

Though drafted by provincial congresses

rather than popular conventions, the state constitutions did nevertheless proceed on the assumption that the people are the source of political power. Virginia, the first to complete one, began it with a bill of rights which asserted that "all power is vested in, and consequently derived from, the people; that magistrates are their trustees and servants, and at all times amenable to them." Other states copied this provision and supported it by various devices to prevent their governments from slipping the reins of popular control.

It was of elementary importance that every officer of government be elected directly or indirectly by the people. There must be no office of hereditary right, no king, no house of lords. Some constitutions made express provisions to this effect; others simply specified the term of every office, usually a year except in the case of judges. But even though the new governors and judges were to be elective, there remained a much greater confidence in the legislative branch of government than in the executive or judiciary. The members of the legislature, it was felt, were more intimately connected with the people and more immediately subject to them. The governor was generally not allowed to veto legislative acts. He could not dissolve or prorogue legislative meetings. In many states he was elected by the legislature and could be impeached by it. The colonial assemblies had whittled away at the powers of the royal governors for a century and a half, and when the opportunity came could not resist the temptation to finish the job. Pennsylvania decided that a governor was only a nuisance anyhow and abolished the office altogether; in most other states it might as well have been abolished.

John Adams, the Braintree lawyer who helped the Massachusetts Assembly reject the authority of Parliament, saw that the states were making their executive departments too weak. Now that the governor represented popular rather than royal authority, it would have

New Hampshire Declaration of Rights, 1779. Thanks to pressure from the people of the hill towns, New Hampshire law-makers added this Bill of Rights to the state constitution drafted in 1778. Drawing on English common law and on what the colonists had learned in their struggle with England, the document summarizes the rights and governmental processes Americans thought were indispensable to a free and stable society. (Courtesy of The New York Public Library, Astor, Lenox and Tilden Foundations.)

been safer to give him enough power to check an overambitious legislature. Adams was unable to persuade his countrymen of this, but he was successful in urging another device for limiting the legislature, namely, to split it into two chambers, each of which must agree to every act.

Because America had no titled aristocracy and did not want one, it seemed to many, in-

cluding Benjamin Franklin, that American legislatures should be unicameral, with no upper house. Adams, however, was convinced that an upper house was more than a sanctuary for pampered aristocrats. It was a vantage point from which men of property might slow down the more extravagant schemes of a thoughtless multitude. It was also a place where ambitious men of great prestige might be safely and happily isolated without endangering the liberties of the masses. Though America might grant no titles of nobility, Adams was convinced that every society grows aristocrats as inevitably as a field of corn will grow some large ears and some small. Whether by wealth, birth, or talents, some individuals would gain an influence over the others; the function of the upper house was to furnish a place where their influence might be restrained within defined limits.

Adams was not very clear about the way these natural aristocrats were to be prevented from infiltrating the lower house too, but by letters to influential friends and by a well-timed pamphlet he did succeed in persuading every state except Pennsylvania to make its new legislature bicameral. Since most colonial assemblies had contained an upper house in the form of the Governor's Council, it was easy enough to continue the institution on an elective basis.

While they carried out in these institutions the principle that all power emanates from the people, the constitutions were less consistent in applying another principle which most of them enunciated: that all men are born free and equal. Though power emanated from the people, it did not emanate from all of them equally. Western areas in the colonies from Pennsylvania southward had not enjoyed under royal government a representation in proportion to their population. And though they gained a few seats in the new governments, they still had less than their share, especially in South Carolina. There were also people,

varying in number from state to state, from whom no power emanated at all, because they did not have enough property to vote. The property qualification for voting was reduced everywhere except in Massachusetts, but in no case was the suffrage thrown open to all adult men or any women. In spite of the fact that the Americans had scoffed at the notion of virtual representation, they were still practicing a limited form of it themselves.

In explanation of this failing it should be remembered that except in Virginia and perhaps in South Carolina, where the number of tenant farmers was unusually high, the vast majority of white Americans could probably meet the property qualifications required of them. Moreover, the Revolution had begun as a dispute over the security of property, and it was a common assumption that government existed for the protection of property. Those who had none were thought to have very little stake in society. The Virginia bill of rights displays this supposition in stating that "all men having sufficient evidence of permanent common interest with, and attachment to the community, have the right of suffrage."

That the toleration of these inequalities was inconsistent with the avowed principles of the Revolution did not escape men at the time, and there was much argument about it, but another generation passed before Americans brought their practice into closer adjustment with their principles in this matter. It should be emphasized, however, that the Revolutionary period did see a general reduction in property requirements and an increase in western representation. In some states, notably Pennsylvania, there was a thorough electoral reform that secured all taxpayers the right to vote and provided for keeping representation in harmony with population by periodic reapportionments. In other states there were similar though incomplete reforms, and in still others there had never been either regional inequalities in representation or disbarment of any large numbers

from the suffrage. In no state was representation reduced, and only in Massachusetts was the property qualification increased, and there only slightly.

In failing to establish proportional representation and universal suffrage the Revolutionists showed they were not prepared to follow the principle of equality to its logical political conclusion. We need not, however, conclude that their enunciation of the principle was hypocrisy. Though we still adhere to it and though we have carried it much farther than our ancestors, we are still finding new applications. During the Revolutionary period the men who formulated it could scarcely begin to know where it might take them.

Their original intention had been merely to affirm their equality with Englishmen. When they called upon Locke's philosophy of government to support the affirmation, they did not perceive that they were opening the door to developments that Locke himself would probably have disavowed. Locke had described the state of nature as a state of perfect equality, in which no man enjoyed any kind of right or authority or dignity beyond another. In so doing he had no intention of unseating English dukes and earls from their exalted position in the settled state of English society. Locke's state of nature was purely hypothetical, and he did not suggest that the equality prevailing in it ought to continue in organized society. Nor did the revolution he was defending bring about any upset in the social structure of England.

Most Americans, as we have seen, thought of their revolution in much the same way: they too were beyond the hypothetical state of nature and need not return to it. But in America there was not as wide a gap as in England between the hypothetical state of nature and the actual state of society. Here were no titled nobility and no degraded peasantry. Most people owned land and enjoyed economic independence. They were more nearly equal than

the people of any European country, and with the wilderness beckoning on the other side of the mountains they could easily picture the state of nature as a real thing. Under these circumstances Locke's description of the perfect equality of natural men gradually became an ideal to be preserved in American society. Though there was no radical rebuilding of social institutions at this time, it is nevertheless possible to see the ideal beginning to take shape and operating, if only fitfully, against the grosser social inequalities of the day.

There was a beginning made, for example, in the reform that led Americans to civil war by 1860. Early in the agitation against Great Britain individuals had remarked on the inconsistency of a people holding slaves and at the same time complaining that Parliamentary taxation would reduce them to slavery. As the struggle progressed, more and more Americans came to see the need for casting out this beam. In July, 1774, Rhode Island led the way with a law providing that all slaves imported thereafter should be freed. That the move was prompted by the new equalitarian ideas is evident from the preamble, which states that "those who are desirous of enjoying all the advantages of liberty themselves should be willing to extend personal liberty to others." Under this same impulse the Continental Congress in 1774 agreed to discontinue the slave trade and to boycott those who engaged in it. Connecticut, Delaware, Virginia, Maryland, South Carolina, and North Carolina passed laws in the 1770's and 1780's either forbidding or discouraging the importation of slaves. Jefferson would have included a statement against slavery in the Declaration of Independence had not other members of Congress ruled it out.

In most of the northern states the abolition of the slave trade was followed shortly by the abolition of slavery itself. The case of Massachusetts was most striking. Here the constitution adopted in 1780 declared in its first article,

"All men are born free and equal." Under this clause a Massachusetts slave brought suit in court for his freedom, and the court awarded it to him. As a result all slaves in Massachusetts were thenceforth free. Even the southern states, though they continued to hold slaves, admitted the injustice of doing so and looked for a way of abolishing the evil without bringing about their own economic ruin. They did not find a way, but so many southerners were conscience stricken by their own conduct that in 1782 the Virginia legislature passed a law permitting manumission. This had hitherto been forbidden, but now, in the next eight years, ten thousand Virginia slaves received their freedom by the voluntary action of owners who took the principle of equality literally.

These first assaults on slavery were matched by a similar attack on the most obvious form of special privilege. In 1776 there was an established church receiving exclusive economic support from the government in every colony except Pennsylvania and Rhode Island. In New England the Congregational church enjoyed this privilege; in the other colonies the Anglican church. During the Revolution, partly because of pressure from other denominations, partly because of the new disposition toward equality, the Anglican church was disestablished; but in New England where the vast majority of the population was Congregationalist, that church continued to enjoy state support, in New Hampshire until 1817, in Connecticut until 1818, and in Massachusetts until 1833.

Besides the deliberate extension of equality to slaves and churches, the Revolution brought in its train a host of incalculable accidental and incidental changes in society, many of which tended toward a redistribution of wealth. The war inevitably made new fortunes and ruined old ones. Among the heaviest losers were the merchants. Particularly during the early years of the fighting, their business was disrupted by the British Navy. Cut off from trade routes within the Empire, they were obliged to seek out new ones, and these seldom proved initially as profitable as the old. Many turned their ships to privateering against English vessels and occasionally struck it rich, but this required a special talent and was not nearly as reliable a source of income as regular commerce. Few of the established merchant firms of the colonial period came through the Revolution unscathed.

The big southern planters were also hard hit, for the war interfered with the marketing of their rice and tobacco. It was some time after peace arrived before they recovered, and in tidewater Virginia the great plantations, largely exhausted of their fertility, never did regain the old grandeur.

On the other hand, many small farmers enjoyed a prosperity they had never known before. Armies marched on their stomachs in the American Revolution too, and the farmers who supplied them commanded unheard-of prices. With part of the population in the army, albeit a relatively small proportion, there was more work for the civilians and more profit.

The prosperity of the small man was heightened also by the inflation of the currency in every state. The Revolutionary governments, in spite of the fact that they claimed to be trustees of the people, were at first reluctant to impose the high taxes needed to finance the war, and the Continental Congress had no power to tax at all. Instead of taxes both Congress and the state governments resorted to printing money to supply their needs. The result was a flood of paper bills which sent prices soaring. In such a situation the farmer, who was frequently a debtor, could sell his crops at astronomical prices and pay off his debts at their face value in currency that was worth only a fraction of what it had been when he borrowed it.

The inflation of the currency together with the removal of British authority also made op-

portunities for speculators to amass fortunes. The role of these men in American history has generally been a dishonorable one, and this period no less than others had its shady characters and fast deals. But while he was making his pile, the speculator incidentally was helping his countrymen to a wider distribution of property. He thrived on the estates that were everywhere confiscated from those who opposed the Revolution and professed loyalty to Great Britain. These estates were sometimes very large, and through the speculators they were split and transferred to smaller buyers.

A further distribution of property was brought about by reform of inheritance laws. Hitherto in many states the eldest son of a man who died without a will would receive all his father's land; in some cases he might even be required to pass it on intact to his own eldest son. These customs, known as "primogeniture" and "entail," were originally designed to perpetuate an aristocracy. They were felt to be out of place in the new America and were everywhere abolished during the Revolutionary period.

The changes of these years, both social and political, were not accomplished without disagreements among the Revolutionists themselves. Some wanted to go much farther, others not this far. The disagreements have so impressed recent historians that the Revolution is sometimes interpreted as an internal struggle in which the contest between different classes and parties looms as large as the conflict between England and America. Carl Becker, for example, in examining the origins of the Revolution in New York stated that it was not only a dispute about home rule but also about who should rule at home, and his aphorism has become the theme of many subsequent histories.

It cannot be denied that both disputes existed, but to magnify the internal contest to the same proportions as the revolt against England is to distort it beyond recognition. Both before and after the struggle Americans of every state were divided socially, sectionally, and politically; but these divisions did not with any consistency coincide with the division between patriot and loyalist, nor did they run so deep as to arouse the same intensity of feeling. The Revolution cut across the old lines and plucked loyalists and patriots alike from every class and section. And though an ardent patriotism was often used by one group or another to advance its own political fortunes, no group was able to monopolize the commodity. During the war (as before and after it), in spite of the many opportunities for violence, internal disputes generally found peaceable if noisy settlement within the ordinary framework of politics.

The most radical change produced in Americans by the Revolution was in fact not a division at all but the union of three million cantankerous colonists into a new nation.

10

A Revolution Betrayed

Staughton Lynd

delegates to pass it by or to forget about creating a better union. While some, like Benjamin Franklin and Alexander Hamilton, strongly objected to slavery, the other delegates gave in to Southern demands. So, apart from allowing Congress to abolish the foreign slave trade (which it did in 1808), the Constitution maintained "a conspiracy of silence" regarding the slavery problem. And the central paradox in American history—the existence of slavery in a free society—was left to later generations to resolve.

Staughton Lynd examines the slavery issue and the sectional conflict that surrounded it during the Revolutionary, Confederation, and Constitution periods, challenging many traditional and popular theories as he goes along. His observations will not be acceptable to everyone, but they are presented with a bold and honest mind.

The United States was conceived in idealism, and it was conceived in paradox. America joined the family of nations dedicated to the proposition that all men enjoyed the inalienable rights of life, liberty, and the pursuit of happiness and that all stood as equals in the eyes of the law. These were truths Americans had learned in the Age of Enlightenment, when Western man searched for more rational, humane ways to order his universe. Yet in 1776, this same enlightened America held some 700,000 Negroes in chains, mostly in the South. While white Americans championed the liberty and equality of men, they discriminated against free Negroes—even though several thousand had fought with them against the British—and continued to regard slavery itself as both a labor system and a means of racial control to keep blacks and whites apart. Moreover, some of America's leading Revolutionary democrats were Southerners who owned other human beings. Thomas Jefferson, George Washington, and James Madison all dedicated themselves to the triumph of Republican government and human liberty—and all supported their careers by slave labor. Furthermore, Southern slaveowners who attended the 1787 Federal Convention obstinately refused even to discuss the slavery issue, compelling the other

Sectional conflict, like the ghost in *Hamlet*, was there from the beginning. When in September 1774 at the first Continental Congress Patrick Henry made his famous declaration "I am not a Virginian, but an American," the point he was making was that Virginia would not insist on counting slaves in apportioning representation; Henry's next sentence was: "Slaves are to be thrown out of the Question, and if the freemen can be represented according to their Numbers I am satisfyed." The next speaker, Lynch of South Carolina, protested, and the question was left unsettled. Thus early did South Carolinian intransigence overbear Virginian liberalism.

Again in July 1776, the month of the Declaration of Independence, the problem of slave

From Staughton Lynd, "The Abolitionist Critique of the United States Constitution," in *The Antislavery Vanguard: New Essays on the Abolitionists*, ed. Martin Duberman (copyright © 1965 by Princeton University Press; Princeton Paperback, 1968), pp. 218 through 239. Omission of footnotes. Reprinted by permission of Princeton University Press.

PLAN DU NÉGRIER LA VIGILANTE DE NANTES
saisi à Bonni dans le golfe de Guinée le 15 Avril 1822
copié grandeur de l'original à l'échelle de 0^m128

The international slave trade was such an unspeakably brutal business—especially the trip across the Atlantic—that even Southern slaveholders were anxious to outlaw it. Above is a diagram of a slave ship, showing arrangement and padlocks. In recounting a single night on such a ship, an eye-witness wrote of "400 wretched beings . . . crammed into a hold 12 yards in length . . . and only 3½ feet in height." He described how "the suffocating heat of the hold" drove the Negroes to panic in their attempts to escape to the upper air. The next day, he saw 54 "crushed and mangled corpses" lifted up from the slave deck. (Courtesy of The New York Public Library, The Arents Collection.)

representation was brought before Congress in the debate over the proposed Articles of Confederation. The Dickinson draft of the Articles produced three controversies, strikingly similar to the three great compromises of the subsequent Constitutional Convention: "The equal representation of all the states in Congress aroused the antagonism of the larger states. The apportionment of common expenses according to total population aroused the bitter opposition of the states with large slave populations. The grant to Congress of broad powers over Western lands and boundaries was resisted stubbornly by the states whose charters gave them large claims to the West." In the remainder of its existence the Continental Congress succeeded in solving only the last of these controversies, the question of Western lands, and accordingly emphasis has tended to fall on it in histories of the Confederation. But the other two problems were just as hotly debated, in much the same language as in 1787; and on these questions, as Channing observes, there was a "different alignment in Congress" than on the matter of Western lands: a sectional alignment.

The eleventh article of the Dickinson draft stated that money contributions from the states should be "in Proportion to the Number of Inhabitants of every Age, Sex and Quality, except Indians not paying Taxes." On July 30, 1776, Samuel Chase of Maryland (later a prominent Antifederalist) moved the insertion of the word "white," arguing that "if Negroes are taken into the Computation of Numbers to ascertain Wealth, they ought to be in settling the Representation"; Gouverneur Morris would use this same formula in July 1787 to resolve the deadlock over representation in the House. In the debate which followed, the changes were rung upon several themes of the Constitutional Convention. Wilson of Pennsylvania said that to exempt slaves from taxation would encourage slaveholding; in response to the observation that if slaves were counted, Northern sheep should also be counted, Benjamin Franklin remarked that "sheep will never make any Insurrections"; Rutledge of South Carolina anticipated the August 1787 debate on navigation laws by warning that "the Eastern Colonies will become the Carriers for the Southern. They will obtain Wealth for which they will not be taxed"; and his colleague Lynch again threw down a South Carolina ultimatum: "If it is debated, whether their Slaves are their Property, there is an end of the Confederation."

The war had scarcely ended when the sectional debate resumed. We tend to think of Thomas Jefferson as a national statesman, and of the controversy over whether new states would be slave or free as something subsequent to 1820. How striking, then, to find Jefferson writing from Congress to Governor Benjamin Harrison of Virginia in November 1783 about the Northwest Territory: "If a state be first laid off on the [Great] lakes it will add a vote to the Northern scale, if on the Ohio it will add one to the Southern." This concern would never be out of the minds of Southern politicians until the Civil War. Jefferson did, of course, attempt to exclude slavery from the Territories. But on the ninth anniversary of Lexington and Concord, Congress, on motion of Spaight of North Carolina, seconded by Read of South Carolina, struck this provision from Jefferson's draft proposals.

A principal issue between North and South in these first years of the Critical Period was financial. Southern resistance to Northern financial manipulations did not wait until the 1790's: it began, if one must choose a date, when Delaware, Maryland, Virginia, and both the Carolinas voted against the devaluation plan of March 18, 1780, with every Northern state except divided New Hampshire voting Aye. After the war the issue became still more intense. The Revolutionary campaigns in the South took place largely in the last three years of the war "when neither Congress nor the

states," in the words of E. James Ferguson, "had effective money and the troops were supported by impressments." The result was that of the three major categories of public debt—Quartermaster and Commissary certificates issued to civilians; loan certificates; and final settlement certificates issued to the Continental army—the South held only 16 per cent. The public debt of the South was a state debt, while the various kinds of Federal debt were held by Northerners: as Spaight of North Carolina put it, "the Eastern [i.e., Northern] States . . . have got Continental Securities for all monies loaned, services done or articles impressed, while to the southward, it has been made a State debt." Hence when Congress sought to tax all the states to repay the Federal debt, the South protested; and when Congress further provided that Northern states could meet their Congressional requisitions with securities, so that only the South need pay coin, the South was furious. Madison told Edmund Randolph in 1783 that unless the public accounts were speedily adjusted and discharged "a dissolution of the Union will be inevitable." "The pious New-Englanders," Read of South Carolina wrote in April 1785, "think tis time to carry their long projected Scheme into Execution and make the southern states bear the burthen of furnishing all the actual money."

Sectional considerations underlay many an action of the early 1780's where they might not, at first glance, seem evident. Jefferson's appointment as United States representative in France is an example. Jefferson had been appointed to the commission to negotiate a peace, as had Laurens of South Carolina; but Jefferson did not go and Laurens was captured by the British en route to Europe, so that three Northerners—John Jay, John Adams, and Benjamin Franklin—carried the burden of the peace talks. The treaty completed, the same three men stayed on in Europe to represent American interests there, and it was this that

aroused Southern concern. James Monroe expressed it in March 1784, writing to Governor Harrison. Monroe pointed out that Virginia owed British merchants £2,800,000 in debts, which according to the peace treaty must now be paid. "It is important to the southern States to whom the negotiation of these treaties are committed; for except the fishery and the fur-trade (the latter of w'h Mr. Jeff'n thinks . . . may be turn'd down the Potow'k), the southern States, are as States, almost alone interested in it." In May, with Jefferson's appointment achieved, the Virginia delegates in Congress wrote the governor: "It was an object with us, in order to render the Commission as agreable as possible to the Southern States to have Mr. Jefferson placed in the room of Mr. Jay." The previous arrangement, the Virginians went on, involved "obvious inequality in the Representation of these States in Europe"; had it continued, it would have presented "an insurmountable obstacle" to giving the commission such great powers.

Here in microcosm was the problem of the South until its victory at the 1787 Convention: recognizing the need for stronger Federal powers, it feared to create them until it was assured that the South could control their use.

Even as early as the 1780's the South felt itself to be a conscious minority. This was evident, for example, in the comment of Virginia delegates as to the location of the national capital. "The votes in Congress as they stand at present," wrote the delegates from the Old Dominion, "are unfavorable to a Southern situation and untill the admission of Western States into the Union, we apprehend it will be found impracticable to retain that Body [Congress], any length of time, Southward of the middle States." In the fall of 1786, when the clash over shutting the Mississippi to American commerce was at its height, Timothy Bloodworth of North Carolina remarked that "it is

wel known that the ballance of Power is now in the Eastern States, and they appear determined to keep it in that Direction." This was why such Southerners as Richard Henry Lee, later the nation's leading Antifederalist pamphleteer, were already opposing stronger Federal powers in 1785. "It seems to me clear, beyond doubt," Lee wrote to Madison, "that the giving Congress a power to Legislate over the Trade of the Union would be dangerous in the extreme to the 5 Southern or Staple States, whose want of ships and seamen would expose their freightage and their produce to a most pernicious and destructive Monopoly." This was a strong argument, which would be heard throughout the South till 1861; it was this fear which in all probability caused George Mason and Edmund Randolph of Virginia to refuse to sign the Constitution in 1787. Recognizing the force of Lee's argument, Madison wrote to Jefferson in the summer and fall of 1785 that commercial distress was causing a call for stronger powers in Congress throughout the North, but that the South was divided. Lee was "an inflexible adversary, Grayson [William Grayson, another Virginia Antifederalist in 1788] unfriendly." Animosity against Great Britain would push the South toward commercial regulation, but the high price of tobacco would work against it. "S. Carolina I am told is deliberating on the distresses of her commerce and will probably concur in some general plan; with a proviso, no doubt against any restraint from importing slaves, of which they have received from Africa since the peace about twelve thousand." Madison concluded by telling his comrade in France that he trembled to think what would happen should the South not join the other states in strengthening Congress.

Others beside Madison trembled at this thought: the possibility of disunion was openly and seriously discussed in the 1780's, particularly by those who knew of the fiercely sectional debates in Congress. And if disunion was only the speculation of a few in 1785, the great controversy over the Mississippi in 1786 shook many more from their complacence.

The Mississippi question of the 1780's was a part of the larger question of the destiny of the West which, ultimately, would be the immediate cause of the Civil War. Farrand is less than accurate in his attempt to disengage the question of the admission of new states at the Constitutional Convention from sectional strife. For if there is a single key to the politics of Congress and the Convention in the Critical Period, it is that the South expected the West to be slave rather than free and to tilt the balance of power southward, while in Bancroft's words "an ineradicable dread of the coming power of the Southwest lurked in New England, especially in Massachusetts." That group in Congress recognized as "the Southern Interest (1786), "the southern party" (1787) or "the Southern Delegation" (1788) fought throughout the 1780's to forestall the admission of Vermont until at least one Southern state could be added simultaneously, to hasten the development of the West, and to remove all obstacles to its speedy organization into the largest possible number of new states. It was here that the Mississippi question entered. What was feared if America permitted Spain to close New Orleans to American commerce was not only a separation of the Western states, but a slackening of the southwestward migration which Southerners counted on to assure their long-run predominance in the Union.

"The southern states," wrote the French minister to his superior in Europe,

are not in earnest when they assert that without the navigation of the Mississippi the inhabitants of the interior will seek an outlet by way of the lakes, and will throw themselves into the arms of England. . . . The true motive of this vigorous opposition is to be found in the great preponderance of the northern states, eager to incline the balance toward their side; the southern ne-

glect no opportunity of increasing the population and importance of the western territory, and of drawing thither by degrees the inhabitants of New England. . . . These new territories will gradually form themselves into separate governments; they will have their representatives in congress, and will augment greatly the mass of the southern states.

Otto is abundantly confirmed by the debates of the Virginia ratifying convention, and still more by Monroe's correspondence of late 1786. On August 12, 1786, Monroe wrote from Congress to Patrick Henry:

P.S. The object in the occlusion of the Mississippi on the part of these people so far as it is extended to the interest of their States (for those of a private kind gave birth to it): is to break up so far as this will do it, the settlements on the western waters, prevent any in future, and thereby keep the States southward as they now are—or if settlements will take place, that they shall be on such principles as to make it the interest of the people to separate from the Confederacy, so as effectually to exclude any new State from it. To throw the weight of population eastward and keep it there. . . .

Like many another Southerner in the next seventy-five years, Monroe ended by saying that, if it came to separation, it was essential that Pennsylvania join the South. So forceful was the effect of his letter on Henry, Madison wrote Washington in December, that Henry, who had hitherto advocated a stronger Union, began to draw back. By 1788 he, like Lee, Grayson, and Monroe, would be an Antifederalist.

The effect of the Mississippi squabble was that the long efforts to vest Congress with power over commerce were threatened with failure at the very brink of success. As delegates made their way to the Annapolis Convention in the fall of 1786, Bloodworth of North Carolina wrote that because of debate on the Mississippi "all other Business seem to be out of View at present." "Should the measure proposed be pursued," Grayson told the Congress, "the S. States would never grant those powers which were acknowledged to be essential to the existence of the Union." When Foreign Secretary Jay had instructions authorizing him to give up American insistence on using the Mississippi river adopted by a simple Congressional majority of seven states it stirred in many Southern breasts the fear of being outvoted. Even before the Mississippi question came before Congress, Southerners like Monroe had insisted that, if Congress were to regulate commerce, commercial laws should require the assent of nine or even eleven states. Jay's unfairness (as Southerners saw it) in using a simple majority to push through a measure fundamentally injurious to the South greatly intensified this apprehension. When the Constitutional Convention met, the so-called Pinckney Plan would suggest a two-thirds Congressional majority for commercial laws, and both the Virginia ratifying convention (which voted to ratify by a small majority) and the North Carolina convention (which rejected ratification) would recommend the same amendment.

In the midst of the Mississippi controversy, men hopeful for stronger government saw little chance of victory. Madison wrote Jefferson in August 1786 that he almost despaired of strengthening Congress through the Annapolis Convention or any other; in September, Otto wrote to Vergennes: "It is to be feared that this discussion will cause a great coolness between the two parties, and may be the germ of a future separation of the southern states."

Why then did the South consent to the Constitutional Convention? If the South felt itself on the defensive in the 1780's, and particularly so in the summer and fall of 1786, why did its delegates agree to strengthen Federal

powers in 1787? If a two-thirds majority for commercial laws seemed essential to Southerners in August of one year, why did they surrender it in August of the next? Were Madison and Washington, as they steadfastly worked to strengthen the national government, traitors to the interests of their section, or was there some view of the future which nationalist Southerners then entertained which enabled them to be good Southerners and good Federalists at the same time?

It is Madison, once more, who provides the clue. He saw that if the South were to agree in strengthening Congress, the plan which gave each state one vote would have to be changed in favor of the South. And in letters to Jefferson, to Randolph, and to Washington in the spring of 1787 he foretold in a sentence the essential plot of the Convention drama. The basis of representation would be changed to allow representation by numbers as well as by states, because a change was "recommended to the Eastern States by the actual superiority of their populousness, and to the Southern by their expected superiority."

So it fell out. Over and over again members of the Convention stated, as of something on which all agreed, that "as soon as the Southern & Western population should predominate, which must happen in a few years," the South would be compensated for any advantages wrung from it by the North in the meantime. "He must be short sighted indeed," declared King on July 12,

who does not foresee that whenever the Southern States shall be more numerous than the Northern, they can & will hold a language that will awe them [the Northern States] into justice. If they threaten to separate now in case injury shall be done them, will their threats be less urgent or effectual, when force shall back their demands.

"It has been said," Gouverneur Morris added, "that N.C. [,] S.C. and Georgia only will in

a little time have a majority of the people of America. They must in that case include the great interior Country, and every thing was to be apprehended from their getting the power into their hands."

This false expectation explains why Georgia and the Carolinas who should by present population have been "small" states, considered themselves "large" states at the Convention. This expectation clarifies, it seems to me, why the South gave way in its demand that commercial laws require a two-thirds majority; for would not time and the flow of migration soon provide such a majority without written stipulation? Later, at the Virginia ratifying convention, no one questioned that (as Grayson put it) "God and nature have intended . . . that the weight of population should be on this side of the continent." Antifederalists reasoned from this assumption that Virginia should wait until a Southern majority in Congress made it safe to transfer power from the states to the national government. Federalist Wilson Nicholas reasoned from the identical premise to a contrary conclusion. "The influence of New England, and the other northern states is dreaded," Nicholas said,

there are apprehensions of their combining against us. Not to advert to the improbability and illiberality of this idea it must be supposed, that our population, will in a short period, exceed theirs, as their country is well settled, and we have very extensive, uncultivated tracts. We shall soon out-number them in as great a degree as they do us at this time: therefore this government, which I trust will last to the remotest ages, will be very shortly in our favor.

Nicholas' argument did not convince George Mason. Nicholas showed, stated Mason, "that though the northern states had a most decided majority against us, yet the increase of population among us would in the course of years change it in our favor. A very sound argument

indeed, that we should cheerfully burn our-selves to death in hopes of a joyful and happy resurrection."

The irony, of course, was that the expecta-tion was completely erroneous. The expected Southern majority in the House never mate-rialized, and the Senate, not the House, became the bulwark of the South. In 1790, the popu-lation of the South had been growing more rapidly than the North's population for sev-eral decades, and was within 200,000 of the population north of the Potomac. True to the general expectation in 1787, the Southwest filled up more rapidly than the area north of the Ohio River. In 1820, Ohio, Indiana, Illinois, and Michigan contained a population of almost 800,000, but Missouri, Kentucky, Tennessee, Alabama, Mississippi, Louisiana, and Arkansas held over 1,300,000 persons. Nevertheless, in the original thirteen states the Northern pop-ulation pulled so far ahead of the Southern that by 1820 the white population of Northern states and territories was almost twice that of Southern states and territories. Thus the South never obtained the Congressional ma-jority which statesmen of both sections had anticipated at the time of the Constitutional Convention.

When the dream of a Southern majority in Congress and the nation collapsed, there fell together with it the vision of a Southern com-mercial empire, drawing the produce of the West down the Potomac and the James to "a Philadelphia or a Baltimore" on the Vir-ginia coast. It was not, as it so often seems, an accident that the Convention of 1787 grew from the Annapolis Convention, or that Vir-ginians were the prime movers in calling both. Throughout the 1780's Madison, Jefferson, Monroe, and to an almost fanatical degree, Washington, were intent on strengthening the commercial ties between Virginia and the West. As early as 1784, Jefferson suggested to Madi-son cooperation with Maryland in opening communication to the West, and during that

year and the next both Washington and Mon-roe toured the Western country with their grand plan in mind. Jefferson and Monroe pushed a Potomac location for the national capital partly with the hope that it would "cement us to our Western friends when they shall be formed into separate states" and help Virginia to beat out Pennsylvania and New York in the race for Western trade. Virginia had given up its claims to Western land, but its leaders hoped for a commercial dominion just as satisfactory: as Jefferson put it, "almost a monopoly of the Western and Indian trade." "But smooth the road once," wrote the en-raptured Washington, "and make easy the way for them, and then see what an influx of arti-cles will be poured upon us; how amazingly our exports will be encreased by them, and how amply we shall be compensated for any trouble and expence we may encounter to effect it." The West, then, would not only give the South political predominance but also, as Madison wrote Jefferson, "double the value of half the lands within the Commonwealth, . . . extend its commerce, link with its interests those of the Western States, and lessen the emmigration of its Citizens." This was the castle-in-the-air which Virginians pictured as they worked to bring about the Constitutional Convention, this was the plan for economic development so abruptly and traumatically shattered by Secretary of the Treasury Alex-ander Hamilton.

In the Spring and Summer of 1788, how-ever, as the South with the North moved to ratify the Constitution, few foresaw the clouds on the horizon. The Constitutional Convention, with a Southern majority (in Bancroft's words) "from its organization to its dissolution," seemed to have wrought well for the South. Madison alone, from his vantage-point in Congress, fretted about that body's continued preoccupation with sectional issues. After wrangling all Spring about the admission of Kentucky, Congress turned to that old favorite,

the location of the capital. "It is truly mortifying," Madison wrote to Washington, to see such "a display of locality," of "local and state considerations," at the very "outset of the new Government." The behavior of Congress would give "countenance to some of the most popular arguments which have been inculcated by the southern antifederalists," and "be regarded as at once a proof of the preponderancy of the Eastern strength." "I foresee contentions," he wrote the next Spring, "first between federal and anti-federal parties, and then between northern and southern parties." Before long he would be leading the opposition.

Even this sampling of the printed sources suggests that sectional conflict based (to quote Madison once more) on "the institution of slavery and its consequences" was a potent force in the shaping of the Constitution. The conclusion seems inescapable that any interpretation of the Convention which stresses realty and personality, large states and small states, or monarchy and democracy, but leaves slavery out, is an inadequate interpretation.

Scholarly effort to bring slavery back into the story of the Revolutionary and Early National periods might do worse than begin with those much-maligned exponents of the abolitionist critique, Horace Greeley and Henry Wilson. They, like Beard, believed that a counterrevolution took place, but they saw as its victim the slave rather than the white artisan or farmer. Moreover, they viewed the counterrevolution not as a sudden *coup d'état* in the years 1787–1788, but as a long-drawn-out process which drew strength from the fatal concessions (as Wilson called them) of the Convention, but required such events as the cotton gin and the Louisiana Purchase for its completion.

Crude though they may be, these early abolitionist historians have the power to show us familiar events in a new light. They knew that Adams would have been President in 1800 had the three-fifths clause not existed, and they understood why the Hartford Convention made the abrogation of that clause the first plank of its platform. They viewed the accession of Jefferson as a triumph for slavery; in their accounts the Louisiana Purchase figures not as a diplomatic triumph or an instance of loose Constitutional construction, but as an event by which slavery acquired "a vast extension of its power and influence." They were fully aware of the part which Southern fear of a San Domingo in Cuba played in the genesis of the Monroe Doctrine, and in the American reaction to the Panama Congress. No doubt all these insights are half-truths, but they are half-truths which have been neglected in this century and deserve to be reincorporated into the mainstream of scholarly interpretation.

If it be granted that sectional conflict based on slavery was real and intense long before 1820, our final evaluation of the abolitionist critique of the United States Constitution will still depend on how we answer the question, *Could* the Revolution have abolished slavery?

It came very close. During the Revolutionary War the importation of slaves ceased. In 1779 the Continental Congress agreed unanimously to arm 3,000 slaves in South Carolina and Georgia, with freedom as a reward. In 1784 Congress failed by one vote to prohibit slavery in the Western territories. These facts support von Holst in his remark that "but one more impulse was needed." Jeffrey Brackett, writing in 1889, suggested the sense of lost possibilities that was felt when the South Carolina and Georgia legislatures refused to adopt the plan to enlist slaves of the Deep South against the British:

It was on hearing of the failure of this plan that Washington wrote, that that spirit of freedom which had so strongly marked the beginning of the war, had subsided. It is private not public interest, he added, which influences the generality of mankind.

English version of a Virginia tobacco plantation, showing slaves packing tobacco for shipment. For Southern whites, slavery was both a labor system and a means of racial control to keep blacks and whites apart. Thus, on the issue of slavery Southern whites would never compromise. And their delegates to the Constitutional Convention in 1787 would not permit any meddling with domestic slavery, forcing the other delegates to pass it by or to forget about creating a stronger Union. So, apart from authorizing Congress to abolish the foreign slave trade, the Founding Fathers allowed slavery to continue in the American Republic. (Courtesy of The New York Public Library, The Arents Collection.)

Many abolitionists, concerned to identify their cause with the charisma of the Founding Fathers, contended that at the time of the Convention all public men expected slavery to die a natural death. This was far from the case. As Hildreth observed a century ago, the delegates from Georgia and South Carolina did not expect slavery to end: "S. Carolina & Georgia," Madison reported to Jefferson, "were inflexible on the point of slaves." Nor is it safe to assume that the Upper South looked forward to emancipation. If so, why did every Southern delegation oppose Jefferson's 1784 proposal to prohibit slavery in the West? And if the South was rigid, the North gave way almost without protest. Farrand misses the tragedy of the situation when he says that the majority "regarded slavery as an accepted

institution, as a part of the established order." It would be more accurate to say that almost without exception the Fathers felt that slavery was wrong and almost without exception they failed to act decisively to end it.

Among the obvious reasons for the Revolution's failure to cope with slavery were an inability to imagine a genuinely multi-racial society, and an over-scrupulous regard for private property.

Even the most liberal of the Founding Fathers were unable to imagine a society in which whites and Negroes would live together as fellow-citizens. Honor and intellectual consistency drove them to favor abolition; personal distaste, to fear it. Jefferson said just this when he wrote: "Nothing is more certainly written in the book of fate, than that these people are to be free; nor is it less certain that the two races, equally free, cannot live in the same government." These were also the sentiments of Northerners like Otis, Franklin, and John Quincy Adams. Otis condemned slavery in the abstract, but also prided himself that North America was settled "not as the common people of *England* foolishly imagine, with a compound mongrel mixture of *English, Indian* and *Negro*, but with freeborn *British white* subjects." On the eve of his career as an abolitionist, John Quincy Adams praised Andrew Jackson for destroying the "motley tribe of black, white, and red combatants," the "parti-colored forces" of the "negro-Indian banditti" in Florida. As for Franklin, the future president of the Pennsylvania Abolition Society wrote in 1751:

> . . . the Number of purely white People in the World is proportionably very small. All Africa is black or tawny. Asia chiefly tawny. America (exclusive of the new Comers) wholly so. And in Europe, the Spaniards, Italians, French, Russians and Swedes, are generally of what we call a swarthy Complexion; as are the Germans also, the Saxons only excepted, who with the English, make the principal Body of White People on the Face of the Earth. I could wish their Numbers were increased. And while we are, as I may call it, *Scouring* our Planet, by clearing America of Woods, and so making this Side of our Globe reflect a brighter Light to the Eyes of Inhabitants in Mars or Venus, why should we in the Sight of Superior Beings, darken its People? why increase the Sons of Africa, by Planting them in America, where we have so fair an Opportunity, by excluding all Blacks and Tawneys, of increasing the lovely White and Red?

A second reason why the Fathers turned aside from an attack on slavery was their commitment to private property. Gouverneur Morris was the Convention's most outspoken opponent of slavery, the South Carolina delegates were its frankest defenders; but their identical assumptions about the place of property in society drove them to similar conclusions. Thus, in the Convention debates of July 5 and 6, Morris declared that "life and liberty were generally said to be of more value, than property," but that "an accurate view of the matter would nevertheless prove that property was the main object of Society." This was a view which the South Carolinians could only echo. What it came down to was, as Charles Cotesworth Pinckney put it, that "property in slaves should not be exposed to danger under a Govt. instituted for the protection of property." And so, while Morris stated on July 11 that if compelled to do injustice to human nature or the southern states, he must do it to the latter, that same evening he worked out the formula proportioning representation to direct taxation which proved a "bridge" to the three-fifths compromise; and in August it was he who proposed what he termed a "bargain" between North and South over slave importation.

As late as 1833, Madison could write that the good faith of the North was "sufficiently guaranteed by the interest they have, as mer-

chants, as Ship owners, and as manufacturers, in preserving a Union with the slaveholding states." But apart from interest, the belief that private property was the indispensable foundation for personal freedom made it more difficult for Northerners to confront the fact of slavery squarely.

A third, more subtle reason for the failure of nerve of the Founding Fathers when confronting slavery, was precisely that economic realism which Beard so much admired. Harrington's "balance" warred uneasily in their minds with Locke's law "writ in the hearts of mankind." They knew only too well that "power follows property": when statecraft was defined as the mutual adjustment of existing economic interests, uprooting so substantial a reality as slavery was much to ask. Lee Benson says aptly that Madison presented "an essentially fatalistic theory of politics." Having observed at the Convention how the existence or non-existence of slavery shaped men's politics, Madison became in 1790–1792 a victim of that very process. There was a greater irony. In contending for discrimination between original and subsequent holders of Federal securities he found himself pleading for a justice based not on the letter of the law but on the promptings of the heart: the very logic abolitionists would use to defy the Constitution Madison had helped to form, and to destroy the peculiar institution by which, not just in the last analysis but also in his analysis, Madison's own politics were shaped.

Unable to summon the moral imagination required to transcend race prejudice, unwilling to contemplate social experiment which impinged on private property, too ready to rationalize their failure by a theory of economic determination, the Fathers, unhappily, ambivalently, confusedly, passed by on the other side. Their much-praised deistic coolness of temper could not help them here. The abolitionists were right in seeing the American Revolution as a revolution betrayed.

IV   Figures in the Landscape

11

What, Gracious God, is Man?

Marcus Cunliffe

Do people make history? Or is it the other way around? Determinists contend that historical forces were at work shaping the course and composition of past societies. Humanists, on the other hand, reject such deterministic views of history: they insist that emphasis be placed less on historical "forces" than on the people themselves, that history in truth—as Sir Walter Scott phrased it— is "the essence of innumerable biographies." Part IV of *Portrait of America* follows the humanist view of history and seeks to illustrate Scott's dictum: it attempts to show the course of the United States, from the Articles of Confederation to the Era of Good Feelings, through the lives of some of the leading participants: Washington, Jefferson, Aaron Burr, Tecumseh, Madison, the Western warhawks of 1812, and Chief Justice John Marshall.

The scenes open on George Washington and the "critical period" of the 1780s, when the young Republic had begun to flounder under the Articles of Confederation. Marcus Cunliffe provides rare insight into the character and significance of America's first president, as he recounts Washington's role in these crucial initial years and the turbulent Federalist decade that followed.

Some of Washington's more eulogistic biographers have made his career practically synonymous with American history as a whole during his lifetime, placing him in the center of the stage at every episode. Tracing his story backward, they have seen a direct causal chain of circumstances all the way from his mission to Fort Le Boeuf in 1753 to his statesmanlike plan for the Potomac Company and thence, step by logical step, to the full glory of the Presidency in 1789. See, they proclaim, Washington *is* the Father of His Country; with uncanny prescience and a perfect sense of the true meaning of the Union he guides events, from early manhood to righteous old age.

Now this contention is not entirely wrong. We *can* discern an oddly circumstantial sequence; Washington *does* have a knack of being on hand at the place and moment where history is being made. But, before the Revolutionary War, there is an element of accident in the pattern. In those days he achieved a measure of distinction, but he did not (in the eyes of his contemporaries, at any rate) achieve true greatness. That he accomplished in the war itself. In retirement afterwards, he was a factor in the national scene; whatever he did tended to have national repercussions, and whatever he did not do was also, negatively, a factor of national importance. Washington was well aware of this; and even if he had not been, his experience as president-general of the Cincinnati was well calculated to ram home the lesson.

The problem in considering Washington's

Reprinted from pp. 137–183 in *George Washington, Man and Monument* by Marcus Cunliffe, by permission of Little, Brown & Co. Copyright © 1958 by Marcus Cunliffe.

development between 1783 and 1789 is this: did he achieve further greatness in his own right, or was further greatness thrust upon him, as something he could not avoid? Did he take a lead in re-forming the Union, or was he merely brought in, so to speak, in an honorary capacity? Or does the truth lie somewhere between such extremes? And behind this problem is another one, which still engages historians in vehement debate: what was the actual state of the Union during the years of the Confederation? Was this "the critical period," or was America in fact flourishing? Did the United States really *need* a new instrument of government? And (to come back to our hero) did Washington himself genuinely believe that the Union was in danger? If so, did he make up his own mind, or did others plant the notion?

Perhaps no final answers to such questions are possible. But they are worth raising, to shake our minds free of the conventional, oversimplified picture of George Washington —even if we end up with explanations not wildly dissimilar to the usual ones.

Temperamentally and from his experience as commander in chief, Washington favored a strong national government—or at least one that would be more effectual in moments of emergency than the wartime Congress he had served. This is clear from his Circular to the States, a lengthy memorandum compiled in June 1783, which is condensed to a phrase in the toast he offered at a dinner in Philadelphia, the day before he surrendered his commission: "Competent powers to Congress for general purposes." There is an implication (which, because of his scrupulous modesty, appears only now and then in his letters) that *he* had begun the work, and through example and precept had indicated the path for the new nation to follow. Thus, in a letter to John Jay (Foreign Secretary under the Confederation) Washington speaks a little pontifically of the way in which his fellow countrymen have neglected

his "sentiments and opinions . . . tho' given as a last legacy in the most solumn manner." To this extent did he identify himself with America: his own reputation and hers were inextricably interwoven, and it hurt him that America should present to outsiders a spectacle of disunity. He was especially sensitive to British reactions, and naturally annoyed that the British—the enemy he had beaten—refused to evacuate various Western posts according to their treaty obligations. It was the more galling that the British had some excuse, since several American states had likewise failed to honor their treaty promises.

But the letter to Jay was sent in the summer of 1786 and does not accurately convey Washington's outlook in the previous couple of years. At that period he shrank from involvement. Cato or Cincinnatus, he had played his part and said his piece. He was now a bystander, determined to devote his remaining years to the consolidation of his private fortunes. Though he had no direct heirs, that did not lessen his zeal to have and to hold like any other Virginia dynast. True, he had a sharper sense than most of America's nationhood, real and potential. But it should be noted that the Potomac plan aroused his pride *as a Virginian.* The plan was recommended to him by another Virginian, Jefferson; and after he had assumed control, Washington initially thought in regional rather than national terms. Writing to Northern acquaintances, he stressed the urgency of thwarting Britain; to men of his own area, he disclosed that he was equally concerned with the rivalry of the "Yorkers" and their route to the interior via the Hudson.

This is not to say that Washington behaved dishonestly, but only that in 1784–1785 he was not thinking in grandly Continental terms. His state pride never ran counter to the interests of America as a whole. Yet for a spell these interests receded; they did not dominate his imagination. Friends in Congress kept in touch with him; his bulging post bag brought news

of conditions in most parts of the Union, from Massachusetts to Georgia. But Congress was a long way off, shifting, as it did, away from Annapolis to Trenton, and then further, to New York. Domestically absorbed, anxious to maintain the proprieties of retirement, uncertain as to the true import of what his correspondents told him, sick of dissension, Washington expressed his opinions with oracular vagueness. It was men like John Jay, Henry Lee and James Madison who committed themselves (though also warily), who took the lead in the move for a new government. They wanted to enlist his aid not for his pen or his brain but for his name. To Americans, Washington was victory, rectitude—and, for the moment, something of a cipher. Surely, Jay told him in March 1786, he could not watch the disintegration of America "with the eye of an unconcerned spectator"? Sounding him out, Jay went on: "An opinion begins to prevail, that a General Convention for revising the articles of Confederation would be expedient." Replying, a month later, Washington agreed broadly that the "fabrick" was "tottering"; but he confined himself to cautious generalities.

Again, this is not to accuse Washington of stupidity or irresponsibility, but merely to emphasize that he had no ready solution to offer. Viewed as an agglomeration of farmers and merchants, America was prospering. Congress was not entirely inept; it was the legitimate government of the land. If Congress were not willing to reform itself, could reform be legally imposed by some *ad hoc* convention? What would people say? What would the states say? On the other hand, the Articles of Confederation, in practice, did not admit of firm national government; the states were dangerously indifferent to Congress and antagonistic to one another. *Something* should be done.

Following some way behind the active controversialists, as he had done before 1775, Washington gradually began to sort out his ideas. Thus on August 1, 1786, he wrote three letters. Two went to France, to the Chevalier de la Luzerne and the American minister, Thomas Jefferson. The third was to Jay in New York. The first two were cheerful in tone, the third full of foreboding. Why the discrepancy? In large part because Washington did not wish to discredit America's reputation abroad; even to his bosom friend Lafayette he spoke of America with a perhaps forced optimism. In part, too, because he was divided in his mind, and so reacted differently to different correspondents. So, he frankly acknowledged to the pessimistic Jay, "I cannot feel myself an unconcerned spectator. . . . Your sentiments, that our affairs are drawing rapidly to a crisis, accord with my own."

For Washington, the crisis revealed itself in the shape of Shays's Rebellion in Massachusetts, in the autumn of 1786. It was an abortive and incoherent rising of back-country malcontents. But both the rebellion and the way in which it was handled seemed to Washington symptomatic of profound disorder. Expletives were rare in his letters; now he burst out in alarm: *Are your people getting mad? . . . What is the cause of all this? When and how is it to end? . . . These disturbances—Good God! who besides a tory could have foreseen, or a Briton predicted them? . . . What, gracious God, is man! that there should be such inconsistency and perfidiousness in his conduct? . . . We are fast verging to anarchy and confusion!*

What should he do? For months he worried and hesitated, while more actively engaged Americans laid the groundwork for the Philadelphia convention of May 1787. Would he attend as a Virginia delegate? He was urged to declare himself. One uneasiness was removed early in 1787 when Congress gave the convention its blessing. But Washington was plagued by doubts. He was fifty-five, and felt older, racked with rheumatism, short of funds. He had already declined to attend the triennial meeting of the Cincinnati, which was also to

be held in Philadelphia at the same time as the convention; how could he now disclose that his reasons for nonattendance were mere excuses? Above all, Washington shrank from associating himself with a body that might prove as impotent as the Annapolis convention of September 1786. If the northeastern states again held aloof, as they had done at Annapolis, the Philadelphia delegates would get nothing done. Worse, they might do harm—to the country and to their own reputations. Washington wanted no part in a conspiracy *or* a farce.

Douglas Southall Freeman, Washington's foremost biographer, thinks that his conduct at this period was unpleasantly egocentric. If America was in peril, Freeman wonders, why did he not rush to the rescue? This seems too harsh a verdict. The most that we can say of Washington is that he was, after all, a human being and not a sort of ideal permanent patriot-without-portfolio. His motives were not heroic, but they were understandable. Still, one wonders; can excessive modesty become almost the same thing as its opposite—inordinate vanity? Did it in his case?

Perhaps. The essential fact is that Washington did finally decide to go to Philadelphia. He arrived there in early May, was elected president of the convention by the unanimous wish of the other delegates, and sat in his chair of office through exhausting weeks of argument and maneuver, until the business was concluded in mid-September. There was one lengthy adjournment in August. Washington took advantage of it to visit his old encampment at Valley Forge and the town of Trenton, where he had caught the Hessians unaware. No doubt the interlude refreshed him; one would like to affirm that the glimpse of the past also moved him, but if so, he nevertheless wrote of other things in his diary.

His role in the Philadelphia convention, as it toiled through the hot summer, exactly suited him. Whenever a point was put to the vote, he appears to have stepped down from his chair

to record his preference among the other delegates. Otherwise, he was able to maintain a certain detachment. As he listened, contributing little to the intricate sequence of debate, he could make up his mind at leisure, *in* and yet not exactly *of* the company, arbiter rather than advocate. Only one other man, Benjamin Franklin (who was also present), could have filled the presidential chair with equal appropriateness; but Franklin was past eighty and sick, though still not moribund.

Sometimes Washington voted on the losing side, and usually on what was to be known as the Federalist side; that is, for a strong national government and an effective executive within the government. Little by little, however, the Federalists carried the day. None of the delegates—including Washington—was entirely satisfied with the document that gradually emerged. A number were so disgusted that they withdrew from Philadelphia or would not put their signatures to the finished work. Some regretted the explicit surrender of provincial powers to the federal government. Those from such large states as Virginia and Massachusetts feared the loss of privileges not merely to the federal government, but to such smaller states as Delaware and New Jersey; and men from the smaller states clung to the principle of equal representation that had been granted under the Articles of Confederation. Several times the convention was near deadlock. But by degrees it moved forward; and Washington shared the conviction of a majority of his colleagues that its compromises were workmanlike. Politics was the art of the possible; the new Constitution was the best that could be drawn up in the circumstances.

Washington, at any rate, thought so. He could approve of its provisions for an executive (in the shape of a President), for a Congress (of two houses, a Senate and a House of Representatives) and for a judicial system headed by a federal Supreme Court. Each branch was separated from the others. The arrangement

made sense to him in terms of his own experience; the President would be something like the Governor of Virginia (except that there would be no instructions and vetoes emanating from London), the Senate like the Governor's Council (with two members from each state, it would be a compact group of twenty-six seasoned counselors) and the House of Representatives comparable to the Virginia General Assembly. Indeed, Virginia would have an influential voice in its proceedings, since she as the most populous state would have more members—ten, for example, as against only one for lowly Rhode Island—than any other.

While the individual states would retain a degree of autonomy, the Constitution pleased Washington by putting teeth into the federal government. It would exercise in practice powers that Congress had hitherto wielded only in theory; and it gained new powers. It would be able to present a united front to foreigners, to collect its revenues, to regulate its finances, and in general to ease the way for every law-abiding American, be he planter, farmer, manufacturer or merchant.

Washington could ride home in his coach to Mount Vernon that September with the conviction that he had done his duty. His own house was almost finished; as a final touch, an ironwork dove of peace was being added to Mount Vernon's cupola as a weathervane. But the new Constitution was still unfinished until it had been ratified by state conventions and put into effect. Washington's life entered a new phase, with almost as much distress and uncertainty as in the months before he set out for Philadelphia. He was committed to support the Constitution, and did what he could. Certainly in his own Virginia his influence helped to tip the balance. But he was disturbed by the protests in state after state. The delegates at Philadelphia were accused (with some justice) of having exceeded their instructions. They had met in secret, not allowing their decisions to be announced until the end. They were intriguers,

aristocrats. They were in too much of a hurry; let there be another convention to review the proposals of the first one. Such were some of the arguments against the Constitution makers. Radical Rhode Island had not even sent delegates to Philadelphia, and ratification seemed uncertain in several other states. It was not only debtors and paper-money men who attacked the Founding Fathers (or were they the Foundering Fathers?). There was enmity from disgruntled men of substance: Governor Clinton in New York, Governor John Hancock in Massachusetts, and—in Washington's own state—Patrick Henry, Richard Henry Lee, Edmund Randolph, even his old friend and neighbor George Mason.

Nine out of thirteen states had to approve the Constitution for it to be adopted. By January 1788 five states had ratified. In February Massachusetts came in by a narrow margin, swayed by the Federalist intimation to Hancock that he might be Vice-President, or even (if Virginia failed to ratify and Washington was thereby excluded) President under the new government. Hancock was won over. What was more, he introduced a valuable formula that was followed by other states: Massachusetts would accept the Constitution on the understanding that amendments would subsequently be adopted that would meet the criticisms raised against the document. These would amount to a Bill of Rights, similar to the provisions already incorporated in various state constitutions.

Two more states came in, making a total of eight; and Virginia, the most crucial of all, came in at the end of June after a tense struggle. Better still, it was learned in Virginia that New Hampshire had already ratified. Ten states were in, one more than the necessary minimum. Alexander Hamilton and other ardent Federalists in New York used the glad news to disarm opposition in that state. A year after the delegates dispersed from Philadelphia, the Constitution they had drawn up was sanctioned, with

or without reservations, by eleven out of thirteen states. Only North Carolina and Rhode Island stood outside. Their obstinacy, though unfortunate, was not fatal.

What next? For the nation as a whole, it remained for Congress to wind itself up and for a new Congress to be chosen. There was a squabble over the seat of the future government, ending in the tentative agreement that it should remain temporarily at New York. For Washington, there was the virtual certainty that he would be elected President. His name had been freely used by Federalists in the debates over ratification. Someone had suggested that the Federalists should be known "by the name of Washingtonians," and that the Anti-Federalists should be named Shaysites after Daniel Shays, the Massachusetts rebel. Once the terms of the Constitution were published, Washington seemed the obvious candidate for the Presidency. Only he was known, respected and trusted in all the states. Only he, apart from the aged Franklin, had the requisite magic, glory, prestige (there is no adequate word for this quality) demanded of those who are to fill the great offices of government. So the newspapers told him; so his friends insisted. "In the name of America, of mankind at large, and your own fame," Lafayette wrote in January 1788, "I beseech you, my dear General, not to deny your acceptance of the office of President for the first years. You only can settle that political machine."

Washington's own emotions were mixed. He was gratified, embarrassed and alarmed. The honor proposed was immense. But how could he discuss it until it became actual? A foregone conclusion was not quite the same thing as an election. If he were offered the Presidency, he must accept. But if he accepted, how could he endure four more years of the strain of life in the pitiless limelight? No one else was better prepared, certainly, to undertake the task. But was he himself well enough prepared? "I should," he said, "consider myself

as entering upon an unexplored field, enveloped on every side with clouds and darkness." However, at the time that he wrote thus, in the autumn of 1788, it was taken for granted by his acquaintances that he would be President. All through the winter they reminded him briskly of his duty, while he without enthusiasm thought of his coming trial. In April 1789, waiting at Mount Vernon for the news that was bound to come, Washington told his old friend Henry Knox, in confidence:

> My movements to the chair of Government will be accompanied by feelings not unlike those of a culprit who is going to the place of his execution: so unwilling am I, in the evening of a life nearly consumed in public cares, to quit a peaceful abode for an Ocean of difficulties, without that competency of political skill, abilities and inclination which is necessary to manage the Helm. I am sensible, that I am embarking the voice of my Countrymen and a good name of my own, on this voyage, but what returns will be made for them, Heaven alone can foretell.

First Administration: 1789–1793

A fortnight later the suspense, though not the apprehension, was over. Washington had received every vote in the electoral college, Congress informed him; and John Adams of Massachusetts had got enough to qualify as his Vice-President. Washington set out at once for New York. All along the road—a muddy road that took eight days to travel—he met with a tumultuous reception: flowers, banners, triumphal arches, addresses of welcome, militia escorts, extravagant newspaper tributes to "our adored leader and ruler."

To the beholder he was a magnificent figure. Inwardly, he was full of dread. His popularity could not be doubted in face of such lavish proofs. But each fresh demonstration deepened

George Washington's first inauguration at Federal Hall in New York City. Though widely admired throughout the Republic, Washington was filled with dread about his presidency—and troubled by personal matters as well. As he gave his inaugural address, he seemed agitated and embarrassed. "He trembled," noted one observer, "and several times could scarce make out to read." (Courtesy of Culver Pictures.)

his anxiety; his countrymen, in praising him as superhuman, would also make superhuman demands upon him. How correspondingly terrible would his crash be, if he failed in a task that he could not even adequately define to himself! Thirteen disparate states, two of them still outside the Union of a Constitution that was still in the hazard, all jealous for their "darling sovereignty," stretching up the Atlantic seaboard for fifteen hundred miles; a population of less than four million (the exact figure was unknown), of whom nearly one in

five were Negro slaves; a nation new to nationality, undertaking the experiment of federal republicanism, burdened by debt, menaced by external enemies—what might happen if the worst should come to the worst?

However, it must be counted among Washington's major virtues that he never lost his nerve. In some men, anxiety causes a general paralysis of the will or onsets of sudden directionless energy. In Washington it induced a certain extra caution, but also an extra, dogged adherence to the job in hand.

A sour critic at the time—and there were one or two whose skepticism touched even the majestic figure of Washington in 1789—could feel that at this tremendous moment in America's history the Chief Executive did not quite fulfill expectation. Bothered by private matters —his debts, the proper care of Mount Vernon during his absence, the furnishing of his house in New York, points of protocol, the need to vindicate himself against the charge (which no one was making) that he had been false to his previous pledges of retirement—all these made him appear a trifle wooden. At least, they did in the eyes of such a witness as William Maclay, a caustic and irreverent senator from Pennsylvania. Half awed and half derisive, Maclay noted of Washington's inaugural address:

> This great man was agitated and embarrassed more than ever he was by the leveled cannon or pointed musket. He trembled, and several times could scarce make out to read, though it must be supposed he had often read it before.

His gestures were maladroit, Maclay said; and his costume could also have been thought odd, since Washington wore a worsted suit of American manufacture together with the dress sword and white silk stockings of European court ceremony. Nor was there anything particularly memorable in the actual text of his address. It was ponderous, official; satisfactory, but not overwhelming.

Yet, unlike Maclay, most of the crowd who saw Washington inaugurated that April day were deeply stirred. If he was a little awkward, they forgave him and even trusted him the more. Washington was to discover what he no doubt already suspected: that his unique standing in the nation was a priceless asset. Other elements were on his side. He was not an expert on finance, or a nimble political tactician, or a constitutional theorist, or a diplomatist acquainted at firsthand with foreign affairs.

But as commander in chief and as president of the Constitutional Convention he had gained some familiarity with these and other aspects of government, not to mention what he had learned in earlier days at Williamsburg and elsewhere. Whatever he might lack in the higher arts of polity, he was an honest, canny and methodical administrator. Thus, he had been deluged with requests from men seeking appointments under the new government. With his usual blunt good sense he had refused to commit himself to any of them. He came to New York with a heavy heart but with clean hands.

Fortunately, no immediate crisis threatened in the summer of 1789. Congress was slow to assemble and occupied itself for a while mainly with minor problems of procedure and so on. All was not sweetness and light in Congress. The prolonged squabbles over the site for the permanent seat of the federal government revealed that sectional jealousies were still very much alive; and there were signs of more fundamental dissension. Even so, Congress and the nation as a whole accepted the new Constitution with remarkably little fuss. The necessary amendments to form a Bill of Rights were drawn up, submitted to the states and ratified without much trouble. North Carolina and Rhode Island thereupon both entered the Union. A Judiciary Act, to fill out the constitutional provision for a federal court system, was also passed in 1789. Within a few months of Washington's inauguration, the document conceived at Philadelphia was taking on a life of its own. It was being accepted without demur as the given frame of reference. Indeed, while Washington was venerated as one symbol of American union, the Constitution was likewise assuming an almost sacred character as a second and more permanent symbol of that union. Much as Americans respected George Washington, even more did they respect the notion of representative government. They interpreted the notion in different ways. The de-

bates in Congress were rancorous at times and petty at others. But they were carried on within the frame of reference—the parliamentary frame, in which Americans were at home through long experience. The Constitution was workable because a majority of Americans wished it to work. Without that vital element of habitual skill and harmony, all of Washington's labors and exhortations would have been in vain.

His way was made easier also in that the new government in 1789 inherited tangible features of the old one; there was a degree of continuity in actual institutions. The President benefited in personal terms by being able to add William Jackson, the former secretary of the Continental Congress, to his own small group of secretaries—Tobias Lear, David Humphreys and other knowledgeable, articulate men. More largely, he benefited from the survival of the old executive departments, some of whose heads had been closely associated with Washington in the past. Under the Constitution, the departments were mentioned only obliquely. But Congress passed the necessary legislation to renew them and, after some argument, conceded that the President should have the right —a crucial one—to remove his executive officers as well as to appoint them.

He retained Henry Knox of Massachusetts, his former artillery chief, as Secretary of War. John Jay of New York, who had been Secretary of Foreign Affairs since 1784, became the first Chief Justice of the Supreme Court. In Jay's place, at the head of the redesignated Department of State, Washington put his brilliant Virginia friend Thomas Jefferson. Another Virginian, Edmund Randolph (who had in the meantime overcome his scruples with regard to the Constitution), was given office as Attorney General. As for the Treasury, which ranked in importance with the State Department, this had recently been administered by a small committee. Washington, instead, entrusted it to one man, Alexander Hamilton of

New York, who, though still in his early thirties, had already made his mark as soldier, lawyer and theorist. Finally, the postal organization that Benjamin Franklin had once directed was given to Postmaster General Samuel Osgood, a former member of the Treasury board. All prominent men, all more or less familiar with their new functions. Indeed, New York was thronged with men who had contributed to American independence and union in one way or another. James Madison, for example, though kept out of the Senate by opposition in Virginia, was a leading figure in the House of Representatives.

So far, Washington was merely implementing legislation contrived in Congress to amplify what was already sketched in the Constitution. Many matters were still left in doubt. Among these was the precise nature of the Presidency. Washington and his contemporaries were in broad agreement that the Chief Executive should, while sharing certain powers and duties with the two branches of Congress, nevertheless stand somewhat aloof. In the Constitutional Convention, Franklin spoke against a salary for the President, on the grounds that (as British politics dreadfully revealed) a "Post of Honour" that was also a "Place of Profit" was calculated to bring out the worst excesses of ambition and avarice. Washington had taken no salary, but merely his expenses, while commander in chief; and now in his inaugural address he proposed the same rule. He might well have ruined himself if the suggestion had been adopted. Happily for himself and his successors, Congress fixed the President's annual salary at $25,000. For 1789 it was a most substantial income, lifting him far above the Secretary of State and Treasury Secretary with their $3500 apiece, or above members of Congress with their six dollars a day.

He was expected, then, to maintain a fairly high style. But (in the words of the old riddle) how high was high? There was no perfect answer. To live in splendor was to risk the hos-

tility of men like Maclay, who were still suspicious that some Americans hankered after monarchy; to practice undue economy was to expose the Presidency to contempt. Washington's compromise pleased most of his countrymen. It was the compromise implicit in his inaugural costume, when he wore the apparel of a gentleman who was nevertheless unmistakably an American gentleman. Dignity and common sense were his guides. What should his title be? John Adams, presiding over the Senate, made himself a little ridiculous by insisting on kingly designations. "His Highness, the President of the United States of America, and Protector of their Liberties" was the formula suggested by the Senate. The House, however, wanted the plain title "President of the United States"; and Washington (though he is often said to have preferred "His Mightiness, the President of the United States") had the wisdom to let the argument die a natural death, until by general usage he was simply "Mr. President."

Common sense, too, determined his policy on entertaining and on public visits. At Mount Vernon he had kept open house. That was impossible in New York; so, taking advice beforehand, he established a system of weekly levees, at which formal calls could be paid, and of dinner parties (usually in the late afternoon, when the levee ended). He accepted no private invitations, though—indulging his fondness for plays—he frequently relaxed among guests at the theater. Taking advice again, he decided to travel in different parts of the Union. And again he sought a balance; if he toured New England in 1789, he paid his respects to the Southern states two years later.

Perhaps it was all a little on the stiff side. Certainly this could be said of his relations with Congress. Both were on their best behavior; and best behavior is not easy behavior. His addresses produced formal replies, which in turn brought forth replies to the replies. One result, unforeseen by the Founding Fathers,

was that the President and the Senate drew apart. Perhaps it was inevitable, since all branches of the new government were so tensely aware of their own privileges and of the precedents that were being created at every step. But some coldness and bewilderment were caused. Instead of becoming his inner council, the Senate maintained its distance from Washington. Only once did he come to the Senate in person, to confer on foreign policy—an area in which the Executive and Senate were supposed to share responsibility. The occasion was dismally unsuccessful. If Maclay is to be believed, Washington was haughty and impatient, and departed irritably when the Senate was unwilling to give immediate assent to his wishes.

However, even Maclay admits that when Washington came back after the adjournment, he seemed perfectly good-humored. If he never repeated the experiment, neither did he persist in what might have been a disastrous relationship. In any case, Washington was not short of advice. During the first years his closest ties were with James Madison. Madison came to see him, prepared papers for him and gave constitutional opinions. When Washington planned to retire at the end of his first term, it was Madison who in 1792 wrote the initial draft of what was to emerge four years afterward as the celebrated Farewell Address. He leaned heavily, too, upon Alexander Hamilton and—somewhat less—upon John Jay and Vice-President Adams. Gradually he came to rely more and more on the heads of the executive departments. It was an unplanned process, for no one had envisaged the President as Prime Minister. Yet, in effect, by the end of Washington's first administration, he was equipped with a "cabinet." The word was in use, and the idea in embryonic being.

By then, also unplanned, Washington was confronted by something like a party system. Indeed, he was the center of acute antagonisms, so that—for example—he and Madison

fell almost completely out of step with one another. Madison, in his prescient way, had realized that "the spirit of party and faction" was bound to exist in any civilized nation, and that the reconciliation of such interest groups would, inevitably, be among the tasks of Congress and the Chief Executive. Washington too had recognized, before he became President, that—in addition to the usual provincial rivalries—the country was seriously divided over the new Constitution. He thought it quite likely that the Anti-Federalists would vote against him in the electoral college.

Washington and many others with him were dismayed to find that the adoption of the Constitution focused argument rather than ended it. In general, those who had actively supported the Constitution in 1787–1788 were ranged against those who had had misgivings. They continued to call themselves Federalists and Anti-Federalists, and to quarrel noisily over the desired shape of their infant nation. There was no neat division. Some men, such as Madison and Randolph, changed their minds. Differences of opinion were met within the same family; Fisher Ames of Massachusetts, the Federalists' most eloquent champion in the House of Representatives, had no fiercer enemy than his own brother Nathaniel, who even refused to attend Fisher's funeral some years later—alleging that it was being staged as a piece of Federalist propaganda. Roughly, though, the Federalists (the "prigarchy," in Nathaniel Ames's view) were men of substance: merchants, lawyers and the like, Easterners, for the most part. Their opponents ("mobocrats," as against "monocrats," in the terminology of the time) were in opposition for various reasons. Some still disliked the idea of a strong national government, or even the principle of administrative authority. Government, for them as for Tom Paine, was "the lost badge of innocence." Others, especially in the West and South, objected to the Federalists as a clique of selfish businessmen.

The struggle that resulted was, for at least four reasons, intensely distasteful and disturbing to Washington. First, it pained him that the stability of the Union should be threatened at all. Second, the battle was fought within his own executive branch of the government. Third, it extended to the field of foreign policy. Fourth, it directly involved his own reputation.

When Washington took office in 1789, he believed—not out of arrogance but because so many Americans had told him so—that he was needed at the helm. Or, if we must use a nautical metaphor, it is better to say that he was needed on the bridge. America's primary requirement, as he saw it, was confidence. *Crescit eundo*—She grows as she goes—could well have been the Union's official motto. In the words of his Farewell Address, "time and habit are at least as necessary to fix the true character of government as of other human institutions." Let the Union be set on the right lines and all else would follow. Let there be a small navy and army, and a suitable militia organization to keep the peace; let the revenues be collected, the laws obeyed, native pride encouraged; let things run in their own fashion thereafter. This was his philosophy. America and the Union were potentially sound, potentially great. It was not a doctrine that he expressed lyrically or analyzed with much subtlety. But he was not whistling to keep his spirits up. It was an article of faith, something that he *felt*.

This being so, Washington—as far as legislation was concerned—acted as Chief Magistrate rather than as Chief Executive. Alexander Hamilton, his Treasury Secretary, was much more positive. To Hamilton the Constitution was "a fabric which can hardly be stationary, and which will retrograde if it cannot be made to advance." It was, he argued, quoting Demosthenes, the duty of a statesman to "march at the head of affairs" and "produce the *event*." Confidence, then, was something to be contrived, nurtured—in fact, created. And by "a

statesman" Hamilton meant himself.

Hamilton is one of the most fascinating figures in American history. If Washington puzzles us because he seems too good to be true, the mystery of Hamilton is by contrast that of an amazingly diverse and inconsistent personality. By turns devoted and self-seeking, meticulous and slovenly, shrewd and reckless, cynical and righteous, practical and visionary, he would have been a handful for any President in any period. At a time when the details of government were still unsettled, this supremely confident and extraordinarily able young man threatened to dominate the executive and to emerge as a kind of Prime Minister, with Washington as a kind of limited constitutional monarch.

Ambitions aside, Hamilton had some grounds for defining his position thus. In contemporary Britain (whose affairs he studied closely and whose constitution he revered), William Pitt, even more youthful than Hamilton, was both Prime Minister and Chancellor of the Exchequer. Some regulation of American finances was in any case essential; Hamilton's plans were therefore bound to figure prominently in Washington's first administration. Moreover, Hamilton's appointment was worded so as to suggest that, among the executive heads, he might have a special function as an intermediary between President and Congress. Finally, the other chief executive head, Thomas Jefferson, did not take office until six months after Hamilton—six vital months during which Hamilton's advice was constantly sought on all major problems, including foreign policy, and unfailingly given.

The consequences were almost catastrophic, since Jefferson and Hamilton were soon at loggerheads. It is possible to overstress the Hamiltonian-Jeffersonian polarity as a fundamental division in the story of America. The ideological gulf between them was less extreme than that of many other episodes in history. Yet there is no denying the sharpness of their con-

flict or the tumult of American faction that they typified. As great a figure as Hamilton, perhaps even greater, Thomas Jefferson was less pugnacious. Unlike Hamilton, he hated to become personally involved in controversy and had little of Hamilton's passion to be at the top; the high dangerous places did not beckon him. Hamilton had led troops in battle (storming a redoubt at Yorktown) and was eager to risk his hand again (incidentally, he could not resist doing the Secretary of War's job, when he got the chance, as well as his own and the Secretary of State's). Jefferson had never been a soldier and made no pretense of martial quality.

Nevertheless, the two men clashed, angrily and often. Jefferson was well enough pleased with the Constitution, once the Bill of Rights was incorporated in it. But, in the eyes of Jefferson, Madison and many others, Hamilton's policies were ultra-Federalist, viciously so. These policies were sanctioned by Washington; most of them were adopted; and they now seem such commonplaces of America's heritage that it takes an imaginative effort to see why they stirred up so much protest.

The main reason is, of course, that Hamilton's proposals appealed strongly to the conservative and mercantile elements in the Union and were correspondingly antipathetic to other, radical and agrarian groups. It was difficult in the circumstances to arrive at any compromise; one set of interests or the other was bound to be dissatisfied. The initial problem, which Hamilton tackled in 1790, was that of America's debts. These, which had been incurred during the Revolutionary War, amounted to about eighty million dollars, of which twenty-five million were owed by individual states. Hamilton proposed to honor them in full, though the paper securities which represented the various debts were greatly depreciated. He proposed, that is, to fund the national debt at face value and to assume the state debts as a national liability, almost at par. Hamilton won

the debate, basing his case on national honor and national confidence—both arguments that seemed sound to Washington. The arguments against funding and assumption were varied; but perhaps the most heated was that of Hamilton's scheme to enrich the speculator: the usual holder of paper securities was not the original owner, who had bought them for patriotic reasons and sold them through necessity at a discount, but the crafty Easterner who was thereby subsidized by the Federal Government. Hamilton himself was well aware of the process, but he saw its implications in a different light. His measures would (he rightly predicted) "cement" the Union by attaching to it every group that acquired a financial stake in its well-being.

As Hamilton's plans unfolded, Jefferson became the more enraged, because he had been persuaded to support funding and assumption —and bring his influence to bear in Congress —by a compromise that had nothing to do with finance. Hamilton, he felt, had tricked him in a piece of horse trading. By it, Hamilton's Northern friends in Congress voted with the Southerners on the vexed issue of the national capital. With these votes the South was able, so to speak, to pull the projected site down as far as the Potomac instead of merely to Philadelphia, where Congress was to move until 1800, when it was expected that the new "Federal City" would be ready for occupation. True, this was a concession to the South—and, moreover, a source of quiet pleasure to Washington, whose home would be only a few miles away along the river. But it seemed an empty victory to set against Hamilton's Federalist molding of the Constitution.

Early in 1791 the Treasury Secretary and the Secretary of State clashed violently in front of the President. Hamilton wished to establish a national bank, under governmental auspices, and had reported so to the House of Representatives in one of his masterly documents. The measure aroused such an outcry that Washington asked his executive heads to submit their written opinions, not as to whether a national bank would be desirable but whether it would be constitutional. Hamilton naturally answered, again in masterly fashion, that it was. Jefferson, with equal brilliance, contended that the Constitution could not be stretched so far. What should Washington do? The two opinions were diametrically opposed. Neither seemed to him entirely tenable. Yet, since Congress had passed the bill, it remained to him only to sign or veto. As it was Hamilton's brain child, not Jefferson's, he decided to sign. Soon afterward he approved an excise bill that Hamilton had likewise recommended, in order to augment the separate revenues derived from import duties. The excise was to be levied on distilled liquor, which formed the main livelihood for many Western farmers. Hence another division of opinion.

Funding, assumption, a national bank, the excise tax: all seemed to Madison and Jefferson to prove that Hamilton was in power and would corrupt America if he continued to win. Gone would be the prospect of a tranquil land of enlightened agrarians. Instead, the "monocrats" would consolidate their hold and turn America into a plausible imitation of Europe. Congress would be packed with placemen; and if the poison spread, America would revert to hereditary dynastic rule. The remedy, if any, was to combat Hamilton. Jefferson was reluctant to take the lead; like Washington, he longed to be a private citizen again in his native Virginia. But events had a momentum of their own. Little by little, Jefferson, Madison and a few associates emerged as the spokesmen of those Americans who thought of themselves as Anti-Federalists. As their loose and somewhat accidental coalition became more self-aware, it adopted a new name: its members called themselves Democratic-Republicans, or Republicans for short.

One symptom of the growing rift was the establishment in October 1791 of a Republican

paper, the *National Gazette*. While not the first newspaper to attack the Federalists, it was the first to offer an effective—in fact, a devastating—challenge at the national level to the Federalist *Gazette of the United States*, which had come into existence with the new government in 1789, under the editorship of John Fenno, and which unfailingly supported Hamilton. Fenno's rival editor, the poet Philip Freneau, was a college friend of Madison, and an ardent Republican. A much more enterprising journalist than Fenno, he was also employed as a part-time translator in the Department of State. Since Freneau was getting the better of the argument in 1792, Hamilton (writing for Fenno under a variety of pen names) accused the poet of being Jefferson's lackey. Freneau countered with equal ferocity.

To a later generation the situation may seem fantastic. Washington's two most important cabinet members were engaged, by clandestine means that deceived nobody, in a bitter and fundamental quarrel. The other executive heads were tending to take sides, Knox with Hamilton and Randolph with his fellow Virginian Jefferson. Hamilton was still actively (if secretly) concerning himself with foreign affairs. Nor were clear lines drawn in other directions. Hamilton took over the postmaster-general's organization, which would have been more suitably entrusted to the Department of State; and the new federal mint, which ought logically to have been put under the Treasury, was instead put under Jefferson. Was it all muddle and antagonism?

Not at the time, as Washington's age saw it. The "cabinet" had as yet little coherence; nor had the alignment of "parties." Only in a rough and undefined sense were the programs of the executive heads taken to be those of the President himself, still less of a unanimous Administration. Both Hamilton and Jefferson respected the President and believed they were loyal to him and to their different ideas of the Union. In his presence they did not squabble.

Their grievances were directed at one another, not at Washington; and each, it must be said, admired the other while distrusting him. Though there was a feud, there was not a hopeless crisis. If Washington was a somewhat remote figure who did not actively devise and promote legislation, he was not a fool or a weakling. During his first term no one seriously accused him of being Hamilton's dupe. He had known Hamilton intimately for four years in the Revolutionary War, when Hamilton was an aide-de-camp. He had heard Hamilton's conservative views on government expressed at the Philadelphia convention in 1787. He had had ample opportunity to read what Freneau and others thought of Hamilton's "system." No doubt he was deeply impressed by the young man's intellectual ability. Perhaps he knew from wartime conversations with his aide that even as far back as 1776 Hamilton was already fascinated by problems of finance and trade. No doubt, also, he realized the flaws in Hamilton's temperament—a knowledge he must have gained at least as early as 1781, when Hamilton, after an imagined slight, withdrew from Washington's headquarters in a fit of pique.

Nevertheless, 1792 was an uneasy year for the President. Until the summer, he fully intended to retire from an office that he had not enjoyed. He had suffered two serious illnesses—a tumor on the thigh in 1789 and a bout of pneumonia in 1790; and in his letters we find several references to his weakening powers of memory. He was aging, and Mount Vernon seemed increasingly dear to him, as Monticello did to Jefferson. He managed to live there when Congress was not in session, and when away, sent long, minutely specific instructions to his overseers.

Was retirement feasible? The Union was prospering, despite perpetual troubles with the Indians along the frontier. But Federalist-Republican controversy was spreading, not diminishing. In a confidential talk, Madison urged

Washington not to abandon the Presidency; no other figure—not even Madison's close friend Jefferson—could preserve unity. John Adams, the Vice-President, was suspect as a Federalist, a snob and a New Englander. John Jay, though he had fewer enemies, was also too much of a Federalist. Hamilton was out of the question, as the Arch-Federalist. Though Madison did not mention himself, he likewise, as a prominent Republican, was out of the running. Only Washington would do.

It was a disagreeable reflection. We cannot tell at what point Washington finally resigned himself to his fate. Possibly he clung to the notion that some candidate could be found, if only he could heal the breach between Hamilton and Jefferson. At any rate he took pains to clarify the situation. Jefferson supplied him with a list of no fewer than twenty-one charges against Hamilton, "the corrupt squadron of paper dealers" and Federalist tendencies in general ("The ultimate object of all this is to prepare the way for a change, from the present republican form of Government, to that of a monarchy; of which the British Constitution is to be the model"). Washington copied the items out and passed them on to Hamilton, without mention of Jefferson, implying that they were a summary of criticisms that had reached him from various sources. In due course Hamilton replied, angrily, eloquently and circumstantially, denying every one of the charges.

Washington persevered, urging both men in tactful language to sink their differences for the common good. Their answers were disappointingly truculent. Jefferson reiterated his previous charges and added fresh ones. Hamilton laid all the blame on Jefferson and would not undertake to drop his campaign against the Republicans. There was nothing much that Washington could do further, except renew his appeal for a spirit of mutual tolerance and persuade Jefferson not to retire from the Secretaryship of State. He did not wish to lose

the services of either, for they were men of rare ability whose advice was almost indispensable to him. He may also have realized that out of office they would be equally active and more reckless.

And perhaps it occurred to Washington that, in office, they balanced one another to some extent. A "cabinet" without Jefferson would encourage Hamilton to spread himself. It would give color to the argument that a monarchy was in the making. Washington did not take this argument seriously. He had been a little shocked, and possibly bewildered, when a group of officers had hinted to him in 1783 that with their aid he could become King of the United States; there is little to suggest, though, that he believed such a scheme conceivable, in terms of himself or of any other American. Unlike Jefferson, he appears to have seen no harm in the fact that under the Constitution a President could in theory be re-elected several times. Yet if there were suspicions of monarchy, he was ready to allay them. As for a "cabinet" without Hamilton, this might encourage the Republicans to undo what Washington regarded as a Hamiltonian system of proven merit. Moreover, if a sectional and occupational bias could be attributed to Hamilton, the same could be said of Jefferson, who had declared his determination to uphold the South.

In short, Washington must retain his executive chiefs, and he must remain President (it was quite obvious that the electors would choose him in 1792, unless he begged them not to). If he needed the two factions to cancel one another out, he might have derived an ironical satisfaction from the thought that they needed him. Both Jefferson and Hamilton (as well as Randolph, Madison and others close to him) implored Washington to do his duty by the nation. Once more he was committed, and John Adams with him, to four years of lonely grandeur—one might almost say of penal servitude, so bleak was the prospect. He

would uphold the Constitution at the expense of his own constitution. Must the road lead always away from Mount Vernon?

Second Administration: 1793–1797

Whether or not Washington guessed it, his second administration was to expose him to more criticism than he had suffered in his entire life. He had already, as President, been perturbed by faction in the country as a whole and faction within the government in particular. Now, as grave issues of foreign policy divided the nation, the discord was to become strident.

Not long after Washington's first inauguration in 1789, revolution broke out in France. In the autumn of 1792, while Washington was endeavoring to reconcile Hamilton and Jefferson, France proclaimed herself a republic. She had, in the eyes of sympathetic Americans, followed the example set by the United States —though with certain regrettable excesses; France's Declaration of the Rights of Man was lineally descended from Jefferson's Declaration of Independence; America was no longer the only democratic republic in the world. But a few weeks before Washington's second inauguration in March 1793, the French sent their former king, Louis XVI, to the guillotine and added Britain to the list of countries with which they were at war.

Here indeed was a crisis for infant America. She has never found neutrality easy to maintain; in fact, it has throughout her history proved almost impossible in the case of major European conflicts. In 1793 the situation was extraordinarily tense and delicate. On the one hand, France was America's late ally. Gratitude for Yorktown prompted the thought that the New World should rally to the republican cause in the Old. So did more precise obligations, since the United States was still bound to France by a treaty of alliance. Confronted

by the spectacle of tyrannical Britain, her late enemy, at grips with egalitarian France, how could she fail to show her preference?

On the other hand, America had even more intimate ties with Britain. Until the War of Independence, the colonies, like the mother country, regarded France as the hereditary enemy. The winning of independence did not mean the severing of all connections with Britain. To many Americans (Hamilton prominent among them) the land of George III and William Pitt was still, with all her faults, a near relation. The bulk of American overseas trade was with the British Empire; if it were suspended, Hamilton's revenue system would collapse. Again, republicanism in America was a different proposition from republicanism in Europe, where it was ushered in by bloody revolution. American Tories were merely tarred and feathered; French *aristos*, like their king, perished on the scaffold. For a while Washington's dear friend Lafayette was among the leaders in France, until he fell into disgrace in 1792 and lay for four years in the dubious sanctuary of an Austrian jail. At that, he was luckier than most of his comrades.

America's obvious course, as Washington saw it and as even his quarreling advisers agreed at the outset, was to remain neutral; and this was the policy he promptly announced in a proclamation. As a polite concession to French opinion (and to Jefferson, who urged the point) he did not actually use the word "neutrality" in the document. He signified approval of the new French government by preparing to receive its minister, Citizen Genêt. So much was clear and precise; then for a while everything in America appeared to be an angry chaos. For if America was officially neutral, individual Americans were not. They had tended to take sides from the very outbreak of the French Revolution; now their enthusiasms were inflamed to an astonishing degree. "Gallomen" made Tom Paine's *Rights of Man* their Bible, damned aristocracy and

hurrahed for liberty, formed themselves into Democratic clubs and gave Genêt a tremendous welcome when he arrived on the scene. "Anglomen" watched in horror, and denounced their opponents as subversive madmen.

Even at a distance of a century and a half it is hard for us to see these events in perspective, or properly estimate Washington's part in them. To all but the extreme Federalists, he was both a hero and an emblem: the prestige of his name was their ultimate appeal in all argument. To all but moderate Republicans he became something of a tarnished warrior, the embodiment—willingly or unwillingly—of Federalist schemes and machinations. In 1793, for the first time in his long career, Washington was the target of sustained and open criticism. "God save great Washington," Americans had sung in 1789 (to the tune of "God save our Gracious King"). In 1793 they were reminding one another in Republican newspapers that he was no demigod, but a fallible mortal who had surrounded himself with "court satellites" and "mushroom lordlings." Two years later a Philadelphia journalist called Washington "a man in his political dotage" and "a supercilious tyrant." "If ever a nation was debauched by a man," the same journalist remarked at the end of 1796, "the American Nation has been debauched by Washington."

The bulk of contemporary comment was more respectful in tone. Yet these examples are a gauge of the passions of the era. The Republicans felt that the Chief Magistrate was being transformed into a party chieftain, and that under the guise of disinterested patriotism the Federalists were playing into the hands of the British. They admitted that France's conduct was puzzling, and even reprehensible; Genêt, for example, behaved so wildly that Jefferson was forced to concur with Washington in demanding his withdrawal. But they nevertheless preferred France to Britain, as they preferred the future to the past. They saw America cold to her true friend and deferential to her real enemy. With rage they heard in 1794 that Washington was sending John Jay, a known Federalist and Anglophile, to London to negotiate a settlement of outstanding differences. Their worst suspicions were confirmed in March 1795, when details of the treaty he had signed reached America.

Instead of asserting America's rights, he seemed to have given way meekly. True, the British pledged themselves to evacuate the various western posts on American soil that they still held, and from which they were stirring up the Indians. But this was the only notable concession; and after all, the British were only undertaking to carry out a promise made more than ten years before. Otherwise the concessions seemed to be on the American side. And several vital matters were deferred for future negotiation. The Anglomen were selling America's birthright; Jay was a traitor (they burned him in effigy); Federalists were villains; Washington was a "political hypocrite," not the Father but the "Step-Father" of His Country. Wrangling over Jay's Treaty went on through 1795 and part of 1796, long after the Senate ratified and Washington signed the document. In vain—the treaty came into effect and Jay was upheld. By contrast, the American envoy to France, James Monroe, a Virginian and a Republican, was recalled in disgrace by Washington in 1796, apparently for failure in the impossible task of convincing the French that Jay's Treaty was an American rather than a Federalist measure.

Such was the Republican view of foreign policy in Washington's second administration. At home they detected other evidence of Federalist malice. Hamilton's "odious" excise law (as Jefferson called it) provoked so much indignation that in 1792 Washington tried to reinforce it in a severely worded proclamation. Two years later, persuaded by Hamilton that the "whiskey rebels" of western Pennsylvania were threatening the safety of the Union, he called out a large militia force and sent it to the scene of the trouble, after inspecting the

troops at their rendezvous. There was no fighting because—according to the Republicans—there was no real rebellion, only a phantom conjured up by Hamilton for his own purposes. A hundred and fifty Pennsylvanians were arrested; two were condemned to death. Washington pardoned them, yet he seemed to be converted to Hamilton's views. The game, in Madison's opinion, was "to connect the Democratic Societies with the odium of the insurrection—to connect the Republicans in Congress with those societies—to put the President ostensibly at the head of the other party." Jefferson, a year earlier, had actually told the President that Hamilton's intention was "to dismount him from being the head of the nation and to make him the head of a party." When Washington went so far as to lay the blame for the rebellion on "certain self-created societies," in his annual address to Congress of November 1794, Madison thought he had made "perhaps the greatest error of his political life."

So much for the Republican interpretation of events. What of Washington's standpoint? He was neither Angloman nor Galloman. This was a continuation of the war for independence, but must be fought without resort to war. The main threat to America's stability was external, for to a humiliating degree she still lacked an effective will of her own. America was not yet fully independent or mature. Like the adolescent heroine of some melodrama, she was heiress to a fortune of which false guardians struggled to deprive her, either by forcing her into matrimony or—if necessary—by murder.

Of the two self-appointed guardians France was the more dangerous. Britain was surly and contemptuous, flouting neutral rights in her typical style. But America could not afford to challenge Britain; the aim was to preserve trading relations and improve them, to get the redcoats out of the western forts, to avoid close commitments and in general to play for time. Though Washington was disappointed in Jay's

performance, he recognized that America held too weak a hand to achieve miracles.

As for France, the menace was more subtle, and harder to combat. Washington's emphasis was on *neutrality*; the French stress was on *friendly* neutrality. They did not choose to invoke the existing treaty of alliance, because they expected to profit from the ambiguities of their link with the United States. They would get supplies. More important, they could employ America as a base for privateers and perhaps for imperial adventures in the Caribbean and the American hinterland. Genêt had both possibilities actively in mind, and like his successors, he assumed that he could depend on revolutionary sentiment in America to bolster him. If Washington and the Federalists stood in the way, France would appeal beyond them to the American people. In fact, by 1796 French agents in America were doing their best to ensure a Republican victory at the polls.

Washington's problems were complicated by partisan intrigue. Hamilton with deliberate indiscretion confided in British diplomatic representatives, while the Republicans (though Jefferson himself was less at fault) tended to treat the French as full allies. Though Jefferson resigned from office at the end of 1793 and Hamilton at the beginning of 1795, their influence on national affairs continued to be felt. Hamilton in particular maintained his hold—partly, it must be admitted, at Washington's invitation. He contrived, while running a law practice in New York, to remain as a sort of invisible cabinet member. Jefferson's successor as Secretary of State, Edmund Randolph, had to be dismissed in 1795 in peculiar circumstances. Rightly or wrongly, Washington thought him guilty of conspiring with the French minister against Jay's Treaty.

However, despite intrigues, blandishments and frank abuse, Washington stuck to his policy. We must conclude that in the light of subsequent history—a light, of course, denied him—he was right, and that the extreme Republicans, at any rate, who would have pulled

America into the French orbit, were wrong, even if for worthy motives. He was wise, he was courageous; if he now and then lost his temper, he did not lose his grip. Nor was his diplomacy entirely negative in its results. The meager gains of Jay were handsomely offset in Thomas Pinckney's treaty with Spain in 1795, by which at long last America won acceptance of the claim to free navigation of the Mississippi (whose outlet was in Spanish territory) and of the recognition of the Mississippi as her western boundary. An Indian treaty of the same year, following a decisive victory won by General Anthony Wayne in what is now Ohio, brought additional security to the northwestern frontier. "With me," Washington was to reiterate in his Farewell Address, "a predominant motive has been, to endeavor to gain time to our country to settle and mature its yet recent institutions, and to progress without interruption to that degree of strength and consistency, which is necessary to give it humanly speaking, the command of its own fortunes."

Given these conditions, the country could not fail to forge ahead. Washington saw proofs of growth and prosperity all around him. By the end of his second administration three new states—Vermont, Kentucky and Tennessee—had joined the Union, and others would follow. Turnpike roads were under construction; coal deposits had been found in Pennsylvania; though progress was slow, the Potomac Company was still alive, as were other improvement schemes; and the Federal City (in which Washington took a keen interest) was being laid out, in a mingled atmosphere of grandeur and pettiness that may have set the tone of the place for ever afterward.

For these accomplishments Washington is entitled to take much of the credit—although he did not claim it—since a less consistent foreign policy would have jeopardized them all. With the passage of Jay's Treaty the French became increasingly hostile, until the tension at home and abroad was almost unendurable.

The Vice-President's son, John Quincy Adams, writing from Holland (where he was American minister), said at the end of 1795 that "if our neutrality be still preserved, it will be due to the President alone. Nothing but his weight of character and reputation, combined with his firmness and political intrepidity, could have stood against the torrent that is still tumbling with a fury that resounds even across the Atlantic."

If we grant that Washington revealed fine powers of leadership in these years of crisis, is it true that he did so as leader of a political party—the Federalists—rather than as a dispassionate Chief Magistrate? We have noted that, in common with most of his contemporaries, he considered parties as undesirable phenomena; that he saw the President as above politics; and that above all he wished to establish law and order in the Union. The vigor of Republican opposition was an unpleasant surprise, though he felt able to hold the balance so long as Republican attacks were concentrated upon Hamilton. But during his second administration, as political controversy grew and as he himself came under fire, Washington's opinions gradually hardened. "I think," said Jefferson, "he feels those things more than any other person I ever met with." Washington burst out, at a cabinet meeting in 1793, that Freneau was a "rascal" who ought to be stopped. Freneau's newspaper did cease publication later in the year, but other Republican sheets kept up the offensive. Resenting criticism, as always, and believing with some reason that the Republicans were irresponsible and malevolent, Washington came at length to share the Federalist view that their opponents were not the *other* party, but simply "party," or "faction"; not the "opposition" who might one day justly inherit the reins of government, but opposition as sedition, conspiracy, Gallomania. Hence his too sweeping condemnation of the Democratic societies, most of which were harmless political clubs; hence his indignant comment in a letter of 1798 that

"you could as soon scrub the blackamore white, as to change the principles of a profest Democrat," and that such a man "will leave nothing unattempted to overturn the Government of this Country." His final cabinet was entirely Federalist in composition.

From this it was only a step—a step that, nevertheless, he probably took unconsciously—to acknowledging that he himself was a Federalist. In 1799, the last year of his life, when he had been out of office for two years, Washington was urged to stand as a candidate in the presidential election of 1800, on the grounds that the Union was in grave danger. He refused, explaining that "principle, not men, is now, and will be, the object of contention." Even if he put himself forward, "I should not draw a *single* vote from the Antifederal side; and of course, should stand upon no stronger ground than any other Federal well supported." He was not quite ready to concede that the Republicans were a legitimate group; yet from his letter as a whole ("any *other* Federal") we see that he was beginning to grasp the altered basis of American politics.

If he had still been in office, he might not have been willing to label himself a Federalist; he might have maintained that the President must still strive to stand aloof. Certainly no serious blame attaches to him; but on this issue he did not achieve the lofty and prescient calm that some biographers have acclaimed in him. Only by seeing the decade entirely through Washington's or through Federalist eyes can we agree that he justly formulated the political equation.

The Last Retirement

These are speculative matters. Whatever else is doubtful, though, there can be no doubt that Washington was profoundly glad to relinquish the Presidency. Many expected him to accept a third term, and everyone knew that he could be re-elected with ease. Despite some hostile comment, he was still by far the most admired of Americans. But he had had enough—more than enough. His successor, John Adams, while flattered by the honor, was under no illusion as to what lay ahead. "A solemn scene it was indeed," Adams wrote to his wife, describing the inauguration in March 1797, "and it was made affecting to me by the presence of the General, whose countenance was as serene and unclouded as the day. He seemed to enjoy a triumph over me. Methought I heard him say, 'Ay! I am fairly out and you fairly in! See which of us will be the happiest!' . . . In the chamber of the House of Representatives was a multitude as great as the space would contain, and I believe scarcely a dry eye but Washington's." Washington had been deeply moved on other great occasions—as when he said good-by to his officers at Fraunces' Tavern in 1783. No tears now; all that he noted in his diary, under the inaugural date, was, "Much such a day as yesterday in all respects. Mercury at 41."

It was not that he handed over office in a sulk, but that nothing and no one could now convince him that he was indispensable to America. He had just celebrated his sixty-fifth birthday (or rather, it had just been celebrated for him, at an "elegant entertainment" where twelve hundred Philadelphians squeezed in to applaud him) and did not expect to enjoy many more. The few years that were left he meant to spend at Mount Vernon. His adult life had been splendid; yet the passage of time and the demand of public service had consumed too much. Most of his old friends were dead. One of the Fairfaxes had come back to Virginia, but Belvoir was a ruin and Sally Fairfax had never returned from England. Lafayette was free again (Washington had sent funds to his wife, with habitual generosity), but an ocean away. There remained Mount Vernon and the cheerful companionship of Martha and some of their young relatives.

If biography could be made as shapely as a good play, we could ring the curtain gently

down on Washington, leaving him in white-haired tranquillity. His existence, however, was not cast in such a pattern. The curtain was always jerking up again, the music awakening suddenly from some lulling coda. So it was to be again with him in 1798. In a way, it was his own fault. He would have been left alone if he had seemed senile. Instead, he appeared as vigorous as ever, whether in superintending his farms, in offering hospitality, or in dealing with correspondence. His letters, in fact, seem more pungent—perhaps because he now felt more at liberty to speak his mind, whereas hitherto official caution had hedged him in. At any rate, he was summoned back into uniform in 1798. French conduct had grown so outrageous that she was virtually at war with the United States. At naval war, that is. America had no army, except for the tiny nucleus of regulars that Washington had struggled to retain. He was now required to raise an army and assume command. The prospect made him groan. When Hamilton predicted that another summons to action would reach him, Washington replied that he would go "with as much reluctance from my present peaceful abode, as I should do to the tomb of my ancestors." He was displeased when President Adams nominated him as commander in chief without previous consultation. He was worried, as before in his career, that opponents might interpret his return to authority as a piece of ambition or—in view of his Farewell Address—hypocrisy. But the obligation was not to be evaded. Brisk, sensible, conscientious, he set about the task. As before, the ubiquitous Alexander Hamilton was promptly on hand, arranging things behind the scenes, securing for himself an appointment that would make him Washington's second-in-command. It was a hectic time, especially for poor John Adams. In his place, Washington would probably have come in for similar vilification. But we can be fairly sure that Washington would have avoided some of Adams's tactical blunders in the business of administration. A detailed comparison of his Presidency with Washington's would do much to bring out the solid, sober merit of the latter.

However, there was no war in 1798 or in 1799. Washington's life resumed its normal tempo. The months wheel by in the jog-trot entries of his diary. Hot days, cool days, rain, snow. Surveying, riding, visitors, dinners, a baby daughter born to his niece Betty Lewis. Then the diary stops on December 13, with a note that the thermometer has dropped to a slight frost. Then, indeed, the curtain comes down with a rush. Washington has caught a chill; he has a sore throat; the doctors bleed him, bleed him again, to no avail. At ten in the evening of December 14 he is dead, without a climax (save for that invented posthumously by Parson Weems), without a memorable final utterance; in pain, a sacrifice to the well-meaning but barbarous medical treatment of his day.

With less primitive care he could have survived a few more years. He could have witnessed the removal of the federal government to Federal City (christened Washington, D.C.), which would have pleased him, or the inauguration of Thomas Jefferson in 1801, following a Republican victory that would not have pleased him. He could have read of the Louisiana Purchase, and of Hamilton's death in a duel—a medley of bright news and dark news. But would he have wanted much more? His century was over, and he with it. Spenser's quiet lines fit his end better than many of the sonorous phrases that orators and scribes (including Freneau) were soon declaiming throughout the enormous, ramshackle, thriving Union:

Sleep after toyle, port after stormie seas,
Ease after warre, death after life does greatly
    please.

12

Thomas Jefferson: The Aristocrat as Democrat

Richard Hofstadter

When John Adams replaced Washington as president in 1796, Federalist leaders were extremely apprehensive about the French Revolution and the anarchy and violence which seemed to characterize it. Might the French virus not spread to America as it appeared to be spreading across Europe? Might not a conspiracy already be underway in the United States to fan the flames of revolution, to unleash the American mob on Federalist leaders, to destroy the order and stability they had worked so hard to establish? Since 1793, when Citizen Genêt had tried to enlist American men and privateers for the French cause, the Federalists had feared revolution in their midst. Champions of a strong government to maintain order, apostles of elitist rule and the sanctity of private property, the Federalists soon equated the Republicans under Madison and Jefferson with revolution, chaos, and destruction. After all, did the Republicans not support the French? Did they not defend the mob here at home? Did they not call for more democracy in government (although many of their leaders paradoxically were Southern slaveowners)? The harried Federalists barely beat off a Republican attempt to seize the government in 1796, when Adams defeated Jefferson by only three votes in the electoral college. Then, as though the Republican threat were not bad enough, trouble broke out with Revolutionary France. In the notorious X, Y, Z Affair, French agents tried to extract a bribe from American representatives sent to negotiate about deteriorating Franco-American relations. Many Americans thought the nation's honor had been besmirched and demanded a war of revenge. In response, the Federalists undertook an undeclared sea war against France that lasted from 1798 to 1800. Using the war as a pretext to consolidate their power, bridle the Republicans, and prevent revolution in the United States, the Federalists passed the alien and sedition acts. These, they declared, were necessary for the nation's security in the war with France. The alien acts severely restricted the rights and political influence of immigrants, who usually joined the Republicans after they were naturalized and who might be carrying the French virus. The sedition act made hostile criticism of Federalist policies punishable by fine and imprisonment. The Republicans, decrying such government censorship, launched a counterattack against Federal "despotism." The Federalists were so discredited by the alien and sedition laws, and so divided by an irreconcilable feud between Adams and Hamilton, that the Republicans swept to power in 1801. Their victory marked the decline and eventually the end of the Federalist Party as a national political organization.

Jefferson's rise to power has often been described as "the revolution of 1800." But was it really a revolution? Were the Jeffersonians actually that different from the Federalists they displaced? How many Federalist measures did the Jeffersonians rescind? How many political and social changes did they bring about? And was Jefferson himself, at any time in his career, a true revolutionary democrat? Richard Hofstadter explores these questions in what still ranks as one of the most perceptive accounts of Jefferson and his era in American historical literature.

The sheep are happier of themselves, than under the care of the wolves.

THOMAS JEFFERSON

The mythology that has grown up around Thomas Jefferson is as massive and imposing as any in American history. Although the bitterly prejudiced views of Federalist historians have never had wide acceptance, the stereotype perpetuated by such adherents of the Jeffersonian tradition as Claude Bowers and the late V. L. Parrington has been extremely popular. Jefferson has been pictured as a militant, crusading democrat, a Physiocrat who repudiated acquisitive capitalistic economics, a revolutionist who tore up the social fabric of Virginia in 1776, and the sponsor of a "Revolution of 1800" which destroyed Federalism root and branch. Although there is fact enough to give the color of truth to these notions, they have been torn down by shrewd Jefferson scholars like Charles A. Beard, Gilbert Chinard, and Albert J. Nock, and it is certainly not lack of good criticism that accounts for the dominant Jefferson legend. The issues of his time have been overdramatized, and Jefferson has been overdramatized with them.

It would have been strange if Jefferson had become one of those bitter rebels who live by tearing up established orders and forcing social struggles to the issue. He was born into an eminent place in the Virginia aristocracy. Peter Jefferson, his father, was a self-made man, but through his mother, Jane Randolph, who came from the distinguished Virginia family, he had an assured social position. Peter Jefferson died in 1757, leaving his son, then fourteen, over 2,700 acres and a large number of bondsmen. During most of his mature life Thomas Jefferson owned about 10,000 acres and from one to two hundred Negroes. The leisure that made possible his great writings on human liberty was supported by the labors of three generations of slaves.

Jefferson was a benevolent slavemaster, and his feeling for the common people was doubtless affected by an ingrained habit of solicitude for the helpless dependents who supported him. He prided himself on not being overprotective, once writing Dupont that the difference between their affections for the people was that Dupont loved them as infants who must be nursed, while he loved them as adults who could govern themselves. But no aristocrat, reared in a society rent by such a gulf between rich and poor, learned and unlearned, could be quite the democrat Jefferson imagined himself. As Charles M. Wiltse puts it, "He remains always quite aloof from the masses, and if he claims equality for all men, it is not because he feels that men are equal, but because he reasons that they must be so." An element of gentle condescension is unmistakable in his democracy; its spirit is caught in one of his letters to Lafayette:

It will be a great comfort to you to know from your own inspection, the condition of all the provinces of your own country, and it will be interesting to them at some future day, to be known to you. This is, perhaps, the only moment of your life in which you can acquire that knowledge. And to do it most effectually, you must be absolutely incognito, you must ferret the people out of their hovels as I have done, look into their kettles, eat their bread, loll on their beds under pretense of resting yourself, but in fact, to find if they are soft. You will feel a sublime pleasure in the course of this investigation, and a sublimer one hereafter, when you shall be able to apply your knowledge to the softening of their beds, or the throwing of a morsel of meat into their kettle of vegetables.

Jefferson was educated at the College of William and Mary at Williamsburg, where in spite of his youth he was immediately accepted by the most brilliant and enlightened society. After graduation he fell into the expected pattern of the Virginia gentry, among whom polit-

From pp. 18–43 in *The American Political Tradition* by Richard Hofstadter. Copyright 1948 by Alfred A. Knopf. Reprinted by permission of the publisher.

ical leadership was practically a social obliga-tion. At twenty-four he was admitted to the bar, at twenty-six elected to a seat in the House of Burgesses, which he held for six years. At twenty-nine, a successful but unenthusiastic consulting lawyer, he married a young widow and settled at Monticello. His marriage brought large landholdings to add to his patrimony, but also a debt of four thousand pounds. Like many other Virginia planters, he developed from his own relations with British creditors a bilious view of the province's economic sub-ordination to England and fell in with the anti-British group among the Burgesses. The ring-ing phrases he had learned from English re-publican philosophers began to take on more vivid meaning for him. In 1774 he wrote a bold tract applying the natural-rights doctrine to the colonial controversy, which won immediate at-tention throughout the colonies and gave him the reputation for literary craftsmanship that later made him the draftsman of the Declara-tion of Independence.

The Revolution found Jefferson in the prime of life and at the full flush of his reforming en-thusiasm; during its first few years he did some of the most creative work of his life. Under his leadership the Virginia reformers abolished primogeniture and entail and laid the base for freedom of thought and religion by disestab-lishing the Anglican Church and forbidding legal or political disabilities for religious dis-sent. They also attempted, with paltry results, to found a good common-school system. Jeffer-son wrote the bills destroying primogeniture and entail, and on behalf of the bill for religious freedom drafted one of the most brilliant and trenchant pleas for free thought in the history of literature.

The accomplishments of this reform move-ment were considerable, but they have been subject to fantastic exaggeration by historians and biographers who look upon Jefferson and his colleagues as revolutionists putting through a sweeping program of social reform, destroy-

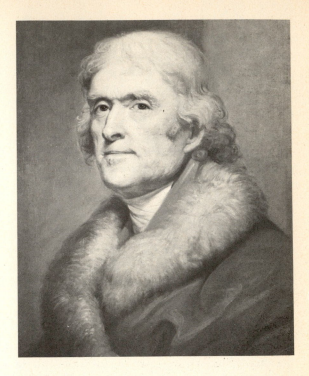

Thomas Jefferson, an oil painting done in 1805 by Rembrandt Peale. Jefferson was tall and slender, with a freckled face, gray eyes, and short, pow-dered, red hair. The color of his hair inspired one correspondent to salute him as "You red-headed son of a bitch." Despite his aristocratic upbringing, he was largely indifferent about his clothes, which rarely fit him. A Federalist senator once mistook Jefferson for a servant, observing with a sniff that his shirt was dirty. (Courtesy of The New York Historical Society.)

ing the Virginia aristocracy, and laying the foundations for democratic government. Even Jefferson, who was usually modest and accu-rate about his achievements, claimed too much when he said that these reforms "laid the axe" to the root of the Old Dominion's aristocracy. If the changes were actually so important, one would expect bitter resistance. The truth is that, with the exception of the bill for religious freedom (which, Jefferson testified, gave rise to "the severest contests in which I have ever been engaged"), the old institutions fell almost

without a push. Jefferson wrote to Franklin that "this important transformation" was accomplished with the most remarkable ease; only "a half-dozen aristocratic gentlemen, agonizing under the loss of pre-eminence," had opposed it, and they "have been thought fitter objects of pity than of punishment."

The explanation of this "revolution by consent" is simple: there was no revolution. Primogeniture in the full meaning of the word did not really exist in Virginia. It was never mandatory upon the landowner. It applied only when he died without leaving a will disposing of his land. It was not regularly practiced by the landed families of the Old Dominion, for Virginians usually did leave wills dividing their land among their sons, and sometimes even among their daughters. Entail was actually a nuisance to the aristocracy because it interfered with the sale of estates they often found inconvenient to hold. During the years before 1776 petition after petition came into the Virginia legislature from leading families asking that their lands be exempted from entail.

Much has been made by rapt biographers of Jefferson's interest in abolishing slavery at this time. As a member of a committee to revise the legal code, he did draft a law for gradual emancipation, but never presumed to introduce it. "It was found," he explained, "that the public mind would not bear the proposition. . . . Yet the day is not distant when it must bear and adopt it, or worse will follow." Trying to force through any law, however desirable, which "the public mind would not bear" would have been thoroughly uncharacteristic of Jefferson's pragmatic political temperament.[1]

After a most unhappy experience as war Governor of Virginia, Jefferson, at thirty-eight,

[1] Jefferson was characteristically circumspect about attacking slavery in his own state, but more aggressive in intercolonial affairs when he could expect Northern backing. Thus he included a bitter attack upon the slave trade in the Declaration of Independence—which was struck out—and tried to get slavery banned from the Northwest Territory in his Ordinance of 1784.

was eager for permanent retirement from politics, but the death of his wife drove him away from Monticello and back into furiously active service for the Congress. From 1785 to 1789 he was American Minister to France, where his experience may have been crucial in determining the direction of his political thinking. While his friends at home were watching the failure of the Articles of Confederation, looking anxiously upon the political advances of the dirt farmers, and turning rightward in their politics, he was touring Europe, taking the measure of feudal and monarchical institutions, observing the bitter exploitation of the workers of England and the peasantry of France, and confirming his republicanism. Appalled at the extremes of wealth and misery in European countries, he found kings, nobles, and priests "an abandoned confederacy against the happiness of the mass of the people," saw in the royalty of Europe only "fools" and "idiots," and described the treatment of the English laboring classes in the bitterest language. Europe fortified his conviction that America, with its republican government, broad distribution of landed property, agrarian economy, and oceanic isolation, was the chosen spot of the earth. Although he found much to admire in the European common people, they too brought him back to the political superiority of America. A lifelong prejudice is summed up in a few words from one of his letters to Lafayette: "The yeomanry of the United States are not the *canaille* of Paris."

In France during the early days of the French Revolution, Jefferson was naturally consulted by the moderate leaders of its first phase. Once he committed the indiscretion of allowing Lafayette and a few friends to meet at his house. He promptly apologized to the French Foreign Minister, Montmorin; but Montmorin, who evidently understood Jefferson well, answered that he hoped Jefferson "would habitually assist at such conferences, being sure I would be useful in moderating the warmer spirits and promoting a wholesome and practicable refor-

mation only." When the King showed the first signs of a conciliatory state of mind, appearing in public with the popular cockade on his head, Jefferson concluded that the time had come for a compromise with the crown. But the draft of terms which he gave to his revolutionary friends was rejected—because it was too moderate.

What of the notion that Jefferson was an impractical visionary, that he was, as Charles Carroll of Carrollton called him, "a theoretical and fanciful man"? There is a sense in which this was true, but it has little to do with his public activity or his cast of mind. He *was* fatally generous, borrowed funds to give to beggars, entertained with a lavishness far beyond the capacities of his purse, and in his last years gave his declining fortunes the *coup de grâce* by signing the note of a floundering neighbor.

But did his mind run naturally to high abstractions? Did he spend his spare moments on them? On the contrary, when he found time to write at length, he turned his energies to such matter-of-fact projects as the encyclopedic *Notes on Virginia*, a parliamentary manual for the use of the Senate, a study of Indian languages, and his autobiography. He never attempted to write a systematic book of political theory—which was well, because he had no system and lacked the doctrinaire's compulsion to be consistent. Although he found time and energy for everything from epistemology to the mechanical arts, it was the latter that interested him most. He had an almost compulsive love of counting, observing, measuring. ("Not a sprig of grass shoots uninteresting to me," he once wrote to his daughter.) His standard of values was eminently practical. ("The greatest service which can be rendered any country is to add an useful plant to its culture.") He was the architect of his own home, ran his farm on a fairly self-sufficient basis, and made elaborate efficiency studies of his slaves' work. He invented a hempbeater, worked out the formula for a moldboard plow of least resistance, for which the French Institute of Agriculture of the Department of Seine-et-Oise gave him a prize, devised a leather buggy top, a swivel chair, and a dumbwaiter. He kept elaborate journals about the farms, gardens, social conditions, and natural phenomena he saw on his travels. Albert Jay Nock concludes that he "examined every useful tree and plant in western Europe and studied its cultivation." For long periods he kept daily thermometric and barometric readings. He was constantly studying new plows, steam engines, metronomes, thermometers, elevators, and the like, as well as the processing of butters and cheeses. He wrote a long essay for Congress on standards of weights and measures in the United States, and an excellent critique of the census returns, with detailed suggestions for collecting more minute information. On his travels he procured the plans of twelve large European cities, which he was able to lend L'Enfant to help him lay out the scheme of Washington. He conceived the American decimal system of coinage, demonstrating on this score his superiority to the financier Robert Morris. Such are the contributions to practical arts of this "theoretical and fanciful man."

What of the Jefferson who said that the tree of liberty must be watered periodically with the blood of tyrants, who thought that a rebellion every twenty years was an excellent thing, and who urged throughout his life that constitutions should be completely remade every twenty-five or thirty years? What of the Jefferson who was considered dangerous by so many conservative contemporaries, who was everywhere understood to be a strongheaded doctrinaire?

Jefferson was a complex person who must be measured in whole, not in part, in action as well as thought. There were deep ambiguities in his thinking, which made any effort at con-

sistency impossible. Although Federalist historians have cited these ambiguities as evidence of a moral taint, a constitutional shiftiness of mind, they may in fact be traced to a continuously ambivalent personal and political history. He valued much more highly the achievements of his father, whom he intensely admired, than the high social status of his mother, whose influence he never acknowledged; but from the beginning he was aware of both the assurance of the aristocracy and the real merits and talents of men who came from unknown families. In his autobiography he remarked dryly of the Randolph genealogy: "They trace their pedigree far back in England and Scotland, to which let everyone ascribe the faith and merit he chooses." When he came to maturity, Jefferson was a slaveowner and yet a revolutionist, who could say that man's rights were "unalienable" at the very moment when he owned several dozen souls. All his life he circulated among men of wealth, learning, and distinction, and as befitted one who disliked acrimony he learned to accommodate himself to them—but he also absorbed the most liberal and questionable opinions of his age and associated on congenial terms with men like Thomas Paine and Joel Barlow. In American politics he became a leader of yeomen farmers —but also of great planters. He was the head of a popular faction that stood against the commercial interests—but it was also a propertied faction with acquisitive aspirations of its own. Well read in the best philosophical literature of his century, he accepted broad cosmopolitan ideas, but he was also an ardent American patriot. He was a pacifist in personal temperament and philosophy, a nationalist by training, and yet a Virginian with strong parochial loyalties. He wanted with all his heart to hold to the values of agrarian society, and yet he believed in progress. Add to all this the fact that he lived an unusually long life, saw many changes, and tried to adapt his views to changing circumstances.

Jefferson had warm impulses. His cosmopoliton mind refracted the most advanced and liberating ideas of his time. He believed in those ideas, and rephrased and reiterated them in language that has become classic; but he was not in the habit of breaking lances trying to fulfill them. The generous and emancipating thoughts for which his name is so justly praised are to be found almost entirely in his *private* correspondence; after he wrote the Declaration of Independence and the Virginia Statute for Religious Freedom he avoided expressing his more unacceptable ideas in public. He understood that in the workday world of public activity his most lofty ideals were chiefly valuable to indicate the direction in which society should be guided. He never really expected them to be realized in his time and preferred to place his hopes in progress, in the promise that mankind would consummate his ideals in some magnificent future. ("Your taste is judicious," John Adams once taunted him, "in liking better the dreams of the future than the history of the past.")

Jefferson's practical activity was usually aimed at some kind of minimum program that could be achieved without keen conflict or great expenditure of energy. He hated vigorous controversy, shrank from asserting his principles when they would excite the anger of colleagues or neighbors. He tried to avoid a wide circulation of his *Notes on Virginia* because he did not want Virginians to read his bitter remarks on slavery and a few tart observations on the province's Constitution. Jefferson did not lack courage—his futile embargo policy, carried out under bitter protest from every part of the country, proves that—but rather that hardihood of spirit which makes a political fight bearable. Although he had strong political prejudices and sometimes violent animosities, he did not enjoy power and could not bear publicity. He was acutely sensitive to criticism, admitting to Francis Hopkinson in 1789: "I find the pain of a little censure, even when it is un-

founded, is more acute than the pleasure of much praise." Abnormally shy and troubled by a slight speech defect, he found it impossible to read his messages in person to Congress as Washington and Adams had done. He had not the temperament of an agitator, hardly even of a leader in the qualities that leadership requires under modern democracy. Not once did he deliver an exciting speech. His private life was one of enormous variety and interest, and there were many times when he would have been happy to desert public service to enjoy his farm, his family, and his books.

2

Jefferson's Federalist opponents feared, above all, power lodged in the majority. Jefferson feared power lodged anywhere else. In his First Inaugural Address he asked concerning the common observation "that man cannot be trusted with the government of himself"; "Can he, then, be trusted with the government of others?" He would have agreed with Madison that power is "of an encroaching nature," and he was sure that power corrupts those who possess it. "If once the people become inattentive to the public affairs," he wrote Edward Carrington from Paris, "you and I and Congress and Assemblies, Judges and Governors, shall all become wolves. It seems to be the law of our general nature, in spite of individual exceptions."

Admitting that a majority will often decide public questions wrongly, Jefferson argued that "the duperies of the people are less injurious" than the self-interested policies of kings, priests, and aristocrats. He refused to be alarmed by popular uprisings like the Shays Rebellion. In the safety of his private correspondence he felt free to say that "honest republican governments" should be "so mild in their punishment of rebellions as not to discourage them too much." "A little rebellion

now and then is a good thing, and as necessary in the political world as storms in the physical." The people are not always well informed, but it is better that they have misconceptions that make them restless than that they be lethargic —for lethargy in the people means death for republics.

Again and again Jefferson urged that the people be educated and informed through a broad common-school system and a free press. Although he had small faith in the power of republics to resist corruption and decay, he hoped that mass education would stem this degenerative process.[2] Education not only would give stability and wisdom to the politics of a commonwealth, but would widen opportunities, bring out the natural talents that could be found in abundance among the common people. Throughout Jefferson's life there runs this humane concern for "the pursuit of happiness," for the development of the individual without regard to limitations of class.

By and large, however, when Jefferson spoke warmly of the merits and abilities of "the people" he meant "the farmers." He did not see a town until he was almost eighteen, and he believed deeply that rural living and rural people are the wellspring of civic virtue and individual vitality, that farmers are the best social base of a democratic republic. "Those who labor in the earth are the chosen people of God, if ever he had a chosen people," he proclaimed in his *Notes on Virginia*. "Corruption of morals in the mass of cultivators is a phenomenon of which no age nor nation has furnished an example."[3]

[2] In his Bill for the More General Diffusion of Knowledge (1779) he declared that "experience hath shewn, that even under the best forms [of government] those entrusted with power have, in time, and by slow operations perverted it into tyranny. . . ."

[3] In 1787 he wrote: "I think our governments will remain virtuous for many centuries; as long as they remain chiefly agricultural; and this will be as long as there shall be vacant lands in any part of America. When they get piled upon one another in large cities, as in Europe, they will become corrupt as in Europe."

. . . generally speaking, the proportion which the aggregate of the other classes of citizens bears in any State to that of its husbandmen, is the proportion of its unsound to its healthy parts, and is a good enough barometer whereby to measure its degree of corruption. While we have lands to labor then, let us never wish to see our citizens occupied at a work bench or twirling a distaff. . . . Let our workshops remain in Europe.

The American economy, then, should be preserved in its agricultural state. Manufacturers, cities, urban classes, should be held at a minimum. So Jefferson believed, at any rate, until the responsibilities of the White House and the conduct of foreign policy caused him to modify his views. He once went so far as to say that he hoped the United States would remain, with respect to Europe, on the same economic footing as China. Commerce he would encourage—it supplied the needs of agriculture—but this was the extent of his early concessions to the urban classes.

Thus far Jefferson, with his faith in the farmers, his distrust of the urban classes, and his belief in the long-range value of rebellions and social disturbances, seems at the opposite pole from the Constitution-makers—and so he might have been if his political theory had been elaborated into a coherent system. But he had more in common with the conservative thinkers

of his age than is usually recognized. His differences with the political theory of the Constitution-makers were differences of emphasis, not of structure. He shared their primary fears. He did not think that political constitutions could safely rely on man's virtue. In a letter to Mann Page in 1795 he declared that he could not accept the idea of the Rochefoucaulds and Montaignes that "fourteen out of fifteen men are rogues." "*But I have always found that rogues would be uppermost,* and I do not know that the proportion is too strong for the higher orders and for those who, rising above the swinish multitude, always contrive to nestle themselves into the places of power and profit." It was the upper, not the lower orders of society that he thought especially unregenerate—but it was Jefferson, too, who could use words like "canaille" and "swinish multitude."

Jefferson, of course, accepted the principle of balanced government and the idea that the people must be checked. "It is not by the consolidation, or concentration of powers, but by their distribution that good government is effected," he wrote in his autobiography. He designed a constitution for Virginia in 1776 which employed the principle of checks and balances and required property qualifications of voters.[4] Of the two houses of the legislature, only the lower was to be elected by the people: the senate was to be chosen by the house, as was the governor, so that two of the three parts of the lawmaking body were at one remove from the citizens. Five years later, criticizing the Constitution that had been adopted by Virginia instead of his own, he complained primarily of its lack of checks: the Senate and the House of Delegates were too much alike because both were chosen by the voters in the

---

After he had observed the machinations of the Federalists, his faith in the husbandman's monopoly on civic virtue became even more rigid than before, and a shrill note rang through his letters: "Farmers, whose interests are entirely agricultural . . . are the true representatives of the great American interest, and are alone to be relied on for expressing the proper American sentiments."

In his belief that one economic class, the freeholding farmers, had more political virtue than the other orders, Jefferson made a significant breach in the abstract conception that human nature is everywhere the same, but he does not seem to have developed the implications of this insight.

[4] And yet in his *Notes on Virginia* he voiced his displeasure with the limited suffrage of the state: "The majority of the men in the State who pay and fight for its support, are unrepresented in the legislature, the roll of freeholders entitled to vote not including generally the half of those on the roll of the militia, or of the taxgatherers."

same way. *"The purpose of establishing different houses of legislation is to introduce the influence of different interests or different principles."* He continued:

> All the powers of government, legislative, executive, and judiciary, result to the legislative body. The concentrating these in the same hands is precisely the definition of despotic government. It will be no alleviation that these powers will be exercised by a plurality of hands and not by a single one. One hundred and seventy-three despots would surely be as oppressive as one. . . . As little will it avail us that they are chosen by ourselves. An *elective despotism* was not the government we fought for, but one which should not only be founded on free principles, but in which the powers of government should be so divided and balanced among several bodies of magistracy, as that no one could transcend their legal limits without being effectually checked and restrained by the others.

This would have been accounted sound doctrine at the Philadelphia Convention of 1787. A government that does not divide and balance powers in a system of checks is precisely what Jefferson means by despotic; the fact that the governing body is chosen by the people does not qualify his complaint; such a government, without checks, is merely "an elective despotism." Jefferson, then, refused to accept simple majority rule, adopting instead the idea that "different interests or different principles" should be represented in government.

All this sounds close to the theories of Madison and Adams. In fact, Jefferson did not differ with them strongly enough to challenge their conservative writings of the constitutional period. In 1788 he wrote to Madison praising the *Federalist* as "the best commentary on the principles of government which ever was written." Two years later, advising his nephew Thomas Mann Randolph on a course of reading, Jefferson praised Locke's work as being "perfect as far as it goes," and then added: "Descending from theory to practice, there is no better book than the Federalist." In 1787 he told John Adams that he had read his *Defence* "with infinite satisfaction and improvement. It will do great good in America. Its learning and its good sense will, I hope, make it an institute for our politicians, old as well as young."[5]

When the text of the federal Constitution of 1787 reached him in France, Jefferson confessed to Adams that he was staggered at what had been attempted, but soon recovered his composure. He informed Madison that he saw many good features in it, but objected strongly to two things: the absence of a bill of rights (later included in the first ten amendments), and the eligibility of the president for more than one term. In the end he gave it a substantial endorsement: "It is a good canvas, on which some strokes only want retouching." His regard for it grew with the years.

As much as Madison or Morris, Jefferson disliked the idea of city mobs—"the panders of vice and the instruments by which the liberties of a country are generally overturned"—but he believed that they would not emerge in the calculable future because America's lands would be open to make substantial farmers of the ragged and discontented. In his First Inaugural he said that the land would last the American people "to the hundredth and thousandth generation"! The United States would be a nation of farmers, tilling their own soil, independent, informed, unexcitable, and incorruptible. Such a national destiny, he must have felt, would be secured by the Louisiana Purchase.

---

[5] Later he also endorsed heartily John Taylor's *An Inquiry into the Principles and Policy of the Government of the United States* (1814), which was in large part a headlong assault on Adams's theories. This of course was after the Federalist-Republican antagonism had ripened.

The future, then, would be founded on a propertied class in a propertied nation. Jefferson leaned strongly to the idea that a propertied interest in society is necessary to a stable political mentality. In 1800 he wrote a friend that he had always favored universal manhood suffrage; but this was one of those theoretical notions to which he was not firmly wedded. "Still I find some very honest men," he added, "who, thinking the possession of some property necessary to give due independence of mind, are for restraining the elective franchise to property." His 1776 draft of a constitution for Virginia had required that voters own either a freehold estate of twenty-five acres in the country or one fourth of an acre in town, or pay taxes within two years of the time of voting. Never did Jefferson try to introduce universal manhood suffrage anywhere.[6]

The outstanding characteristic of Jefferson's democracy is its close organic relation to the agrarian order of his time. It seems hardly enough to say that he thought that a nation of farmers, educated, informed, and blessed with free institutions, was the best suited to a democratic republic, without adding that he did not think any *other* kind of society a good risk to maintain republican government. In a nation of large cities, well-developed manufactures and commerce, and a numerous working class, popular republicanism would be an impossibility—or at best an improbability.

Certainly the balance of Jefferson's good society is a tenuous thing: the working class is corrupt; merchants are corrupt; speculators are corrupt; cities are "pestilential"; only farmers are dependably good. Sunder human nature from its proper or "natural" nourishment in the cultivation of the soil and the ownership of real property, and he profoundly distrusts it. Sunder democracy from the farm and how much more firmly does he believe in it than John Adams? Yet this is just what the relentless advance of modern industrial capitalism has done: it has sundered four fifths of society from the soil, has separated the masses from their property, and has built life increasingly on what Jefferson would have called an artificial basis—in short, has gradually emptied the practical content out of Jefferson's agrarian version of democracy. This process had its earliest beginnings during Jefferson's lifetime, and, as we shall see, he yielded a good part of his agrarian prejudices (like the pragmatic, undoctrinaire soul that he was) without sacrificing his democratic preferences. But although he clung to his humane vision of democracy, he left it without the new economic rationale that it required.

3

In after years Jefferson declared that the struggle between his party and the Federalists was one between those who cherished the people and those who distrusted them. But he had been associated with a number of men like Elbridge Gerry, Pierce Butler, Charles Pinckney, and Edmund Randolph who did not cherish the people in the least, and the differences in abstract principle were hardly intense enough to account for the fierceness of the conflict or for the peculiar lines along which it was drawn. Although democratically minded Americans did stand with Jefferson, the line of division was essentially between two kinds of property, not two kinds of philosophy.

The Federalists during Hamilton's service as Secretary of the Treasury had given the govern-

[6] It is important to add, however, that in 1776 Jefferson proposed that Virginia grant fifty acres of land to every white of full age who had less than that amount. This would have made suffrage practically universal. It also illustrates his belief in broadening economic opportunities where free land made the policy possible, as well as the vital linkage in his mind between landed property and democracy. He was, at this time, more democratic in his conception of the economic *base* of government than in his conception of the *structure* of government.

ment a foundation of unashamed devotion to the mercantile and investing classes. Through his method of funding the national debt, through his national bank, and through all the subsidiary policies of the government, Hamilton subsidized those who invested in manufactures, commerce, and public securities, throwing as much of the tax burden as possible on planters and farmers. The landed interests, however, were in a majority, and it was only a matter of time before they could marshal themselves in a strong party of their own. Jefferson's party was formed to defend specific propertied interests rather than the abstract premises of democracy, and its policies were conceived and executed in the sober, moderate spirit that Jefferson's generation expected of propertied citizens when they entered the political arena.

When Jefferson was elected in 1800, the more naïve Federalists, frightened to the marrow by their own propaganda, imagined that the end of the world had come. Fisher Ames anticipated that he would soon scent "the loathsome steam of human victims offered in sacrifice." Among those who knew the President-elect, however, there was no such hysteria—especially not among insiders who had private knowledge of the circumstances under which he had been chosen.

The election of 1800 was unique in American history. Because no distinction had yet been made in the Constitution between ballots cast for presidential and vice-presidential candidates, Jefferson and his running mate, Aaron Burr, won the same number of votes in the electoral college. The tied contest was thrown into the House of Representatives, where it fell to Federalist Congressmen to choose between two Republicans. To some this seemed merely a choice of executioners; others, looking upon Jefferson as their supreme enemy, gravitated naturally toward Burr. Not so Alex-

ander Hamilton, who had long been Burr's political rival in New York. In a remarkable letter to a Federalist Representative, Hamilton gave a shrewd estimate of Jefferson's character. He admitted that his old foe's views were "tinctured with fanaticism; that he is too much in earnest with his democracy." But it is not true, he continued, in an appraisal that is as penetrating in substance as it is unfair in phrasing,

> that Jefferson is zealot enough to do anything in pursuance of his principles which will contravene his popularity or his interest. He is as likely as any man I know to temporize—to calculate what will be likely to promote his own reputation and advantage; and the probable result of such a temper is the preservation of systems, though originally opposed, which, being once established, could not be overturned without danger to the person who did it. To my mind a true estimate of Mr. Jefferson's character warrants the expectation of a temporizing rather than a violent system. . . . Add to this that here is no fair reason to suppose him capable of being corrupted, which is a security that he will not go beyond certain limits.

Not entirely satisfied with Hamilton's advice, Federalist leaders sought for assurance from Jefferson. The Virginian refused to commit himself in response to direct approach, but a friend who sounded him out informally was able to convey to the Federalists the comforting knowledge that Jefferson's intentions were moderate. That Jefferson abandoned any of his original plans, and in that sense bargained away any principles to win the office, is extremely unlikely; but when he entered the White House it was after satisfying the Federalists that he and they had come to some kind of understanding.

A little thought on the difficult position in which Jefferson now found himself should convince anyone that for a man of his moderate

temperament there was small choice in fundamental policy. The Hamiltonian system, now in operation for twelve years, had become part of the American economy. The nation was faring well. To unscramble Hamilton's system of funding, banks, and revenues would precipitate a bitter struggle, widen the breach between the classes, and drive moderates out of the Republican ranks; it might bring a depression, perhaps even rend the Union. And when the strife was over, there would always be the need of coming to terms with the classes that carried on commerce and banking and manufactures. Further, even if the landed interests were charged with the burden of Hamilton's debts, there was always the probability that they were better off when the system was working smoothly than they would be after a ruinously successful assault upon it. Jefferson, in short, found himself in a position much like that of modern social-democratic statesmen who, upon attaining power, find themselves the managers of a going concern that they fear to disrupt. Just as they have been incapable of liquidating capitalism, so Jefferson found himself unable to keep it from growing and extending its sway over the agrarian masses. Instead he wisely confined himself to trimming carefully at the edges of the Hamiltonian system.

Jefferson's First Inaugural Address was a conciliatory document contrived to bind up the wounds of the bitter period from 1798 to 1800 and to attract moderate Federalists to his support. "We are all republicans—we are all federalists," he declared. Soon the President was writing to Dupont de Nemours in words that show how well Hamilton had taken his measure:

When this government was first established, it was possible to have kept it going on true principles, but the contracted, English, half-lettered ideas of Hamilton destroyed that hope in the bud. We can pay off his debts in 15 years: but we can never get rid of his financial system. It mortifies me to be strengthening principles which I deem radically vicious, but this vice is entailed on us by the first error. In other parts of our government I hope we shall be able by degrees to introduce sound principles and make them habitual. What is practicable must often control what is pure theory.

Jefferson kept his promises to friends and enemies alike. So successfully did he whittle away at the Federalist machinery by reducing expenditures that he was able to abolish the hated excise duties that had stirred up the Whisky Rebellion and still make great inroads on the public debt. He tried hard to tame the federal judiciary—the last arm of the national government still under Federalist control —but to little effect. Through the Louisiana Purchase he widened the area for agrarian expansion. In 1811, two years after his terms were over, his party also allowed the First Bank of the United States to die upon the expiration of its charter.

But no attack was made upon other vital parts of the Hamiltonian system. No attempt was made to curb such abuses as speculation in public lands; nor did the well-organized Republican machines try hard to democratize the mechanics of government in the states or the nation. Limitations on the suffrage, for example, were left untouched. Professor Beard observes that the Republican states were "no more enamored of an equalitarian political democracy" than the Federalist states. Had Jefferson suggested a broad revision of the suffrage, many of his state leaders who had no use for theoretical democracy would have looked at him askance; if he had been the crusading democrat of Jeffersonian legend he could not have been so successful a machine leader.

Since his policies did not deviate too widely from those of the Federalists, Jefferson hoped to win over the moderates from their ranks and planned to use the patronage in doing so. "If

we can hit on the true line of conduct which may conciliate the honest part of those who were called federalists," he wrote to Horatio Gates soon after taking office, "and do justice to those who have so long been excluded from [the patronage], I shall hope to be able to obliterate, or rather to unite the names of federalists and republicans."

In politics, then, the strategy was conciliation; in economics it was compromise. Soon the Republican machines began flirting with the financial interests they had sworn to oppose. Republican state legislatures issued charters liberally to local banks, which, in turn, tended to cleave to the Republican Party in politics. Jefferson gave his benediction to this process of mutual accommodation. When the Bank of Baltimore applied to the administration for assistance, he wrote to Secretary of the Treasury Albert Gallatin:

It is certainly for the public good to keep all the banks competitors for our favors by a judicious distribution of them and thus to engage the individuals who belong to them in support of the reformed order of things or at least in an acquiescence under it.

And:

. . . I am decidedly in favor of making all the banks Republican by sharing deposits among them in proportion to the disposition they show. . . . It is material to the safety of Republicanism to detach the mercantile interest from its enemies and incorporate them into the body of its friends. A merchant is naturally a Republican, and can be otherwise only from a vitiated state of things.

John Adams, in the quiet of his retirement at Quincy, might have been amused to see a new elite, closely linked to the fiscal interests, emerging in the heart of the Republican Party, but the militant agrarian John Taylor was deeply discouraged. In 1811 he wrote:

. . . those who clearly discerned the injustice and impolicy of enriching and strengthening the federalists by bank or debt stock, at the publick expense, will seldom refuse to receive a similar sinecure. In short, a power in the individuals who compose legislatures, to fish up wealth from the people, by nets of their own weaving . . . will corrupt legislative, executive and judicial publick servants, by whatever systems constituted.

The inability of the Republicans to follow a pure policy of democratic agrarianism was matched by their inability to fashion a positive theory of agrarian economics. The predominant strain in their economic thinking was laissez-faire, their primary goal essentially negative— to destroy the link between the federal government and the investing classes. Acute and observant, their economic writing was at its best in criticism, but it offered no guide to a specific agrarian program. They had no plan; indeed, they made a principle of planlessness.

Jefferson has been described as a physiocrat by many writers—among them V. L. Parrington—but there is little more substance to this notion than there is to the preposterous idea that he was influenced chiefly by French thought. He was naturally content to remain an eclectic in economics. "No one axiom," he wrote to J. B. Say in 1815, "can be laid down as wise and expedient for all times and circumstances." Their defense of free trade was responsible for whatever appeal the physiocrats had for Jefferson; but after he read *The Wealth of Nations* he became a convert to the doctrines of Adam Smith.[7]

Like other theorists of the "natural law" era, Jefferson was quite ready to believe that the "natural" operations of the system of self-seeking private enterprise were intrinsically beneficent and should not normally be dis-

---

[7] Ultimately he came to prefer J. B. Say's adaptations of Smith as more lucid and readable, and showed much admiration for the work of Destutt de Tracy.

turbed by government. In his First Inaugural he called for "a wise and frugal government, which shall restrain men from injuring one another, *which shall leave them otherwise free to regulate their own pursuits of industry and improvement,* and shall not take from the mouth of labor the bread it has earned."[8] In a letter to Joseph Milligan, April 6, 1816, in which he discussed the proper limits of taxation, he concluded that the state ought not be aggressive in redistributing property:[9]

> To take from one, because it is thought his own industry and that of his fathers has acquired too much, in order to spare to others, who, or whose fathers have not exercised equal industry and skill, is to violate arbitrarily the first principle of association, "the *guarantee* to everyone a free exercise of his industry and the fruits acquired by it."

John Taylor, perhaps the cleverest of the agrarian writers, likewise believed that "it is both wise and just to leave the distribution of property to industry and talents."

This conception of state policy was not anticapitalist but anti-mercantilist. Jefferson and his followers had seen the unhappy effects of British governmental interference in American economic affairs, and they regarded Hamilton's system of state economic activity ("the contracted, English, half-lettered ideas of Hamilton") as merely a continuation at home of English economic ideas. Hamilton had set the government to helping the capitalists at the expense of the agrarians. The Jeffersonian response was not to call for a government that would help the agrarians at the expense of the capitalists, but simply for one that would let things alone. Where modern liberals have looked to government interference as a means of helping the poor, Jefferson, in common with other eighteenth-century liberals, thought of it chiefly as an unfair means of helping the rich through interest-bearing debts, taxation, tariffs, banks, privileges, and bounties. He concluded that the only necessary remedy under republican government would be to deprive the rich of these devices and restore freedom and equality through "natural" economic forces. Because he did not usually think of economic relationships as having an inherent taint of exploitation in them, he saw no necessity to call upon the state to counteract them. It was not the task of government to alter the economic order: the rich were not entitled to it and the poor would not find it necessary.

Jefferson rejected from his political philosophy the idea that one man has any intrinsic superiority over another; but he implicitly and perhaps unwittingly took it back again when he accepted competitive laissez-faire economics with its assumption that, so long as men were equal in law, and government played no favorites, wealth would be distributed in accordance with "industry and skill." Such a philosophy seemed natural enough to American farmers and planters who were in their own rights entrepreneurs, businessmen, exporters, and often, in a small way, speculators with a weather eye on land values—men accustomed to stand on their own feet.

In due time, of course, Jeffersonian laissez-faire became the political economy of the most conservative thinkers in the country. Fifty years after Jefferson's death men like William Graham Sumner were writing sentences exactly like Jefferson's and John Taylor's to defend enterprising industrial capitalists and railroad barons from government regulation and reform. And one hundred years after the Jeffersonians first challenged John Adams at the

---

[8] In his Second Inaugural, when he listed the things government should do, he asserted that it should maintain "that state of property, equal or unequal, which results to every man from his own industry or that of his fathers."

[9] He added that if an individual's wealth becomes so overgrown that it seems a danger to the State, the best corrective would not be discriminatory taxation but a law compelling equal inheritance in equal degree by all the heirs.

polls, William Jennings Bryan, leading the last stand of agrarianism as an independent political power, was still striving to give his cause the color of respectability by showing that, after all, the farmer too was a businessman!

4

The practical conduct of foreign relations forced the Jeffersonians into a position no less frustrating than the maintenance of Hamilton's domestic system. In the East they found themselves almost as dependent on foreign commerce as were the sea traders of New England; their cheapest manufactured goods were bought abroad, and abroad their surplus was sold. In the West, where they looked about hungrily for new lands, fear of the Indians and of the closure of their trade outlet at New Orleans intensified their expanionist appetites. Expansion of their export market on the land and defense of it on the sea finally started them on a headlong retreat from Jeffersonian principles.

Jefferson himself was both a fierce patriot and a sincere pacifist. During the Napoleonic Wars, when England and France began to prey upon American commerce, he tried to retaliate by a pacifist policy of economic coercion. In December 1807 Congress passed his drastic Embargo Act, which simply confined American ships to port. His aim was to bring both sides to terms by withholding food and other supplies. This was the one doctrinaire and impractical measure of his career, and it proved a miserable failure. The Embargo not only failed to force Britain and France to respect American rights on the high seas, but also brought economic paralysis to the trading cities of the Northeast and the farms and plantations of the West and South. Jefferson finally admitted that the fifteen months of its operation cost more than a war. At the close of his second term the Embargo was replaced by a Nonintercourse Act, which opened trade with the rest of Europe but continued the costly ban on England and France.

Although Jefferson's successor, James Madison, continued to be harried by the maritime controversy, it was expansionism—what John Randolph called "agrarian cupidity"—rather than free trade that in the end brought the War of 1812. Southern planters wanted the Floridas and Northern farmers wanted Canada. Jefferson, always an ardent expansionist, approved of both aims and accepted the popular clichés with which expansion was justified. ("The possession of Canada," he wrote Adams in the summer of 1812, "secures our women and children forever from the tomahawk and scalping knife, by removing those who excite them.") As Julius W. Pratt has shown, enthusiasm for war with England raged along the broad arc of the frontier; resistance to war was hottest in the old Federalist and mercantile sections.

But if the United States was to withdraw from Europe economically, as under Jefferson, or to lose its best market through war, as under Madison, it had to find a way of employing its energies and supplying its people with manufactured goods. Accordingly, capital, cut off from its normal investment outlet in overseas commerce, began to turn to manufacturing. The period of the Embargo and the War of 1812 proved to be the seedtime of American industrialism; Henry Adams remarked on the ironic fact that "American manufactures owed more to Jefferson than to northern statesmen who merely encouraged them after they were established."

Jefferson, of course, realized the immediate implications of his desire to pursue an independent economic course and as early as 1805 became a convert to the development of manufactures. "The spirit of manufacture has taken deep root among us," he wrote Dupont in 1809, "and its foundations are laid in too great expense to be abandoned." "Our enemy," he wailed to William Short in 1814, "has indeed the consolation of Satan on removing our first

parents from Paradise: from a peaceable and agricultural nation he makes us a military and manufacturing one." To another he wrote: "We must now place the manufacturer by the side of the agriculturist." If the United States was to be peaceful, it must be self-sufficient, must end its dependence on foreign goods and overseas trade. The Napoleonic Wars destroyed the Jeffersonian dream of an agrarian commonwealth. Since Jeffersonian democracy, as embodied in measures of public policy, was entirely dependent on the agrarian order, these wars also erased the practical distinction between Republicans and Federalists.

Manufactures, if they were to be maintained, needed tariffs, especially when British capitalists, hoping to crush their new competitors at once, began dumping goods in the American market at the close of the war. In 1816 the Republicans passed a much higher tariff than Hamilton's. They, not the Federalists, began the American protective system.

And war must be financed. Hard hit by the economic drain of military operations and the financial sabotage of the Northeast, the Republicans were confronted with a bitter dilemma: either they must go begging to the fiscal interests for support, or they must charter a new national bank to fill the vacuum they had created by letting Hamilton's bank expire. They chose the second course—and soon Republican newspapers were reprinting Alexander Hamilton's arguments in favor of the constitutionality of the First Bank of the United States! In vain did Jefferson rage in his letters against the banking system. A second bank, similar in structure to Hamilton's, was chartered by the Republicans in 1816. By the end of that year Jefferson's party had taken over the whole complex of Federalist policies—manufactures, bank, tariffs, army, navy, and all—and this under the administration of Jefferson's friend, neighbor, and political heir, James Madison. As Josiah Quincy complained, the Republicans had "out-Federalized Federalism." By 1820 they

had driven the rival party completely off the field, but only at the cost of taking over its program. Federalism, Jefferson wrote to Albert Gallatin in 1823, "has changed its name and hidden itself among us . . . as strong as it has ever been since 1800." Nathaniel Macon, one of the last of the intransigent agrarians, lamented: "The opinions of Jefferson and those who were with him are forgot."

And Jefferson himself? He lived through his last years without bitterness or anger, certainly without a sense of defeat. His country, in spite of one short-lived depression, was growing and flourishing, and as he looked down upon it from his mountaintop he predicted hopefully that the process of civilization would continue to sweep across the continent from east to west "like a cloud of light." He busied himself answering his voluminous correspondence, interpreting for inquirers the history of his times, trading opinions with scientists and inventors, trying to steady his failing fortunes, and laying the foundations of the University of Virginia, which gave him special pride. He renewed his old friendship with John Adams, and once again argued with him the case of democracy. At the age of seventy-eight he wrote to the old man at Quincy: "I shall not die without a hope that light and liberty are on steady advance." When Adams asked if he would choose to live his life over again, he replied in the affirmative, at least for the greater part of it. "From twenty-five to sixty, I would say yes; and I might go further back, but not come lower down." "I enjoy good health," he went on, "I am happy in what is around me, yet I assure you I am ripe for leaving all, this year, this day, this hour. Nothing proves more than this that the Being who presides over the world is essentially benevolent."

Here speaks the antithesis of the tragic temperament. Through all Jefferson's work there runs like a fresh underground stream the deep

conviction that all will turn out well, that life will somehow assert itself. Wherever he was, he managed to find it good, and in these last years he never felt the need of moving more than a few miles from Monticello. Life had always come more than halfway to meet him, just as visitors now came from everywhere in the Western World to find him out on his mountain. For him no defeat could ever be more than a temporary interruption in the smooth flow of things toward their beneficent end. It was not, after all, a system of economics or politics that he was leaving, not even a political party, but an imperishable faith expressed in imperishable rhetoric. It did not matter that his agrarianism was in retreat, that his particularism was falling into the hands of proslavery apologists whom he would have detested, that his individualism would become the doctrine of plutocrats and robber barons. His sense of values would survive. Men like Hamilton could argue that manufactures ought to be promoted because they would enable the nation to use the labor of women and children, "many of them at a tender age," but Jefferson was outraged at such a view of humanity. Hamilton schemed to get the children into factories; Jefferson planned school systems. While Hamilton valued institutions and abstractions, Jefferson valued people and found no wealth more important than life. If he had gone astray as to means, he had at least kept his eyes on his original end—the pursuit of happiness.

One of the last survivors among the founders, Jefferson lived to see himself become an object of veneration, and as his life ebbed out he might easily have observed with the dying Roman Emperor: "I feel myself becoming a god." But he had no desire that he and his contemporaries should become oracles to future generations. "The earth," he was fond of saying, "belongs to the living." The world changes, and truths cannot be embalmed.

Some men look at constitutions with sanctimonious reverence, and deem them like the ark of the covenant, too sacred to be touched. They ascribe to the preceding age a wisdom more than human, and suppose what they did to be beyond amendment. I knew that age well; I belonged to it and labored with it. It deserved well of its country. It was very like the present, but without the experience of the present; and forty years of experience in government is worth a century of book-reading; and this they would say themselves, were they to rise from the dead. I am certainly not an advocate for frequent and untried changes in laws and institutions. . . . But I know also, that laws and institutions must go hand in hand with the progress of the human mind. As that becomes more developed, more enlightened, as new discoveries are made, new truths disclosed, and manners and opinions change with the change of circumstances, institutions must advance also, and keep pace with the times. We might as well require a man to wear still the coat which fitted him when a boy, as civilized society to remain ever under the regime of their barbarous ancestors.

Two years before his death he wrote: "Nothing then is unchangeable but the inherent and unalienable rights of man."

13

The Gods Invite Us to Glory

John Dos Passos

Aaron Burr was an unusual, charismatic, many-sided man. As the editors of *American Heritage* put it, "No one who met him ever forgot him. His charm captivated beautiful women, his eloquence moved the United States Senate to tears, his political skills carried him to the very threshold of the White House. Yet while still Vice President he was indicted for murder, and was already dreaming the dreams of empire that would bring him to trial for treason." John Dos Passos, who achieved eminence both as a novelist and an historian, tells Burr's story with such dramatic impact, with such a feel for character and a sense for tragicomedy, that his account stands as a supreme example of history as a literary art.

About eleven o'clock on the night of February 18 or 19, he never could remember which, in the year of our Lord 1807, a backwoods lawyer named Nicholas Perkins who headed the federal land office in Mississippi Territory left the group around the fire in Sheriff Theo-

dore Brightwell's log tavern and went to the door for a breath of fresh air. It was a night of clear frosty moonlight. Perkins could see far down the rutted road. Though he was described as a fearless giant of a man, and a major in the territorial militia, Perkins was startled to see two horsemen come riding up out of the forest.

The smaller of the horsemen rode right past. He was a shabby-looking little fellow lost under a broad-brimmed beaver hat. His companion reined in his horse and asked Perkins the way to Major Hinson's. His name, it turned out, was Major Robert Ashley.

Perkins told Ashley that the major was away from home, and added that, on account of a freshet, the flooding of the creeks would make it hard for a stranger to reach the Hinson house that night. The sensible thing would be to put up at the tavern, where there was refreshment for man and beast. Ashley insisted they must push on, so Perkins told him the best places to ford the streams. While he was talking to Ashley, Perkins kept staring at the first traveller, who had pulled up his horse thirty or forty yards up the road. Something about the man aroused his suspicions.

Perkins had read President Jefferson's proclamation warning of a treasonous conspiracy on the Mississippi, and the territorial governor's proclamation that followed it offering a reward of two thousand dollars for the apprehension of the former Vice President of the United States, Colonel Aaron Burr. Colonel Burr was said to have jumped his bail at Natchez, 200 miles to the west, two weeks before. Perkins scratched his head as he walked to the fire. These men were up to no good. Mightn't the little man with the hatbrim flapped over his face be Aaron Burr himself?

Right away Perkins routed the sheriff, who was related to Mrs. Hinson, out of bed. They

saddled their horses and rode off after the travellers. They found Ashley in the Hinson's front room. When she heard voices she knew, Mrs. Hinson, who'd been hiding in the back of the house in a fright ever since the strangers walked in, let herself be seen, and started to fry up some supper for her visitors.

The small man sat warming himself beside the kitchen fire, his hat still pulled down over his face. Perkins observed him narrowly. He wore a boatman's ragged pantaloons and a coarse blanket wrap-around belted in by a strap. The hat that had once been white was stained and shabby, but the riding boots on his very small feet were elegant and new. Perkins caught one quick glance of his eyes from under the brim of the hat and was convinced that the man must be Colonel Burr. Everybody spoke of how Burr could look clear through you with his lustrous black eyes.

He took Ashley aside and asked him point-blank if his companion was Colonel Burr. Ashley became agitated and walked out of the house without a word.

Perkins began to feel the two thousand dollars almost in the palm of his hand, but he had to move with circumspection. The little colonel was held in great respect in the western country —and he was known to be a dead shot. Mumbling a misleading excuse, Perkins rode off in a hurry, borrowed a canoe, and went speeding down the flooding Tombigbee River to a palisade named Fort Stoddert, the last American fortification before the frontier of Spanish West Florida.

Arriving there about daybreak, he roused Lieutenant Edmund P. Gaines, commander of the federal detachment, and told him he had the traitor Burr in his grasp. Right at this moment Burr would be starting down the trail to Pensacola; there was no way to cross the river except at Mrs. Carson's ferry. The lieutenant ordered out a file of mounted soldiers, and they galloped off to intercept him.

They found Burr and his companion on the

Aaron Burr. Although he was the son of a president of Princeton University, black-eyed and hawk-faced Aaron Burr was a consummate manipulator, adventurer, and visionary with an instinct for intrigue. (Courtesy of The Library of Congress.)

trail of the ferry. The sheriff, whom Burr seemed to have completely fascinated in a few minutes' conversation, was acting as their guide to the Spanish border. Colonel Burr pointed out to the young lieutenant the risk he took in making an arrest without a warrant. The lieutenant brought out the President's proclamation and that of the territorial governor. Burr declared both were illegal and unconstitutional. The lieutenant insisted that he was an officer in the United States Army and had to do his duty. Colonel Burr would be treated with all the respect due a former Vice President of the United States—if he made no effort to escape. The little colonel was conducted back to the fort and shut up in a room. Dinner was served him in solitary state. Sentries were posted at the windows and doors. Ashley meanwhile had managed to disappear into the woods.

Lieutenant Gaines and Perkins started racking their brains as to how they could get their

prisoner safely to Washington, D.C. The weather was freezing and drizzly. There were no roads yet through the enormous woodlands of Mississippi Territory. The country abounded in Indians of doubtful loyalty. Rumors had enormously magnified the size of Burr's expedition. For all Gaines and Perkins knew, the back country was full of partisans grouping to rescue their leader.

There was nothing for it but for Lieutenant Gaines to take the little colonel into his family under a sort of parole. Gaines' brother, who was government factor to the Choctaw nation, was ill in bed. Burr showed himself the soul of tact and courtesy. Explaining that he'd picked up a certain amount of medical information on his travels, he helped nurse the brother back to health. Meanwhile, he sat at his bedside keeping him amused with sprightly talk about Indian quirks and customs. At the table he fascinated the family with his knowledge of books and pictures and the great world. He fixed his black eyes on the ladies with respectful attention. He played chess with Mrs. Gaines. So long as he stayed at Fort Stoddert not a word passed his lips about the failure of his western project, or about his arrest or his plans.

Lieutenant Gaines was counting the hours until he should see the last of his charming prisoner, whose friends had spread the story that the aim of Burr's thwarted expedition was to drive the Spaniards out of West Florida. As that was the dearest wish of every settler in the Mississippi Territory, expressions of sympathy were heard on every hand. "A week longer," Gaines wrote to his commander, "[and] the consequences would have been of a most serious nature."

At last the floods subsided to the point where Gaines felt it would be safe to try to take his prisoner up the Alabama River. The party was rowed in a government boat. When they stopped at John Mills' house on the Tensaw River, the ladies of the family all wept over the sorrows of Colonel Burr. Indeed a certain Mrs.

Johnson was so moved by his plight that when a boy was born to her some months later, she named him Aaron Burr. "When a lady does me the honor to name me the father of her child," Burr was wont to remark, "I trust I shall always be too gallant to show myself ungrateful for the favor."

At a boat yard at the head of navigation on the Alabama, Gaines turned his prisoner over to Perkins, Perkins' friend Thomas Malone, and a guard of six men, including two federal soldiers with muskets, to be conducted to Washington, D.C. Gaines sent them off under the strictest injunction not to speak to their prisoner or listen to his blandishments, and to shoot to kill at his first effort to escape.

The lieutenant had found them good horses. Riding thirty or forty miles a day, avoiding the settlements, they hurried their prisoner along Indian traces through drowned woodlands. It was a rainy March. The nights were cold. Wolves howled about their campfires. Half the time they were drenched to the skin. Burr's fortitude amazed his guards. Never a word of complaint. Never a sign of fatigue. He rode his fine horse with as much style, so one of the guards told his friends, as if he were at the head of his New York regiment.

They crossed the rivers in Indian canoes, swimming their horses alongside. At last, on the Oconee River in the state of Georgia, they found a ferry and an inn not far beyond. For the first time since leaving the Alabama country they slept under a roof. When they crossed into South Carolina, Perkins redoubled his precautions. He knew that Joseph Alston, the husband of Burr's beloved daughter, Theodosia, was a member of the legislature. Public sentiment there was supposed to be strong for Burr. Perkins arranged his cavalcade in a square with Burr in the middle. Two riders went ahead of him, two on either flank, and two behind. They passed through towns and villages at a brisk trot.

In the village of Chester, about fifty miles

south of the North Carolina border, they rode past an inn. From inside came a sound of music and dancing, and a crowd had gathered to look in the windows. The prisoner suddenly jumped from his horse and cried out to the bystanders that he was Aaron Burr under military arrest, and must be taken to a magistrate. Perkins dismounted at one leap with a pistol in either hand and ordered Burr to remount.

"I will not," cried Burr.

Perkins, a man of enormous strength, dropped his pistols and, grabbing the little colonel round the waist, lifted him back on his horse as if he were a child. Malone grabbed Burr's reins, pulled them over his horse's head, and led him off as fast as he could while the guards formed up around him. Before the astonished villagers could open their mouths the cavalcade was lost in the dust. Aaron Burr broke into a flood of tears. Malone, who rode beside him, was so distressed at his prisoner's humiliation that he found tears streaming down his own face. It was the man's eyes that moved him so, Malone told his friends afterward: his eyes were like stars.

Aaron Burr, at fifty-one, had reached the end of his rope.

If ever a man was born to eminence it was Aaron Burr. On both sides of his family he was descended from clergymen, the aristocrats of colonial New England. Burr's father, though a Connecticut man, was the second president and virtual founder of the College of New Jersey, later Princeton University. His mother's father was the famous Jonathan Edwards, who preached predestined damnation so vividly that once a congregation ran out of the church in terror. On both sides there were strains of madness among the eminent divines. Burr early showed that he had inherited the family brains —and certain idiosyncrasies as well. He was only sixteen when he was graduated with honors from Princeton. While his classmates

declaimed against taxation without representation, young Aaron graced the commencement with an Addisonian essay on building castles in the air.

After a winter's study of his grandfather's theology, he borrowed the best horse in his tutor's stable and rode off for Connecticut, declaring that predestined damnation was an unchristian doctrine. While a student at the Litchfield Law School, he put in more time piercing the hearts of the village girls with his intense black gaze than in memorizing Coke's Littleton. At the outbreak of the Revolutionary War he hurried to Cambridge in hopes of a commission. General Washington turned him down, so it was as a gentleman volunteer that in 1775 he joined Benedict Arnold's expedition against Quebec.

In view of his delicate frame his hardihood surprised his mates. He met privations fearlessly. Having at last procured a captain's commission from General Richard Montgomery, he walked beside the tall, laughing Irishman on the snowy night when they attempted to assault the lower city of Quebec. When the vanguard was cut down by a burst of grapeshot, Captain Burr distinguished himself by trying to drag the huge carcass of his fallen chief back to the American lines. Before reaching twenty he was counted a national hero.

Washington invited him to join his staff. Young Burr made sport of his Commander in Chief's spelling, and criticized his handling of the New York campaign. At Valley Forge he was one of the grumblers, and, for all his services, the highest rank he attained was that of lieutenant colonel. At Monmouth he disobeyed orders and led his regiment into a British ambush. His horse was shot from under him. Shock and frustration brought on an illness which eventually caused him to resign from the service in the spring of 1779. If Colonel Burr did not appreciate General Washington, it had also become clear that General Washington did not appreciate Colonel Burr.

Burr was nursed back to health by a motherly lady named Theodosia Prevost. Though she was the wife of a British army officer, Mrs. Prevost entertained so charmingly during lulls in the war in the Jerseys that her stone house at Paramus became popular with George Washington and his staff. Her husband died in 1779. In July of 1782 Burr induced her to marry him, though she was ten years older than he. A year later they settled in New York, where he took up the law in earnest. The city was a paradise for young lawyers who had served in the Continental Army, since all Tory attorneys had been disbarred. Soon Burr had a practice rivalled only by Alexander Hamilton's.

The law led to politics. Burr climbed fast. He cast his lot with Jefferson's Democratic-Republicans when Governor Clinton made him attorney general of the state of New York. He served the Clinton faction so well they sent him to the United States Senate. During the years of the growth of the Jeffersonian party, he built himself a strong political machine in New York City. His wife died, leaving him a daughter he adored.

It was young Theodosia, hardly into her teens, who presided at Burr's great dinners at Richmond Hill, his country place on the outskirts of Greenwich Village, the same house which Washington had made his headquarters and which John Adams occupied as Vice President. Meanwhile Burr's ambitions became national. Though outwardly friends, Burr and Hamilton were now bitter rivals for the control of ward politics in the city. Gossip claimed they were rivals too for the favors of a young woman named Eliza Bowen, who was one of the city's better-known harlots. But setting the best table and pouring the choicest wines in New York cost a great deal, and Burr was dangerously in debt.

In the bitter presidential campaign of 1800, which brought about the defeat of Adams and the Federalists, Burr and his "Little Band"—a group of young hotspurs he had gathered around him—were instrumental in holding New York in the Republican column. By a fluke in the procedure, though nobody seems to have intended Burr for the Presidency, the vote in the Electoral College was a tie: seventy-three for Jefferson and seventy-three for Burr. After thirty-six ballots the House of Representatives finally chose Jefferson, and Burr was elected Vice President.

Just before the long stalemate in the House, Burr presided over the wedding of his darling Theodosia to Joseph Alston, member of a wealthy and powerful family of South Carolina planters. Friends of his daughter in New York wondered whether Aaron Burr had bartered Theodosia's hand for the eight votes from South Carolina that helped cause the tie. In any event, his connection with the wealthy Alstons certainly helped keep his creditors at bay.

Though Burr was an able presiding officer in the Senate, President Jefferson, like General Washington before him, soon began to show a lack of confidence in him. The New York Burrites were disappointed by the small share of federal patronage that went their way. The Louisiana Purchase, by threatening to upset the balance of power among the original states, stung some extreme Federalists in New England into agitating for secession and thereafter Burr's politics began to change. Jefferson's control of the Republican Party would bar his way to renomination. Plainly, Burr's future now lay with the Federalists.

Burr's ambitions began to build him a castle in the air. If he could get himself elected governor of New York, when the time was ripe he might swing that state into a New England federation. As scion of two great New England families, he would be in line for the presidency of a new government. The Little Band went to work with a will.

Hamilton, who had been instrumental in trying to swing votes away from Burr to Jefferson in the House of Representatives, again stood

in the way. He was letting it be known he considered Burr "the Catiline of America." And Burr, having lost the support of the upstate Republicans, needed the Federalists to win. In the June, 1804, gubernatorial election he carried New York City, but upstate the various Republican factions combined to snow him under. In bitter frustration he challenged Hamilton to a duel.

The bullet that killed Alexander Hamilton that early July morning on the Weehawken shore put an end to Aaron Burr's political career. By a strange ricochet Hamilton's death also ruined the plans of the New England secessionists: Republicans and Federalists united to mourn the great man dead. Burr was denounced as a murderer. Proceedings were instituted to indict him in New York and New Jersey, and in spite of his office the Vice President became a fugitive from justice.

He made off to Philadelphia. From there he wrote Theodosia that he was retiring to a friend's plantation to the southward. Only the risk of crossing the lowlands in the malarial season kept him from paying her a visit. Already her little son, Aaron Burr Alston, was the center of his grandfather's ambitious dreams.

He kept her posted on his prospects of marrying a wealthy woman. "If any male friend of yours should be dying of ennui, recommend to him to engage in a duel and a courtship at the same time. . . ." She must ignore stories of attempts to assassinate him: "Those who wish me dead prefer to keep at a very respectful distance. . . . I am very well and not without occupation and amusement."

The Plotters

The occupation Aaron Burr found so amusing in Philadelphia was plotting a dream castle even more breathtaking than the one that had just collapsed. He found a kindred spirit in his old friend Jonathan Dayton, U.S. Senator from New Jersey. The two dreamers turned their eyes far from Philadelphia, looking to exciting prospects both in Europe and the new American West.

Bonaparte's successes in Europe were tantalizing every ambitious schemer of the age. His victory over the Spanish Bourbons had knocked the props out from under the Spanish dominions in the New World. Out of the weakening of Spanish power in Mexico and the restless land hunger of the American settlers beyond the Alleghenies, men with a knack for leadership should be able to build themselves a Napoleonic empire on the Mississippi. Burr and Dayton would mask the early stages of their enterprise behind a perfectly reasonable project to build a canal around the falls of the Ohio opposite Louisville.

Since anyone who summered in Washington City was thought to be risking his life from malaria, most of the diplomatic corps spent the hot months in Philadelphia. Waiting on the British minister, Anthony Merry, was Colonel Charles Williamson, with whom Burr had been associated in land deals in upstate New York. Though Williamson had assumed American citizenship in order to take title to real estate, he was a retired British army officer and a long-term agent of the Foreign Office. Williamson had for years been urging on His Majesty's government a scheme to curb the growing power of the United States by spreading British influence down the Mississippi. The Louisiana Purchase had ruined these plans. When Burr let drop the suggestion that the settlers on the western waters might be induced to secede from the Union, Williamson caught fire.

Mr. Merry, who had nothing but scorn for President Jefferson and his levelling democratic tendencies, could hardly conceal his pleasurable astonishment when Burr declared to him outright that, given a naval force and financial backing, he would "effect the separation of the western part of the United States." Burr could

speak with authority: after all, he was still Vice President.

On August 6, 1804, Merry urged consideration of Burr's plan in a dispatch to the Foreign Office. Colonel Williamson, soon to set sail for England, would explain the details. Though Merry admitted "the profligacy of Mr. Burr's character" and acknowledged that he had been "cast off as much by the democratic as by the Federal Party," he insisted that Burr "still preserves connections with some people of influence, added to his great ambition and a spirit of revenge against the present Administration." These factors, he wrote, "may possibly induce him to exert the talents and activity which he possesses with fidelity to his Employers."

With the Hamilton murder indictments still hanging over his head, Burr had to keep out of the way of the sheriff. He wangled an invitation from one of the Georgia senators to visit his plantation on St. Simon Island. With a follower named Sam Swartwout in attendance, he set out in high spirits on a coastal vessel. While the ship beat its way down the coast against light summer breezes, he had plenty of time to indulge himself with the glorious prospects of his great scheme.

First he would establish a government at New Orleans, and then he would launch a two-pronged expedition against Spanish Mexico. One army would advance overland while a naval expedition would disembark at Veracruz or the Rio Pánuco. All this would cost a great deal of money, but his interview with the British minister had opened up the prospect of a copious source of funds. With British help Burr would conquer Mexico. The Mexicans would flock to his standard. He was already counting all the fresh silver dollars that would flow from the Mexican mint.

The dream swelled to grand dimensions. There would be no more republican nonsense. Mexico would proclaim him emperor. He would govern with the aid of a council of worthies made up of the best brains in the land. Theodosia would be empress apparent, and little Gamp (Burr and his grandson each called the other Gamp) heir to the throne.

But by early December Burr was back in Washington presiding with his usual punctilious gravity over the Senate. Senator William Plumer of New Hampshire, the diarist of the session, found him changed. "He appears to have lost those easy graceful manners that beguiled the hours away last session—He is now uneasy, discontented & hurried.—So true it is 'great guilt ne'er knew great joy at heart.'" Plumer set to wondering what Burr's future would be. "He can never I think rise again. But surely he is a very extraordinary man & is an exception to all rules. . . . And considering of what materials the mass of men are formed—how easily they are gulled—& considering how little restraint laws human or divine have on his mind, it is impossible to say what he will attempt—or what he may obtain."

Burr's last appearance before Congress wound up all business on March 2, 1805, was impressive. He delivered the most effective address of his career. "This house is a sanctuary," he declaimed, "a citadel of law, of order, and of liberty; it is here—it is here in this exalted refuge, here, if anywhere, will resistance be made to the storms of political phrenzy and the silent arts of corruption; and if the Constitution be destined ever to perish by the sacrilegious hands of the demagogue or the usurper, which God avert, its expiring agonies will be witnessed on this floor."

When he walked out of the hushed chamber, many senators were in tears.

The Paths of Glory

Two weeks later Burr was back in Philadelphia telling Anthony Merry that the French inhabitants of Louisiana were ready to revolt against the United States and to ask for the protection of Great Britain. He suggested that

the Foreign Office send as consul at New Orleans a confidential agent who spoke French, and arrange for a flotilla of two or three frigates and some smaller vessels to blockade the mouth of the river when Burr established his government there. For himself he requested an immediate loan of one hundred thousand pounds.

The same day that Mr. Merry transmitted this remarkable request for the consideration of his government, Burr wrote Theodosia that he was off for the West. He found the trip down the Ohio River a tonic to his spirits. Below Marietta he stopped at an island that was one of the showplaces of the region. A rich immigrant named Harman Blennerhassett had built himself a mansion there with gardens and parklands in the English style, almost ruining himself in the process. Blennerhassett, a graduate of Trinity College, Dublin, was a big, gangling, nearsighted man with some learning but not a trace of common sense. To the settlers up and down the Ohio he was known, half in affection, half in derision, as "Blanny." Blanny was away during Burr's first visit, but Burr was entertained by Mrs. Blennerhassett, described as an accomplished and well-educated woman who was pining for talk of music and books on that far frontier. Colonel Burr had at his tongue's tip all the fashionable conversation of the age. One contemporary historian claimed that Burr played Ulysses to Mrs. Blennerhassett's Calypso. Be that as it may, from that moment on, the Blennerhassetts, man and wife, were as fascinated by the little colonel as a pair of cuckoos by a snake.

By mid-May Burr was in Cincinnati, being entertained by Jonathan Dayton's colleague in the Senate, a busy Jack-of-all-trades named John Smith, who was storekeeper, land speculator, Baptist preacher, and politician. Dayton joined them. The three men put their heads together. The plan took shape.

Leaving his boat to follow the curves of the river, Burr rode briskly across country into Tennessee. The early summer weather was fine.

He enjoyed the riding. No word in public of secession, only of a coming war with Spain; that was his posture. His progress became a personal triumph. Without quite saying so he managed to give the impression that his good friend Henry Dearborn, the Secretary of War, was only waiting for a declaration of war to put him in command of an expedition against the Spanish possessions. In Nashville he was tendered a public dinner. Andrew Jackson grasped him warmly by the hand and took him home to the Hermitage.

An enthusiastic duellist himself, Jackson considered the hue and cry against Burr over the death of Hamilton damnable persecution. And an expedition against the Dons had his hearty approval. General Jackson furnished Burr a boat to take him down the Cumberland River to Fort Massac, on the lower Ohio near present-day Cairo, Illinois, where he was to pick up his own boat again. There Burr at last caught up with an old acquaintance he had determined on as his second in command. This was Brigadier General James Wilkinson, General in Chief of the small Army of the United States.

The General in Chief

Wilkinson was then nearing fifty, short, red-faced, and corpulent from high living; grown gray before his time, so he liked to put it, in the service of his country. Like Burr he had served under Arnold in the botched Canadian expedition, but unlike Burr he had found promotion quick and easy.

Luck always seemed to be with young Wilkinson. By a series of fortunate chances he caught Washington's eye in a lucky moment at Trenton. General Horatio Gates, to whose headquarters staff he had transferred, found him pliable and sympathetic, a young officer adept at scrounging up a meal or a drink or a wench. In 1777 Wilkinson was promoted to

deputy adjutant-general and brevetted brigadier general. In his memoirs he took credit for
choosing General Gates' fine position on Bemis
Heights and so bringing about Burgoyne's surrender.

Wilkinson had just turned twenty-one when
he married Ann Biddle, the attractive daughter
of a Quaker innkeeper rising in Philadelphia
society. Because of some association with the
discredited anti-Washington "Conway Cabal,"
Wilkinson had thought it prudent to resign
from active service, but the young man had a
way of ingratiating himself. Plump, popeyed,
and convivial, he somehow slipped in and out
of scrapes and scandals without leaving bad
feelings behind. Finding a living hard to come
by on the Bucks County farm he took over from
a dispossessed Tory, he sold it in 1784, piled
his wife and two children into a carriage and
his household goods into a Conestoga wagon,
and set out for Kentucky. As agent for the
Philadelphia firm of Barclay, Moylan and Co.,
he opened a general store in Lexington.

In Kentucky he was in his element. Store-
keepers were making fortunes. Speculation in
military land grants held out prospects of
wealth to every settler. Politics was a hive of
intrigue. Not many months passed before
young Wilkinson had outrun George Rogers
Clark as the spokesman for the grievances of
the frontiersmen along the Ohio.

When the Spanish attempted to close the
Mississippi to American commerce in 1786, it
could have meant ruin to the Kentuckians,
especially Wilkinson, who invested in everything. He dealt in land. He speculated in cargoes
for export. His livelihood depended on trade
through New Orleans. Along with his business
associate, Judge Harry Innes, he promoted the
notion that the future of Kentucky depended
on accommodation with the Spaniards, and he
developed a real knack for dealing with them.

In the spring of 1787 he made his way down
the Mississippi. His handsome gifts, such as
the pair of blooded horses he presented to the
commander at Natchez, opened every door.

During the two months he spent in New Orleans, he and the Spanish governor, Don Esteban Miró, became thick as thieves. Wilkinson
confided in Don Esteban that though he had a
poor head for figures he had noticed that
tobacco which could be bought for two dollars
a hundredweight in Kentucky sold for nine
and a half at the royal warehouse in New Orleans. Why not let him have the monopoly of
the traffic down the Mississippi?

Don Esteban was no mean horse trader. Joining in the monopoly of the tobacco trade would
require a somewhat hazardous interpretation of
the royal regulations. He demanded a *quid pro
quo*. Wilkinson intimated that there might be
services he could perform for His Most Catholic Majesty.

Always an eager penman, Wilkinson set to
work to draft a memorial setting forth for the
Spanish officials the benefits that would accrue
to them from a separation of the western settlements from the Atlantic states. Don Esteban
was eager for news of disaffection in Kentucky.
He pointed out that it would be a graceful gesture, as a mere formality between men of the
world, if the General would sign an oath of
allegiance to the Spanish sovereign. That grateful monarch furnished pensions to his retainers.
Wilkinson signed, and his name was entered
in the secret ledgers of the Ministry for the
Colonies as Agent Number Thirteen. Two
thousand silver dollars a year was mentioned
as a suitable honorarium.

The tobacco monopoly failed to prove as
lucrative as Wilkinson expected. His Spanish
pension appeared intermittently. By 1790, high
living and careless speculation had reduced him
to bankruptcy. He applied for a commission in
the new Army of the United States that President Washington was organizing to protect
the frontier, and soon attained his old rank of
brigadier. When Burr became Vice President,
Wilkinson felt he had a friend at court. They
had become intimate as young men in the days
of the Conway Cabal, and occasionally corresponded in a private cipher. He had every rea-

son for feeling cordial toward Burr, whose influence was thought by some to have brought Wilkinson the appointment, in 1805, as governor of the Territory of Louisiana. Furthermore, Burr's elimination of Hamilton left Wilkinson the ranking general officer in the United States Army.

Now, in June of 1805, the congenial pair spent four days together at Fort Massac tracing out the trails to Mexico on their maps. With Wilkinson's help, Burr believed, his project was certain of success.

The War Department, Tennessee, Kentucky, Ohio—all were in the palm of his hand. Now he must sound out the Creoles, the French-speaking natives of New Orleans, who were restive under the new regulations—and taxes—imposed by the Americans since the Louisiana Purchase. Wilkinson may have had his doubts, but if Burr did manage his coup, he wanted to be in on the loot. He offered Colonel Burr every civility.

"The general and his officers," Burr wrote Theodosia, "fitted me out with an elegant barge, sails, colours and ten oars, with a sergeant and ten able faithful hands."

In New Orleans Colonel Burr was soon the toast of the Vieux Carré. He was dined by the very Jeffersonian governor of Orleans Territory, W. C. C. Claiborne, and set up to grand turnouts by members of the Mexican Association, made up of buccaneering characters on fire to make their fortunes by promoting a new revolution in Mexico. He fluttered the hearts of the Creole beauties with his mysterious charm. He became fluent in bad French. He was attentive to the Catholic bishop, who like much of the local Spanish clergy was disgusted with the subjection of his homeland to the infidel French and eager for the independence of Mexico. As Burr told the story, the bishop sent off three Jesuit priests to prepare the Mexicans for Colonel Burr's expedition.

New Orleans seemed so ripe for Burr's plans that he felt he had to have fresh interviews with Andrew Jackson and General Wilkinson.

After leaving New Orleans and spending a few days in Natchez ("and saw some tears of regret as I left it"—he kept boasting of his conquests in his letters to his daughter), he rode north along the Natchez Trace, "drinking the nasty puddle-water, covered with green scum, and full of animalculae—bah!" into the clear air of the Tennessee mountains.

From Nashville he wrote Theodosia: "For a week I have been lounging at the house of General Jackson, once a lawyer, after a judge, now a planter; a man of intelligence, and one of those prompt, frank, ardent souls I love to meet." To Andrew Jackson he said not a word about secession or funds from the British, but talked long of Santa Fe and his contacts with the Mexican patriots. He declared that the Mexican Association in New Orleans was behind him to a man.

A new project was rising on his horizon as a cover-up for his secret plan. While Louisiana was still under the control of the Dons, the Spanish governor had granted an enormous area—1,200,000 acres—of fertile land on the Ouachita River to a certain Baron de Bastrop. This tract was now, supposedly, on the market. Burr would find funds to buy it.

Burr's physical energy was inexhaustible. From Nashville he rode 250 miles to St. Louis for a second conference with General Wilkinson, who had now taken up his post as governor of the Louisiana Territory. As usual the two men enjoyed each other's company. Wilkinson was a great trencherman and amusing over his wine. Now Burr could report to him amid considerable merrymaking that General Jackson would march for Mexico at the drop of a hat. The Bastrop lands, which by this time Burr felt he virtually owned, would make them all rich, if everything else failed. They reached the point of drawing up lists of officers for their army.

By mid-November Burr was back in Washington, D.C., calling on Anthony Merry. Mr. Merry had disappointing news. His first dispatches had been lost at sea when a British

packet was captured by the French. Duplicates had so far elicited no response from the Foreign Office. Jonathan Dayton, whom Burr had hoped would be on hand during the summer to fan Mr. Merry's enthusiasm for the scheme, had been delayed by illness and had only just arrived.

Though Merry wrote the Foreign Office on November 25, 1805, that Burr showed every sign of distress at the bad news, it didn't take the little colonel long to rally his spirits. He refused to be discouraged. He now demanded £110,000 and three ships of the line as well as the several frigates and smaller vessels to cruise off the mouth of the Mississippi. He set March of 1806 for the beginning of operations. The revolution in New Orleans would follow in April or May. He told Merry he had found a deposit there of ten thousand stand of arms and fifty-six pieces of artillery abandoned by the French. He must have "pecuniary aid" by February.

He held out a glittering prospect to the Foreign Office. As a result of the *coup d'état* to set up a western federation, "the Eastern States will separate themselves immediately from the Southern:—and . . . thus the immense power which has risen up with such rapidity in the Western Hemisphere will, by such a division, be rendered at once informidable."

A few days later Colonel Burr dined with President Jefferson. It didn't take much conversation to discover another check to his plans. Jefferson believed his envoys in Paris were about to accomplish a deal through Talleyrand to purchase the Floridas. He had dropped any project for a war with Spain.

Burr Writes a Letter

News of Burr's goings and comings could hardly be kept out of the newspapers. For all his successful intriguing, Wilkinson was famous for his indiscretions when he'd had too much to drink, and that was almost every time

the wine was uncorked after dinner. Burr too, usually enigmatic in his utterances, was so intoxicated by the prospects of grandeur that he allowed himself to be overhead making jeering remarks about the need for a change in Washington. Rumors circulated and multiplied.

On December 1, 1805, President Jefferson received an anonymous letter warning him against Burr's conspiracy. "You admit him to your table, and you held a long and private conference with him a few days ago *after dinner* at the very moment he is meditating the overthrow of your Administration. . . . Yes, Sir, his abberations through the Western states *had no other object.* . . . Watch his connections with Mr. M—y and you will find him a British pensioner and agent."

Actually, Burr's difficulties at that moment stemmed from the fact that he hadn't succeeded in becoming a British pensioner. It was only with the help of the Alstons that he paid his travelling expenses. Jonathan Dayton too was flat broke; and despite extraordinary efforts, was able to raise only a few thousand dollars from the Spanish minister by selling him the details of a rival expedition against the Spanish dominions. For the moment, Theodosia's husband remained the conspirators' chief banker. Meanwhile, Burr was no more successful in his efforts to recruit prominent American naval and military officers for his enterprise. He approached men he knew had some grievance against the Jefferson administration—Thomas Truxtun, Stephen Decatur, William Eaton—but they all thumbed him down when they realized the illicit character of Burr's plans. Still, Burr had Harman Blennerhassett under his spell.

Blanny proved even more credulous than Alston. He wrote Colonel Burr that his island estate was up for sale and that he was looking for a profitable way to invest his capital. He offered his services as a lawyer. Burr answered that he could offer Mr. Blennerhassett not only fortune but fame. He congratulated him on giving up "a vegetable existence" for a life of

activity. He explained that he couldn't go into the details of his plans until they met face to face. His letter left Blanny panting to give his all.

Burr had gone too far now to turn back. He must act the part to the end. He recruited a German secretary and the services of a down-at-the-heels French officer named Julien de Pestre to act as chief of staff. Burr and Dayton were now dropping the fiction of the Ohio canal. The young men enlisted for service on the Mississippi were being told instead that in accordance with the secret policy of the administration they were to establish an armed settlement on Colonel Burr's lands up the Ouachita River. Each man was to have a hundred acres for his own.

Though many old Philadelphia friends turned Burr down, the famous Dr. Erich Bollman swallowed his scheme hook, line, and sinker. Bollman was the German physician who had been subsidized by Americans in London to try to free Lafayette from prison at Olmütz, in Austria. He was desperate for money. Burr told him he would send him to Europe as his diplomatic representative.

Somehow during the next few months he did scrape up funds to ship Bollman to New Orleans by sea, while Sam Swartwout and Peter Ogden of the Little Band started off across country to join forces with General Wilkinson. Each man carried a copy of a cipher letter that was soon to become famous. With its dispatch, Burr burned all his bridges.

". . . At length I have obtained funds and have actually commenced. The Eastern detachments, from different points and under different pretenses, will rendezvous on the Ohio 1st November. . . . Naval protection of England is secured. Truxtun is going to Jamaica to arrange with the [British] admiral on that station. It will meet us at the Mississippi. England, a navy of the United States, are ready to join, and final orders are given to my friends and followers. It will be a host of choice spirits. Wilkinson shall be second to Burr only. . . .

Burr will proceed westward 1st August, never to return. With him goes his daughter; the husband will follow in October, with a corps of worthies. . . . Our object, my dear friend, is brought to a point so long desired. Burr guarantees the result with his life and honor, with the lives and honor and the fortunes of hundreds, the best blood of our country. Burr's plan of operation is to move down rapidly from the Falls [of the Ohio] on the 15th of November, with the first five hundred or a thousand men, in light boats now constructing for that purpose; to be at Natchez between the 5th and 15th of December, there to meet you; there to determine whether it will be expedient to seize or pass by Baton Rouge. . . . The gods invite us to glory and fortune. . . ."

General Wilkinson Turns on a Friend

It is not till early October, 1806, that Sam Swartwout, after many hundreds of miles of weary riding, finds the General in camp at Natchitoches on the Red River, and delivers the cipher message. His companion, Ogden, hands Wilkinson an even more extravagant communication from Jonathan Dayton, warning him that he is to be put out of office by Jefferson at the next session of Congress: "You are not a man to despair, or even despond, especially when such prospects offer in another quarter. Are you ready? Are your numerous associates ready? Wealth and glory! Louisiana and Mexico!"

In the solitude of his tent, with the help of a pocket dictionary that furnishes the key, the General sits up half the night deciphering the hieroglyphics. Food for thought indeed. Wilkinson is a gentleman with the profoundest regard for the safety of his own skin. It strikes him at once that the conspiracy in its present form is crack-brained.

Burr is lying to him. Wilkinson knows that the administration has decided against war with Spain. His orders are to patch up a truce with

the Spanish force which has advanced across Texas to meet a rumored American invasion, and to agree to the Sabine River as a provisional boundary.

Furthermore, even to this distant outpost news has come of Pitt's death and of the appointment of Charles James Fox, the most pro-American of British statesmen, as Foreign Minister. Wilkinson has no way of knowing that one of Fox's first acts in office was to recall the eager Mr. Merry, thereby putting a quietus on any hope of British help for Burr, but it is obvious that Fox is no man to back an insurrection against the United States. By now Wilkinson knows too that the western settlers are "bigotted for Jefferson," as he put it a few months later, and that the conspiracy has no backing among the people.

The General decides that the safest thing for him to do is to turn state's evidence on Dayton and Burr. Once that decision is made, he lashes himself up into a frenzy of righteous indignation. He writes the President in heroic vein: He will defend the Union with his life. He writes Governor Claiborne in New Orleans to be on his guard: "You are surrounded by dangers of which you dream not and the destruction of the American Union is seriously menaced. The Storm will probably burst on New Orleans, when I shall meet it & triumph or perish."

Not a word to Swartwout and Ogden; they must be deceived into believing that he is still one of them. But among his officers, in the privacy of the wine after dinner, he swells like a bullfrog. He is the man who will stamp out this foul conspiracy, so help him God. How better can he squelch the libellous rumors of his being on the Spanish payroll than by saving New Orleans for the Union? He and his little force will stand like the Spartans at Thermopylae.

After further cogitation the General hits on a scheme that he feels will not only keep him in good odor with the administration in Washington but will produce a handsome bonus from his Spanish employers. He knows that President Jefferson is agog for exploration of the West. Wilkinson already has Lieutenant Zebulon Pike searching out the trails to Santa Fe. Now he sends off his aide, Walter Burling, to Mexico City—ostensibly to buy mules, but actually on a mission to the viceroy. For Washington his story will be that Burling is making a survey of roads and fortifications. For the viceroy he drafts a letter, picturing himself, again like Leonidas holding back the Persian hordes, as averting an attack on Mexico. He respectfully demands the sum of $121,000 in payment for these services.

Burr Sets the Plot in Motion

Never suspecting that his plans have been betrayed, Burr meanwhile is building his dream castle with the help of the doting Theodosia, Alston, and little Gampillo in the crisp air of Bedford Springs in the Pennsylvania mountains. They are already living in the imagined splendors of Montezuma's court under Aaron the First. They will put the Emperor Napoleon to shame. No title has yet been found for Joseph Alston. He announces that he will earn one by his deeds "in council and in the field."

Leaving the Alstons to follow by slow stages, Burr, attended by his secretary and chief of staff, rides off to Pittsburgh. There he sets up his headquarters at O'Hara's Tavern and starts recruiting young men of mettle. He contracts for twenty thousand barrels of flour and five thousand barrels of salt pork. He pays for everything with his own bills of exchange, guaranteed by the infatuated Alston.

Burr talks so big in Pittsburgh that a number of military men become alarmed and send warnings to Washington. Burr has already gone down river. On Blennerhassett's island he conquers all hearts. Poor nearsighted Blanny is transfigured by the prospect of glory. He sets

to work collecting fowling pieces and muskets, and whiskey by the barrel. He has his hands build a kiln for drying Indian meal. They roll out tubs of salt pork and corned beef. Mrs. Blennerhassett packs her trunks, and when Theodosia arrives, pronounces her the loveliest woman she has ever met.

Blanny mortgages what is left of his fortune to raise funds. Alston has told him he will guarantee every dollar. They sign a contract for fifteen boats with the Woodbridges at Belpre, across from the island. Blanny writes his name on every bill of exchange Burr puts under his nose. He retires to his study to prepare four articles for the *Ohio Gazette* advocating the secession of the western states.

Burr moves on in a fever of activity. He can't stay in one place long enough to complete his arrangements. Leaving Blennerhassett and Alston to recruit riflemen and to follow with the provisions when the boats are ready, he hurries to Cincinnati. On the way, at Wilmington, a mob denouncing disunion and treason surrounds Burr's lodgings. When fife and drum play "The Rogue's March," Colonel Burr declares coolly that there is nothing he enjoys more than martial music. The outcry can't refer to him because his plans are all for the honor and glory of the United States. His disclaimer is so plausible that he is tendered an apology and the mob goes home.

Mobs or senators, Burr pulls the wool over all eyes. John Adair, an old Indian fighter associated with Wilkinson in his wars against the Miamis, now a senator from Kentucky, joins Burr and lends a willing ear to his Mexican project. They ride through Kentucky in company.

Back in Nashville, Burr finds the Republican part of the population in a fever to march on the Spaniards. General Jackson has alerted his militia, but he still has occasional doubts. When he confronts Burr with rumors of secessionist talk drifting down river from Ohio, Burr is said to have shown him a blank commission signed by Jefferson. To cap that, he produces $3,500 in Kentucky banknotes to pay for the boats that Jackson's partner, John Coffee, is building at Clover Bottom. He has already paid five thousand (in his own paper) to a Colonel Lynch for his claims on the Bastrop lands. He draws sight drafts on all and sundry. According to the newspapers he is spending $200,000 on boats and provisions. Blanny's money flows like river water. Thoroughly reassured, Andrew Jackson puts on his best uniform to introduce Burr to the citizens of Nashville at a public ball.

To certain parties in Kentucky, this is all a red flag to a bull: the Spanish conspiracies all over again. Humphrey Marshall, Federalist brother-in-law of Jefferson's Chief Justice, has set up a newspaper named *The Western World* to expose the old Spanish intrigue to separate Kentucky from the Union; in it he charges that Wilkinson's old associate, Innes, is implicated. Joseph Daveiss, United States District Attorney, another brother-in-law of the Chief Justice, has been writing President Jefferson all summer warning him that Wilkinson and Burr are engaged in plots dangerous to the Union. On November 8, 1806, he presents an affidavit in federal court, charging Aaron Burr and John Adair with illegally promoting an expedition against Mexico. The presiding judge is none other than Harry Innes, under attack in *The Western World* as a pensioner of Spain. Motion dismissed.

Aaron Burr, ever eager to assume the role of injured innocence, rides back to Lexington and demands an inquiry. Popular sentiment in Kentucky is still with him. He has induced a rising young lawyer named Henry Clay to act as his counsel. When a grand jury is impanelled to hear Daveiss' charges, Daveiss is unable to present them because his key witness is absent on business. Daveiss has to ask for a postponement. Burr makes an address to the court and walks out in triumph.

He is heard by a bystander to remark that Daveiss must think him a great fool if, suppos-

ing he did have an unlawful enterprise in view, he should conduct it in such a manner as to give anyone an opportunity of proving it.

Andrew Jackson is assailed by doubts again. On November 12 he writes his old friend Governor Claiborne in New Orleans one of his tempestuous epistles:

". . . I fear treachery is become the order of the day . . . Put your Town in a State of Defence organize your Militia, and defend your City as well against internal enemies as external . . . keep a watchful eye upon our General [Wilkinson]—and beware of an attack, as well from your own Country as Spain . . . your government I fear is in danger, I fear there are plans on foot inimical to the Union . . . —beware the month of December—I love my Country and Government, I hate the Dons —I would delight to see Mexico reduced, but I will die in the last ditch before I would yield a part to the Dons or see the Union disunited. This I write for your own eye and your own safety, profit by it and the Ides of March remember. . . ."

On November 25, in Frankfort this time, the District Attorney renews his motion for Burr's indictment. When Henry Clay demands an assurance from his client that Burr's expedition has no treasonable intent, Burr hands him the same written statement he has already sent to his old friend Senator Smith of Ohio, denying any intention of subverting the Union by force. Clay is convinced and declares to the court that he pledges his own honor on Burr's innocence. A second grand jury refuses to find a true bill. The Republicans of Frankfort honor the little colonel with another ball.

Meanwhile, President Jefferson and his Cabinet have been startled into activity by General Wilkinson's first warning of the conspiracy, which the General dispatched from Natchitoches some twelve days after he received Burr's cipher letter. Hitherto they seem to have discounted Daveiss' warnings as expressions of party spite by pestiferous Federal-

ists. Now the Secretary of War and the Secretary of the Navy send out messengers to alert their forces, and on November 27 President Jefferson issues his proclamation that "sundry persons . . . are conspiring and confederating together to begin a military expedition or enterprise against the dominions of Spain," and enjoining "all faithful citizens who have been led without due knowledge or consideration to participate in the said unlawful enterprises to withdraw from the same without delay. . . ."

During this period a private emissary of the President gives information he has collected about the conspiracy to Governor Edward Tiffin of Ohio. Tiffin informs the legislature, then in session in Chillicothe. A bill is rushed through authorizing the militia to seize Burr's boats and supplies.

Tatterdemalion troops take possession of the boats being built at Belpre. They descend on Harman Blennerhassett's island paradise, break into the wine cellar, plunder the kitchens, trample the flowerbeds, slaughter the sheep, and break up the fence rails for campfires. Blanny himself escapes by boat into a snowy night, while, according to one witness' story, the levelled muskets of his recruits hold off the militia officer come to arrest him.

Mrs. Blennerhassett follows in a big flatboat manned by a group of youngsters from Pittsburgh. From then on, the expedition is a race between the speed of the current and the couriers distributing the President's proclamation.

Almost two weeks go by before the Blennerhassetts get news of their leader. Taking refuge one late December evening from the chop and the storm in the mouth of the Cumberland, they are met by a skiff with a letter. Colonel Burr is anchored a couple of miles upstream and requests five hundred dollars in paper and fifty in silver. Next day the whole flotilla pushes off downstream.

For Burr it is just in time. A certain Colonel

Hardin of South Carolina is already on his way down the Cumberland with the announced intention of shooting him on sight. The President's proclamation has thrown Nashville into a fury. The citizens have hardly read it before they get ready to burn Burr in effigy. General Jackson musters his militia. He almost breaks down with patriotic emotion when the elderly veterans of the Revolutionary War, who have formed a corps known as the Invincibles, ride up to tender their lives in defense of the Union. Days before, Jackson's man John Coffee has returned to Colonel Burr $1,725.62, which represents the unfinished boats that Burr had to abandon in his haste to depart. Accounts are closed between them, except for a note for $500 that Jackson unwisely put his name to, which eventually was to come back protested.

Unopposed except by cold rain and high winds and an occasional floating log, Burr's flotilla, amounting now to thirteen boats manned by some sixty men, drifts down the Ohio to Fort Massac. The lieutenant in command there, who has not heard of the proclamation or of orders to apprehend Burr, exchanges civilities with the little colonel, and, believing Burr to be leading a group of settlers to the Bastrop lands, gives one of his sergeants a furlough to go along as guide.

New Year's Day, 1807, finds the flotilla comfortably beached at New Madrid, on the Mississippi, in Louisiana Territory. According to one account, forty new recruits join Burr's party. Other witnesses were to speak of cannon, and of two gunboats building there. Some were to accuse Blennerhassett of trying to buy arms and ammunition from the army post. Next morning they push off. Still keeping ahead of the hue and cry, they are borne swiftly southward on the current of the enormous brown river. As they glide along, Blanny and Burr follow their boats' progress on their maps. Blanny is later to declare that it is when the boats sweep past what seems to him the logical landing from which they should have proceeded overland to the Bastrop lands that he first suspects an imposture.

Burr for his part seems to have forgotten all about the Bastrop settlement. His talk now is of Baton Rouge. This outpost of Spanish West Florida is supposedly so ill-defended that even the peaceable Governor Claiborne of Orleans Territory is said to have suggested jokingly over the wine after dinner that he and his guests drive up the levee in their carriages some evening and take it.

The weather has cleared. The little colonel is in high spirits. He appoints officers and noncoms. Muskets are brought out of a packing case, and he puts some of the boys through the manual of arms on one of the big flatboats as they drift down the river. At his friend Judge Peter Bruin's plantation some thirty miles above Natchez he is confidently expecting news from General Wilkinson, whom he believes to be waiting in New Orleans for the word.

Burr is so anxious to reach Judge Bruin that he has himself rowed ahead of the flotilla in a keelboat. He reaches Bayou Pierre the morning of January 10. Judge Bruin has the reputation of being a hard drinker. Burr finds him in a state. Burr is shown the President's proclamation. He is told that Acting Governor Cowles Mead of Mississippi has called out the militia with orders to arrest him. He is handed an issue of the *Mississippi Messenger* containing a transcription of his cipher message. For the first time Burr learns that Wilkinson has betrayed him.

He slips back into the role of injured innocence. Skillfully he fences for terms with Cowles Mead. Mead later declared that Burr's statements were so strange he doubted his sanity. After surrendering on terms to the civil authority, Burr lets himself be taken to Natchez. Friends stand bail.

Again Burr finds himself the toast of Federalist dinners. The ladies ply him with dainties. In Natchez he has a host of defenders. Another grand jury refuses to find him guilty of an in-

dictable offense and furthermore issues a presentment against General Wilkinson's illegal arrests of suspected persons in New Orleans.

The presiding judge, Thomas Rodney, an administration supporter, has a different view. His son Caesar Augustus has just been appointed Attorney General of the United States. Judge Rodney refuses to lift Burr's bond.

News comes of the apprehension of Bollman and Swartwout. General Wilkinson has offered five thousand dollars for Burr's capture, living or dead. Burr knows the General well enough to be sure that, with all he knows, Wilkinson would much prefer to have him dead. Panic seizes the usually imperturbable conspirator. Nothing for it but to jump his bail and vanish into the wilderness.

From hiding, Burr tries to send a last message to his men. It is a note stitched into the Colonel's old overcoat worn by a slave boy. "If you are yet together keep together and I will join you tomorrow night—in the mean time put *all* your arms in perfect order. Ask the bearer no questions but tell him all you may think I wish to know.—He does not know this is from me, nor where I am."

The boy is apprehended, the note discovered. Immediately Acting Governor Mead encircles Burr's camp with militia and arrests every man he can lay hands on.

Burr, with Major Robert Ashley for a guide, is already riding desperately off through the forest toward the Spanish border—and to capture at Carson's Ferry.

Attorney for the Defense

Theodosia had hurried back to South Carolina with her husband and little Gampillo as soon as it became clear that her father's castle in the air had collapsed. On March 27 Burr wrote her from Richmond: "My military escort having arrived at Fredericksburg on our way to Washington, there met a special messenger,

with orders to convey me to this place. . . . I am to be surrendered to the civil authority tomorrow, when the question of bail is to be determined. In the mean time I remain at the Eagle Tavern."

While all Richmond buzzed with the excitement of his arrival, Burr was busy with a tailor rigging him more suitable apparel than the boatman's trousers and floppy felt hat that were already notorious. The consummate actor was preparing to play his greatest role. He managed somehow to secure funds and to get in touch with well-wishers willing to stand bail. Around noon on March 30, in a private room of the Eagle Tavern, he was brought before Chief Justice John Marshall for pre-trial examination.*

The government's case was in the hands of an ardent Republican, George Hay, United States District Attorney for Virginia, since Blennerhassett's island on the Ohio, the chief scene of the alleged crimes, was within the confines of that enormous commonwealth.

On behalf of Burr appeared two of the most esteemed members of the Richmond bar: portly Edmund Randolph, one-time governor of Virginia, and John Wickham, a Long Island man, accused by the Republicans of Tory antecedents.

George Hay presented a copy of the evidence on which the Attorney General had based his charges against Bollman and Swartwout when they appeared in Washington, shipped north under armed escort by General Wilkinson. Nicholas Perkins told a plain tale of Burr's arrest. Hay moved forthwith that the prisoner be committed on the charge of high misdemeanor in preparing a military expedition against the dominions of the king of Spain. Further, he contended that the prisoner had committed acts of treason in gathering a force

---

* Until 1891, Justices of the Supreme Court, including the Chief Justice, regularly heard cases in the federal circuit courts as well.

of armed men with the intention of seizing the city of New Orleans, fomenting a revolt in the Orleans Territory, and separating the western states from the Union. Hay referred to the interpretation of treason promulgated by the Supreme Court in the Chief Justice's own words only a month before, when Bollman and Swartwout were freed on a writ of habeas corpus. This decision seemed to describe the assembling of armed men for a treasonable purpose as treason. Since argument by counsel would be necessary on this motion, all parties agreed to move the proceedings up the hill to the courtroom in the state's new Ionic capitol, designed by Thomas Jefferson.

Next morning the Chief Justice appeared betimes on the bench. William Wirt, who was himself soon to join the prosecution, had described John Marshall a couple of years before as "in person tall, meagre and emaciated. His head and face are small in proportion to his height, his complexion swarthy, the muscles of his face relaxed . . . his countenance has a faithful expression of great good humor and hilarity; while his black eyes . . . possess an irradiating spirit which proclaims the imperial powers of his mind. . . . His voice is hard and dry; his attitude . . . often extremely awkward; as it was not unusual for him to stand with his left foot in advance, while all his gesture proceeded from his right arm. . . . His eloquence consists in the apparently deep selfconviction, and emphatic earnestness of his manner."

Attorney General Rodney was waiting to address the court before leaving for Washington. Burr's lawyers were eager to begin the defense. The crowded courtroom waited, breathless. Colonel Burr appeared half an hour late, announcing with a debonair smile that he had mistaken the hour.

Since the stairways and lobbies were packed with Richmonders trying to get in, proceedings were adjourned to the hall of the House of Delegates. Burr's lawyers launched into their argument: intent was no basis for a charge of treason; according to the Constitution the crime of treason had to be an overt act, sworn to by two witnesses. Colonel Burr rose and in his most courtly manner pointed out that he had already been acquitted of all these charges in Kentucky and Mississippi; that in each case he himself had sought an investigation; that he had not forfeited his bond by fleeing the jurisdiction of any court, but had merely retired to avoid the illegal seizure of his person and property by a military force.

Burr had failed as a revolutionist, but he remained matchless as a courtroom lawyer. As the proceedings advanced, he regained all his aplomb. This was a world he knew how to deal with. Attack was the best defense. His safety depended on turning the case into a political wrangle between Federalists and Republicans. President Jefferson was personally directing the prosecution from Washington. The leading Federalists were rushing to Burr's defense. The prosecution's case must rest on Wilkinson. Burr now felt that the ranting Commanding General, whom a few weeks back he had relied on as his partner in high adventure, would be the easiest man in the world to discredit. Burr knew that the Chief Justice hated Jefferson as hard as he himself did. If he could attack Jefferson through Wilkinson, he could not help winning John Marshall's sympathy. On the whole, in the crucial game that was about to be played, Burr held a good hand of cards.

The Chief Justice declared he preferred at this point not to commit Burr for treason, but that he felt the evidence sufficient to commit him for high misdemeanor. In explaining his decision, John Marshall pointed out what was to be the nub of the defense: As he interpreted the wording of the cipher letter, admitting that that document should turn out to be genuine, it pointed to an attack against the Spanish dominions instead of to a treasonable enterprise against New Orleans. Therefore, until the government presented more evidence he

would hold Colonel Burr for misdemeanor only. Treason had to be proved by two witnesses. As to the proof of treason: "More than five weeks have elapsed since the opinion of the supreme court has declared the necessity of proving the fact if it exists. Why is it not proved?"

Treason would not have been a bailable charge, but misdemeanor was. Bail was set at ten thousand dollars, and later in the afternoon Colonel Burr presented five securities, entered into recognizance for that sum to appear before the circuit court on May 22, and walked out a free man.

Aaron Burr emerged from this first phase of his trial the hero of all the Federalist mansions scattered along the hilltops of Richmond, where detestation of Jefferson was becoming the password to social acceptance. Invitations poured in. The afternoon he dined with John Wickham in celebration of the initial victories of the defense, John Marshall was of the party. Wickham and the Chief Justice were warm and confidential friends. Wickham had been thoughtful enough to warn Marshall that the dinner was for Aaron Burr. Marshall, who loved a good dinner, said he'd come anyway. According to his friends he did sit at the other end of the table, had no direct communication with the accused man, and left early. But this incident did not pass unnoticed by the Republican press, which denounced the Chief Justice's conduct as "grossly indecent."

The President's Dilemma

Jefferson was anxiously studying every letter and newspaper that came in from Richmond. He could see right away that George Hay was no match for Burr's Federalist lawyers. Besides Randolph and Wickham, the little colonel had engaged two of the brightest of the younger Virginia attorneys, Benjamin Botts and John Baker. The President had heard too that Luther Martin, one of his bitter personal enemies, was on his way from Annapolis to join the defense counsel. The ablest lawyers, it seemed, tended to be Federalists. The President had to make do with what Republicans he could collect. He arranged to have Alexander McRae, a gruff Scot who was lieutenant governor of Virginia, assist in the prosecution, and got off an express to William Wirt, who was trying a case in Williamsburg, engaging him for the government. Young Wirt was generally thought of as a coming man.

Jefferson was exasperated by the difficulties the Chief Justice was putting in the way of the prosecution. From Monticello he wrote William B. Giles, the administration leader in the Senate, commenting testily on "the newborn zeal for the liberties of those whom we would not permit to overthrow the liberties of their country." Against Burr personally, he added, "I never had one hostile sentiment. I never indeed thought him an honest, frank-dealing man, but considered him as a crooked gun, or other perverted machine, whose aim or shot you could never be sure of."

Burr, on his side, was taking high ground in his letters to Theodosia: "Was there in Greece or Rome a man of virtue and independence, and supposed to possess great talents, who was not the object of vindictive and unrelenting persecution?"

Burr complained that the panel from which a grand jury was to be selected was composed of twenty Republicans and only four Federalists. A few days later William Wirt, still stoutly maintaining that John Marshall was a fair-minded man, was facing the fact that by insistence on a technicality the court had limited the number of grand jurors to sixteen, "and consequently the chance of the concurrence of 12 in finding a Bill was reduced to a minimum," as he explained when he got time to write an account of the trial to his foster brother Ninian Edwards in Kentucky. "Burr and his counsel were filled with triumph at the pros-

pect that there would be no Bill found—they displayed their triumph very injudiciously."

After all challenges were exhausted, the list of grand jurors selected turned out to be a roster of some of the ablest men in Virginia. When the Chief Justice chose John Randolph of Roanoke as foreman, the Federalist dinner tables rocked with satisfaction. Nobody could accuse Marshall of bias; he had chosen a Republican; but of all Republicans, John Randolph was the least friendly to Jefferson. The erstwhile administration leader in the House was now making a career of opposition to the man he was coming to jeer at as "St. Thomas of Cantingbury."

As May wore on, Richmond filled to overflowing with curious visitors. The Burr trial was the greatest show in the history of the commonwealth. Every bed in every inn was taken. Every house was stuffed with guests sleeping on truckle beds in the attics. Every stable and shed had its complement of horses and gigs. Coaches and carriages encumbered the inn yards. Families of country people came in covered wagons and camped in the open lots. The streets were brilliant with uniforms of the Army and Navy and of various militia organizations. The ladies all wore their best.

Though many Republicans were wagering that Colonel Burr would jump his bail again, on the morning of May 22 the little colonel was seen flitting among his lawyers, cool as a cucumber, wearing a neat suit of black silk, with his hair carefully powdered and tied in a queue. Judge Cyrus Griffin, George Washington's appointee to the Virginia district court, joined the Chief Justice on the bench.

From day to day the crowds were disappointed. The trial marked time. The Chief Justice would not allow the grand jury to start examining witnesses until General Wilkinson arrived. Aaron Burr's friends scoffed loudly as May passed into June. The General would never dare show his face. While the grand jurors sat idly deploring their wasted days,

counsel for both sides entertained the courtroom with rambling arguments over the nature of treason and the amount of the prisoner's bail.

On May 28 the session was enlivened by the appearance of Luther Martin on behalf of Colonel Burr. Martin had been carrying on a vendetta with Thomas Jefferson for years. A great wassailer and brandy-drinker, fast drifting into helpless alcoholism, Luther Martin was a prey to violent hatreds and affections. But he was also the leading lawyer of his native Maryland, and he had taken a fancy to Aaron Burr.

When Burr, who never let an opportunity pass of playing up to the Chief Justice, did the handsome thing to end the dispute over bail by offering to raise his security to twenty thousand dollars "so that the court should not be embarrassed," Luther Martin stood up and offered himself as one of the sureties.

Confrontation at the Bar

On June 13, a Saturday, the news spread that General Wilkinson with a suite of witnesses had disembarked from a U.S. Navy schooner and was on his way to Richmond. George Hay reported to the court that only the fatigue of the journey prevented the General from presenting himself that very day.

The General in Chief had every reason to be fatigued. For three months Wilkinson had been charging about New Orleans in a state of frenzy. To clear his own skirts he had blown up such a bogey out of Burr's schemes that he ended by frightening himself. He kept the city under martial law. He set his troops to digging earthworks and building palisades. He sent out squads to arrest Burr's associates. Though Burr himself had slipped through his fingers, Wilkinson pounced on an old friend, John Adair, in town by prearrangement with the conspirators, and marched him off from his dinner table at the inn to the city prison. Wil-

kinson could not rest easy until every man jack who knew of his complicity in Burr's conspiracy was behind bars.

In February the General's wife died at the house of a hospitable Creole planter who was serving as the General's aide. Shattered with grief, Wilkinson lingered on in New Orleans in spite of insistent requests from Washington that he come north immediately to testify in Burr's trial. Meanwhile he tried to distract the administration from the clamor against his arbitrary acts by thundering letters about the torrent of Burrites that was about to descend on him.

Finally, with his son James for an aide and in company with a large band of witnesses under subpoena, he embarked May 20, 1807, for Hampton Roads.

As soon as the news of General Wilkinson's safe arrival was confirmed, the court began to swear witnesses for the grand jury. Two veterans of the naval war with France, Commodore Truxtun and Captain Decatur, led the way, along with Benjamin Stoddert, who had been John Adams' Secretary of the Navy. When Erich Bollman's turn came, George Hay tried rather clumsily to hand him the presidential pardon he had so eagerly sought in return for the information he gave during an interview with Jefferson and Madison back in Washington. But Bollman had changed his mind. He had been feted by the Richmond Federalists as a minor hero of Burr's odyssey. Emboldened by the atmosphere of success in Burr's camp, he now refused to accept any pardon. Luther Martin hastily explained that Bollman preferred to rely on the constitutional guarantee that no man would be forced to testify against himself. The court sent him in to the grand jury anyway.

On Monday, June 15, the halls and lobbies of the capitol were jammed with people. General Wilkinson was on his way up the hill. Crowds stumbled panting after him. Men and boys hung from the window ledges and climbed the great trees on the eroded slope, craning their necks for a glimpse of the actors in the grand confrontation.

Men's accounts of the scene in the Hall of Delegates varied according to their political persuasions. Washington Irving, who reported the trial for a Burrite newspaper in New York, said Wilkinson "strutted into court . . . swelling like a turkey cock." David Robertson, the stenographer, described the General's countenance as "calm, dignified and commanding while that of Colonel Burr was marked by a haughty contempt."

Wirt's description in his letter to Ninian Edwards was possibly more discerning. "In the midst of all this hurly-burly came Wilkinson and his suite, like Pope's fame 'unlooked for' at least by Burr's partisans. It was curious to mark the interview between Burr and Wilkinson. There was no nature in it—they had anticipated the meeting and resolved on the countenance which they would wear—Wilkinson had been some time within the bar before Burr would look towards him affecting not to know he was there until Hay introduced him by saying to the court: 'It is my wish that General Wilkinson, who is now before the court, should be qualified and sent up to the Grand Jury.' At the words 'who is now before the court,' Burr started in his chair, turned quickly and fastened a look of scorn and contempt on Wilkinson—Wilkinson bowing to the court on his introduction did not receive Burr's first glance; but his bow finished, he turned his face down on Burr and looked with all the sullenness and protervity of a big black bull—Burr withdrew his eyes composedly and that was the end of it."

Wilkinson himself described the scene in a letter to President Jefferson in his own inimitable style. "I saluted the Bench & in spite of myself my eyes darted a flash of indignation at the little Traitor on whom they continued

fixed until I was called to the Book—The Lyon hearted Eagle Eyed Hero, sinking under the weight of conscious guilt, with haggard Eye, made an Effort to meet the indignant salutation of outraged Honor, but it was in vain, his audacity failed Him, He averted his face, grew pale & affected passion to conceal his perturbation."

As soon as Wilkinson had taken the oath, he was sent to the grand jury. He had dressed in his best in the commanding general's uniform of his own devising. His enormous gold epaulets glittered in the light pouring through the tall windows. He wore his famous gold spurs, and his heavily encrusted sword trailed on the ground. John Randolph, the foreman, immediately piped up that the marshal must take that man out and disarm him.

It was soon clear that the jurymen were set to give the General a hard time. John Randolph had discovered that the copies of Burr's and Dayton's cipher messages which had been in the General's hands had been tampered with. Phrases had been erased, words written in. The grand jurors kept asking the General why, since he claimed he'd first learned of Burr's plot from Swartwout in October, he had let a whole month go by before warning Governor Claiborne that an attack on New Orleans was imminent? In fact, wasn't Wilkinson guilty too? And when the grand jury came to vote its indictments, a motion to add Wilkinson's name to the list of defendants was just barely lost, seven to nine.

John Randolph was furious: "But the mammoth of iniquity escaped," he wrote a friend; "not that any man pretended to think him *innocent*, but upon certain wire-drawn distinctions that I will not pester you with. W——n is the only man that I ever saw who was from the bark to the very core a villain."

While the grand jury was closeted day after day in one part of the capitol, at the public sessions in the Hall of Delegates Burr and his lawyers hammered on a similar theme—that the true traitor of the piece was Wilkinson; instead of being a witness for the prosecution he should be in the prisoners' dock.

On Wednesday, June 24, Burr's attorney's brought in a motion for the attachment of the person of General Wilkinson. While this motion was being argued, word went around that the grand jury was about to bring in an indictment. Every man who could puffed up the hill to the capitol. At two o'clock that afternoon, as one of Burr's lawyers was arguing for the attachment of General Wilkinson (who, since he had emerged from his ordeal, was sitting brazen with self-righteousness among the government lawyers), John Randolph led his sober-faced jurors into court and laid several indictments on the clerk's table.

The clerk read out the endorsements: True bills against Burr and Blennerhassett for treason and misdemeanor.

In his letter to Ninian Edwards, Wirt described with relish the consternation in the camp of the defense: "When the grand-jury came down with the Bills against Burr and Blennerhassett, I never saw such a group of shocked faces. The chief justice, who is a very dark man, shrunk back with horror upon his seat and turned black. He kept his eyes fixed on Burr with an expression of sympathy so agonizing and horror so deep & overwhelming that he seemed for two or three seconds to have forgotten where & who he was. I observed him & saw him start from his reverie under the consciousness that he was giving away too much of his feelings and look around upon the multitude to see if he had been noticed. . . ."

The Chief Justice had no choice but to order Burr to the public jail, although he was moved the following day to a comfortable guarded room in a private house where Luther Martin lodged. Meanwhile the grand jury was deliberating further indictments, and John Ran-

dolph asked the court's assistance in obtaining a copy of a letter postmarked May 13, 1806, written by James Wilkinson, to which Burr's cipher letter was thought to be an answer. The members of the grand jury were aware that they could not ask the accused to present material which might incriminate him but hoped he would facilitate their inquiry into the facts. John Randolph was hinting that the letter might incriminate Wilkinson.

The Chief Justice replied dryly that the jurors were quite right in their opinion that the accused could not be required to incriminate himself.

Colonel Burr rose and in his most disarming manner declared that it would be impossible for him "to expose any letter which had been communicated to him confidentially." He added, with that suggestion of the steel claw under the velvet glove of which he was a master, that he was not then prepared to decide "how far the extremity of circumstances might impel him to such action."

Mr. McRae of the prosecution interposed that General Wilkinson had informed him that he wished to have the whole of the correspondence between Colonel Burr and himself exhibited before the court. Wilkinson was referring to other letters in his possession even more damaging to Burr.

Burr replied sarcastically that the General was "welcome to all the éclat which he may expect to derive from his challenge," but that the letter postmarked May 13 would not be produced. "The letter is not at this time in my possession and General Wilkinson knows it."

Even in their deadly grapple a curious intimacy persisted between the two men. Each knew how the other's mind worked. Each was telegraphing to the other that he held in his possession the evidence needed to convict him. Whoever produced any more damaging correspondence would do so at his own risk.

The grand jury promptly returned with a new set of indictments presenting ex-Senator Jonathan Dayton of New Jersey and Senator John Smith of Ohio, along with Comfort Tyler, Israel Smith, and Davis Floyd, who had been Burr's agents in organizing the expedition, as guilty of treason and of levying war against the United States on Blennerhassett's island in Wood County, Virginia, on December 13, 1806.

A few days later Burr was removed to the penitentiary which Benjamin Latrobe, the architect of the south wing of the U.S. Capitol, had designed and recently completed for the commonwealth of Virginia.

Burr seems to have been happy under the cool, vaulted ceilings of his new quarters. It was at least a protection from his creditors, who were getting ready to place Colonel Burr in debtors' prison whenever they could lay hands on him.

"I have three rooms in the third story of the penitentiary," Burr wrote Theodosia, "making an extent of a hundred feet. My jailer is quite a polite and civil man—altogether unlike the idea one would form of a jailer. You would have laughed to have heard our compliments last evening."

The jailer apologized for having to keep the door locked after dark. Burr replied that he would prefer it, to keep out intruders. When the jailer told him lights would have to be extinguished at nine, Colonel Burr said that was quite impossible because he never went to bed before midnight. "As you please, Sir," said the jailer.

Under the plea that travelling back and forth between the penitentiary and the capitol would be too great a tax on the accused and his lawyers during the sessions of the trial, Burr, accompanied by his seven guards, was again removed in the first days of August to a private house. His suite at the prison was promptly occupied by the chief victim of his impostures, Harman Blennerhassett.

Poor Blanny had been taken into custody by the federal marshal in Kentucky, where he had

already fallen into the clutches of Burr's creditors, bent on attaching his person and property. He called in Henry Clay as his counsel and with Clay's help held off the bailiffs by producing a letter from Joseph Alston which promised to assume at least part of the indebtedness. Mrs. Blennerhassett meanwhile was struggling to exist with their two boys in Natchez.

When the Alstons arrived they took over Burr's old quarters in Luther Martin's house. "I want an independent and discerning witness to my conduct and to that of the government," Burr had written Theodosia. ". . . I should never invite anyone, much less those so dear to me, to witness my disgrace. I may be immured in dungeons, chained, murdered in legal form, but I cannot be humiliated or disgraced. If absent you will suffer much solicitude. In my presence you will feel none, whatever be the *malice* or the *power* of my enemies. . . ."

People were beginning to lose interest in Burr's machinations. It was the prospect of a war with England that worried them now. Late in June the British frigate *Leopard* had made an unprovoked attack on the American frigate *Chesapeake* off Cape Henry, and indignation was sweeping the country. The government witnesses had scattered to the hills.

The trial proper began on August 3. When Chief Justice Marshall appeared on the bench at noon, George Hay for the prosecution was forced shamefacedly to confess that he had not the witnesses on hand he needed to present his case. Again court was adjourned. It was not till the following Monday that enough government witnesses assembled to justify impanelling a jury. A number of jurors were rejected because they admitted having formed an opinion, like a certain Mr. Bucky, that whether treason were proved or not, Colonel Burr ought to be hung.

George Hay's prosecution never recovered its impetus, even though the people in general agreed with Mr. Bucky. In spite of William Wirt's flights of oratory, his fanciful description of the beauties of Blennerhassett's island before Burr arrived like the serpent in Eden, Burr and his lawyers retained the offensive.

President Jefferson could give only half his mind to the Burr trial. Yet the conviction of Burr had become an idea so fixed that it clouded his judgment. At one point he wrote Hay, after reading some particularly intemperate remarks by Luther Martin, that if "Old Brandy Bottle," as Martin was popularly called, was such a good friend of Burr's, maybe he should be indicted himself.

The administration was in a dilemma. To make a proper case against Burr they had to inculpate Wilkinson, and yet the President and his two advisers, Secretary of State James Madison and Secretary of the Treasury Albert Gallatin, had decided that the state of affairs in New Orleans demanded that, come what may, they support the General. The prosecution's case against Burr—though a procession of witnesses from the rank and file of those whom Burr had deceived produced evidence enough to convict him of all sorts of other crimes—depended on John Marshall's broad definition of treason as the assembling of armed men— the definition advanced by the Chief Justice in the habeas corpus proceedings against Bollman and Swartwout. George Hay made no effort to prove that Aaron Burr was present when the overt acts were committed by his armed forces assembled on Blennerhassett's island.

But on August 31, John Marshall seemed to shift his ground. Admitting that there were times when the Supreme Court might be called upon to reconsider its judgments, he explained away the phrases in his previous definition of treason which might imply that conspiracy to assemble armed men was sufficient to establish guilt. "The present indictment charges the prisoner with levying war against the United States, and alleges an overt act of levying war. That overt act must be proved, according to the mandates of the constitution

and of the act of congress, by two witnesses. It is not proved by a single witness."

The Chief Justice furthermore ruled that since the overt act had not been proved, "corroborative or confirmatory testimony" was not admissible. This ruling by one scratch of the pen threw out all the testimony as to Burr's performances on the Mississippi and the Ohio which the prosecution had gone to such pains to collect. As was his wont, the Chief Justice presented his opinion in writing, and at great length.

The court adjourned to give District Attorney Hay time to read it over. Next morning he threw up the case. His swarm of witnesses had been ruled out unheard. He would leave it to the jury.

After twenty-five minutes the jury returned to the hall. The verdict was read by the foreman, this time the much-respected Colonel Edward Carrington. "We of the jury say that Aaron Burr is not proved to be guilty under this indictment by any evidence submitted to us."

Burr immediately objected to the form of the verdict. Luther Martin asked if the jury intended to censure the court for suppressing testimony. Members of the jury, as politely as they could, made it clear that that was exactly what they did intend. The Chief Justice, in his offhand manner, ended the imbroglio by suggesting that the verdict stand as written but that "Not guilty" be entered in the record.

The Case Falls Apart

The threat of the gallows was lifted, but the sun had not come out for Aaron Burr. He was no sooner freed of the indictment for treason than he found himself attached for debt in a civil suit. Somehow he managed to find surety to the amount of $36,000.

Emboldened by the favorable verdict in Burr's case, Jonathan Dayton emerged from hiding and appeared in court with an affidavit to the effect that he had not been on Blennerhassett's island in December, 1806. Hay entered a nolle prosequi. And when Harman Blennerhassett was brought into court the next day, his case was treated in the same way.

There was still the "misdemeanor" charge, the considerable misdemeanor of mounting an expedition against Spanish territories. Burr and the rest were admitted to bail on that. And while they waited, Blanny dogged Burr's footsteps; he kept writing the little colonel begging for an explanation. He and his family were penniless. Colonel Burr must propose some plan for repaying the money he owed him. Whenever he managed to see Burr, that gentleman was surrounded by friends and remarkably inattentive to talk of a financial settlement. Blennerhassett then sought out Alston. All Alston would talk about was how he himself was fifty thousand dollars in the hole. At last Burr granted Blanny a private interview. Burr wanted to know which influential men Blanny could introduce him to in England.

To his diary Blennerhassett confided his hopes that in exchange for letters to people of rank Burr might be induced to start repaying the money he owed, but when Blanny hinted at this *quid pro quo*, Burr would talk only of his projects. The new aggressive mood showing itself at the British Foreign Office would provide just the climate he needed for getting backing for his plan of disunion. "He is as gay as usual," Blanney noted, "and as busy in speculations on reorganizing his projects for action as if he had never suffered the least interruption."

The misdemeanor trial proved to be more of a trial of General Wilkinson than of Aaron Burr. The lawyers for the prosecution had lost heart. Important papers were mislaid. They had only the most perfunctory assistance from the Attorney General, and the result was another series of verdicts of Not Guilty. Other charges in Ohio were never pressed.

Aaron Burr departed for Philadelphia. Already he was trying to recruit young men to form his suite on his projected journey to England. Blennerhassett followed in his trail, still hopeful of a settlement of his claims.

A mob threatening tar and feathers caused them to hurry through Baltimore. In Philadelphia Blanny noted that the Colonel as usual moved in the best circles. Finding himself one of a crowd of creditors whom Burr always managed to avoid, Blanny gave up. Travelling under assumed names and under strange disguises, Aaron Burr managed to shake loose from his creditors long enough to get himself smuggled aboard a packet boat for England. One of his last acts in New York was to borrow a few dollars from his German cook, who, knowing his master, made him leave the deed to a trunkload of personal effects as security.

The Last Years

Burr's wanderings during his years of exile in Europe were as puzzling as his performances on the western waters. In England he ingratiated himself with Jeremy Bentham, the political economist whose utilitarian theories Burr claimed to find admirable. Bentham put him up and furnished him with funds while the little colonel tried to interest the government in the conquest of Mexico. When Lord Liverpool's administration turned his proposition down, and sought to expel him from Great Britain, Burr had the effrontery to claim that, having been born under King George, he was a British subject. He ran up so many bills that he had to take it on the run, nevertheless, to escape imprisonment for debt, and retired to Sweden. There he panhandled his way from nobleman's seat to nobleman's seat, keeping all the while, expressly for the eyes of Theodosia and little Gampillo, his grandson, one of the most extraordinary journals in the history of the human mind.

Using a curious code compounded of German and English and Swedish and French, he noted, for the edification of the only two people he loved in the world, every single detail of an existence dedicated to a conscienceless depravity without match in confessional literature. He noted every subterfuge he indulged in to cadge a meal or a handout; every time he drank too much; his efforts to ease the vacant spirit with opium; every success with a woman, were she duchess or chambermaid; the price he paid his harlots and whether they were worth it or not. Intermingled were sparkling descriptions of weather and places, shrewd estimates of people, philosophical disquisitions on the meaninglessness of life, but never a word or a phrase that betrayed a moment's escape from the strait jacket of self-worship.

When he wore out his welcome in Sweden and Germany, he made his way to Paris. There he presented to the Emperor Napoleon's foreign office a fanciful scheme involving the reconquest of Louisiana and Canada for France. The response of Burr's old idol was to have him watched by the police.

In the end Burr somehow managed to shake down the French foreign office for his passage home. In June of 1812 he slipped back into New York in disguise and was sheltered by such members of the Little Band as still retained political influence. He even ventured to open a law office on Nassau Street. He had barely settled in practice before a distracted letter reached him from Theodosia. His grandson was dead. He would never see Gampillo again. Desperate with grief, Theodosia could think only of rejoining her father. Too ill to travel by land, she tried to run the British blockade and was lost at sea on the pilot boat *Patriot*.

Friends remarked how nobly Burr bore his affliction. Stoicism amid total disaster fitted into his philosophy. He managed to make a living at the law, surrounded himself with a new

family of outcasts, unfortunate women and foster children, some of whom were reputed to be his own bastards and whose education he supervised with pedantic care. He lived on for years as one of New York's minor notorieties. Men pointed him out on the street to their sons as the wickedest man alive.

To the end he protested that his strange schemes were never intended to be detrimental to the United States. In 1833, at the age of seventy-seven, he married a woman to whom his name had been linked by gossip forty years before. As Mme. Jumel, the wife of a successful French wine merchant for twenty-eight years, Eliza Bowen had attained a certain respectability. Now she was reputed to be one of the wealthiest widows in New York. They had been married barely a year before Mme. Jumel sued him for divorce on the charge of adultery. Burr had laid his hands on large sums of her money to invest in the Texas land schemes of a beautiful young woman named Jane McManus. The decree was granted, on the testimony of a housemaid, the day Burr died. The end had come, after a series of strokes, at a hotel on the Staten Island shore to which friends had carried him on a stretcher —partly because he loved the sea breezes and partly to escape the persecution of clergymen who wanted to take the credit for the deathbed conversion of the wickedest man alive.

In a batch of Burr papers that turned up recently in the possession of the New-York Historical Society appear the court records of a proceeding for perjury brought against the housemaid who testified to his adultery. With Aaron Burr, in small things as in great, one can never be quite sure.

14

The West
in the War of 1812

Ray Allen Billington

Too often, in explaining the origins of the War of 1812, textbooks stress Anglo-American tensions on the high seas and ignore or play down the crucial role of Westerners in the coming of that conflict. Here, in an exhilarating narrative, Ray Allen Billington demonstrates how Western Indian troubles and outright land hunger, combined with Southern expansionism *and* the need to protect American honor on the seas, brought about the second war with England. Billington also recounts the major campaigns, shows how the nation became divided with anti-war dissent, and reminds us that while the war was not a United States victory, it had major significances nevertheless.

The issues that plunged the United States into its second war with England seemingly were of little interest to frontiersmen. Why should they grow wrathful over a distant death struggle between Britain and the newly risen colossus of the Continent, Napoleon? What matter to them that both warring powers confiscated American cargoes or that England's navy impressed British deserters (and a few United States citizens) from American ships? As loyal Jeffersonians, westerners could be expected to applaud their President's efforts to keep peace and to support his application of economic sanctions to both belligerents. As ardent nationalists they would certainly boil with indignation at each new attack on their country's shipping or each added insult to its honor. But neither partisanship nor patriotism seemed sufficient to send the West along the road to war.

Yet frontier demands, coupled with those of the South, forced the War of 1812 on a reluctant East, frontier arms accounted for the few American victories, and frontier ambitions dictated the peace. The answer to this apparent paradox can be found in both the practical problems facing the West in 1812 and the psychological attitudes persistent there. A serious depression engulfed the back country, fur traders were engaged in a losing battle with intruders, an Indian war ravaged outlying settlements, and a younger generation of revolutionists bristled with each new sullying of the national honor. The average westerner believed that England was responsible for all his troubles, and that only a war with that power would allow the conquest of Canada which was the sole means of their solution. Such a conquest would automatically solve the fur-trading problem and end Indian attacks; then at war's end the plundered colony could be offered to England as the price for respecting America's neutral shipping rights. With freedom of the seas guaranteed, the West could shake off the depression by again exporting its surpluses to a hungry Europe.

This depression that shackled the Ohio Valley between 1808 and 1812 underlay all other

Reprinted with permission of The Macmillan Company from pp. 268–289 in *Westward Expansion* by Ray Allen Billington. Copyright © by The Macmillan Company, 1967.

grievances. Its cause was the unsound economy forced on the Ohio Valley by its inadequate transportation system. The bulky farm goods produced there could be marketed only in New Orleans. Western farmers had to select their cargoes for export in the light of price information a month old, spend another month and a large sum of money reaching the market, and compete with dozens of other sellers who arrived at the same time. Often backwoodsmen who had braved snags and pirates in the tortuous journey down the Mississippi were so overawed by the bustling strangeness of teeming New Orleans or so afraid of contracting tropical fevers that they sold their cargoes hurriedly at ridiculously low prices. Only the fortunate few were able to sell at a profit under those conditions.

The West did not feel the full impact of its economic maladjustment until 1808, for until that time the influx of new immigrants not only absorbed agricultural surpluses but kept the frontier supplied with ready cash. Thus the depression coincided with England's blockade, and to frontiersmen the two events were intimately connected. So long as American ships reached Europe the Ohio Valley enjoyed prosperity; when Britain closed that market hard times followed. Prosperity would only return when the English fleet allowed the United States to trade with the Continent once more. Westerners, reasoning in that fashion, solidly supported the Embargo of 1807, objected strenuously when eastern pressure forced Congress to adopt the less stringent Non-Intercourse Act in 1809, and adopted a belligerent I-told-you-so attitude when hard times grew more acute in the next three years. By 1812 frontiersmen agreed that war was necessary to restore prosperity. "The true question," said one of their congressional representatives, ". . . is the right of exporting the productions of our soil and industry to foreign markets."

This goal could be achieved, westerners agreed, only by using a conquered Canada as a hostage to force England to her knees. This was Britain's only vulnerable spot; not even the most optimistic patriot could hope that the few American vessels could challenge the might of the world's dominant naval power on the high seas. But poorly protected Canada could be easily taken, then dangled before England in return for the promise to allow American ships freedom to trade wherever they pleased. To the frontiersmen, this was all-important. Wealthy Boston or New York shipowners could afford to lose two vessels in every three to Britain's raiders and still count a respectable profit; even greater losses could be sustained so long as their cash reserves and ready credit held out. To these easterners war spelled disaster, for they well knew that all their trade would end at once. The pioneers of the Ohio Valley, however, had no such fears. With their near-marginal economy, they were convinced that the export of only five or ten per cent of their surpluses to starving Europe would lift them from their depression and assure them perpetual prosperity. Maritime rights and neutral trade were more important to them than to New England's merchants, despite their relatively small stake in European commerce.

To western expansionists, then, the overrunning of Canada was not an end—frontiersmen were aware that the nation's supply of unoccupied lands would suffice for generations to come—but a means through which they would restore prosperity and avenge the sullied national honor. That this was the case was amply demonstrated by the correlation between belligerency and inadequate trade outlets. The farmers of northern New York and Vermont, long accustomed to exporting their grain and potash to Montreal via the St. Lawrence River, not only opposed war but persisted in their trade after the 1807 Embargo made such trade illegal. On the other hand the planters of South Carolina and Georgia, where glutted cotton

markets sent prices tumbling, and the farmers of the Ohio Valley, where a faulty marketing system doomed prosperity, were the most violent spokesmen for conflict.

Southerners had another reason for war, for a conflict with England and that nation's ally, Spain, would allow the conquest of Spanish Florida. This would open new trade routes to the Gulf along the Alabama, Pearl, and Apalachicola rivers and end chaotic conditions along the southern borderland where renegades, runaway slaves, and lawless Indians took advantage of Spain's preoccupation at home to roam about unmolested. The South's appetite for this tempting prize had been whetted by a series of events that had taken place in the decade preceding 1812. Chief among these were the gradual infiltration of Americans into West Florida and growing official interest in the region. Settlers, lured southward by Spain's liberal land policy, drifted into the region west of the Pearl River in such large numbers that by 1809 nine-tenths of the district's inhabitants were loyal to the United States. Their presence encouraged President James Madison to make a bold bid for the whole region. Taking advantage of Spain's absorption in the Napoleonic Wars, President Madison advanced the theory that West Florida was part of the Louisiana Purchase. The Treaty of 1803, he pointed out, gave the United States Louisiana "with the same extent that it now has in the hands of Spain, and that it had when France possessed it." Actually those two provisions were irreconcilable; the eastern boundary of Louisiana under Spain was the Iberville River, while under France in 1763 the province extended on to the Perdido. Madison's determination to secure West Florida by claiming the latter boundary was an invitation to Americans there to take matters into their own hands.

They acted in September, 1810, when a group of revolutionists formed an army, seized the Spanish fort at Baton Rouge, and captured the governor. Three days later a convention of insurrectionists formally requested annexation by the United States. President Madison responded on October 27, 1810, when he issued a proclamation annexing the region between the Iberville and Perdido rivers. This order was carried into West Florida by Governor David Holmes of Mississippi Territory with a detachment of regular troops; no resistance was encountered and on December 10 the American flag was raised over Baton Rouge. Mobile, however, remained in Spanish hands, nor did the President dare use force to oust its strong garrison so long as the United States remained at peace. The promise of that rich prize, which controlled the trade of the Alabama Valley, helped to create a western demand for war with Spain and her English ally.

The war spirit was fanned in the Southeast by demands for East Florida, although there the situation was slightly different. The many Americans living in that province were not only well satisfied with Spanish rule but realized that annexation would stop the importation of slaves and end the smuggling of foreign imports across St. Mary's River—a trade that brought prosperity to northern Florida after passage of the Embargo Act. North of the border, however, desire for East Florida was strong, inspired partly by land hunger, partly by a desire to end turbulent border conditions, partly by the success of the West Florida revolution, and partly by the enthusiasm of an ardent expansionist, George Mathews, a former governor of Georgia who began building up a revolutionary party in the autumn of 1810. That winter Mathews laid his plans before President Madison with such success that when he returned to Georgia in the spring of 1811 he carried an official proclamation authorizing him to secure East Florida for the United States either by negotiation or, if any foreign power threatened to take possession, by force. With him too, in all probability, went the President's assurance of aid should Mathews succeed in stirring up a rebellion. Certainly the

troops and warships that Madison dispatched to the Georgia border indicated a plan for armed intervention on the slightest excuse.

Mathews spent the rest of 1811 building up a revolutionary party among Americans in East Florida. By March, 1812, he was ready to act. With a following of two hundred volunteers he fell first on the Spanish town of Fernandina on Amelia Island, then started a march on St. Augustine, followed closely by American troops who refused to take part in actual fighting but occupied each conquered town. By mid-April the Florida capital was under siege and Mathews was dispatching urgent messages to Madison asking authority to use the regular army for its reduction. The President dared not go that far in face of Spain's vigorous protests and the criticism from the antiwar faction in Washington. Instead he dismissed Mathews, ordered the army back to the St. Mary's River, and placed control of border relations in the hands of the Georgia governor. News of this step aroused resentment throughout the southern borderland from Savannah to Nashville. Expansionists, with East Florida snatched from their grasp, believed war with England and Spain necessary before they could complete a conquest they considered rightfully theirs.

In the Northwest expansionist sentiment was stimulated by a desire for Canada. Neither land hunger nor hope for new trade routes was responsible; plentiful lands still awaited the westward marching pioneers while the St. Lawrence route to the sea, although closed to Americans, was too roundabout to be coveted. Instead conquered Canada promised two important benefits: it would end an irritating dispute over the fur trade, and check a serious Indian outbreak then well underway.

The trading dispute was more imagined than real. Since the drafting of Jay's Treaty Canadians roamed the country south of the border, operating from posts at Green Bay, Prairie du Chien, and other strategic spots. Zebulon M. Pike, an army officer sent to explore the Mississippi headwaters in 1805, found them everywhere in the northern woods, entirely unaware that they were on American soil. Their presence alarmed westerners who not only resented the drain of peltry northward, but believed Canadian trappers armed and incited the Indians. Those fears were not shared by the men most affected—the American traders. United States trade was dominated by John Jacob Astor's American Fur Company which, after a period of cutthroat competition with the Canadian North West Company, agreed in 1811 to divide the trade of the West with its rival. The American Fur Company, operating through a subsidiary corporation known as the South West Company, was given exclusive trading rights east of the Rockies, while the Canadian concern was awarded the far-western area. Astor was well satisfied with that arrangement and shied from a war that would upset his carefully worked out plans. Frontiersmen, however, knowing nothing of those international agreements, believed a conflict with England desirable if only to wipe out the clauses of Jay's Treaty that allowed Canadian traders to operate south of the border.

Far more important in sending the West along the road to war was the Indian unrest that boiled through the back country by 1812. Responsible for this were land-grabbing treaties, forced upon the natives by avaricious frontier officials. Thomas Jefferson, whose frontier background transcended his well-known humanitarianism, was to blame for these. Under his administration Indian agents were instructed either to convert western tribesmen to agriculture or move them to unwanted lands beyond the Mississippi. Those harsh orders invited trouble in both South and North. The principal southern agent, a sincere friend of the red men named Benjamin Hawkins, made an honest attempt to transform his charges into farmers, but when this failed he had no choice but to begin absorbing their lands. Between 1802, when the Creeks ceded territories east of

the Oconee and north of the St. Mary's rivers, and 1806, millions of acres in central Georgia, southern Tennessee, and Mississippi Territory were taken from the Cherokee, Choctaw, and Chickasaw, leaving the Indians dissatisfied within their restricted hunting grounds.

Conditions in the Northwest were even worse. Jefferson's agent there was Governor William Henry Harrison of Indiana Territory whose avaricious desire for Indian lands was tempered by neither sympathy nor humanitarianism. He showed his colors first in 1802 when he called representatives of the Kickapoo, Wea, and Delaware tribes together at Vincennes to adjust disputes growing out of the Greenville Treaty line surveys across Indiana. To their amazement Harrison not only proposed to define that boundary, but demanded they cede the territory supposedly purchased by the Wabash Land Company a quarter of a century before. When the chiefs indignantly refused, the governor assured them the lands already belonged to the United States and would be occupied by force unless they backed down. This threat, together with bribes and cajolery, proved effective, although the cession was smaller than Harrison wished.

The Treaty of Vincennes set a pattern that was duplicated time and time again over the next seven years. Conferences were called almost yearly, some at the insistence of the Indians to protest illegal cessions, others by Harrison to correct an alleged wrong done the red men. In each the result was the same, for the natives were powerless before the governor's bribes and threats of force. In 1803 he persuaded the weakened Kaskaskia to surrender their flimsy title to the Illinois country by promising them aid in a threatened war with the Potawatomi. A year later the Sauk and Foxes gave up 15,000,000 acres south of the Wisconsin River in return for annuities and the surrender of a tribesman accused of murdering a white man. When native objections to these tactics reached Harrison's ears he called

a conference at Grouseland, his newly completed mansion at Vincennes, then pitted the assembled tribes against each other to extract another 2,000,000 acres from them. Those treaties, together with smaller cessions from the Delawares and Piankashaw and a giant grant arranged by Governor William Hull of Michigan territory, gave the United States control of eastern Michigan, southern Indiana, and most of Illinois by the close of 1807.

Indian resentment at Harrison's land-grabbing activities would probably have subsided eventually had not two unforeseen events altered the situation. One was the advance of the powerful upper-Mississippi tribes—the Sioux and Chippewa—into the Wisconsin country in search of peltry. There they formed an impenetrable barrier; Great Lakes Indians, no longer able to move westward to new hunting grounds, must fight to maintain their homes. The other was the rise of two leaders for the red men: a Shawnee chieftain, Tecumseh, and his brother, The Prophet. Tecumseh saw that his people suffered because small tribes bowed to Harrison's pressure. If all natives were united in a confederation, with members pledged to make no land cessions without the consent of all, they could resist American demands. That was the message Tecumseh began spreading through the Northwest in 1805, aided by The Prophet, a one-eyed, epileptic medicine man believed by the natives to possess supernatural powers. Together they traveled among the tribes, preaching the need of unity and urging Indians to give up the foibles and firewater of the white man that they might gain strength to win back their lands.

Harrison first heard of their spreading influence in 1806, and although not greatly alarmed, decided to warn the natives against their newly risen prophet. "If he is really a prophet," the governor wrote the Delawares, "ask him to cause the sun to stand still, the moon to alter its course, the rivers to cease to flow." Unfortunately word of this message

reached The Prophet, who had heard from the whites that a total eclipse of the sun was to take place on June 16, 1806. By forecasting this, he realized, his reputation would be forever made. From that time on the word of both Tecumseh and his brother was accepted as law by the Indians; had they not accepted Harrison's challenge to blot out the sun? As tribe after tribe aligned itself with their confederation, the two conspirators were encouraged to take two significant steps during 1808. One was to found the village of Prophetstown at the junction of the Wabash River and Tippecanoe Creek where they could extend their influence over Illinois and Wisconsin tribes. The other was to visit the British post, Ft. Malden, established on the Canadian shore of the Detroit River after Jay's Treaty had forced the evacuation of Detroit. Tecumseh was warmly received by the skilled agent in charge, Captain Mathew Elliott, for the English expected war to follow the controversy over impressment and welcomed a chance to build Indian alliances. At a great council Elliott urged the red men to unite and expressed concern over their loss of lands, but cautioned them not to strike the first blow. Tecumseh, however, was convinced that he could count on British aid.

In the meantime, Harrison, blissfully unaware of this forest intrigue, went ahead with plans for another land-grabbing treaty. The occasion was the creation of Illinois Territory in 1809; many of the earlier cessions were in what was now Illinois and the inhabitants of Vincennes professed alarm at a demarcation line only twenty miles from their doors. Runners spread word of the conference so widely that 1,100 natives were assembled at Fort Wayne when the governor lighted the council fire in September, 1809. Again one tribe was played off against another, particularly after Harrison found the Delawares and Potawatomi anxious to increase their annuities by selling some of their territories; again bribes and pres-

ents were dangled before wavering chiefs. In the end the Treaty of Fort Wayne transferred 3,000,000 acres of Indiana land to the United States, in return for $7,000 in cash and an annuity of $1,750.

That was the final blow. Since the turn of the century nearly 110,000,000 acres of choice hunting land had been wrung from the natives by bribery, threats, and treaties with tribal fragments. Tecumseh, hurrying to Vincennes with a small group of followers, recited his people's grievances in a great open-air council. The land, he told Harrison, was the common property of all the red men; no one tribe had a right to sell. Hence the Treaty of Fort Wayne was invalid, and any attempt to occupy the territory would be resisted. Harrison replied that the lands were acquired legally and would be settled by force if need be. The issue was now clear and war certain.

Attacks on outlying settlements began in the spring of 1810. By autumn, when 6,000 Indians visited Ft. Malden to plead for arms, a border war was in full swing. Major General Isaac Brock, governor general of Upper Canada, was thoroughly alarmed by these developments, fearing England would be blamed for inciting the natives, but his pleas for peace came too late. Young warriors, their fear of the dreaded "Long Knives" forgotten, passed war belts through the forests during the winter of 1810–11 or boasted about council fires that their new unity would drive the whites back to the sea. Tecumseh, however, worked frantically to restrain his over eager braves so long as Harrison made no attempt to occupy the Fort Wayne Treaty lands. In July, 1811, he visited Vincennes with news that he was on his way to enlist southern tribes in his confederacy, and to assure the governor that war could still be avoided if the disputed territory were left alone. When Harrison reiterated his determination to carry on surveys, the two men parted in an atmosphere of mutual distrust.

Tecumseh, with twenty-four Shawnee fol-

lowers, continued south to meet the Creeks, Cherokee, and Choctaw in a conference on the banks of the Tallapoosa River. There, with his face painted the black war color, he urged his 5,000 listeners to join in a to-the-death attack on their oppressors. "Burn their dwellings," he shouted. "Destroy their stock. The red people own the country. . . . War now. War forever. War upon the living. War upon the dead; dig their very corpses from the grave; our country must give no rest to a white man's bones." His fiery plea won over the Creeks, but the Choctaw and Cherokee preferred to wait the actual American invasion of their lands before they risked annihilation.

In the meantime hostilities began in the North. When Tecumseh left Vincennes on August 5, 1811, Harrison recognized a golden opportunity. A march on Prophetstown would goad young warriors, freed from their chief's restraining influence, into an attack that would allow him to administer a crushing defeat. With a thousand troops from Washington and Kentucky he started northward along the Wabash on September 26, 1811. Pausing on the way to erect two strong fortifications, Ft. Harrison at the site of Terre Haute, and a log blockhouse at the mouth of the Vermillion River, the army reached Prophetstown on November 6 and camped three-quarters of a mile from the town, choosing a ten-acre triangle of level land bounded by a thick marsh, a creek, and heavy woods. That night the men slept on their arms, while in the neighboring village The Prophet performed magic rites to render the enemy impotent and his own warriors invincible.

Just before daylight on the morning of November 7 the Indians moved forward through a cold, slow-falling rain to surround the sleeping Americans. Before they attacked, however, one of Harrison's guards detected a movement in the bushes and fired. With this the red men rushed pell-mell into the camp, sweeping past the outposts and into tents where soldiers were still asleep. No surprise could overawe the

seasoned fighters Harrison had assembled. Within a few minutes they beat off the first attack, formed solid lines, and began pouring a murderous fire into the savages. The Indians, disheartened by resistance from soldiers supposedly made helpless by The Prophet's magic, first fell back, then broke completely when Harrison's cavalry charged upon them from two directions. The commander, unable to believe victory was his, kept his men erecting breastworks until November 8 when scouts brought back word that Prophetstown was deserted. The village was destroyed before the American army started back to Vincennes.

The Battle of Tippecanoe was no decisive victory. Harrison's men, who outnumbered the enemy by almost three hundred, held their ground, but their losses were as large as those of the Indians, each side counting thirty-eight killed and 150 wounded. Nor did the victory end the Indian menace in the West. Instead Tecumseh, on his return, sent his followers storming against American outposts with fire and tomahawk. Tippecanoe only scattered Prophetstown fanatics along the frontier to launch the Northwest on a serious Indian war. By the spring of 1812 settlers were fleeing from outlying cabins and fear was sweeping even the thickly settled regions of Ohio and Kentucky.

Hostilities, every westerner believed, could be laid directly at England's door. British agents lured the savages to Ft. Malden, supplied them with guns and ammunition, and drove them forth to murder American backwoodsmen! Harrison reflected the popular view when he wrote: "The whole of the Indians on this frontier have been completely armed and equipped from the British King's stores at Malden." The solution seemed equally simple. The United States must conquer Canada, wipe out Ft. Malden, and end forever the unholy alliance between red coats and red men. The conquest would not only end Indian attacks, but would lift the depression by forcing Britain

to respect American shipping as the price for the return of her colony. Little wonder that westerners drank toasts to "the starry flag of 1812" which would soon "float triumphant over the ramparts of Quebec," or that western representatives assured Congress that "the militia of Kentucky are alone competent to place Montreal and upper Canada at your feet." "We have heard but one word," wrote a disgusted easterner, "—like the whip-poor-will, but an eternal monotonous tone—Canada! Canada! Canada!"

The West wanted war, but that thinly peopled region was too under-represented in Congress to inflict its will on the nation. This became clear when the elections of 1810 sent to Washington a noisy band of "War Hawks," as they were derisively labeled by their enemies. These fire-eaters took control in the House, naming Henry Clay of Kentucky their speaker, packing committees with their numbers, and flooding Congress with petitions and reports demanding heavier military expenditures. Westerners were prominent among the War Hawks, but they were more noticeable for the shrillness of their demands than the weight of their numbers. Of the 61 delegates in the House of Representatives who consistently favored war measures, only 7 were from the West, while 10 were from New England, 15 from the Middle States, and 29 from the South. Clearly hard times in the Ohio Valley or Indian raids along the frontiers were of only remote concern to the majority of the War Hawks. They supported a declaration of war because they believed that the only alternative was humiliating submission to the British colonial and commercial system, and the surrender of the national honor. Their pressure forced a war message from the reluctant Madison. Congress responded on June 18, 1812, by declaring a state of war to exist between the United States and England.

Seldom had a nation been so poorly prepared for a major conflict. Half a dozen warships, an ill-trained army of 6,700 men led by two inept major generals, Henry Dearborn and Thomas Pinckney, an overly cautious President, a people generally indifferent to or, in the case of most New Englanders, openly hostile to war—these were the assets on which the United States relied to win victory from the world's mightiest military power. Nor did public apathy dissolve when fighting began; an appeal for an $11,000,000 loan brought in only $6,000,000, while a call for volunteers was so disappointing that for the rest of the war reliance was placed on state militia. Yet westerners were not discouraged. Canada was defended by only 4,500 troops, and Florida poorly guarded; both would surely fall to American arms before the year was out.

Those dreams were rudely shattered. Within a few months after fighting began even the cocksure Ohio frontiersmen found themselves on the defensive rather than engaged in a spectacular conquest of Canada. The first blow fell when one of their own outposts, Ft. Mackinac, was surprised by a superior British force from nearby St. Joseph Island on July 17, 1812, and forced to surrender without a shot being fired. This disappointment was forgotten amidst plans for an invasion of Canada which would not only recapture Ft. Mackinac but reduce Ft. Malden as well. Westerners could not know that their very enthusiasm for the war ruined their nation's chance for victory. Proper American strategy called for a drive against Montreal through the Champlain Valley, cutting Canada in two, stopping the flow of British supplies to western Indians, and forcing Upper Canada to surrender. Such a campaign was impossible. Only the West would provide men and materials needed for a Canadian invasion, and the West demanded the immediate capture of Ft. Malden. Hence American strategists decided to direct their principal attack against that distant fortification.

General William Hull, the sixty-year-old governor of Michigan Territory named commander of the western army, realized the hopelessness of his task. His force, he pointed out, must be

supplied from Ohio. Food, ammunition, and other essentials could be shipped to Detroit either across Lake Erie or along the banks of the Detroit River. Neither route could be used; English gunboats controlling the lake menaced shore roads, while land transportation was made additionally difficult by the Black Swamp, a tangled morass along the Maumee River lying squarely across the American path. Ft. Malden could never be taken, Hull insisted, until the United States controlled Lake Erie, but like every good soldier he obeyed his orders. Raising 2,000 men, he marched rapidly to Detroit which was reached on July 7, 1812. After a brief pause, the army crossed the Detroit River to Canadian soil where the overly cautious Hull hesitated before launching his attack. General Isaac Brock, British commander in Upper Canada, seized on this opportunity. A small British force was dispatched by water to capture the little village of Brownstown which lay squarely athwart American supply lines on the lower Detroit River. Hull was terrified. When an attempt to dislodge the Brownstown captors failed, he fell back to Detroit, then, as his supplies dwindled, sent one-quarter of his men southward to by-pass his troublesome enemies and reopen communication lines.

That was the moment chosen by General Brock for his attack. On August 16 the entire English army crossed the Detroit River to storm the town's defenses. Hull, his supplies dwindling and his force weakened, had no choice but surrender. The first Canadian invasion resulted not only in defeat but the loss of Detroit to the enemy! Nor did disasters end there, for just as Hull surrendered, another western outpost, Ft. Dearborn, fell. The garrison of that fort, marching to join the defenders of Detroit, was ambushed by Indians amidst the sand dunes of lower Lake Michigan; twenty-six men were killed outright and nine others tortured to death in the "Dearborn Massacre."

Even now the West was not discouraged. The energetic William Henry Harrison, who succeeded Hull in command, had no difficulty raising troops for a fall attack on Canada. Before the Americans could march, they found themselves, to their surprise, on the defensive as British and Indian raiding parties swept down from Detroit against the Ohio forts. Harrison was forced to spend the summer beating off attacks on Ft. Wayne and Ft. Harrison rather than leading a triumphant army northward. When he was finally ready to march in October, 1812, the Black Swamp was impassable and he set his men building military roads across its treacherous surface. Thus ended the glorious dreams of the expansionists in that winter of 1812–13, with their army grubbing its way through the mud of an Ohio swamp and both Canada and three of their own forts in British hands.

Nor did the 1812 campaigns on the New York frontier succeed any better. Two invasions of Canada were planned for that autumn, one across the Niagara River, the other along Lake Champlain. The former was launched on October 18, 1812, when the commander of the state militia at Ft. Niagara threw 6,000 men across the river to capture the heights surrounding the strong British fort of Queenston. Reinforcements needed to turn this initial triumph into a victory never arrived, for Brigadier General Alexander Smyth, commander of the regular army at Niagara, refused to let his men cross the river, insisting that a militia action was no concern of his. As more British troops were rushed into action the outnumbered militiamen fell back slowly until they reached the rushing waters of the Niagara where they surrendered. Petty jealousies and weak discipline cost the United States an army. Equally disheartening was the American failure at Lake Champlain. There General Henry Dearborn drilled 5,000 troops until mid-November, then marched northward. At the Canadian boundary the militia refused to go on, insisting they were to fight only in their own state. Dearborn, who was old and weak, bowed to the mutineers and led his men back to winter quarters at Plattsburg. He alone among the American com-

manders saved his army, but only by keeping it well away from the enemy.

Events in the southern theater during the first year of war were slightly more favorable. When hostilities began only Mobile and Pensacola remained in Spanish hands in West Florida, while in East Florida the American army of occupation, commanded by Governor D. B. Mitchell of Georgia, controlled the country west of the St. John's River and held St. Augustine in a state of siege. Every expansionist was certain that a formal declaration of war would be followed by a rapid conquest of the whole region by the regular army. Spain, however, refused to play into their hands, for her officials, recognizing their country's weakness, steadfastly refused to abandon their neutrality. President Madison, sorely disappointed, was forced to leave the situation to Governor Mitchell and his small army of "patriots." Even they fared badly after St. Augustine officials encouraged the Florida Indians to take to the war path. So many American soldiers scurried off to protect their homes that the remainder, fearing an attack on their thin supply lines, gave up the siege of St. Augustine and fell back to Georgia soil. In November, 1813, disappointed expansionists in that state's legislature grumblingly informed Congress that unless troops were sent against East Florida they would take matters into their own hands.

President Madison, certain that this show of feeling would persuade Congress to authorize an attack on Spanish possessions, hurried word to Andrew Jackson, commander of the Tennessee militia, to raise 1,500 men for a march on Mobile, Pensacola, and St. Augustine as soon as congressional approval was secured. With preparations made, the President in January, 1813, asked Congress for authority to annex both Floridas, charging that negotiations with Spain had broken down and that England or France would occupy the strategic territories if the United States did not. His proposal was decisively defeated on February 2, 1813, by a combination of northern and Federalist votes,

leaving Madison no choice but to dismiss Jackson's army. Southern expansionists were only partly placated when Congress did authorize the occupation of Mobile and West Florida, a move carried out by General James Wilkinson during the next months.

Disheartening as were these events, the Americans were destined to still more trying days before they tasted the sweets of victory. The winter of 1812–13 in the Northwest was spent preparing for a march across the ice to Ft. Malden. That expedition was abandoned when a thousand of Harrison's men, disregarding his orders, struck out on their own to capture Frenchtown, a little settlement on the Raisin River. There they were surprised by a war party of British and Indians on the morning of January 22, 1813. The River Raisin Massacre not only cost the Americans 250 dead and 500 prisoners, but ended all hope of a Canadian invasion. Instead Harrison devoted himself to strengthening Ohio's defenses, knowing the jubilant British could now count on aid from most of the western Indians. Nor was he mistaken. While his men labored on the stout walls and blockhouses of a well-located new fort, Ft. Meigs, skilled English agents scoured the forests between Georgian Bay and the Mississippi for native recruits. By spring a thousand warriors were camped about Ft. Malden, waiting the signal to attack from Colonel Henry Proctor, who succeeded to the western command when General Isaac Brock was killed at the Battle of Queenston.

This came in mid-April, 1813, when Proctor led his thousand regulars and an equal number of Indians southward to lay siege to Ft. Meigs. From April 28 to May 7 British batteries hammered at the American works, but Harrison's defenses were so well planned that the cannon balls buried themselves harmlessly in earthen barricades protecting the fort's wooden walls. When 350 frontiersmen braved enemy fire on May 6 to spike the English guns, the attackers lost heart; the next day they silently dismantled their cannon and vanished into the forest. Three

months later they were back again, this time with 1,400 Indians recently arrived from the Wisconsin country. Harrison, sure that Ft. Meigs could care for itself, left its defense to subordinates while he moved his main force to the Sandusky River country. Two forts commanded that valley: Ft. Stephenson on the lower river and Ft. Seneca several miles to the south. Deciding the former was too weak to withstand a serious attack, Harrison concentrated his men at Ft. Seneca, leaving only 150 militia under a twenty-one-year-old stripling, Major George Croghan, at Ft. Stephenson. The American commander diagnosed the situation correctly; on July 29, 1813, the British abandoned their siege of Ft. Meigs to descend on the Sandusky Valley, marching first against the poorly defended lower fort. Major Croghan, instead of burning the palisade and retreating, decided to make a stand. Loading his one cannon with grapeshot and arranging his handful of followers carefully about it, he waited until the enemy rushed through a breach in the walls, then raked them with a deadly fire from point-blank range. Those not killed broke for the woods where they encountered a strong force under Harrison that had started north at the sound of gunfire. Within a few hours the thoroughly beaten attackers were slinking back toward Ft. Malden, their spirits broken by two failures to penetrate American defenses.

The victory gave Harrison a chance to turn to a task more to his liking: a new attack on Detroit and Ft. Malden. Preparations were already under way. Washington officials, finally realizing that control of Lake Erie was essential to a successful western campaign, had entrusted twenty-seven-year-old Oliver Hazard Perry with the task of building a fleet strong enough to defeat the British gunboats. Perry's sturdy vessels, painstakingly built at Erie of materials transported from the East by wagon train, sailed westward on August 12, 1813, in search of the British force, which was anchored under the guns of Ft. Malden. Not daring to engage the enemy amidst the treacherous cur-

rents of the lower Detroit River, the Americans waited at Put-in-Bay Harbor on South Bass Island, knowing the enemy would have to attack or lose control of Lake Erie by default. On September 10, 1813, the two fleets met in a furious three-hour engagement that ended in complete victory for the superior American force. Harrison heard the good news a day later when a small boat rowed furiously up the Sandusky River bearing an officer who delivered Perry's famous message scribbled on the back of an old envelope: "We have met the enemy and they are ours."

The imposing task of ferrying the whole United States army—recently augmented by the arrival of 3,500 Kentucky militia—to the Canadian shore began at once, and on the afternoon of September 27 a landing was made three miles below Ft. Malden. There word reached Harrison that the British, acting on the sound assumption that it was better to lose a province than an army, had started east along the Thames River. The pursuit began at once, with 3,000 picked men leading the way and supplies following on river boats—an advantage that allowed the Americans to gain rapidly on the slow-moving enemy. On October 5, when only a few miles separated the two armies, General Proctor decided to make a stand. The battle ground selected was a level plain between the Thames River and a dense swamp. There Proctor posted his scanty force: four hundred regulars spread between the swamp and river in two thin lines, six hundred Indians under Tecumseh scattered through the swamp to pour fire upon the attackers.

These elaborate preparations were in vain. At 2:30 on that quiet afternoon Harrison ordered a charge. His Kentucky cavalrymen, yelling like demons, swept through the flimsy British lines, slaughtering as they went, while the infantry plunged into the swamp after the outnumbered Indians. A few minutes of furious fighting and all was over; the entire English force was either killed or captured, Tecumseh dead, and Proctor fleeing toward the neighbor-

Tecumseh, as Billington writes in the text, allied his Indian forces with the British in the War of 1812. He was killed in the crucial battle of the Thames in October 1813, as shown in this painting. (Library of Congress, Courtesy Life.)

ing village of Moravian Town. The Battle of the Thames was one of the decisive victories of the War of 1812, for it broke Indian power in the Ohio and Wabash country, scattered Tecumseh's confederation, and convinced the red men they could not depend on their English allies. To make matters even worse from the Indian point of view a second American army, made up of 1,400 Illinois and Missouri militia and commanded by General Benjamin Howard, at the same time spread a path of destruction through Illinois. By the winter of 1813 all the Northwest was in American hands, with the exception of a few British-held posts.

On other fronts the United States enjoyed less success during 1813. Minor skirmishing along the New York frontier accomplished nothing. In the Southwest a new British ally, the Creek tribe, took to the warpath during the spring, and by midsummer frontiersmen in the whole southern borderland were scurrying into hastily built blockhouses for protection. One rude fortification, built by Samuel Mims on the lower Alabama River, held 553 persons on August 30, 1813, when a horde of yelling savages swarmed through the gates before the surprised defenders could protect themselves. The Ft. Mims Massacre not only brought home the seriousness of the Creek War, but forced the southern states into action.

Although the two small armies that marched west from Georgia accomplished little, a third

column from Tennessee was more successful. This was commanded by Andrew Jackson and composed of 5,000 militiamen who assembled at Fayetteville on October 4, 1813. Marching rapidly south to save Huntsville from a rumored attack, the Tennesseans moved into the heart of the Creek country, pausing only to construct a well-guarded supply road between the Tennessee and Coosa rivers. From the fort at the southern end of that portage route, Ft. Strother, Jackson sent a series of raiding parties to destroy Creek villages; Tallushatchee was wiped out with its two hundred defenders and Talladega subdued with three hundred more. By that time winter ended operations except for one unsuccessful January raid on the Creek town of Tohopeka at Horse Shoe Bend on the Tallapoosa River. Even that defeat reacted in Jackson's favor, as the Indians, convinced this village was impregnable, flocked there in large numbers during the next months. The Americans had only to wait until spring to strike a decisive blow at the whole Creek tribe.

By March 27, 1814, 3,000 troops were camped before Tohopeka where a thousand braves awaited them behind a zigzag log barricade that protected a hundred-acre peninsula. Jackson turned his cannon against the fortification at once, but before his six-pounders opened a breach, a number of friendly Indians swam the Tallapoosa River to attack the defenders from the rear. Instantly all was confusion within the village. Jackson seized the opportunity to order a charge which sent his shouting infantry swarming over the barricade and into the midst of the outnumbered Indians. None attempted to escape; none asked quarter. For hours the slaughter went on; when the Battle of Horseshoe Bend was over eight hundred warriors lay dead on the battlefield. Jackson ordered the few survivors to appear at newly built Ft. Jackson to draw up a treaty of peace. There, on August 1, 1814, the Tennessee commander dictated the terms: the Creeks must surrender sites for military roads and

posts, stop all trade with the Spaniards of Florida, and give up about half their lands—an L-shaped plot lying between their hunting grounds and those of the Choctaw and Chickasaw. The bewildered red men protested in vain; Jackson was adamant and on August 9, 1814, the Treaty of Ft. Jackson was signed. Indian power in the Southwest was broken.

Along the northern borderland the Americans enjoyed less success during 1814, the last year of fighting. A small force of frontiersmen, mindful that the peace treaty might award each nation the lands in its possession when the war ended and aware of the importance of the Wisconsin-Fox River portage route to the fur trade, succeeded in capturing the British-held post of Prairie du Chien in June, 1814, but a larger English party from Mackinac recaptured the fort a month later. Nor did an effort to subdue Mackinac fare any better, for an attempt to land there in August, 1814, was beaten off. Fighting ended with both those strategic outposts in British hands.

On the Niagara frontier the record of dismal defeats also continued. Ft. George, a Canadian outpost captured by a United States naval force early in 1813, was recaptured by the English in December of that year. From that time on they harried Americans constantly; expeditions that crossed on the Niagara River during the winter of 1813–14 destroyed Ft. Niagara, burned Buffalo, and ravaged the countryside. Not until March, 1814, when two able generals, George Izard and Jacob Brown, replaced inefficient commanders did the tide turn. After whipping an army into shape, Brown led his men across the river in July to best British defenders at the Battles of Chippewa and Lundy's Lane before returning to American soil. The summer of skirmishing accomplished little but did prevent an invasion of New York at that point.

Fighting on the Lake Champlain frontier was more serious, as that was the route chosen by British authorities for the final attack on the

United States that would end the war. There they concentrated the seasoned veterans released for American service by Napoleon's defeat; by September 18,000 trained troops stood poised at the northern end of Lake Champlain, waiting the signal to advance. Opposing them at Plattsburg were 3,300 American regulars and militiamen commanded by General George Izard. In this apparently hopeless situation only one factor favored the United States. The British must gain naval control of Lake Champlain before they could attack, and a sufficient powerful American fleet might turn the scales toward victory. All that summer of 1814 skilled shipbuilders labored at the southern lake ports, while in the north English workers fashioned vessels for their commanders. By September 3 the Canadian general, Sir George Prevost, was ready. His fleet of sixteen vessels and his army, reduced to 11,000 men when no more appeared necessary, started south.

At Plattsburg fourteen American gunboats waited them. Their brilliant young commander, Captain Thomas Macdonough, knowing he was outnumbered and must make every shot tell, prepared for the onslaught by providing his anchored vessels with devices that allowed them to swing about quickly. This proved the deciding factor. When the English fleet sailed into Plattsburg Harbor Macdonough's gunboats were able to exchange broadside for broadside, then as British fire weakened, warp about to bring freshly loaded cannon to bear. A few hours of this crippled the strongest enemy ships and forced the remainder to surrender. The Battle of Lake Champlain was decisive, for when Prevost heard of the defeat he turned his army back toward Canada. New York, and perhaps the whole nation, was saved by a young commander's strategy.

Only one more battle remained to be fought, and that in the Southwest. There the English, hoping to secure control of strategic ports against a possible peace treaty that would award spoils to the victors, began an offensive in August, 1814, by landing at Pensacola as a prelude to attacking Mobile. Andrew Jackson, whose triumph at Horse Shoe Bend had been rewarded by a generalship in the regular army, managed to beat off the assault on Mobile but the worst was yet to come. While those maneuvers absorbed American attention a British expedition of fifty ships bearing 10,000 troops set out from Jamaica for New Orleans. News of this new threat sent Jackson west at the head of 12,000 Tennessee volunteers. On December 1, 1814, he began preparing the city for attack, building forts along the lower river and at the entrance to Lake Ponchartrain, throwing up earthworks along the Chef Menteur Road that offered the one land approach, and clogging the bayous along Lake Borgne with fallen trees.

Unfortunately the English hit upon the one flaw in those defenses. On December 22 a landing party found the Bayou Bienvenue was not yet blocked; by noon of the next day several thousand redcoats were drawn up below the city. Jackson, although caught napping, threw the enemy into confusion by an immediate attack, then used the time gained to build earthworks between the British and New Orleans. That delay cost the English leader, Sir Edward Pakenham, the battle, for by the time he turned to the assault the Americans were too well entrenched to be dislodged. A frontal attack failed first, then a heavy bombardment that scarcely marred Jackson's stout defenses. Finally on January 7, 1815, Pakenham adopted the one device that might have succeeded: he sent part of his army across the Mississippi to turn captured American batteries against Jackson's earthworks while his own infantry stormed forward. A sudden fall in the river that night delayed the troops assigned the task of crossing the Mississippi; at the time agreed on for attack on the morning of January 8 they were still far below the American batteries. Pakenham, unaware of this, ordered his men to charge. Wave after wave swept forward, to

be met with the steady fire of the frontiersmen. By nightfall Pakenham and 2,000 of his men lay dead on the battlefield, while Jackson had lost only six men. A few days later the British force straggled back to its ships. The War of 1812 was over, Jackson the new hero of the West.

The Battle of New Orleans did not affect the outcome, for two weeks before Jackson's victory the peace treaty had been signed. Negotiations were begun at Ghent in August, 1814, just as American fortunes were at their lowest ebb; Mackinac, Niagara, and eastern Maine were in British hands, the capitol and White House recently burned, and two powerful English armies preparing to invade the United States through Lake Champlain and New Orleans. From this debacle of wrecked hopes the able American commissioners—John Quincy Adams, Albert Gallatin, Henry Clay, James A. Bayard and Jonathan Russell—must gain what concessions they could. Little wonder that few informed men on either side of the Atlantic expected them to emerge with one, let alone both, of their avowed objectives: a specific English agreement to respect American maritime rights in the future, and the abrogation of the sections of Jay's Treaty which gave Canadian traders the right to operate south of the border. The victorious British would scarcely back down on those two points.

Preliminary negotiations convinced the American agents they had no hope of securing both their demands and that peace could only be secured if they gave ground on one. This one, they saw, must concern neutral rights, partly because the English would never compromise on that issue, partly because frontiersmen would rebel against a treaty unfavorable to their section. Hence they informed the British negotiators that the United States would accept a treaty that did not mention neutral rights—a tacit admission that England's stand

was accepted—if the British would agree to their contentions on the West. For a time negotiations hung in the balance as commissioners deliberated this offer, but time was on the side of the Americans. Word that Prevost's Lake Champlain expedition had failed helped convince the English; so did mounting pressure for peace from taxpayers tired of twenty years of war, and the realization that the United States could never be conquered until Lake Erie and Lake Champlain were controlled. England did not dare begin that slow and expensive task when her crumbling European alliances made a new continental war seem possible. Hence her agents agreed to back down in their western demands for a barrier state, a renewal of Jay's Treaty, and a boundary revision giving Mackinac, Prairie du Chien, and the head of the Mississippi River to Canada. With those mutual concessions, the Treaty of Ghent was signed on December 24, 1814.

Its provisions were far from happy for the United States: a restoration of all territorial conquests by both nations, and a tacit recognition, by omission, that the United States accepted England's provisions concerning neutral rights, while Britain gave up all claims to trade south of the Canadian border. Only one section referred to the Indians and this, although promising them all rights enjoyed in 1811, was so vaguely worded that it meant little. Technically the United States lost the war, as none of the objectives for which it fought was attained. Actually the peace spelled victory, particularly for the West. By signing a treaty of *status quo ante bellum* the British signified their intention of abandoning the Indians to land-hungry frontiersmen. No longer could the red men count on aid from Canadian trappers, or rally behind a prophet who promised them English aid. The way was cleared for a new era of westward expansion that would carry the frontier to the Mississippi.

15

The Chief Justice

George Dangerfield

After the War of 1812, most American leaders insisted that the United States must avoid any further economic or political entanglements with Europe. To do so, America had to become completely self-sufficient. By 1815, many Republicans —Madison among them—sounded like the old Federalists as they talked about the measures necessary to achieve national self-sufficiency: a protective tariff to stimulate American industry, another national bank to stabilize the country's financial system, and government-subsidized internal improvements to unite the sections and facilitate the flow of trade. The name they gave this neo-Federalist program was the American system; its chief architects were Henry Clay of Kentucky and John C. Calhoun of South Carolina, at this time an ardent nationalist who scolded the states for encroaching on the federal government's exclusive power to regulate currency. To implement the American system, Congress in 1816 not only established the Second United States Bank but enacted the first protective tariff in American history. Because of constitutional scruples, Madison vetoed a third measure—Calhoun's cherished "Bonus Bill," which would have given federal funds to the states for internal improvements. By the time James Monroe entered the presidency in 1816, the American system was under way, with the states themselves building their own canals and railroads.

Monroe supposedly inaugurated a period of Republican tranquility, a time of one-party rule called the "Era of Good Feelings." It was misnamed, for the period was marked by bank wars, panics, a sectional crisis over slavery in Missouri, an expansionistic foreign policy which produced the Adams-Oñis Treaty and the Monroe Doctrine, and vicious Republican infighting over the election of 1824 which brought grim and imperious John Quincy Adams to power. Adams, too, was a neo-Federalist. He extracted money from Congress for internal improvements and even went beyond Clay in demanding that the federal government underwrite scientific expeditions, astronomical observatories, and a national university.

Chief Justice John Marshall, however, was the most influential champion of Federalist doctrine during the period. One of John Adams' "midnight appointments," Marshall made the court a bastion of Federalism, and read its basic tenets into American constitutional law: the sanctity of contracts, the protection of property rights, the supremacy of the nation over the states, and the superiority of business over agriculture.

While Marshall and constitutional law may sound like forbidding subjects, George Dangerfield, a Pulitzer Prize-winning historian, not only provides a lively analysis of Marshall's far-reaching decisions but brings him to life both as a judge and a man.

The Washington of Monroe's day generated a good deal of energy, but it was largely personal. The two-party system has rarely if ever produced two distinct parties; in Monroe's time it produced no parties at all. A few old Fed-

eralists still moved around the capital, like statues or mummies; their prestige was great, but their power was chiefly the power of locomotion, and the time would soon come when they would move no more. All ambitious men called themselves Republicans, or sought, without undergoing a public conversion, to attach themselves to whatever Republican faction would best serve their interests. The party boss and the political convention were still local phenomena, and national politics arranged themselves around personalities.

The Era of Good Feelings was pre-eminently the era of the personal myth. The nation's destiny was still uncertain: now one man seemed to personify it, now another. Idiosyncrasies still counted for something, and important figures loomed—at least in their own estimation—a little larger than life size. There was a certain innocence in all but the most opprobious of their transactions: they really believed that what they said and did might have some value, not only for future Americans, but for all mankind. For a few years, the tide in the affairs of men was poised at the flood. Anything might happen to anyone. Even the scramble for the succession to the Presidency, which is one of the most disagreeable features of Monroe's regime, was not altogether a scramble for place or power: it was also a scramble for immortality.

When men are thus challenged to exert themselves, the exertions may take some unusual forms. As an example of personal energy, there are few events in American history to equal that great *Report on Weights and Measures* which John Quincy Adams compiled in such time as he could spare from the management of an understaffed department. When he arrived in Washington in 1817, he found upon his desk a resolution of Congress, requiring him to examine the regulations and standards for weights and measures in the several states, and the proceedings in foreign countries for establishing uniformity in weights and meas-

ures, and to suggest "the course proper to be adopted by the United States." Congress, like the British Parliament, had been stirred by the new French metric system. Coinage depended upon weights, trade upon measures; did the secret of uniformity and peace lie in the French system? The demands of Congress were certainly not modest. What, for example, was the relation of the foot to the meter? Even a well-trained mathematician and physicist, armed with every appliance and supplied with every facility for research, might have confessed himself baffled by such a question. Mr. Adams was an amateur; and Washington provided neither appliances nor books. For a pair of scales upon which to test his theories, he was obliged to go to the Washington branch of the Bank of the United States; and the scales he borrowed were rusty and unregulated. On another occasion, he could find no one who could tell him the content of an ordinary hogshead of Bordeaux. He was expected, of course, to hand the job over to some underling, who would concoct a précis of the available authorities; no one supposed that he would do the work himself, still less that he would produce a masterpiece.

The Report, which was considered by its author to be his chief claim to renown, contained an historical survey of English, Greek, Hebrew, Roman, and French weights and measures, and a "philosophical account of the moral principles involved in the consideration of weights and measures, and of the extent and limitation of its connection with the binal, decimal, and duodecimal arithmetic." It is a major generalization from history, philosophy, and physics; and its essentially dramatic approach to a subject bristling with technicalities reminds the modern reader that its author was the grandfather of Henry and Brooks Adams. The villain of the piece was King Edward I of England, who coined the pound sterling into 243 silver pennies, and thus took away the standard of all the weights and of all the vessels of measure, liquid or dry, throughout his king-

dom. The heroes were the French who, in spite of the "fanatical paroxym" of their revolution, had produced a system of metrology which alone approached perfection. The Secretary doubted whether it would be advisable to disturb the prevailing uniformity between the United States and Great Britain, laden though it was with the crimes of Edward I and the curious mistakes of the Act of 1496. But if the Congress deemed its powers competent and its duties imperative to establish uniformity in its most comprehensive sense, then there was nothing to equal the Definitive French System as established on December 10, 1799. "If the Spirit of Evil," he informed the Congress, "is, before the final consummation of things, to be cast down from his dominion over men, and bound in the chains of a thousand years, the foretaste here of man's eternal felicity, then . . . the metre will surround the globe in use as well as in multiplied extension; and one language of weights and measures will be spoken from the equator to the poles." From the meter to the millennium—what other statesman would have lectured the legislative branch of his government in quite such a way!

What Congress would have made of all this will never be decided; for Congress never bothered to read the *Report.* During Adams's lifetime only one man—an obscure colonel of the Royal Engineers—seems actually to have perused it from beginning to end. He thought it a work of genius, and wrote to say so. Long after Adams's death, Professor Charles Davies and Sir Sandford Flemming reached a similar conclusion. To the observer of Monroe's America it is a singular example of the energy that could be generated by Monroe's Washington. It was published on the very day upon which the great Transcontinental Treaty with Spain was finally proclaimed—February 22, 1821.

Thus, while he was engaged upon this monumental task, Mr. Adams had also been rearranging the continent on Melish's map. At the same time, it was seriously doubted whether Congress could or could not construct a yard of road or dig a foot of canal. The energy contained in Washington can be measured as well by these considerations as in any other way. As has been shown, in the case of Jackson's invasion of Florida, no line of force can be discovered between the capital and the frontier; nor could it have been supplied by an electric telegraph, if one had existed. If the General had been in daily or hourly contact with the War Department, it is still extremely improbable that he could have been restrained from assaulting Pensacola. What influenced him, besides his fervent nationalism, and his inability to distinguish between a campaign and a duel, was the prevailing concept of the powers of the general government. To what extent could it interfere; or, conversely, to what extent could it be disregarded? The General had answered the question in so downright a fashion as to satisfy neither the supporters nor the opponents of strong central government; but the question was of vital significance. It was settled, or its settlement was at any rate adumbrated, in a basement room in the North Wing of the Capitol, where in March 1819 Chief Justice John Marshall delivered his judgment in the case of *McCulloch v. Maryland.* This judgment is at least as extraordinary an example of personal energy as that presented by John Quincy Adams in his *Report on Weights and Measures;* it was also less elevated, and far more influential.

2

Chief Justice John Marshall was a gift sardonically presented to his successor by President John Adams, whose Secretary of State Marshall had been. By nominating Marshall in the last month of his Administration President Adams made it certain that the Federalist cause —defeated in Cabinet and Congress—would at least be maintained upon the Supreme

Bench: nor was he disappointed. John Marshall became the great link between the aristocracy of the eighteenth century and the capitalism of the nineteenth. For one brief moment in 1805, during the impeachment of Justice Chase, it seemed as if Marshall himself would fall victim to the just wrath of his opponents: as if disgrace, and worse than disgrace, would be his portion. Marshall himself trembled; but the crisis passed. From then on "the wise, the rich, and the good" knew that, whatever inroads democracy might make upon two of the coordinate branches of the government, the third was safe from its invasion.

In 1819, John Marshall was at the very height of his powers; and it is to this year that we must look for the most concentrated expression of his Constitutional views. In February he declared, in his decision on the case of *Sturges v. Crowninshield,* that a New York State bankruptcy law violated the contract clause of the Constitution; and thereupon drew upon his head the objurgations of every debtor in the country. A few days later, in his judgment on the case of *Dartmouth College v. Woodward,* he announced that a corporation charter should be regarded as a private contract, immune from all legislative control. In March, in the case of *McCulloch v. Maryland,* he pronounced the national Constitution and the laws thereof to be superior in every instance to the constitutions and laws of the respective states. To the business community, all this was balm from Gilead.

Of the great figures of Monroe's America, John Marshall has been the one most often wrested out of the context of his times. He then becomes the robed servant of the moneyed interests and the business community; and, of course, to a very great extent he was. There is a close connection between constitutionalism and capitalism; and Marshall has done as much as any man to call attention to it. As Justice Holmes has said, Marshall was not one of the originators of transforming thought: he did not

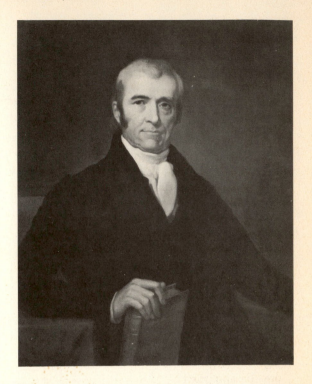

John Marshall, Chief Justice of the United States Supreme Court from 1801–1835. There was a "terrible disparity," Dangerfield writes, "between the great mistrusting Federalist judge and the friendly human being who hid himself beneath those judicial robes." As a judge, Marshall read the basic tenets of Federalist doctrine into American constitutional law. As a man, though, Marshall loved to mix with drinkers at wayside taverns, where people often mistook him for an old farmer. "His black eyes gleamed with good humor and his characteristic expression was one of great benevolence." (Courtesy of The National Portrait Gallery, Smithsonian Institution.)

make those decisions which have in them the germ of some wider theory, and therefore of some profound interstitial change in the very tissue of the law. His thought did not transform; it merely sanctioned transformation. It seems to be little more than a judicial gloss upon those doctrines which we commonly associate with the name of Alexander Hamilton.

Powerful but unscholarly, olympian but redundant, his decisions inform us that nothing could prevent the advance of capitalism into the empty spaces of America during the early nineteenth century; and that the national Constitution was the very means by which this advance could be expedited. These decisions are so clearly formulated that even the layman can pick his way through them without undue difficulty; but he is apt to find the experience a chilly one. Marshall was no humanitarian. He often had occasion to mention "the people"; but, with very few exceptions, his "people" have neither hearts nor sensibilities nor tears, neither appetites nor satisfactions: they are simply a function of power.

Yet at this point it is necessary to return him to the context of his times. That he was a Virginian Federalist; that he worshiped his father and was obliged, as eldest son, himself to be father surrogate to a large family of brothers and sisters; that his favorite early reading was Pope's *Essay on Man*; that he learned, as a soldier at Valley Forge, to distrust the good faith of the individual states; that he regarded Burke's *Reflections on the Revolution in France* as almost a sacred text—all these were important factors in the life of a man who was a strict, one might almost say a relentless, paternalist, and who strove to inject into the American Constitution a strong dose of English conservative thought. With such a background and such mentors was it likely that John Marshall, when the choice was offered him, would prefer the agrarian to the capitalist? And the choice was offered him over and over again.

At the same time one has to recognize that the business community for whom John Marshall seems so faithfully to have labored was still in its infancy; though it had, to be sure, already given the world some remarkable evidences of an extreme precocity. It would be foolish to assume that the corporation, which Marshall so plentifully blessed in *Dartmouth College v. Woodward*, was the unit of business enterprise it has since become. It could still be regarded as a humble but useful device in the development of a system of free enterprise which was, itself, as yet no more than an eventuality. To Marshall, therefore, the business community was the agent of order and of progress.

There were some men, it is true, to whom the notion of the businessman as a revolutionary, a person capable of subverting society in order to further his own ends, had already presented itself in the most forcible manner: but these men were usually slave-holders, and therefore potential revolutionaries themselves. The prevailing ethos of Marshall's times would have rejected such a notion, because this ethos made it quite impossible for men to sift the evidence that supported it. Land speculation was the focus for financial activity in Marshall's day; and the history of early land-titles is one long record of subverted law, of weird fraudulence, of corrupted legislatures. Marshall's inspection stopped at the legislatures, which he regarded with an extreme suspicion as the repositories of democracy and disorder, two words that were to his way of thinking practically synonymous. He condemned, as it were, the flotsam on the waterline, but not the flood that had deposited it there. He was, indeed, himself still damp from bathing in those waters. He had once been deeply engaged in land speculation, and the consequent litigation pursued him even on to the Supreme Bench. Yet in *Fletcher v. Peck* (1810) he declared that a contract was sacred, regardless of its ethics, and thus appeared to encourage all that was vicious in the land business and to condone much that was dubious in his own past. This was clearly not evident to him; and the fact that it was not evident indicates how deeply land speculation had eaten into the moral fiber of America.

It is true that Marshall subsequently raised the sanctity of contract into a *mystique*, in which Contract appears as a great principle, "anterior to and independent of society"; and

that even his obedient colleagues could not follow him into this legal Manichaeism—this effort to provide the business community with a tutelary demon. But Marshall would never have seen things in this light. To him the sanctity of contract was not an ingenious device for transferring the property of the many into the hands of the few, but the very cornerstone of economic stability. It was when he was most mystical that he was also most nationalist.

Indeed, when one attempts to restore him to the context of his times, it becomes exceedingly difficult to separate the business-minded judge from the nationalist statesman. His nationalism was not lovable; it was based on a mistrust of the human *dynamis* of the nation which it strove to create. It was founded upon a defense of artificial property: but it is only just to admit that it did not carry this defense to extremes. In his decision on the case of *Gibbons v. Ogden,* Marshall struck down a steamboat monopoly, and did as much as any single man could do to make the steamboat free upon the western rivers; and the steamboat was not merely an essential factor in the development of the internal market, it was also the very symbol of democracy. Moreover, it was in his judgment in this important case that Marshall, for all his boldness, showed a great deal of caution. The question at the very heart of *Gibbons v. Ogden* was this: Did the mere grant of a power to Congress to regulate commerce "among the several states" automatically prohibit a state from creating a steamboat monopoly? The question was exceedingly difficult, and Marshall himself, in *Sturges v. Crowninshield,* had declared that "the mere granting of a power to Congress did not imply a prohibition on the states to exercise the same power." But he immediately qualified this statement by declaring that whenever the nature of the power required that it should be exercised exclusively by Congress, "the subject is as completely taken from the state legislatures as if they had been expressly forbidden to act on

it." Was the nature of the power granted in the commerce clause such that it should be exercised exclusively by Congress? If it was—or rather if the Supreme Court declared it to be—of such a nature, then it was clear that a vast and subtle change had taken place in the relationship between the general government and the individual states. Marshall never answered the question directly. He gained much popularity from his decision, and he might have established the "dormant" power of the commerce clause—that is to say, its *implicit* veto upon state legislation—without too much disagreement from the rest of the Court. Instead, he merely suggested—and in terms that may have been deliberately confused—the existence of the dormant power. He seemed to think that too open a declaration of federal authority would arouse in time an irresistible opposition, and he may well have reminded himself that his own doctrine was, after all, a double-edged affair. If the state authority could be limited by the Court in the interests of the nation, might not the national authority also be limited by the Court in the interests of the states? The Tenth Amendment—not one of Marshall's favorites—always made this possible. Marshall even went further, and began to restore to the states, in the form of a "police power," some of the authority he had elsewhere taken from them. "We must never forget," he once said, "that it is a constitution we are expounding" . . . something organic, capable of growth, susceptible to change.

Indeed his vaguely defined notion that political activity must be coextensive with economic activity suggests that if he had been born into a late instead of an early stage of liberal capitalism, he might have been as anxious to check the exuberance of business enterprise as he was in fact eager to encourage it. His nationalism was not lovable; but how readily, in another age, under other circumstances, might its terms have been changed!

In 1819, however, his nationalism seemed to

place the Constitution at the service of the moneyed interests, and to express a profound mistrust in the ability of the masses to govern themselves—for it was in the state legislatures, in those days, that men chiefly looked for a manifestation of the art of self-government.

It is for this reason that John Marshall with all his advantages—intelligence, conviviality, a prodigious gusto for the simple pleasures of life—has left but a frosty imprint upon American history. There is a perplexing, indeed a terrible disparity between the great mistrusting Federalist judge and the friendly human being who hid himself beneath those judicial robes. John Marshall was a tall man, thin to emaciation, with a head rather too small for his body, and joints so loosely put together that he shambled around like a marionette. His black eyes gleamed with good humor and his characteristic expression was one of great benevolence. As he lounged among the drinkers at a wayside tavern, with his tousled hair and his soiled and shabby clothes, one might have mistaken him —and many people did—for a simple old farmer. There are numberless stories attesting him the most democratic of men: stories of Marshall ambling to market with a basket on his arm and stopping to gossip at every stall; or riding out to his country farm with a stray child on his saddlebow, or with his thumb in a jug of whisky of which he had lost the cork; or crawling on the ground with a straw in his mouth to make some nice decision in a game of quoits; or shouting out a chorus at one of his famous suppers. His chivalry towards women was exalted, even for a Southern gentleman; and Richmond long remembered his romantic devotion towards his poor, distracted wife. Often enough at night he would go downstairs in his bare feet to drive away from their house some errant cow or pig which threatened to disturb her sleep. Or he would send her out for a long country drive while he himself, in his shirtsleeves with a bandanna twisted round his head, would lead the ser-

vants in a thorough scrubbing of the house. The contrast between the man and the judge is so extreme that one is almost forced into mythology for a similar metamorphosis. Does he not resemble the Ovidian Jove, approaching the maiden Democracy in all sorts of agreeable disguises and then only, in the moment of possession, revealing himself as the Thunderer?

Such was the Chief Justice who on March 6, 1819, in his little basement room, pronounced his judgment in the case of *McCulloch v. Maryland*.

3

The facts in the case of *McCulloch v. Maryland* were as follows: Congress had authorized the incorporation of the Second Bank of the United States, and this great institution had set up a branch at Baltimore. In an Act of February 11, 1818, the legislature of Maryland required all banks doing business within her borders, and holding charters she had not granted, to pay an annual tax of fifteen thousand dollars, and to issue notes only of certain denominations. If such banks preferred not to pay the tax, then they must print their notes only upon stamped paper purchased from the Treasurer of the Western Shore. The Baltimore branch of the Bank of the United States, however, declined to pay the tax, and with complete insouciance continued to issue its notes upon unstamped paper. Whereupon the Treasurer of the Western Shore, John James, sued the cashier of the branch Bank, James W. McCulloch, for the recovery of the prescribed penalties—which, at five hundred dollars an offense, probably ran into many hundreds of thousands.

The Baltimore County Court gave judgment for the state, as did the Maryland Court of Appeals, which then permitted the case to be brought to the Supreme Court of the United States upon a writ of error. Like many other cases involving a Constitutional issue, this was

"arranged"; and it was even suggested that there was some collusion in it, and that the Maryland counsel had not presented their strongest arguments.

However this may have been, the issues involved were of great and grave consequence. If one construed the Constitution loosely, then Congress had the right to charter a bank; if one construed it strictly, then Congress had no such right. Obviously, the true significance of the controversy over loose and strict construction lay in the uses to which they could be put by economic interests. The new industrial capitalism needed, or thought that it needed, a national bank in order to send fresh money circulating through all the arteries and veins of trade; while the moneyed interests of New York and New England, though somewhat jealous of the national bank, would not frown on a judicial decision that threw around financial activity the protecting cloak of loose construction.

A national bank! The words had a distressing sound for all good agrarians, who believed that the industrialists and financiers were out to crush them with protective tariffs, and corrupt them with internal improvements. Had not Alexander Hamilton's child, the First Bank of the United States, been a deliberate effort to ally the national government with the moneyed interests? And was there any reason to believe that James Madison's child, the Second Bank of the United States, would be more pure? Mr. Madison, it is true, had fathered the bank with some reluctance, but the country's fiscal needs were so pressing, and the currency was in such disorder, that the government had either to create a national institution or to throw itself on the mercy of the private bankers. On April 10, 1816, therefore, the Second Bank of the United States came into existence. It was far more closely wedded to the government than was the Bank of England, the Bank of France, or any other similar contemporary institution. The federal government owned one fifth of its

stock, whereas the capital of other central banks was wholly private. The President of the United States appointed five of the twenty-five directors. No man who disliked the connection between government and banking could possibly approve of such an institution.

It is a little difficult to separate the bank's main functions from the press of incidental powers surrounding them; from the vast amount of private business it transacted; from its ability to loan the public money to politicians and newspaper editors; from its control of foreign exchange and its alliance with foreign banking. But its utility as a keeper of the public deposits and a transferer of the public funds could hardly be denied; and it was probably true that it alone possessed the power of restoring some kind of order to the national currency. The government's receipts were principally from taxes paid by importers to customs collectors. These tax payments were generally made in the notes of private banks, for such notes provided most of the money in circulation in the United States. By receiving these notes on deposit from the customs collectors, and presenting them to the private banks for payment, the Bank of the United States became the creditor of the banks. Thus a private bank that extended credit in a proper manner, and maintained an adequate gold and silver reserve, could always meet its obligations, and a bank that overextended itself could not. The Bank of the United States, therefore, by maintaining a constant pressure upon the private banks could restrict their lending and their issue of notes, and curb their tendency to lend too much and so depreciate their circulation. In short, its regulatory powers were exactly the opposite of those now existing under the Federal Reserve Act. Under the present system, private banks maintain balances with the Federal Reserve Banks, and are their creditors; in those days, the private banks were the debtors of the Bank of the United States. It has been maintained that this system, though it would not be prac-

ticable in our complicated economy, was well suited to those simpler times.

Obviously, the private banks disliked this situation—this dependence upon an institution with headquarters in Philadelphia and with four fifths of its board of directors elected by the stockholders of that city, and with all the powers of the national government behind it. Those who examine the doctrine of State Rights in the hopes of finding a rich deposit of idealism in it are generally obliged to confess that this deposit is extraordinarily elusive and sporadic. In the case of *McCulloch v. Maryland* did the state of Maryland propose to tax the branch bank at Baltimore out of existence because it believed such a bank to be a dangerous invasion of its sovereignty, or could the pressure of private bankers have been responsible?

In any case, it is true that the private banks offered very little assistance to the Second Bank of the United States when it first came into being. Its purpose was to create a stable currency, and this in turn could only be effected if the private banks would agree to resume specie payments, if they would consent to contract their credit dealings sternly enough to support the fiction that their paper was convertible upon demand into gold or silver. Since they were making large profits out of inconvertible paper, they were naturally unwilling to make this contraction; and a convention of the associated banks of New York, Philadelphia, Baltimore and Richmond only agreed to do so if the Bank of the United States would extend its credit dealings while they contracted theirs. This was a very harsh, and very early declaration of the view that it is the duty of the central bank to act as lender of the last resort. The bank needed all its caution if it was to discount six million dollars before it called in the balances accumulating against the private banks.

And the bank, as it happened, used no caution at all during the first two years of its existence, with the inevitable result, as will be shown, that when it began to put its affairs in order it was obliged to inflict the country with a ruinous contraction of credit. Thereafter, it performed its functions with a praiseworthy efficiency. And yet there was something dangerous and menacing about it. The strict members of the Republican Party could not forgive James Madison for signing the bill which incorporated the Second Bank of the United States. Had he not fought the first bank tooth and nail? And was there any difference between the first bank and the second? They could not see that, since the monetary policy was national, the means for putting it into effect must be national too; their criticism was just, but it did not go far enough, and it moved in the wrong direction. What was dangerous about the Second Bank of the United States was that it was far too free from government control. The Republicans who created it in 1816 were themselves suspicious of strong government, and they allowed this suspicion fatally to weaken the relation between the government and the bank. Nicholas Biddle, the bank's third president, in those moments of infatuated exuberance to which he was so unfortunately given, made this clear enough; but he made it clear, too, in his sober moments. Writing to Monroe in 1824, he said that certain suggestions of the Secretary of the Treasury "will be most respectfully considered by the Board of Directors, and cheerfully agreed to, *if not inconsistent with their duties to the institution.*" What might not be expected from a national bank that would follow the suggestions of the government only when these suggestions did not conflict with the interests of its stockholders?

All this was still in the future. In 1819, the Second Bank of the United States was fighting for its life against the efforts of certain states to destroy it with taxes; while at the same time the nation at large, plunged deep in an economic depression, was beginning to regard the bank as the chief engineer of its misfortunes.

It was in this atmosphere that John Marshall was called upon to decide between the bank and the state of Maryland; and this decision permits us to hear, full and resonant, the strange and dangerous voice of early economic nationalism.

4

The Supreme Court of the United States sat in the city of Washington for one brief term of six or eight weeks every year. Marshall and his associates lived at the same boarding house, where the Chief Justice seemed, says his biographer, to be "the head of a family as much as he was chief of a court." At these close quarters, his singular combination of intelligence, charm, and iron will worked its magic upon his colleagues. The Court was "Marshall's Court," it was said. As the years passed, the political complexion of the justices had changed: a majority of the Court was now Republican. But—it was odd and it was disturbing—these Republicans had scarcely taken their seats before they changed their views. Justice Joseph Story might have been forgiven for such a defection—he was young when he joined the Court, he was impressionable, he came from Massachusetts, and his Republicanism had always been doubtful. But what could one say for William Johnson of South Carolina, once "strongly imbued with the principles of southern democracy," whose leaning towards Federalism now became so pronounced that in some instances—notably in his interpretation of the commerce clause—he seemed to out-Herod Herod himself? Marshall's great decisions, it may safely be said, were generally the result of long discussion between himself and his brethren—they have been described as orchestral rather than solo performances; but there could never be any doubt as to who was the conductor. In legal scholarship, and indeed in richness of mind, men like Story and John-

son were far superior to Marshall; what they lacked was the power to resist his will. Towards the end of Marshall's reign, when nationalism sought to divorce itself from its marriage with private wealth, his Court grew restive; but even after his death there was a Marshall group which, under Justice Story, fought bitterly against the democratic tendencies of Chief Justice Taney.

A Court thus dominated, and by a man who used the "people" as a conceptual means of defeating what little could be ascertained of the people's will, was naturally a dramatic affair. During the hearing of *McCulloch v. Maryland* the Supreme Court basement in the Capitol was "full almost to suffocation, and many went away for lack of room." Probably most people knew that the Chief Justice would declare for the bank and carry the Court with him; what took the country by surprise was the magistral fashion in which he did so. The denouement, then, as far as the bank was concerned, was already known; the drama was prearranged; and what summoned the spectators was a classic interest in the quality of the performance.

Ladies as well as gentlemen elbowed their way into the modest room beneath the Capitol; for Washington was culturally famished and the Supreme Court represented a kind of theater. An eminent counsel had been known to stop in the middle of an argument when ladies appeared, and ask permission to repeat what he had said, but in simpler and more amusing language; nor was permission denied him. For the acting out of *McCulloch v. Maryland* a most distinguished cast had been assembled: for the bank, Mr. William Pinkney, Mr. Daniel Webster, and Attorney-General Wirt; for the state of Maryland, Mr. Luther Martin, Mr. Joseph Hopkinson, and Mr. Walter Jones. Luther Martin, "the Thersites of the law," short, broad-shouldered, slovenly, seventy-one years old, whose wit had confronted the dull world with conviviality but not with gladness, and whose face was purple from fifty years of

brandy-drinking, brought into that room the lurid memories of Justice Chase and of Aaron Burr. Everybody was interested in Luther Martin, who happened also to be making his last appearance before any bar in this world. But the most popular actors were Daniel Webster and William Pinkney. Mr. Webster had already made his reputation as a lawyer and an orator in his arguments before the Court in *Dartmouth College v. Woodward.* His mind had, it is true, not yet revealed its barometric character—its almost perfect registration of the climate of opinion among men of wealth and power. He was not yet a famous man, but much was expected of him. He had at least founded—it is the fate of most orators—a reputation that was to be composed almost exclusively of perorations. At the end of his speech in the Dartmouth College case he had paused, apparently groping for the words that, with a characteristic economy, he had already used in a lower Court. "It is, Sir," he faltered out at last, "as I have said, a small College. And yet, there are those who love it." His voice choked with sobs; the audience reached for its handkerchiefs; and even Chief Justice Marshall began to cry. "Business enterprise," says one disillusioned commentator, "has never had more useful mercenaries than the tears Daniel Webster and John Marshall are reputed to have shed that March day." Such was Webster's magic that the true issue—the demand of private corporations to be immune from legislative interference—temporarily disappeared, and the image of a small college, dedicated to the instruction of the sons of poor men, superimposed itself upon this huge pretension. Certainly, Mr. Webster would go far. His appearance was formidable—the craggy head, the smouldering black eyes, the solid body correctly encased in the blue cut-away with big brass buttons. His opening argument in *McCulloch v. Maryland* was not long, but one would have liked to hear that deep, that thrilling voice as it pronounced the words "the power to tax is the power to destroy"—an argument that Marshall used in his decision and that still booms, very usefully though with less conviction, across the years. He was followed in due time by William Pinkney, the leading actor—one might almost say the leading juvenile—in that gifted cast. The old rip, with his corsets and his cosmetics and his preposterously youthful clothes, was a great favorite with the ladies: when they were present he never failed to scatter little complimentary allusions along the dusty trail of the law. But it so happened that he had one of the finest minds in the profession; and when he spoke—which, on this occasion, he did for three days—the flowery tropes and hircine postures did not interfere with what was, first and last, a masterly exposition of Hamiltonian law. At the end of nine days the audience retired, well satisfied with the performance, and left the Chief Justice to recite, almost to an empty theater, his resounding epilogue.

John Marshall was a master of deductive exposition. No man was happier with a syllogism than he—no man was more adept at separating the "irrelevant" elements from the "significant" facts of the case, and then discovering that this particular case had already been provided for in a general rule of law. Thus it was easy for him to deduce from the "necessary and proper" clause of the Constitution the power of Congress to incorporate a bank, since this power was clearly "incidental" to the great enumerated powers: "to lay and collect taxes; to borrow money; to regulate commerce; to declare and conduct a war; and to raise and support armies and navies." It was, therefore, "the unanimous and decided opinion" of the Court that the Bank Act of February 10, 1816, was Constitutional. The establishment of a branch bank at Baltimore was also Constitutional. Since some of his opponents resolutely refused to believe that the

judiciary had the power to declare an Act of Congress either Constitutional or not Constitutional, this announcement was audacious enough. It was nothing, however, to what came after. For in declaring that the Act of the state of Maryland, which taxed the branch bank, was repugnant to the national Constitution, John Marshall readily admitted that the power of taxation was retained by the states and not abridged by the grant of a similar power to the general government. But he went on to say, with all the emphasis at his command, that the Constitution was of so paramount a character that "its capacity to withdraw any subject from the action of even this power, is admitted." In other words, the national government might withdraw from state taxation *any* taxable subject, and not merely those subjects which the Constitution specifically withdraws. And this argument, or assertion, was sustained, not on the language of the Constitution, but on the "great principle that the constitution and the laws thereof are supreme; that they control the constitution and laws of the respective states, and cannot be controlled by them."

Nationalism could go no farther.

Marshall always maintained, as a fundamental premise, that it was possible to fathom the purposes of the framers of the Constitution; and neither his friends nor his opponents disagreed with him. In 1819, it is true, very little was known about the purposes of the framers of the Constitution. The Journal of their Convention had not yet been published; and Mr. Madison's invaluable notes still lay buried in his private archives. None the less, everybody agreed that if one examined the Constitution in the right light one would inevitably descry the purposes of its framers. The great document itself was marvelously brief: even in the late 1880's an English admirer was able to exclaim that it was about half as long as St. Paul's first epistle to the Corinthians, and one fortieth as long as the Irish Land Act of 1881. Few instruments in history have laid down such momentous rules, on such a vast range of subjects, and in so few words. The only question remained—in what light was one to examine it?

Obviously, so much had occurred between the framing of the Constitution in 1787 and the attack on the bank in 1819 that the purposes of the framers, even if they could be discovered, had already become irrelevant. They could not have foreseen the invention of the cotton gin, or the awakening of industrial enterprise under the Embargo. No doubt they intended the Constitution to bestow upon Congress "the capacity to avail itself of experience, to exercise its reason, and to accommodate its legislation to circumstances." Marshall said that they did; and few men in the country could have disagreed with him. Whether Congress should accommodate its legislation to the special needs of bankers and industrialists— that was the question. Marshall carried his generalization one step further. He announced that the framers of the Constitution, when they granted certain specific powers to Congress, did not intend to impede the exercise of those powers by withholding a choice of means. "Let the end be legitimate," he said, "let it be within the scope of the constitution, and all means which are appropriate, which are plainly adapted to that end, which are not prohibited, but consist with the letter and spirit of the constitution, are constitutional." In other words, while Marshall's opponents contended that the national government might only do what it was expressly permitted to do, Marshall himself declared that it might do anything it was not expressly forbidden to do.

What would the framers of the Constitution, with their grave suspicion of the caprice of the majority, have said to *that*? As it happened, one of the Founding Fathers was sitting in Marshall's presence, in the rather saurian shape of Mr. Luther Martin. Mr. Martin, it is true,

was not exactly a Father—he had left the Constitutional Convention in a rage, because it seemed to him to be paying too little heed to the claims of the small states. He had subsequently become a Federalist. He was now, once again, pleading the cause of State Rights. If one had asked him what were the purposes of the framers of the Constitution, one would have received a rather confusing answer; but his presence in Marshall's court, as an attorney for the state of Maryland against the bank, suggested that Marshall's interpretation was open to some doubt. On the other hand, no man had more claim to interpret the intentions of the Fathers than had James Madison; and in Number 44 of *The Federalist* Madison himself had written: "No axiom is more clearly established in law, or in reason, than that wherever the end is required, the means are authorized; wherever a general power to do a thing is given, every particular power necessary for doing it is included." Marshall himself had said no more than that.

No sooner had Marshall's decision been published than the attack upon it was commenced; and it was impossible for James Madison to remain uninvolved. He was asked by Judge Spencer Roane for an opinion upon Marshall's decision. "Is there a legislative power, in fact," he replied, "not expressly prohibited by the Constitution, which might not, according to the doctrine of the court, be exercised as a means of carrying into effect some specified power? . . . It was anticipated, I believe, by few, if any, of the friends of the Constitution, that a rule of construction would be introduced as broad and pliant as what has occurred." This was perspicuously stated, as one might expect from that keen and copious mind: it revealed the weak link in Marshall's logic. Whether or not the furibund Roane was satisfied with such an answer has not been recorded; but Madison can scarcely have written it without some misgivings. He can hardly have forgotten Number 44 of *The Federalist*. Moreover, he had signed the

bill that incorporated the bank, and his attitude towards Marshall's decision, which protected the bank, must have been, to say the least, ambivalent.

And so it became clear that when the Constitution was challenged by a specific set of circumstances, there would be little comfort in the Fathers, living or dead.

5

The Court's decision in the case of *McCulloch v. Maryland* was read by Marshall on March 6, 1819. The bank was saved. The Chief Justice had said little that had not already been said by Alexander Hamilton in his opinion on the Constitutionality of the first bank, written in 1791. It was not the originality of Marshall's decision that counted: it was its audacity and its resonance. The doctrine of nationalism had been shouted from the highest court in the land; and those who believed, either as ideologists or as economists, that salvation lay with the action of state legislatures, were equally loud in their rebuttal. Even Hezekiah Niles took up the cudgels in his *Register*. Spencer Roane—inadequately disguised as "Amphictyon" and as "Hampden"—pummeled the Chief Justice in the columns of the *Richmond Enquirer*. Judge Roane threatened that Virginia might employ force, if other measures failed her, and Mr. Niles gave it as his opinion that "certain nabobs" in New York, Boston, Philadelphia, and Baltimore had fairly purchased the souls of Congressmen with money in order to secure the passage of the Bank Act. He called upon all the people who hated monopolies and privileged orders to rise in their might and "purge our political temple of the money-changers and those who sell doves." The attack spread. The legislatures of Pennsylvania, Tennessee, Ohio, Indiana, and Illinois voiced their disapproval, asking for an amendment to the Constitution forbidding Congress to incorporate a bank. The

Chief Justice was severely shaken; and though he gave his support to the business community in decision after decision thereafter, he never again offered this support in such resounding nationalist terms. It may well be that the reception given to his decision in *McCulloch v. Maryland* taught him a valuable lesson in the art of statecraft, and urged him to pay more attention to the value of local autonomy in his nationalist scheme. For, with all his chilling predilections, Chief Justice John Marshall was a great man.

V Freedom's Ferment

16

Andrew Jackson and the Rise of Liberal Capitalism

Richard Hofstadter

The Age of Jackson was a turbulent era—an era of boom and bust, of great population shifts into the cities and out to the frontier, of institutionalized violence and racial antagonisms, of utopian communities, reform movements, the Abolitionist Crusade, and the "Great Southern Reaction." It was also a time of graft and corruption, of machine politics and ruthless political bosses. But above all it was an age of the self-made man, a time when privilege and elitist rule gave way to the vestiges of popular democracy (at least for white males). Between the 1820s and 1840s, America witnessed the rise of universal manhood suffrage for whites, long ballots, national nominating conventions, and grass-roots political parties.

But what of Jackson himself? Was he a great Democrat who led the common man to power in 1828? Or was he merely a symbol for an age? Richard Hofstadter portrays him as rather more complex than that. As he explores Jackson's character and career, he offers trenchant insights into the meaning and consequences of the Jacksonian movement itself.

Could it really be urged that the framers of the constitution intended that our Government should become a government of brokers? If so, then the profits of this national brokers' shop must inure to the benefit of the whole and not to a few privileged monied capitalists to the utter rejection of the many. ANDREW JACKSON

The making of a democratic leader is not a simple process. Because Andrew Jackson came into prominence on the Tennessee frontier, he has often been set down as typical of the democratic frontiersman; but many patent facts about his life fit poorly with the stereotype. From the beginning of his career in Tennessee he considered himself to be and was accepted as an aristocrat, and his tastes, manners, and style of life were shaped accordingly. True, he could not spell, he lacked education and culture, but so did most of those who passed as aristocrats in the old Southwest during the 1790's and for long afterward; even many Virginians of the passing generation—George Washington among them—spelled no better. Since Virginians and Carolinians of the upper crust seldom migrated, the Southwestern aristocracy came mainly from middle- or lower-class migrants who had prospered and acquired a certain half-shod elegance. Jackson, the mid-Tennessee nabob, was typical, not of the Southwest's coonskin democrats, but of its peculiar blend of pioneer and aristocrat.

Jackson was born in 1767 on a little farm in the Carolinas some months after the death of his father. He enlisted in the Revolution at thirteen, was captured and mutilated by British troops at fourteen, and lost his entire family in the war when one brother was killed, another succumbed to smallpox in prison, and his mother was carried off by "prison fever" while nursing captured American militiamen. From

From pp. 44–66 in *The American Political Tradition* by Richard Hofstadter. Copyright 1948 by Alfred A. Knopf. Reprinted by permission of the publisher.

his family he inherited a farm-size plot of land in North Carolina, from the Revolution a savage and implacable patriotism. For six months Jackson was apprenticed to a saddler. Then, although his own schooling had been slight and irregular, he turned for a brief spell to schoolteaching. When a relative in Ireland left him a legacy of over three hundred pounds, he moved to Charleston, where, still in his teens, he aped the manners of the seaboard gentry and developed a taste for gambling, horses, and cockfighting. When he was not playing cards or casting dice for the rent with his landlord, Jackson studied law. At twenty, knowing little about jurisprudence but a great deal about making his own way, he was admitted to the bar of North Carolina. A year later, tradition says, he turned up in Jonesboro, Tennessee, owning two horses, a pack of foxhounds, and a Negro girl.

Before long Jackson made what he intended to be a brief visit to the growing settlement of Nashville. The one established lawyer in the vicinity was retained by a syndicate of debtors, leaving creditors legally helpless. Jackson went to work for the creditors, collected handsome fees, and earned the gratitude and friendship of local merchants and moneylenders. From a fellow Carolina law student he also accepted an appointment as public solicitor. He soon fell in with the machine of William Blount, a powerful territorial land speculator and political patron, and began to consolidate his position among the budding aristocrats, the owners of slaves and horses, the holders of offices and titles. With his salary and fees he began to buy land and Negroes.

Thus far Jackson's story was by no means unusual, for the one-generation aristocrat was a common product of the emerging South.[1] Because of the ease and rapidity with which the shrewd and enterprising farmer might become a leader of the community, and hence a gentleman, during the decades when the cotton economy was expanding into the uplands, the upper classes of the Southwest came to combine the qualities of the frontier roughnecks and the landed gentry. The sportsmanlike, lawless, individualistic, quick-tempered, brawling nature of the first was soon sublimated into the courtly, sentimental, unreflective, touchy spirit of the second. As slaveholding, horsemanship, patriarchal dignities, money, and the deference of the community deepened the ex-frontiersman's sense of pride, the habit of command was added and the transformation was complete. The difference between the frontiersman's readiness to fight and the planter's readiness to defend his "honor" is not so much a difference of temperament as of method, and there is no better exemplar of the fact than Jackson. It is not recorded that the master of the Hermitage, a justice in the state courts and a major general of the militia, ever engaged in a brawl—although one encounter with the Bentons has so been called—or had a wrestling match such as a commoner like Abraham Lincoln enjoyed on the Illinois frontier. Nor did it occur to Jackson to use his fists, although it is true that he threatened at least one social inferior with a caning. Insulted by anyone who technically qualified as a gentleman, he resorted to the code duello; his quarrels are classic in the history of that institution in the South. Charles Dickinson insulted Jackson over a horse race in 1806, and went to his grave for it; and Jackson carried from the encounter a bullet close to his heart. The same violent, self-assertive subjectivism of the duelist can be found in Old Hickory's conduct as a public man. "I have an opinion of my own on all subjects," he wrote in 1821, "and when that opinion is formed I persue it *publickly*, regardless of who goes with me." Historians have never been certain how much his policies were motivated by public considerations and how much by private animosities.

Yet in his calmer moods Jackson's manner

[1] There is a superb account of these emergent aristocrats in W. J. Cash's *The Mind of the South*, pp. 14–17.

ripened quickly into gentleness and gravity. Measured against the picture of the "cotton snob" painted by more than one sympathetic observer of the Old South, where, as F. L. Olmsted put it, "the farce of the vulgar rich" was played over and over again, Jackson was a man of gentility and integrity. In 1824 Daniel Webster could say of him: "General Jackson's manners are more presidential than those of any of the candidates." Mrs. Trollope, who admitted finding precious few gentlemen in America, saw him on his way to Washington in 1829 and reported that he "wore his hair carelessly but not ungracefully arranged, and in spite of his harsh, gaunt features looked like a gentleman and a soldier." With the common citizen he had a patient and gracious air.

The frontier, democratic in spirit and in forms of government, was nevertheless not given to leveling equalitarianism. The ideal of frontier society, as Frederick Jackson Turner has remarked, was the self-made man. And the self-made man generally received a measure of casual deference from the coonskin element, which itself was constantly generating new candidates for the local aristocracies. Keen class antagonisms were not typical of frontier politics, and class struggles did not flourish in a state like Tennessee until the frontier stage was about over.[2] The task of fighting the Indians gave all classes a common bond and produced popular heroes among the upper ranks. The cotton economy, as it spread, also brought its own insurance against bitter antagonisms, for the presence of a submerged class of slaves gave the humbler whites a sense of status and all whites a community of interest. Frontiersmen may have resented alien Eastern aristo-

crats—as Jackson did himself—but felt otherwise about those bred in their own community, as they thought, out of competitive skill rather than privilege. Even in those states and territories where suffrage was broadly exercised, men who owned and speculated in land and had money in the bank were often accepted as natural leaders, and political offices fell to them like ripe fruit. Such beneficiaries of popular confidence developed a stronger faith in the wisdom and justice of popular decisions than did the gentlemen of the older seaboard states, where class lines were no longer fluid and social struggles had venerable histories. A man like Jackson who had been on the conservative side of economic issues in Tennessee could become the leader of a national democratic movement without feeling guilty of any inconsistency. When we find a planter aristocrat of this breed expressing absolute confidence in popular judgment, it is unfair to dismiss him as a demagogue. He became a favorite of the people, and might easily come to believe that the people chose well.

Offices, chiefly appointive, came quickly and easily to Jackson in the territory and youthful state of Tennessee. He was a solicitor at twenty-two, United States Attorney at twenty-three, a Congressman at twenty-nine, a United States Senator at thirty, and justice of the Supreme Court of Tennessee at thirty-one—all this without particularly strong political ambitions, for he applied himself casually to all these offices except the judgeship and resigned them readily after brief tenure. He accepted them, it seems clear, more as symbols of status than as means of advancement. Jackson's persistent land speculations, business ventures, and military operations suggest that he aspired more urgently to have wealth and military glory than political power.

It was, in fact, his achievements as a fighter of Indians and Englishmen that brought Jackson his national popularity.

Jackson's victory in January 1815 over the

---

[2] Thomas Perkins Abernethy points out that in Tennessee during the 1790's "no strong and universal antagonism existed . . . between the rich and the poor. In fact, political office was rarely sought even on the frontier by any but the natural leaders of society, and they secured the suffrage of their neighbors by reason of their prestige, without resorting to electioneering methods."

British forces besieging New Orleans, the crowning triumph of his military career, made him a national hero almost overnight. Americans had already developed their passion for victorious generals in politics. The hero of New Orleans was instantly acclaimed as another Washington, and in 1817 the first campaign biography appeared. But Jackson soon experienced severe political criticism for the conduct of his postwar campaigns in Florida, and he feared the effect of political prominence on his domestic happiness; at first he was slow to rise to the bait of presidential ambition. "I am wearied with public life," he wrote President Monroe in 1821. "I have been accused of acts I never committed, of crimes I never thought of." When a New York newspaper editor commented on the ambition of his friends to put him in the White House, the general grew impatient. "No sir," he exclaimed. "I know what I am fit for. I can command a body of men in a rough way: but I am not fit to be President."

2

The rise of Andrew Jackson marked a new turn in the development of American political institutions. During the period from 1812 to 1828 the two-party system disappeared and personal, local, and sectional conflicts replaced broad differences over public policy as the central fact in national politics. As the presidency declined from its heights under the leadership of Washington and Jefferson, the contest for the presidential seat resolved into a scramble of local and sectional princelings for the position of heir apparent. The Virginia dynasty's practice of elevating the forthcoming president through the vice-presidency or cabinet seemed to have become a set pattern. Presidential nominations, made by party caucuses in Congress, were remote from the popular

will, and since the elections of 1816 and 1820 were virtually uncontested, nomination by "King Caucus" was equivalent to being chosen president. Since the days of Jefferson there had been no major turnover in the staff of officeholders, whose members were becoming encrusted in their posts.

However, the people, the propertyless masses, were beginning, at first quietly and almost unobtrusively, to enter politics. Between 1812 and 1821 six western states entered the Union with constitutions providing for universal white manhood suffrage or a close approximation, and between 1810 and 1821 four of the older states substantially dropped property qualifications for voters.[3] As poor farmers and workers gained the ballot, there developed a type of politician that had existed only in embryo in the Jeffersonian period—the technician of mass leadership, the caterer to mass sentiment; it was a coterie of such men in all parts of the country that converged upon the prominent figure of Jackson between 1815 and 1824. Generally subordinated in the political corporations and remote from the choicest spoils, these leaders encouraged the common feeling that popular will should control the choice of public officers and the formation of public policy. They directed popular resentment of closed political corporations against the caucus system, which they branded as a flagrant usurpation of the rights of the people, and spread the conviction that politics and administration must be taken from the hands of a social elite or a body of bureaucratic specialists and opened to mass participation. Success through politics, it was implied, must

---

[3] In 1824, the first election on which we have statistics, there were only 355,000 voters, chiefly because the triumph of a particular candidate—e.g., Jackson in Tennessee and Pennsylvania, Adams in Massachusetts, Crawford in Virginia—was so taken for granted in most states that voters lost interest. By 1828, when interest was greatly heightened, 1,155,000 voted. Between 1828 and 1848 the vote trebled, although the population did not quite double.

become a legitimate aspiration of the many.[4] Jackson expressed the philosophy of this movement in his first annual message to Congress, December 1829, when he confidently asserted:

> The duties of all public offices are, or at least admit of being made, so plain and simple that men of intelligence may readily qualify themselves for their performance, and I can not but believe that more is lost by the long continuance of men in office than is generally to be gained by their experience. . . . In a country where offices are created solely for the benefit of the people no one man has any more intrinsic right to official station than another.

Rotation in office, he concluded, constituted a "leading principle in the Republican creed."

The trend toward popular activity in politics was heightened by the panic of 1819, which set class against class for the first time since the Jeffersonian era. A result of rapid expansion, speculation, and wildcat banking, the panic and ensuing depression fell heavily upon all parts of the country, but especially upon the South and West, where men had thrown all their resources into reckless buying of land. The banks, which had grossly overextended themselves, were forced to press their debtors to the wall, and through the process of foreclosure the national bank particularly became a great absentee owner of Western and Southern property. "All the flourishing cities of the West," complained Thomas Hart Benton, "are mortgaged to this money power. They may be devoured by it at any moment. They are in the jaws of the monster!" This alien power was resented with particular intensity in the West,

where, as the New York *American* put it, "a wild son of Tennessee who has been with Jackson could ill brook that his bit of land, perhaps his rifle, should be torn from him by a neighboring shopkeeper, that the proceeds may travel eastward, where the 'sceptre' of money has fixed itself." The panic brought a cruel awakening for thousands who had hoped to become rich. John C. Calhoun, talking with John Quincy Adams in the spring of 1820, observed that the last two years had produced "an immense revolution of fortunes in every part of the Union, enormous multitudes in deep distress, and a general mass of disaffection to the Government not concentrated in any particular direction, but ready to seize upon any event and looking out anywhere for a leader."

Calhoun's "general mass of disaffection" was not sufficiently concentrated to prevent the re-election, unopposed, of President Monroe in 1820 in the absence of a national opposition party; but it soon transformed politics in many states. Debtors rushed into politics to defend themselves, and secured moratoriums and relief laws from the legislatures of several Western states. State legislatures, under pressure from local banking interests, waged tax wars against the Bank of the United States. A popular demand arose for laws to prevent imprisonment for debt, for a national bankruptcy law, and for new tariff and public-land policies. For the first time many Americans thought of politics as having an intimate relation to their welfare. Against this background Jackson's star rose. But, curiously, the beneficiary of this movement not only failed to encourage it, but even disapproved. The story of his evolution as a national democratic leader is a strange paradox.

North Carolina, the scene of Jackson's childhood, had been a Jeffersonian stronghold, and Jackson was nurtured on Jeffersonian ideas. In

[4] Jackson wrote to an editor of the Richmond *Enquirer* in 1829: "The road to office and preferment, being accessible alike to the rich and poor, the farmer and the printer, honesty, probity, and capability constituting the sole and exclusive test will, I am persuaded, have the happiest tendency to preserve, unimpaired, freedom of action."

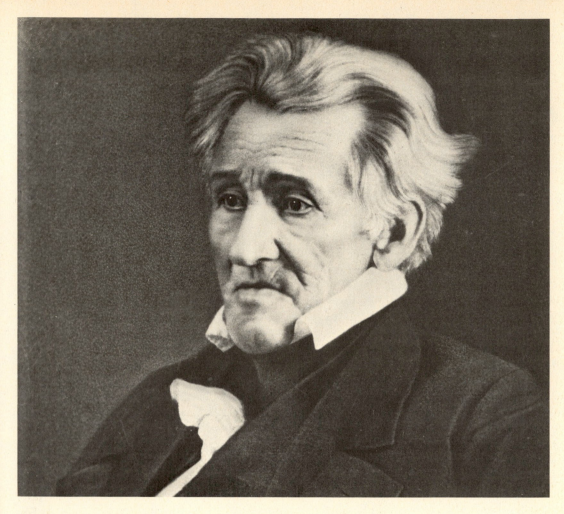

Andrew Jackson in 1845, as photographed by Matthew Brady. A self-made planter of considerable wealth, Jackson "wore his hair carelessly but not ungracefully arranged, and in spite of his harsh, gaunt features looked like a gentleman and a soldier." (Courtesy of Culver Pictures.)

1796 and 1800 the young Tennessean voted for the sage of Monticello. Except for his nationalism, Jackson's politics chiefly resembled agrarian Republicanism of the old school, which was opposed to banks, public debts, paper money, high tariffs, and federal internal improvements. When the Burr trial and Jefferson's pacificism disillusioned him with Jefferson, Jackson did not become a convert to Federalism but rather adhered to the Randolph-Macon school of intransigent Republicans.

Jackson's personal affairs shed much light on his ambiguous political evolution from 1796 to 1828. An event of 1796 that had a disastrous

effect on his fortunes may have sown in him the seeds of that keen dislike of the Eastern money power and "paper system" which flowered during his presidency. Jackson had gone to Philadelphia to sell several thousand acres of land to a rich merchant and speculator, David Allison; he accepted notes from Allison, which he endorsed and promptly used to pay for supplies he planned to use in opening a general-merchandise store in Nashville. Allison failed, and defaulted on his notes; Jackson became liable. In order to pay the notes as they fell due, he was forced to retrench, give up the estate on which he lived, move to a smaller one built of logs, and sell many of his slaves. Subsequently his store enterprise turned out badly and he was obliged to sell out to his partners. Jackson seems never to have whined about his misfortune, but he lived for nineteen years in its shadow, remaining in debt from 1796 to 1815, when at last his military pay and allowances brought him into the clear. In the fall of 1815 he had a cash balance of over twenty-two thousand dollars at the Nashville bank, was again heavily committed in land speculations, and was building the fine new estate that has become famous as the Hermitage. Just at this time, when he was so vulnerable, the panic of 1819 struck.

The general distress of Tennessee debtors led, as in many other places, to a movement for relief. Felix Grundy, elected to the state Senate on a "relief" platform, brought forth a proposal to establish a state loan office to help debtors out of the state treasury.[5] Creditors who refused to accept notes of the loan bank in payment of debts would have their collections suspended for two years. Jackson's own obligations forced him to press his debtors hard, and he instituted a single lawsuit against

one hundred and twenty-nine of them at once. One of the few men in middle Tennessee to stand against Grundy's relief program, he sent a protest to the state legislature, which was rejected on the ground that its language was disrespectful. Having learned from the Allison episode to feel for the luckless entrepreneur, Jackson was now learning to see things from the standpoint of the local moneyed class. The emergence of class conflict in Tennessee found him squarely on the side of the haves. In 1821, when General William Carroll ran for the governorship of the state on a democratic economic program, Jackson supported Carroll's opponent, Colonel Edward Ward, a wealthy planter who had joined Jackson in fighting Grundy's scheme. Carroll was elected, and proceeded to put through a program of tax revision and constitutional and humanitarian reform, which has many elements of what historians call "Jacksonian" democracy. At the moment when Jackson was pitting himself against Carroll in Tennessee, his friends were bringing him forward as a presidential candidate. None of this prevented Grundy and Carroll from later joining the Jackson bandwagon.

Had Jackson's record on popular economic reform been a matter of primary importance, he might never have been President. But by 1824, when he first accepted a presidential nomination, prosperity had returned, hostility to banks and creditors had abated, and breaking up established political machines seemed more important to the parvenu politician and the common citizen. As chief "issues" of the campaign the caucus system shared honors with the defense of New Orleans.[6] An outsider to the Congressional machines, a man of humble birth whose popularity was based on military achievement and whose attitude toward economic questions was unknown and of little

---

[5] Grundy's history makes it clear that he represented what may be called entrepreneurial rather than lower-class radicalism. In 1818 he was a leader in a movement to bring a branch of the second United States Bank to Nashville.

[6] Actually only one of the four candidates, William H. Crawford, was nominated by the customary Congressional caucus; the others were nominated by state legislatures.

interest to the average voter, Jackson had a considerable edge with the new electorate.

The consequences of the campaign of 1824 settled all doubt in Jackson's mind about the presidency. Far stronger in the popular vote than any of his three rivals, John Quincy Adams, Clay, and Crawford, he still fell short of the necessary majority in the electoral college, and the election was thrown into the House of Representatives. There the position of Clay became decisive, and Clay threw his support to Adams. Subsequently, when President Adams named Clay his Secretary of State, a bitter cry went up from the Jackson following. Jackson himself was easily persuaded that Clay and Adams had been guilty of a "corrupt bargain" and determined to retake from Adams what he felt was rightfully his. The campaign of 1828 began almost immediately with Adams's administration. For four years the President, a man of monumental rectitude but a career politician of the dying order par excellence, was hounded by the corrupt-bargain charge and subjected by the Jackson professionals to a skillful campaign of vilification, which culminated in the election of 1828. In Jackson's second presidential campaign the bank was hardly mentioned. The tariff was played for what it was worth where men cared especially about it; but a series of demagogic charges about Adams's alleged monarchist, aristocratic, and bureaucratic prejudices served the Jackson managers for issues. Jackson got 647,000 votes, Adams 508,000.

The election of 1828 was not an uprising of the West against the East nor a triumph of the frontier: outside of New England and its colonized areas in the West, Federalist Delaware, New Jersey, and Maryland, Jackson swept the country. Nor was his election a mandate for economic reform; no financial changes, no crusades against the national bank, were promised. The main themes of Jacksonian democracy thus far were militant nationalism and equal access to office. Jackson's election was more a

result than a cause of the rise of democracy, and the "revolution of 1828" more an overturn of personnel than of ideas or programs. Up to the time of his inauguration Jackson had contributed neither a thought nor a deed to the democratic movement, and he was elected without a platform. So far as he can be said to have had a popular mandate, it was to be different from what the people imagined Adams had been and to give expression to their unformulated wishes and aspirations. This mandate Jackson was prepared to obey. Democrat and aristocrat, failure and success, debtor and creditor, he had had a varied and uneven history which made it possible for him to see public questions from more than one perspective. He was a simple, emotional, and unreflective man with a strong sense of loyalty to personal friends and political supporters; he swung to the democratic camp when the democratic camp swung to him.

3

For those who have lived through the era of Franklin D. Roosevelt it is natural to see in Jacksonian democracy an earlier version of the New Deal, for the two periods have many superficial points in common. The Jacksonian movement and the New Deal were both struggles of large sections of the community against a business elite and its allies. There is a suggestive analogy between Nicholas Biddle's political associates and the "economic royalists" of the Liberty League, and, on the other side, between the two dynamic landed aristocrats who led the popular parties. Roosevelt himself did not fail to see the resemblance and exploit it.

But the two movements differed in a critical respect: the New Deal was frankly based upon the premise that economic expansion had come to an end and economic opportunities were disappearing; it attempted to cope with the situation by establishing governmental ascendancy

over the affairs of business. The Jacksonian movement grew out of expanding opportunities and a common desire to enlarge these opportunities still further by removing restrictions and privileges that had their origin in acts of government; thus, with some qualifications, it was essentially a movement of laissez-faire, an attempt to divorce government and business. It is commonly recognized in American historical folklore that the Jackson movement was a phase in the expansion of democracy, but it is too little appreciated that it was also a phase in the expansion of liberated capitalism. While in the New Deal the democratic reformers were driven to challenge many assumptions of traditional American capitalism, in the Jacksonian period the democratic upsurge was closely linked to the ambitions of the small capitalist.

To understand Jacksonian democracy it is necessary to recreate the social complexion of the United States in the 1830's. Although industrialism had begun to take root, this was still a nation of farms and small towns, which in 1830 found only one of every fifteen citizens living in cities of over 8,000. Outside the South, a sweeping majority of the people were independent property-owners. Factories had been growing in some areas, but industry was not yet concentrated in the factory system; much production was carried out in little units in which the employer was like a master craftsman supervising his apprentices. The development of transportation made it possible to extend trade over large areas, which resulted in a delay in collections and increased the dependence of business upon banks for credit facilities. The merchant capitalist found it easier to get the necessary credits than humbler masters and minor entrepreneurs, but the hope of growing more prosperous remained intensely alive in the breast of the small manufacturer and the skilled craftsman.

The flowering of manufacturing in the East, the rapid settlement of the West, gave to the spirit of enterprise a large measure of fulfillment. The typical American was an expectant capitalist, a hardworking, ambitious person for whom enterprise was a kind of religion, and everywhere he found conditions that encouraged him to extend himself. Francis J. Grund, an immigrant who described American social conditions in 1836, reported:

> Business is the very soul of an American: he pursues it, not as a means of procuring for himself and his family the necessary comforts of life, but as the fountain of all human felicity. . . . It is as if all America were but one gigantic workshop, over the entrance of which there is the blazing inscription, "No admission here, except on business."

More than one type of American, caught up in this surge of ambition, had reason to be dissatisfied with the United States Bank. Some farmers were more interested in the speculative values of their lands than in their agricultural yield. Operators of wildcat banks in the South and West and speculators who depended upon wildcat loans shared the farmers' dislike of Biddle's bank for restraining credit inflation. In the East some of the heads of strong, sound state banks were jealous of the privileged position of the national bank—particularly the bankers of New York City, who resented the financial supremacy that the bank brought to Philadelphia.[7] In Eastern cities the bank was also widely disliked by workers, craftsmen, shopkeepers, and small business people. Labor was hard hit by the rising cost of living, and in many cases the workmen's agitation was directed not so much against their immediate employers as against the credit and currency system. Small business and working men felt

[7] State-bank men were prominent in Jackson's councils. Roger Brooke Taney had been a lawyer for and stockholder in the Union Bank of Maryland. Two key members of the kitchen cabinet, Amos Kendall and Francis Preston Blair, were recruits from the famous relief war in Kentucky, and the former had been president of the Commonwealth Bank of Kentucky.

that banks restricted competition and prevented new men from entering upon the avenues of enterprise.[8]

The prevalent method of granting corporation charters in the states was a source of enormous resentment. The states did not have general laws governing incorporation.[9] Since banks and other profit-making businesses that wished to incorporate had to apply to state legislatures for individual acts of incorporation, the way was left open for favoritism and corruption. Very often the corporation charters granted by the legislatures were, or were construed to be, monopolies. Men whose capital or influence was too small to gain charters from the lawmakers were barred from such profitable and strategic lines of corporate enterprise as banks, bridges, railroads, turnpikes, and ferries. The practice was looked upon as an artificial closure of opportunity: laborers often blamed it for the high price of necessities.[10] The practice of granting economic privileges was also considered a threat to popular government. Jackson, explaining in one of his presidential messages why "the planter, the farmer,

the mechanic, and the laborer" were "in constant danger of losing their fair interest in the Government," had a standard answer: "The mischief springs from the power which the moneyed interest derives from a paper currency, which they are able to control, from the multitude of corporations with exclusive privileges which they have succeeded in obtaining in the different States."

Among all the exclusive privileged monopolies in the country the Bank of the United States was the largest, the best-known, and the most powerful. It became a symbol for all the others, and the burden of many grievances for which it was not really responsible fell upon it. As a national institution it was doubly vulnerable: it was blamed by Western inflationists for deflationary policies and by Eastern hard-money men for inflation. One certain accomplishment of Jackson's war on the bank was to discharge the aggressions of citizens who felt injured by economic privilege.

Jackson himself was by no means unfamiliar with the entrepreneurial impulse that gave Jacksonian democracy so much of its freshness and vitality. An enterpriser of middling success, he could spontaneously see things from the standpoint of the typical American who was eager for advancement in the democratic game of competition—the master mechanic who aspired to open his own shop, the planter or farmer who speculated in land, the lawyer who hoped to be a judge, the local politician who wanted to go to Congress, the grocer who would be a merchant. He had entered the scramble himself in a variety of lines, as a professional man, a merchant, a land speculator, a planter, an office-holder, and a military chieftain. He understood the old Jeffersonian's bias against overgrown government machinery, the Westerner's resentment of the entrenched East, the new politician's dislike of the old bureaucracy, and the aspiring citizen's hatred of privilege. Years before his presidency, he recalled, when a few Tennesseans proposed in 1817 to

---

[8] Workingmen had a special grievance against banks. Employers often paid them in the notes of distant or suspected banks, which circulated below par value. They were thus defrauded of a portion of their pay. Although the United States Bank was not responsible for such practices, it had to share in the general odium that attached to banks. "I was not long in discovering," remembered the Whig politician Thurlow Weed, "that it was easy to enlist the laboring classes against a 'monster bank' or 'monied aristocracy.' . . . The bank issue 'hung like a millstone' about our necks."

[9] There were exceptions. New York in 1811 and Connecticut in 1817 adopted laws permitting general incorporation for certain types of manufacturing enterprises.

[10] "We cannot pass the bounds of the city," complained one of the left-wing Jacksonian leaders in New York, "without paying tribute to monopoly; our bread, our meat, our vegetables, our fuel, all, all pay tribute to monopolists." William Leggett of the New York *Post* declared: "Not a road can be opened, not a bridge can be built, not a canal can be dug, but a charter of exclusive privileges must be granted for the purpose. . . . The bargaining and trucking away chartered privileges is the whole business of our lawmakers."

bring a branch of the bank to Nashville, he had opposed it on the ground that the bank "would drain the state of its specie to the amount of its profits for the support and prosperity of other places, and the Lords, Dukes, and Ladies of foreign countries who held the greater part of its stock—no individual but one in our state owning any of its stock." In 1827, when a branch of the bank was finally created at Nashville, and its agent, General Thomas Cadwalader, coyly hinted to Jackson that its patronage could be turned over to the Jackson party, he was rebuffed.

Looking at the bank from the White House, Jackson saw an instrument of great privilege and power ruled by a man of uncommon force and intelligence. As a fiscal agency it was comparable in magnitude to the government itself. It issued about one fourth of the country's bank paper; because of its power over the discounts of innumerable smaller banks, especially in the West and South, it was the only central instrument in the United States that could affect the volume of credit. A private agency performing a major public function, it was yet substantially free of government control.[11] As Hezekiah Niles put it, the bank had "more power than we would grant to any set of men unless responsible to the people." Nicholas Biddle, boasting of the forbearance with which he ran the bank, once stated in a Congressional investigation that there were "very few banks which might not have been destroyed by an exertion of the powers of the Bank." "As to mere power," he wrote to Thomas Cooper in 1837, "I have been for years in the daily exercise of more personal authority than any President habitually enjoys." Understandably the

bank's critics regarded it as a potential menace to democratic institutions.

As an economic instrument, there was a great deal to be said for the bank. Under Biddle it had done a creditable job in stabilizing the currency and holding in check inflationary pressure from the wildcatters. Before Jackson's election Biddle had also been concerned to keep the bank out of partisan politics and, as he wrote Webster, "bring it down to its true business character as a Counting House." But the bank inspired too many animosities to stay out of political life. After 1829 it had large loans outstanding to a great number of prominent politicians and influential newspaper editors, and Biddle was well aware how great its power would be if it should be employed directly in corruption. "I can remove all the constitutional scruples in the District of Columbia," he arrogantly informed a correspondent in 1833. "Half a dozen Presidencies—a dozen Cashierships—fifty Clerkships—a hundred Directorships—to worthy friends who have no character and no money."

Since the bank's charter was to expire in 1836, and since a second term for Jackson was probable, it seemed necessary that a renewal of the charter be secured under Jackson. Biddle attempted at first to be conciliatory, made earnest efforts to answer Jackson's grievances against the bank, appointed Jacksonian politicians to several branch directorships, and sent the President a not ungenerous proposal for assistance in discharging the government's indebtedness in return for recharter. Yet in the fall or winter of 1829–30, when Biddle and Jackson had an amicable interview, the general frankly said: "I do not dislike your Bank any more than all banks. But ever since I read the history of the South Sea bubble I have been afraid of banks." By December 1830, when Jackson questioned the bank's expediency and constitutionality, it was clear that he would not consent to renew its life. Biddle, reluctantly,

---

[11] Five of its twenty-five directors were appointed by the federal government. Nicholas Biddle, who actually ran the bank without interference, was one of the government directors; before the bank controversy began, his appointment had been renewed by Jackson himself.

uncertainly, and under prodding from Whig politicians, decided in the summer of 1832 to ask Congress for recharter before the presidential election. "The bank," said Jackson to Van Buren, "is trying to kill me, *but I will kill it!*" To the frontier duelist the issue had instantly become personal.

Jackson lost no time in returning the recharter bill to Congress with his[12] famous veto message, described by Biddle as "a manifesto of anarchy, such as Marat and Robespierre might have issued to the mob." The body of the message was an argument against the bank's constitutionality. The social indictment of the bank was inclusive: it was a monopoly, a grant of exclusive privilege; the whole American people were excluded from competition in the sale of the privilege, and the government thus received less than it was worth; a fourth of the bank's stock was held by foreigners, the rest by "a few hundred of our citizens, chiefly of the richest class"; it was a menace to the country's liberty and independence. At the end the President launched into a forthright statement of the social philosophy of the Jacksonian movement:

It is to be regretted that the rich and powerful too often bend the acts of government to their selfish purposes. Distinctions in society will always exist under every just government. Equality of talents, of education, or of wealth cannot be produced by human institutions. In the full enjoyment of the gifts of Heaven and the fruits of superior industry, economy, and virtue, every man is equally entitled to protection by law; but when the laws undertake to add to these natural and just advantages artificial distinctions, to grant titles, gratuities, and exclusive privileges, to make the rich richer and the potent more powerful, the humble members of society—the farmers, mechanics, and laborers—who have neither the time nor the means of securing like favors to themselves, have a right to complain of the injustice of their Government. There are no necessary evils in government. Its evils exist only in its abuses. If it would confine itself to equal protection, and, as Heaven does its rains, shower its favors alike on the high and the low, the rich and the poor, it would be an unqualified blessing.

Certainly this is not the philosophy of a radical leveling movement that proposes to uproot property or to reconstruct society along drastically different lines. It proceeds upon no Utopian premises—full equality is impossible, "distinctions will always exist," and reward should rightly go to "superior industry, economy, and virtue." What is demanded is only the classic bourgeois ideal, equality before the law, the restriction of government to equal protection of its citizens. This is the philosophy of a rising middle class; its aim is not to throttle but to liberate business, to open every possible pathway for the creative enterprise of the people. Although the Jacksonian leaders were more aggressive than the Jeffersonians in their crusades against monopoly and "the paper system," it is evident that the core of their philosophy was the same: both aimed to take the grip of government-granted privileges off the natural economic order.[13] It was no coinci-

[12] The message was composed with the assistance of Amos Kendall, Andrew J. Donelson, Roger B. Taney, and Levi Woodbury.

[13] This was the position not only of the regular Jacksonians but also of the more "radical" Locofoco school. For example, William Leggett, who was considered to be a hound of anarchy by New York conservatives, believed implicitly in free trade and was extremely solicitous of the rights of property when divorced from special privilege. He looked upon a general law of incorporation as "the very measure to enable poor men to compete with rich." "My creed," said Isaac Smith, a prominent Locofoco candidate, "is to leave commercial men to manage their own affairs." And Martin Van Buren: "I have ever advocated . . . limiting the

dence that Jacksonians like William Leggett and Thomas Hart Benton still venerated John Taylor, a thinker of what Jackson affectionately called "the old republican school."

4

Pursuing the bank war to its conclusion, Jackson found defeat in victory. Re-elected overwhelmingly on the bank issue in 1832, he soon removed all United States funds from the bank. Biddle, in the course of a fight to get the federal deposits back, brought about a short-lived but severe depression through restriction of credit, which ended only when the business community itself rebelled. No sooner did this artificial depression end than an inflationary movement began. The federal deposits that Jackson had taken from Biddle were made available to several dozen state banks; these promptly used their new resources to start a credit boom, which broke disastrously in 1837. This had been no part of Jackson's original intention, nor that of his hard-money followers. "I did not join in putting down the Bank of the United States," complained Thomas Hart Benton, "to put up a wilderness of local banks." By destroying Biddle's bank Jackson had taken away the only effective restraint on the wildcatters,

and by distributing the deposits had enlarged the capital in the hands of inflationists. He was opposed to both privilege and inflation, but in warring on one he had succeeded only in releasing the other. In killing the bank he had strangled a potential threat to democratic government, but at an unnecessarily high cost. He had caused Biddle to create one depression and the pet banks to aggravate a second, and he had left the nation committed to a currency and credit system even more inadequate than the one he had inherited.

Biddle, from 1823, when he took control of the bank, to 1833, when removal of the deposits provoked him to outrageous retaliation, had followed a policy of gradual, controlled credit expansion, which was well adapted to the needs of the growing American economy. Had Jackson not yielded to archaic hard-money theories on one hand and the pressure of interested inflationary groups on the other,[14] it might have been possible—and it would have been far wiser—for him to have made a deal with Biddle, trading recharter of the bank for more adequate government control of the bank's affairs. It would have been possible to safeguard democratic institutions without such financial havoc but the Jacksonians were caught between their hostility to the bank and their unwillingness to supplant it with adequate federal control of credit. The popular hatred of

---

interference of the Government in the business concerns of the People to cases of actual necessity, and [have been] an enemy to monopoly in any form." "The people, the democracy," asserted Ely Moore, the New York labor leader, "contend for no measure that does not hold out to individual enterprise proper motives for exertion." William Gouge, the most popular economic writer of the period, declared that his hard-money policy would mold a society in which "the operation of the natural and just causes of wealth and poverty will no longer be inverted, but . . . each cause will operate in its natural and just order, and produce its natural and just effect—wealth becoming the reward of industry, frugality, skill, prudence, and enterprise, and poverty the punishment of few except the indolent and prodigal."

[14] There was a division of purpose among those who supported the bank war. The hard-money theorists wanted to reduce all banks to the functions of discount and deposit and deny them the right to issue currency notes; they believed that overissue of bank notes was an essential cause of booms and depressions. The inflationary groups, including many state banks, objected to the Bank of the United States because it restrained note issues. Caught between these two forces, Jackson pursued an inconsistent policy. Deposit of federal funds with state banks pleased the inflationists. The Specie Circular and the Independent Treasury policy adopted under Jackson's successor, Van Buren, was more consonant with the views of the hard-money faction.

privilege and the dominant laissez-faire ideology made an unhappy combination.

The bank war flared up, died, and was forgotten, its permanent results negative rather than positive. But the struggle against corporate privileges which it symbolized was waged on a much wider front. In the states this struggle bore fruit in a series of general incorporation acts, beginning with Connecticut's in 1837 and spreading to the other states in the two decades before the Civil War. By opening the process of incorporation to all comers who could meet state requirements, legislators progressively sundered the concept of the corporate form of business from its association with monopoly privilege and for many decades made it an element in the growth of free enterprise—a contribution to the development of American business that can hardly be overestimated. The same was done for banking. In 1838 New York, the center of the Locofoco agitation against bank monopolies, passed a free banking law that permitted banking associations to operate under general rules without applying for specific acts of incorporation. A precedent for similar laws in other states, it has been described by one authority, Bray Hammond, as "the most important event in American banking history."

While the state legislatures were writing Jacksonian ideals into the law of corporations, a Jacksonian Supreme Court under Chief Justice Taney was reading them into the clauses of the Constitution. Taney, appointed by Jackson in 1836, sat on the Court until his death in 1864, and during his long tenure the Court propagated the Jacksonian view of business without privilege. Professor Benjamin F. Wright, in his study of *The Contract Clause of the Constitution*, has pointed out that as a result of the Court's work under Taney the contract clause "was a more secure and broader base for the defense of property rights in 1864 than it had been in 1835." Taney's most startling case, as symbolic of the fight against privilege in the juridical sphere as the bank war had been in politics, was the Charles River Bridge case. The majority decision, prepared by Taney, which represented a long forward step in detaching from the corporation the stigma of monopoly, stands as a classic statement of the Jacksonian faith.

The Charles River Bridge had been erected in the 1780's by Harvard College and prominent Bostonians under a Massachusetts charter. As the population of Boston and Cambridge grew, business flourished, traffic mounted, and the par value of the bridge's stock shot upwards. A share bought in 1805 at $444 was worth $2,080 in 1814. Since a new bridge was badly needed, the state legislature in 1828 chartered another, the Warren Bridge, to be built very close to the original, and to be free after sufficient tolls were collected to pay for its construction. Anxious to prevent a development that would destroy the value of their stock, the proprietors of the older bridge attempted to restrain the new builders from erecting the Warren Bridge. When Taney began sitting as Chief Justice in 1837, the issue was still pending before the Supreme Court. The case clearly involved a conflict between vested rights on one side and new entrepreneurs and the rest of the community on the other. Four distinguished Massachusetts lawyers, including Daniel Webster, represented the promoters of the Charles River Bridge. They argued that the legislative grant to the original bridge company was a contract, and that implicit in such a ferry or bridge franchise was a promise on the part of the state not to break the contract by granting another competing franchise that would lower the value of the original.

The Court decided for the new bridge, five to two. Since the two dissenting justices, Story and Thompson, were holdovers from the pre-

Jackson period and the five majority judges were all Jackson appointees, the decision may accurately be called a Jacksonian document. Story's dissent, which expressed horror at "speculative niceties or novelties" and invoked the interests of "every stockholder in every public enterprise of this sort throughout the country," was reasoned in the language of entrenched capital, of monopoly investors who abhorred risk. Taney's majority decision was a plea for the public interest, for technological progress and fresh enterprise.[15]

The object of all government, Taney asserted, is to promote the happiness and prosperity of the community, and it could never be assumed that a government intended to curtail its own powers in this respect. "And in a country like ours, free, active, and enterprising, continually advancing in numbers and wealth," new channels of communication and travel are continually found necessary; an abandonment of the state's power to facilitate new developments should not be construed from contracts that do not contain an explicit statement of such intent.

What would happen, Taney asked, if the idea of an implied monopoly in charters should be sustained by the Court? What would become of the numerous railroads established on the same line of travel with old turnpike companies? He thought he knew: if these old corporations were given an "undefined property in a line of travelling," they would awaken from their sleep and call upon the Court to put down new improvements to protect their vested interests. The "millions of property" that had been invested in railroads and canals upon lines of travel once occupied by turnpike corporations

would be endangered. Until obsolete claims were settled, the community would be deprived of the benefits of invention enjoyed by every other part of the civilized world. The rights of property, Taney conceded, should be "sacredly guarded," but "we must not forget that the community also have rights, and that the happiness and well being of every citizen depends upon their faithful preservation."

To the Whig press and conservative lawyers like Kent and Story this opinion appeared as another "manifesto of anarchy," comparable to Jackson's bank veto message. In fact, as Charles Warren observes in his history of the Court, it gave encouragement to "all business men who contemplated investments of capital in new corporate enterprise and who were relieved against claims of monopoly concealed in ambiguous clauses of old charters."

In the Congressional session of 1823–4, at the beginning of the Jackson era, Daniel Webster had observed: "Society is full of excitement: competition comes in place of monopoly; and intelligence and industry ask only for fair play and an open field." No friend of Jacksonian democracy expressed more accurately than this opponent the historic significance of the Jackson movement. With Old Hickory's election a fluid economic and social system broke the bonds of a fixed and stratified political order. Originally a fight against political privilege, the Jacksonian movement had broadened into a fight against economic privilege, rallying to its support a host of "rural capitalists and village entrepreneurs." When Jackson left office he was the hero of the lower and middling elements of American society who believed in expanding opportunity through equal rights, and by the time of his death in 1845 the "excitement" Webster had noticed had left a deep and lasting mark upon the nation. "This," exulted Calvin Colton, "is a country of self-made men, than which there can be no better in any state of society."

---

[15] Taney's moderate and balanced view of state policy toward corporations is most clearly brought out by his deft decision in *Bank of Augusta* v. *Earle* (1839). For this and his continuing friendliness to the non-monopoly corporation, see Carl Brent Swisher's *Roger B. Taney*, Chapter xviii.

17

"Woe if it comes with storm and blood and fire"

Ralph Korngold

In the Jacksonian era, slavery remained the central paradox of American society. Now it was even more tragic, because while white men enjoyed greater opportunity and more political rights, while the nation attempted to mold itself into a popular democracy, two-and-a-half million Southern blacks remained in chains. Moreover, most Northern states either retained or now enacted black codes that discriminated against free Negroes, denying them the right to vote, hold political office, work at skilled jobs, live in white neighborhoods, or attend public schools (even though blacks had to pay school taxes). Only in Massachusetts and a few other New England states did Negro citizens enjoy more or less the same rights as white people. But white racial hostility often flared up in New England, too. In fact, hundreds of race riots broke out all over the North during the age of Jackson; in many of the riots, angry whites—including leaders of the community—burned Negro ghettos and beat up and killed Negro people.

It was inevitable that some whites would become upset about such injustice to Negroes, would become distressed and then angered about the contradiction of slavery and racial discrimination in a self-proclaimed free and just society. Some Americans—Southern and Northern Quakers particularly—had, in fact, opposed slavery since the colonial period. But it was in the 1820s, a decade of religious and political ferment, a decade when the struggle began for universal manhood suffrage, that antislavery truly became a movement. The American Colonization Society, founded in 1816, distributed pamphlets and gathered petitions that called for the abolition of slavery and the colonization of all Negroes in Africa. Quakers and free Negroes also collected antislavery petitions and sent them to Congress (where intimidated Southerners had them tabled); and Benjamin Lundy, a Baltimore Quaker, not only started publishing *The Genius of Universal Emancipation*, but organized antislavery societies in the South itself. At this time, most antislavery whites (a distinct minority of the population) were both gradualists and colonizationists. But by the 1830s some would emphatically change their minds, would champion immediate emancipation, organize a national antislavery society, and start an Abolitionist crusade that would haunt the American conscience and arouse latent racism everywhere in the land.

The best-known leader of the crusade was William Lloyd Garrison, an intense, bespectacled young man who came from a broken home (his father ran away) and whose mother raised him as an ardent Baptist. Later he became a radical Christian perfectionist. Initially, Garrison too was a gradualist and a colonizer. But in 1829, after he went to work for Lundy's paper, Garrison renounced colonization and came out for immediate emancipation. Ralph Korngold speculates that he was influenced by the Abolitionist writings of James Duncan and the Rev. George Bourne, who denounced slavery as a sin and demanded that Negroes be freed at once. At any rate, in the columns of Lundy's paper, Garrison conducted a stunning moral attack against slavery and anybody who condoned or perpetuated it. For example, when he learned that a ship belonging to a man from Newburyport, Massachusetts (Garrison's home town), was taking a cargo of slaves from Baltimore to New Orleans, Garrison castigated

him as a highway robber and a murderer. The man, a highly respected citizen and a church deacon, slapped Garrison with a $5,000 libel suit. The court decided against Garrison and fined him $50, but he couldn't pay and had to go to jail. Korngold's narrative opens with Garrison in prison. It follows his career as he founded the *Liberator* and not only crusaded against slavery but championed the rights of free Negroes as well.

While in prison Garrison had prepared three lectures. The first contrasted the program of the Colonization Society with his own; the second gave a vivid description of the slavery system; the third showed the extent to which the North shared responsibility for the "peculiar institution." After his release he left Baltimore for the North, intending to make a lecture tour of several months' duration and then launch an antislavery weekly in Washington. If he later chose Boston, it was because Lundy moved the *Genius* to the National Capital. Garrison had become convinced the North needed enlightenment even more than the South. In the first issue of his new paper he was to write:

"During my recent tour for the purpose of exciting the minds of the people by a series of discourses on the subject of slavery, every place that I visited gave fresh evidence of the fact, that a greater revolution in public sentiment was to be effected in the free States—*and particularly in New England*—than at the South. I found contempt more bitter, opposition more active, detraction more relentless, prejudice more stubborn, and apathy more frozen, than among slave-owners themselves."

He delivered his lectures in Philadelphia, where he was the guest of James and Lucretia

From pp. 42–64 in *Two Friends of Man* by Ralph Korngold, published by Little, Brown & Co., 1950. Reprinted by special permission of Mrs. Ralph Korngold.

Mott, whose influence was to be largely responsible for his abandonment of religious orthodoxy. "If my mind has since become liberalized in any degree, (and I think it has burst every sectarian trammel)," he wrote, "if theological dogmas which I once regarded as essential to Christianity, I now repudiate as absurd and pernicious,—I am largely indebted to them for the changes." When he reached Massachusetts he decided that his native Newburyport should be the first to hear his message. But he had reckoned without Mr. Todd, whose influence was sufficiently great to have the trustees of the Presbyterian Church intervene when the minister offered Garrison the use of the church auditorium. The pastor of the Second Congregational Church came to the rescue and he was able to deliver his first lecture. Then again Todd intervened. Garrison made no further attempt to enlighten his native town, and left for Boston.

2

In Boston Garrison took lodgings as usual at Parson Collier's, and then called on the Reverend Lyman Beecher, hoping to enlist his moral support. Dr. Beecher, however, was not the man to identify himself with an unpopular cause. ("True wisdom," he said in one of his Seminary lectures, "consists in advocating a cause only so far as the community will sustain the reformer.") He now excused himself, saying: "I have too many irons in the fire already."

"Then," replied the young zealot, "you had better let them all burn than to neglect your duty to the slave."

Dr. Beecher did not think so. "Your zeal," he said, "is commendable, but you are misguided. If you will give up your fanatical notions and be guided by us [the clergy] we will make you the Wilberforce of America."

When not looking for a hall in which to deliver his message Garrison wrote letters to

public men imploring them to declare themselves for immediate emancipation. He wrote to Channing, to Webster and to several others, but received no reply. His search for a meeting place likewise remained unrewarded. Finally he inserted the following advertisement in the Boston *Courier:*

WANTED—For three evenings, a Hall or Meetinghouse (the latter would be preferred), in which to vindicate the rights of TWO MILLIONS of American citizens who are now groaning in servile chains in this boasted land of liberty; and also to propose just, benevolent, and constitutional measures for their relief. As the addresses will be gratuitous, and as the cause is of public benefit, I cannot consent to remunerate any society for the use of its building. If this application fails, I propose to address the citizens of Boston in the open air, on the Common.   Wm. Lloyd Garrison
No. 30, Federal Street, Oct. 11, 1830

The advertisement attracted the attention of sexagenarian Abner Kneeland, founder of the First Society of Free Enquirers. Kneeland was an atheist, and his society made war on religion. A few years later he was to be indicted for having published in his paper, the Boston *Enquirer*, a "scandalous, injurious, obscene, blasphemous and profane libel of and concerning God." His society was the lessee of Julian Hall, on the northwest corner of Milk and Congress Streets. He had no sooner read Garrison's advertisement than he offered him the use of the hall.

It was only a couple of years since Garrison had written about "the depravity and wickedness of those . . . who reject the gospel of Jesus Christ," but he now saw no reason why he should "reject the co-operation of those who . . . make no pretense to evangelical piety" when "the religious portion of the community are indifferent to the cries of suffering humanity."

William Lloyd Garrison, celebrated Abolitionist and editor of the controversial Liberator. "I will be as harsh as truth, and as uncompromising as justice," wrote Garrison in his manifesto in the first issue of the Liberator. On the subject of slavery, "I do not wish to think, or speak, or write, with moderation. . . . I am in earnest—I will not equivocate—I will not excuse—I will not retreat a single inch—AND I WILL BE HEARD." (Courtesy of The Library of Congress.)

3

The hall was filled. Dr. Beecher and other notables were present. Three men were there who were destined to become Garrison's staunch friends and supporters. They had come together and were seated side by side. The eldest was Samuel J. May, a Unitarian minister from Brooklyn, Connecticut, who was visiting his father, Colonel Joseph May, a prosperous Boston merchant. His friends called him "God's

chore boy," for while far less combative than Garrison, he was just as ready to rush to the succor of anyone in need of assistance. Sitting beside him was his brother-in-law, Bronson Alcott, whose daughter Louisa May Alcott was to become a popular novelist. He was a philosopher and a mystic who combined great profundity with great extravagance of thought. The Sage of Concord has called him "the most refined and the most advanced soul we have ever had in New England," and "the most remarkable and the highest genius of his time." Along with gems of thought worthy of Aristotle, Alcott propounded such absurdities as that the atmosphere surrounding the earth was the accumulated exhalation of mankind, and that the weather was fair or foul depending on whether good or evil thought predominated! He would say in all seriousness to a friend: "Men must have behaved well to-day to have such fine sunshine." The third man was May's cousin, Samuel E. Sewall, a Boston attorney and a direct descendant of the judge of that name who a hundred and thirty years before had written the first antislavery pamphlet in America.

When the speaker had finished, May turned to his two companions and said: "That is a providential man; he is a prophet; he will shake our nation to its center, but he will shake slavery out of it. We ought to know him, we ought to help him. Come, let us go and give him our hands." When they had done so, May said to the young lecturer: "Mr. Garrison, I am not sure that I can endorse all you have said this evening. Much of it requires careful consideration. But I am prepared to embrace you. I am sure you are called to a great work, and I mean to help you."

Alcott suggested that all come home with him. They accepted and remained in animated conversation until after midnight. Garrison told his new friends of his plan to launch an antislavery paper in Boston, which he intended to call the *Liberator*. Sewall thought the name too

provoking and suggested the *Safety Lamp*. Garrison would not hear of it. "Provoking!" That was exactly what he meant it to be. Slavery in the United States had now lasted over two hundred years. During nearly three quarters of that time the Quakers had agitated against it in their inoffensive, conciliatory fashion. What had been accomplished? There were now more than four times as many slaves as when they began their propaganda. New Slave States had been added to the Union. The slave laws were more oppressive than ever. He meant to agitate. He meant to call hard names. He meant to make it impossible for any man to confess without shame that he was the owner of slaves. He was prepared for any sacrifice: "A few white victims must be sacrificed to open the eyes of this nation and show the tyranny of our laws. I expect and am willing to be persecuted, imprisoned and bound for advocating African rights; and I should deserve to be a slave myself if I shrunk from that duty or danger."

May was so fascinated by the young man's enthusiasm that the following morning, immediately after breakfast, he called on him at his boardinghouse and remained until two in the afternoon. Before the week was over he and Sewall had made arrangements for Garrison to repeat his lectures at Athenæum Hall.

The Sunday following, May occupied the pulpit at "Church Green," in Summer Street. So filled was he with Garrison's message that he interpolated his sermon with frequent references to slavery and finished with an appeal to the congregation to help abolish the institution before it destroyed the Republic. He was aware of the mounting uneasiness among his listeners, and having pronounced the benediction, said: "Every one present must be conscious that the closing remarks of my sermon have caused an unusual emotion throughout the church. I am glad. . . . I have been prompted to speak thus by the words I have heard during the past week from a young man hitherto unknown, but who

is, I believe, called of God to do a greater work for the good of our country than has been done by any one since the Revolution. I mean William Lloyd Garrison. He is going to repeat his lectures the coming week. I advise, I exhort, I entreat—would that I could compel!—you to go and hear him."

The following day May's father, Colonel Joseph May, was walking down State Street when a friend rushed up to him and impulsively grasped his hand.

"Colonel," he said, "you have my sympathy. I cannot tell you how much I pity you."

The old man looked at him astounded. "Sympathy? Pity? For what?"

The other appeared embarrassed. "Well," he said, "I hear your son went mad at 'Church Green' yesterday."

4

In a small chamber, friendless and unseen,
    Toiled o'er his types one poor, unlearned
        young man;
The place was dark, unfurnitured and mean,
    Yet there the freedom of a race began.

Help came but slowly; surely, no man yet
    Put lever to the heavy world with less;
What need of help? He knew how types
        were set,
    He had a dauntless spirit and a press.

James Russell Lowell, the author of these lines, has availed himself of the usual poetic license. The room on the third floor of Merchants' Hall, in Boston, where on January 1, 1831, Garrison launched the *Liberator*, was not particularly small, being eighteen feet square, and not one, but two unlearned young men "toiled over the types," for he and Isaac Knapp of Newburyport had joined forces. Later they were aided by a Negro apprentice. The windows were grimy and spattered with printer's ink, as were the dingy walls. There was a press, picked up at a bargain, a couple of composing stands with worn secondhand type, a few chairs and a long table covered with exchanges, at which the editor attended to his correspondence. In a corner of the room was a mattress on which the two friends slept, for they could not afford the luxury of a boarding-house. They lived on bread, milk and a little fruit, sharing the first two with a cat who, when Garrison sat down to write, would jump on the table and rub her fur caressingly against his bald forehead. Although the paper advocated temperance as well as abolition, Knapp found it impossible to wean himself from his craving for strong drink, a weakness which eventually led to his undoing.

In the literature of social protest few lines are more stirring than the following paragraph from Garrison's salutatory to the public in the first number of the *Liberator*:

"I am aware that many object to the severity of my language; but is there not cause for severity? I *will be* as harsh as truth, and as uncompromising as justice. On this subject, I do not wish to think, or speak, or write, with moderation. No! No! Tell a man whose house is on fire to give a moderate alarm; tell him to moderately rescue his wife from the hands of the ravisher; tell the mother to gradually extricate her babe from the fire into which it has fallen;—but urge me not to use moderation in a cause like the present. I am in earnest—I will not equivocate—I will not excuse—I will not retreat a single inch—AND I WILL BE HEARD."

The last statement proved prophetic. The *Liberator* never paid expenses, never had over three thousand subscribers, but its message became known from coast to coast and across the Atlantic. The paper had a fertilizing influence that caused the sprouting of various forms of opposition to slavery, of most of which Garrison disapproved, but for all of which he was directly or indirectly responsible. There were to be Abolitionists who formed political

Masthead of Garrison's Liberator. (Courtesy of The New-York Historical Society.)

parties and others who abstained from voting; those who were orthodox churchmen and those who set out to destroy organized religion; those who believed in nonresistance and those who advocated armed intervention; those who wished to arouse the slaves to revolt and those who opposed this; those determined to remain within constitutional limits and those who scoffed at the Constitution. The Liberty Party, the Free-Soil Movement, the Republican Party —all, to a greater extent than their leaders cared to acknowledge, owed their existence to Garrison. He was the sower who went forth to sow and whose seed fell onto fertile ground, blossoming forth in a variety of shapes. He was the spiritual father of innumerable children, most of whom disowned him. He shamed a reluctant nation into doing what it did not wish to do, and the nation has never forgiven him. In 1853, Wendell Phillips said:

"The community has come to hate its reproving Nathan so bitterly, that even those whom the relenting part of it is beginning to regard as standard-bearers of the antislavery host think it unwise to avow any connection or sympathy with him. I refer to some of the leaders of the political movement against slavery. . . . They are willing to confess privately, that our movement produced theirs, and

that its continued existence is the very breath of their life. But, at the same time, they would fain walk on the road without being soiled by too close contact with the rough pioneers who threw it up. . . . If you tell me that they cherished all these principles in their own breasts before Mr. Garrison appeared, I can only say, if the antislavery movement did not give them their ideas, it surely gave them the courage to utter them."

5

"Why so hot my little man?" wrote Ralph Waldo Emerson; and at another time: "There is a sublime prudence which, believing in a vast future, sure of more to come than is yet seen, postpones always the present hour to the whole life." But now see Emerson, returning from Boston in 1850, a copy of the Fugitive Slave Law in his pocket, writing in his Journal: "This filthy enactment was made in the nineteenth century—I will not obey it—by God!" What has become of the "sublime prudence"? To refuse to obey the Fugitive Slave Law meant to incur a thousand dollar fine and be liable to pay another thousand to the claimant of the fugitive, not to speak of a possible six months in

jail. Was it that Emerson had come to agree with Whittier that a civilized man could no more obey the Fugitive Slave Law, even when a Lincoln set out to enforce it, than he could become a cannibal?

Garrison never worried about keeping cool. He agreed with Burke that "To speak of atrocious crimes in mild language is treason to virtue," with Luther that "Those things that are softly dealt with, in a corrupt age, give people but little concern, and are presently forgotten." Samuel J. May once said to him: "O, my friend, do try to moderate your indignation, and keep more cool; why, you are all on fire." His friend replied: "Brother May, I have need to be *all on fire*, for I have mountains of ice about me to melt."

Was the method effective? That it made it well-nigh impossible to spread the gospel of emancipation in the South admits of no doubt. But except among Southern Quakers such propaganda had borne no fruit. Indeed, while at one time the slaveholders had been willing to concede that slavery was an evil and a curse, foisted upon the South by the mother country, after years of propaganda by Quakers and others they had arrived at the conclusion that it was the best of all possible labor systems, far superior to that prevailing in the North. This change of outlook was clearly perceptible at the time of the Missouri Compromise, long before the appearance of the *Liberator*. It was due to the fact that the invention of the cotton gin had made slavery far more profitable.

When Garrison began publication of his paper nearly all opposition to slavery had disappeared, North as well as South. Albert Bushnell Hart, in a profound study of the subject, wrote: "When Jackson became President in 1829, anti-slavery seemed, after fifty years of effort, to have spent its force. The voice of the churches was no longer heard in protest; the abolitionist societies were dying out; there was hardly an abolitionist militant in the field. . . . In Congress there was only one anti-slavery man and his efforts were without avail." But in 1839 the managers of the Massachusetts Anti-Slavery Society were able to declare: "Ten years ago a solitary individual stood up as the advocate of immediate and unconditional emancipation. Now, that individual sees about him hundreds of thousands of persons, of both sexes, members of every sect and party, from the most elevated to the humblest rank of life. In 1829 not an Anti-Slavery Society of a genuine stamp was in existence. In 1839 there are nearly two thousand such societies swarming and multiplying in all parts of the free States. In 1829 there was but one Anti-Slavery periodical in the land. In 1839 there are fourteen. In 1829 there was scarcely a newspaper of any religious or political party which was willing to disturb the 'delicate' question of slavery. In 1839 there are multitudes of journals that either openly advocate the doctrine of immediate and unconditional emancipation, or permit its free discussion in their columns. Then scarcely a church made slave-holding a bar to communion. Now, multitudes refuse to hear a slave-holder preach, or to recognize one as a brother. Then, no one petitioned Congress to abolish slavery in the District of Columbia. Now, in one day, a single member of the House of Representatives (John Quincy Adams) has presented one hundred and seventy-six such petitions in detail; while no less than seven hundred thousand persons have memorialized Congress on that and kindred subjects."

Garrison was to say: "In seizing the trump of God, I had indeed to blow a 'jarring blast'—but it was necessary to wake up a nation then slumbering in the lap of moral death. . . . What else but the *Liberator* primarily, (and of course instrumentally,) has effected this change? Greater success than I have had, no man could reasonably desire, or humbly expect."

When in 1837 Dr. William Ellery Channing complimented James G. Birney on the reasonableness and moderation of his antislavery paper, in contrast with the *Liberator*, which

he accused of being "blemished by a spirit of intolerance, sweeping censure and rash, injurious judgment," the former Kentucky slaveholder and Solicitor General of Alabama replied: "Our country was asleep, whilst slavery was preparing to pour its 'leprous distilment' into her ears. So deep was becoming her sleep that nothing but a rude and almost ruffian-like shake could rouse her to a contemplation of her danger. If she is saved, it is because she has been thus treated." He left no doubt about whom he had in mind when he said on another occasion: "My anti-slavery trumpet would never have roused the country—Garrison alone could do it."

Another former Kentucky slaveholder, the famous Cassius Marcellus Clay, who while a student at Yale heard Garrison speak and became a convert, wrote: "There is one saying of his [Garrison's] traducers, and the traducers of those who act with him, . . . that 'they have set back the cause of emancipation by agitation'! Nothing is more false. The cause of emancipation advances only with agitation: let that cease and despotism is complete."

6

Garrison did not expect to convert the slaveholders. He considered such an attempt a waste of time. In 1837 he wrote to Elizabeth Pease: "I have relinquished the expectation that they [the slaveholders] will ever, by mere moral suasion, consent to emancipate their victims." In 1840 he wrote to Elizabeth's brother Joseph: "There is not any instance recorded either in sacred or profane history, in which the oppressors and enslavers of mankind, except in individual cases, have been induced, by mere moral suasion, to surrender their despotic power, and let the oppressed go free; but in nearly every instance, from the time that Pharaoh and his hosts were drowned in the Red Sea, down to the present day, they have persisted in their

evil course until sudden destruction came upon them, or they were compelled to surrender their ill-gotten power in some other manner."

Others were of the same opinion. Cassius M. Clay wrote: "The slaveholders have just as much intention of yielding up their slaves as the sum of the kings of the earth have of laying down, for the benefit of the people, their sceptres." In August, 1855, Abraham Lincoln was to write to George Robertson of Kentucky that the Tsar of Russia would abdicate and free his serfs sooner than American slaveholders would voluntarily give up their slaves. "Experience has demonstrated, I think, that there is no peaceful extinction of slavery in prospect for us."

Garrison feared, like Lincoln, that slavery would never be abolished except by force of arms, but he believed there was one other method worth trying. When Jesus of Nazareth called the Pharisees "fools," "hypocrites," "devourers of widows' houses," "serpents," "generation of vipers"—and asked, "How can ye escape the damnation of hell?"—he was obviously not using moral *suasion*, but moral *pressure*. This was the method Garrison had decided to adopt. Shortly after he founded the *Liberator*, he told Samuel J. May: "Until the term 'slaveholder' sends as deep a feeling of horror to the hearts of those who hear it applied to any one as the term, 'robber,' 'pirate,' 'murderer' do, we must use and multiply epithets when condemning the sins of him who is guilty of 'the sum of all villainies.' " He hoped to arouse such a feeling of abhorrence and storm of disapproval in the North (and in fact throughout the civilized world) that the South would be forced to yield. That the method offered some hope of success was acknowledged by General Duff Green, who wrote: "We believe that we have most to fear from the organized action upon the conscience and fears of the slaveholders themselves. . . . It is only by alarming the consciences of the weak and feeble, and diffusing among our own people a

morbid sensibility on the question of slavery, that the abolitionists can accomplish their object."

The method did not succeed any more than it had succeeded in Christ's time; but who will say that it was not worth trying? Nor can it be said that it produced no results. If Garrison failed to shame and intimidate the South, he yet succeeded in arousing such an aversion to, and fear of, slavery in the North that war seemed preferable to allowing it to spread. Archibald H. Grimké has well said: "The public sentiment which Lincoln obeyed, [Garrison and] Phillips created."

7

About a year before the appearance of the *Liberator,* David Walker, a Boston Negro who made a living as an old-clothes man, published a pamphlet entitled *Walker's Appeal.* He boldly called upon the slaves to revolt. "If you commence," he wrote, "make sure work—do not trifle, for they will not trifle with you—they want us for their slaves, and think nothing of murdering us in order to subject us to that wretched condition—therefore, if there is an attempt made by us, kill or be killed." There were three editions of the pamphlet, copies of which found their way into the Slave States. The consternation these produced in the South bordered on the ridiculous and was eloquent testimony of the fear that lurked under the South's brave exterior. Governors sent special messages to Legislatures. Repressive laws were hastily passed. Incoming ships and trains were searched. Colored seamen were taken from Northern ships entering Southern ports and imprisoned. "How much is it to be regretted," declared *Niles' Weekly Register,* "that a negro dealer in old clothes, should thus excite two states to legislative action." Walker, however, died in June, 1830, and the South breathed a sigh of relief.

Then, in January, 1831, again in the city of Boston, appeared the *Liberator,* and in an early issue of the paper a poem from the editor's pen warning of the danger of a slave uprising if emancipation were delayed. One stanza read:

> Woe if it come with storm, and blood,
>   and fire,
> When midnight darkness veils the earth and
>   sky!
>   Woe to the innocent babe—the guilty
>   sire—
> Mother and daughter—friends of kindred
>   tie!
>   *Stranger and citizen alike shall die!*
> Red-handed slaughter his revenge shall feed,
>   And Havoc yell his ominous death-cry;
> And wild Despair in vain for mercy plead—
>   While Hell itself shall shrink, and sicken
>   at the deed!

The slave uprising in the French colony of San Domingo towards the close of the eighteenth century proved there were reasons for the warning. Garrison, however, did not advise the slaves to revolt. He had condemned *Walker's Appeal* in the *Genius,* and the last stanza of his poem read:

> Not by the sword shall your deliverance be;
>   Not by the shedding of your masters'
>   blood,
> Not by rebellion—or foul treachery,
>   Upspringing suddenly, like swelling flood:
> Revenge and rapine ne'er did bring forth
>   good.
>   God's *time is best!*—nor will it long delay:
> Even now your barren cause begins to bud,
>   And glorious shall the fruit be!—Watch
>   and pray,
> For, lo! the kindling dawn, that ushers in
>   the day!

Shortly after the appearance of this poem, on August 22, 1831, there took place in Southampton County, Virginia, the most sanguinary slave uprising in the annals of American

slavery. A Negro mystic named Nat Turner, a slave belonging to a small planter, gathered a band of followers variously estimated at from forty to two hundred, and after killing his master and the latter's family, moved from plantation to plantation, slaughtering between fifty and sixty persons, men, women and children. Bands of white men and the state militia finally subdued the rebels, but not without committing outrages upon innocent Negroes surpassing in cruelty anything of which Turner had been guilty. Finally, the Negro leader and nineteen of his followers were hanged. The uprising was responsible for a sensational debate in the Virginia Legislature during which slavery was condemned in language as violent as any Garrison had ever used. For a while indeed it seemed that what years of propaganda by the Quakers had failed to accomplish would come as a result of Turner's bloodletting. Governor John Floyd of Virginia noted in his diary: "Before I leave this Government I will have contrived to have a law passed gradually abolishing slavery in this state." But the people and the authorities eventually got over their fright and began looking about for a scapegoat. Walker was read, but there was Garrison and his paper. Turner and his confederates had denied that they had read either *Walker's Appeal* or the *Liberator,* and no evidence to the contrary was introduced; but Governor Floyd wrote to Governor James Hamilton of South Carolina that black preachers had read from the pulpit the inflammatory writings of Walker and Garrison, which may or may not have been true. Anyway, Harrison Gray Otis, Mayor of Boston, received letters from the Governors of Virginia and Georgia "severally remonstrating against an incendiary newspaper published in Boston, and, as they alleged, thrown broadcast among their plantations, inciting to insurrection and its horrid results."

Mayor Otis was puzzled. Although the *Liberator* had now been published in Boston for nearly a year, he had never seen a copy or even heard of the paper's existence. "It appeared on enquiry," he wrote, "that no member of the city government, nor any person of my acquaintance, had ever heard of the publication. Some time afterward, it was reported to me by the city officers that they had ferreted out the paper and its editor; that his office was an obscure hole, his only visible auxiliary a negro boy, and his supporters a very few insignificant persons of all colors. This information, with the consent of the aldermen, I communicated to the above-named governors, with an assurance of my belief that the new fanaticism had not made, nor was likely to make, proselytes among the respectable classes of our people. In this, however, I was mistaken."

Neither the Mayor of Boston nor the Governor of Massachusetts felt he possessed the power to stop publication of the *Liberator,* though both regretted that shortcoming in the law. The South was indignant. The Columbia (South Carolina) *Telescope* believed the matter called for armed intervention. "They [the people of Massachusetts] permit a battery to be erected upon their territory, which fires upon us, and we should be justified in invading that territory to silence their guns," the editor declared. A Vigilance Committee in Columbia offered a reward of fifteen hundred dollars for the arrest and conviction of any person "distributing or circulating the *Liberator* or any other publication of a seditious nature." Georgetown, District of Columbia, passed a law forbidding any colored person to take the *Liberator* from the post-office on pain of twenty dollars' fine and thirty days' imprisonment. In Raleigh, North Carolina, the grand jury found a true bill against Garrison and Knapp in the hope of extraditing them. A correspondent in the Washington *National Intelligencer* proposed that the President of the United States or the Governor of Virginia demand Garrison's extradition, and in case of refusal by the Governor of Massachusetts "the people of the South offer an adequate reward to any person

who will deliver him dead or alive, into the hands of the authorities of any State South of the Potomac." He did not have long to wait. On November 30, 1831, the Senate and the House of Representatives of Georgia appropriated five thousand dollars to be paid by the Governor "to any person or persons who shall arrest, bring to trial and prosecute to conviction, under the laws of the State, the editor or publisher of a certain paper called the *Liberator*, published in the town of Boston and State of Massachusetts."

Garrison was not in the least intimidated and wrote defiantly: "A price upon the head of a citizen of Massachusetts—for what? For daring to give his opinion of the moral aspect of slavery! . . . Know this, ye Senatorial Patrons of kidnappers! that we despise your threats as much as we deplore your infatuation; nay, more—know that a hundred men stand ready to fill our place as soon as it is made vacant by violence."

8

On his last visit to the United States, General Lafayette expressed his astonishment at the increase in racial prejudice. He recalled that in Washington's army, white and black had fought side by side and had messed together in harmony. Now, however, in the Free as well as in the Slave States, free Negroes were despised, persecuted, deprived of most of the prerogatives of the freeman, permitted to earn a living only at the most menial and ill-paid employments.

A glance at some of the laws governing the free people of color leaves no doubt concerning the tenuous nature of the freedom they enjoyed. In Maryland a Justice of the Peace could order a free Negro's ears cropped for striking a white man even in self-defense. A free Negro entering that State incurred a penalty of fifty dollars for every week spent within its borders, and if unable to pay was sold into slavery. In Georgia the penalty for teaching a free Negro to read or write was five hundred dollars if the offender was white, if colored he was fined and flogged at the discretion of the court. In Virginia and South Carolina any Justice of the Peace could disband a school where free Negroes or their offspring were taught to read or write, fine the teacher five hundred dollars and have twenty lashes administered to each pupil. In Louisiana a fine of like amount awaited the zealous Christian who taught a free Negro in Sunday School. In Mississippi and the District of Columbia a Negro unable to prove his legal right to freedom could be sold into slavery. In South Carolina a Negro who "entertained" a runaway slave by giving him as much as a crust of bread was fined fifty dollars, and if unable to pay was sold. In several Slave States free Negroes were not permitted to assemble for religious purposes unless white people were present, and they were forbidden to preach. In Ohio a white man who hired a Negro or mulatto even for a day made himself liable for his future support. In the Free States, Negro children could not attend public school and little or no provision was made for their instruction. In several Free and of course in all the Slave States, free people of color were denied the right of suffrage.

Custom solidified this edifice of injustice. It made it well-nigh impossible for an artisan, mechanic or shopkeeper to employ a colored apprentice. In the North as well as in the South, Negroes were required to travel in the steerage of a boat or on the outside of a stagecoach, when they were not barred altogether. When a convention of colored people in Philadelphia made a brave attempt to establish a manual labor school for Negroes in New Haven, Connecticut, the Mayor called a mass meeting of the citizens, and such a hue and cry arose that the plan had to be abandoned. When Noyes Academy, in Canaan, New Hampshire, admitted a few colored students, three hundred

citizens with a hundred yoke of oxen dragged the building from its foundation and deposited it outside the town. In church, Negroes had to sit in separate pews—which in the Baptist Church at Hartford, Connecticut, were boarded up and provided with peepholes. When in Houghton, Massachusetts, a colored man acquired a white man's pew, the church authorities had the floor removed in that part of the edifice.

The case of Prudence Crandall, in which Garrison was involved, deserves special attention.

9

In 1832, Miss Crandall invested her small capital in a house in Canterbury, Connecticut, and established a "Female Boarding School." She was a capable teacher and had no difficulty in having girls entrusted to her care. One day a mulatto girl of seventeen, Sarah Harris, came to her with a humble request. If she boarded at home, would she be allowed to attend classes, "to get a little more learning—enough if possible to teach colored children"? Miss Crandall laid the matter before her pupils. Several had attended district school with Sarah and knew her to be neat, modest and well-mannered. They voted unanimously that she be admitted.

But they had reckoned without their elders. Tongues wagged. . . . A colored girl attending a private school for young ladies! What was the world coming to! . . . The wife of the Episcopal clergyman called on Miss Crandall to voice the disapproval of respectability. If Miss Crandall persisted in her course she would lose her pupils, she told her. "Then," replied the teacher, "the school must sink, for I won't turn her out." The minister's wife departed in a dudgeon, and soon after most of Miss Crandall's pupils were called home by their parents.

Miss Crandall, who occasionally read the

Liberator, wrote to the editor: "I have been for some months past determined if possible during the remaining part of my life to benefit the people of color. Will you be so kind as to write by the next mail and give me your opinion on the subject; and if you consider it possible to obtain 20 or 25 young ladies of color to enter the school for the term of one year at the rate of $25 per quarter, including board, washing and tuition, I will come to Boston in a few days and make arrangements about it."

She came and met Garrison at the Marlboro Hotel. He gave her letters to colored friends in Boston and New York and published her advertisement in his paper, with favorable comment.

A colored girl attending a school for young ladies was bad enough; but a private school for colored girls—it was too much! No sooner had Miss Crandall's intention become known than leading citizens of Canterbury called a mass meeting. Garrison wrote to his friend George W. Benson, in the neighboring town of Brooklyn: "If possible, Miss C. must be sustained at all hazards. If we suffer the school to be put down in Canterbury, other places will partake of the panic, and also prevent its introduction in their vicinity. We may as well, 'first and last,' meet the prescriptive spirit and conquer it."

Benson and Samuel J. May went to the meeting, which a thousand people attended. "Should the school go into operation," Andrew T. Judson, a Democratic politician and Colonizationist, roared from the platform, "our sons and daughters will be forever ruined and property no longer safe." Garrison's friends attempted to reply, but were shouted down. A committee called on Miss Crandall and informed her that "by putting your design into operation you will bring ruin and disgrace upon us all."

Garrison published an account of the meeting under the caption "Heathenism Outdone," and pilloried Judson and his fellow agitators in these terms: "We put the names of the prin-

cipal disturbers in black letters,—black as the infamy which will attach to them as long as there exists any recollection of the wrongs of the colored race. To colonize these shameless enemies of their species in some desert country would be a relief and a blessing to society." So vehement was he that Miss Crandall begged him to moderate his tone: "Permit me to entreat you to handle the prejudices of the people of Canterbury with all the mildness possible, as everything severe tends to heighten the flame of malignity amongst them."

But for all her mildness she remained resolute, and the following month a score of colored girls arrived from Boston, New York, Philadelphia and Providence. Canterbury struck back. Shopkeepers refused to trade with her. The doctor declined to call. The church closed its doors against her and her pupils. Her house was smeared with filth and her well filled with manure. An old vagrancy law was invoked and her pupils threatened with ten lashes upon the bare back if they did not depart.

Miss Crandall's friends now rushed to the rescue. May and others gave bond for the pupils, making it impossible to invoke the vagrancy law. A local Quaker furnished water from his well; others helped to obtain provisions from neighboring towns. So Canterbury appealed to the Legislature. A law was rushed through forbidding schools in Connecticut to admit nonresident colored pupils. When news of its passage reached Canterbury there was rejoicing. The cannon, brought into action only on festive occasions, was noisily fired, church bells tolled; for had not Canterbury's sons and daughters been saved from "everlasting ruin"?

Not yet! Miss Crandall refused to obey the law. The case assumed national importance. Arthur Tappan wrote to May: "Consider me your banker. Spare no necessary expense. Command the services of the ablest lawyers. See to it that the great case shall be thoroughly tried, cost what it may. I will cheerfully honor your draft to enable you to defray the cost."

The courts were now asked to pronounce on Miss Crandall's guilt and the constitutionality of the law. At the first trial the jury disagreed, at the second she was convicted. Appeal was taken to the highest court in the State, which sidestepped the issue by dismissing the case on a technicality.

Canterbury's patience was now exhausted. An attempt was made to set fire to the school, but the flames did little damage. Then a mob assembled armed with sticks and stones and shattered every window. As the teacher herded her pupils where they would be safe from hurtling stones and flying glass, she decided not to put their lives in jeopardy and closed the school.

10

Garrison championed the free people of color as fervently as the slaves. "This then is my consolation," he wrote on one occasion: "if I cannot do much in this quarter towards abolishing slavery, I may be able to elevate our free colored population in the scale of society." Speaking before a colored convention in Philadelphia he said with feeling: "I never rise to address a colored audience without feeling ashamed of my color; ashamed of being identified with a race of men who have done you so much injustice and yet retain so large a portion of your brethren in servitude."

No matter how pressing his work, he would lay it aside when invited to address a colored audience. He did not flatter his listeners, but urged them to be worthy of liberty, to be temperate, industrious and to surpass the white man in virtue, which, he assured them, was no difficult task. They must not resort to violence, but should incessantly petition to be permitted to vote, to send their children to public school and to exercise every other right of the freeman. "If your petition is denied seven times, send it seventy times seven."

His influence was great among them. Once in Boston, when he had addressed them on temperance, they immediately formed a temperance society, which within a few days counted one hundred and fifty members. "Such acts as these, brethren, give me strength and boldness in your cause," he assured them. Henry E. Benson, in a letter to Isaac Knapp, described a scene that took place in Providence, Rhode Island, after Garrison had addressed a colored audience. "After the meeting," he wrote, "the poor creatures wept and sobbed like children—they gathered round him anxious to express their gratitude for what he had done for them, and tell him how well they loved him."

So persistent was he in their defense that some believed him to be colored, and when he advocated the repeal of the Massachusetts law against intermarriage, the rumor spread that he meant to marry a Negress. No resentment at the rumor is noticeable in this mild denial he published in the *Liberator:* "We declare that our heart is neither affected *by*, nor pledged *to*, any lady, black or white, bond or free."

11

If "the style is the man," then one might have expected Garrison in his maturity to have been a scowling, brusque, bitter, opinionated individual. Such in fact was the mental image formed by many. The reality confounded Buffon's maxim. Josiah Copley, editor of a religious paper in Pittsburgh, Pennsylvania, happening to be in Boston in 1832, called on Garrison after some hesitation. "I never was more astonished," he wrote. "All my preconceptions were at fault. My ideal of the man was that of a stout, rugged, dark-visaged desperado—something like we picture a pirate. He was a quiet, gentle and I might say handsome man—a gentleman indeed, in every sense of the word."

William H. Herndon, Lincoln's law partner, who visited Garrison in the latter's old age, wrote: "I had imagined him a shriveled, cold, selfish, haughty man, one who was weak and fanatically blind to the charities and equities of life, at once whining and insulting, mean and miserable, but I was pleasantly disappointed. I found him warm, generous, approachable, communicative; he has some mirth, some wit, and a deep abiding faith in coming universal charity. I was better and more warmly received by him than by any man in Boston."

Harriet Martineau, famous British authoress, who met Garrison in 1835, declared: "His aspect put to flight in an instant what prejudices his slanderers had raised in me. I was wholly taken by surprise. It was a countenance glowing with health and wholly expressive of purity, animation and gentleness. I did not now wonder at the citizen who, seeing a print of Garrison at a shop window without a name to it, went in and bought it and framed it as the most saintlike of countenances. The end of the story is, that when the citizen found whose portrait he had been hanging in his parlor, he took the print out of the frame and huddled it away."

The preponderance of opinion is that his conversation was the very opposite of his writing—mild, tolerant, disarming. Miss Martineau wrote: "Garrison had a good deal of a Quaker air; and his speech is deliberate like a Quaker's but gentle as a woman's. . . . Every conversation I had with him confirmed my opinion that sagacity is the most striking attribute of his conversation. It has none of the severity, the harshness, the bad taste of his writing; it is as gladsome as his countenance, and as gentle as his voice."

Harriet Beecher Stowe, who had confided to one of Garrison's sons that she was "dreadfully afraid" of his father, having made the editor's acquaintance, wrote to him: "You have a remarkable tact at conversation."

Ralph Waldo Emerson, who for a long time

had been prejudiced against him, in 1844 wrote in his Journal: "The haters of Garrison have lived to rejoice in that grand world movement which, every age or two, casts out so masterly an agent for good. I cannot speak of the gentleman without respect."

12

In the first number of the *Liberator,* where appeared Garrison's immortal challenge to the slaveholders, one may read these lines from the editor's pen:

"An attempt has been made—it is still making—we regret to say, with considerable success—to inflame the minds of our working classes against the more opulent, and to persuade them that they are contemned and oppressed by a wealthy aristocracy. That public grievances exist, is unquestionably true; but they are not confined to any one class of society. Every profession is interested in their removal—the rich as well as the poor. It is in the highest degree criminal, therefore, to exasperate our mechanics to deeds of violence, or to array them under a party banner; for it is not true, that, at any time, they have been the objects of reproach . . . We are the friends of reform; but that is not reform, which, in curing one evil, threatens to inflict a thousand others."

The reason for this outburst was an attempt by Seth Luther and others to organize a Working Men's Party and to form labor unions.

In the fifth number of the paper a correspondent pointed out to Garrison that he was wrong in trying to discourage labor's attempts to organize:

"Although you do not appear to have perceived it, I think there is a very intimate connexion between the interests of the working men's party and your own . . . In the history of the origin of slavery is to be found the explanation of the evils we deplore and seek to remove, as well as those you have attacked.

. . . We seek to enlighten our brethren in the knowledge of their rights and duties. . . . It is a duty owed by working men to themselves and the world to exert their power through the ballot-box."

Garrison replied: "There is a prevalent opinion that . . . the poor and vulgar are taught to consider the opulent as their natural enemies. Where is the evidence that our wealthy citizens, as a body, are hostile to the interests of the laboring classes? It is not in their commercial enterprises, which whiten the ocean with canvas and give employment to a useful and numerous class of men. It is not found in the manufacturing establishments, which multiply labor and cheapen the necessities of the poor. It is not found in the luxuries of their tables, or the adornments of their dwellings, for which they must pay in proportion to their extravagance. . . . Perhaps it would be the truth to affirm, that mechanics are more inimical to the success of each other, more unjust toward each other, than the rich are toward them."

Yet in 1831, and for a long time thereafter, the hours of labor in New England factories were from five in the morning until seven-thirty in the evening—the working day being thirteen and one half hours. The two half hours allowed for breakfast and midday dinner were as tiring as any, since the workers had to hurry home, bolt their food and hasten back to the factory to escape a fine. In 1849 a report submitted to the American Medical Association by one of its members contained the statement that "there is not a State's prison, or house of correction in New England, where the hours of labor are so long, the hours for meals so short, or the ventilation so much neglected, as in all the cotton mills with which I am acquainted." In Boston Irish workmen were forced to labor fifteen hours a day, including Sunday. The death rate among them was so appalling that it was claimed the Irish lived on an average only fourteen years after reaching Boston. The Cochee Manufacturing Company required its

workers to sign an agreement to "conform in all respects to the regulations which are now, or may be hereafter adopted . . . and to work for such wages as the company may see fit to pay." Workers were commonly required to buy at the company store and were usually in debt to their employers. If they attempted to leave their employment without paying what they owed they were imprisoned. In 1831 there were over fifteen hundred people imprisoned for debt in Boston alone, more than half of whom owed less than twenty dollars. It may therefore be said that a system of veritable peonage prevailed.

Strikes were frequent, but prior to 1860 not a single strike was won in Massachusetts, and not until 1874 did that State have any legal restriction on the number of hours adult wage-workers could be required to work. Employers in other parts of the country often gave working conditions in New England as an excuse for not improving labor's lot.

In view of all this, how could a man ready for almost any sacrifice for the sake of the Negro have remained indifferent to the lot of white wageworkers?

Garrison was an individualist. In his opinion, if a man was not a chattel, he was master of his own fate. If he was poor the fault was his. In the days of handicraft, poverty had indeed usually been the result of shiftlessness; but the poverty of the factory worker was more often due to the greed of the employer. The handicraftsman, having finished his apprenticeship, looked forward to being his own master. If he worked long hours he was buoyed up by the hope of getting ahead in the world. But later, only the exceptional man could hope to become a factory owner or even a foreman. Garrison, grown to maturity in a transition period, failed to grasp that the average wageworker's only hope of improving his lot was to unite with his fellows.

When Garrison wrote "Mechanics are more inimical to the success of each other, more un-just toward each other than the rich are towards them," he failed to comprehend that fear was at the bottom of this. Yankee workmen feared the competition of Irish immigrants and sometimes rioted against them. White workmen were hostile to Negroes for the same reason and opposed emancipation fearing it would result in hordes of Negroes from the South invading the North and lowering their standard of living, already sufficiently low. Southern leaders shrewdly exploited this fear. In 1843, Henry Clay wrote to the Reverend Calvin Colton, urging him to prepare a popular tract whose "great aim and object . . . should be to arouse the laboring classes of the free States against abolition. The slaves, being free, would be dispersed throughout the Union; they would enter into competition with the free laborer; with the American, the Irish, the German; reduce his wages; be confounded with him, and affect his moral and social standing. And as the ultras go for both abolition and amalgamation, show that their object is to unite in marriage the laboring white man and the laboring black man, and to reduce the white laboring man to the despised and degraded condition of the black man."

The situation required shrewd and careful handling. Most of all it required a thorough understanding of the problem. Garrison lacked that understanding, and antagonized his natural allies. As a result American wageworkers remained indifferent, if not hostile, to Abolition. Some regarded it as a plot of the employers to lower wages. Others saw it as a scheme of professional philanthropists. The editor of the *Chronicle*, a Massachusetts weekly devoted to the interests of labor, wrote: "Philanthropists may speak of negro slavery, but it would be well first to emancipate the slaves at home. Let us not stretch our ears to catch the sound of the lash on the flesh of the oppressed black, while the oppressed in our midst are crying in thunder tones, and calling upon us for assistance."

18

The Making of a Black Militant

Frederick Douglass

Negroes were involved in the Abolitionist crusade from the beginning. The most eminent was Frederick Douglass, a mulatto who had run away from a Maryland plantation, married a free black woman, befriended Garrison, and lectured to white audiences up and down New England. In 1845, he made a lecture tour in England, where friends raised money to buy his freedom. On his return, he decided to establish a black abolitionist newspaper, but Garrison and other whites objected. Douglass went ahead anyway, eventually breaking with the Garrisonians. Here, in an excerpt from his autobiography, Douglass describes these events and goes on to explain why he moved from nonviolent to militant abolitionism.

Prepared as I was to meet with many trials and perplexities on reaching home, one of which I little dreamed was awaiting me. My plans for future usefulness . . . were all settled, and in imagination I already saw myself wielding my pen as well as my voice in the great work of renovating the public mind, and building up a public sentiment, which should send slavery to the grave, and restore to "liberty and the pursuit of happiness" the people with whom I had suffered.

My friends in Boston had been informed of what I was intending, and I expected to find them favorably disposed toward my cherished enterprise. In this I was mistaken. They had many reasons against it. First, no such paper was needed; secondly, it would interfere with my usefulness as a lecturer; thirdly, I was better fitted to speak than to write; fourthly, the paper could not succeed. This opposition from a quarter so highly esteemed, and to which I had been accustomed to look for advice and direction, caused me not only to hesitate, but inclined me to abandon the undertaking. All previous attempts to establish such a journal having failed, I feared lest I should but add another to the list, and thus contribute another proof of the mental deficiencies of my race. Very much that was said to me in respect to my imperfect literary attainments I felt to be most painfully true. The unsuccessful projectors of all former attempts had been my superiors in point of education, and if they failed how could I hope for success? Yet I did hope for success, and persisted in the undertaking, encouraged by my English friends to go forward.

I can easily pardon those who saw in my persistence an unwarrantable ambition and presumption. I was but nine years from slavery. In many phases of mental experience I was but nine years old. That one under such circumstances and surrounded by an educated people, should aspire to establish a printing press, might well be considered unpractical, if not ambitious. My American friends looked at me with astonishment. "A wood-sawyer" offering himself to the public as an editor! A slave, brought up in the depths of ignorance, assum-

From Frederick Douglass, *Life and Times*. Hartford, Conn.: Park Publishing Co., 1882.

ing to instruct the highly civilized people of the North in the principles of liberty, justice, and humanity! The thing looked absurd. Nevertheless, I persevered. I felt that the want of education, great as it was, could be overcome by study, and that wisdom would come by experience, and further (which was perhaps the most controlling consideration) I thought that an intelligent public, knowing my early history, would easily pardon the many deficiencies which I well knew that my paper must exhibit. The most distressing part of it all was the offense which I saw I must give my friends of the old antislavery organization, by what seemed to them a reckless disregard of their opinion and advice. I am not sure that I was not under the influence of something like a slavish adoration of these good people, and I labored hard to convince them that my way of thinking about the matter was the right one, but without success.

From motives of peace, instead of issuing my paper in Boston, among New England friends, I went to Rochester, N.Y., among strangers, where the local circulation of my paper *The North Star*—would not interfere with that of the *Liberator* or the *Anti-Slavery Standard*, for I was then a faithful disciple of Wm. Lloyd Garrison, and fully committed to his doctrine touching the pro-slavery character of the Constitution of the United States, also the non-voting principle of which he was the known and distinguished advocate. With him, I held it to be the first duty of the non-slaveholding states to dissolve the union with the slaveholding states, and hence my cry, like his, was "No union with slaveholders." With these views I went into western New York, and during the first four years of my labors there I advocated them with pen and tongue to the best of my ability. After a time, a careful reconsideration of the subject convinced me that there was no necessity for dissolving the union between the northern and southern states, that to seek this dissolution was no part of my duty as an aboli-

tionist, that to abstain from voting was to refuse to exercise a legitimate and powerful means for abolishing slavery, and that the Constitution of the United States not only contained no guarantees in favor of slavery, but, on the contrary, was in its letter and spirit an antislavery instrument, demanding the abolition of slavery as a condition of its own existence as the supreme law of the land.

This radical change in my opinions produced a corresponding change in my action. To those with whom I had been in agreement and in sympathy, I came to be in opposition. What they held to be a great and important truth I now looked upon as a dangerous error. A very natural, but to me a very painful thing, now happened. Those who could not see any honest reasons for changing their views, as I had done, could not easily see any such reasons for my change, and the common punishment of apostates was mine.

My first opinions were naturally derived and honestly entertained. Brought directly, when I escaped from slavery, into contact with abolitionists who regarded the Constitution as a slaveholding instrument, and finding their views supported by the united and entire history of every department of the government, it is not strange that I assumed the Constitution to be just what these friends made it seem to be. I was bound, not only by their superior knowledge, to take their opinions in respect to this subject, as the true ones, but also because I had no means of showing the unsoundness of these opinions. But for the responsibility of conducting a public journal, and the necessity imposed upon me of meeting opposite views from abolitionists outside of New England, I should in all probability have remained firm in my disunion views. My new circumstances compelled me to re-think the whole subject, and to study with some care not only the just and proper rules of legal interpretation, but the origin, design, nature, rights, powers, and duties of civil governments, and also the rela-

A handsome, bewhiskered man, with full hair and stern, frowning eyes, Frederick Doug-lass became the most eminent black leader of his generation. (Courtesy of The Library of Congress.)

tions which human beings sustain to it. By such a course of thought and reading I was conducted to the conclusion that the Constitution of the United States—inaugurated to "form a more perfect union, establish justice, insure domestic tranquility, provide for the common defense, promote the general welfare, and secure the blessings of liberty"—could not well have been designed at the same time to maintain and perpetuate a system of rapine and murder like slavery, especially as not one word can be found in the Constitution to authorize such a belief. Then, again, if the declared purposes of an instrument are to govern the meaning of all its parts and details, as they clearly should, the Constitution of our country is our warrant for the abolition of slavery in every state of the Union. It would require much time and space to set forth the arguments which demonstrated to my mind the unconstitutionality of slavery, but being convinced of the fact, my duty upon this point in the further conduct of my paper was plain.

The North Star was a large sheet, published

weekly, at a cost of $80 per week, and an average circulation of 3,000 subscribers. There were many times when, in my experience as editor and publisher, I was very hard pressed for money, but by one means or another I succeeded so well as to keep my pecuniary engagements, and to keep my antislavery banner steadily flying during all the conflict from the autumn of 1847 till the union of the states was assured and emancipation was a fact accomplished.

.   .   .

Of course there were moral forces operating against me in Rochester, as well as material ones. There were those who regarded the publication of a Negro paper in that beautiful city as a blemish and a misfortune. The New York *Herald,* true to the spirit of the times, counselled the people of the place to throw my printing press into Lake Ontario and to banish me to Canada, and, while they were not quite prepared for this violence, it was plain that many of them did not well relish my presence amongst them. This feeling, however, wore away gradually, as the people knew more of me and my works. I lectured every Sunday evening during an entire winter in the beautiful Corinthian Hall, then owned by Wm. R. Reynolds, Esq., who, though he was not an abolitionist, was a lover of fair play, and was willing to allow me to be heard. If in these lectures I did not make abolitionists, I did succeed in making tolerant the moral atmosphere in Rochester—so much so, indeed, that I came to feel as much at home there as I had ever done in the most friendly parts of New England. I had been at work there with my paper but a few years before colored travelers told me that they felt the influence of my labors when they came within fifty miles. I did not rely alone upon what I could do by the paper, but would write all day, then take a train to Victor, Farmington, Canandaigua, Geneva, Waterloo, Batavia, or Buffalo, or elsewhere, and speak in the evening,

returning home afterwards or early in the morning, to be again at my desk writing or mailing papers. There were times when I almost thought my Boston friends were right in dissuading me from my newspaper project. But looking back to those nights and days of toil and thought, compelled often to do work for which I had no educational preparation, I have come to think that, under the circumstances, it was the best school possible for me. It obliged me to think and read, it taught me to express my thoughts clearly, and was perhaps better than any other course I could have adopted. Besides, it made it necessary for me to lean upon myself, and not upon the heads of our antislavery church—to be a principal, and not an agent. I had an audience to speak to every week, and must say something worth their hearing or cease to speak altogether. There is nothing like the lash and sting of necessity to make a man work, and my paper furnished this motive power. More than one gentleman from the South, when stopping at Niagara, came to see me, that they might know for themselves if I could indeed write, having, as they said, believed it impossible that an uneducated fugitive slave could write the articles attributed to me. I found it hard to get credit in some quarters either for what I wrote or what I said. While there was nothing very profound or learned in either, the low estimate of Negro possibilities induced the belief that both my editorials and my speeches were written by white persons. I doubt if this scepticism does not still linger in the minds of some of my democratic fellow-citizens.

.   .   .

One important branch of my antislavery work in Rochester, in addition to that of speaking and writing against slavery, must not be forgotten or omitted. My position gave me the chance of hitting that old enemy some telling blows, in another direction than these. I was on the southern border of Lake Ontario, and

the Queen's dominions were right over the way—and my prominence as an abolitionist, and as the editor of an antislavery paper, naturally made me the station-master and conductor of the underground railroad passing through this goodly city. Secrecy and concealment were necessary conditions to the successful operation of this railroad, and hence its prefix "underground." My agency was all the more exciting and interesting, because not altogether free from danger. I could take no step in it without exposing myself to fine and imprisonment, for these were the penalties imposed by the fugitive-slave law for feeding, harboring, or otherwise assisting a slave to escape from his master; but, in face of this fact, I can say I never did more congenial, attractive, fascinating, and satisfactory work. True, as a means of destroying slavery, it was like an attempt to bail out the ocean with a teaspoon, but the thought that there was *one* less slave, and one more freeman—having myself been a slave, and a fugitive slave—brought to my heart unspeakable joy. On one occasion I had eleven fugitives at the same time under my roof, and it was necessary for them to remain with me until I could collect sufficient money to get them on to Canada. It was the largest number I ever had at any one time, and I had some difficulty in providing so many with food and shelter, but, as may well be imagined, they were not very fastidious in either direction, and were well content with very plain food, and a strip of carpet on the floor for a bed, or a place on the straw in the barnloft.

The underground railroad had many branches, but that one with which I was connected had its main stations in Baltimore, Wilmington, Philadelphia, New York, Albany, Syracuse, Rochester, and St. Catherines (Canada). It is not necessary to tell who were the principal agents in Baltimore; Thomas Garrett was the agent in Wilmington; Melloe McKim, William Still, Robert Purvis, Edward M. Davis, and others, did the work in Philadelphia; David

Ruggles, Isaac T. Hopper, Napolian, and others, in New York City; the Misses Mott and Stephen Myers were forwarders from Albany; Revs. Samuel J. May and J. W. Loguen were the agents in Syracuse; and J. P. Morris and myself received and dispatched passengers from Rochester to Canada, where they were received by Rev. Hiram Wilson. When a party arrived in Rochester it was the business of Mr. Morris and myself to raise funds with which to pay their passage to St. Catharines, and it is due to truth to state that we seldom called in vain upon whig or democrat for help. Men were better than their theology, and truer to humanity than to their politics, or their offices.

On one occasion while a slave master was in the office of a United States commissioner, procuring the papers necessary for the arrest and rendition of three young men who had escaped from Maryland (one of whom was under my roof at the time, another at Farmington, and the other at work on the farm of Asa Anthony, just a little outside the city limits), the law partner of the commissioner, then a distinguished democrat, sought me out, and told me what was going on in his office, and urged me by all means to get these young men out of the way of their pursuers and claimants. Of course no time was to be lost. A swift horseman was dispatched to Farmington, eighteen miles distant, another to Asa Anthony's farm, about three miles, and another to my house on the south side of the city, and before the papers could be served all three of the young men were on the free waves of Lake Ontario, bound to Canada. In writing to their old master, they had dated their letter at Rochester, though they had taken the precaution to send it to Canada to be mailed, but this blunder in the date had betrayed their whereabouts, so that the hunters were at once on their tracks.

. . .

My pathway was not entirely free from thorns in Rochester, and the wounds and pains

inflicted by them were perhaps much less easily borne, because of my exemption from such annoyances while in England. Men can in time become accustomed to almost anything, even to being insulted and ostracized, but such treatment comes hard at first, and when to some extent unlooked for. The vulgar prejudice against color, so common to Americans, met me in several disagreeable forms. A seminary for young ladies and misses, under the auspices of Miss Tracy, was near my house on Alexander Street, and desirous of having my daughter educated like the daughters of other men, I applied to Miss Tracy for her admission to her school. All seemed fair, and the child was duly sent to Tracy Seminary, and I went about my business happy in the thought that she was in the way of a refined and Christian education. Several weeks elapsed before I knew how completely I was mistaken. The little girl came home to me one day and told me she was lonely in that school, that she was in fact kept in solitary confinement, that she was not allowed in the room with the other girls, nor to go into the yard when they went out, that she was kept in a room by herself and not permitted to be seen or heard by the others. No man with the feeling of a parent could be less than moved by such a revelation, and I confess that I was shocked, grieved, and indignant. I went at once to Miss Tracy to ascertain if what I had heard was true, and was coolly told it was, and the miserable plea was offered that it would have injured her school if she had done otherwise. I told her she should have told me so at the beginning, but I did not believe that any girl in the school would be opposed to the presence of my daughter, and that I should be glad to have the question submitted to them. She consented to this, and to the credit of the young ladies not one made objection. Not satisfied with this verdict of the natural and uncorrupted sense of justice and humanity of these young ladies, Miss Tracy insisted that the parents must be consulted, and

if one of them objected she should not admit my child to the same apartment and privileges of the other pupils. One parent only had the cruelty to object, and he was Mr. Horatio G. Warner, a democratic editor, and upon his adverse conclusion my daughter was excluded from Tracy Seminary. Of course Miss Tracy was a devout Christian lady after the fashion of the time and locality, in good and regular standing in the church.

My troubles attending the education of my children were not to end here. They were not allowed in the public school in the district in which I lived, owned property, and paid taxes, but were compelled, if they went to a public school, to go over to the other side of the city to an inferior colored school. I hardly need say that I was not prepared to submit tamely to this proscription, any more than I had been to submit to slavery, so I had them taught at home for a while by Miss Thayer. Meanwhile I went to the people with the question, and created considerable agitation. I sought and obtained a hearing before the Board of Education, and after repeated efforts with voice and pen the doors of the public schools were opened and colored children were permitted to attend them in common with others.

There were barriers erected against colored people in most other places of instruction and amusement in the city, and until I went there they were imposed without any apparent sense of injustice and wrong, and submitted to in silence, but one by one they have gradually been removed, and colored people now enter freely, without hindrance or observation, all places of public resort. This change has not been wholly effected by me. From the first I was cheered on and supported in my demands for equal rights by such respectable citizens as Isaac Post, Wm. Hallowell, Samuel D. Porter, Wm. C. Bloss, Benj. Fish, Asa Anthony, and many other good and true men of Rochester.

Notwithstanding what I have said of the adverse feeling exhibited by some of its citizens

at my selection of Rochester as the place in which to establish my paper, and the trouble in educational matters just referred to, that selection was in many respects very fortunate. The city was and still is the center of a virtuous, intelligent, enterprising, liberal, and growing population. The surrounding country is remarkable for its fertility, and the city itself possesses one of the finest waterpowers in the world. It is on the line of the New York Central Railroad—a line that, with its connections, spans the whole country. Its people were industrious and in comfortable circumstances—not so rich as to be indifferent to the claims of humanity, and not so poor as to be unable to help any good cause which commanded the approval of their judgment.

.   .   .

About the time I began my enterprise in Rochester I chanced to spend a night and a day under the roof of a man whose character and conversation, and whose objects and aims in life, made a very deep impression upon my mind and heart. His name had been mentioned to me by several prominent colored men, among whom were the Rev. Henry Highland Garnet and J. W. Loguen. In speaking of him their voices would drop to a whisper, and what they said of him made me very eager to see and to know him. Fortunately, I was invited to see him in his own house. At the time to which I now refer this man was a respectable merchant in a populous and thriving city, and our first place of meeting was at his store. This was a substantial brick building on a prominent, busy street. A glance at the interior, as well as at the massive walls without, gave me the impression that the owner must be a man of considerable wealth. My welcome was all that I could have asked. Every member of the family, young and old, seemed glad to see me, and I was made much at home in a very little while. I was, however, a little disappointed with the appearance of the house and its location. After

seeing the fine store I was prepared to see a fine residence in an eligible locality, but this conclusion was completely dispelled by actual observation. In fact, the house was neither commodious nor elegant, nor its situation desirable. It was a small wooden building on a back street, in a neighborhood chiefly occupied by laboring men and mechanics—respectable enough, to be sure, but not quite the place, I thought, where one would look for the residence of a flourishing and successful merchant. Plain as was the outside of this man's house, the inside was plainer. Its furniture would have satisfied a Spartan. It would take longer to tell what was not in this house than what was in it. There was an air of plainness about it which almost suggested destitution.

My first meal passed under the misnomer of tea, though there was nothing about it resembling the usual significance of that term. It consisted of beef soup, cabbage, and potatoes —a meal such as a man might relish after following the plow all day or performing a forced march of a dozen miles over a rough road in frosty weather. Innocent of paint, veneering, varnish, or tablecloth, the table announced itself unmistakably of pine and of the plainest workmanship. There was no hired help visible. The mother, daughters, and sons did the serving, and did it well. They were evidently used to it, and had no thought of any impropriety or degradation in being their own servants. It is said that a house in some measure reflects the character of its occupants; this one certainly did. In it there were no disguises, no illusions, no make-believes. Everything implied stern truth, solid purpose, and rigid economy. I was not long in company with the master of this house before I discovered that he was indeed the master of it, and was likely to become mine too if I stayed long enough with him. He fulfilled St. Paul's idea of the head of the family. His wife believed in him, and his children observed him with reverence. Whenever he spoke his words commanded

earnest attention. His arguments, which I ventured at some points to oppose, seemed to convince all; his appeals touched all, and his will impressed all. Certainly I never felt myself in the presence of a stronger religious influence than while in this man's house.

In person he was lean, strong, and sinewy, of the best New England mold, built for times of trouble and fitted to grapple with the flintiest hardships. Clad in plain American woolen, shod in boots of cowhide leather, and wearing a cravat of the same substantial material, under six feet high, less than 150 pounds in weight, aged about fifty, he presented a figure straight and symmetrical as a mountain pine. His bearing was singularly impressive. His head was not large, but compact and high. His hair was coarse, strong, slightly gray, and closely trimmed, and grew low on his forehead. His face was smoothly shaved, and revealed a strong, square mouth, supported by a broad and prominent chin. His eyes were bluish-gray, and in conversation they were full of light and fire. When on the street, he moved with a long, springing, race-horse step, absorbed by his own reflections, neither seeking nor shunning observation.

Such was the man whose name I had heard in whispers—such was the spirit of his house and family—such was the house in which he lived—and such was Captain John Brown, whose name has now passed into history, as that of one of the most marked characters and greatest heroes known to American fame.

After the strong meal already described, Captain Brown cautiously approached the subject which he wished to bring to my attention, for he seemed to apprehend opposition to his views. He denounced slavery in look and language fierce and bitter, thought that slaveholders had forfeited their right to live, that the slaves had the right to gain their liberty in any way they could, did not believe that moral suasion would ever liberate the slave, or that political action would abolish the system. He said that he had long had a plan which could accomplish this end, and he had invited me to his house to lay that plan before me. He said he had been for some time looking for colored men to whom he could safely reveal his secret, and at times he had almost despaired of finding such men, but that now he was encouraged, for he saw heads of such rising up in all directions. He had observed my course at home and abroad, and he wanted my cooperation. His plan as it then lay in his mind had much to commend it. It did not, as some suppose, contemplate a general rising among the slaves, and a general slaughter of the slave-masters. An insurrection, he thought, would only defeat the object, but his plan did contemplate the creating of an armed force which should act in the very heart of the South. He was not averse to the shedding of blood, and thought the practice of carrying arms would be a good one for the colored people to adopt, as it would give them a sense of their manhood. No people, he said, could have self-respect, or be respected, who would not fight for their freedom. He called my attention to a map of the United States, and pointed out to me the far-reaching Alleghenies, which stretch away from the borders of New York into the southern states. "These mountains," he said, "are the basis of my plan. God has given the strength of the hills to freedom; they were placed here for the emancipation of the Negro race; they are full of natural forts, where one man for defense will be equal to a hundred for attack; they are full also of good hiding-places, where large numbers of brave men could be concealed, and baffle and elude pursuit for a long time. I know these mountains well, and could take a body of men into them and keep them there despite of all the efforts of Virginia to dislodge them. The true object to be sought is first of all to destroy the money value of slave property, and that can only be done by rendering such property insecure. My plan, then, is to take at first about twenty-five picked men, and begin on a

small scale—supply them with arms and ammunition and post them in squads of fives on a line of twenty-five miles. The most persuasive and judicious of these shall go down to the fields from time to time, as opportunity offers, and induce the slaves to join them, seeking and selecting the most restless and daring."

He saw that in this part of the work the utmost care must be used to avoid treachery and disclosure. Only the most conscientious and skillful should be sent on this perilous duty. With care and enterprise he thought he could soon gather a force of one hundred hardy men, men who would be content to lead the free and adventurous life to which he proposed to train them; when these were properly drilled, and each man had found the place for which he was best suited, they would begin work in earnest: they would run off the slaves in large numbers, retain the brave and strong ones in the mountains, and send the weak and timid to the North by the underground railroad. His operations would be enlarged with increasing numbers and would not be confined to one locality.

When I asked him how he would support these men, he said emphatically that he would subsist them upon the enemy. Slavery was a state of war, and the slave had a right to anything necessary to his freedom. "But," said I, "suppose you succeed in running off a few slaves, and thus impress the Virginia slaveholders with a sense of insecurity in their slaves, the effect will be only to make them sell their slaves further south." "That," said he, "will be what I want first to do; then I would follow them up. If we could drive slavery out of *one county*, it would be a great gain—it would weaken the system throughout the state." "But they would employ bloodhounds to hunt you out of the mountains." "That they might attempt," said he, "but the chances are, we should whip them, and when we should

have whipped one squad, they would be careful how they pursued." "But you might be surrounded and cut off from your provisions or means of subsistence." He thought that this could not be done so they could not cut their way out, but even if the worst came he could but be killed, and he had no better use for his life than to lay it down in the cause of the slave. When I suggested that we might convert the slaveholders, he became much excited, and said that could never be, he knew their proud hearts and that they would never be induced to give up their slaves, until they felt a big stick about their heads. He observed that I might have noticed the simple manner in which he lived, adding that he had adopted this method in order to save money to carry out his purposes. This was said in no boastful tone, for he felt that he had delayed already too long, and had no room to boast either his zeal or his self-denial. Had some men made such display of rigid virtue, I should have rejected it, as affected, false, and hypocritical, but in John Brown, I felt it to be real as iron or granite.

From this night spent with John Brown in Springfield, Mass, 1847, while I continued to write and speak against slavery, I became all the same less hopeful of its peaceful abolition. My utterances became more and more tinged by the color of this man's strong impressions. Speaking at an antislavery convention in Salem, Ohio, I expressed this apprehension that slavery could only be destroyed by bloodshed, when I was suddenly and sharply interrupted by my good old friend Sojourner Truth with the question, "Frederick, is God dead?" "No," I answered, "and because God is not dead slavery can only end in blood." My quaint old sister was of the Garrison school of non-resistants, and was shocked at my sanguinary doctrine, but she too became an advocate of the sword, when the war for the maintenance of the Union was declared.

19

Thunderbolts of Protest: The Struggle for Women's Rights

Alice Felt Tyler

The Jacksonian Age was a time of great humanitarian crusades, a time not only of abolitionist ferment but of zealous reform movements to eradicate war, modernize education, and remodel the prison system. At the same time, American women launched a women's rights movement designed to break the shackles of strict domesticity and to expand their activities. In doing so, they challenged the all-pervasive attitude of America's male-dominated social order—that the only place for the True Woman was her home. Most men and a great many women in those days stoutly contended that the ideal woman was pious, pure, submissive, and domesticated, caring for her husband and rearing her children with a fragile, unquestioning sweetness. As Barbara Welter has wryly observed, "it was a fearful obligation, a solemn responsibility, which the nineteenth-century American woman had—to uphold the pillars of the temple with her frail white hand." And those who nurtured the cult of True Womanhood raged at dissidents who denounced the old virtues, branding them all as enemies of God, of the Republic, of civilization itself.

Yet a number of women did reject the subservient position society arbitrarily assigned them because of their sex. As Alice Felt Tyler demonstrates in the sprightly narrative that follows, Abigail Adams early spoke out against male domination. And as the Abolitionist Crusade and other reform movements sprang up in Jacksonian America, many women protested their own enslavement in a patriarchal society. On the lecture circuit, Scottish-born Frances Wright inveighed against the tyrannies of marriage as well as chartered monopolies. In the 1840s, brilliant and articulate Margaret Fuller published *Woman in the Nineteenth Century,* a slashing indictment of male supremacy and a ringing demand that all occupations be thrown open to women. But with most American institutions and popular prejudice arrayed against them, the crusaders for women's rights faced a long, uphill struggle in their quest for sexual equality.

In every phase of the American experiment much had depended upon the cooperation of the women. A biography of Mrs. Daniel Boone would be as thrilling an adventure tale as any of the accounts of her intrepid husband, for the frontier woman played no secondary role in the winning of the "dark and bloody ground" of Kentucky and of the newer lands farther West. Each woman who gave up her easier and more sheltered life in the seaboard communities and went with her husband to make a new home beyond the mountains, each woman who packed her household equipment into a covered wagon and ventured out upon the prairies, each emigrant woman who bade farewell to family and friends and crossed the Western ocean to a new life in a new world took on an enhanced value from the frontier.

Something of the equalitarianism of Western philosophy affected woman's status. Although the political equality her menfolk demanded

From Alice Felt Tyler, *Freedom's Ferment.* University of Minnesota Press, Minneapolis. Copyright 1944, 1972 by Alice Felt Tyler.

was not accorded her, the omission may have been due, in part at least, to her willingness to consider politics a field outside her interests. In frontier church and camp meeting and school women took their place with scarcely a comment. And the West in general did not forget that on the frontier there had been equality between the sexes, as men and women had faced together the hardships and loneliness of the wilderness, where there had been no pedestal upon which women could be placed and few circumstances in which masculine superiority could be demonstrated.

The Status of Women in the Young Republic

In the late colonial era and the days of the young republic the American woman lost something of her pioneer equality and independence in becoming a "lady." The new standards for women were a composite of English and European practices with an admixture of Calvinistic teachings in the North and a strong flavor of romanticism in the South. North and South alike expected her to be irreproachable in conduct, tireless in pursuit of domestic virtues, strong in religious faith, spotless in purity, and ignorant of the evils of the world about her.

Of course there was always great disparity between the theory of woman's place and the reality of her actual participation in the life of the family and the community, and occasionally an exceptional woman made her influence so felt that she was accorded recognition far beyond that given her sex in general. Before the Revolution Eliza Lucas came to South Carolina from Antigua and, marrying a member of the Pinckney family, settled there as mistress of a plantation. She introduced indigo culture in the colony and was for many years one of the leaders in the economic development of the lower South. In Massachusetts Mercy Otis Warren, the sister of James Otis, ranked high in the councils of the

Revolutionary patriots, and her house was their resort in the stirring days preceding the Declaration of Independence; indeed, she may well have been the first person to urge separation from England upon the Massachusetts delegates to the Continental Congress. Her correspondence with Jefferson and with John Adams continued throughout the Revolution.

John Adams' wife, Abigail, was another feminine advisor to the statesmen, and she early made the connection between the principles for which Americans were contending and the improvement of the legal status of women. In writing to her husband in March 1776, Mrs. Adams expressed quite plainly her feeling that women had a stake in the Revolutionary movement:

> . . . in the new code of laws which I suppose it will be necessary for you to make, I desire you would remember the ladies, and be more generous to them than your ancestors. Do not put such unlimited power in the hands of husbands. Remember, all men would be tyrants if they could. If particular care and attention are not paid to the ladies, we are determined to foment a rebellion, and will not hold ourselves bound to obey the laws in which we have no voice or representation.

Hannah Lee Corbin of Virginia in 1778 wrote her brother, Richard Henry Lee, protesting the taxation of women unless they were allowed to vote, and he replied that "women were already possessed of that right." Women did vote for a time in Virginia, and in New Jersey for more than thirty years. But after the Revolution had been won, these tentative concessions were forgotten, and state and national constitutions were drafted without mention of the rights of women. When suffrage was denied to a majority of the men of nearly every state, it was, perhaps, inevitable that none should protest the consignment of women to a legal status similar to that of the Negro.

For more than fifty years women were legally

considered perpetual minors: if unmarried, the wards of male relatives; if married, a part of their husbands' chattels. An unmarried woman or a widow was allowed a certain independence in the ownership of property and in earning her own living, although few, indeed, were the occupations she might enter. As late as 1860 the eminent jurist, David Dudley Field, summarized the laws relating to married women thus:

A married woman cannot sue for her services, as all she earns legally belongs to the husband, whereas his earnings belong to himself, and the wife legally has no interest in them. Where children have property and both parents are living, the father is the guardian. In case of the wife's death without a will, the husband is entitled to all her personal property and to a life interest in the whole of her real estate to the entire exclusion of her children, even though this property may have come to her through a former husband and the children of that marriage still be living. If a husband dies without a will, the widow is entitled to one-third of the personal property and to a life interest in one-third only of the real estate. In case a wife be personally injured, either in reputation by slander, or in body by accident, compensation must be recovered in the joint name of herself and her husband, and when recovered it belongs to him. . . . The father may by deed or will appoint a guardian for the minor children, who may thus be taken entirely away from the jurisdiction of the mother at his death. . . .

This poor creature was given certain logical and interesting immunities. Her lack of separate legal identity was recognized in laws that held her husband solely responsible for offenses and crimes she might commit in his presence or with his consent. But the value of this recognition is doubtful, for wife beating "with a reasonable instrument" was legal in almost every state as late as 1850. In Massachusetts Judge Buller defined the legal instrument as a "stick no thicker than my thumb," and in New York the courts upheld a worthy Methodist exhorter who beat his wife with a horsewhip every few weeks in order to keep her in proper subjection and prevent her scolding.

In legal status servile and incompetent, by social canon revered and closely guarded, in cold fact a vitally necessary part of a dynamic economic and social system, the American woman of the early nineteenth century, without opportunity of voicing any dissatisfaction outside the domestic circle, was considered by most observers to be content and favored beyond the women of other countries. But Captain Basil Hall, whose own wife accompanied him on all his travels, expressed a note of disapproval that must have surprised American readers. He said the whole level of American society was lowered by the poor position assigned to women. Kindness and politeness were accorded them, but there was no real companionship with men. Social events, therefore, were dull and uninteresting, there was little stimulating conversation, business was discussed interminably, and all the finer social arts were neglected.

The result of all my observations and enquiries [he wrote] is that the women do not enjoy that station in society which has been allotted to them elsewhere; and consequently much of that importance and habitual influence which, from the peculiarity of their nature, they alone can exercise over society in more fortunately arranged communities, seem to be lost.

Serious-minded though they were, the young De Tocqueville and De Beaumont obviously missed the conversation, the gaiety, the possibility of innocent flirtation and light persiflage that European society afforded. Other European visitors commented upon the prudishness and affectation of the "genteel female," as well as upon the general dullness of American social intercourse. Mrs. Trollope thought the life of the American lady most uninteresting, while

Harriet Martineau was alarmed by what she called "the political non-existence of women" in America and called attention to its denial of democratic principles. Even Jefferson, she said, had classed women with children and slaves and thus had repudiated the principle of equal rights identified with his name.

•   •   •

Frances Wright, the brilliant Scotswoman, condemned the married women's property law as "absolute spoilation," permitting "robbery, and all but murder, against the unhappy female who swears away, at one and the same moment, her person and her property." Since marriage imposed such onerous restrictions, she renounced the institution in entirety for her settlement at Nashoba, laying down the rule, "No woman can forfeit her individual rights or independent existence and no man assert over her any rights or power whatsoever beyond what he may exercise over her free and voluntary affections."

These strictures did not go unnoticed by American women themselves. Eliza Farnham wrote a treatise on the subject which she called *Woman and Her Era,* and in 1832 Lydia Maria Child published a two-volume *History of the Condition of Woman in All Ages.* The general trend of the 1820's and 1830's made women conscious of their own lack of opportunities and of their right to develop as persons. Women as well as men experienced the emotions and aspirations of the religious revivals and were imbued with perfectionist ideas. They, too, felt the urge toward humanitarian reform. Made conscious of themselves and their status by the work of such women as Frances Wright and Mrs. Child, and made aware of the needs of other human beings through contact with the humanitarians, American women were ready to advance through participation in many reform movements to an effort to improve their own status as a prerequisite to their real effectiveness in any social work.

Women made up the rank and file of the peace crusade and carried on extensive correspondence with women of other societies in the United States, in England, and in European countries. In the women's temperance societies and auxiliaries and in the women's antislavery societies they became adept at organization and adroit in political manipulation and the direction of public opinion. Their local, state, and national organization was government in miniature. Auxiliary and subsidiary to the controlling men's organization it was, in origin and in the minds of the masculine leaders; but the women's help was essential for success, and once they were trained to equal effectiveness, the fiction of masculine superiority would be hard to maintain and the barrier of masculine domination might be assailed.

Pioneers in the Professions

Women early insisted upon their right to equal opportunities for education. In urging that the new Constitution be distinguished for its encouragement of learning, Abigail Adams wrote, "If you complain of education in sons, what shall I say in regard to daughters, who every day experience the want of it? . . . If we mean to have heroes, statesmen, and philosophers, we should have learned women.". . .

For many years Abigail Adams' plea for education for women was unanswered, but early in the nineteenth century, when educational reforms won constant hearing, women came to the fore in advancing the education of their own sex. . . . In the Emma Willard school for girls in Troy, New York, and at Mount Holyoke many of the women later well known in the women's rights movement were trained. As assistant matron in the women's prison at Sing Sing, Georgiana Bruce Kirby, the English governess who aided in the school at Brook Farm, taught those in her charge to read and write, read aloud to them as they worked, built up the prison library, and corrected the exercises written on

slates and pushed out to her under the doors of the cells after working hours.

It made little difference in what line of interest, business or professional, women of the early nineteenth century became interested, everywhere they met the same prejudice against their participation and the same reluctance to open the way for their proper training. Ministers declaimed about the inferior position of women, made as by an afterthought from Adam's rib and ordained by God as the subordinate and helpmate of man. The sanctity of the home, the purity of womanhood, the delicacy and fragility of feminine charm, were the texts of innumerable exhortations against removing any of the restrictions that hemmed in the cherished creatures. Biblical and biological arguments and illustrations drawn from history were backed by fulsome tributes to contemporary examples of domestic virtues. But little by little women doggedly bored from within, added a slight concession in one field to a gain in another, and finally won a measure of honest consideration on their merits as individuals.

Margaret Fuller, Transcendentalist, author, and editor, was educated by her father as a son would have been and always resented the thought that a woman's mind was different from or inferior to that of a man. In the early 1840's she wrote *The Great Law Suit or Man vs. Woman*, which was republished in 1845 under the more familiar title of *Woman in the Nineteenth Century*, the first logical statement of the position of women to be written by an American.

Miss Fuller condemned the laws that gave men rights over their wives and children and advocated throwing open every occupation to women. "What woman needs," she wrote, "is not as a woman to act or rule, but as a nature to grow, as an intellect to discern, as a soul to live freely and unimpeded, to unfold such powers as were given her when we left our common home." Minds and souls, she said, are neither masculine nor feminine, genius has no sex, and intellectual merit deserves recognition whatever the sex of its possessor. Many a woman of later generations could read with fellow-feeling the Boston bluestocking's plea that women be accepted intellectually and advanced professionally without discrimination because of sex.

Women had long been regarded as the natural teachers of little children, and progress toward a measure of equality in the teaching profession came steadily although slowly. One of the greatest of the advocates of women's rights, Susan B. Anthony, began her career as a teacher. Of Quaker parentage, she always had the Quaker's conception of the equality of the sexes before God and never could understand the ideas current in her youth in regard to the inferiority of women. At seventeen she wrote angrily, "What an absurd notion that women have not intellectual and moral faculties sufficient for anything but domestic concerns." In 1853 she caused consternation in a teachers' convention by a request to enter a debate, which had already lasted for three days, on the question as to why the profession of teacher was less respected than that of lawyer, minister, or doctor. Never before had a woman spoken in such a gathering, and the dignified but determined young Quakeress was kept standing for half an hour while the question of her right to speak was hotly debated. Eventually the president, Professor Davies of West Point, complete in full dress, buff vest, blue coat, and gilt buttons, reluctantly announced, "The lady can speak," and Miss Anthony made this brief and lucid address:

It seems to me, gentlemen, that none of you quite comprehend the cause of the disrespect of which you complain. Do you not see that so long as society says a woman is incompetent to be a lawyer, minister, or doctor, but has ample ability to be a teacher, that every man of you who chooses that profession tacitly acknowledges that he has no more brains than a woman? . . . Would you exalt your profession, exalt those who labor with you. Would you make it more lucrative, in-

crease the salaries of the women engaged in the noble work of educating our future Presidents, Senators, and Congressmen.

In medicine the opposition was much more violent, and intrepid indeed was the young woman of the pre-Civil War period who dared express a desire to be a physician. Those few who were able to break through the barriers raised against them were justly famous in their own day and quite logically became leaders in the feminist crusade; they knew all too well the restrictions and prejudices that hampered their sex.

Dr. Harriot K. Hunt was one of the earliest woman physicians, beginning her practice in 1835. Her training was very sketchy, and her practice seems to have been along lines of general hygiene, hydrotherapy, and psychotherapy rather than medicine, but she was quite successful. She was twice refused admission to Harvard Medical School and was apparently frowned upon by medical men. She lectured on temperance, phrenology, the evils of tobacco, and sex hygiene. She was a woman of wealth and so strongly resented the discrimination against women that she sent an annual protest to the treasurer of Boston against being compelled to pay taxes when she was not represented in the government.

Dr. Hunt was joined in the late 1840's by Elizabeth Blackwell, whose name became of much more significance in the medical world. Miss Blackwell belonged to a large and remarkable Ohio family. Of five sisters two became physicians, one was a musician, one an artist and author of some note, while the fifth—reputed to be the most brilliant—was kept from public life by ill-health. No one of the five married, but they adopted and reared a number of children. One of their brothers married Lucy Stone, a prominent antislavery lecturer and feminist, and another became the husband of Antoinette Brown, one of the earliest woman preachers.

After being refused entry to the medical schools of Philadelphia, Elizabeth Blackwell appeared at Geneva College in western New York, presented evidence of adequate preparation, and asked for admission to the medical school. The authorities were shocked, but, scarcely knowing how to refuse her, they referred the question to the medical students. The young men took the whole matter as a joke and voted her in, fully expecting that after a sad failure she would withdraw, but in 1849 she graduated at the head of her class. Her sister Emily soon acquired a similar degree, and the two went abroad to study. In Paris there was some difficulty over admission to classes and hospitals, and it was suggested that Elizabeth don male dress as a prerequisite to entry. She refused flatly, saying that she would not alter so much as a bonnet string, and the authorities eventually gave way and permitted her to take the work she desired.

In 1857 the sisters opened the New York Infirmary for Women and Children, which they successfully administered for many years. Dr. Emily Blackwell was later dean of the Women's Medical College of New York, and Dr. Elizabeth organized a unit of field nurses during the Civil War. In 1869 she went to England, where she was the first woman to be admitted to the British Medical Registry and where she served for many years as professor of gynecology in the London School of Medicine for Women.

In the middle 1840's a quiet, determined girl appeared before the officials of Oberlin College and demanded that she be allowed to enter the theological course. No woman had ever been admitted to the closed corporation of the clergy, but, adamant against all adverse comment, Antoinette Brown refused to give up her desire to be a minister and finally won the reluctant consent of the college authorities. One kindly professor, aghast at the thought of a woman in the pulpit, told her that, despite his hearty disapproval of her course, he would endeavor to teach her the required subjects, but that he could not surrender the hope that he might

persuade her to change her mind. He failed to do so, and Antoinette Brown graduated with the theology class of 1850, although Oberlin tried to hide its shame by omitting her name from the class list. She could obtain neither ordination nor a church to preach in, but in 1853 she acquired renown as the woman delegate refused the right to speak at the World Temperance Convention in New York City and was asked by the indignant supporters of women's rights to preach in Metropolitan Hall. A few days later she was ordained and was called to a church in a little town at the munificent salary of three hundred dollars a year. Miss Brown won the hearts of her liberal parishioners and felt free to invite her college friend, Lucy Stone, to speak in her church. The doughty little clergywoman left the church a little later to become a social worker. Still later she turned minister again, this time as a Unitarian. She married a brother of Dr. Elizabeth Blackwell and lived to the good old age of ninety-six.

Lucy Stone was the eighth of nine children in the family of a New England farmer, and her childhood was filled with work—cooking, cleaning, weaving, sewing, and shoemaking. An extremely observant and sensitive child, she was so horrified at the lot of women that she wanted to die, crying, "Is there anything that will put an end to me?" Finding no answer to that question, she made up her mind to go to college to find out whether the biblical texts quoted to justify woman's degradation were translated correctly and then to devote her life to improving the condition of her sex.

No one encouraged her in this unusual ambition, but her persistence in attempting to vote in church meetings, despite the fact that her vote was never counted, shows that she never lost sight of her objective. At sixteen she taught a district school, saving all that she could of her pittance, but she was twenty-five before she was able to go to college, and then it was Oberlin she chose. Older than most college students, without money, working every available hour,

and boarding herself at fifty cents a week, Lucy Stone managed to become a leader in college affairs. She was prominent in the peace society and in the antislavery group; she organized a girl's debating club and taught classes of colored students. When the time of graduation came she was chosen to write a commencement oration, which, by college regulation, must be read for her by a man. Lucy Stone then made her first sacrifice for the cause of women's rights by refusing to accept the honor at all if she could not read the paper she had written.

Her college degree obtained, she alarmed her family by announcing that her chosen profession was that of lecturer in behalf of any good cause she might espouse. Her first public address on women's rights was given in 1847 in a church in Gardner, Massachusetts, where her brother was the minister. A year later she was employed as agent or lecturer for the American Anti-Slavery Society and toured New England with Parker Pillsbury. She was mobbed several times, was stunned by a book hurled by an angry listener, was deluged with cold water, was dropped from her church—in general received the treatment accorded the proponents of an unpopular cause. She never forgot the status of women and was admonished by the officers of the antislavery society for mixing too much women's rights in her discussions of the evils of slavery.

After a time she gave up other reforms and concentrated on the status of women, becoming her own manager and agent, writing her own publicity, and, since she refused to charge admission, passing the hat herself after each lecture. A tiny woman, weighing about one hundred pounds, she had a marvelous voice and was a most effective speaker. Touring the country to lecture on the political, social, and industrial disabilities of women, she spoke to audiences of sufficient size and generosity to yield her seven thousand dollars in three years. Early in her career as a public speaker, she met Henry Blackwell, another brother of the sister

physicians, who finally persuaded her to marry him. His pledge to accept the idea of complete equality was sincere and was expressed in the famous Protest, which he wrote and they both signed when, in 1853, they were married by Thomas Wentworth Higginson. After acknowledging their mutual affection, they repudiated the laws of marriage that gave the husband "injurious and unnatural superiority, investing him with legal powers which no honorable man would exercise, and which no man should possess." The Protest ended wth a condemnation of "the whole system by which the legal existence of the wife is suspended during marriage."

The *Boston Post* jubilantly hailed the marriage of Lucy Stone in derisive verse, concluding with

A name like Curtius' shall be his,
    On Fame's loud trumpet blown,
Who with a wedding kiss shuts up
    The mouth of Lucy Stone!

But the hopes of the *Post* were blasted, for marriage had no such effect. The first American woman to retain her maiden name, "Mrs. Stone" continued to lecture and to attend women's rights conventions. Even in the contentment of a happy marriage, she kept alive her protest against the disabilities of women by permitting her household goods, even her baby's cradle, to be sold for the taxes she refused to pay because she was not represented in the government!

Women Writers and Editors

Almost every contemporary commentator on the American scene in the second quarter of the nineteenth century called attention to the tremendous increase in the number of books, magazines, and newspapers being printed in the United States. Every town and hamlet, every church and reform society had its press; pamphlets, tracts, newssheets, and books of all descriptions on every possible subject poured forth

to urge support of the innumerable parties and causes to which Americans were devoting their attention.

In this flood of ephemeral publication there was opportunity for women to acquire training in the art of self-expression. Countless little stories and poems were written by women for the annual gift books sponsored by the temperance advocates, and women were largely responsible for the children's periodicals and Sunday school library books devoted to the cause of temperance. An occasional woman among these writers won fame among her contemporaries and some sort of recognition from posterity. Margaret Fuller as editor of the *Dial* was without doubt the most important of the galaxy, but several others had a wide contemporary reputation. Anne Royall of Baltimore was editor of the *Huntress* for twenty-five years. Lydia Maria Child published a paper for children, the *Juvenile Miscellany*, was one of the most prolific writers of antislavery pamphlets, and in 1841 became the editor of the *Anti-Slavery Standard* in New York. Amelia Bloomer, postmistress in a little New York town, was the editor of the *Lily*, a temperance magazine, and achieved immortal fame through her advocacy of a "reform dress" for women, a part of which yet bears her name.

Two of the women who edited newspapers in the period were intensely interested in furthering the claims of their sex. Neither made any one contribution to the cause equal to Margaret Fuller's *Woman in the Nineteenth Century*, but each persistently for many years kept the issue before a wide public.

The fame of *Godey's Lady's Book* as America's first woman's fashion magazine has been revived with the interest in its charming colored illustrations and designs, but the name of its editor, Sarah Josepha Hale, has barely escaped oblivion. And yet Mrs. Hale was an extraordinarily interesting woman with a wide influence upon the thinking of her own day. In all outward things she was Victorian and conservative,

intensely feminine and conventional. Her personality and career belong distinctively to the period and the environment in which she lived, and yet her mind and point of view were essentially modern, and her achievements along the lines she serenely marked out for herself are astonishing. Born in 1788, she had the limited formal education of the day but was privately instructed by a devoted Dartmouth brother so that she kept pace with his college studies. She married and had five children, was left a penniless widow when the oldest child was seven years of age, and made a precarious living as a seamstress. She was always writing and eventually had a novel published that won her some renown. When she was forty, she was summoned by Louis Godey, whom she always called the "Prince of Publishers," to be the editor of his *Lady's Book*.

In that editorship, which lasted for nearly fifty years, Mrs. Hale had opportunity to further numerous causes and to reach a wider public in their behalf than could any of the editors of publications devoted to reform measures, for the *Lady's Book* circulation of more than a hundred and fifty thousand put all other subscription lists to shame. Mrs. Hale is said to have "cajoled" the American public into approval of reform measures; she certainly managed to carry on the work of reformer and promoter without shocking her public or diminishing the financial returns of the magazine. She gave Mary Lyon and Mount Holyoke College a vast amount of free publicity, and she was little short of a press agent for Emma Willard. About equal educational and professional opportunities for women, she made statements so radical that only the popularity of *Godey's* other features could have sugar-coated the feminism.

When Elizabeth Blackwell was making her fight for a medical education, Mrs. Hale answered in a series of editorials all the arguments of the opposition. To the query, "What will women doctors do, when it is impossible for them to go out at all times and to all places?"

she answered, "Just what male doctors do when they are called for and cannot go. Stay at home!" And when she reached the familiar argument that women would drive men out of employment, she sturdily came back with, "They may as well starve as the women. And if men cannot cope with women in the medical profession let them take an humble occupation in which they can." With unprecedented frankness, Mrs. Hale condemned unlicensed midwifery and advocated the training of women specialists in obstetrics and pediatrics. She helped in establishing the Female Medical College in Philadelphia in 1849 and worked to provide trained nurses for hospitals to which women doctors might take patients.

The editor of the *Lady's Book* advocated public playgrounds for city children as early as 1840, urged education in methods of preventing disease, and, by assuming that all right-minded and well-bred people agreed with her, made effective campaigns against such varied evils as pie for breakfast, airless sleeping rooms, tight corsets, and the Saturday night bath. She made swimming and horseback riding fashionable and established the popularity of the "pic-nic."

Although Mrs. Hale was too conservative, or perhaps too conscious of the subscription list, to advocate suffrage reform, earlier than any of the other feminists she agitated against the restrictions upon married women. But her feminism sometimes took amusing lines. The "reform dress" would not, of course, have been good business, but the word *female* was her pet abomination, and she often campaigned against its use. When her friend Matthew Vassar proposed to found a college for women, her pleasure in the prospect was chilled by word that the institution was to be called Vassar Female College, and she wrote the founder:

Female! What female do you mean? Not a female donkey? Must not your reply be, "I mean a female woman?" Then . . . why degrade the feminine sex to the level of animals?

. . . I write thus earnestly because I wish to have Vassar College take the lead in this great improvement in our language.

Whether or not because of Mrs. Hale's demands, the obnoxious word was deleted, and where it had appeared on the original college building the victory was commemorated by a broad blank stone, leaving the inscription, "VASSAR ———— COLLEGE."

Working in an environment far removed from that of the elegant editor of the *Lady's Book*, Jane Grey Swisshelm also made a significant contribution to the cause of women's rights. Born in Pittsburgh, Jane Grey Cannon had only an elementary education. At fourteen she was teaching in a country school, and at twenty-one she married James Swisshelm, with whom she lived most unhappily for twenty years. He was a petty domestic tyrant, ruled by a dominating mother who aided him in making Jane's life miserable. In her autobiography, *Half a Century*, Jane described her sacrifice of literary and artistic tastes, her hard work to help support her household, the constant friction and persecution in a home where not even the pittance she made at dressmaking could be called her own. Bitterly she wrote of her husband:

> I knew from the first that his education had been limited, but thought the defect would be easily remedied as he had good abilities, but I discovered he had no love for books. His spiritual guides derided human learning and depended on inspiration. My knowledge stood in the way of my salvation, and I must be that odious thing—a superior wife—or stop my progress, for to be and appear were the same thing. I must be the mate of the man I had chosen; and if he would not come to my level, I must go to his. So I gave up study, and for years did not read one page in any book save the Bible.

After many years of subordination, Mrs. Swisshelm's personality and abilities began to assert themselves, partly, perhaps, because it was necessary for her to contribute to the family income. Her mother died, leaving her property in trust for the daughter whose husband she disliked, and that daughter gained firsthand acquaintance with the legal disabilities of married women when her husband sued the estate for the money he said was due him for the time Mrs. Swisshelm had spent nursing her mother in her last illness. It was little wonder that Jane Grey Swisshelm fought for equal legal rights for women. She believed in coeducation, sought the removal of all legal disabilities, and advocated equality of opportunity, but she was surprisingly moderate about political rights. She felt that women should not weaken their cause by impracticable demands. "Take one step at a time," she wrote. "Get a good foothold in it and advance carefully."

Residence for a time in Kentucky made Mrs. Swisshelm an uncompromising abolitionist, and in the 1840's she wrote articles for a succession of antislavery papers in Pittsburgh. When the last of these ceased publication, she started her own newspaper, the *Saturday Visiter*, and thus initiated a career as editor that was to last for many years. In the *Visiter* she attacked the Fugitive Slave Law, condemned Webster's Seventh of March speech, excoriated the slave catchers, and, in general, did all in her power to further the antislavery cause—and, incidentally, to enrage the opposition. When George D. Prentice, a Kentucky editor equally well known for his proslavery and his nativistic opinions, angrily accused Mrs. Swisshelm of being a man, "all but the pantaloons," she pertly retorted,

> Perhaps you have been busy
> Horsewhipping Sal or Lizzie
> Stealing some poor man's baby,
> Selling its mother, maybe.
> You say—and you are witty—
> That I—and, 'tis a pity—
> Of manhood lack but dress;
> But you lack manliness,

A body clean and new,
A soul within it, too.
Nature must change her plan
Ere you can be a man.

After a legal and permanent separation from her husband, Mrs. Swisshelm went out to the Territory of Minnesota, where she had relatives. In the little town of St. Cloud, she established another newspaper and carried on for many years a constant battle for the reforms in which she was interested.

• • •

Women in the Antislavery Movement

The Grimké sisters, Sarah and Angelina, became Quakers after they left their South Carolina home and went North to aid in the antislavery cause. They soon found that, although their aid was eagerly accepted, they were criticized and disliked by many abolitionists and were howled down by the riffraff of many audiences solely because they were women venturing into a sphere heretofore reserved for men. The correspondence of the able and spirited sisters throws much light on the difficulties that faced the women who desired to give their support to humanitarian reforms and who were thereby brought face to face with the restrictions on their sex.

Theodore Weld, who later married Angelina, assured the sisters that he had always believed in the equality of the sexes, but he urged them not to let advocacy of the rights of women divert them from the much more important and immediate issue of the sorrows of the Negro slave.

Let us all [he wrote] *first* wake up the nation to lift millions of slaves of both sexes from the dust, and turn them into MEN and then when we all have our hand in, it will be an

easy matter to take millions of females from their knees and set them on their feet, or in other words transform them from *babies* into *women*.

And that, with a few exceptions, was the cold comfort women received from the men who sought their aid in the cause of reform. That there was anything incongruous in seeking this aid in the fight for the slaves while women were themselves on their knees seems not to have occurred to Weld or his associates.

• • •

In the years after the organization of the American Anti-Slavery Society women formed numerous auxiliary societies to raise money and arouse public opinion. There they learned valuable lessons in the business of organization and propaganda, although, as one of them said, when they first began the work "there was not a woman capable of taking the chair and organizing the meeting in due order, and they had to call in a man to aid them." Once trained, however, they were unexpectedly successful, and the leaders of the parent society wished to use their efforts more extensively. With a little experience in a broader sphere, women of ability began to feel that the "Ladies" societies with their fairs and prayer meetings were childish and that they should participate in all antislavery work on an equal basis. In 1840, however, came two momentous defeats to their ambitions in this direction.

In the convention of the American Anti-Slavery Society in New York, the radical Garrison faction proposed a woman for membership on the executive committee and carried the proposition by a narrow majority. The conservative members at once left the convention and organized a separate national society pledged to distinctly non-Garrisonian principles. After 1840, therefore, only in the ranks of the Garrisonian abolitionists could women find rec-

ognition; and, although that group had had a majority in the convention, it was very apparent that it was a decreasing minority in antislavery ranks as a whole.

The second blow fell in London later in the same year. The British issued a call for a World's Anti-Slavery Convention without specifying that all delegates should be men, and the Pennsylvania and Massachusetts societies sent large delegations that included some eight or nine prominent women. Lucretia Mott and her husband James, Philadelphia Quakers, were both delegates, as were Wendell Phillips and his bride Ann.

Mrs. Mott was a woman of ability and of remarkable character and spirit. Everywhere in her own country men and women had honored and loved her. Her clear, serene eyes, her quiet Quaker dress, and her mild but assured manner had won her the respect even of the mobs that heckled the meetings at which she spoke. Her home was a refuge for fugitive slaves, her advice was sought by Hicksite Quakers everywhere, and her calm judgment was appreciated by the leaders of all the reform movements in which she worked. Her husband adored her, and his chuckle as he once admonished a speaker whose points Lucretia had criticized, saying, "If she thinks thee is wrong, thee had better look it over again," indicated his delight in her wit and wisdom.

Mrs. Mott and her fellow women delegates were uncertain as to their reception in London, but welcomed the opportunity for testing both their status in the reform movements and the strength of the support to be accorded them by the masculine American delegation.

Ann Green Phillips told her husband, "No shilly-shallying, Wendell! Be brave as a lion!" and he prepared to lead the fight for the admission of the women delegates. Many of his fellows from the United States were eager to vote against it and had counseled the English conservatives to stand firm. Phillips opened battle with a motion that a committee be ap-

pointed to prepare a list of the members of the convention, with instructions to include in the list "all persons bearing credentials from any Anti-Slavery body." With that the debate was on, and it raged for hours. An English clergyman made a touching appeal to the American women to defer to British prejudice and withdraw their credentials voluntarily, thus permitting the convention to avoid the discourtesy of refusing them. Biblical arguments were hurled at them and ministers of conflicting views quoted texts in a confusing exchange. When eventually the vote was taken, the women were excluded by an overwhelming majority—only to receive the added insult of being asked to attend the meetings in a curtained enclosure and to have "no unpleasant feelings over the outcome."

Garrison was delayed in leaving the United States and did not reach London until the question of the women delegates had been settled, but he expressed his disapproval of their exclusion by refusing to participate in the convention. Sitting with the rejected women or in the gallery, he looked down upon the convention—much to the chagrin of the triumphant men, for, despite the division of opinion in the United States about his leadership, in British antislavery circles he was considered a figure of major importance.

At the London conference, too, were Henry Stanton of New York and his bride, Elizabeth Cady Stanton. The young husband was a Lane Seminary friend of Theodore Weld and a member of the conservative faction of the antislavery society. The bride was the daughter of an eminent lawyer and the cousin of Gerrit Smith. Elizabeth Cady had been interested in the rights of women ever since, as a wide-eyed little girl, she had sat in the office of her adored father and listened to him sadly explaining to women clients that their husbands had legal right to their children and their property. In London Mrs. Stanton began a lifelong friendship with Mrs. Mott and the other women whose credentials had been rejected. These women were left

Eloquent and irrepressible, Elizabeth Cady Stanton ranked with Susan B. Anthony as one of the leading feminists of the nineteenth century. Stanton not only campaigned for women's rights—including the right to vote—but condemned slavery, advocated free divorce, and attacked organized religion for discriminating against women. (Courtesy of Culver Pictures.)

with few illusions as to their position in any organization dominated by men, and they grew steadily more convinced that they must organize in an effort to secure the rights and privileges denied them.

• • •

Women Organize in Their Own Behalf

Realizing at last that they were faced with persistent discrimination along all lines—educational, professional, legal, political, even humanitarian —women began to organize for a campaign in their own behalf. Initiated in one locality by a small group, the movement spread wherever interest could be aroused. A few leaders would issue a call for a state convention, where arrangements were made for closely knit local societies. When sufficient interest was aroused and enough states had been organized, national conventions were held. Speeches, newspaper publicity, letters, platforms, petitions to other organizations and to legislatures—no known agency of propaganda was neglected. Women's rights newspapers were established and women joined in the barrage of pamphlets, printed addresses, and campaign dodgers that had been a part of the tactics of the humanitarians.

This organization of the movement was not of sudden or spectacular origin. In 1840 Mrs. Mott and Mrs. Stanton had talked in London of the possibility of a convention to consider the disabilities of women. But in the following years Mrs. Mott was occupied with the anti-slavery movement and with the problems of the liberal Quakers, and Mrs. Stanton was busy with household cares and with one baby after another. After all, as Sarah Grimké wrote to an English friend, "it is plainly the duty of woman to nurse her offspring; it cannot be the duty of man because God has not furnished him with the nourishment necessary for the infant."

In the 1840's, also, Antoinette Brown and Lucy Stone were struggling to obtain professional training against obstacles placed in their way even at liberal Oberlin, and Elizabeth Blackwell and her sister were overcoming obstinate prejudice in the field of medicine. Susan Anthony was running up against discrimination in the teaching profession, and both she and Mrs. Stanton were finding difficulties in their work for temperance. The decision to organize was the result of this long and painful experience.

In the summer of 1848 Lucretia and James Mott went to Waterloo, New York, for a yearly meeting of the Friends. Mrs. Mott went on to

visit her sister at Auburn and there met, for the first time since their London experience in 1840, Elizabeth Cady Stanton, who was then living in the near-by town of Seneca Falls. As a result of some cogitation over the teacups, there appeared in the *Seneca Falls County Courier* on July 14 the following announcement:

Seneca Falls Convention

Woman's Rights Convention—a Convention to discuss the social, civil, and religious condition and rights of woman, will be held in the Wesleyan Chapel, at Seneca Falls, N.Y., on Wednesday and Thursday, the 19th and 20th of July, current; commencing at 10 o'clock A.M. During the first day the meeting will be exclusively for women, who are earnestly invited to attend. The public generally are invited to be present on the second day, when Lucretia Mott, of Philadelphia, and other ladies and gentlemen, will address the Convention.

When July 19 arrived, a large number of people, almost as many men as women, appeared at the doors of the Wesleyan Chapel, only to find them locked. A small boy was lifted through an open window, however, and the convention opened according to schedule with James Mott in the chair, an evidence of the inexperience or timidity of the women who had called the convention. With the meeting once opened, the women read their prepared speeches; Lucretia Mott presented the purpose of the convention, and Mrs. Stanton read the Declaration of Sentiments over which the committee had expended much effort.

The women had used the Declaration of Independence as a model, substituting *Man* for *King George* and listing some eighteen familiar grievances as the basis for their demand for reform. Of these the last was a general arraignment of man's treatment of woman: "He has endeavored, in every way that he could, to destroy her confidence in her own powers, to

lessen her self-respect, and to make her willing to lead a dependent and abject life." In view of all these injustices, those "aggrieved, oppressed, and fraudulently deprived of their most sacred rights" asked immediate admission to all the rights and privileges pertaining to citizens of the United States and called upon women everywhere to organize, to petition, to employ agents, to circulate tracts, and hold conventions.

The Declaration was followed by a series of twelve resolutions in accord with its sentiments. These were all passed unanimously except the ninth, which stated that "it is the duty of the women of this country to secure to themselves their sacred right to the elective franchise." A part of the committee had disapproved this resolution, feeling that in asking too much the women might make their cause ridiculous, but Mrs. Stanton had her way, and with the assistance of Frederick Douglass, the Negro abolitionist, she was able to obtain the acceptance of the resolution by a small majority. Its inclusion was perhaps a mistake, however, for many of the one hundred men and women who signed the Declaration at Seneca Falls withdrew their names when the storm of ridicule broke.

In August 1848 a second women's rights convention was held in Rochester, New York, and with that event the organization of women in their own cause may fairly be said to have begun. Conventions were held in the next two or three years in Massachusetts, Ohio, Pennsylvania, and Indiana, and before the end of a decade the movement had spread through all the Northern states and as far West as Wisconsin and Kansas. Annual national conventions were held beginning in 1850. Nearly every woman who had managed to win recognition in any profession gave aid in the work, and the more liberal masculine leaders of other reform movements all spoke at conventions and kept in touch with the women leaders.

And a fight it was, for it was difficult even to win over the women whom the crusade was designed to benefit. Meetings were often attended

by those who desired only to break them up. At the New York convention in 1853, for example, the session had to be closed after hoodlums had filled the air with shouts of "Sit down," "Get out," "Bow-wow," "Go it, Susan," accompanied by hisses and catcalls, while police looked on in apparent approval. And only the *Tribune* and the *Evening Post* condemned the action of the mob.

Lack of funds was another deterrent. Married women had little to call their own, and the salaries of the valiant spinsters left much to be desired. Most of the work was done by voluntary contributions of time and energy. Much of the publicity was free and adverse, but those who could spoke, wrote, and published for the good of the cause. Somehow they managed to get together funds for a few agents to circulate petitions and to hold the local organizations in line. A few women lecturers were well enough known so that admission fees could be charged when they appeared on the program, and some of the country's best known masculine lecturers contributed their services and their fees.

It was uphill work and depended always upon the utter devotion of a few tireless women. In 1849 Richard Henry Dana, a prominent member of literary circles in Brahmin Boston, delivered a lecture throughout the country ridiculing the new demand of American women for greater rights and privileges. He held up Shakespeare's docile, tender, loving women— Desdemona, Juliet, and Ophelia—as examples to be studied and imitated. He did not mention Portia. Lucretia Mott answered his strictures in a "Discourse on Woman" given in the Assembly Hall in Philadelphia and later printed for wide distribution. In remarkably clear, hard-hitting sentences she knocked the props from under Dana's argument, showed its shallowness and sentimentality, and established firmly the bases of the demands made by women. Stating that man-made restrictions had enervated the minds and powers of women, she denied that the sex was willing to be the plaything or the slave of man, and asked that women be allowed

to develop as moral, responsible beings. She went into the history of the discrimination against women, analyzed the legal status that women wanted to improve, and demanded equal rights in education, in the professions, in the business world, and before the law. Mrs. Mott's inflexible Quaker principles appeared in the stern statement:

> Far be it from me to encourage women to vote, or to take an active part in politics in the present state of our government. Her right to the elective franchise, however, is the same, and should be yielded to her, whether she exercise that right or not. Would that man, too, would have no participation in a government recognizing the life-taking principle; retaliation and the sword. It is unworthy of a Christian nation. But when in the diffusion of light and intelligence a Convention shall be called to make regulations for self-government on Christian principles, I can see no good reason why women should not participate in such an assemblage, taking part equally with man.

Another strong force in defense of women's rights was Ernestine Rose, born Siismund Potoski in Pyeterkow, Poland. Her father had been a Jewish rabbi, and she had been brought up in the strictest observance of their religious faith. As a young woman she rebelled against both religious restrictions and absolutism in government and left Poland, living in France and later in England. In the 1830's she became a friend of Elizabeth Fry and Robert Owen and devoted herself to social reforms. She married a liberal Englishman, William Rose, and came with him to New York, where she at once became interested in the antislavery movement and others. Handsome and cultivated, an able speaker with great dignity and quick wit, she became one of the most valuable of the suffragist lecturers, speaking often and before large audiences in every Northern state. She was chosen to present petitions to legislatures and to give the keynote speeches at conventions, and in general played

remarkable. Neither was subordinate to the other; both were vital to the cause. Mrs. Stanton wrote and talked easily and well, and for many years she wrote the speeches for which Miss Anthony collected the material. Henry Stanton once said, "You stir up Susan and she stirs the world," and Mrs. Stanton herself admitted that she "forged the thunder bolts" and Susan fired them. What Susan thought is more difficult to ascertain. There are letters extant that show her rage when matrimony and maternity robbed her of able lieutenants, and other letters urging Mrs. Stanton to put family activities aside and write the call for a convention or the address to accompany a legislative petition. There are plaintive letters from Elizabeth, also, complaining that the demands upon her time are too great, saying that she will not write a single address while nursing the current infant, and once even threatening, "As soon as you all begin to ask too much of me, I shall have a baby! Now, be careful, do not provoke me to that step!"

Susan it was who brought down upon herself the reproaches of many friends of the cause by deliberately assisting a desperate mother to kidnap her child from the husband who had cruelly denied it to her. The woman was the wife of a state senator of Massachusetts and the sister of a United States senator from New York, so the case aroused much comment. Even Phillips and Garrison were horrified and urged that the child be returned to its father. When asked if she did not realize that she was violating the law, Susan calmly replied,

> Yes, I do know it, and does not the law of the United States give the slave holder the ownership of the slave? And don't you break the law every time you help a slave to Canada? Well, the law which gives the father the sole ownership of the children is just as wicked, and I'll break it just as quickly. You would die before you would deliver a slave to his master, and I will die before I will give up that child to its father.

In 1848 the legislature of the state of New York, after twelve years of discussion, passed a Married Women's Property Law that gave to women certain limited rights in the control of their own property. From that time women in all the older states where restrictive laws existed worked for their repeal, and in New York petitions were circulated for a law to grant married women full control of their own wages, incomes, and property. One at a time other states followed the example of New York, and in 1860 the New York laws were amended to give women joint guardianship of children, the right to sue and be sued, the right to their own wages, incomes, and real and personal property.

In the matter of more liberal divorce legislation, women made some headway. Even the reformers were horrified at Mrs. Stanton's proposal in 1860 that drunkenness be considered due cause for divorce, and Phillips and Greeley refused to give her their support. But out in Indiana Robert Dale Owen came to her defense, writing letters to the *Tribune* in a published debate with Horace Greeley. As a member of the Indiana legislature, Owen pushed through a bill adding habitual drunkenness to the legal causes for divorce.

In the meantime, men were growing more used to the idea of women in the professions and made many concessions. Women were still a long way from equality there or in the matter of higher education, but the breach had been made and the battle had turned ever so slightly their way. In the matter of suffrage itself there were no gains, nor was success to be achieved for many years. Little could be done as long as the majority of men agreed with the author of an article in *Harper's New Monthly Magazine* in November 1853:

> If nothing else, however, should give it [woman suffrage] consequence, it would demand our earnest attention from its intimate connection with all the radical and infidel movements of the day. A strange affinity

a large part in the work she had chosen. Cosmopolitan in attitude, she brought a broader vision into the American movement.

Clarina Howard Nichols was another of the same caliber. It was she who organized the women of Vermont, and later, moving west with her family, she worked for the cause in Wisconsin, in Kansas, and in Missouri. She knew every suffrage leader, attended many conventions, and lectured wherever she went. In Massachusetts Paulina Wright Davis, who had shocked the fastidious by her health lectures in an earlier day, called the first national convention, edited the suffrage paper *Una*, and led the local women's rights organization. Out in Ohio Frances D. Gage was a pillar of strength. She had long been a leader in humanitarian and literary circles in Ohio, a correspondent of Harriet Martineau, and a friend of those prominent in the antislavery movement. In 1851 she was made president of the Ohio Women's Convention, which met in Akron, and was joined in leading it by Maria Giddings, daughter of Joshua Giddings, the Congressional defender of the right of petition, and Jane Grey Swisshelm, who was soon to leave Pittsburgh for St. Cloud, Minnesota.

At this Akron convention appeared Sojourner Truth, an old Negress, born a slave in New York, who had long been a worker in the abolition cause. The entry of the tall, gaunt black woman in her gray dress and white turban caused consternation in the convention, for the women were finding it rough going in the storm of protest and criticism raised by members of the clergy who had invaded the meeting and were monopolizing the discussion. But Sojourner delivered them from their adversaries. After listening to the reverend gentlemen patiently for some hours, the old colored woman rose slowly from her seat on the pulpit steps and spoke in deep tones to a suddenly hushed audience:

Wall, chilern, whar dar is so much racket dar must be somethin' out o' kilter. I tink dat 'twixt de niggers of de Souf and de womin at de Norf, all talkin' bout rights, de white men will be in a fix pretty soon. But what's all dis here talkin' 'bout?

Dat man ober dar say dat womin needs to be helped into carriages and lifted ober ditches, and to hab de best place everywhar. Nobody eber helps me into carriages, or ober mud-puddles, or gibs me any best place! And a'n't I a woman? Look at my arm! I have ploughed, and planted and gathered into barns, and no man could head me! And a'n't I a woman? I could work as much and eat as much as a man—when I could get it—and bear de lash as well! And a'n't I a woman? I have borne thirteen chilern, and seen 'em mos' all sold off to slavery, and when I cried out with my mother's grief, none but Jesus heard me! And a'n't I a woman? . . . Den dat little man in black dar, he say women can't have as much rights as men, 'cause Christ wan't a woman! Whar did your Christ come from? Whar did your Christ come from? From God and a woman! Man had nothin' to do wid Him!

When the deep voice was still and the outstretched arms had fallen and the old Negress sank once more to the pulpit step, the clerical hecklers were silent.

Two names stand out beyond all others in the crusade for women's rights. Elizabeth Cady Stanton and Susan B. Anthony were central figures in its organization period before 1860, and in the next half century they were largely responsible for its continuance to a successful conclusion. Dogged, persistent, capable, and hard-working, the spinster Susan tramped up and down New York in all weathers, organizing, circulating petitions, speaking, and in general fanning the breath of life into a movement that might otherwise have died from opposition or from lack of interest in the rank and file. Mrs. Stanton had a little more of genius and tact, a touch of humor and zest, and an invaluable compound of charm and magnetism.

The friendship between the two women was

seems to bind them all together. . . . the claim of woman's rights presents not only the common radical notion which underlies the whole class, but also a peculiar enormity of its own; in some respects more boldly infidel, or defiant both of nature and revelation, than that which characterizes any kindred measure. It is avowedly opposed to the most time-honoured propensities of social life; it is opposed to nature; it is opposed to revelation. . . . This unblushing female Socialism defies alike apostles and prophets. In this respect no kindred movement is so decidedly infidel, so rancorously and avowedly anti-biblical. . . . It is equally opposed to nature and the established order of society founded upon it.

With such opinions accepted in the realm of the "benevolent empire," it was to be expected that in the South, where woman was romantically placed on a pedestal and treated with a sentimentality far removed from the arena of politics, there should be nothing but ridicule for the suffragist. The *Southern Literary Messenger* found welcome amusement in wartime in these verses reprinted from an English magazine:

Short-Skirt-Opathy

Take a pretty girl,
The prettier the better,
Give her naught to read
But novel and love-letter,
Let her go to plays,

Circuses and dances,
Fill her heart with love,
Murder and Romances.

Furnish her with beaux
Too numerous to mention,
Send her to attend
Each "Woman's Rights" Convention,
Humor her to death
When e'er she has the vapors,
Verses let her write
For magazines and papers.

Tell her of her charms
On every occasion,
Make her "talents" rare
The theme of conversation;
Let "affairs of state"
And politics be taught her—
And she'll wear "short skirts and pants,"
Or at least she "orter."

When their most strenuous efforts met with such response, it was no wonder that success did not attend all action. In Mrs. Stanton's words, "no power could have met the prejudice and bigotry of that period more successfully than they did who so bravely and persistently fought and conquered." Fully realizing the justice of their cause and aware of the strength of the forces pitted against them, the women of the early nineteenth century courageously did their share to establish institutions that should be in accord with the American democratic faith.

20

The Great Oneida Love-in

Morris Bishop

The Jacksonian Age was also a time of cults and utopias, most of them with religious origins. There were the visionary Millerites who founded a church on the prediction that the world would come to an end in 1843 and that the true believers, waiting on mountain tops, would witness the return of Christ and would ascend with Him into Heaven. There were the Mormons who searched for Zion out on the Utah desert. There were the celibate Rappites who resided in a community of harmony and equality at the mouth of the Wabash River in Ohio. There were the Shakers who renounced sex, championed the equality of women, nonresistance, and human perfectibility, and hailed the approach of the millennium, when Christ would return to rule a thousand years. And there were the followers of John Humphrey Noyes, who established a communistic society on Oneida Lake, in upstate New York, where they shared everything—including their marital partners.

Sin, the conviction of sin, the assurance of punishment for sin, pervaded pioneer America like the fever and ague, and took nearly as many victims. Taught that in Adam's fall we had sinned all, threatened with hell-fire by revivalist preachers, tortured by the guilt of intimate offenses, earnest youths whipped themselves into madness and suicide, and died crying that they had committed the sin against the Holy Ghost, which is unforgivable, though no one knows quite what it is.

The year 1831 was known as the Great Revival, when itinerant evangelists powerfully shook the bush and gathered in a great harvest of sinners. In September of that year John Humphrey Noyes, a twenty-year-old Dartmouth graduate and a law student in Putney, Vermont, attended such a revival. He was in a mood of metaphysical despair, aggravated by a severe cold. During the exhortings the conviction of salvation came to him. Light gleamed upon his soul. "Ere the day was done," he wrote later, "I had concluded to devote myself to the service and ministry of God."

Noyes was a young man of good family. His father was a Dartmouth graduate, a successful merchant in Putney, and a congressman. John was a bookish youth, delighting in history, romance, and poetry of a martial character, such as lives of Napoleon or of the Crusaders or Sir Walter Scott's *Marmion*. He was red-haired and freckled, and thought himself too homely ever to consider marriage. But when he began preaching his face shone like an angel's; one of his sons later averred that "there was about him an unmistakable and somewhat unexpected air of spiritual assurance." According to his phrenological analysis, his bumps of amativeness, combativeness, and self-esteem were large, his benevolence and philoprogenitiveness very large. His life confirmed these findings.

From "The Great Oneida Love-in" by Morris Bishop. © Copyright 1969 by American Heritage Publishing Co., Inc. Reprinted by permission from *American Heritage*, February 1969, pp. 14, 16, 86–92.

After his mystical experience in Putney, Noyes spent a year in the Andover Theological Seminary (Congregational). He found his teachers and companions lukewarm in piety, and devoted himself to an intensive study of the New Testament, most of which he could recite by heart. A divine direction—"I know that ye seek Jesus which was crucified. He is not here"—sent him from Andover to the Yale Theological Seminary in New Haven. There he came in contact with the doctrine of perfectionism and was allured by it.

Perfectionism asserted that men may be freed from sin and attain in this life the perfect holiness necessary to salvation. It rejected therefore the consequences of original sin and went counter to the Calvinistic dogma of total depravity. Perfectionism took shape early in the nineteenth century and found lodgment among adventurous groups in New Haven, Newark, Albany, and in villages of central New York, "the burned-over district," where religion smote with a searing flame. Perfectionism was likely to develop into antinomianism, the contention that the faithful are "directly infused with the holy spirit" and thus free from the claims and obligations of Old Testament moral law. And antinomianism led readily to scandal, as when three perfectionist missionaries, two men and a sister of one of them, were tarred and feathered for sleeping together in one bed.

Though suspected of perfectionist heresy, Noyes was licensed to preach in August, 1833. At about the same time, he made a sensational discovery: Jesus Christ had announced that He would return during the lifetime of some of His disciples. Jesus could not have been mistaken; therefore the Second Coming of Christ had taken place in A.D. 70. The "Jewish cycle" of religious history then ended and a "Gentile cycle" began, in which the Church has improperly usurped the authority of the apostles. We live no longer in an age of prophecy and promise, but in an age of fulfillment. Perfect holiness is attainable in this life, as well as guaranteed deliverance from sin.

Noyes found this revelation by fasting, prayer, and diligent search of the Scriptures. At divine command he announced it in a sermon to the Free Church of New Haven on February 20, 1834. "I went home with a feeling that I had committed myself irreversibly, and on my bed that night I received the baptism which I desired and expected. Three times in quick succession a stream of eternal love gushed through my heart, and rolled back again to its source. 'Joy unspeakable and full of glory' filled my soul. All fear and doubt and condemnation passed away. I knew that my heart was clean, and that the Father and the Son had come and made it their abode."

This was all very well, but next day the word ran through New Haven, "Noyes says he is perfect!" with the inevitable corollary, "Noyes is crazy!" The authorities promptly expelled him from the seminary and revoked his license to preach. But the perfect are proof against imperfect human detractors. "I have taken away their license to sin, and they keep on sinning," said Noyes. "So, though they have taken away my license to preach, I shall keep on preaching." This he did, with some success. His first convert was Miss Abigail Merwin of Orange, Connecticut, with whom he felt himself sealed in the faith.

Nevertheless his way was far from smooth. He had yet to pass through what he called "the dark valley of conviction." He went to New York and wandered the streets in a kind of frenzy, catching a little sleep by lying down in a doorway, or on the steps of City Hall, or on a bench at the Battery. He sought the most ill-famed regions of the city. "I descended into cellars where abandoned men and women were gathered, and talked familiarly with them about their ways of life, beseeching them to believe on Christ, that they might be saved

from their sins. They listened to me without abuse." Tempted by the Evil One, he doubted all, even the Bible, even Christ, even Abigail Merwin, whom he suspected to be Satan in angelic disguise. But after drinking the dregs of the cup of trembling he emerged purified and secure. He retreated to Putney for peace and shelter. His friends, even his sister, thought him deranged. But such was the power of his spirit that he gathered a little group of adepts, relatives, and friends to accept his revelation.

Miss Abigail Merwin, however, took fright, married a schoolteacher, and removed to Ithaca, New York. Noyes followed her there—a rather ungentlemanly procedure. After a few months she left her husband, but not for Noyes's arms —only to return to her father in Connecticut.

Noyes was delighted with the pretty village of Ithaca, with his lodging in the Clinton House, and especially with the broad-minded printers, unafraid of publishing heresies and liberal with credit. On August 20, 1837, he established a periodical, the *Witness*, for a subscription rate of one dollar, or, if a dollar should be inconvenient, for nothing. The issue of September 23 reverberated far beyond the subscription list of faithful perfectionists. Noyes had written a private letter expressing his radical views on marriage among the perfect. By a violation of confidence, this had reached the free-thinking editor of a paper called the *Battle-Axe*. Noyes, disdaining evasion, acknowledged in the *Witness* his authorship of the letter and reiterated his startling conclusions. The essential of "the *Battle-Axe* letter" lies in the concluding words: "When the will of God is done on earth as it is in heaven, *there will be no marriage*. The marriage supper of the Lamb is a feast at which *every dish is free to every guest*. Exclusiveness, jealousy, quarreling, have no place there, for the same reason as that which forbids the guests at a thanksgiving dinner to claim each his separate dish, and quarrel with the rest for his rights. In a holy community, there is no more reason

why sexual intercourse should be restrained by law, than why eating and drinking should be— and there is as little occasion for shame in the one as in the other. . . . The guests of the marriage supper may each have his favorite dish, each a dish of his own procuring, and that without the jealousy of exclusiveness."

Ungallant as this statement is in its characterization of women as dishes to pass, it states a reasonable protest against the egotisms of marriage. One may readily perceive in it also a secret resentment against the unfaithful Abigail Merwin. One may even interpret it as the erotic outburst of repressed impulse. Noyes, an impassioned, amorous type, was still a virgin.

Noyes was soon vouchsafed a sign, almost a miracle. When he was eighty dollars in debt to an Ithaca printer, he received from a disciple in Vermont, Miss Harriet A. Holton of Westminster, a letter enclosing a gift of exactly eighty dollars. He paid his bill, returned to Putney, and after a decent interval, forgetting the perfectionist views of the *Battle-Axe* letter, proposed exclusive marriage to Miss Holton. The two were formally united in Chesterfield, New Hampshire, on June 28, 1838. For a honeymoon they drove to Albany to buy a second-hand printing press, with more of Harriet's money.

Thus began the Putney Community, which at first consisted only of Noyes and his wife, several of his brothers and sisters, and a small cluster of converts from the neighborhood. They lived in a group, sharing possessions and duties. Their chief occupations were spiritual exercises in pursuit of holiness and the printing of the *Witness* on their own press. Noyes had no great liking for sheer honest toil for its own sake; he wished to secure for all the freedom for spiritual development. The women prepared one hot meal a day—breakfast. Thereafter the hungry had to help themselves in the kitchen.

Noyes was restless in the monotonous peace

of Putney. His wife inherited $9,000 in 1844; Noyes was provoked to fantastic visions. He wrote his wife: "In order to subdue the world to Christ we must carry religion into money-making." He proposed first a theological seminary for perfectionism, then agencies in Boston and New York to distribute their spiritual goods. "Then we must advance into foreign commerce, and as our means enlarge we must cover the ocean with our ships and the whole world with the knowledge of God. This is a great scheme, but not too great for God. . . . Within ten years we will plant the standard of Christ on the highest battlements of the world."

Though allured by such shimmering visions, he had to deal with present problems. An urgent personal problem was that of sex. His wife was pregnant five times in six years. She endured long agonies ending in four stillbirths. The only surviving child was Theodore, born in 1841. John Noyes suffered with his wife, and he protested against cruel nature, perhaps against God. Surely women were not made to suffer so. Surely there was a better way. A perfectionist could not brook flagrant imperfection. Noyes's habit was to seek and find a better way, and then sanctify it. The better way turned out to be male continence.

Noyes had been trained in the Puritan ethic, which did not regard marital sex as unholy. Nevertheless the consequences of male egotism horrified him. "It is as foolish and cruel to expend one's seed on a wife merely for the sake of getting rid of it," he wrote, "as it would be to fire a gun at one's best friend merely for the sake of unloading it." After his wife's disasters he lived for a time chaste by her side. But chastity proving to be no solution at all, he embraced male continence, of which the definition embarrasses the chaste pen. When embarrassed, the chaste pen may decently quote. One of the community disciples, H. J. Seymour, thus defined the practice: "checking the flow of amative passion before it reaches the point of

exposing the man to the loss of virile energy, or the woman to the danger of undesired child-bearing." Or, with Latin decorum, *coitus reservatus*; or, more colloquially, everything but.

This was not actually the beginning of birth-control advocacy. In 1832 a Boston physician, Charles Knowlton, published *The Fruits of Philosophy; or the Private Companion of Young Married People*, pointing to the menace of excessive child-bearing and eventual over-population, and recommending contraception. Dr. Knowlton and his publisher were accused of blasphemy. Their case was carried to the Supreme Court, and they were condemned to several months in jail. Robert Dale Owen, the reformer of New Harmony, Indiana, supported by Miss Frances Wright, "the Priestess of Beelzebub," carried on the work. In his *Moral Physiology* (1836), Owen recommended *coitus interruptus*, which Noyes scored as substituting self-indulgence for self-control.

"Amativeness is to life as sunshine is to vegetation," wrote Noyes twelve years later in his *Bible Argument Defining the Relation of the Sexes in the Kingdom of Heaven*. "Ordinary sexual intercourse (in which the amative and propagative functions are confounded) is a momentary affair, terminating in exhaustion and disgust. . . . Adam and Eve . . . sunk the spiritual in the sensual in their intercourse with each other, by pushing prematurely beyond the amative to the propagative, and so became ashamed." In the future society, "as propagation will become a science, so amative intercourse will become one of the 'fine arts.' Indeed it will rank above music, painting, sculpture, &c.; for it combines the charms and the benefits of them all."

All this is very noble and high-minded; but we are trained to look for—and we usually find —a casuistical serpent in the gardens, who is able to transform impulse into ideals, even into new theologies. The serpent in this case was Mary Cragin, who with her husband, George, had joined the Putney Community. Mary was

a charmer, and, to put it baldly, sexy. (Do not condemn her; some are, some aren't. This is a well-known fact.) Noyes feared that she might "become a Magdalene" if he did not save her. One evening in the woods, Noyes and Mary discovered that they were united by a deep spiritual bond. "We took some liberty of embracing, and Mrs. George distinctly gave me to understand that she was ready for the full consummation." But Noyes insisted on a committee meeting with the respective spouses. "We gave each other full liberty, and so entered into marriage in quartette form. The last part of the interview was as amiable and happy as a wedding, and a full consummation . . . followed."

This was Noyes's first infidelity, according to the world's idiom. He found a more grandiloquent term for it—complex marriage, to contrast with the restrictiveness of simple marriage. Heaven beamed on the participants. "Our love is of God; it is destitute of exclusiveness, each one rejoicing in the happiness of the others," said Mary. The Putney Community, in general, applauded; some, under direction, adopted the new cure for marital selfishness. It appears that some puritan wives, as well as husbands, were secretly weary of the "scanty and monotonous fare" provided by monogamy.

But righteous Putney soon had hints of the goings-on and uprose in anger. On October 26, 1847, Noyes was arrested, charged with adultery, and released, pending trial, in $2,000 bail. Noyes declared himself guiltless, insisting that in common law no tort has been committed if no one is injured. "The head and front and whole of our offense is communism of love. . . . If this is the unpardonable sin in the world, we are sure it is the beauty and glory of heaven." But in fear of mob violence from "the barbarians of Putney" he thought it well to jump bail, following the counsel of the highest authority: "When they persecute you in this city, flee ye into another."

A refuge awaited the persecuted saints in the burned-over district of central New York, a region familiar to Noyes. A group of perfectionists offered the Putneyans a sawmill and forty acres of woodland on Oneida Creek, halfway between Syracuse and Utica. It was a bland, fertile, welcoming country, suitable for an Eden. By good omen, the spot was the exact geographical center of New York, if one overlooked Long Island.

In mid-February of 1848, "the year of the great change," the pilgrims began to arrive. Defying the upstate winter, lodging in abandoned cabins, they set to with a will to build a community dwelling and workshops. Some of the neighbors looked at them askance; most welcomed these honest, pious, industrious newcomers, and some even were converted to perfectionism and threw in their lot with the colony.

The early years were the heroic age of Oneida. All worked together, cutting and sawing timber, digging clay for bricks, building simple houses, clearing land for vegetable gardens. Everyone took his or her turn at the household tasks. All work was held in equal honor, without prestige connotations. Noyes recognized that most American experiments in communal life had foundered because they were established on the narrow base of agriculture; his communism would live on industry. Thus Oneida marketed canned fruits and vegetables, sewing silk, straw hats, mop sticks, travelling bags, and finally, silver tableware. Its traps for animals, from rodents to bears, became famous as far as Alaska and Siberia. The cruelty of traps seldom occurred to the makers, who were frontiersmen as well as perfectionists. Sympathy with suffering beasts and the conservation of wildlife were concepts still undeveloped. To a critic, Noyes replied that since God had covered the earth with vermin, Oneida simply helped to cleanse it. Salesmen, known only as peddlers, were sent out to

market the wares. On their return, they were given a Turkish bath and a sharp examination on faith and practice, a spiritual rubdown to expunge the stains of the unregenerate world.

The Oneida Community prospered. The numbers of the faithful rose. The great Mansion House, the community home, was begun in 1860 and completed a dozen years later. It is a far-wandering red-brick building or group of buildings, standing on a knoll amid magnificent fat trees. Harmoniously proportioned, with its towers, mansard roofs, and tall French windows, it is a superb example of mid-nineteenth-century architecture. Its message is security, peace, and material comfort. The interior is graced with fine woodwork and decorations. The parlors, the excellent library, the lovely assembly hall, are redolent with memories, jealously preserved and proudly recounted. Here live a number of descendants of the original Oneidans, together with some lodgers, still regarded with kindly pity as "foreign bodies."

The memories, second-hand though they are, are all of a happy time, of a golden age long lost. John Humphrey Noyes, affectionately referred to by his grandchildren as "the Honorable John," was a cheerful person, and imposed happiness on his great family. The story is told of a visitor who asked her guide: "What is the fragrance I smell here in this house?" The guide answered: "It may be the odor of crushed selfishness." There was no money within the Oneida economy, no private possession, no competition for food and shelter, and hence little rivalry.

All worked and played together. Whenever possible, work was done on the "bee" system; thus a party of men and women would make handbags on the lawn, while a dramatic voice read a novel aloud. Classes were conducted in such recondite subjects as Greek and Hebrew. Dances and respectable card games, like euchre and whist, were in favor. Amateur theatricals were a constant diversion. The productions of

The Merchant of Venice, The Merry Wives of Windsor, and especially of *H.M.S. Pinafore,* were famous as far as Utica and Syracuse. Music was encouraged, with an orchestra and much vocalization. Music, Noyes mused, was closely related to sexual love; it was an echo of the passions. However, music contained a menace; it gave rise to rivalries, jealousies, and vanities, to what Noyes reproved as "prima donna fever."

Noyes had strong views on dress. He called the contrast of men's and women's costumes immodest, in that it proclaimed the distinction of sex. "In a state of nature, the difference between a man and a woman could hardly be distinguished at a distance of five hundred yards, but as men and women dress, their sex is telegraphed as far as they can be seen. Woman's dress is a standing lie. It proclaims that she is not a two-legged animal, but something like a churn, standing on castors. . . . Gowns operate as shackles, and they are put on that sex which has most talent in the legs."

From the beginning at Oneida, a new dress for women was devised, loose skirts to the knee with pantalets below, thus approximating a gentleman's frock coat and trousers. Some visitors were shocked, some were amused; few were allured. Indeed, the specimens remaining in the community's collections and the representations in photographs hardly seem beautiful. But the wearers rejoiced in their new freedom of movement. They cut their hair, in despite of Saint Paul. It was asserted they looked and felt younger.

For thirty years the community, a placid island amid the stormy seas of society, lived its insulated life. It numbered, at its peak, three hundred members. It was undisturbed, except by invasions of visitors brought on bargain excursions by the railroads. As many as a thousand appeared on a single day, picnicking on the grounds, invading the workshops and private

quarters. They were welcomed; but on their departure all the Oneidans turned to in order to collect the scatterings, to scrub out the tobacco stains on the parquet floors.

The structure, the doctrine, the persistence of Oneida made a unique social phenomenon. It was consciously a family, with Noyes as father. As Constance Noyes Robertson says, it substituted "for the small unit of home and family and individual possessions the larger unit of group-family and group-family life." Its faith was "Bible Communism." Though it held aloof from all churches and deconsecrated the Sabbath, it was pietistic in demanding the regeneration of society by rejecting competition, a money economy, and private ownership, whether of goods or persons. But it was not Marxian, for it made no mention of class warfare, of a revolution to come, of proletarian dictatorship.

The internal organization of the community was loose and vague, depending largely on the will of Noyes. Justice and discipline were administered informally, if at all. To provide correction, Noyes trusted chiefly to a procedure known as mutual criticism. Saint Paul had said: "Speak every man truth with his neighbor; for we are members one of another"; and the Apostle James: "Confess your faults one to another." When an individual offered himself for criticism, or was designated from above, a committee prepared his "trial," but any member might join in the proceedings. The trial was a game, though a serious one. The subject was informed of his secret faults, of shortcomings he had not suspected. He learned that his very virtues, on which he had flattered himself, were only disguised vices. The critics would pounce on an unpopular fellow-member with glee, seizing the opportunity to reveal to him some home truths, at the same time revealing their hidden rancors. A transcript of the proceedings was posted and often printed. The subject of this primitive psychoanalysis was likely to suffer dreadfully from his new self-knowledge.

"I was shaken from center to circumference," said one. "I was metaphorically stood upon my head and allowed to drain until all the self-righteousness had dripped out of me." Afterward the subject felt enlightened, purified, happy. "Mutual criticism," said Noyes, "subordinates the I-spirit to the We-spirit." It also made the subjects, mostly brooding introspectives, for a time the center of interest and concern for the whole community. Mutual criticism, under the name of "krinopathy," was even used as a therapeutic device to cure children's colds, with, it was said, remarkable success.

Of the various Oneida institutions, the most fascinating to the prurient observer is the organization of sex behavior. Since the community was a single great family, there could be within it no marrying and giving in marriage. Each was married to all, Noyes insisted; every man was husband and brother to every woman. Love, far from being a sin, was holy, a sacrament; in the sexual experience one escaped from egotism and selfhood into the ecstasy of communion. Every effort must be to "abound" —one of Noyes's favorite words. One must spend, not hoard. The human heart seldom realizes its possibilities; it "is capable of loving any number of times and any number of persons; the more it loves the more it can love." One had only to look at surrounding society to recognize the evils of exclusive marriage, the chains binding unmatched natures, the secret adulteries, actual or of the heart, the hate-filled divorces, women's diseases, prostitution, masturbation, licentiousness in general.

Noyes maintained that sexual love was not naturally restricted to pairs, that second marriages were often the happiest. "Men and women find universally (however the fact may be concealed) that their susceptibility to love is not burned out by one honeymoon, or satisfied by one lover." The body should assert its rights; religion should make use of the senses as helpers of devotion. Sexual shame, the con-

John Humphrey Noyes, founder of the Oneida Community, seated (center right) with some of his followers around him. Noyes was a strong-minded man whose firmness and sense of purpose kept the community together. (From Oneida Community: An Autobiography, 1851–1876, *Constance Noyes Robertson, ed. (Syracuse University Press, 1970), by permission of Constance Noyes Robertson.)*

sequence of the fall of man, was factitious and irrational. "Shame ought to be banished from the company of virtue, though in the world it has stolen the very name of virtue. . . . Shame gives rise to the theory that sexual offices have no place in heaven. Anyone who has true modesty would sooner banish singing from heaven than sexual music." Beware, said Noyes, of one who proclaims that he is free from sexual desire, beware of religious teachers with fondling hands. Beware especially of Dr. Josiah Gridley of Southampton, Massachusetts, who boasts that he could carry a virgin in each hand

without the least stir of passion. In short, "you must not serve the lusts of the flesh; if you do you will be damned. You must not make monks of yourself; if you do you will be damned."

One might suspect that these doctrines would have led to outright antinomianism and to general orgies. Nothing of the sort occurred, thanks to the watchful care of Noyes and thanks to the character of the Oneidans, devout and rather humorless seekers for perfection. The system of complex marriage, or pantagamy, begun in Putney, was instituted. A man might request the privilege of a private visit with a lady, or

a lady might take the initiative, for "in all nature the female element invites and the male responds." The request was submitted to a committee of elders, headed by Noyes, who gave the final approval or disapproval. The mate besought had the right of refusal. It was recommended that older women initiate young men, and vice versa. Thus the young men were expertly guided in the practice of male continence, while the maturer men undertook without complaint the education of the maidens. The committee was also concerned to break up "exclusive and idolatrous attachments" of two persons of the same age, for these bred selfishness. We are assured that complex marriage worked admirably, and that for many life became a continuous courtship. "Amativeness, the lion of the tribe of human passions, is conquered and civilized among us." But the records are unwontedly reticent on the details of the system's operation. Only one scandal is remembered, when an unworthy recruit tried to force his attentions on the women, and was expelled through a window into a snowdrift. One suspects that in spite of all the spiritual training, there were heartaches and hidden anger, and much whispering and giggling at the sound of midnight footsteps on the stairs.

The flaw in the system of continence was the threatening sterilization of the movement—the fate of the Shakers. Noyes recognized the danger, and in his *Bible Argument* of 1848 had proposed scientific propagation to replace random or involuntary propagation. But the time was not yet ripe. In the difficult early years of Oneida, Noyes discouraged childbearing, and his docile followers produced only forty-four offspring in twenty years. Then increasing prosperity permitted him to take steps for the perpetuation of his community. Early in 1869, he proposed the inauguration of stirpiculture, or the scientific improvement of the human stock by breeding. "Every race-horse, every straight-backed bull, every premium pig tells us what we can do and what we must do for men." Oneida should be a laboratory for the preparation of the great race of the future.

The Oneidans, especially the younger ones, greeted the proposal with enthusiasm. Fifty-three young women signed these resolutions:

1. That we do not belong to ourselves in any respect, but that we do belong to *God*, and second to Mr. Noyes as God's true representative.
2. That we have no rights or personal feelings in regard to childbearing which shall in the least degree oppose or embarrass him in his choice of scientific combinations.
3. That we will put aside all envy, childishness and self-seeking, and rejoice with those who are chosen candidates; that we will, if necessary, become martyrs to science, and cheerfully resign all desire to become mothers, if for any reason Mr. Noyes deem us unfit material for propagation. Above all, we offer ourselves "living sacrifices" to God and true Communism.

At the same time thirty-eight young men made a corresponding declaration to Noyes:

The undersigned desire you may feel that we most heartily sympathize with your purpose in regard to scientific propagation, and offer ourselves to be used in forming any combinations that may seem to you desirable. We claim no rights. We ask no privileges. We desire to be servants of the truth. With a prayer that the grace of God will help us in this resolution, we are your true soldiers.

Thus began the first organized experiment in human eugenics. For several years Noyes directed all the matings, on the basis of physical, spiritual, moral, and intellectual suitability. In 1875 a committee of six men and six women was formed to issue licenses to propagate. The

selective process bore some bitter fruit. The eliminated males particularly were unhappy, unconsoled by the reflection that in animal breeding one superior stud may serve many females. Noyes relented in his scientific purpose so far as to permit one child to each male applicant. There was also some covert grumbling that Noyes, then in his sixties, elected himself to father nine children, by several mates. Eugenically, to be sure, he was entirely justified; there could be no doubt of his superiority.

The results of the stirpicultural experiment have not been scientifically studied, though an article by Hilda Herrick Noyes, prepared in 1921, offered some valuable statistical information. About one hundred men and women took part; eighty-one became parents, producing fifty-eight living children and four stillborn. No mothers were lost during the experiment; no defective children were produced The health of the offspring was exceptionally good; their longevity has far surpassed the average expectations of life. The children, and the children's children, constitute a very superior group, handsome and intelligent. Many have brilliantly conducted the affairs of their great manufacturing corporation; others have distinguished themselves in public service, the arts, and literature.

The integration of the children into the community caused some difficulties. The mother kept her child until he was weaned and could walk; then he was transferred to the Children's House, though he might return to his mother for night care. Noyes, with his ideal of the community family, disapproved of egotistic, divisive "special love"; the mothers were permitted to see their children only once or twice a week. The children were excellently educated in the nursery school, the kindergarten, and the grammar school, by teachers chosen for their competence and natural liking for the young. If the children cried for their mothers, they were severely reproved for "partiality" or

"stickiness." One graduate of the Children's House remembered that when he was forbidden to visit his mother he went berserk. Another recalled her agony when she caught sight of her mother after a fortnight's enforced separation. The child begged her mother not to leave her —and the mother fled for fear of a penalty of an additional week's separation from her child.

The atmosphere of the Children's House was, in short, that of a friendly orphanage. If the disruption of the family units had any bad psychic effects on the children, they have not been recorded. Children accept their world as it is; they know no other. The memories of the Oneida boys and girls are mostly of happy schooldays under kind teachers, days of laughter, play, and delightful learning. The judgment of one eminent product, Pierrepont B. Noyes, is surely correct, that the community system was harder on the mothers than on the children.

The fathers were more remote from their children than were the mothers. Pierrepont Noyes admitted: "Father never seemed a father to me in the ordinary sense." The system reflected indeed the character of John Humphrey Noyes. He was the Father of his people, the semidivine begetter of a community, and he loved the community communally. He saw no reason to encourage family bonds, "partiality," among the faithful, at cost to the community spirit. He seems to have shown little personal affection for his sons after the flesh. No doubt a phrenologist would have noted that his bump of parental love was small. One is tempted to go further, to see in his disregard for his children a certain horror of paternity, a deep-implanted remembrance of his four stillborn babies, of his wife's sufferings and his own.

The rumors of strange sex practices roused the righteous and the orthodox, already angered by Oneida's nonobservance of the Sabbath and rejection of church affiliations. A professor at

Hamilton College, John W. Mears, still the bogeyman of Oneida after a hundred years, began in 1873 a long campaign to destroy the community and its band of sinners. Though most of the inhabitants and newspaper editors of the region defended Noyes and his followers, though local justice could find no grounds for prosecution, the churches demanded action against "the ethics of the barnyard," and sought enabling legislation from the state. The menace mounted until, in June, 1879, Noyes fled to Canada, as, thirty-one years before, he had fled from Vermont. From a new home in Niagara Falls, Ontario, he continued to advise and inspire his old companions until his death, on April 13, 1886.

With the Father's departure the community system collapsed. In August, 1879, complex marriage was abandoned. Most of the Oneidans paired off and married, to legitimize their children. There were distressing cases of mothers whose mates were already taken, of the children of Noyes himself, left high and dry. In the reorganization into conventional families, it was necessary to establish rights of private property. As Noyes had foreseen, the demons of greed, self-seeking, jealousy, anger, and uncharitableness invaded the serene halls of the Mansion House.

The Oneida industries were converted into a joint-stock company, the shares distributed to the members of the community. After a period of drifting and fumbling, the widely varied enterprises came under the inspired management of Pierrepont Noyes and became models of welfare capitalism, or the partnership of owners and workers. To the present day, high wages are paid, profits are shared, schools, country clubs, aids for home-building, are provided. Oneida is the leading producer of stainless-steel flatware, the second largest producer of silver-plated ware in the United States. It has over three thousand employees in the Oneida plants, and many more in the factories in Canada, Mexico, and the United Kingdom. Its net sales in 1967 amounted to fifty-four million dollars, with net profits of two and a half million.

This outcome is not the least surprising feature of the Oneida story. Nearly all other communistic experiments in this country have long since disappeared, leaving nothing more than a tumble-down barracks or a roadside marker. Oneida found a transformation into the capitalist world. It did so at the cost of losing its religious and social doctrines; but it has never lost the idealism, the humanitarianism, and the communitarian love of John Humphrey Noyes.

VI   Beyond the Mississippi

21

A Passage to India

Henry Nash Smith

After the War of 1812, as Ray Allen Billington pointed out, America turned away from Old World entanglements and sought to extend her "natural sphere of influence" westward, her pioneers moving in sporadic waves out to the Mississippi River and beyond. Jefferson had made this westward movement possible by purchasing the vast Louisiana Territory from France in 1803. He had also begun American dreams of a transcontinental empire when he sent Lewis and Clark out to the Pacific and back. In the next two decades, Americans occupied the fertile Mississippi Valley, creating the new states of Louisiana, Indiana, Mississippi, Illinois, Alabama, and Missouri. At the same time, army explorers and scientists undertook expeditions up the Arkansas and Missouri rivers, finding that the complex river systems offered tremendous possibilities for commerce and trade. Then, during the Era of Good Feelings, Secretary of State John Quincy Adams—an uninhibited expansionist—not only extended United States hegemony in the Caribbean and South America (he helped conceive the Monroe Doctrine) but paved the way for transcontinental expansion in the Adams-Oñis Treaty with Spain. In it, the United States acquired Florida, agreeing in exchange to assume $5,000,000 worth of debts which Spain owed to American citizens. But more significantly, in return for clear title to Texas, Spain gave the United States her claims to the Oregon country, an expansive region lying north of the Red and Arkansas Rivers and the forty-second parallel. After Mexico revolted from Spain in 1822, the Mexican Republic also ratified the Adams-Oñis Treaty, thus clearing the way for an American march to the Pacific.

American fur companies, operating out of St. Louis and Independence, had already sent trappers and traders out into the awesome Rocky Mountains. These fabled mountain men blazed trails and explored rich mountain valleys across the Oregon country, reporting back that the region was excellent for settlement. In the 1830s and 1840s, Americans from the fringes of the South and the old Northwestern states headed across the trails the mountain men had blazed, establishing American outposts in Oregon and California. Meanwhile, other settlers—most of them from the Border South—migrated into Mexican-held Texas, where they eventually revolted and set up an independent republic. Many of these Western pioneers were honest people who wanted to start new lives on the frontier. But others were greedy speculators, unscrupulous promoters, and adventurous riff-raff who saw the frontier as a business windfall and went there to make fortunes any way they could.

In the 1840s—an era of unprecedented westward expansion—the United States virtually doubled her territory. She annexed the Republic of Texas, drove the British out of Oregon with threats of violence, and wrested California and the rest of the Southwest in a highly controversial war with Mexico.

The "glacial inexorability" of this westward sweep, as T. H. Watkins phrased it, gave birth to a faith called "Manifest Destiny," a belief that the United States had a natural, God-given right to expand her superior institutions and way-of-life across the continent. And woe indeed to anybody —British, Indians, or Mexicans—who stood in the way. Still, as Bernard DeVoto has reminded us, there were other energies at work behind America's westward thrusts. Some Southerners, for example, desired the empty lands for Southern

expansion, in order to maintain an equilibrium of power between slave and free states in Washington. There was, moreover, the need of both Southern and Northern interests to control the Middle West for political and economic gain. And there was the "blind drive" of American industrial interests to establish ports on the West coast, thereby opening the Pacific Ocean and distant Asia to United States commercial expansion.

In the latter respect, the United States was drawn by the romantic lure of Asia just as were Columbus and scores of other New World explorers in the fifteenth and sixteenth centuries. For some American expansionists, as Henry Nash Smith shows, the trans-Mississippi West was "a passage to India," one that might allow the United States to develop a great commercial empire in Asia, just as Portugal and Spain had dreamed of before.

Passage to India: Thomas Hart Benton and Asa Whitney

When Lewis and Clark reached the shore of the Pacific in 1804 they reactivated the oldest of all ideas associated with America—that of a passage to India. Columbus had been seeking the fabled wealth of the Orient when he discovered that a New World lay between Europe and Asia. Since his day, explorers of many nationalities had engaged in an almost continuous search for a route through or around this obstacle without traversing the Spanish possessions in America. Several expeditions were organized in Virginia during the seventeenth century "to find out the East India Sea," as Governor William Berkeley wrote in 1669 concerning his own plans. The distance was at

Reprinted by permission of the publishers from Chapters I, II, and IV of Henry Nash Smith, *Virgin Land: The American West as Symbol and Myth.* Cambridge, Mass.: Harvard University Press, Copyright, 1950, by the President and Fellows of Harvard College.

that time not believed to be very great—perhaps ten days' journey beyond the Alleghenies. But as men gradually realized the enormous bulk of North America, they had given up this project in favor of an equally unavailing search for a northwest passage around the continent by sea.

Until the very end of the eighteenth century the West beyond the Mississippi was so shadowy and remote that it could be pictured in almost any guise that might occur to a writer's imagination. Nevertheless, some of these fantasies bear faint marks of purposiveness and a continuing tradition. The Freneau-Brackenridge commencement poem of 1771, for instance, in elaborating the idea of a westward course of empire, predicts that analogues of various imperial capitals of the Old World will spring up in the America of the future: a St. Petersburg amid the snows of the far north, a Babylon in Mexico, a Nineveh on the Orinoco in South America. In the Far West the future reveals

> A new Palmyra or an Ecbatan
> And sees the slow pac'd caravan return
> O'er many a realm from the Pacific shore,
> Where fleets shall then convey rich Persia's silks,
> Arabia's perfumes, and spices rare
> Of Philippine, Cœlebe and Marian isles,
> Or from the Acapulco coast our India then,
> Laden with pearl and burning gems of gold.

If this is hardly more than a pretty conceit, one can find in as sober a writer as Thomas Hutchins the notion that North America would eventually dominate the trade of the Orient.

That Jefferson fully grasped the relation of the Pacific Northwest to Asia is evident in his plan for John Ledyard to approach the American coast by way of Siberia, and in the emphasis he gave to finding a trade route "between the higher parts of the Missouri and the Pacific ocean" in the instructions he prepared for Michaux. This document was composed in

January, 1793. By that time enterprising American ship captains sailing out of Atlantic ports around Cape Horn had developed a lucrative trade between the Pacific Northwest and China by way of the Sandwich Islands, so that Jefferson could hardly have discussed the possibility of a transcontinental route without having the China trade in mind. The idea was current in the American press: in February, 1795 the *Kentucky Gazette* picked up from a New York paper a notice that Alexander Mackenzie had reached the Pacific overland. "This circumstance," the dispatch noted, "will, in the course of time, be of the utmost consequence to this country, as it opens a direct communication with China, and may doubtless lead to further discoveries."

It is true that Jefferson himself nowhere dwells on the value of the Asiatic trade. Perhaps his desire for maintaining a simple agricultural society in the United States prevented him from growing enthusiastic over this commercial possibility. But his private instructions to Meriwether Lewis probably took for granted the importance of trade with the Orient:

> The object of your mission is to explore the Missouri river, & such principal stream of it as, by it's course & communication with the waters of the Pacific Ocean, may offer the most direct & practicable communication across this continent, for the purposes of commerce.

Furthermore, Lewis's confidential letter to Jefferson from St. Louis immediately after his return from the expedition seems to refer to a previous discussion of access to the Far East:

> We vew this passage across the continent as affording immence advantages to the fir trade but fear that advantages wich it offers as a communication for the productions of the East Indias to the United States and thence to Europe will never be found equal on an extensive scale to that by the way of

the Cape of good hope. still we beleive that many articles not bulky brittle nor of a perishable nature may be conveyed to the U'. States by this rout with more facility and less expence than by that at present practiced.

This plan, however, could hardly be taken seriously in view of Lewis's rather lame suggestion that freight could be carried from the head of navigation on the Missouri to the head of navigation on the Columbia by means of horses, which could be procured "in immence numbers and for the most trivial considerations from the natives."

It is not clear what means of transport John Jacob Astor intended to use along the overland route to Astoria, the trading post he built in 1811 near the mouth of the Columbia. He meant to supply his fort mainly by sea, but he sent Wilson P. Hunt westward from the Missouri in the hope of finding a better route than Lewis's proposed combination of river boating and a packhorse portage. Hunt's men had an even worse time getting over the Rockies than Lewis and Clark, but a party of returning Astorians led by Robert Stuart discovered South Pass in 1813. Ten years later William Ashley's demonstration that wagons could be driven through the Pass suggested an overland wagon road to Oregon and revived the old dream of Asiatic trade. Caleb Atwater of Ohio declared in 1829 with stout Western confidence: "That this will be the route to China within fifty years from this time, scarcely admits of a doubt." He foresaw a dense population all along the way, with corresponding wealth, grandeur, and glory for the American people. It was nevertheless a long haul for wagons from Independence, Missouri, to the Columbia. The hardy frontiersman might learn how to plow it through with his family and household goods in four or five months, if he had luck, but Asa Whitney, an early propagandist for a Pacific railway, was justified in pouring scorn on the notion that the

Oregon Trail was any better than the Lewis and Clark route as a highway for Oriental imports. "I presume no man," he exclaimed, "will think of an overland communication with teams through a wilderness and desert of more than two thousand miles in extent!" Only in the 1840's, when a transcontinental railroad began to be seriously discussed, did the notion of bringing Asiatic goods eastward across the continent come to deserve practical consideration.

Yet the idea of a passage to India, with its associated images of fabulous wealth, of ivory and apes and peacocks, led a vigorous existence on the level of imagination entirely apart from its practicability. So rich and compelling was the notion that it remained for decades one of the ruling conceptions of American thought about the West. It was almost an obsession with Thomas Hart Benton of Missouri, who during the thirty years following the death of Jefferson was the most conspicuous and best-informed champion of westward expansion in Congress. Benton's public career extended from the beginnings of the Santa Fé Trail and the heyday of the Rocky Mountain fur trade to the eve of the Civil War. During all this time he was indefatigable in analyzing the problems of the West and urging the cause of expansion. Defeated for the Senate in 1850 because of his free-soil views, he returned to the House of Representatives in 1854 and threw his energies into the cause of a Pacific railway. Almost to the day of his death in 1858 he was making speeches in behalf of the railway and the general development of the West.

Benton was a devoted follower of Thomas Jefferson. He believed, according to his daughter Jessie Benton Frémont, that a visit he paid to the aged statesman at Monticello late in 1824 was the occasion of a laying on of hands, a ceremony at which Benton received the mantle of the first prophet of American expansionism. So strong was Benton's piety, in fact, that he read into Jefferson ideas of his own which were not there, or at most were present

in an embryonic state. The point is not of great significance, but it is suggestive enough to warrant passing notice. In his *Thirty Years' View* Benton wrote that Jefferson sent Lewis and Clark out to open commercial communication with Asia. "And thus Mr. Jefferson," he added, "was the first to propose the North American road to India, and the introduction of Asiatic trade on that road; and all that I myself have either said or written on that subject . . . is nothing but the fruit of the seed planted in my mind by the philosophic hand of Mr. Jefferson." Jessie Benton is even more explicit concerning Jefferson's conception of the Lewis and Clark expedition. Paraphrasing this passage from her father's memoirs, she says that Jefferson told Congress the Lewis and Clark expedition

> would 'open overland commercial relations with Asia; and enlarge the boundaries of geographical science'—putting as the first motive a North-American road to India, and the introduction of Asiatic trade over that road.

The words enclosed in quotation marks do not occur in Jefferson's message to Congress proposing the expedition, or indeed in any other statement of Jefferson known to me. The notion of trade with Asia was so strong in the Benton tradition eighty years after the message was delivered that it actually colored Jessie Benton's memory.

Benton's interest in the passage to India grew out of an elaborate philosophy of westward expansion. After a childhood and youth in North Carolina and Tennessee, he served under Jackson with the Tennessee militia in 1812. His daughter says that this experience determined him to identify himself with the West, the vast basin of the Mississippi, and to repudiate "the exclusively English and seaboard influences to which he had been born and in which he had been trained." The Atlantic coast, for father and daughter alike, is identified with European

tradition: it is "the English seaboard," and is viewed as an influence stifling the development of the American personality by imposing deference to precedent and safe usage. By contrast, access to Asia becomes a symbol of freedom and of national greatness for America. Benton adopts the role of a Moses leading his people out of bondage. Jessie Benton cites the inscription on her father's statue in St. Louis: "There is the East; there lies the road to India," a quotation from a speech he made in the Senate in 1825 favoring military occupation of Oregon.

The image of Asia became for Benton the key to all modern history, which he saw as a series of conflicts between Britain and her successive rivals for world dominance. Jessie Benton asserts that when her father moved to St. Louis after the War of 1812,

> he found himself confronting English aggression in another form. The little French town so far in the centre of our continent found itself direct heir to the duel of a century between England and France for the New World and the Asiatic trade, and, France having withdrawn, was meeting the added resentment of English feeling against her late subjects, who now replaced France in that contest.

Defeated in the struggle for the Mississippi Valley, the English still hoped by controlling San Francisco to dominate the Asiatic trade across the Pacific. American seizure of California would thus be an act of defiance to England rather than to Mexico, and would mean a great deal more than a mere occupation of territory.

Benton's thought concerning the passage to India and the related theme of Anglo-American rivalry can be traced through almost four decades of public discussion: (1) in a series of editorials written for the St. Louis *Enquirer* in 1818–1819, before the admission of Missouri as a state; (2) in his famous speech on the Oregon question, delivered in the Senate in 1825;

(3) in his fostering of the exploring expeditions of his son-in-law, Lieutenant John Charles Frémont, during the 1840's; and (4) in his concern with the proposed railway to the Pacific during the 1850's.

The editorials in the *Enquirer* were occasioned by the Treaty of 1818 with Britain providing for joint occupation of Oregon, and the Spanish Treaty of 1819 establishing the Sabine and the Red River as the boundary between Spanish and American possessions in the Southwest. Benton's position is that John Quincy Adams, who negotiated the Spanish treaty, and Albert Gallatin, who negotiated the treaty with Britain, had made outrageous concessions to foreign powers at the expense of westward expansion. He insists upon the value of the western half of the Mississippi Valley and the inevitability of American commercial expansion toward the Pacific. Elaborating the theory of the course of empire, he declares that westward advance has been throughout recorded time "the course of the heavenly bodies, of the human race, and of science, civilization, and national power following in their train." This vast perspective suggests grandiose reflections. Soon the American pioneers will complete "the circumambulation of the globe" when they reach the Pacific and look out toward that Asia in which their first parents were originally planted. The Arkansas, the Platte, and the Yellowstone rivers, their sources interlocking with those of streams emptying into the western ocean, will become for the people of the United States "what the Euphrates, the Oxus, the Phasis, and the Cyrus were to the ancient Romans, lines of communication with eastern Asia, and channels for that rich commerce which, for forty centuries, has created so much wealth and power wherever it has flowed."

For thousands of years merchants loaded with gold and silver have traversed the deserts on camels or the trackless sea in ships, in quest of the rich productions of the East. From the

ancient Phoenicians to the English, the nation which has commanded the trade of Asia in each successive era has been the leader of the world in civilization, power, and wealth. It is her monopoly of this trade that has enabled England to triumph single-handed over the combined powers of Europe and to impress her policy upon every quarter of the globe. American mariners have already made inroads upon the English monopoly; and this enterprise, embryonic though it may be, forms the richest vein of American commerce. What then would be the consequences if Americans could perfect their own route to Asia, shorter than that open to the English?

Lewis and Clark have demonstrated that such a route exists, by way of the Columbia River. Nothing is wanted but a second Daniel Boone to lead the way through the wilderness. Benton translates maritime commerce, which had always been carried on by wealthy merchants, into Jacksonian terms. The shortness of the American road to India will make it easy for men of moderate means to embark in the trade, which, by being made more accessible to all classes of the community, will be more valuable to the nation. Most important of all is the prospect that trade with the Orient will emancipate the United States from its dependence on Europe. No longer will Americans be "servile copyists and imitators," branded with Buffon's stigma of biological inferiority. They have built their own system of government; let them go on to nationalize their character by establishing a system of commerce adapted to their geographical position and free from European interference.

Five years later Benton returned to the theme of contact with Asia in his speech on the occupation of Oregon. He had now become more fully aware of the agricultural resources of the Pacific coast, and predicted that within one hundred years a population greater than that of the present United States would exist beyond the Rocky Mountains. American pioneers would bring science, liberal principles in government, and the true religion to the peoples of Asia, and the oldest and the newest, the most despotic and the freest of nations might become friends united in opposition to a Europe which was determined to dominate and exploit them both.

Yet despite Benton's exuberant expansionism his fidelity to Jeffersonian tradition exerted a markedly conservative influence on his thinking. Still cherishing the old fear, stemming from Montesquieu, that republican government could not survive too great an extension of its boundaries, he considered it inevitable and desirable that the descendants of Americans who would settle the Pacific Coast should form an independent nation. The Rocky Mountains were a convenient, natural, and everlasting western boundary for the United States. There "the statue of the fabled god, Terminus, should be raised . . . , never to be thrown down." Such a delimitation of territory would in no way hamper American commercial expansion into the Orient because the new Pacific republic would stand beside the United States against the combined powers of the Old World.

The next phase of Benton's interest in Far Western expansion was the most significant of his career. By 1841 emigrants from the Missouri frontier, encouraged by the passage of a Senate bill donating 640 acres of land in Oregon to every settler (even though the bill failed to pass the House), were beating a broad path up the valley of the Platte River and through South Pass to Fort Hall and Oregon. The following year Benton was able to secure passage of a bill authorizing his son-in-law, John Charles Frémont of the Topographical Corps, to map the trail as far as South Pass. Publication of Frémont's report of the expedition, in a form owing much to the literary flair of Jessie Benton, fostered an increased migration out the Oregon Trail in succeeding summers. The further expeditions of Frémont, leading him eventually into California at the outbreak of the

Mexican War, were a conspicuous and carefully publicized phase of the burst of expansionism that extended the boundaries of the United States to the Pacific by 1848.

Out of the war grew yet another development of Benton's program for the West, again in the spirit of his emphasis on westward movement, on the passage to India. On February 7, 1849, he introduced a bill to appropriate a part of the proceeds from the sales of public lands for building a Central National Road from the Pacific Ocean to the Mississippi River. As a forerunner of the eventual federal subsidy for a Pacific railway, Benton's plan has an air of archaism. He favored construction of a railway as far as practicable, but was prepared for reliance upon sleighs through the snowy passes. The railway was to be built by the federal government and then leased to contractors who would operate trains over it. And throughout the entire length of the highway was to be built "a plain old English road, such as we have been accustomed to all our lives—a road in which the farmer in his wagon or carriage, on horse or on foot, may travel without fear, and without tax—with none to run over him, or make him jump out of the way."

This homespun conception, with its imaginative fusion of the Cumberland Road across the Alleghenies, the actual Oregon Trail with its covered wagons, and the Union Pacific Railway of the future, was balanced in Benton's speech by one of the grandiose historical parallels with which he habitually dignified his remarks on westward expansion. He quotes Gibbon on the Roman roads that connected the remotest provinces of the Empire. Like these ancient highways, the road to the Pacific would facilitate sending troops to protect the frontiers. It would foster political unity by connecting the Atlantic and the Pacific states. (Benton has dropped the idea of the god Terminus at the Continental Divide.) But commercial considerations were most important of all, for here was Benton's ancient and preferred theme, the passage to

India. Each time he returned to this notion he added fresh ornaments to it. As he said, it was always for him "a boundless field, dazzling and bewildering the imagination from its vastness and importance." A pageant of universal history opened before him portraying the events which would follow completion of a transcontinental highway:

The trade of the Pacific Ocean, of the western coast of North America, and of Eastern Asia, will all take its track; and not only for ourselves, but for posterity. That trade of India which has been shifting its channels from the time of the Phoenicians to the present, is destined to shift once more, and to realize the grand idea of Columbus. The American road to India will also become the European track to that region. The European merchant, as well as the American, will fly across our continent on a straight line to China. The rich commerce of Asia will flow through our centre. And where has that commerce ever flowed without carrying wealth and dominion with it? Look at its ancient channels, and the cities which it raised into kingdoms, and the populations which upon its treasures became resplendent in science, learning, and the arts. Tyre, Sidon, Balbec, Palmyra, Alexandria, among its ancient emporiums, attest the power of this commerce to enrich, to aggrandize, and to enlighten nations. Constantinople, in the middle ages, and in the time of the crusades, was the wonder of Western Europe; and all, because she was then a thoroughfare of Asiatic commerce. Genoa and Venice, mere cities, in later time, became the match of kingdoms, and the envy of kings, from the mere divided streams of this trade of which they became the thoroughfare. Lisbon had her great day, and Portugal her preëminence during the little while that the discovery of the Cape of Good Hope put her in communication with the East. Amsterdam, the city

Wagon train heading West in a storm. For many Americans, the vast, unsettled frontier was a splendid place to start a new and better life. For others, the West was what Henry Nash Smith calls "a passage to India," one that would facilitate American expansion across the Pacific to Asia. (Courtesy of Harper's Weekly.)

of a little territory rescued from the sea, and the Seven United Provinces, not equal in extent to one of our lesser States, became great in arms, in letters, in wealth, and in power; and all upon the East India trade. And London, what makes her the commercial mistress of the world—what makes an island no larger than one of our first class States—the mistress of possessions in the four quarters of the globe—a match for half of Europe—and dominant in Asia? What makes all this, or contributes most to make it, but this same Asiatic trade? In no instance has it failed to carry the nation, or the people which possessed it, to the highest pinnacle of wealth and power, and with it the highest attainments of letters, arts, and sciences.

This imperial destiny, like the eighteenth-century dream of an American Empire, had two different aspects which seldom received equal emphasis at a given moment. There was on the one hand the world-historical mission of dominion over the seven seas, like that of Venice, or Amsterdam, or London, which could

carry a nation to greatness without regard to its internal resources and population. The theme of the passage to India, as Benton developed it during most of his career, belongs to this aspect of the notion of empire. The economic basis which it emphasizes is that of ocean-borne commerce. But the highway to the Pacific was potentially more than a means of connecting the wharves of the seaport with the warehouses of merchants in the interior. It was not only an instrument of distribution: it could also become an instrument of production, or at least of creating facilities for production, in the area through which it passed. In the conclusion of his speech of 1849 Benton for the first time took cognizance of the internal development of the West which the highway would bring about. "An American road to India through the heart of our country," he declared, "will revive upon its line all the wonders of which we have read—and eclipse them. The western wilderness, from the Pacific to the Mississippi, will start into life under its touch."

This puts the problem in an entirely new light. It is no longer a question merely of extending the maritime commerce of the United States, but also of developing the trans-Mississippi region: the transition has begun from an outward-looking to an introspective conception of empire. The idea of gaining access to the trade of Asia had served as a rationale of American expansion to the Pacific, but with the formal acquisition of Oregon in 1846 and California in 1848, expansionism had reached the natural boundary of the ocean. Its goal had been achieved and the impulse itself was ceasing to be a major concern of American society. The debate was now to become one over federal policy concerning the development of the vast new area which had been added to the national domain.

Beyond the Missouri there was no natural equivalent for the network of navigable rivers that had so magnificently furthered the agricultural occupation of the eastern half of the Mississippi Valley. The Far Western farmer would evidently have to depend on railroads to get his crops to market. But how should the railroads be built?

In this phase of the discussion Benton was joined by a man who for a five-year-period, without holding office or commanding any established organ for reaching the public, made himself a national figure through the sole agency of his thinking on the subject of a Pacific railway. This crusader was Asa Whitney, a New York merchant of New England origins who, after failing in business in the Panic of 1837, went out to the Orient as a mercantile agent and returned in 1844 with a fortune which gave him a comfortable income for the rest of his life. In January, 1845, Whitney laid before Congress a request for a gigantic land grant to finance the construction of a railway from Lake Michigan to the Pacific. The audacity of the proposal—he asked for a tract of land sixty miles wide throughout the distance to be traversed by his road—together with the spectacular publicity campaign he conducted, aroused an interest which temporarily obscured the impractical nature of his scheme.

When Whitney first entered the discussion, Benton, after twenty-five years' fervent devotion to the memory of Thomas Jefferson, was finding it difficult to understand the importance of the railroad. In a speech on the Oregon question delivered in May, 1846, which Whitney quoted with justifiable delight in a later altercation, Benton declared with all the emphasis of his momentous rhetoric: "Lewis and Clarke were sent out to discover a commercial route to the Pacific Ocean; and so judiciously was their enterprise conducted that their return route must become, and forever remain, the route of commerce. . . ." The implication was that once Jefferson had made up his mind, the geography had jolly well better get into line. Benton was willing to concede something to the wagon road of his friends the St. Louis fur traders—"the route further south, through the South Pass . . .

will be the travelling road"—but nothing could be conceded to New Yorkers and technological innovation: "commerce will take the water line . . . crossing the Rocky Mountains in latitude 47, through the North Pass." The reason why Benton showed such a monumental inability to understand the revolution in transport that was under way was that he thought in terms of a tradition, a century of preoccupation with the network of natural waterways overspreading the Mississippi Valley. St. Louis, his home, was the metropolis of the trans-Mississippi trade because it dominated the Missouri, having the same relation to that river that New Orleans had to the Mississippi. The imaginary American East India merchant of the future (a significantly old-fashioned figure who dominates Benton's thinking until near the end of his career), having come by boat up the Columbia and then by an overland portage which may just conceivably depend upon the "steam car" for a short distance in the mountains, stands at last beside the Great Falls of the Missouri, head of steamboat navigation upstream from St. Louis. Here his troubles are over. Before him he sees a thousand markets inviting his approach, each readily accessible along the rivers. What place had the railroad in such a panorama?

Yet Whitney was right in insisting that the railroad must be the technological basis both for the Asiatic trade and for large-scale settlement in the trans-Mississippi. The rivers of the Far West could not compare with those of the eastern Mississippi Valley as commercial routes. The country could not be developed by any other means than the railroad. Benton himself finally conceded the point. As we have seen, for four or five years between 1848 and 1853 he advocated a railway to the Pacific constructed by the federal government. But he opposed Whitney's scheme on the very sensible ground that no individual could safely be trusted with the power conveyed by so vast a land grant. Convinced at last that sectional rivalries made federal action to build the road impossible, Benton turned to the private capitalists he had once so strongly criticized and threw his weight into promoting a Pacific railroad corporation headed by Abbott Lawrence of Massachusetts.

A discourse which Benton delivered before the Boston Mercantile Library Association in December, 1854 (and repeated in substance before a Baltimore audience and on the floor of the House of Representatives) sets forth the final state of his thinking about westward expansion. Its most remarkable feature is its attention to the internal development of the trans-Mississippi as contrasted with the theme of the passage to India: Benton was at last renouncing his lifelong devotion to an archaic mercantilist point of view and was beginning to confront the theme of the "garden of the world" which was destined to supplant it in the main stream of American thought about the West. He brings to this new conception as contagious an enthusiasm as he had brought to the older one. Benton was not the man to do this sort of thing by halves; and the cause was one for which he was, as he said, perfectly capable of becoming a Peter the Hermit to wander about preaching a crusade. Proclaiming that a line of states will be created between the Missouri frontier and California as great as the line stretching from the Atlantic to the Mississippi, he demonstrates how each proposed far-western commonwealth abounds in natural resources. Kansas has a soil "rich like Egypt and tempting as Egypt would be if raised above the slimy flood, waved into gentle undulations, variegated with groves and meadows, sprinkled with springs, coursed by streams. . . ." In similar fashion he deals with Colorado, the lyrically beautiful parks of the Rocky Mountains, and the Interior Basin beyond, emphasizing iron and coal when he can not manage to praise the fertility of the soil, and citing the ease of irrigation by artesian wells when he concedes an inadequate rainfall.

The same procedure enables him to say of a route through the Rockies of southern Colorado still considered impracticable for a railroad, that there was "Not a tunnel to be made—a mountain to be climbed—a hill to be crossed—a swamp to be seen—or desert, or movable sand to be encountered, in the whole distance." One feels a kind of awe in the presence of a faith so triumphantly able to remove mountains; but a more appropriate attitude would be that which greets the ecstatic lover praising his mistress. For Benton was in love with the Far West. He had never seen it, except vicariously, through the delegated eyes of Frémont; but perhaps his love was only the more intense for being ideal and Platonic. We may leave him as he bedecks his mistress with jewels, fabulous cities-to-be strung upon the thread of the railway from St. Louis to San Francisco—

> the channel of Asiatic commerce which has been shifting its bed from the time of Solomon, and raising up cities and kingdoms wherever it went—(to perish when it left them)—changing its channel for the last time—to become fixed upon its shortest, safest, best, and quickest route, through the heart of our America—and to revive along its course the Tyres and Sidons, the Balbecs, Palmyras, and Alexandrias, once the seat of commerce and empire; and the ruins of which still attest their former magnificence, and excite the wonder of the oriental traveller.

Coming into the field more than twenty years after Benton had begun proclaiming the value of Oriental trade, Whitney took over Benton's main positions and added to them the fruits of two years' residence in China. Like Benton he declared that the commerce of Asia had been the foundation of all commerce since the earliest ages, controlling the rise and fall of nations, and furnishing the basis of Britain's greatness. He touched the familiar theme of how the Asiatic trade would in turn bring the United States to a peak of unexampled and permanent grandeur. "Here we stand forever," he exclaimed; "we reach out one hand to all Asia, and the other to all Europe, willing for all to enjoy the great blessings we possess, claiming free intercourse and exchange of commodities with all, seeking not to subjugate any, but *all* . . . tributary, and at our will subject to us."

A controversy between Whitney and Stephen A. Douglas, embodied in a public exchange of letters in 1845, brought out an interesting and basic disagreement between the Easterner Whitney and this emerging western leader concerning the development of the trans-Mississippi. Speaking in behalf of the frontier farmer with his half-anarchic individualism, Douglas refused to endorse Whitney's plan because it was too contrived, too consciously planned from above, too little adapted to what Douglas conceived to be the way all American frontiers must advance. A Pacific railway, he agreed, was necessary and would eventually be built. But not all at once, and not according to any rational blueprint. A Pacific railway constructed according to the principle of "squatter sovereignty," as Douglas's doctrine came to be called later when he applied it to the problem of slavery in the territories, would be the work of years. It would have to

> progress gradually, from east to west, keeping up a connected chain of communication, and following the tide of emigration, and the settlement of the country. In addition to the India and China trade, and the vast commerce of the Pacific ocean, which would pass over this route, you must create a further necessity for the road, by subduing the wilderness, and peopling it with a hardy and industrious population, who would soon have a surplus produce, without the means of getting it to market, and require, for their own consumption, immense quantities of goods and merchandize [*sic*], which they

could not obtain at reasonable rates, for want of proper facilities of transportation.

Douglas, spokesman for the West, considered the individual farmer with his primitive agriculture to be the ultimate source of social values and energies—an assumption derived, however remotely, from the agrarian tradition of Franklin and Jefferson. On the other hand, the New York merchant, Whitney, set out from the assumption that the prime source of social values and achievements is commerce. The notion seems at first glance hardly applicable to an agricultural frontier. But Whitney was as consistent as Douglas. If Douglas insisted that the individual farmer would create the Pacific railway, Whitney was as certain that only the railway could create the far-western farmer, in the sense of making him a useful member of society. The settler in the trans-Mississippi, Whitney pointed out, had no way of getting produce to market. In the wilderness, remote from civilization, destitute of comforts, he was but a "demi-savage." It was true that his labor produced food from the earth: in this limited sense the ideal of subsistence farming was valid. But since he could not "exchange with the different branches of industry," that is, had no place in the commercial system, he was not a source of wealth or power to the nation, and from the mercantilist point of view could hardly be said to exist. It was in this fashion that Whitney conceived what his friend and supporter Senator John M. Niles of Connecticut called "the *creative* power of a railroad." The railroad was the only means by which the wilderness from the Great Lakes to the Pacific could ever be developed. Without it, this immense area must remain forever useless to mankind, "being the greater part without timber, and without navigable streams to communicate with civilization or markets." Whitney was in fact so little disposed to count upon Douglas's squatters that he planned to import European laborers to construct his railway.

Walt Whitman and Manifest Destiny

Walt Whitman, the poet who gave final imaginative expression to the theme of manifest destiny, was a native and lifelong resident of the Atlantic seaboard. He was drawn into contact with the Western intellectual tradition not through firsthand experience—for he had not even traveled beyond the Mississippi when he wrote his principal poems—but through his burning conviction that the society and the literature of the United States must be adapted to the North American continent. This obsession led him to declare with Benton (and of course also with Emerson) that America must turn away from the feudal past of Europe to build a new order founded upon nature:

> I swear there is no greatness or power that does not emulate those of the earth!
> I swear there can be no theory of any account, unless it corroborate the theory of the earth!

He wrote in the preface to the first edition of *Leaves of Grass* in 1855 that the poet of America "incarnates its geography and natural life and rivers and lakes":

> Mississippi with annual freshets and changing chutes, Missouri and Columbia and Ohio and Saint Lawrence with the falls and beautiful masculine Hudson, do not embouchure where they spend themselves more than they embouchure into him. . . . When the long Atlantic coast stretches longer and the Pacific coast stretches longer he easily stretches with them north or south. He spans between them also from east to west and reflects what is between them.

As this statement implies, Whitman originally set out to sing the whole continent, East and West, North and South; and intermittently throughout his life he returned to the impartial celebration of all the regions. But the Atlantic

seaboard after all represented the past, the shadow of Europe, cities, sophistication, a derivative and conventional life and literature. Beyond, occupying the overwhelming geographical mass of the continent, lay the West, a realm where nature loomed larger than civilization and where feudalism had never been established. There, evidently, would grow up the truly American society of the future. By 1860 Whitman had become aware that his original assumptions logically implied the Western orientation inherent in the cult of manifest destiny. "These States tend inland, and toward the Western sea," he wrote, "and I will also." He made up his mind that his future audience would be found in the West: "I depend on being realized, long hence, where the broad fat prairies spread, and thence to Oregon and California inclusive." It was in inland America that he discovered the insouciance, the self-possession, the physical health which he loved. He declared that his *Leaves* were made for the trans-Mississippi region, for the Great Plains and the Rocky Mountains and the Pacific slope, and dwelt with ecstasy upon "a free original life there . . . simple diet, and clean and sweet blood, . . . litheness, majestic faces, clear eyes, and perfect physique there. . . ." Above all, he foresaw "immense spiritual results, future years, inland, spread there each side of the Anahuacs."

At the same time, Whitman had become interested in the conception of a fated course of empire leading Americans to the shores of the Pacific and bringing them into contact with Asia. In "Enfans d'Adam" he gives the ancient idea a vivid restatement:

Inquiring, tireless, seeking that yet unfound,
I, a child, very old, over waves, toward the house of maternity, the land of migrations, look afar,
Look off over the shores of my Western sea —having arrived at last where I am—the circle almost circled;

For coming westward from Hindustan, from the vales of Kashmere,
From Asia—from the north—from the God, the sage, and the hero;
From the south—from the flowery peninsulas, and the spice islands,
Now I face the old home again—looking over to it, joyous, as after long travel, growth, and sleep;
But where is what I started for, so long ago?
And why is it yet unfound?

The plaintive question at the end of this passage does not belong to the jubilant Western tradition and indeed represents but a passing moment of melancholy in Whitman himself. Three poems in the collection *Drum-Taps*, published in 1865, return to the course of empire with an optimism more appropriate to Whitman's philosophy as a whole and to the intimations of manifest destiny. "Pioneers! O Pioneers," his most celebrated although not his best poem about the westward movement, depicts the march of the pioneer army in phrases that often suggest Gilpin's description of the Great Migration to Oregon. The peoples of the Old World are weakening; the youthful and sinewy pioneers take up the cosmic burden. Having conquered the wilderness and scaled the mighty mountains, they come out upon the Pacific coast. Their advent inaugurates a new era in the history of mankind: "We debouch upon a newer, mightier world . . ."

"Years of the Unperform'd" (the title may echo Gilpin's phrase, "the *untransacted* destiny of the American people") launches the westward-moving pioneer out upon the waters of the Pacific and equips him with the weapons of a developing technology:

Never was average man, his soul, more energetic, more like a God;
Lo, how he urges and urges, leaving the masses no rest;
His daring foot is on land and set every-

where—he colonizes the Pacific, the
    archipelagoes;
With the steam-ship, the electric telegraph,
    the newspaper, the wholesale engines of
    war,
With these, and the world-spreading fac-
    tories, he interlinks all geography, all
    lands. . . .

And the idea of an American empire in the
Pacific is carried even farther in "A Broadway
Pageant," celebrating the arrival of the first
Japanese embassy in New York in 1860:

I chant the world on my Western Sea; . . .
I chant the new empire, grander than any
    before—As in a vision it comes to me;
I chant America, the Mistress—I chant a
    greater supremacy;
I chant, projected, a thousand blooming cities
    yet, in time, on those groups of sea-
    islands; . . .
I chant commerce opening, the sleep of ages
    having done its work—races, reborn, re-
    fresh'd. . . .

For the long circuit of the globe is drawing to
its close: the children of Adam have strayed
westward through the centuries, but with the
arrival of the American pioneers in the Pacific
a glorious millennium begins.

Elaborate as these ideas are, Whitman was
not yet done with the theme of the course of
empire. He returned to it in 1871 in "Passage
to India," which he said was an expression of
"what, from the first, . . . more or less lurks in
my writings, underneath every page, every line,
every where." Again he depicts the myriad
progeny of Adam and Eve moving westward
around the globe, "wandering, yearning, curious . . . with questionings, baffled, formless,
feverish—with never-happy hearts. . . ." God's
purpose, hidden from men through countless
ages, is revealed at last when the Suez Canal,
the Atlantic submarine cable, and especially

the Pacific railway connect the nations of the
earth with a single network:

The people [are] to become brothers and
    sisters,
The races, neighbors, to marry and be given
    in marriage,
The oceans to be cross'd, the distant brought
    near,
The lands to be welded together.

But the new era begun with the closing of the
cycle of history meant even more than the
mingling of peoples: it was to restore man's
lost harmony with nature. The secret of impassive earth was to be uttered at last. The
"strong, light works of engineers" encircling
the globe were to lead man into a full understanding of nature and a permanently satisfying communion with her:

All these hearts, as of fretted children, shall
    be sooth'd,
All affection shall be fully responded to—
    the secret shall be told;
All these separations and gaps shall be
    taken up, and hook'd and link'd together;
The whole earth—this cold, impassive,
    voiceless Earth, shall be completely justi-
    fied; . . .
Nature and Man shall be disjoin'd and dif-
    fused no more,
The true Son of God shall absolutely fuse
    them.

This is a mysticism difficult for the twentieth
century to follow, but it moves in a straight line
from Benton's first intimation that the course
of empire would lead the American people
westward to fabulous Asia. In view of the less
attractive inferences that other thinkers have
drawn from the notion of an American empire
in the Pacific, one is grateful for the intrepid
idealism that so triumphantly enabled Whitman to see in the march of the pioneer army a
prelude to peace and the brotherhood of
nations.

22

Roaring California

T. H. Watkins

The westward march of America's pioneers, of course, was not quite the prelude to peace and brotherhood that Walt Whitman envisioned. Instead, it was all too often a prelude to chaos and unbridled violence, as conflicts broke out in all directions between rival promoters, between whites and Indians, whites and Mexicans, lynch mobs and law-breakers, and sheriffs and desperadoes. Confrontation and violence became central themes of America's frontier experience, a place where a man was a man only when he could out-fight and outshoot his rival.

Another central theme was the search for wealth which produced so much of the violence—that unquenchable human dream of striking it rich in a single, fabulous windfall and then living on easy street for the rest of one's life. Nowhere was this more strikingly true than in the Great Gold Rush, which brought thousands of money happy forty-niners to California in a mighty human stampede. T. H. Watkins, a native Californian, vividly recreates the drama of the Gold Rush, set against the background of America's "Roaring Forties."

"The farmers have thrown aside their plows, the lawyers their briefs, the doctors their pills, the priests their prayerbooks, and all are now digging gold."

It was a time for large excitements. The American 1840s was a decade as filled with tumult, change, and contrast as any in the nation's history. Ferment of one kind or another touched every area of life. Politically, the Whig Party —born as the last gasp of Federalism—was steadily crumbling, shaking down its components into what would become the Republican Party in the mid-1850s and, with startling regularity, alternating power with the Democratic Party, itself struggling in a welter of factionalism. The slavery issue began to take on the overtones of the emotional battleground it would become, as politicians of every ilk set up a cacophony over the question of the annexation of Texas and its effect on the balance of power between North and South. And in the great cities mechanics of political corruption, of votes bought and sold, of payoffs and graft at all levels were a harbinger of days to come.

It was a decade that saw America's first large push across the great unknown of the trans-Mississippi West to hopeful Edens in Oregon and California. By 1845 the American population in Oregon alone had reached six thousand, with another two thousand in California. Pioneers in the true sense, entire families had yanked up their eastern roots and replanted them in a new land with an eye toward building the country—and, not incidentally, increasing their lot in this world. The emigration combined with a time of national muscle, the nation's first thrust toward continentalism. With a combination of belligerence and negotiation, the expansionistic Polk Administration

From *Gold and Silver in the West* by T. H. Watkins. © 1971 by The American West Publishing Company. Used by permission of Crown Publishers, Inc.

carved the Oregon Territory out of British land in 1846; and in May of that year, the United States commenced war with Mexico, ostensibly because American lives had been taken at Matamoros, near the Texas-Mexican border, but in fact as a deliberate extension of the expansionist policies of James K. Polk and his supporters; they called it "Manifest Destiny."

Two years, one hundred million dollars, and eleven thousand American lives later (and no one knows how many dead Mexicans), the United States owned most of what would come to be known as the American West, including California. It did not come without cost to America's self-satisfied image as a nonaggressive nation; Ulysses S. Grant, who had fought on the plains of Mexico, echoed a wide base of opinion when he said, "I do not think there was ever a more wicked war than that waged by the United States on Mexico." But it was done, dissent notwithstanding, and no one was about to give the West back.

Economically, the country was in a miasma of confusion. Banking and currency had never quite recovered from the assaults of the administration of Andrew Jackson in the 1830s, when he set out to cripple the Bank of the United States on antimonopolistic grounds. Moreover, a rising industrialism was beginning to challenge the dominance of agriculture in American life, a conflict reflected in the question of the tariff, which was picked up and booted about by politicians. Speculation in land, stocks, and bonds flourished almost without restriction, lending an air of generalized hysteria to the economic scene; bubbles burst all around, and bankruptcies of entire states were the order of the day.

Adding to the confusion was the country's first significant experience in mass immigration, as refugees from Old World agonies, most of them Irish and German, poured into the cities of the Atlantic seaboard. Annual immigration into the country during the 1840s frequently exceeded 100,000, and in 1848, the

year of the Irish potato famine, more than 296,000 arrived—this in a country with a population of only a little over twenty million. The Irish in particular had little to offer their new homeland but muscle, and labor was a glut on the market. Those who could not make their way to the Old Northwest, where employment waited, clustered in enclaves of poverty in New York, Boston, Philadelphia, and Washington, exchanging one misery for another; ghetto was not yet an American word, but it was a reality.

Amid this tangle of political and economic conditions, social ferment sputtered like the witches' cauldron in *Macbeth*. Virulent heresies assaulted the tenets of respectable Protestantism; Wesleyism proliferated and Millerites stood on a hill in baskets, waiting for God to pluck them up to heaven like so many bushels of grapes. Mesmerism, phrenology, and any odd number of supernatural manifestations excited the public imagination, and reformers promulgated the restructuring of civilization, chief among them the Fourierites, who advocated the redivision of society into phalanxes of not less than three hundred persons and not more than eighteen hundred.

More significant agitation, however, was brought to bear on such questions as prison reform, welfare, medicine, elimination of the death penalty, abolition of slavery, and women's rights, with varying degrees of success. Perhaps the most dramatic of all the social phenomena exhibited in these years was the anti-Catholic Native American movement, a reaction to Irish immigration that produced a dismal series of riots throughout the urbanized East, culminating in the Philadelphia riots of 1844, in which thirteen people died.

Accelerating more rapidly than could be chronicled, alternatively arrogant and insecure, confused and purposeful, the American civilization was experiencing a kind of adolescence in the 1840s, making a painful transition from the agrarian age to the industrial age. It would be a mistake to assume—as some historians

have done—that the unsettled nature of life in this period somehow "caused" the California Gold Rush, that it would not have been a catharsis on so grand a scale had it occurred at a more stable period. Given the amount of gold that the new territory provided, and given man's long history of dreaming out the golden fleece, the Gold Rush would have been a phenomenon to alter history no matter when it occurred. It is fitting, however, that its excitement rounded out one of the most profoundly complex decades in American history.

It was the climax of an era—and the beginning of another.

It was a January morning in 1848, one of those bitter, crackling-cold mornings typical of winter in the Sacramento Valley. James Marshall, an itinerant carpenter who was constructing a sawmill on the South Fork of the American River for Johann Augustus Sutter, was taking his usual walk along the new millrace when he spotted "something shining in the bottom of the ditch," as he later recalled it. "I reached my hand down and picked it up; it made my heart thump, for I was certain it was gold. The piece was about half the size and the shape of a pea. Then I saw another piece in the water. After taking it out, I sat down and began to think right hard." After thinking, he took the gold and showed it to his workmen. "Boys," he said, "I believe I have found a gold mine!"

A few days later he rode down to New Helvetia, Sutter's walled outpost of empire near the confluence of the Sacramento and American rivers. Sutter, a Swiss emigré who had persuaded the Mexican authorities to grant him a stupendous amount of land in the valley, was nearly as excited as Marshall, but fearful that news of the discovery would inundate his land with eager hopefuls. He attempted to enforce some kind of secrecy on the whole business, but could not resist prattling about it himself to his servants. By March, the news was out—

and was greeted by a thundering skepticism. On May 20 the *California Star*, one of San Francisco's two minuscule newspapers, said, with regrettable grammar and spelling, that it was all a "sham, a supurb takein as was ever got up to guzzle the gullible."

After all, this was not California's first gold discovery. In 1842, one Francisco Lopez, who had studied mining in Mexico City, had discovered gold in San Feliciano Canyon in the San Fernando Valley, causing a minor rush from Sonora, Mexico. But the deposits in the San Fernando hills had been so shallow that they were worked out in three years. Surely, Marshall's discovery would prove just another flash-in-the-pan.

But it didn't, and by the end of May attitudes had changed considerably. One of the reasons may well have been Sam Brannan, an entrepreneur and Mormon backslider who had started a small general store near New Helvetia and who knew a good thing when he saw it. One day near the end of the month, legend has it, Brannan came galloping into San Francisco, waving a bottle full of nuggets over his head and shouting, "Gold! Gold on the American River!" The story has the ring of apocrypha, but *something* had certainly occurred. San Francisco and Monterey witnessed an exodus of hysterical proportions as able-bodied gold-seekers laid hands on whatever was available for getting at the stuff and headed for the American River. Walter Colton, the *alcalde* at Monterey, remarked in disgust that "the farmers have thrown aside their plows, the lawyers their briefs, the doctors their pills, the priests their prayerbooks, and all are now digging gold."

Sutter's nervous fears were justified by the middle of July, as more than three thousand miners trampled what he liked to think of as his land. Colonel Richard B. Mason, interim military governor of California, investigated the situation in that month, and described one of the diggings in a dispatch to the Secretary

Sluice mining in California in 1852. "This gold digging is no child's play," one miner recorded, "but down right hard labor, and a man to make anything must work harder than any day laborer in the States." The Chinese immigrants at right probably came to California during the great boom of 1849 and 1850. By 1851 there were over 25,000 in California, most of them looking for gold like the whites. The Chinese usually indentured themselves to get to California, only to encounter widespread anti-Chinese feeling by the whites there. From 1851 on, the Chinese were systematically discriminated against in California, having to pay a monthly tax levied on "immigrant miners" and suffering sporadic lynchings and semi-pogroms. (Courtesy of the California State Library.)

of War in Washington: "The hill sides were thickly strewn with canvass tents and bush arbours; a store was erected, and several boarding shanties in operation. The day was intensely hot, yet about two hundred men were at work in the full glare of the sun, washing for gold." As word spread down the coast, thousands more streamed into California from Mexico and South America, until by the end of the year there were at least thirteen thousand scrambling over the foothills like so many beetles on a corpse.

They were chasing no gossamer fable. The gold was there in quantities never before heard of on the American continent. Men were hauling out of the ground as much as eight hundred

dollars a day in such locations as Woods' Dry Diggings, near the present town of Auburn northeast of Sacramento, and it has been estimated that by the end of 1848 no less—and possibly more—than six million dollars had been grubbed out by the fortunate early arrivals. This was the stuff of empire, and the military authorities in California made haste to send word east to Washington.

In July, Commodore Thomas ap Catesby Jones sent Naval Lieutenant Edward F. Beale across Mexico with letters and a sample of California gold. In August, Colonel Mason sent Army Lieutenant Lucien Loeser from San Francisco with similar letters—and a tea caddy packed with 230 ounces of gold. Beale made it to the states first, arriving in Mobile, Alabama, in early September, after a wild and frequently dangerous journey. Somewhat more casually, Loeser sailed around the Horn and arrived in New Orleans in late November. Beale went on to Washington in plenty of time to pass along his report before President James K. Polk's annual message to Congress on December 5, and Polk was able to give official sanction to rumors already spreading like a cholera epidemic: "The accounts of the abundance of gold in that territory are of such an extraordinary character as would scarcely command belief, were they not corroborated by the authentic reports of officers in the public service. . . ." A few days later, Loeser arrived with his 230 ounces of gold, worth at least $3,500 on the open market. The combination was irresistible; the dream was revived.

The California Gold Rush was a national experience rarely matched in American history—and in the nineteenth century only the Civil War surpassed its impact. It was a kind of madness, a thirst for treasure, which such critics of the movement as Henry David Thoreau characterized as nothing more or less than simple-minded greed. Throughout the winter and spring of 1849, newspaper columns throughout the country fairly screamed news of California and its gold, together with comment on the effect it was having. "The coming of the Messiah, or the dawn of the Millenium," one editor exclaimed in awe, "would not have excited anything like the interest." And James Gordon Bennett's New York *Herald*, the most influential paper in the country, proclaimed as early as January that "men are rushing head over heels towards the El Dorado on the Pacific—that wonderful California, which sets the public mind almost on the highway to insanity. . . . Every day, men of property and means are advertising their possessions for sale, in order to furnish them with means to reach that golden land."

They were, indeed. In December and January, thousands of easterners streamed into seaport towns, booking passage on anything that would float—and not a few on tubs whose seaworthiness was questionable at best. Between December 14, 1848, and January 18, 1849, 61 ships with an average of 50 passengers each sailed for California from New York City, Boston, Salem, Philadelphia, Baltimore, and Norfolk. Ships in ports all over the world, encountering news of the rush, canceled their commitments and sailed for the east coast of the United States, eager to grab off their share of the passenger explosion. In February, 60 ships sailed from New York alone, and 70 from Philadelphia. In that same month, a Pacific Mail Company steamship entered the Golden Gate with 365 passengers, the first argonauts; not long afterwards, one day saw no less than 45 shiploads of passengers anchor off Yerba Buena Cove, and by the end of the year more than 700 ships had arrived, bearing a total of at least 45,000 gold-seekers.*

* The demand for transportation during these months provided a good living for New York cartoonists, who lampooned the obsession by coming up with any number of outlandish devices for travel, including enormous rubber bands and miniature rocket ships, but at

Those who went by sea had two basic choices. The first was to board a ship at one or another eastern port, sail to Chagres or Aspinwall on the east coast of the Isthmus of Panama, cross the Isthmus by foot, muleback, and *bungoes* poled by natives through the boggy, mosquito-ridden interior, arrive at the venerable white city of Panama, gleaming like a mirage above the ocean, and finally catch a San Francisco-bound steamer for the last leg of the journey. Thousands chose this route, on the conviction that it was the quickest way to the California mines—and everyone was in a crashing hurry, as Bayard Taylor, one of the travelers in late 1849, reported in *El Dorado; or, Adventures in the Path of Empire.* At Chagres, he wrote, a returning Californian had just arrived "with a box containing $22,000 in gold-dust, and a four-pound lump in one hand. The impatience and excitement of the passengers, already at a high pitch, was greatly increased by his appearance. Life and death were small matters compared with immediate departures from Chagres. Men ran up and down the beach, shouting, gesticulating and getting feverishly impatient at the deliberate habits of the natives, as if their arrival in California would thereby be at all hastened."

Hurry, at this point, was wasted effort, as most of them learned on arrival in Panama City. Hundreds of anxious, waiting goldseekers clustered in and about the city, living in scraps of tents and watching their precious pokes being eaten away to nothing as the weeks passed. The experience of one of them, Howard C. Gardiner, was typical. He left New York on March 15, 1849, with eight hundred other pas-

sengers and $475; he arrived in San Francisco on July 26 with exactly six dollars left—most of the rest having disappeared during his six-week delay in Panama City. Delay was more than frustrating, however—it was dangerous. Panama City was a death-trap. The creeping horror of cholera, which would haunt all the land and sea routes of the Gold Rush, took its toll of both Panamanians and travelers throughout the late spring and summer of 1849, adding its grisly impetus to the generalized anxiety, as Bayard Taylor noted: "There were about seven hundred emigrants waiting for passage when I reached Panama. All the tickets the steamer could possibly receive had been issued and so great was the anxiety to get on, that double price, $600, was frequently paid for a ticket to San Francisco. . . . I was well satisfied to leave Panama at that time; the cholera, which had already carried off one-fourth of the native population, was making havoc among the Americans, and several . . . lay at the point of death."

The second route was entirely by sea, south to Cape Horn at the tip of South America and north to San Francisco—through some of the meanest and most unpredictable waters then known to navigation. It was an 18,000-mile voyage and took anywhere from six to eight months (it would be several years before the great clipper ships cut it down to a little over three months). Many of the vessels were in foul condition, a matter blithely ignored by shipowners hungry for the passenger trade, as historian John Bach McMaster reported: "Every ship, brig, schooner, sloop that was half fit to go to sea was scraped, painted, fitted with bunks or cabins, and advertised as an A-1 fast-sailing, copper-bottomed, copper-nailed vessel, bound for San Francisco. . . ." They were inadequately rigged for long journeys, displayed a tendency to roll badly in heavy seas (and called "butter tubs" for that reason), possessed a collection of leaks that kept pumps busy for months, and were manned by crews patched

least one inventor, Rufus Porter, quite seriously proposed the construction of what he called an "Aerial Transport," a dirigible-like airship which, he maintained, would "have a capacity to carry from 50 to 100 passengers, at a speed of 60 to 100 miles per hour. . . . The Transport is expected to make a trip to the gold region and back in seven days." For one reason or another, including the utter impossibility of the whole thing, Porter's airship was never built.

together with hopelessly inexperienced hands whose only visible qualification was a desire to get their hands on gold the minute anchor was dropped in San Francisco Bay (a few thousand did precisely that, or attempted to; by the end of 1849, the bay was jammed with some six hundred ships whose crews had lit out for the foothills, sometimes with their captains a step or two ahead of them).

Conditions on board these floating incompetents were dismal in the extreme. Passengers were crammed into every available crevice; hundreds were booked passage on ships designed for scores. Food was as primitive as expedience could make it, and there was rarely enough, even for those willing and able to pay extra. Water supplies invariably reached the point of rationing long before sight of the Golden Gate. Overcrowding, hunger, thirst, scurvy, dysentery, seasickness, and the dark presence of cholera combined with boredom and frustration to give most ships the characteristics of a purgatory; for most, only the hope of gold enabled them to tolerate a situation that otherwise would have disintegrated their nerves.

For overland travelers, conditions were no better, although a man was somewhat less at the mercy of the elements and usually subject to no one's incompetence but his own. At least half, and probably more, of those who came to California in 1849 journeyed by one or another of several land routes. One took them through the Southwest, over the Santa Fe Trail to Santa Fe, then west across the deserts to the Gila River, down that to its juncture with the Colorado, across another desert to San Diego, and finally north to the mines. Probably fewer than ten thousand made this journey.

One of the three routes across Mexico attracted others: in the north, from Brownsville, Texas, across the states of Tamaulipas, Nuevo Leon, Coahuila, Chihuahua, and Sonora to the Colorado River; in the center, from Vera Cruz or Tampico to Mexico City, then up the Central Plateau; or in the south, across the continent to the western seaports of Acapulco, San Blas, or Mazatlán, where sea passage to California might (and, too often, might not) be obtained. Until recent years, it has been assumed that very few took any of the Mexican routes, but in *The El Dorado Trail*, historian Ferol Egan estimates that at least fifteen thousand trekked across the broken desert stretches of Mexico.

Most land travelers, however, followed the old Emigrant Trail that had taken land-seeking pioneers to Oregon and California during the previous fifteen years. From various jumping-off points on the Missouri River, this followed the valley of the Platte River to the North Fork, crossed to Chimney Rock and Fort Laramie, then past Independence Rock, through the Devil's Gate and South Pass to Fort Bridger.

Here, the emigrant had two choices for getting to the Humboldt River in northern Nevada: he could take the Hastings Cut-off along the south shore of the Great Salt Lake, across the desert, around the Humboldt Mountains, and down the south branch to the main river; or he could go from Fort Hall, down the Snake or Lewis River to the headwaters of the Humboldt, then down that to its sink (some left the river at the great bend and headed north through Lassen's Pass to the Pitt River and the Sacramento Valley). Like those who used the Hastings Cut-off, they then headed west across the forty-mile stretch of desert to the Truckee River, and finally across the Sierra Nevada into the land of yellow promise.

In the spring, thousands poured into outfitting points on the Missouri River—Independence, Westport, St. Joseph, St. Louis—clamoring in the narrow streets and gladdening the mercantile hearts of tradesmen in wagons, horses, mules, oxen, guns, powder, broadcloth, salt pork, bacon, flour, sugar, tobacco, picks, pans, shovels, and miserably complicated and utterly useless contraptions peddled as sure-fire gold

extractors. Some came as individual adventurers, but most as members of traveling companies formed in their hometowns (in some cases practically depopulating towns of their eligible bachelors), representing a geographical spectrum from New England, through the Old Northwest, the Mississippi Valley, and the South.

The names they gave these companies matched the grandiloquence of their dreams. Typical were the Congress and California Mutual Protective Association and the Sagamore and California Mining and Trading Company, both of which were armed and uniformed and operating under strict military rules (which, also typically, tended to disintegrate under the pressures of the trail, leaving most wagon companies riven by strife and bickering of feline dimensions).

Estimates on the number of wagons that crossed over the Missouri throughout the month of May and the first two weeks of June vary considerably; the Missouri *Republican* announced the total as nearly 5,800—but another contemporary observer estimated it at 12,000 for the month of May alone. Since each wagon generally had a complement of four men (and in very rare cases, women and children), these figures would put the total of emigrants somewhere between 23,000 and 48,000.

Whatever the total was, it was enough to make this the greatest transcontinental migration in American history. It was three to five months of brutal travel by wagon, over deserts, rivers, and mountains of a magnitude unknown to the pioneer experience. Thirst, hunger, and simple exhaustion all took their toll, and while the Indians proved to be less of a problem than many had anticipated, they did have the unnerving habit of picking off stragglers. More emigrants, however, died as victims of their own inexperience; the number of drownings and accidental shootings reached appalling heights. The greatest killer of them all, of

course, was cholera, carried west from the disease-ridden valley of the Mississippi. At least two thousand, and perhaps as many as five thousand, died of this agony before they ever reached the Continental Divide at South Pass in Wyoming.

The trail to California was a great highway, crowded with a sea of wagons. The prairies two hundred miles west of St. Joseph, one observer reported, were "glittering with wagons, carriages, tents, and animals." And they left behind far more than ruts to mark their passing. Among the other stupidities put forward as cold fact by dozens of so-called "guide" books thrown together by publishing sharks and purchased by the fistful, were lists of necessary equipment for the overland traveler. Some of these smacked of something straight out of *Alice in Wonderland*, noted Ray Allen Billington (in the August 1967 issue of *The American West*); many of these mendacious pamphlets, he says, "encouraged the natural proclivity of the emigrants to overload their wagons with nonessentials; travelers were advised not only to burden themselves with excessive quantities of flour and bacon, but to take an alcohol stove for use when buffalo chips were wet, a sheet iron stove, two India-rubber boats large enough to float a wagon across swollen streams, wading boots, mosquito bars, an air mattress, a rubber cloth to protect the wagon during rains, a fly trap, and even (in one English guide book) an Etna stove large enough to boil water for two cups of tea, 'the most refreshing thing possible after a long and fatiguing day's journey.'"

The result of all this was highway littering on a scale that passes belief, even in this age of discarded beer cans and abandoned automobiles. The farther they went, the more they threw away; for three thousand miles, the trail was cluttered with boxes, barrels, trunks, wagon wheels, cooking utensils, stoves, gridirons, carpenter's tools, anvils, crowbars, picks, shovels, gold-washing machines and bake-

ovens, together with abandoned and burned wagons, rotting food, including great piles of rancid bacon slabs, and the carcasses of hundreds and hundreds of dead animals—enough, in fact, that a blind man might have been able to make it to California with nothing but the stench to show him the way. "If I had the property which has been sacrificed within 50 miles of here by those who followed the directions of the 'Guides,'" one traveler commented, "I would never go on to California."

By the time most of them did arrive, they had gone through the closest thing to hell on earth that any would ever experience, as suggested by the letter of one J. L. Stephens, an emigrant from Marietta, Ohio, who had survived long enough to write from Sacramento in September: "The hardships of the overland route to California are beyond conception. Care and suspense, pained anxiety, fear of losing animals and leaving one to foot it and pack his 'duds' on his back, begging provisions, fear of being left in the mountains to starve and freeze to death, and a thousand other things which no one thinks of until on the way, are things of which I may write and you may read, but they are nothing to the reality."

Whether they came by sea or land, then, the trip to California was for most of the forty-niners a desperate adventure, one that took an incredible toll of their physical, mental, and financial resources. "One prime wonder of the California gold rush," historian David Lavender has written, "is that so many people survived it." Having survived it, what the ninety thousand or more found waiting at the end of their painful journeying was enough to wither any man's dream.

The problem was simple enough: too many people and not enough gold. The loose surface gold, whose gleaming accessibility had given rise to the great rush in the first place, had been so thoroughly picked over by early 1849 that there simply was not enough to go around by the time intoxicated easterners could make it to the new Golconda. Their bitterness, understandably enough, was profound. "The greater part that you read in relation to this country," one disappointed miner wrote as early as September, 1849, "is *false;* and this everyone . . . will testify. The gold is here, but no man ever *dug* a dollar who did not earn it—the gold digging is a lottery sure enough. Some men make a fortune in a short time, but others in ten years would not make a cent. Of those who will leave here, the proportion will be scarcely one in five who will leave with any money. . . ."

And another remembered that "sudden disappointment on reaching the mines not only did sink the heart but sometimes the minds of the gold seekers. The abrupt dashing of expectations—the sudden wrecking of gorgeous visions that possessed and illumined the imagination—were as falling resurrectionless like Lucifer from gilded Heaven into the gulf of dark despair."

Still, the dream was hard to abandon, and at least forty thousand stubborn hopefuls made their way to the mining region, which spread throughout the lumpy, rolling foothills of the Sierra Nevada, from the Feather River in the north to the Merced in the south, an area virtually crawling with miners, who went from one tangled ravine to another, one river and creek bed to another, convinced that treasure lay just over the next hogback ridge; they were wanderers with the light of tomorrow in their eyes. They sought wealth that could be picked up, in Mark Twain's phrase, "with a long-handled shovel," but what most of them found was little more gold than could keep them in grub for a day at a time—and this obtained only after back-breaking effort.

"This gold digging is no child's play," one wrote in his journal, "but down right hard labor, and a man to make anything must work harder than any day laborer in the States." Another gave a graphic picture of the marginal

nature of the whole business: "My diggings were about eighteen inches of bedrock. I managed to crevice and dig out about a dozen pans full per day from which about an ounce was daily realized. Out of this it required about $10 per day to supply my food, which was usually beef or pickled pork, hard bread, and coffee. By extra economy I sometimes managed to subsist on $8 per day."

Since the price of gold had been fixed at sixteen dollars the ounce, the chances of a man making a profit of more than five or six dollars a day were pretty anemic—and while this was as much as twice the salary he could expect to make as a laborer in the States, it was hardly enough to justify the dreams of Golconda that had led him west.

The civilization these wanderers erected was as ephemeral as the wisps of dream. Bustling little camps popped up like mushrooms at every real or imagined "strike," cheapjack municipalities whose existence had all the geographic relevance of a village erected in *Gulliver's Travels*, as noted by one man who had spent five years in the gold country: "What a contrast do these funny little villages present, to the eye of one habituated to the sleepy agricultural towns of other countries; built of all kinds of possible materials, shapes and sizes, and in any spot, no matter how inconvenient, where the first store-keeper chose to pitch himself. Sometimes they are found on a broad flat with no suburb visible, squeezed together as though the land had originally been purchased by the inch, the little streets so crooked and confined, a wheelbarrow could scarcely be made to go through them; sometimes again, they are made up of detached buildings, forming an extended village two or three miles long. . . . Some, too, are quite invisible until you discover them at your feet buried in a deep chasm."

The frequently ludicrous names these towns were given suggests their transient nature— Jimtown, Hangtown, Bedbug, Shinbone Peak, Poker Flat, Murderer's Gulch, Delirium Tre-

mens, Whiskey Diggings, Rough and Ready, You Bet—for they were hostages to uncertain fortune, to be taken no more seriously than the outsized practical jokes typical of men among whom the juices of life ran strong.*

They were at the mercy of more than their own dreams. One of the things men learned relatively early was that there was more gold to be had from the goldseekers than from the Sierran hills. Not only the rapidly-building metropolises of San Francisco and Sacramento, but every mining camp scattered through the Mother Lode was a mecca for entrepreneurs with an eye out for the main chance—which, more often than not, meant skinning the miner for all he was worth. More than one observer remarked at the "crowds of lawyers, small tradesmen, mechanics, and others, who swarm in every little camp, even of the most humble description, soliciting the patronage of the public—of whom they often form at least one half."

It was a seller's market par excellence; the simple necessities of life went for fabulous prices, and such amenities as eggs could bring as much as seventy-five cents each. Other appetites possessed by generally womanless, lonely young men far away from home could also be satisfied—and at suitably accelerated prices. Saloons, dance halls, gambling dens, and bordellos were as much a part of the proper mining camp as an assay office or a volunteer fire department. Any man with seemly respect for the laws of supply and demand could amass a comfortable estate, and some of the most permanent fortunes in California history were built on a mercantile foundation—of one kind or another.

For such as these, and for those few who had come early enough—or coming late, had been

---

* A remarkable number have survived, however— either in bits and pieces or as such nearly-intact relics as Columbia, surely one of the most successful examples of wholesale preservation west of Williamsburg, Virginia.

lucky enough, to gather sufficient capital to exploit to the full the potential of the state's mineral wealth—the California Gold Rush was a smashing success. For innumerable others, it was little short of personal tragedy, as suggested by the journal entry of one Ananias Rogers, who wrote in despair from the mines in 1852: "I am solitary & alone. Am I never to see my loved ones again? If I had determined to make a permanent residence in this valley [the Sacramento] I might now have been well off . . . but my whole anxiety was to make a sudden raise and return to my family. This I undertook to do by mining. This is certainly the most uncertain of any business in the world. . . . Indeed I do not know what to do. Oh that I could once more be with my family. Alas, I fear this may never be. Oh me, I am weak in body & I fear worse in mind. . . ."

No one knows what happened to Ananias Rogers. It may be that he did make his way back to his family. If so, he returned, like thousands of others (twenty-three thousand in 1852 alone), broken in spirit and perhaps in body. They had arrived in California young; most of them returned, like men from the agonies of war, sobered and perhaps matured by the follies of greed that had led them west. Those who remained—by choice or simply because they could not afford to return—found themselves victimized by geology. The bulk of the gold remaining after the early placer regions had been worked over (and there was a great deal of it) was at the bottom of rivers whose courses had to be changed to make it available, imbedded in hills that had to be washed away with powerful streams of water, or locked in quartz veins in the earth, where only deep mining could get it out—all processes that required a considerable capital investment, sophisticated technology, and an extensive labor force.

The American Everyman had none of these, and many were forced to compromise their dreams by joining the working classes, employed by mining companies whose owners resided in the red plush luxury of San Francisco, or as itinerant laborers for farmers who had staked out sweeping vistas of farmland in the coastal and interior valleys, or as clerks for merchants who had been canny enough to keep their hands off the shovel and their eyes on the till.

Others continued to wander the pockets and crannies of the west for years, refusing to give up their hopes and, in their "prospecting," giving birth to a name and a tradition. And others, we will never know how many, were driven to suicide or to the slow death of alcoholism and the netherworld of the half-life.

This is a dismal picture, certainly, and one not wholly representative of California life in the early years. Yet it is a picture that has too often been obscured by the electric excitement of the Gold Rush—a kind of lesson in the ironies of something for nothing.

The year 1852 is generally considered to be the "end" of the California Gold Rush. By then, the fact that gold was not exactly lying about on the ground for any fool to pick up had become obvious even in the East. The frantic emigration that had raised California's population from about 14,000 in 1848 to 223,856 in 1852 had begun to taper off by the end of the year, although the period between 1852 and 1860 would still see an average of more than 30,000 people a year enter the state.

In the four years after its discovery, California's mines produced more than $220,000,000 in gold—more than twice the cost of the Mexican War, and more than enough to establish the state as a powerful economic force in the nation. That power would continue. Between 1849 and 1900, production in the state's mines never fell below $11,200,000 per year, bringing its total production to more than $1,300,000,000 in that half century. If she had possessed no other assets but gold, that pro-

ductivity alone would have guaranteed California a voice in the affairs of the nation at a time when most of the trans-Mississippi West was but little removed from *terra incognita*.

In fact, California gold changed the course of American history. The slow, steady movement toward the West that had characterized the previous seventy-five years of the nation's life was interrupted violently by a sudden leap to the western edge of the continent. Motives and methods that had typified the Westward Movement were distorted; those who came to California were light-years removed from the kind of pioneers described by Henry Clay in 1842: "Pioneers of a more adventurous character, advancing before the tide of emigration, penetrate into the uninhabited regions of the West. They apply the axe to the forest, which falls before them, or the plough to the prairie, deeply sinking its share in the unbroken wild grasses in which it abounds. They build houses, plant orchards, enclose fields, cultivate the earth, and rear up families around them."

The forty-niners couldn't have cared less about cultivating anything except their own purses. Rank amateurs in the techniques of the Westward Movement, they were not settlers, but gamblers with a single obsession: to strike it rich in California and return to their homes in the East with a stake to take them through the rest of life in ease and luxury. The dream was very nearly a moral imperative; in the eyes of most of them, it would have been a crime against themselves, their families, and their futures to have ignored the lorelei of gold.

They came from all walks of life—and from most of the major countries of the Western world: there were Mexicans, Chileans, Peruvians, Frenchmen, Australians, Russians, and Germans among them, not to mention Chinese —a veritable grab bag from all the recesses of the civilized world. They were young, most of them in their twenties, and a startling number of them in their teens. Most came from solid, if not affluent backgrounds; after all, it took money, quite a bit of money for the time, to get to California. It was an investment in the future, an act of faith similar to that of today's suburbanite, who buys stock on margin and hocks himself to the teeth in the anticipation of rewards to come.

For too many, anticipation ended in the misery of ruined hopes. Yet it doesn't really matter. California gold was real, profoundly real, and it reinforced all the dreams that men had dreamed since Coronado.

23

To Sing a Song of Death

Dee Brown

Perhaps the most unhappy chapter in the history of the West was the way white Americans treated the Indians. American Indian policy, though, must be seen in the context of the entire European conquest of the New World, a conquest that began with Columbus who gave the people the name "Indios" and kidnapped ten San Salvador Indians, taking them back to Spain so they could learn the white man's ways. In the ensuing four centuries, as Dee Brown wrote in *Bury My Heart at Wounded Knee,* "several million Europeans and their descendants undertook to enforce their ways upon the people of the New World," and when these people would not accept European ways, they were fought, enslaved, or exterminated.

Whites in North America joined the conquest in the colonial period, when they drove the eastern tribes back into the interior, a pattern of "Indian removal" that was continuously repeated in the eighteenth and nineteenth centuries. When Jefferson came to power, as Ray Allen Billington observed in his narrative of the War of 1812, he began an official United States policy of Indian removal either by treaty or outright warfare. But the most impassioned champion of removal was Andrew Jackson, whom the Indians called "Sharp

Knife." Jackson was an incorrigible Indian hater; in his frontier years he had waged war against the Five Civilized Tribes (the Cherokees, Choctaws, Chickasaws, Creeks, and Seminoles), but they still clung to their tribal lands in the South when Jackson took office. At once he announced that these tribes must be sent away to "an ample district west of the Mississippi," and Congress responded with a law which embodied Jackson's recommendations. In a subsequent act, passed in 1830, Congress guaranteed that all that part of the United States west of the Mississippi "and not within the states of Missouri and Louisiana or the Territory of Arkansas" would constitute a permanent Indian frontier.

But settlers moved into Indian country before Washington could put the law into effect. So United States policy makers were obliged to shift the "permanent Indian frontier" from the Mississippi to the ninety-fifth meridian, again promising that everything west of this imaginary line would belong to the Indians "for as long as trees grow and water flows." In the years that followed, eastern and western tribes alike suffered from the inexorable westward march of the American whites. In the late 1830s, United States soldiers rounded up the civilized Cherokees and herded them west into Indian country, on an icy winter trek in which one of four Indians died. They called it their "trail of tears." But scarcely had the Cherokees and the other eastern tribes settled behind their permanent frontier when United States soldiers marched across it on their way to fight Mexico. At the same time, scores of pioneers crossed it as well, heading over the Oregon and Santa Fe trails to find new lives for themselves. To justify these breaches of the permanent Indian frontier, white Americans invoked Manifest Destiny, contending that they were the dominant race and so were responsible for the Indians— "along with their lands, their forests, and their mineral wealth." God wished the white men to have all the lands of the West, because they knew how to use the soil and the pagan Indians did not. Any pagans who challenged the white man's "destined use of the soil" deserved the retribution of Christian violence.

In truth, white-Indian relations from the 1850s to 1890 were rife with violence. After gold was

334

discovered in California, forty-niners literally exterminated the Digger Indians who got in their way. And prospectors who raced to gold strikes in Colorado did the same to Indians in that mountainous region. By the 1860s—the decade of the Civil War—the whites had penetrated both the southern and northern flanks of the "permanent Indian frontier" and white miners had occupied the center. At this time there were about 300,000 Indians in the United States, most of them living west of the Mississippi. It is estimated that their numbers had diminished from one-half to two-thirds since the first settlers had arrived in Virginia and New England. The remaining Indians were now trapped between white populations in the East and on the Pacific coast. During and after the Civil War, running battles broke out between the Indians and the expanding white populations, which resulted in the near liquidation of the red men.

One episode in those Indian conflicts took place in Colorado and involved the Cheyennes. In the old days, these people had lived in Minnesota. But with the coming of the white man, they divided, the Northern Cheyennes moving west to share the Bighorn and Powder River country with the Teton Sioux. The Southern Cheyennes drifted below the Platte River, erecting villages on the Kansas and Colorado plains. Dee Brown recounts what happened to these Southern Cheyennes when the whites came there in the 1850s and 1860s.

———————

In 1851 the Cheyennes, Arapahos, Sioux, Crows, and other tribes met at Fort Laramie with representatives of the United States and agreed to permit the Americans to establish roads and military posts across their territory. Both parties to the treaty swore "to maintain good faith and friendship in all their mutual intercourse, and to make an effective and last-

From Chapter 4 in *Bury My Heart at Wounded Knee* by Dee Brown. Copyright © 1970 by Dee Brown. Reprinted by permission of Holt, Rinehart and Winston, Inc.

ing peace." By the end of the first decade following the treaty signing, the white men had driven a hole through the Indian country along the valley of the Platte River. First came the wagon trains and then a chain of forts; then the stagecoaches and a closer-knit chain of forts; then the pony-express riders, followed by the talking wires of the telegraph.

In that treaty of 1851 the Plains Indians did not relinquish any rights or claims to their lands, nor did they "surrender the privilege of hunting, fishing or passing over any of the tracts of country heretofore described." The Pike's Peak gold rush of 1858 brought white miners by the thousands to dig yellow metal out of the Indian's earth. The miners built little wooden villages everywhere, and in 1859 they built a big village which they called Denver City. Little Raven, an Arapaho chief who was amused by the activities of white men, paid a visit to Denver; he learned to smoke cigars and to eat meat with a knife and fork. He also told the miners he was glad to see them getting gold, but reminded them that the land belonged to the Indians, and expressed the hope they would not stay around after they found all the yellow metal they needed.

The miners not only stayed, but thousands more of them came. The Platte Valley, which had once teemed with buffalo, began to fill with settlers staking out ranches and land claims on territory assigned by the Laramie treaty to Southern Cheyennes and Arapahos. Only ten years after the treaty signing, the Great Council in Washington created the Territory of Colorado; the Great Father sent out a governor; and politicians began maneuvering for a land cession from the Indians.

Through all of this the Cheyennes and Arapahos kept the peace, and when United States officials invited their leaders to gather at Fort Wise on the Arkansas River to discuss a new treaty, several chiefs responded. According to later statements of chiefs of both tribes, what they were told would be in the treaty and what

was actually written into it were quite different. It was the understanding of the chiefs that the Cheyennes and Arapahos would retain their land rights and freedom of movement to hunt buffalo, but that they would agree to live within a triangular section of territory bounded by Sand Creek and the Arkansas River. Freedom of movement was an especially vital matter because the reservation assigned the two tribes had almost no wild game upon it and was unsuited to agriculture unless irrigated.

The treaty making at Fort Wise was a gala affair. Because of its importance, Colonel A. B. Greenwood, Commissioner of Indian Affairs, put in an appearance to pass out medals, blankets, sugar, and tobacco. The Little White Man (William Bent), who had married into the Cheyenne tribe, was there to look after the Indians' interests. When the Cheyennes pointed out that only six of their forty-four chiefs were present, the United States officials replied that the others could sign later. None of the others ever did, and for that reason the legality of the treaty was to remain in doubt. Black Kettle, White Antelope, and Lean Bear were among the signers for the Cheyennes. Little Raven, Storm, and Big Mouth signed for the Arapahos. Witnesses to the signatures were two officers of the United States Cavalry, John Sedgwick and J. E. B. Stuart. (A few months later Sedgwick and Stuart, who urged the Indians to peaceful pursuits, were fighting on opposite sides in the Civil War, and by one of the ironies of history they died within a few hours of each other in the battles of the Wilderness.)

During the first years of the white man's Civil War, Cheyenne and Arapaho hunting parties found it increasingly difficult to stay clear of Bluecoat soldiers who were scouting southward in search of Graycoats. They heard about the troubles of the Navahos, and from friends among the Sioux they learned of the awful fate of the Santees who dared challenge the power of the soldiers in Minnesota. Cheyenne and Arapaho chiefs tried to keep their young men busy hunting buffalo away from the white men's routes of travel. Each summer, however, the numbers and arrogance of the Bluecoats increased. By the spring of 1864, soldiers were prowling into remote hunting grounds between the Smoky Hill and Republican rivers.

When the grass was well up that year, Roman Nose and quite a number of the Dog Soldier Cheyennes went north for better hunting in the Powder River country with their Northern Cheyenne cousins. Black Kettle, White Antelope, and Lean Bear kept their bands below the Platte, however, and so did Little Raven of the Arapahos. They were careful to avoid soldiers and white buffalo hunters by staying away from forts and trails and settlements.

Black Kettle and Lean Bear did go down to Fort Larned (Kansas) that spring to trade. Only the year before the two chiefs had been invited on a visit to see the Great Father, Abraham Lincoln, in Washington, and they were sure the Great Father's soldiers at Fort Larned would treat them well. President Lincoln gave them medals to wear on their breasts, and Colonel Greenwood presented Black Kettle with a United States flag, a huge garrison flag with white stars for the thirty-four states bigger than glittering stars in the sky on a clear night. Colonel Greenwood had told him that as long as that flag flew above him no soldiers would ever fire upon him. Black Kettle was very proud of his flag and when in permanent camp always mounted it on a pole above his tepee.

In the middle of May, Black Kettle and Lean Bear heard that soldiers had attacked some Cheyennes on the South Platte River. They decided to break camp and move northward to join the rest of the tribe for strength and protection. After one day's march they went into camp near Ash Creek. Next morning, as was the custom, the hunters went out early for game, but they soon came hurrying back. They

had seen soldiers with cannons approaching the camp.

Lean Bear liked excitement, and he told Black Kettle he would go out and meet the soldiers and find out what they wanted. He hung the medal from the Great Father Lincoln outside his coat and took some papers that had been given him in Washington certifying that he was a good friend of the United States, and then rode out with an escort of warriors. Lean Bear rode up on a hill near camp and saw the soldiers approaching in four bunches of cavalry. They had two cannons in the center and several wagons strung out in the rear.

Wolf Chief, one of the young warriors escorting Lean Bear, said afterward that as soon as the Cheyennes were seen by the soldiers, the latter formed a line front. "Lean Bear told us warriors to stay where we were," Wolf Chief said, "so as not to frighten the soldiers, while he rode forward to shake hands with the officer and show his papers. . . . When the chief was within only twenty or thirty yards of the line, the officer called out in a very loud voice and the soldiers all opened fire on Lean Bear and the rest of us. Lean Bear fell off his horse right in front of the troops, and Star, another Cheyenne, also fell off his horse. The soldiers then rode forward and shot Lean Bear and Star again as they lay helpless on the ground. I was off with a party of young men to one side. There was company of soldiers in front of us, but they were all shooting at Lean Bear and the other Cheyennes who were near to him. They paid no attention to us until we began firing on them with bows and guns. They were so close that we shot several of them with arrows. Two of them fell backward off their horses. By this time there was a great deal of confusion. More Cheyennes kept coming up in small parties, and the soldiers were bunching up and seemed badly frightened. They were shooting at us with the cannon. The grapeshot struck the ground around us, but the aim was bad."

In the midst of the fighting, Black Kettle appeared on his horse and began riding up and down among the warriors. "Stop the fighting!" he shouted. "Do not make war!" It was a long time before the Cheyennes would listen to him. "We were very mad," Wolf Chief said, "but at last he stopped the fight. The soldiers ran off. We captured fifteen cavalry horses, with saddles, bridles, and saddle bags on them. Several soldiers were killed; Lean Bear, Star, and one more Cheyenne were killed, and many were wounded."

The Cheyennes were sure that they could have killed all the soldiers and captured their mountain howitzers, because five hundred Cheyenne warriors were in the camp against a hundred soldiers. As it was, many of the young men, infuriated by the cold-blooded killing of Lean Bear, chased the retreating soldiers in a running fight all the way to Fort Larned.

Black Kettle was bewildered by this sudden attack. He grieved for Lean Bear; they had been friends for almost half a century. He remembered how Lean Bear's curiosity was always getting him into trouble. Sometime before, when the Cheyennes paid a friendly visit to Fort Atkinson on the Arkansas River, Lean Bear noticed a bright shiny ring worn by an officer's wife. Impulsively he took hold of the woman's hand to look at her ring. The woman's husband rushed up and slashed Lean Bear with a big whip. Lean Bear turned and jumped on his horse and rode back to the Cheyenne camp. He painted his face and rode through the camp, urging the warriors to join him in attacking the fort. A Cheyenne chief had been insulted, he cried. Black Kettle and the other chiefs had a hard time calming him down that day. Now Lean Bear was dead, and his death had stirred the warriors to a far deeper anger than the insult at Fort Atkinson.

Black Kettle could not understand why the soldiers had attacked a peaceful Cheyenne camp without warning. He supposed that if anyone would know, it would be his old friend the Little White Man, William Bent. More than

thirty years had passed since the Little White Man and his brothers had come to the Arkansas River and built Bent's Fort. William had married Owl Woman, and after she died he married her sister, Yellow Woman. In all those years the Bents and the Cheyennes had lived in close friendship. The Little White Man had three sons and two daughters, and they lived much of the time with their mother's people. That summer two of the half-breed sons, George and Charlie, were hunting buffalo with the Cheyennes on Smoky Hill River.

After some thought about the matter, Black Kettle sent a messenger on a fast pony to find the Little White Man. "Tell him we have had a fight with the soldiers and killed several of them," Black Kettle said. "Tell him we do not know what the fight was about or for, and that we would like to see him and talk with him about it."

By chance Black Kettle's messenger found William Bent on the road between Fort Larned and Fort Lyon. Bent sent the messenger back with instructions for Black Kettle to meet him on Coon Creek. A week later the old friends met, both concerned over the future of the Cheyennes, Bent especially worried about his sons. He was relieved to learn that they were hunting on the Smoky Hill. No trouble had been reported from there, but he knew of two fights that had occurred elsewhere. At Fremont's Orchard north of Denver, a band of Dog Soldiers was attacked by a patrol of Colonel John M. Chivington's Colorado Volunteers who were out looking for stolen horses. The Dog Soldiers were herding a horse and a mule picked up as strays, but Chivington's soldiers opened fire before giving the Cheyennes an opportunity to explain where they had obtained the animals. After this engagement Chivington sent out a larger force, which attacked a Cheyenne camp near Cedar Bluffs, killing two women and two children. The artillery soldiers who had attacked Black Ket-

tle's camp on May 16 were also Chivington's men, sent out from Denver with no authority to operate in Kansas. The officer in command, Lieutenant George S. Eayre, was under orders from Colonel Chivington to "kill Cheyennes whenever and wherever found."

If such incidents continued, William Bent and Black Kettle agreed, a general war was bound to break out all over the plains. "It is not my intention or wish to fight the whites," Black Kettle said. "I want to be friendly and peaceable and keep my tribe so. I am not able to fight the whites. I want to live in peace."

Bent told Black Kettle to keep his young men from making revenge raids, and promised he would return to Colorado and try to persuade the military authorities not to continue on the dangerous road they were taking. He then set out for Fort Lyon.

"On my arrival there," he later testified under oath, "I met Colonel Chivington, related to him the conversation that had taken place between me and the Indians, and that the chiefs desired to be friendly. In reply he said he was not authorized to make peace, and that he was then on the warpath—I think were the words he used. I then stated to him that there was great risk to run in keeping up the war; that there were a great many government trains traveling to New Mexico and other points; also a great many citizens, and that I did not think there was sufficient force to protect the travel, and that the citizens and settlers of the country would have to suffer. He said the citizens would have to protect themselves. I then said no more to him."

Late in June the governor of Colorado Territory, John Evans, issued a circular addressed to the "friendly Indians of the plains," informing them that some members of their tribes had gone to war with the white people. Governor Evans declared that "in some instances they have attacked and killed soldiers." He made no mention of soldiers attacking Indians, although

this was the way all three fights with the Cheyennes had begun. "For this the Great Father is angry," he went on, "and will certainly hunt them out and punish them, but he does not want to injure those who remain friendly to the whites; he desires to protect and take care of them. For this purpose I direct that all friendly Indians keep away from those who are at war, and go to places of safety." Evans ordered friendly Cheyennes and Arapahos to report to Fort Lyon on their reservation, where their agent, Samuel G. Colley, would furnish them with provisions and show them a place of safety. "The object of this is to prevent friendly Indians from being killed through mistake. . . . The war on hostile Indians will be continued until they are all effectually subdued."

As soon as William Bent learned of Governor Evans' decree he started immediately to warn the Cheyennes and Arapahos to come in to Fort Lyon. Because the various bands were scattered across western Kansas for their summer hunts, several weeks passed before runners could reach all of them. During this period clashes between soldiers and Indians steadily increased. Sioux warriors, aroused by General Alfred Sully's punitive expeditions of 1863 and 1864 into Dakota, swarmed down from the north to raid wagon trains, stagecoach stations, and settlers along the Platte route. For these actions the Southern Cheyennes and Arapahos received much of the blame, and most of the attention of the Colorado soldiers. William Bent's half-breed son George, who was with a large band of Cheyennes on the Solomon River in July, said they were attacked again and again by the troops without any cause, until they began retaliating in the only way they knew how—burning the stage stations, chasing the coaches, running off stock, and forcing the freighters to corral their trains and fight.

Black Kettle and the older chiefs tried to stop these raids, but their influence was weakened by the appeal of younger leaders such as Roman Nose and by the members of the *Hotamitanio,* or Dog Soldier Society. When Black Kettle discovered that seven white captives—two women and five children—had been brought into the Smoky Hill camps by the raiders, he ransomed four of them from the captors with his own ponies so that he could return them to their relatives. About this time, he finally received a message from William Bent informing him of Governor Evans' order to report to Fort Lyon.

It was now late August, and Evans had issued a second proclamation "authorizing all citizens of Colorado, either individually or in such parties as they may organize, to go in pursuit of all hostile Indians on the plains, scrupulously avoiding those who have responded to my call to rendezvous at the points indicated; also to kill and destroy as enemies of the country wherever they may be found, all such hostile Indians." The hunt was already on for all Indians not confined to one of the assigned reservations.

Black Kettle immediately held a council, and all the chiefs in camp agreed to comply with the governor's requirements for peace. George Bent, who had been educated at Webster College in St. Louis, was asked to write a letter to agent Samuel Colley at Fort Lyon, informing him that they wanted peace. "We heard that you have some prisoners in Denver. We have seven prisoners of yours which we are willing to give up, providing you give up yours. . . . We want true news from you in return." Black Kettle hoped that Colley would give him instructions as to how to bring his Cheyennes across Colorado without being attacked by soldiers or roving bands of Governor Evans' armed citizens. He did not entirely trust Colley; he suspected the agent of selling part of the Indians' allotment of goods for his own profit. (Black Kettle did not yet know how deeply involved Colley was with Governor Evans and Colonel Chivington in their scheme to drive the

Plains Indians from Colorado.) On July 26, the agent had written Evans that they could not depend on any of the Indians to keep the peace. "I now think a little powder and lead is the best food for them," he concluded.

Because of his distrust of Colley, Black Kettle had a second copy of the letter written out and addressed to William Bent. He gave the separate copies to Ochinee (One-Eye) and Eagle Head, and ordered them to ride for Fort Lyon. Six days later, as One-Eye and Eagle Head were approaching the fort, they were suddenly confronted by three soldiers. The soldiers took firing positions, but One-Eye quickly made signs for peace and held up Black Kettle's letter. In a few moments the Indians were being escorted into Fort Lyon as prisoners and handed over to the commanding officer, Major Edward W. Wynkoop.

Tall Chief Wynkoop was suspicious of the Indians' motives. When he learned from One-Eye that Black Kettle wanted him to come out to the Smoky Hill camp and guide the Indians back to the reservation, he asked how many Indians were there. Two thousand Cheyennes and Arapahos, One-Eye replied, and perhaps two hundred of their Sioux friends from the north who were tired of being chased by soldiers. Wynkoop made no reply to this. He had scarcely more than a hundred mounted soldiers, and he knew the Indians knew the size of his force. Suspecting a trap, he ordered the Cheyenne messengers imprisoned in the guardhouse and called his officers together for a council. The Tall Chief was young, in his mid-twenties, and his only military experience was one battle against Texas Confederates in New Mexico. For the first time in his career he was faced with a decision that could mean disaster for his entire command.

After a day's delay, Wynkoop finally decided that he would have to go to the Smoky Hill—not for the sake of the Indians, but to rescue the white prisoners. No doubt it was for this reason that Black Kettle had mentioned the prisoners in his letter; he knew that white men could not abide the thought of white women and children living with Indians.

On September 6 Wynkoop was ready to march with 127 mounted troops. Releasing One-Eye and Eagle Head from the guardhouse, he told them that they would be serving as both guides and hostages for the expedition. "At the first sign of treachery from your people," Wynkoop warned them, "I will kill you."

"The Cheyennes do not break their word," One-Eye replied. "If they should do so, I would not care to live longer."

(Wynkoop said afterward that his conversations with the two Cheyennes on this march caused him to change his long-held opinions of Indians. "I felt myself in the presence of superior beings; and these were the representatives of a race that I heretofore looked upon without exception as being cruel, treacherous, and bloodthirsty without feeling or affection for friend or kindred.")

Five days later, along the headwaters of the Smoky Hill, Wynkoop's advance scouts sighted a force of several hundred warriors drawn up as though for battle.

George Bent, who was still with Black Kettle, said that when Wynkoop's soldiers appeared the Dog Soldiers "got ready for a fight and rode out to meet the troops with bows strung and arrows in their hands, but Black Kettle and some of the chiefs interfered, and requesting Major Wynkoop to move his troops off to a little distance, they prevented a fight."

Next morning Black Kettle and the other chiefs met Wynkoop and his officers for a council. Black Kettle let the others speak first. Bull Bear, a leader of the Dog Soldiers, said that he and his brother Lean Bear had tried to live in peace with white men, but that soldiers had come without cause or reason and killed Lean Bear. "The Indians are not to blame for the fighting," he added. "The white men are foxes and peace cannot be brought about with them; the only thing the Indians can do is fight."

Little Raven of the Arapahos agreed with Bull Bear. "I would like to shake hands with the white men," he said, "but I am afraid they do not want peace with us." One-Eye asked to speak then, and said he was ashamed to hear such talk. He had risked his life to go to Fort Lyon, he said, and pledged his word to Tall Chief Wynkoop that the Cheyennes and Arapahos would come in peacefully to their reservation. "I pledged the Tall Chief my word and my life," One-Eye declared. "If my people do not act in good faith I will go with the whites and fight for them, and I have a great many friends who will follow me."

Wynkoop promised that he would do everything that he could to stop the soldiers from fighting the Indians. He said he was not a big chief and could not speak for all the soldiers, but that if the Indians would deliver the white captives to him, he would go with the Indian leaders to Denver and help them make peace with the bigger chiefs.

Black Kettle, who had been listening silently through the proceedings ("immovable with a slight smile upon his face," according to Wynkoop), arose and said he was glad to hear Tall Chief Wynkoop speak. "There are bad white men and bad Indians," he said. "The bad men on both sides brought about this trouble. Some of my young men joined in with them. I am opposed to fighting and have done everything in my power to prevent it. I believe the blame rests with the whites. They commenced the war and forced the Indians to fight." He promised then to deliver the four white prisoners he had purchased; the remaining three were in a camp farther north, and some time would be required to negotiate for them.

The four captives, all children, appeared to be unharmed; in fact, when a soldier asked eight-year-old Ambrose Archer how the Indians had treated him, the boy replied that he "would just as lief stay with the Indians as not."

After more parleying it was finally agreed that the Indians would remain camped on the Smoky Hill while seven chiefs went to Denver with Wynkoop to make peace with Governor Evans and Colonel Chivington. Black Kettle, White Antelope, Bull Bear, and One-Eye represented the Cheyennes; Neva, Bosse, Heaps-of-Buffalo, and Notanee the Arapahos. Little Raven and Left Hand, who were skeptical of any promises from Evans and Chivington, remained behind to keep their young Arapahos out of trouble. War Bonnet would look after the Cheyennes in camp.

Tall Chief Wynkoop's caravan of mounted soldiers, the four white children, and the seven Indian leaders reached Denver on September 28. The Indians rode in a mule-drawn flatbed wagon fitted with board seats. For the journey, Black Kettle mounted his big garrison flag above the wagon, and when they entered the dusty streets of Denver the Stars and Stripes fluttered protectively over the head of the chiefs. All of Denver turned out for the procession.

Before the council began, Wynkoop visited Governor Evans for an interview. The governor was reluctant to have anything to do with the Indians. He said that the Cheyennes and Arapahos should be punished before giving them any peace. This was also the opinion of the department commander, General Samuel R. Curtis, who telegraphed Colonel Chivington from Fort Leavenworth that very day: "I want no peace till the Indians suffer more."

Finally Wynkoop had to beg the governor to meet with the Indians. "But what shall I do with the Third Colorado Regiment if I make peace?" Evans asked. "They have been raised to kill Indians, and they must kill Indians." He explained to Wynkoop that Washington officials had given him permission to raise the new regiment because he had sworn it was necessary for protection against hostile Indians, and if he now made peace the Washington politicians would accuse him of misrepresentation. There was political pressure on Evans from

Coloradans who wanted to avoid the military draft of 1864 by serving in uniform against a few poorly armed Indians rather than against the Confederates farther east. Eventually Evans gave in to Major Wynkoop's pleadings; after all, the Indians had come four hundred miles to see him in response to his proclamation.

The council was held at Camp Weld near Denver, and consisted of the chiefs, Evans, Chivington, Wynkoop, several other Army officers, and Simeon Whitely, who was there by the governor's order to record every word said by the participants. Governor Evans opened the proceedings brusquely, asking the chiefs what they had to say. Black Kettle replied in Cheyenne, with the tribe's old trader friend, John S. Smith, translating:

"On sight of your circular of June 27, 1864, I took hold of the matter, and have now come to talk to you about it. . . . Major Wynkoop proposed that we come to see you. We have come with our eyes shut, following his handful of men, like coming through the fire. All we ask is that we may have peace with the whites. We want to hold you by the hand. You are our father. We have been traveling through a cloud. The sky has been dark ever since the war began. These braves who are with me are willing to do what I say. We want to take good tidings home to our people, that they may sleep in peace. I want you to give all these chiefs of the soldiers here to understand that we are for peace, and that we have made peace, that we may not be mistaken by them for enemies. I have not come here with a little wolf bark, but have come to talk plain with you. We must live near the buffalo or starve. When we came here we came free, without any apprehension, to see you, and when I go home and tell my people that I have taken your hand, and the hands of all the chiefs here in Denver, they will feel well, and so will all the different tribes of Indians on the plains, after we have eaten and drunk with them."

Evans replied: "I am sorry you did not respond to my appeal at once. You have gone into an alliance with the Sioux, who are at war with us."

Black Kettle was surprised. "I don't know who could have told you this," he said.

"No matter who said this," Evans countered, "but your conduct has proved to my satisfaction that was the case."

Several of the chiefs spoke at once then: "This is a mistake; we have made no alliance with the Sioux or anyone else."

Evans changed the subject, stating that he was in no mood to make a treaty of peace. "I have learned that you understand that as the whites are at war among themselves," he went on, "you think you can now drive the whites from this country, but this reliance is false. The Great Father at Washington has men enough to drive all the Indians off the plains, and whip the Rebels at the same time. . . . My advice to you is to turn on the side of the government, and show by your acts that friendly disposition you profess to me. It is utterly out of the question for you to be at peace with us while living with our enemies, and being on friendly terms with them."

White Antelope, the oldest of the chiefs, now spoke: "I understand every word you have said, and will hold on to it. . . . The Cheyennes, all of them, have their eyes open this way, and they will hear what you say. White Antelope is proud to have seen the chief of all the whites in this country. He will tell his people. Ever since I went to Washington and received this medal, I have called all white men as my brothers. But other Indians have been to Washington and got medals, and now the soldiers do not shake hands, but seek to kill me. . . . I fear that these new soldiers who have gone out may kill some of my people while I am here."

Evans told him flatly: "There is great danger of it."

"When we sent our letter to Major Wynkoop," White Antelope continued, "it was like going through a strong fire or blast for Major

Wynkoop's men to come to our camp; it was the same for us to come to see you."

Governor Evans now began to question the chiefs about specific incidents along the Platte, trying to trap some of them into admitting participation in raids. "Who took the stock from Fremont's Orchard," he asked, "and had the first fight with the soldiers this spring north of there?"

"Before answering that question," White Antelope replied boldly, "I would like for you to know that this was the beginning of the war, and I should like to know what it was for. A soldier fired first."

"The Indians had stolen about forty horses," Evans charged. "The soldiers went to recover them, and the Indians fired a volley into their ranks."

White Antelope denied this. "They were coming down the Bijou," he said, "and found one horse and one mule. They returned one horse before they got to Gerry's to a man, then went to Gerry's expecting to turn the other one over to someone. They then heard that the soldiers and Indians were fighting down the Platte; then they took fright and all fled."

"Who committed depredations at Cottonwood?" Evans demanded.

"The Sioux; what band, we do not know."

"What are the Sioux going to do next?"

Bull Bear answered the question: "Their plan is to clean out all this country," he declared. "They are angry, and will do all the damage to the whites they can. I am with you and the troops, to fight all those who have no ears to listen to what you say. . . . I have never hurt a white man. I am pushing for something good. I am always going to be friends with whites; they can do me good. . . . My brother Lean Bear died in trying to keep peace with the whites. I am willing to die the same way, and expect to do so."

As there seemed little more to discuss, the governor asked Colonel Chivington if he had anything to say to the chiefs. Chivington arose.

He was a towering man with a barrel chest and a thick neck, a former Methodist preacher who had devoted much of his time to organizing Sunday schools in the mining camps. To the Indians he appeared like a great bearded bull buffalo with a glint of furious madness in his eyes. "I am not a big war chief," Chivington said, "but all the soldiers in this country are at my command. My rule of fighting white men or Indians is to fight them until they lay down their arms and submit to military authority. They [the Indians] are nearer to Major Wynkoop than anyone else, and they can go to him when they are ready to do that."

And so the council ended, leaving the chiefs confused as to whether they had made peace or not. They were sure of one thing—the only real friend they could count on among the soldiers was Tall Chief Wynkoop. The shiny-eyed Eagle Chief, Chivington, had said they should go to Wynkoop at Fort Lyon, and that is what they decided to do.

"So now we broke up our camp on the Smoky Hill and moved down to Sand Creek, about forty miles northeast of Fort Lyon," George Bent said. "From this new camp the Indians went in and visited Major Wynkoop, and the people at the fort seemed so friendly that after a short time the Arapahos left us and moved right down to the fort, where they went into camp and received regular rations."

Wynkoop issued the rations after Little Raven and Left Hand told him the Arapahos could find no buffalo or other wild game on the reservation, and they were fearful of sending hunting parties back to the Kansas herds. They may have heard about Chivington's recent order to his soldiers: "Kill all the Indians you come across."

Wynkoop's friendly dealings with the Indians soon brought him into disfavor with military officials in Colorado and Kansas. He was reprimanded for taking the chiefs to Denver without authorization, and was accused of "letting the Indians run things at Fort Lyon."

On November 5, Major Scott J. Anthony, an officer of Chivington's Colorado Volunteers, arrived at Fort Lyon with orders to relieve Wynkoop as commander of the post.

One of Anthony's first orders was to cut the Arapahos' rations and to demand the surrender of their weapons. They gave him three rifles, one pistol, and sixty bows with arrows. A few days later when a group of unarmed Arapahos approached the fort to trade buffalo hides for rations, Anthony ordered his guards to fire on them. Anthony laughed when the Indians turned and ran. He remarked to one of the soldiers "that they had annoyed him enough, and that was the only way to get rid of them."

The Cheyennes who were camped on Sand Creek heard from the Arapahos that an unfriendly little red-eyed soldier chief had taken the place of their friend Wynkoop. In the Deer Rutting Moon of mid-November, Black Kettle and a party of Cheyennes journeyed to the fort to see this new soldier chief. His eyes were indeed red (the result of scurvy), but he pretended to be friendly. Several officers who were present at the meeting between Black Kettle and Anthony testified afterward that Anthony assured the Cheyennes that if they returned to their camp at Sand Creek they would be under the protection of Fort Lyon. He also told them that their young men could go east toward the Smoky Hill to hunt buffalo until he secured permission from the Army to issue them winter rations.

Pleased with Anthony's remarks, Black Kettle said that he and the other Cheyenne leaders had been thinking of moving far south of the Arkansas so that they would feel safe from the soldiers, but that the words of Major Anthony made them feel safe at Sand Creek. They would stay there for the winter.

After the Cheyenne delegation departed, Anthony ordered Left Hand and Little Raven to disband the Arapaho camp near Fort Lyon. "Go and hunt buffalo to feed yourselves," he told them. Alarmed by Anthony's brusqueness,

the Arapahos packed up and began moving away. When they were well out of view of the fort, the two bands of Arapahos separated. Left Hand went with his people to Sand Creek to join the Cheyennes. Little Raven led his band across the Arkansas River and headed south; he did not trust the Red-Eyed Soldier Chief.

Anthony now informed his superiors that "there is a band of Indians within forty miles of the post. . . . I shall try to keep the Indians quiet until such time as I receive reinforcements."

On November 26, when the post trader, Gray Blanket John Smith, requested permission to go out to Sand Creek to trade for hides, Major Anthony was unusually cooperative. He provided Smith with an Army ambulance to haul his goods, and also a driver, Private David Louderback of the Colorado Cavalry. If nothing else would lull the Indians into a sense of security and keep them camped where they were, the presence of a post trader and a peaceful representative of the Army should do so.

Twenty-four hours later the reinforcements which Anthony said he needed to attack the Indians were approaching Fort Lyon. They were six hundred men of Colonel Chivington's Colorado regiments, including most of the Third, which had been formed by Governor John Evans for the sole purpose of fighting Indians. When the vanguard reached the fort, they surrounded it and forbade anyone to leave under penalty of death. About the same time a detachment of twenty cavalrymen reached William Bent's ranch a few miles to the east, surrounded Bent's house, and forbade anyone to enter or leave. Bent's two half-breed sons, George and Charlie, and his half-breed son-in-law Edmond Guerrier were camped with the Cheyennes on Sand Creek.

When Chivington rode up to the officers' quarters at Fort Lyon, Major Anthony greeted him warmly. Chivington began talking of "collecting scalps" and "wading in gore." Anthony

responded by saying that he had been "waiting for a good chance to pitch into them," and that every man at Fort Lyon was eager to join Chivington's expedition against the Indians.

Not all of Anthony's officers, however, were eager or even willing to join Chivington's well-planned massacre. Captain Silas Soule, Lieutenant Joseph Cramer, and Lieutenant James Connor protested that an attack on Black Kettle's peaceful camp would violate the pledge of safety given the Indians by both Wynkoop and Anthony, "that it would be murder in every sense of the word," and any officer participating would dishonor the uniform of the Army.

Chivington became violently angry at them and brought his fist down close to Lieutenant Cramer's face. "Damn any man who sympathizes with Indians!" he cried. "I have come to kill Indians, and believe it is right and honorable to use any means under God's heaven to kill Indians."

Soule, Cramer, and Connor had to join the expedition or face a court-martial, but they quietly resolved not to order their men to fire on the Indians except in self-defense.

At eight o'clock on the evening of November 28, Chivington's column, now consisting of more than seven hundred men by the addition of Anthony's troops, moved out in column of fours. Four twelve-pounder mountain howitzers accompanied the cavalry. Stars glittered in a clear sky; the night air carried a sharp bite of frost.

For a guide Chivington conscripted sixty-nine-year-old James Beckwourth, a mulatto who had lived with the Indians for half a century. Medicine Calf Beckwourth tried to beg off, but Chivington threatened to hang the old man if he refused to guide the soldiers to the Cheyenne-Arapaho encampment.

As the column moved on, it became evident that Beckwourth's dimming eyes and rheumatic bones handicapped his usefulness as a guide. At a ranch house near Spring Bottom, Chiving-ton stopped and ordered the rancher hauled out of his bed to take Beckwourth's place as guide. The rancher was Robert Bent, eldest son of William Bent; all three of Bent's half-Cheyenne sons would soon be together at Sand Creek.

The Cheyenne camp lay in a horseshoe bend of Sand Creek north of an almost dry stream bed. Black Kettle's tepee was near the center of the village, with White Antelope's and War Bonnet's people to the west. On the east side and slightly separated from the Cheyennes was Left Hand's Arapaho camp. Altogether there were about six hundred Indians in the creek bend, two-thirds of them being women and children. Most of the warriors were several miles to the east hunting buffalo for the camp, as they had been told to do by Major Anthony.

So confident were the Indians of absolute safety, they kept no night watch except of the pony herd which was corralled below the creek. The first warning they had of an attack was about sunrise—the drumming of hooves on the sand flats. "I was sleeping in a lodge," Edmond Guerrier said. "I heard, at first, some of the squaws outside say there were a lot of buffalo coming into camp; others said they were a lot of soldiers." Guerrier immediately went outside and started toward Gray Blanket Smith's tent.

George Bent, who was sleeping in the same area, said that he was still in his blankets when he heard shouts and the noise of people running about the camp. "From down the creek a large body of troops was advancing at a rapid trot . . . more soldiers could be seen making for the Indian pony herds to the south of the camps; in the camps themselves all was confusion and noise—men, women, and children rushing out of the lodges partly dressed; women and children screaming at sight of the troops; men running back into the lodges for their arms. . . . I looked toward the chief's

Painting by Robert Lindeux of the Sand Creek massacre, Colorado Territory, 1864. The American flag Black Kettle raised can be seen (right center). A white man who saw the massacre recorded that "there seemed to be an indiscriminate slaughter of men, women, and children. . . . Every one I saw dead was scalped." (Courtesy of The State Historical Society of Colorado.)

lodge and saw that Black Kettle had a large American flag tied to the end of a long lodgepole and was standing in front of his lodge, holding the pole, with the flag fluttering in the gray light of the winter dawn. I heard him call to the people not to be afraid, that the soldiers would not hurt them; then the troops opened fire from two sides of the camp."

Meanwhile young Guerrier had joined Gray Blanket Smith and Private Louderback at the trader's tent. "Louderback proposed we should go out and meet the troops. We started. Before we got outside the edge of the tent I could see soldiers begin to dismount. I thought they were artillerymen and were about to shell the camp.

I had hardly spoken when they began firing with their rifles and pistols. When I saw I could not get to them, I struck out; I left the soldier and Smith."

Louderback halted momentarily, but Smith kept moving ahead toward the cavalrymen. "Shoot the damned old son of a bitch!" a soldier shouted from the ranks. "He's no better than an Indian." At the first scattered shots, Smith and Louderback turned and ran for their tent. Smith's half-breed son, Jack, and Charlie Bent had already taken cover there.

By this time hundreds of Cheyenne women and children were gathering around Black Kettle's flag. Up the dry creek bed, more were

coming from White Antelope's camp. After all, had not Colonel Greenwood told Black Kettle that as long as the United States flag flew above him no soldier would fire upon him? White Antelope, an old man of seventy-five, unarmed, his dark face seamed from sun and weather, strode toward the soldiers. He was still confident that the soldiers would stop firing as soon as they saw the American flag and the white surrender flag which Black Kettle had now run up.

Medicine Calf Beckwourth, riding beside Colonel Chivington, saw White Antelope approaching. "He came running out to meet the command," Beckwourth later testified, "holding up his hands and saying 'Stop! stop!' He spoke it in as plain English as I can. He stopped and folded his arms until shot down." Survivors among the Cheyennes said that White Antelope sang the death song before he died:

Nothing lives long
Only the earth and the mountains.

From the direction of the Arapaho camp, Left Hand and his people also tried to reach Black Kettle's flag. When Left Hand saw the troops, he stood with his arms folded, saying he would not fight the white men because they were his friends. He was shot down.

Robert Bent, who was riding unwillingly with Colonel Chivington, said that when they came in sight of the camp "I saw the American flag waving and heard Black Kettle tell the Indians to stand around the flag, and there they were huddled—men, women, and children. This was when we were within fifty yards of the Indians. I also saw a white flag raised. These flags were in so conspicuous a position that they must have been seen. When the troops fired, the Indians ran, some of the men into their lodges, probably to get their arms. . . . I think there were six hundred Indians in all. I think there were thirty-five braves and some old men, about sixty in all . . . the rest of the men were away from camp, hunting. . . . After the firing the warriors put the squaws and children together, and surrounded them to protect them. I saw five squaws under a bank for shelter. When the troops came up to them they ran out and showed their persons to let the soldiers know they were squaws and begged for mercy, but the soldiers shot them all. I saw one squaw lying on the bank whose leg had been broken by a shell; a soldier came up to her with a drawn saber; she raised her arm to protect herself, when he struck, breaking her arm; she rolled over and raised her other arm, when he struck, breaking it, and then left her without killing her. There seemed to be indiscriminate slaughter of men, women, and children. There were some thirty or forty squaws collected in a hole for protection; they sent out a little girl about six years old with a white flag on a stick; she had not proceeded but a few steps when she was shot and killed. All the squaws in that hole were afterwards killed, and four or five bucks outside. The squaws offered no resistance. Every one I saw dead was scalped. I saw one squaw cut open with an unborn child, as I thought, lying by her side. Captain Soule afterwards told me that such was the fact. I saw the body of White Antelope with the privates cut off, and I heard a soldier say he was going to make a tobacco pouch out of them. I saw one squaw whose privates had been cut out. . . . I saw a little girl about five years of age who had been hid in the sand; two soldiers discovered her, drew their pistols and shot her, and then pulled her out of the sand by the arm. I saw quite a number of infants in arms killed with their mothers."

(In a public speech made in Denver not long before this massacre, Colonel Chivington advocated the killing and scalping of all Indians, even infants. "Nits make lice!" he declared.)

Robert Bent's description of the soldiers' atrocities was corroborated by Lieutenant James Connor: "In going over the battleground the next day I did not see a body of man, woman, or child but was scalped, and in many instances

their bodies were mutilated in the most horrible manner—men, women, and children's privates cut out, &c; I heard one man say that he had cut out a woman's private parts and had them for exhibition on a stick; I heard another man say that he had cut the fingers off an Indian to get the rings on the hand; according to the best of my knowledge and belief these atrocities that were committed were with the knowledge of J. M. Chivington, and I do not know of his taking any measures to prevent them; I heard of one instance of a child a few months old being thrown in the feedbox of a wagon, and after being carried some distance left on the ground to perish; I also heard of numerous instances in which men had cut out the private parts of females and stretched them over the saddle-bows and wore them over their hats while riding in the ranks."

A trained and well-disciplined regiment of soldiers undoubtedly could have destroyed almost all of the defenseless Indians at Sand Creek. Lack of discipline, combined with heavy drinking of whiskey during the night ride, cowardice, and poor marksmanship among the Colorado troops made it possible for many Indians to escape. A number of Cheyennes dug rifle pits below high banks of the dry creek, and held out until nightfall. Others fled singly or in small groups across the plain. When the shooting ended, 105 Indian women and children and 28 men were dead. In his official report Chivington claimed between four and five hundred dead warriors. He had lost nine killed, 38 wounded, many of the casualties resulting from careless firing by the soldiers upon each other. Among the dead chiefs were White Antelope, One-Eye, and War Bonnet. Black Kettle miraculously escaped by running up a ravine, but his wife was badly wounded. Left Hand, although shot down, also managed to survive.

Captives at the end of the fighting totaled seven—John Smith's Cheyenne wife, the wife of another white civilian at Fort Lyon and her three children, and the two half-breed boys, Jack Smith and Charlie Bent. The soldiers wanted to kill the half-breed boys because they were wearing Indian dress. Old Medicine Calf Beckwourth rescued Charlie Bent by concealing him in a wagon with a wounded officer, later turning him over to his brother Robert. But Beckwourth could not save Jack Smith's life; a soldier shot the trader's son by firing at him through a hole in the tent where the boy was being held prisoner.

The third Bent son, George, became separated from Charlie early in the fighting. He joined the Cheyennes who dug rifle pits under the high banks of the creek. "Just as our party reached this point," he said, "I was struck in the hip by a bullet and knocked down; but I managed to tumble into one of the holes and lay there among the warriors, women, and children." After nightfall the survivors crawled out of the holes. It was bitter cold, and blood had frozen over their wounds, but they dared not make fires. The only thought in their minds was to flee eastward toward the Smoky Hill and try to join their warriors. "It was a terrible march," George Bent remembered, "most of us being on foot, without food, ill-clad, and encumbered with the women and children." For fifty miles they endured icy winds, hunger, and pain of wounds, but at last they reached the hunting camp. "As we rode into that camp there was a terrible scene. Everyone was crying, even the warriors, and the women and children screaming and wailing. Nearly everyone present had lost some relatives or friends, and many of them in their grief were gashing themselves with their knives until the blood flowed in streams."

As soon as his wound healed, George made his way back to his father's ranch. There from his brother Charlie he heard more details of the soldiers' atrocities at Sand Creek—the horrible scalpings and mutilations, the butchery of

children and infants. After a few days the brothers agreed that as half-breeds they wanted no part of the white man's civilization. They renounced the blood of their father, and quietly left his ranch. With them went Charlie's mother, Yellow Woman, who swore that she would never again live with a white man. They started north to join the Cheyennes.

It was now January, the Moon of Strong Cold, when Plains Indians traditionally kept fires blazing in their lodges, told stories through the long evenings, and slept late in the mornings. But this was a bad time, and as news of the Sand Creek massacre spread across the plains, the Cheyennes, Arapahos, and Sioux sent runners back and forth with messages calling for a war of revenge against the murdering white men.

By the time Yellow Woman and the young Bent brothers reached their relatives on the Republican River, the Cheyennes were supported by thousands of sympathetic allies— Spotted Tail's Brulé Sioux, Pawnee Killer's Oglala Sioux, and large bands of Northern Arapahos. Cheyenne Dog Soldiers (now led by Tall Bull) who had refused to go to Sand Creek were there, and also Roman Nose and his following of young warriors. While the Cheyennes mourned their dead, the leaders of the tribes smoked war pipes and planned their strategy.

In a few hours of madness at Sand Creek, Chivington and his soldiers destroyed the lives or the power of every Cheyenne and Arapaho chief who had held out for peace with the white men. After the flight of the survivors, the Indians rejected Black Kettle and Left Hand, and turned to their war leaders to save them from extermination.

At the same time, United States officials were calling for an investigation of Governor Evans and Colonel Chivington, and although they must have known it was too late to avoid a general Indian war, they sent Medicine Calf Beckwourth as an emissary to Black Kettle to see if there was any possibility of peace.

Beckwourth found the Cheyennes but soon learned that Black Kettle had drifted off somewhere with a handful of relatives and old men. The leading chief was now Leg-in-the-Water.

"I went into the lodge of Leg-in-the-Water," Beckwourth said. "When I went in he raised up and he said, 'Medicine Calf, what have you come here for; have you fetched the white man to finish killing our families again?' I told him I had come to talk to him; call in your council. They came in a short time afterwards, and wanted to know what I had come for. I told them I had come to persuade them to make peace with the whites, as there was not enough of them to fight the whites, as they were as numerous as the leaves of the trees. 'We know it,' was the general response of the council. 'But what do we want to live for? The white man has taken our country, killed all of our game; was not satisfied with that, but killed our wives and children. Now no peace. We want to go and meet our families in the spirit land. We loved the whites until we found out they lied to us, and robbed us of what we had. We have raised the battle axe until death.'

"They asked me then why I had come to Sand Creek with the soldiers to show them the country. I told them if I had not come the white chief would have hung me. 'Go and stay with your white brothers, but we are going to fight till death.' I obeyed orders and came back, willing to play quits."

In January, 1865, the alliance of Cheyenne, Arapaho, and Sioux launched a series of raids along the South Platte. They attacked wagon trains, stage stations, and small military outposts. They burned the town of Julesburg, scalping the white defenders in revenge for the scalping of Indians at Sand Creek. They ripped out miles of telegraph wire. They raided and

plundered up and down the Platte route, halting all communications and supplies. In Denver there was panic as food shortages began to grow.

When the warriors returned to their winter camp in the Big Timbers on the Republican, they had a big dance to celebrate their first blows for revenge. Snow blanketed the Plains, but the chiefs knew that soldiers would soon come marching from all directions with their big-talking guns. While the dances were still going on, the chiefs held a council to decide where they should go to escape the pursuing soldiers. Black Kettle was there, and he spoke for going south, below the Arkansas, where summers were long and buffalo were plentiful. Most of the other chiefs spoke for going north across the Platte to join their relatives in the Powder River country. No soldiers would dare march into that great stronghold of the Teton Sioux and Northern Cheyennes. Before the council ended, the alliance agreed to send runners to the Powder River country to tell the tribes there that they were coming.

Black Kettle, however, would not go, and some four hundred Cheyennes—mostly old men, women, and a few badly wounded warriors—agreed to follow him southward. On the last day before the camp moved out, George Bent said farewell to this last remnant of his mother's people, the Southern Cheyennes. "I went around among the lodges and shook hands with Black Kettle and all my friends. These lodges under Black Kettle moved south of the Arkansas and joined the Southern Arapahos, Kiowas, and Comanches."

With about three thousand Sioux and Arapahos, the Cheyennes (including Yellow Woman and the Bent brothers) moved northward, exiled into a land that few of them had seen before. Along the way they had fights with soldiers who marched out from Fort Laramie, but the alliance was too strong for the soldiers, and the Indians brushed them off as though they were coyotes snapping at a mighty buffalo herd.

When they reached the Powder River country, the Southern Cheyennes were welcomed by their kinsmen, the Northern Cheyennes. The Southerners, who wore cloth blankets and leggings, traded from white men, thought the Northerners looked very wild in their buffalo robes and buckskin leggings. The Northern Cheyennes wrapped their braided hair with strips of red-painted buckskin, wore crow feathers on their heads, and used so many Sioux words that the Southern Cheyennes had difficulty understanding them. Morning Star, a leading chief of the Northern Cheyennes, had lived and hunted so long with the Sioux that almost everyone called him by his Sioux name, Dull Knife.

At first the Southerners camped on the Powder about half a mile apart from the Northerners, but there was so much visiting back and forth that they soon decided to camp together, pitching their tepees in an old-time tribal circle with clans grouped together. From that time on, there was little talk of Southerners and Northerners among these Cheyennes.

In the spring of 1865, when they moved their ponies over to Tongue River for better grazing, they camped near Red Cloud's Oglala Sioux. The Cheyennes from the south had never seen so many Indians camped all together, more than eight thousand, and the days and nights were filled with hunts and ceremonies and feasts and dances. George Bent later told of inducting Young-Man-Afraid-of-His-Horses, a Sioux, into his Cheyenne clan, the Crooked Lances. This indicated how close the Sioux and Cheyennes were in that time.

Although each tribe kept its own laws and customs, these Indians had come to think of themselves as the People, confident of their power and sure of their right to live as they pleased. White invaders were challenging them on the east in Dakota and on the south along

the Platte, but they were ready to meet all challenges. "The Great Spirit raised both the white man and the Indian," Red Cloud said. "I think he raised the Indian first. He raised me in this land and it belongs to me. The white man was raised over the great waters, and his land is over there. Since they crossed the sea, I have given them room. There are now white people all above me. I have but a small spot of land left. The Great Spirit told me to keep it."

Through the springtime the Indians sent scouting parties down to watch the soldiers who were guarding the roads and telegraph lines along the Platte. The scouts reported many more soldiers than usual, some of them prowling northward along Bozeman's Trail through the Powder River country. Red Cloud and the other chiefs decided it was time to teach the soldiers a lesson; they would strike them at the point where they were farthest north, a place the white men called Platte Bridge Station.

Because the Cheyenne warriors from the south wanted revenge for the relatives massacred at Sand Creek, most of them were invited to go along on the expedition. Roman Nose of the Crooked Lances was their leader, and he rode with Red Cloud, Dull Knife, and Old-Man-Afraid-of-His-Horses. Almost three thousand warriors formed the war party. Among them were the Bent brothers, painted and dressed for battle.

On July 24 they reached the hills overlooking the bridge across the North Platte. At the opposite end of the bridge was the military post —a stockade, stage station, and telegraph office. About a hundred soldiers were inside the stockade. After looking at the place through their field glasses, the chiefs decided they would burn the bridge, cross the river at a shallow ford below, and then lay siege to the stockade. But first they would try to draw the soldiers outside with decoys and kill as many as possible.

Ten warriors went down in the afternoon, but the soldiers would not come out of their stockade. Next morning another set of decoys lured the soldiers out on the bridge, but they would come no farther. On the third morning, to the Indians' surprise, a platoon of cavalrymen marched out of the fort, crossed the bridge, and turned westward at a trot. In a matter of seconds, several hundred Cheyennes and Sioux were mounted on their ponies and swarming down the hills toward the Bluecoats. "As we went into the troops," George Bent said, "I saw an officer on a bay horse rush past me through the dense clouds of dust and smoke. His horse was running away from him . . . the lieutenant had an arrow sticking in his forehead and his face was streaming with blood." (The fatally wounded officer was Lieutenant Caspar Collins.) A few of the cavalrymen escaped and reached a rescue platoon of infantrymen on the bridge. Cannon from the fort broke off further pursuit by the Indians.

While the fighting was going on, some of the Indians still on the hills discovered why the cavalrymen had marched out of the fort. They had been riding to meet a wagon train approaching from the west. In a few minutes, the Indians had the wagon train surrounded, but the soldiers dug in under the wagons and put up a stubborn fight. During the first minutes of the fighting, Roman Nose's brother was killed. When Roman Nose heard of this, he was angry for revenge. He called out for all the Cheyennes to prepare for a charge. "We are going to empty the soldiers' guns!" he shouted. Roman Nose was wearing his medicine bonnet and shield, and he knew that no bullets could strike him. He led the Cheyennes into a circle around the wagons, and they lashed their ponies so that they ran very fast. As the circle tightened closer to the wagons, the soldiers emptied all their guns at once, and then the Cheyennes charged straight for the wagons and killed all the soldiers. They were disappointed

by what they found in the wagons; nothing was there but soldiers' bedding and mess chests.

That night in camp Red Cloud and the other chiefs decided they had taught the soldiers to fear the power of the Indians. And so they returned to the Powder River country, hopeful that the white men would now obey the Laramie treaty and quit prowling without permission into the Indians' country north of the Platte.

Meanwhile, Black Kettle and the last remnants of the Southern Cheyennes had moved south of the Arkansas River. They joined Little Raven's Arapahos, who by this time had heard of the Sand Creek massacre and were mourning friends and relatives lost there. During the summer (1865) their hunters found only a few buffalo below the Arkansas, but they were afraid to go back north where the big herds grazed between the Smoky Hill and Republican rivers.

Late in the summer, runners and messengers began coming from all directions looking for Black Kettle and Little Raven. Suddenly they had become very important. Some white officials had journeyed from Washington to find the Cheyennes and Arapahos and tell them the Great Father and his Council were filled with pity for them. The government officials wanted to make a new treaty.

Although the Cheyennes and Arapahos had been driven from Colorado, and settlers were claiming their lands, it seemed that the titles to the lands were not clear. By the law of the old treaties it could be proven that Denver City itself stood upon Cheyenne and Arapaho land. The government wanted all Indian land claims in Colorado extinguished so that white settlers would be certain they owned the land once they had claimed it.

Black Kettle and Little Raven would not agree to meet with the officials until they heard from the Little White Man, William Bent. He told them that he had tried to persuade the United States to give the Indians permanent rights to the buffalo country between the Smoky Hill and Republican, but the government refused to do this because a stage line and later a railroad would pass through that country, bringing more white settlers. The Cheyennes and Arapahos would have to live south of the Arkansas River.

In the Drying Grass Moon, Black Kettle and Little Raven met the commissioners at the mouth of the Little Arkansas. The Indians had seen two of these treaty makers before—Black Whiskers Sanborn and White Whiskers Harney. They believed Sanborn to be a friend, but they remembered Harney had massacred the Brulé Sioux at the Blue Water in Nebraska in 1855. Agents Murphy and Leavenworth were there, and a straight-talking man, James Steele. Rope Thrower Carson, who had separated the Navahos from their tribal lands, was also there. Gray Blanket Smith, who had endured the ordeal of Sand Creek with them, came to translate, and the Little White Man was there to do the best he could for them.

"Here we are, all together, Arapahos and Cheyennes," Black Kettle said, "but few of us, we are one people. . . . All my friends, the Indians that are holding back—they are afraid to come in; are afraid they will be betrayed as I have been."

"It will be a very hard thing to leave the country that God gave us," Little Raven said. "Our friends are buried there, and we hate to leave these grounds. . . . There is something strong for us—that fool band of soldiers that cleared out our lodges and killed our women and children. This is hard on us. There at Sand Creek—White Antelope and many other chiefs lie there; our women and children lie there. Our lodges were destroyed there, and our horses were taken from us there, and I do not feel disposed to go right off to a new country and leave them."

James Steele answered: "We all fully realize

that it is hard for any people to leave their homes and graves of their ancestors, but, unfortunately for you, gold has been discovered in your country, and a crowd of white people have gone there to live, and a great many of these people are the worst enemies of the Indians—men who do not care for their interests, and who would not stop at any crime to enrich themselves. These men are now in your country —in all parts of it—and there is no portion where you can live and maintain yourselves but what you will come in contact with them. The consequences of this state of things are that you are in constant danger of being imposed upon, and you have to resort to arms in self-defense. Under the circumstances, there is, in the opinion of the commission, no part of the former country large enough where you can live in peace."

Black Kettle said: "Our forefathers, when alive, lived all over this country; they did not know about doing wrong; since then they have died, and gone I don't know where. We have all lost our way. . . . Our Great Father sent you here with his words to us, and we take hold of them. Although the troops have struck us, we throw it all behind and are glad to meet you in peace and friendship. What you have come here for, and what the President has sent you for, I don't object to, but say yes to it. . . . The white people can go wherever they please and they will not be disturbed by us, and I want

you to let them know. . . . We are different nations, but it seems as if we were but one people, whites and all. . . . Again I take you by the hand, and I feel happy. These people that are with us are glad to think that we have peace once more, and can sleep soundly, and that we can live."

And so they agreed to live south of the Arkansas, sharing land that belonged to the Kiowas. On October 14, 1865, the chiefs and head men of what remained of the Southern Cheyennes and Arapahos signed the new treaty agreeing to "perpetual peace." Article 2 of the treaty read: "It is *further agreed* by the Indian parties hereto . . . that henceforth they will, and do hereby, relinquish all claims or rights . . . in and to the country bounded as follows, viz: beginning at the junction of the north and south forks of the Platte River; thence up the north fork to the top of the principal range of the Rocky Mountains, or to the Red Buttes; thence southwardly along the summit of the Rocky Mountains to the headwaters of the Arkansas River; thence down the Arkansas River to the Cimarone crossing of the same; thence to the place of beginning; which country they claim to have originally owned, and never to have relinquished the title thereto."

Thus did the Cheyennes and Arapahos abandon all claims to the Territory of Colorado. And that of course was the real meaning of the massacre at Sand Creek.

VII   A Militant South

24

This Cargo
of Human Flesh

William Wells Brown

through the eyes of both blacks and whites. We feel what life in servitude was like, as William Wells Brown, a slave who ran away to the North, describes his experiences "under the lash" in a widely read slave narrative. We also follow Nat Turner on his blood-drenched slave insurrection in Virginia; and then we look at this event—and at developments in the North—as Southerners saw them, in an attempt to understand what they were afraid of and why they ultimately seceded from the Union.

Sectional conflict over slavery, as Staughton Lynd observed, existed from the very beginning of the nation. It continued through the Federalist, Jeffersonian, and Jacksonian era, becoming especially acute with the rise of the Abolitionist Crusade in the 1830s. Then, in the era of expansion and the Mexican War, the debate over slavery shifted to the Western territories, which slave and free-soil elements alike sought to control for their own political interests. The decade of the 1850s was a time of spiraling violence over the slavery issue as the nation spun inexorably toward Southern secession and Civil War.

Southerners themselves generated much of the suspicion and violence that divided the United States, for they increasingly saw their region as a lonely slave outpost in a hostile world. As a consequence, Southerners sought to dominate the Federal government in order to protect their peculiar institution, an institution which was the cornerstone of the South's racist and class-conscious social order. At the same time, Southern leaders became more repressive and reactionary at home, too, as they made slavery defense the *sine qua non* of Southern patriotism. We begin with a kaleidoscopic picture of the antebellum South, as seen

My master owned about forty slaves, twenty-five of whom were field hands. He removed from Kentucky to Missouri, when I was quite young, and settled thirty or forty miles above St. Charles, on the Missouri, where, in addition to his practice as a physician, he carried on milling, merchandizing and farming. He had a large farm, the principal productions of which were tobacco and hemp. The slave cabins were situated on the back part of the farm, with the house of the overseer, whose name was Grove Cook, in their midst. He had the entire charge of the farm, and having no family, was allowed a woman to keep house for him, whose business it was to deal out the provisions for the hands.

A woman was also kept at the quarters to do the cooking for the field hands, who were summoned to their unrequited toil every morning at four o'clock, by the ringing of a bell, hung on a post near the house of the overseer. They were allowed half an hour to eat their breakfast, and get to the field. At half past four, a horn was blown by the overseer, which was the signal to commence work; and every one that was not on the spot at the time, had to receive

---

From *Narrative of William W. Brown, A Fugitive Slave*, second edition, enlarged, by William Wells Brown. Boston: Published at the Anti-Slavery Office, 1848.

ten lashes from the negro-whip, with which the overseer always went armed. The handle was about three feet long, with the butt-end filled with lead, and the lash six or seven feet in length, made of cowhide, with platted wire on the end of it. This whip was put in requisition very frequently and freely, and a small offence on the part of a slave furnished an occasion for its use. During the time that Mr. Cook was overseer, I was a house servant—a situation preferable to that of a field hand, as I was better fed, better clothed, and not obliged to rise at the ringing of the bell, but about half an hour after. I have often laid and heard the crack of the whip, and the screams of the slave. My mother was a field hand, and one morning was ten or fifteen minutes behind the others in getting into the field. As soon as she reached the spot where they were at work, the overseer commenced whipping her. She cried, "Oh! pray —Oh! pray—Oh! pray"—these are generally the words of slaves when imploring mercy at the hands of their oppressors. I heard her voice, and knew it, and jumped out of my bunk, and went to the door. Though the field was some distance from the house, I could hear every crack of the whip, and every groan and cry of my poor mother. I remained at the door, not daring to venture any farther. The cold chills ran over me, and I wept aloud. After giving her ten lashes, the sound of the whip ceased, and I returned to my bed, and found no consolation but in my tears. It was not yet daylight.

2

My master being a political demagogue, soon found those who were ready to put him into office, for the favors he could render them; and a few years after his arrival in Missouri, he was elected to a seat in the Legislature. In his absence from home, everything was left in charge of Mr. Cook, the overseer, and he soon became more tyrannical and cruel. Among the slaves on the plantation, was one by the name of Randall. He was a man about six feet high, and well-proportioned, and known as a man of great strength and power. He was considered the most valuable and able-bodied slave on the plantation; but no matter how good or useful a slave may be, he seldom escapes the lash. But it was not so with Randall. He had been on the plantation since my earliest recollection, and I had never known of his being flogged. No thanks were due to the master or overseer for this. I have often heard him declare, that no white man should ever whip him—that he would die first.

Cook, from the time that he came upon the plantation, had frequently declared, that he could and would flog any nigger that was put into the field to work under him. My master had repeatedly told him not to attempt to whip Randall, but he was determined to try it. As soon as he was left sole dictator, he thought the time had come to put his threats into execution. He soon began to find fault with Randall, and threatened to whip him, if he did not do better. One day he gave him a very hard task, —more than he could possibly do; and at night, the task not being performed, he told Randall that he should remember him the next morning. On the following morning, after the hands had taken breakfast, Cook called out to Randall, and told him that he intended to whip him, and ordered him to cross his hands and be tied. Randall asked why he wished to whip him. He answered, because he had not finished his task the day before. Randall said that the task was too great, or he should have done it. Cook said it made no difference,—he should whip him. Randall stood silent for a moment, and then said, "Mr. Cook, I have always tried to please you since you have been on the plantation, and I find you are determined not to be satisfied with my work, let me do as well as I may. No man has laid hands on me, to whip me, for the last ten years, and I have long since come to the conclusion not to be whipped

by any man living." Cook, finding by Randall's determined look and gestures, that he would resist, called three of the hands from their work, and commanded them to seize Randall, and tie him. The hands stood still;—they knew Randall—and they also knew him to be a powerful man, and were afraid to grapple with him. As soon as Cook had ordered the men to seize him, Randall turned to them, and said— "Boys, you all know me; you know that I can handle any three of you, and the man that lays hands on me shall die. This white man can't whip me himself, and therefore he has called you to help him." The overseer was unable to prevail upon them to seize and secure Randall, and finally ordered them all to go to their work together.

Nothing was said to Randall by the overseer, for more than a week. One morning, however, while the hands were at work in the field, he came into it, accompanied by three friends of his, Thompson, Woodbridge and Jones. They came up to where Randall was at work, and Cook ordered him to leave his work, and go with them to the barn. He refused to go; whereupon he was attacked by the overseer and his companions, when he turned upon them, and laid them, one after another, prostrate on the ground. Woodbridge drew out his pistol, and fired at him, and brought him to the ground by a pistol ball. The others rushed upon him with their clubs, and beat him over the head and face, until they succeeded in tying him. He was then taken to the barn, and tied to a beam. Cook gave him over one hundred lashes with a heavy cowhide, had him washed with salt and water, and left him tied during the day. The next day he was untied, and taken to a blacksmith's shop, and had a ball and chain attached to his leg. He was compelled to labor in the field, and perform the same amount of work that the other hands did. When his master returned home, he was much pleased to find that Randall had been subdued in his absence.

3

Soon afterwards, my master removed to the city of St. Louis, and purchased a farm four miles from there, which he placed under the charge of an overseer by the name of Friend Haskell. He was a regular Yankee from New England. The Yankees are noted for making the most cruel overseers.

My mother was hired out in the city, and I was also hired out there to Major Freeland, who kept a public house. He was formerly from Virginia, and was a horse-racer, cock-fighter, gambler, and withal an inveterate drunkard. There were ten or twelve servants in the house, and when he was present, it was cut and slash —knock down and drag out. In his fits of anger, he would take up a chair, and throw it at a servant; and in his more rational moments, when he wished to chastise one, he would tie them up in the smokehouse, and whip them; after which, he would cause a fire to be made of tobacco stems, and smoke them. This he called *"Virginia play."*

I complained to my master of the treatment which I received from Major Freeland; but it made no difference. He cared nothing about it, so long as he received the money for my labor. After living with Major Freeland five or six months, I ran away, and went into the woods back of the city; and when night came on, I made my way to my master's farm, but was afraid to be seen, knowing that if Mr. Haskell, the overseer, should discover me, I should be again carried back to Major Freeland; so I kept in the woods. One day, while in the woods, I heard the barking and howling of dogs, and in a short time they came so near, that I knew them to be the bloodhounds of Major Benjamin O'Fallon. He kept five or six, to hunt runaway slaves with.

As soon as I was convinced that it was them, I knew there was no chance of escape. I took refuge in the top of a tree, and the hounds

were soon at its base, and there remained until the hunters came up in a half or three quarters of an hour afterwards. There were two men with the dogs, who, as soon as they came up, ordered me to descend. I came down, was tied, and taken to St. Louis jail. Major Freeland soon made his appearance, and took me out, and ordered me to follow him, which I did. After we returned home, I was tied up in the smoke-house, and was very severely whipped. After the Major had flogged me to his satisfaction, he sent out his son Robert, a young man eighteen or twenty years of age, to see that I was well smoked. He made a fire of tobacco stems, which soon set me to coughing and sneezing. This, Robert told me, was the way his father used to do to his slaves in Virginia. After giving me what they conceived to be a decent smoking, I was untied and again set to work.

Robert Freeland was a "chip off the old block." Though quite young, it was not unfrequently that he came home in a state of intoxication. He is now, I believe, a popular commander of a steamboat on the Mississippi River. Major Freeland soon after failed in business, and I was put on board the steamboat Missouri, which plied between St. Louis and Galena. The commander of the boat was William B. Culver. I remained on her during the sailing season, which was the most pleasant time for me that I had ever experienced. At the close of navigation, I was hired to Mr. John Colburn, keeper of the Missouri Hotel. He was from one of the Free States; but a more inveterate hater of the negro, I do not believe ever walked on God's green earth. This hotel was at that time one of the largest in the city, and there were employed in it twenty or thirty servants, mostly slaves.

Mr. Colburn was very abusive, not only to the servants, but to his wife also, who was an excellent woman, and one from whom I never knew a servant to receive a harsh word; but never did I know a kind one to a servant from

her husband. Among the slaves employed in the hotel, was one by the name of Aaron, who belonged to Mr. John F. Darby, a lawyer. Aaron was the knife-cleaner. One day, one of the knives was put on the table, not as clean as it might have been. Mr. Colburn, for this offence, tied Aaron up in the wood-house, and gave him over fifty lashes on the bare back with a cowhide, after which, he made me wash him down with rum. This seemed to put him into more agony than the whipping. After being untied, he went home to his master, and complained of the treatment which he had received. Mr. Darby would give no heed to anything he had to say, but sent him directly back. Colburn, learning that he had been to his master with complaints, tied him up again, and gave him a more severe whipping than before. The poor fellow's back was literally cut to pieces; so much so, that he was not able to work for ten or twelve days.

There was also, among the servants, a girl whose master resided in the country. Her name was Patsey. Mr. Colburn tied her up one evening, and whipped her until several of the boarders came out and begged him to desist. The reason for whipping her was this. She was engaged to be married to a man belonging to Major William Christy, who resided four or five miles north of the city. Mr. Colburn had forbid her to see John Christy. The reason of this was said to be the regard which he himself had for Patsey. She went to meeting that evening, and John returned home with her. Mr. Colburn had intended to flog John, if he came within the inclosure; but John knew too well the temper of his rival, and kept at a safe distance;—so he took vengeance on the poor girl. If all the slave-drivers had been called together, I do not think a more cruel man than John Colburn,—and he too a northern man,—could have been found among them.

While living at the Missouri Hotel, a circumstance occurred which caused me great unhappiness. My master sold my mother, and all

her children, except myself. They were sold to different persons in the city of St. Louis.

4

I was soon after taken from Mr. Colburn's, and hired to Elijah P. Lovejoy, who was at that time publisher and editor of the "St. Louis Times." My work, while with him, was mainly in the printing office, waiting on the hands, working the press, &c. Mr. Lovejoy was a very good man, and decidedly the best master that I had ever had. I am chiefly indebted to him, and to my employment in the printing office, for what little learning I obtained while in slavery.

Though slavery is thought, by some, to be mild in Missouri, when compared with the cotton, sugar and rice growing States, yet no part of our slaveholding country, is more noted for the barbarity of its inhabitants, than St. Louis. It was here that Col. Harney, a United States officer, whipped a slave woman to death. It was here that Francis McIntosh, a free colored man from Pittsburgh, was taken from the steamboat Flora, and burned at the stake. During a residence of eight years in this city, numerous cases of extreme cruelty came under my own observation;—to record them all, would occupy more space than could possibly be allowed in this little volume. I shall, therefore, give but a few more, in addition to what I have already related.

Capt. J. B. Brunt, who resided near my master, had a slave named John. He was his body servant, carriage driver, &c. On one occasion, while driving his master through the city, —the streets being very muddy, and the horses going at a rapid rate,—some mud spattered upon a gentleman by the name of Robert More. More was determined to be revenged. Some three or four months after this occurrence, he purchased John, for the express purpose, as he

said, "to tame the d——d nigger." After the purchase, he took him to a blacksmith's shop, and had a ball and chain fastened to his leg, and then put him to driving a yoke of oxen, and kept him at hard labor, until the iron around his leg was so worn into the flesh, that it was thought mortification would ensue. In addition to this, John told me that his master whipped him regularly three times a week for the first two months:—and all this to *"tame him."* A more noble looking man than he, was not to be found in all St. Louis, before he fell into the hands of More; and a more degraded and spirit-crushed looking being was never seen on a southern plantation, after he had been subjected to this *"taming"* process for three months. The last time that I saw him, he had nearly lost the entire use of his limbs.

While living with Mr. Lovejoy, I was often sent on errands to the office of the "Missouri Republican," published by Mr. Edward Charles. Once, while returning to the office with type, I was attacked by several large boys, sons of slave-holders, who pelted me with snow-balls. Having the heavy form of type in my hands, I could not make my escape by running; so I laid down the type and gave them battle. They gathered around me, pelting me with stones and sticks, until they overpowered me, and would have captured me, if I had not resorted to my heels. Upon my retreat, they took possession of the type; and what to do to regain it I could not devise. Knowing Mr. Lovejoy to be a very humane man, I went to the office, and laid the case before him. He told me to remain in the office. He took one of the apprentices with him, and went after the type, and soon returned with it; but on his return informed me that Samuel McKinney had told him that he would whip me, because I had hurt his boy. Soon after, McKinney was seen making his way to the office by one of the printers, who informed me to the fact, and I made my escape through the back door.

McKinney not being able to find me on his arrival, left the office in a great rage, swearing that he would whip me to death. A few days after, as I was walking along Main Street, he seized me by the collar, and struck me over the head five or six times with a large cane, which caused the blood to gush from my nose and ears in such a manner that my clothes were completely saturated with blood. After beating me to his satisfaction, he let me go, and I returned to the office so weak from the loss of blood, that Mr. Lovejoy sent me home to my master. It was five weeks before I was able to walk again. During this time, it was necessary to have some one to supply my place at the office, and I lost the situation.

After my recovery, I was hired to Capt. Otis Reynolds, as a waiter on board the steamboat Enterprize, owned by Messrs. John and Edward Walsh, commission merchants at St. Louis. This boat was then running on the upper Mississippi. My employment on board was to wait on gentlemen, and the captain being a good man, the situation was a pleasant one to me;—but in passing from place to place, and seeing new faces every day, and knowing that they could go where they pleased, I soon became unhappy, and several times thought of leaving the boat at some landing place, and trying to make my escape to Canada, which I had heard much about as a place where the slave might live, be free, and be protected.

But whenever such thoughts would come into my mind, my resolution would soon be shaken by the remembrance that my dear mother was a slave in St. Louis, and I could not bear the idea of leaving her in that condition. She had often taken me upon her knee, and told me how she had carried me upon her back to the field when I was an infant—how often she had been whipped for leaving her work to nurse me—and how happy I would appear when she would take me into her arms. When these thoughts came over me, I would

resolve never to leave the land of slavery without my mother. I thought that to leave her in slavery, after she had undergone and suffered so much for me, would be proving recreant to the duty which I owed to her. Besides this, I had three brothers and a sister there,—two of my brothers having died.

. . .

A few weeks after, on our downward passage, the boat took on board, at Hannibal, a drove of slaves, bound for the New Orleans market. They numbered from fifty to sixty, consisting of men and women from eighteen to forty years of age. A drove of slaves on a southern steamboat, bound for the cotton or sugar regions, is an occurrence so common, that no one, not even the passengers, appear to notice it, though they clank their chains at every step. There was, however, one in this gang that attracted the attention of the passengers and crew. It was a beautiful girl, apparently about twenty years of age, perfectly white, with straight light hair and blue eyes. But it was not the whiteness of her skin that created such a sensation among those who gazed upon her—it was her almost unparalleled beauty. She had been on the boat but a short time, before the attention of all the passengers, including the ladies, had been called to her, and the common topic of conversation was about the beautiful slave-girl. She was not in chains. The man who claimed this article of human merchandise was a Mr. Walker,—a well known slave-trader, residing in St. Louis. There was a general anxiety among the passengers and crew to learn the history of the girl. Her master kept close by her side, and it would have been considered impudent for any of the passengers to have spoken to her, and the crew were not allowed to have any conversation with them. When we reached St. Louis, the slaves were removed to a boat bound for New

Orleans, and the history of the beautiful slave-girl remained a mystery.

I remained on the boat during the season, and it was not an unfrequent occurrence to have on board gangs of slaves on their way to the cotton, sugar and rice plantations of the South.

Toward the latter part of the summer, Captain Reynolds left the boat, and I was sent home. I was then placed on the farm under Mr. Haskell, the overseer. As I had been some time out of the field, and not accustomed to work in the burning sun, it was very hard; but I was compelled to keep up with the best of the hands.

I found a great difference between the work in a steamboat cabin and that in a corn-field.

My master, who was then living in the city, soon after removed to the farm, when I was taken out of the field to work in the house as a waiter. Though his wife was very peevish, and hard to please, I much preferred to be under her control than the overseer's. They brought with them Mr. Sloane, a Presbyterian minister; Miss Martha Tulley, a niece of theirs from Kentucky; and their nephew William. The latter had been in the family a number of years, but the others were all new-comers.

Mr. Sloane was a young minister, who had been at the South but a short time, and it seemed as if his whole aim was to please the slaveholders, especially my master and mistress. He was intending to make a visit during the winter, and he not only tried to please them, but I think he succeeded admirably. When they wanted singing, he sung; when they wanted praying, he prayed; when they wanted a story told, he told a story. Instead of his teaching my master theology, my master taught theology to him. While I was with Captain Reynolds, my master "got religion," and new laws were made on the plantation. Formerly, we had the privilege of hunting, fishing, making splint brooms, baskets, &c. on Sunday; but this was all stopped. Every Sun-

day, we were all compelled to attend meeting. Master was so religious, that he induced some others to join him in hiring a preacher to preach to the slaves.

5

My master had family worship, night and morning. At night, the slaves were called in to attend; but in the mornings, they had to be at their work, and master did all the praying. My master and mistress were great lovers of mint julep, and every morning, a pitcher-full was made, of which they all partook freely, not excepting little master William. After drinking freely all round, they would have family worship, and then breakfast. I cannot say but I loved the julep as well as any of them, and during prayer was always careful to seat myself close to the table where it stood, so as to help myself when they were all busily engaged in their devotions. By the time prayer was over, I was about as happy as any of them. A sad accident happened one morning. In helping myself, and at the same time keeping an eye on my old mistress, I accidentally let the pitcher fall upon the floor, breaking it in pieces, and spilling the contents. This was a bad affair for me; for as soon as prayer was over, I was taken and severely chastised.

My master's family consisted of himself, his wife, and their nephew, William Moore. He was taken into the family, when only a few weeks of age. His name being that of my own, mine was changed, for the purpose of giving precedence to his, though I was his senior by ten or twelve years. The plantation being four miles from the city, I had to drive the family to church. I always dreaded the approach of the Sabbath; for, during service, I was obliged to stand by the horses in the hot broiling sun, or in the rain, just as it happened.

One Sabbath, as we were driving past the house of D. D. Page, a gentleman who owned

a large baking establishment, as I was sitting upon the box of the carriage, which was very much elevated, I saw Mr. Page pursuing a slave around the yard, with a long whip, cutting him at every jump. The man soon escaped from the yard, and was followed by Mr. Page. They came running past us, and the slave perceiving that he would be overtaken, stopped suddenly, and Page stumbled over him, and falling on the stone pavement, fractured one of his legs, which crippled him for life. The same gentleman, but a short time previous, tied up a woman of his, by the name of Delphia, and whipped her nearly to death; yet he was a deacon in the Baptist church, in good and regular standing. Poor Delphia! I was well acquainted with her, and called to see her while upon her sick bed; and I shall never forget her appearance. She was a member of the same church with her master.

Soon after this, I was hired out to Mr. Walker; the same man whom I have mentioned as having carried a gang of slaves down the river, on the steamboat Enterprize. Seeing me in the capacity of steward on the boat, and thinking that I would make a good hand to take care of slaves, he determined to have me for that purpose; and finding that my master would not sell me, he hired me for the term of one year.

When I learned the fact of my having been hired to a negro speculator, or a "soul-driver" as they are generally called among slaves, no one can tell my emotions. Mr. Walker had offered a high price for me, as I afterwards learned, but I suppose my master was restrained from selling me by the fact that I was a near relative of his. On entering the service of Mr. Walker, I found that my opportunity of getting to a land of liberty was gone, at least for the time being. He had a gang of slaves in readiness to start for New Orleans, and in a few days we were on our journey. I am at a loss for language to express my feelings on that occasion. Although my master had told me that

he had not sold me, and Mr. Walker had told me that he had not purchased me, I did not believe them; and not until I had been to New Orleans, and was on my return, did I believe that I was not sold.

There was on the boat a large room on the lower deck, in which the slaves were kept, men and women, promiscuously—all chained two and two, and a strict watch kept that they did not get loose; for cases have occurred in which slaves have got off their chains, and made their escape at landing-places, while the boats were taking in wood;—and with all our care, we lost one woman who had been taken from her husband and children, and having no desire to live without them, in the agony of her soul jumped overboard, and drowned herself. She was not chained.

It was almost impossible to keep that part of the boat clean.

On landing at Natchez, the slaves were all carried to the slave-pen, and there kept one week, during which time, several of them were sold. Mr. Walker fed his slaves well. We took on board, at St. Louis, several hundred pounds of bacon (smoked meat) and cornmeal, and his slaves were better fed than slaves generally were in Natchez, so far as my observation extended.

At the end of a week, we left for New Orleans, the place of our final destination, which we reached in two days. Here the slaves were placed in a negro-pen, where those who wished to purchase could call and examine them. The negro-pen is a small yard, surrounded by buildings, from fifteen to twenty feet wide, with the exception of a large gate with iron bars. The slaves are kept in the buildings during the night, and turned out into the yard during the day. After the best of the stock was sold at private sale at the pen, the balance were taken to the Exchange Coffee House Auction Rooms, kept by Isaac L. McCoy, and sold at public auction. After the sale of this lot of slaves, we left New Orleans for St. Louis.

6

On our arrival at St. Louis, I went to Dr. Young, and told him that I did not wish to live with Mr. Walker any longer. I was heart-sick at seeing my fellow-creatures bought and sold. But the Dr. had hired me for the year, and stay I must. Mr. Walker again commenced purchasing another gang of slaves. He bought a man of Colonel John O'Fallon, who resided in the suburbs of the city. This man had a wife and three children. As soon as the purchase was made, he was put in jail for safe keeping, until we should be ready to start for New Orleans. His wife visited him while there, several times, and several times when she went for that purpose was refused admittance.

In the course of eight or nine weeks Mr. Walker had his cargo of human flesh made up. There was in this lot a number of old men and women, some of them with gray locks. We left St. Louis in the steamboat Carlton, Captain Swan, bound for New Orleans. On our way down, and before we reached Rodney,* the place where we made our first stop, I had to prepare the old slaves for market. I was ordered to have the old men's whiskers shaved off, and the gray hairs plucked out where they were not too numerous, in which case he had a preparation of blacking to color it, and with a blacking-brush we would put it on. This was new business to me, and was performed in a room where the passengers could not see us. These slaves were also taught how old they were by Mr. Walker, and after going through the blacking process, they looked ten or fifteen years younger; and I am sure that some of those who purchased slaves of Mr. Walker, were dreadfully cheated, especially in the ages of the slaves which they bought.

We landed at Rodney, and the slaves were driven to the pen in the back part of the village.

* Mississippi.

Several were sold at this place, during our stay of four or five days, when we proceeded to Natchez. There we landed at night, and the gang were put in the warehouse until morning, when they were driven to the pen. As soon as the slaves are put in these pens, swarms of planters may be seen in and about them. They knew when Walker was expected, as he always had the time advertised beforehand when he would be in Rodney, Natchez, and New Orleans. These were the principal places where he offered his slaves for sale.

.   .   .

The next day we proceeded to New Orleans, and put the gang in the same negro-pen which we occupied before. In a short time, the planters came flocking to the pen to purchase slaves. Before the slaves were exhibited for sale, they were dressed and driven out into the yard. Some were set to dancing, some to jumping, some to singing, and some to playing cards. This was done to make them appear cheerful and happy. My business was to see that they were placed in those situations before the arrival of the purchasers, and I have often set them to dancing when their cheeks were wet with tears. As slaves were in good demand at that time, they were all soon disposed of, and we again set out for St. Louis.

On our arrival, Mr. Walker purchased a farm five or six miles from the city. He had no family, but made a housekeeper of one of his female slaves. Poor Cynthia! I knew her well. She was a quadroon, and one of the most beautiful women I ever saw. She was a native of St. Louis, and bore an irreproachable character for virtue and propriety of conduct. Mr. Walker bought her for the New Orleans market, and took her down with him on one of the trips that I made with him. Never shall I forget the circumstances of that voyage! On the first night that we were on board the steamboat, he directed me to put her into a stateroom he had provided for her, apart from the other slaves.

I had seen too much of the workings of slavery, not to know what this meant. I accordingly watched him into the state-room, and listened to hear what passed between them. I heard him make his base offers, and her reject them. He told her that if she would accept his vile proposals, he would take her back with him to St. Louis, and establish her as his housekeeper at his farm. But if she persisted in rejecting them, he would sell her as a field hand on the worst plantation on the river. Neither threats nor bribes prevailed, however, and he retired, disappointed of his prey.

The next morning, poor Cynthia told me what had past, and bewailed her sad fate with floods of tears. I comforted and encouraged her all I could; but I foresaw but too well what the result must be. Without entering into any farther particulars, suffice it to say that Walker performed his part of the contract, at that time. He took her back to St. Louis, established her as his mistress and housekeeper at his farm, and before I left, he had two children by her. But, mark the end! Since I have been at the North, I have been credibly informed that Walker has been married, and, as a previous measure, sold poor Cynthia and her four children (she having had two more since I came away) into hopeless bondage!

He soon commenced purchasing to make up the third gang. We took steamboat, and went to Jefferson City, a town on the Missouri river. Here we landed, and took stage for the interior of the State. He bought a number of slaves as he passed the different farms and villages. After getting twenty-two or twenty-three men and women, we arrived at St. Charles, a village on the banks of the Missouri. Here he purchased a woman who had a child in her arms, appearing to be four or five weeks old.

We had been travelling by land for some days, and were in hopes to have found a boat at this place for St. Louis, but were disappointed. As no boat was expected for some days, we started for St. Louis by land. Mr.

Walker had purchased two horses. He rode one, and I the other. The slaves were chained together, and we took up our line of march, Mr. Walker taking the lead, and I bringing up the rear. Though the distance was not more than twenty miles, we did not reach it the first day. The road was worse than any that I have ever travelled.

Soon after we left St. Charles, the young child grew very cross, and kept up a noise during the greater part of the day. Mr. Walker complained of its crying several times, and told the mother to stop the child's d——d noise, or he would. The woman tried to keep the child from crying, but could not. We put up at night with an acquaintance of Mr. Walker, and in the morning, just as we were about to start, the child again commenced crying. Walker stepped up to her, and told her to give the child to him. The mother tremblingly obeyed. He took the child by one arm, as you would a cat by the leg, walked into the house, and said to the lady,

"Madam, I will make you a present of this little nigger; it keeps such a noise that I can't bear it."

"Thank you, sir," said the lady.

The mother, as soon as she saw that her child was to be left, ran up to Mr. Walker, and falling upon her knees begged him to let her have her child; she clung around his legs, and cried, "Oh, my child! my child! master, do let me have my child! oh, do, do, do. I will stop its crying, if you will only let me have it again."

.   .   .

Mr. Walker commanded her to return into the ranks with the other slaves. Women who had children were not chained, but those that had none were. As soon as her child was disposed of, she was chained in the gang.

.   .   .

We finally arrived at Mr. Walker's farm. He had a house built during our absence to put

A Southern slave auction like that described by William Wells Brown. "Before the slaves were exhibited for sale," Brown writes, "they were dressed and driven out into the yard. Some were set to dancing, some to jumping, some to singing, and some to playing cards. This was done to make them appear cheerful and happy. My business was to see that they were placed in those situations before the arrival of the purchasers, and I have often set them to dancing when their cheeks were set with tears. As slaves were in good demand at that time, they were all soon disposed of, and we again set out for St. Louis." (Courtesy of The Library of Congress.)

slaves in. It was a kind of domestic jail. The slaves were put in the jail at night, and worked on the farm during the day. They were kept here until the gang was completed, when we again started for New Orleans, on board the steamboat North America, Capt. Alexander Scott. We had a large number of slaves in this gang. One, by the name of Joe, Mr. Walker was training up to take my place, as my time was nearly out, and glad was I. We made our first stop at Vicksburg, where we remained one week and sold several slaves.

Mr. Walker, though not a good master, had not flogged a slave since I had been with him, though he had threatened me. The slaves were kept in the pen, and he always put up at the best hotel, and kept his wines in his room, for the accommodation of those who called to negotiate with him for the purchase of slaves. One day while we were at Vicksburg, several gentlemen came to see him for this purpose, and as usual the wine was called for. I took the tray and started around with it, and having accidentally filled some of the glasses too full, the gentlemen spilled the wine on their clothes as they went to drink. Mr. Walker apologized

to them for my carelessness, but looked at me as though he would see me again on this subject.

After the gentlemen had left the room, he asked me what I meant by my carelessness, and said that he would attend to me. The next morning, he gave me a note to carry to the jailer, and a dollar in money to give to him. I suspected that all was not right, so I went down near the landing where I met with a sailor, and walking up to him, asked him if he would be so kind as to read the note for me. He read it over, and then looked at me. I asked him to tell me what was in it. Said he,

"They are going to give you hell."

"Why?" said I.

He said, "This is a note to have you whipped, and says that you have a dollar to pay for it."

He handed me back the note, and off I started. I knew not what to do, but was determined not to be whipped. I went up to the jail —took a look at it, and walked off again. As Mr. Walker was acquainted with the jailer, I feared that I should be found out if I did not go, and be treated in consequence of it still worse.

While I was meditating on the subject, I saw a colored man about my size walk up, and the thought struck me in a moment to send him with my note. I walked up to him, and asked him who he belonged to. He said he was a free man, and had been in the city but a short time. I told him I had a note to go into the jail, and get a trunk to carry to one of the steamboats; but was so busily engaged that I could not do it, although I had a dollar to pay for it. He asked me if I would not give him the job. I handed him the note and the dollar, and off he started for the jail.

I watched to see that he went in, and as soon as I saw the door close behind him, I walked around the corner, and took my station, intending to see how my friend looked when he came out. I had been there but a short time, when a colored man came around the corner, and said to another colored man with whom he was acquainted—

"They are giving a nigger scissors in the jail."

"What for?" said the other. The man continued,

"A nigger came into the jail, and asked for the jailer. The jailer came out, and he handed him a note, and said he wanted to get a trunk. The jailer told him to go with him, and he would give him the trunk. So he took him into the room, and told the nigger to give up the dollar. He said a man had given him the dollar to pay for getting the trunk. But that lie would not answer. So they made him strip himself, and then they tied him down, and are now whipping him."

I stood by all the while listening to their talk, and soon found out that the person alluded to was my customer. I went into the street opposite the jail, and concealed myself in such a manner that I could not be seen by any one coming out. I had been there but a short time, when the young man made his appearance, and looked around for me. I, unobserved, came forth from my hiding-place, behind a pile of brick, and he pretty soon saw me and came up to me complaining bitterly, saying that I had played a trick upon him. I denied any knowledge of what the note contained, and asked him what they had done to him. He told me in substance what I heard the man tell who had come out of the jail.

"Yes," said he, "they whipped me and took my dollar, and gave me this note."

He showed me the note which the jailer had given him, telling him to give it to his master. I told him I would give him fifty cents for it, —that being all the money I had. He gave it to me, and took his money. He had received twenty lashes on his bare back, with the negro-whip.

I took the note and started for the hotel where I had left Mr. Walker. Upon reaching the hotel, I handed it to a stranger whom I had not seen before, and requested him to read it to me. As near as I can recollect, it was as follows:—

> Dear Sir:—By your direction, I have given your boy twenty lashes. He is a very saucy boy, and tried to make me believe that he did not belong to you, and I put it on to him well for lying to me.
>
> I remain,
>
> Your obedient servant.

It is true that in most of the slave-holding cities, when a gentleman wishes his servants whipped, he can send him to the jail and have it done. Before I went in where Mr. Walker was, I wet my cheeks a little, as though I had been crying. He looked at me, and inquired what was the matter. I told him that I had never had such a whipping in my life, and handed him the note. He looked at it and laughed;—"and so you told him that you did not belong to me." "Yes, sir," said I. "I did not know that there was any harm in that." He told me I must behave myself, if I did not want to be whipped again.

This incident shows how it is that slavery makes its victims lying and mean; for which vices it afterwards reproaches them, and uses them as arguments to prove that they deserve no better fate. I have often, since my escape, deeply regretted the deception I practised upon this poor fellow; and I heartily desire that it may be, at some time or other, in my power to make him amends for his vicarious sufferings in my behalf.

7

In a few days we reached New Orleans, and arriving there in the night, remained on board until morning. While at New Orleans this time, I saw a slave killed; an account of which had been published by Theodore D. Weld, in his book entitled, "Slavery as it is." The circumstances were as follows. In the evening, between seven and eight o'clock, a slave came running down the levee, followed by several men and boys. The whites were crying out, "Stop that nigger, stop that nigger;" while the poor panting slave, in almost breathless accents, was repeating, "I did not steal the meat —I did not steal the meat." The poor man at last took refuge in the river. The whites who were in pursuit of him, ran on board of one of the boats to see if they could discover him. They finally espied him under the bow of the steamboat Trenton. They got a pike-pole, and tried to drive him from his hiding place. When they would strike at him, he would dive under the water. The water was so cold, that it soon became evident that he must come out or be drowned.

While they were trying to drive him from under the bow of the boat or drown him, he would in broken and imploring accents say, "I did not steal the meat; I did not steal the meat. My master lives up the river. I want to see my master. I did not steal the meat. Do let me go home to master." After punching him, and striking him over the head for some time, he at last sunk in the water, to rise no more alive.

On the end of the pike-pole with which they were striking him was a hook which caught in his clothing, and they hauled him on the bow of the boat. Some said he was dead, others said he was *"playing possum,"* while others kicked him to make him get up, but it was of no use— he was dead.

As soon as they became satisfied of this, they commenced leaving, one after another. One of the hands on the boat informed the captain that they had killed the man, and that the dead body was lying on the deck. The captain came on deck, and said to those who were remaining, "You have killed this nigger; now

take him off of my boat." The captain's name was Hart. The dead body was dragged on shore and left there. I went on board of the boat where our gang of slaves were, and during the whole night my mind was occupied with what I had seen. Early in the morning, I went on shore to see if the dead body remained there. I found it in the same position that it was left the night before. I watched to see what they would do with it. It was left there until between eight and nine o'clock, when a cart, which takes up the trash out of the streets, came along, and the body was thrown in, and in a few minutes more was covered over with dirt which they were removing from the streets. During the whole time, I did not see more than six or seven persons around it, who, from their manner, evidently regarded it as no uncommon occurrence.

During our stay in the city, I met with a young white man with whom I was well acquainted in St. Louis. He had been sold into slavery, under the following circumstances. His father was a drunkard, and very poor, with a family of five or six children. The father died, and left the mother to take care of and provide for the children as best she might. The eldest was a boy, named Burrill, about thirteen years of age, who did chores in a store kept by Mr. Riley, to assist his mother in procuring a living for the family. After working with him two years, Mr. Riley took him to New Orleans to wait on him while in that city on a visit, and when he returned to St. Louis, he told the mother of the boy that he had died with the yellow fever. Nothing more was heard from him, no one supposing him to be alive. I was much astonished when Burrill told me his story. Though I sympathized with him, I could not assist him. We were both slaves. He was poor, uneducated, and without friends; and if living, is, I presume, still held as a slave.

After selling out this cargo of human flesh, we returned to St. Louis, and my time was up with Mr. Walker. I had served him one year, and it was the longest year I ever lived.

25

A Disturbing Institution

William W. Freehling

At no time in American history was slavery on the verge of dying out. While tobacco cultivation may have become unprofitable by the Revolutionary period, the invention of the cotton gin in 1793 stimulated cotton production immeasurably and created a tremendous demand for slave labor. Thanks to the cotton gin, slavery washed over the South in giant human waves, spreading out beyond the rich black belt of Alabama and Mississippi, out to the Kansas-Missouri border, the fringes of western Arkansas, and south and east Texas. Although Congress outlawed the foreign slave trade in 1808 (it simply continued as an illicit traffic), the number of slaves rose impressively over the decades, so that by 1860 there were nearly four million in fifteen slaveholding states, including Delaware and Maryland. Slavery remained profitable, too, as evidenced by the fact that in 1860 a prime field hand sold for $1,250 in Virginia and $1,800 on the auction blocks in New Orleans. A "fancy girl" went for as high as $2,500. Still, from the Southern white's viewpoint, the profitability of slavery was not the crucial issue. If slavery proved too costly in its plantation setting, Southerners would have found other ways to utilize slave labor, other ways to keep the Negroes in chains. For them, slavery was more than a labor device; it was a rigid system of social control to maintain the purity of the white race.

Before 1820, Southerners tended to apologize for the institution, even though it was crucial for preserving the South as a white man's country. They blamed this "necessary evil" not on themselves, but on British, Dutch, and Yankee slave traders who brought all those blacks here in the first place. Gradually, Southerners contended, they had become stuck with the institution, as the northern states eradicated it by law, constitution, or court decree. After the invention of the cotton gin, slavery became "an economic necessity," that ever-ready rationalization for gentleman planters who felt embarrassed about the discrepancy between Jeffersonian liberalism and human bondage, but lacked the courage to do anything about it. While Jefferson and other Virginia statesmen talked a lot about abolishing slavery and colonizing the freed blacks, they never put their words into action. Their racist constituents would never have accepted emancipation anyway. Some planters—Washington among them—did provide for the manumission of their own slaves when they died, but Jefferson, author of all those eloquent statements about human freedom, was obliged by his southern heritage to leave his Negroes indefinitely enslaved after his death. All he could do was to liberate a couple of "faithful retainers."

If Southerners were grudgingly apologetic about slavery in the Jeffersonian era, the events of the 1820s and 1830s changed all that. In those critical decades, two simultaneous developments played dramatically on the fears of white Southerners—especially in South Carolina—and moved them away from the necessary evil argument to an outright defense of slavery as a positive good.

A society reveals its deepest anxieties when it responds hysterically to a harmless attack. The South Carolina lowcountry's morbid sensitivity to the relatively undeveloped abolitionist crusade in the 1820's is a case in point. The

northern antislavery campaign, although slowly gaining strength in the years before the Nullification Controversy, remained a distant threat in 1832. Yet during the prenullification decade, the Carolina tidewater was periodically in an uproar over the slavery issue. In the 1820's lowcountry congressmen delivered fire-eating harangues at any mention of the subject. And in the early 1830's the lowcountry gentry embraced the nullifiers' cause partly to win constitutional protection against a nascent abolitionist crusade. Throughout the period, the discrepancy between the abolitionists' innocuous attack and the slaveholders' frenzied response was a measure of the guilt and fear which made Negro slavery a profoundly disturbing institution in ante bellum South Carolina.

During the years from 1820 to 1832, only the most prescient Americans realized they were witnessing the first signs of a growing crusade against slavery. In the benevolent reform empire which stretched along the eastern seaboard, idealists were more concerned with temperance and Sunday schools than with the plight of American Negroes. Those reformers who were distressed by racial problems usually soothed their consciences by joining the American Colonization Society. The society, dedicated to removing free Negroes from the United States, had at best only a tangential interest in freeing southern slaves.

However, as the twenties progressed a handful of antislavery crusaders initiated the campaign which would convulse the nation's politics in the years ahead. In 1821 Benjamin Lundy began his influential newspaper, *The Genius of Universal Emancipation*. In 1828 young William Lloyd Garrison assumed control

Abridged from pp. 49–53, 64–72, 82–86 in *Prelude to Civil War* by William W. Freehling. Copyright © 1965, 1966 by William Willhartz Freehling. Reprinted by permission of Harper & Row, Publishers, Inc.

of the Bennington (Vermont) *Journal of the Times*, wrote his first antislavery editorial, and collected over 2,000 signatures on his first antislavery petition. In 1829 David Walker, a militant free Negro, published his *Appeal*, urging slaves to revolt against their masters. Finally, on January 1, 1831, Garrison founded his bellicose newspaper, the *Liberator*. By the eve of the Nullification Controversy, the Nat Turner Revolt and its alleged connection with Garrison's writings had made the *Liberator* notorious in the nation's households.

Yet by 1832 Garrison had gained little support for his crusade. When Garrison organized the New England Anti-Slavery Society at the end of 1831, he managed to persuade only eleven disciples to sign the constitution. The founding fathers could contribute little more than their zeal; not one of them could have scraped together over $100. In the ensuing year, the Garrisonian onslaught continued to lack both funds and followers.

A more significant development of the prenullification years was the mounting evidence that the slavery issue could not be kept out of national politics. The 1820's commenced with a long congressional debate over slavery during the Missouri Controversy. Frightened by the savage emotions which the debates revealed, leading American statesmen attempted to bury the issue. But in 1824 the Ohio state legislature raised the subject again by proposing a national program of gradual emancipation. In 1826 a presidential proposal for a delegation to the Panama Congress of Spanish-American nations touched off a stormy discussion. The delegates would have to hobnob with the successful slave conspirators of San Domingo, and the United States might appear to sanction servile insurrection. In 1827 the American Colonization Society's request for congressional aid inspired another ominous dispute over slavery. It was fitting that the famed Hayne-Webster debate of 1830, with its far-ranging discussion of public issues, should focus at last

on the vexing problem which the nation could not avoid.

It must be emphasized again that most Americans—including most southerners—paid little heed to these nagging controversies. The slavery issue would not become a major national political problem until the gag-rule disputes of the mid-1830's. The point is that the South Carolina lowcountry was too uneasy about slavery to tolerate the slightest signs of a growing abolitionist attack. One leading Charlestonian wrote, as early as 1823, "all the engines and all the means and machines, which talent, fanaticism, false charity, fashionable humanity, or jealousy or folly can invent, are in dreadful operation and array."

South Carolinians raged at the first indications of an antislavery crusade partly because they viewed emancipation with dread. Abolition conjured up grotesque specters of plunder, rape, and murder. The slave, too barbaric and degraded to adjust peaceably to freedom, seemed certain to declare race war the moment he threw off his chains. Moreover, in South Carolina alone, $80 million worth of slave property would be wiped out. Upcountry planters, like most slaveholders, could at least hope to salvage landed property from the wreck of emancipation. But tidewater gentlemen feared they would lose their huge investment in improved land as well as a fortune in slave property. Negroes would never work efficiently without bondage and the fatal swamps could never be cultivated without Negroes. "The richest, most productive land in the State, must be forever left waste," wrote Frederick Dalcho, a conservative Charlestonian. ". . . Can we reasonably be expected to submit to this state of things? Certainly not by reasonable men." Abolition posed a greater *economic* threat than the abominations of the highest protective tariff.

The possibility of an abolitionist triumph was enough to make Negro slavery the most explosive issue an American Congress has ever faced. The fear of ultimate emancipation, however, pervaded the South throughout the ante bellum period, and became more intense as the abolitionist crusade grew stronger. The Carolina lowcountry's intransigence in the 1820's was more explicitly a reaction to the first stages of the conflict over slavery. The real issue in the period of transition was not so much whether slavery should be abolished but rather whether slavery could be discussed. If emancipation could unleash a race war, antislavery agitation could inspire a servile insurrection. An abolitionist attack would also force planters to defend slavery, and many of them regarded slavery as an abomination which should never be defended. The tidewater gentry had every reason to tremble at a full-scale discussion of the slavery issue; and its acute anxiety over facing the issue made the era of nullification a time of great crisis along the South Carolina coast.

In the late eighteenth century, such southerners as Thomas Jefferson and James Madison had helped to forge an American liberal philosophy which was still dogma in South Carolina during the years of the Nullification Controversy. Before the 1830's southerners often admitted that slavery had no place in a land which assumed that men had a natural right to life, liberty, and the pursuit of happiness. Moreover, they could never forget that insurrection was legitimate if men were deprived of their natural rights. The sight of a slave listening to a Fourth of July oration chilled the bravest southerner. "The celebration of the *Fourth of July*, belongs *exclusively* to the white population," wrote a leading Charlestonian. ". . . In our speeches and orations, much, and sometimes more than is politically necessary, is said about personal liberty, which Negro auditors know not how to apply, except by running the parallel with their own condition."

Of course abolitionists insisted that the theory which the Fourth celebrates belongs to Negroes as well as whites. That assertion, no

For the most part, slave labor and the cotton gin proved immensely profitable to ante-bellum Southern planters—especially those who raised luxury cotton in the South Carolina low country. The slaves above are preparing cotton for the gin on a plantation at Beaufort, S.C. (Courtesy of The Library of Congress.)

matter how dispassionately presented, made slaveholders consider any abolitionist tract "incendiary" if it reached the eyes of a slave. Thomas Jefferson's felicitous Declaration of Independence seemed almost as dangerous as David Walker's fiery *Appeal*.

The South Carolina tidewater, with its high proportion of slaves and its considerable number of African imports, was always more apprehensive about slave revolts than any other region in the Old South. Thus the lowcountry gentry watched the Missouri debates with con-

siderable concern. Governor John Geddes of Charleston warned the state legislature of 1820 that "the Missouri question . . . has given rise to the expression of opinions and doctrines respecting this specie of property, which tend not only to diminish its value, but also to threaten our safety." He called for measures which would "oppose at the threshold, everything likely in its consequences to disturb our domestic tranquility." The lawmakers responded by enacting laws designed to halt the increase of free Negroes. South Carolina mas-

ters were no longer permitted to free their slaves, and colored freemen were denied the right to enter the state. The legislature also provided heavy penalties for distributing "incendiary" papers. But as South Carolinians soon discovered, these laws were in no way sufficient to keep at least some slaves from taking in deadly earnest the cardinal tenets of the white man's political dogma.

The nullification crusade made many heroes. Still, the man most responsible for bringing South Carolina to the boiling point was not a great planter-politician, such as John C. Calhoun or James Hamilton, Jr., but a lowly Charleston mulatto named Denmark Vesey. The tragic slave conspiracy which Vesey inspired, although completely crushed in 1822, remained in 1832 and long thereafter a searing reminder that all was not well with slavery in South Carolina. . . .

Uneasy, even in decades of calm, because of the heavy concentration of Negroes, lowcountry South Carolina faced four serious slave disturbances in the ten years preceding the Nullification Crisis. These recurrent conspiracies seemed particularly alarming because they followed on the heels of the first signs of an antislavery attack. The Denmark Vesey Conspiracy occurred two years after the Missouri congressional debates; the Nat Turner Revolt occurred less than a year after the appearance of Garrison's notorious *Liberator*. By 1832 the lowcountry gentry understandably believed that a slight growth of antislavery "fanaticism" immediately led to mounting cases of servile insurrection.

In the longer perspective of ante bellum history, the decade which began with Denmark Vesey and ended with Nat Turner emerges as the great period of slave conspiracies in South Carolina. Never before and never again did the slaves conspire so shrewdly, so widely, so often. Perhaps the rising abolitionist crusade influenced bondsmen, and perhaps they sensed

their masters' uneasiness and irresolution in the face of external attack. After 1835, when slaveholders defended slavery as a "positive good" and tightened controls, slaves seldom dared to seek freedom by revolution. By 1860 South Carolinians were probably less apprehensive about servile insurrection. The famous slave conspiracies of the prenullification decade, like the exaggerated fear they helped to create, were products of the period of transition in southern history, when the beleaguered Carolinian tried to find the nerve to defend a system which he regarded as an abomination against outsiders who believed abominations should be abolished.

The grim chronicle of sabotage and conspiracy, however necessary for an understanding of slavery in South Carolina, distorts the peculiar institution. A small minority of slaves were involved in overt rebellions. Moreover, if planters sometimes regarded slaves with fear and trembling, they often viewed "their people" with kindly affection and an abiding sense of parental duty. The gay barbecues, the Christmas holidays, the homecoming celebrations, however exaggerated in the Old South's myth of plantation life, fulfilled a real need to treat one's slaves with warmth and affection. Indeed, the myth of the mellow old plantation and the dutiful, carefree Sambos who worked on it, like all utopian myths, has an important reality of its own. A society's vision of perfection reveals its most acutely frustrated desires. In the myth, southerners expressed their craving for a kindly, paternalistic slave system, without tension or punishment or violence, where master and slave lived together in rich comradeship and intuitive understanding.

Even if plantation life could have approximated the utopian myth, southerners would not have rested easily. The philosophy which planters so enthusiastically celebrated on the Fourth of July would have remained a nagging moral burden. Moreover, the Carolina social

code limited the value of an idyllic master-slave relationship. The drawing-room code, which insisted upon conversation between honorable equals, condemned the fawning slave, while accepting his inferiority with a smile, as a hopelessly degraded human being. Judged by the southerner's own values, a utopian plantation remained an illegitimate form of human exploitation.

Unfortunately plantation reality was rarely so sublime as the flawed utopia of the myth. Of course many southern slaves resembled the Sambo stereotype. Indulgent masters and their dutiful house servants often enjoyed a lifetime of friendship. But every plantation manager had to cope with a significant percentage of troublesome bondsmen. And the attempt to impose discipline on recalcitrant slaves frequently made managing the southern plantation a grim, ugly way of life. As one South Carolinian lamented, slaveholding subjected "the man of care and feeling to more dilemmas than perhaps any other vocation he could follow."

The dilemmas of the scrupulous planter centered around the problems of discipline. As the Denmark Vesey Conspiracy demonstrated, indulged slaves could become archconspirators. And though few slaves emulated the notorious Rolla Bennett, many resisted their chains with devious sabotage and destructive laziness. When masters stopped painting their slaves as banjo-strumming Sambos or bloodthirsty savages, they presented another, equally revealing, stock portrait: the seemingly innocent but cunning laborer who could misunderstand adroitly, loiter diligently, or destroy guilefully. Indulgence and kindness, *by themselves*, could neither avoid rebellions nor produce an efficient labor force. Whipping, deprivation of privileges, and other punishments were accepted everywhere as a necessary part of plantation government. "Were *fidelity* the only security we enjoyed," exclaimed one slaveholder,

". . . deplorable indeed would be our situation. The fear of punishment is the principle to which we must and do appeal, to keep them in awe and order."

Occasionally planters tried to escape from this unpleasant conclusion. In the halcyon days before the Vesey affair, many slaveholders "exulted in what they termed the progress of liberal ideas upon the subject of slavery." Planters experimented with a regime which, like the plantation of the myth, eschewed the lash and other forms of punishment, and relied on incentives, praise, and kindness to keep the slaves in order. Charleston's slaves were permitted "to assemble without the presence of a white person for . . . social intercourse or religious worship." Many bondsmen were given "the facilities of acquiring most of the comforts and many of the luxuries of improved society." Slaves were allowed "means of enlarging their minds and extending their information." But the events of 1822 proved to everyone that the peculiar institution could not endure if only humane treatment was employed. We must proceed "to govern them," Charlestonians concluded sadly, "on the only principle that can maintain slavery, the principle of fear."

Still, employing the lash was distasteful to owners who liked to regard their slaves as personal friends. "We think it a misfortune," wrote William Harper, "that we should be compelled to subject to a jealous police, and to view with distrust and severity, those whom we are disposed to regard with confidence and kindness." The "misfortune," one suspects, seemed most upsetting with indulged house servants, who often had a close personal relationship with their masters, but still needed an occasional whipping. The unpleasant problems of discipline could be most clearly seen in Charleston, where personal servants formed a high percentage of the slave population and masters were forced to inflict stripes personally rather than pass the task on to plantation overseers.

Few ante bellum events are more revealing than the obscure decision of the Charleston city council, in 1825, to erect a treadmill in the city workhouse, thereby relieving sensitive masters of the necessity of whipping their own people. "Such a mode of correction has long been a desideratum with many of our citizens," reported Robert Mills in 1826. Many slaveholders had "been often induced to pass over faults in their slaves demeriting correction, rather than resort to coercive measures with them, who now will, without doing violence to their feelings, be able to break their idle habits."

The large slaveholder, closer to his house servants, probably found disciplining his field hands a less disturbing business. Still, field hands were "his people" as well as his property, and plantation management was fraught with dilemmas. The most successful disciplinarians were so rigid and strict that they rarely had to punish. But even such planters went through a distressing period of frequent punishment when they "broke in" their slaves, and they never escaped the necessity of proving to bondsmen that the system was screwed tight. "When I first began to plant I found my people in very bad subjection," James Hammond explained to a new overseer. ". . . It required of me a year of severity which cost me infinite pain and gained a name which I detest of all others to subdue them. They are now entirely broken in, & . . . it will be seldom necessary to use the lash." But overseers on his plantation could never forgo the lash for long.

Many planters could not emulate Hammond's agonized persistence; rigorous discipline was simply too severe a strain on uneasy consciences. This—not the weather—was the crucial cause of the lazy pace and inefficient practices on many declining plantations. Yet those who could not bear to impose strict plantation rules and punish all transgressions in the end whipped all the more. Spotty discipline encouraged passive resistance, devious

sabotage, and—with the more willful slaves —overt violence. James Edward Calhoun, traveling through the lowcountry in 1826, encountered one unforgettable example of the tension which pervaded the plantation of an inconsistent disciplinarian. James Kirk, a leading Beaufort planter, told Calhoun that "if he lives 10 or 15 yrs. longer" his slaves would "gain ascendency over him . . . is sensible they are gaining on him: confesses whips in a passion & half the time unjustly. . . . Confesses scruples of conscience about slavery."

In the 1820's leading South Carolinians admitted that inconsistent disciplinarians abounded in their state. "The relaxed, sentimental, *covert abolitionist*," lamented the editor of the *Southern Agriculturist*, "first begins by spoiling his slave, next becomes severe, which is followed by running away, this again by enormous depredations . . . a large proportion of our ablest and most intelligent slaves are annually sent out of the State for misconduct arising from the most erroneous notions of discipline." The editor of the *Southern Review* added: "One great evil of the system is its tendency to produce in process of time, laxity of discipline, and consequently, disorders and poverty . . . by the excessive indulgence of careless or too scrupulous masters . . . some of the worst symptoms of the time are owing to this ill-judged, but we fear, inevitable facility and indulgence."

The slaveholder's guilt was thus more than a reaction to the discrepancy between Jefferson's Declaration and southern slavery. It was also a response to the gulf between the plantation myth and the realities of bondage—a gulf evident day after day in the painful dilemmas of discipline. Planters who eschewed fear entirely and relied only on kindness invited economic bankruptcy and servile insurrection. Slaveholders who employed punishment erratically lived with periodic flareups and sometimes faced the unpleasant necessity of having to sell rebellious bondsmen. Planters who im-

posed discipline consistently had the least trouble in the long run, but endured the anxiety of inflicting perpetual punishment during the breaking-in period.

Of course many planters rarely worried about the morality of slavery or the dilemmas of discipline. At the other extreme, a few slave-holders, convinced that profits could be kept up only by a distasteful driving of slaves, sold out their plantations. Many others found solace in treating slaves as kindly as possible within the limits set by proper discipline. Plantations fell apart when control was based entirely on indulgence and incentives. But when punishment and fear were employed, kindness and courtesy effectively produced a more contented, efficient labor force. This, in turn, reduced the necessity to punish. As one astute observer noted, humane planters were "saved from many painful feelings at home and cared less about being traduced abroad." For many planters, however, the acts of kindness and the familial relationships were never quite enough. "I have a just partiality for all our servants from many touching recollections, & expect my residence at home made very comfortable by having them about me," remarked Hugh S. Legaré. "This circumstance is after all sometimes a great compensation for the unquestionable evils attendant upon the institution of slavery."

Just as the unusually heavy concentration of slaves in tidewater Carolina intensified the low-country's fear of slave uprisings, so the special problems of the coastal plantation may have increased the gentry's guilt. As always, the problems centered around the malaria. Paternalistic masters felt compelled to protect their people's health. Yet planters knew that a slave thrust into the swamp was likely to become debilitated with illness and would sometimes prematurely die. Many owners must have pushed the ugly problem out of their minds. Some salved their conscience by employing fine plantation physicians. But for others, providing ex-cellent medical care could not compensate for subjecting the slaves to malarial fever in the first place. The planters betrayed their qualms by incessantly claiming what they knew to be false—that Negroes were immune from the diseases of the swamp. One leading slaveholder even exposed his uneasy conscience in his plantation journal. On James Hammond's Savannah River plantation, slaves were required to cut fodder in river swamps every September:

> September 23, 1833: At plantation all day nursing the sick. Some very low—High grade of bilious fever—Twenty-two on the sick list . . . September 26, 1833: Sick all better and the list reduced to 15—Pulling Fodder today in the Lower Bluff. *Fearful that it will produce more sickness.* . . . September 26, 1834: Saw Dr. Galphin who anticipates cholera here. Ordered all hands to be removed from the river . . . September 29—The cholera has driven almost everybody from the swamp. September 30—hands pulling fodder. Another case of cholera—Eleanor —very severe—It happened in my presence —Left her better—Ordered them to pull no more fodder. . . . October 3—Mr. Dawkins [the overseer] came up this evening and stated that there had been no new cases of cholera. He says he has put the hands to pulling fodder in the swamp again—*Feel uneasy about it.* [Italics mine.]

Later Hammond noted that on his plantation slaves died faster than they were born. "One would think from this statement that I was a monster of inhumanity," he added. "Yet this one subject has caused me more anxiety and suffering than any other in my life."

Disease-ridden swamps led planters to rely on unsupervised overseers, which raised special moral problems. Every contract between owners and overseers contained a clause binding the manager to treat Negroes with moderation and humanity. Overseers were frequently dismissed because they whipped slaves passion-

ately or passed out medicine sparingly. Still, overseers were most often judged by their skill at raising yields. Overseers, like slave-traders, were more involved in the economic, exploitative side of slavery than the personal, paternalistic side; this is one reason they were despised. The incompetent young men who served as overseers on many tidewater plantations, and the absence of the owner's restraining word, undoubtedly increased the severity of slavery. As James Hammond summed up the matter in the midst of a famous proslavery polemic, a "leading" cause of cruelty to slaves was "the absenteeism of proprietors. Agents are always more unfeeling than owners, whether placed over West Indian or American slaves, or Irish Tenantry. We feel the evil greately even here."

Finally, the nature of absentee ownership involved tidewater gentlemen in a curious paradox. On the one hand, they were shielded from observing the unseemly side of plantation slavery during the summer months; in this sense they could ignore the dilemmas of discipline more easily than other planters. On the other hand, aristocrats who owned hundreds of slaves and often left their plantations had few memories of warm relationships with field hands to soften the exploitative aspect of slavery. They also had the detachment, time, and cultivated education to agonize over the morality of owning slaves. Elsewhere, relatively uneducated planters, personally involved day after day with building an economic empire, were less likely to stand back and question the means they were employing. One suspects that reasons like these help to explain why the Charleston aristocracy found is necessary to conduct "liberal" experiments with discipline and to build treadmills to punish slaves.

The diseases of the coastal Negro, the character of lowcountry overseers, and the nature and effects of absentee ownership *might* (for this is speculative) have intensified the guilt of the tidewater planter. Although less important than the lowcountry's particularly intense fear

of slave revolts, this acute guilt may have helped to make slavery at the South Carolina tidewater so peculiarly disturbing. . . .

Thus the proslavery argument of the 1820's, although growing in strength, was still a fragmentary and qualified polemic which was not widely accepted. The few proslavery theorists made almost as little headway convincing the community that slavery was a blessing as the few Carolina abolitionists made in persuading the planters that bondage could be abolished. The huge majority of slaveholders, distressed by slavery but seeing no way out, clung stubbornly to the untenable "necessary evil" position. They did not widely discuss or accept the "positive good" thesis until *after* South Carolina adopted nullification.

The most revealing public reaction to the tensions slavery generated in the 1820's and early 1830's was neither the "necessary evil" nor the "positive good" argument but rather the attempt to repress open debate. The conviction that slavery was an abomination ran too deep to be overcome in a season, and antislavery opponents easily refuted the argument from necessity. If subjected to a barrage of criticism, conscience-stricken planters might become covert abolitionists who would fight half-heartedly for slavery's perpetuation and relax the discipline which kept their slaves in order. Moreover, public debate might increase the restlessness of Negro slaves and would certainly magnify the apprehensions of the white community.

Thus South Carolina profoundly desired to keep the subject buried. The discovery of a copy of Walker's *Appeal*, or an issue of Garrison's *Liberator*, or a handkerchief stamped with Negroes in a state of defiance was enough to start a panic over insurrection. Charleston's newspapers avoided notice of slave conspiracies, and upcountry sheets gave only cursory details. Lowcountry editors trembled at items

that approached the issue and refused to meet the matter head on. Pre-1833 editorials chanted that the evil was necessary and the subject too dangerous to discuss.

In 1832, when the Virginia legislature engaged in a month of searching arguments on the merits of slavery, and Thomas Ritchie's *Richmond Enquirer* doubled the danger by printing the debates, even Carolina unionists were flabbergasted. Benjamin F. Perry, a moderate, refused "to comment on a policy so unwise, and blended with so much madness and fatality"; the sober *Camden Journal* rejected an essay *against* the Virginia experiment with open discussion because "it is a subject that ought not to be agitated at all in this State."

If the unionists fumed, the fire-eaters raged. In Sumter, John Hemphill urged patrols to be on the alert and denounced Ritchie as "the apostate traitor, the recreant and faithless sentinel, the cringing parasite, the hollow-hearted, hypocritical advocate of Southern interests . . . who has scattered the firebrands of destruction everywhere in the South." In Washington, Duff Green proclaimed that Ritchie's heresy was "calculated to unsettle everything—the minds of masters and slaves." The *Charleston Mercury* added: "We cannot too earnestly deprecate the public discussion of such a topic. . . . The very agitation . . . is fraught with evils of the most disastrous kind."

For a moment in early 1832, one Carolina editor dared to broach the forbidden subject. Young Maynard Richardson, son of the Carolina jurist and editor of the Sumterville *Southern Whig*, opened his columns "for a *liberal* and *guarded* discussion of slavery." Southerners invited northern attack, he argued, by their "own sensitiveness. We receive their objections with bitter revilings, nor do we ever deign any answer save the most unqualified contempt and abhorrence. This course augurs badly for us. It implies consciousness of a weak cause, and an unwillingness to undergo scrutiny."

Richardson printed a communication from

"W.E." in the *Southern Whig* "without hesitation" because it merely discussed the "abstract question . . . upon which we . . . are . . . safest." The "W.E." essay was the type of argument which leading southerners wished neither guilty whites nor restless slaves to read. "Is it an argument," asked the correspondent, to assert that slavery is legitimate because northerners abuse their free Negroes? "Is it not rather the retort, 'You do so too'? . . . Is it an argument," inquired "W.E.," to blame slave-traders for the inception of bondage? "Or is it not rather an attempt to cover our own weakness, in yielding to seduction, by throwing the blame on the seducer?" Does the Negro's mental imbecility justify slavery? For

the mental imbecility of the Negro is the result of our own injustice and oppression. Do we not endeavor, by every means in our power, to debase his mind? . . . And why do we act thus towards him? Is knowledge inconsistent with justice and the safety of the majority? . . . Is it an argument when he tells us, that our lands cannot be cultivated without them? Or does it not rather prove that we are resolved, at all hazards, on the gratification of our lust for power?

John Hemphill, editor of the rival *Sumter Gazette*, spoke for a frightened community when he castigated Richardson's policy and called on the patrol for greater vigilance. Still, Hemphill refused to answer "W.E." With "a dense slave population at our own firesides," he wrote, South Carolinians would never allow anyone to "discuss the subject *here*." The value of an essay refuting "W.E." could never justify the danger involved. "Must we free ourselves," asked Hemphill's *Gazette*, "from such misrepresentation at the risk of such appalling mischief?"

Maynard Richardson countered by accusing Hemphill of "the sickly sensitiveness and ridiculous squeamishness, about touching the subject of slavery which have ever been the sub-

ject of our misunderstanding abroad and of which there is not a nervous female who is not thoroughly ashamed." Yet Richardson stopped printing communications on slavery and picked a quarrel with Hemphill to cover his isolation in the community. A vituperative battle royal ensued between the two editors. Newspaper epithets soon gave way to physical violence. On an April day at Sumter Court House, Richardson, armed with a dirk, and Hemphill, equipped with a pistol, scuffled for their honor. Other Sumterites swarmed in the street, wanting to join the brawl, and Judge Richardson plunged into the fray. Before the riot ended, the combatants were marked by bloody heads and torn clothing. And the image of the honorable judge wrestling in the dirt for the pistol comments on the eclipse of Maynard Richardson's rather noble aims and the disturbing nature of slavery in South Carolina.

The Hemphill-Richardson affair was the most dramatic incident in the decade-long Carolina attempt to repress public discussion of slavery. But this policy in South Carolina could hardly be reconciled with the strategy of vigorous defense in Washington. Leading South Carolinians always believed that they

must put down the smallest beginnings of a political antislavery campaign. An incessant abolitionist attack was expected to reach menacing proportions in the North and to provoke servile insurrections in the South. Yet a vigorous proslavery campaign in Congress would flounder without the enthusiastic support of southerners at home. A thoroughgoing propaganda campaign was needed to convince slaveholders to crusade for their institutions. And the incessant discussion of slavery in South Carolina seemed almost as dangerous as a growing abolitionist crusade in the North.

This irreconcilable commitment to both a strategy of militant defense in Washington and a policy of complete repression at home was the essence of South Carolina's dilemma in the 1820's. Desperately anxious to keep the distressing subject buried, the South Carolina congressmen lashed out stridently at the mildest antislavery proposals during the 1820's. And one of the crucial appeals of crusading for nullification on the tariff issue was that a weapon could be won to check the abolitionists without discussing slavery. The event would reveal that South Carolina could not escape the dilemma so painlessly. . . .

26

The Confessions of Nat Turner

Nat Turner
as told to Thomas R. Gray

One of the pivotal events in the emergence of a militant South was the Nat Turner insurrection of 1831. A slave preacher who called himself an instrument of God, Turner unleashed sixty or seventy black insurgents on the unsuspecting whites of Southampton County, Virginia. They shot and hacked some sixty people to death, including women and children, and spread terror and destruction in all directions. At last white militia smashed the rebellion, but not before the whites had slaughtered a number of innocent slaves. Finally, the authorities captured Turner and his surviving followers and took them to Jerusalem, the county seat, where they were tried and hanged. Here is Turner's own account of the uprising, as he allegedly gave it to a white lawyer before he went to the gallows.

To the Public

The late insurrection in Southampton has greatly excited the public mind, and led to a thousand idle, exaggerated and mischievous reports. It is the first instance in our history of an open rebellion of the slaves, and attended with such atrocious circumstances of cruelty and destruction, as could not fail to leave a deep impression, not only upon the minds of the community where this fearful tragedy was wrought, but throughout every portion of our country, in which this population is to be found. Public curiosity has been on the stretch to understand the origin and progress of this dreadful conspiracy, and the motives which influence its diabolical actors. The insurgent slaves had all been destroyed, or apprehended, tried and executed, (with the exception of the leader,) without revealing any thing at all satisfactory, as to the motives which governed them, or the means by which they expected to accomplish their object. Every thing connected with the sad affair was wrapt in mystery, until Nat Turner, the leader of this ferocious band, whose name has resounded throughout our widely extended empire, was captured. This "great Bandit" was taken by a single individual, in a cave near the residence of his late owner, on Sunday, the thirtieth of October, without attempting to make the slightest resistance, and on the following day safely lodged in the jail of the County. His captor was Benjamin Phipps, armed with a shot gun well charged. Nat's only weapon was a small light sword which he immediately surrendered, and begged that his life might be spared. Since his confinement, by permission of the Jailor, I have had ready access to him, and finding that he was willing to make a full and free confession of the origin, progress and consummation of the insurrectory movements of the slaves of which he was the contriver and head; I determined for the gratification of public curiosity to commit his statements to writing, and publish them,

From *The Confessions of Nat Turner, the Leader of the Late Insurrection in Southampton, Va., as Fully and Voluntarily Made to Thomas R. Gray.* Baltimore: Lucas & Deaver, 1831.

with little or no variation, from his own words. That this is a faithful record of his confessions, the annexed certificate of the County Court of Southampton, will attest. They certainly bear one stamp of truth and sincerity. He makes no attempt (as all the other insurgents who were examined did,) to exculpate himself, but frankly acknowledges his full participation in all the guilt of the transaction. He was not only the contriver of the conspiracy, but gave the first blow towards its execution.

It will thus appear, that whilst every thing upon the surface of society wore a calm and peaceful aspect; whilst not one note of preparation was heard to warn the devoted inhabitants of woe and death, a gloomy fanatic was revolving in the recesses of his own dark, bewildered, and over-wrought mind, schemes of indiscriminate massacre to the whites. Schemes too fearfully executed as far as his fiendish band proceeded in their desolating march. No cry for mercy penetrated their flinty bosoms. No acts of remembered kindness made the least impression upon these remorseless murderers. Men, women and children, from hoary age to helpless infancy were involved in the same cruel fate. Never did a band of savages do their work of death more unsparingly. Apprehension for their own personal safety seems to have been the only principle of restraint in the whole course of their bloody proceedings. And it is not the least remarkable feature in this horrid transaction, that a band actuated by such hellish purposes, should have resisted so feebly, when met by the whites in arms. Desperation alone, one would think, might have led to greater efforts. More than twenty of them attacked Dr. Blunt's house on Tuesday morning, a little before day-break, defended by two men and three boys. They fled precipitately at the first fire; and their future plans of mischief, were entirely disconcerted and broken up. Escaping thence, each individual sought his own safety either in concealment, or by returning home, with the hope that his participation might escape detection, and all were shot down in the course of a few days, or captured and brought to trial and punishment. Nat has survived all his followers, and the gallows will speedily close his career. His own account of the conspiracy is submitted to the public, without comment. It reads an awful, and it is hoped, a useful lesson, as to the operations of a mind like his, endeavoring to grapple with things beyond its reach. How it first became bewildered and confounded, and finally corrupted and led to the conception and perpetration of the most atrocious and heart-rending deeds. It is calculated also to demonstrate the policy of our laws in restraint of this class of our population, and to induce all those entrusted with their execution, as well as our citizens generally, to see that they are strictly and rigidly enforced. Each particular community should look to its own safety, whilst the general guardians of the laws, keep a watchful eye over all. If Nat's statements can be relied on, the insurrection in this county was entirely local, and his designs confided but to a few, and these in his immediate vicinity. It was not instigated by motives of revenge or sudden anger, but the results of long deliberation, and a settled purpose of mind. The offspring of gloomy fanaticism, acting upon materials but too well prepared for such impressions. It will be long remembered in the annals of our country, and many a mother as she presses her infant darling to her bosom, will shudder at the recollection of Nat Turner, and his band of ferocious miscreants.

Believing the following narrative, by removing doubts and conjectures from the public mind which otherwise must have remained, would give general satisfaction, it is respectfully submitted to the public by their ob't serv't,

T. R. Gray

. . .

Confession

Agreeable to his own appointment, on the evening he was committed to prison, with permission of the jailer, I visited NAT on Tuesday the 1st November, when, without being questioned at all, he commenced his narrative in the following words:—

SIR,—You have asked me to give a history of the motives which induced me to undertake the late insurrection, as you call it—To do so I must go back to the days of my infancy, and even before I was born. I was thirty-one years of age the 2nd of October last, and born the property of Benj. Turner, of this county. In my childhood a circumstance occurred which made an indelible impression on my mind, and laid the ground work of that enthusiasm, which has terminated so fatally to many, both white and black, and for which I am about to atone at the gallows. It is here necessary to relate this circumstance—trifling as it may seem, it was the commencement of that belief which has grown with time, and even now, sir, in this dungeon, helpless and forsaken as I am, I cannot divest myself of. Being at play with other children, when three or four years old, I was telling them something, which my mother overhearing, said it had happened before I was born—I stuck to my story, however, and related somethings which went, in her opinion, to confirm it—others being called on were greatly astonished, knowing that these things had happened, and caused them to say in my hearing, I surely would be a prophet, as the Lord had shewn me things that had happened before my birth. And my father and mother strengthened me in this my first impression, saying in my presence, I was intended for some great purpose, which they had always thought from certain marks on my head and breast—[a parcel of excrescences which I believe are not at all uncommon, particularly among negroes, as I have seen several with the same. In this case he has either cut them off or they have nearly disappeared]— My grandmother, who was very religious, and to whom I was much attached—my master, who belonged to the church, and other religious persons who visited the house, and whom I often saw at prayers, noticing the singularity of my manners, I suppose, and my uncommon intelligence for a child, remarked I had too much sense to be raised, and if I was, I would never be of any service to any one as a slave— To a mind like mine, restless, inquisitive and observant of every thing that was passing, it is easy to suppose that religion was the subject to which it would be directed, and although this subject principally occupied my thoughts— there was nothing that I saw or heard of to which my attention was not directed—The manner in which I learned to read and write, not only had great influence on my own mind, as I acquired it with the most perfect ease, so much so, that I have no recollection whatever of learning the alphabet—but to the astonishment of the family, one day, when a book was shewn to me to keep me from crying, I began spelling the names of different objects—this was a source of wonder to all in the neighborhood, particularly the blacks—and this learning was constantly improved at all opportunities—when I got large enough to go to work, while employed, I was reflecting on many things that would present themselves to my imagination, and whenever an opportunity occurred of looking at a book, when the school children were getting their lessons, I would find many things that the fertility of my own imagination had depicted to me before; all my time, not devoted to my master's service, was spent either in prayer, or in making experiments in casting different things in moulds made of earth, in attempting to make paper, gun-powder, and many other experiments, that although I could not perfect, yet convinced me

of its practicability if I had the means.* I was not addicted to stealing in my youth, nor have ever been—Yet such was the confidence of the negroes in the neighborhood, even at this early period of my life, in my superior judgment, that they would often carry me with them when they were going on any roguery, to plan for them. Growing up among them, with this confidence in my superior judgment, and when this, in their opinions, was perfected by Divine inspiration, from the circumstances already alluded to in my infancy, and which belief was ever afterwards zealously inculcated by the austerity of my life and manners, which became the subject of remark by white and black. —Having soon discovered to be great, I must appear so, and therefore studiously avoided mixing in society, and wrapped myself in mystery, devoting my time to fasting and prayer— By this time, having arrived to man's estate, and hearing the scriptures commented on at meetings, I was struck with that particular passage which says: "Seek ye the kingdom of Heaven and all things shall be added unto you." I reflected much on this passage, and prayed daily for light on this subject—As I was praying one day at my plough, the spirit spoke to me, saying "Seek ye the kingdom of Heaven and all things shall be added unto you." *Question*—what do you mean by the Spirit. *Ans.* The Spirit that spoke to the prophets in former days—and I was greatly astonished, and for two years prayed continually, whenever my duty would permit—and then again I had the same revelation, which fully confirmed me in the impression that I was ordained for some great purpose in the hands of the Almighty. Several years rolled round, in which many events occurred to strengthen me in this my belief. At this time I reverted in my mind to the remarks made of me in my childhood, and the things that had been shewn me—and as it

* When questioned as to the manner of manufacturing those different articles, he was found well informed on the subject.

had been said of me in my childhood by those by whom I had been taught to pray, both white and black, and in whom I had the greatest confidence, that I had too much sense to be raised, and if I was, I would never be of any use to any one as a slave. Now finding I had arrived to man's estate, and was a slave, and these revelations being made known to me, I began to direct my attention to this great object, to fulfil the purpose for which, by this time, I felt assured I was intended. Knowing the influence I had obtained over the minds of my fellow servants, (not by the means of conjuring and such like tricks—for to them I always spoke of such things with contempt) but by the communion of the Spirit whose revelations I often communicated to them, and they believed and said my wisdom came from God. I now began to prepare them for my purpose, by telling them something was about to happen that would terminate in fulfilling the great promise that had been made to me— About this time I was placed under an overseer, from whom I ranaway—and after remaining in the woods thirty days, I returned, to the astonishment of the negroes on the plantation, who thought I had made my escape to some other part of the country, as my father had done before. But the reason of my return was, that the Spirit appeared to me and said I had my wishes directed to the things of this world, and not to the kingdom of Heaven, and that I should return to the service of my earthly master—"For he who knoweth his Master's will, and doeth it not, shall be beaten with many stripes, and thus have I chastened you." And the negroes found fault, and murmured against me, saying that if they had my sense they would not serve any master in the world. And about this time I had a vision—and I saw white spirits and black spirits engaged in battle, and the sun was darkened—the thunder rolled in the Heavens, and blood flowed in streams— and I heard a voice saying, "Such is your luck, such you are called to see, and let it come rough

or smooth, you must surely bare it." I now withdrew myself as much as my situation would permit, from the intercourse of my fellow servants, for the avowed purpose of serving the Spirit more fully—and it appeared to me, and reminded me of the things it had already shown me, and that it would then reveal to me the knowledge of the elements, the revolution of the planets, the operation of tides, and changes of the seasons. After this revelation in the year of 1825, and the knowledge of the elements being made known to me, I sought more than ever to obtain true holiness before the great day of judgment should appear, and then I began to receive the true knowledge of faith. And from the first steps of righteousness until the last, was I made perfect; and the Holy Ghost was with me, and said, "Behold me as I stand in the Heavens"—and I looked and saw the forms of men in different attitudes—and there were lights in the sky to which the children of darkness gave other names than what they really were—for they were the lights of the Savior's hands, stretched forth from east to west, even as they were extended on the cross on Calvary for the redemption of sinners. And I wondered greatly at these miracles, and prayed to be informed of a certainty of the meaning thereof—and shortly afterwards, while laboring in the field, I discovered drops of blood on the corn as though it were dew from heaven—and I communicated it to many, both white and black, in the neighborhood—and I then found on the leaves in the woods hieroglyphic characters, and numbers, with the forms of men in different attitudes, portrayed in blood, and representing the figures I had seen before in the heavens. And now the Holy Ghost had revealed itself to me, and made plain the miracles it had shown me—For as the blood of Christ had been shed on this earth, and had ascended to heaven for the salvation of sinners, and was now returning to earth again in the form of dew—and as the leaves on the trees bore the impression of the figures I had seen in the heavens, it was plain to me that the Savior was about to lay down the yoke he had borne for the sins of men, and the great day of judgment was at hand. About this time I told these things to a white man, (Etheldred T. Brantley) on whom it had a wonderful effect—and he ceased from his wickedness, and was attacked immediately with a cutaneous eruption, and blood oozed from the pores of his skin, and after praying and fasting nine days, he was healed, and the Spirit appeared to me again, and said, as the Savior had been baptised so should we be also—and when the white people would not let us be baptised by the church, we went down into the water together, in the sight of many who reviled us, and were baptised by the Spirit —After this I rejoiced greatly, and gave thanks to God. And on the 12th of May, 1828, I heard a loud noise in the heavens, and the Spirit instantly appeared to me and said the Serpent was loosened, and Christ had laid down the yoke he had borne for the sins of men, and that I should take it on and fight against the Serpent, for the time was fast approaching when the first should be last and the last should be first. *Ques.* Do you not find yourself mistaken now? *Ans.* Was not Christ crucified? And by signs in the heavens that it would make known to me when I should commence the great work—and until the first sign appeared, I should conceal it from the knowledge of men —And on the appearance of the sign, (the eclipse of the sun last February) I should arise and prepare myself, and slay my enemies with their own weapons. And immediately on the sign appearing in the heavens, the seal was removed from my lips, and I communicated the great work laid out for me to do, to four in whom I had the greatest confidence, (Henry, Hark, Nelson, and Sam)—It was intended by us to have begun the work of death on the 4th July last—Many were the plans formed and rejected by us, and it affected my mind to such a degree, that I fell sick, and the time passed

without our coming to any determination how to commence—Still forming new schemes and rejecting them, when the sign appeared again, which determined me not to wait longer.

Since the commencement of 1830, I had been living with Mr. Joseph Travis, who was to me a kind master, and placed the greatest confidence in me; in fact, I had no cause to complain of his treatment to me. On Saturday evening, the 20th of August, it was agreed between Henry, Hark and myself, to prepare a dinner the next day for the men we expected, and then to concert a plan, as we had not yet determined on any. Hark, on the following morning, brought a pig, and Henry brandy, and being joined by Sam, Nelson, Will and Jack, they prepared in the woods a dinner, where, about three o'clock, I joined them.

Q. Why were you so backward in joining them.

A. The same reason that had caused me not to mix with them for years before.

I saluted them on coming up, and asked Will how came he there, he answered, his life was worth no more than others, and his liberty as dear to him. I asked him if he thought to obtain it? He said he would, or lose his life. This was enough to put him in full confidence. Jack, I knew, was only a tool in the hands of Hark, it was quickly agreed we should commence at home (Mr. J. Travis') on that night, and until we had armed and equipped ourselves, and gathered sufficient force, neither age nor sex was to be spared, (which was invariably adhered to). We remained at the feast, until about two hours in the night, when we went to the house and found Austin; they all went to the cider press and drank, except myself. On returning to the house, Hark went to the door with an axe, for the purpose of breaking it open, as we knew we were strong enough to murder the family, if they were awakened by the noise; but reflecting that it might create an alarm in the neighborhood, we determined to enter the house secretly, and murder them

whilst sleeping. Hark got a ladder and set it against the chimney, on which I ascended, and hoisting a window, entered and came down stairs, unbarred the door, and removed the guns from their places. It was then observed that I must spill the first blood. On which, armed with a hatchet, and accompanied by Will, I entered my master's chamber, it being dark, I could not give a death blow, the hatchet glanced from his head, he sprang from the bed and called his wife, it was his last word, Will laid him dead, with a blow of his axe, and Mrs. Travis shared the same fate, as she lay in bed. The murder of this family, five in number, was the work of a moment, not one of them awoke; there was a little infant sleeping in a cradle, that was forgotten, until we had left the house and gone some distance, when Henry and Will returned and killed it; we got here, four guns that would shoot, and several old muskets, with a pound or two of powder. We remained some time at the barn, where we paraded; I formed them in a line as soldiers, and after carrying them through all the manoeuvres I was master of marched them off to Mr. Salathul Francis', about six hundred yards distant. Sam and Will went to the door and knocked. Mr. Francis asked who was there, Sam replied it was him, and he had a letter for him, on which he got up and came to the door; they immediately seized him, and dragging him out a little from the door, he was dispatched by repeated blows on the head; there was no other white person in the family. We started from there for Mrs. Reese's, maintaining the most perfect silence on our march, where finding the door unlocked, we entered, and murdered Mrs. Reese in her bed, while sleeping; her son awoke, but it was only to sleep the sleep of death, he had only time to say who is that, and he was no more. From Mrs. Reese's we went to Mrs. Turner's, a mile distant, which we reached about sunrise, on Monday morning. Henry, Austin, and Sam, went to the still, where, finding Mr. Peebles, Austin shot him, and the rest of us went to the

On August 21, 1831, Nat Turner met with Hark, Nelson, Sam, Will, Henry, and Jack at the Cabin Pond where they made final plans for their insurrection. This meeting is illustrated above. That night they invaded the Travis house, where they executed Travis himself, his wife, child, and several others. (Courtesy of The Association for the Study of Negro Life and History.)

house; as we approached, the family discovered us, and shut the door. Vain hope! Will, with one stroke of his axe, opened it, and we entered and found Mrs. Turner and Mrs. Newsome in the middle of a room, almost frightened to death. Will immediately killed Mrs. Turner, with one blow of his axe. I took Mrs. Newsome by the hand, and with the sword I had when I was apprehended, I struck her several blows over the head, but not being able to kill her, as the sword was dull. Will turning around and discovering it, despatched her also. A general destruction of property and search for money and ammunition, always succeeded the murders. By this time my company amounted to fifteen, and nine men mounted, who started for Mrs. Whitehead's, (the other six were to go through a by way to Mr. Bryant's, and rejoin us at Mrs. Whitehead's,) as we approached the house we discovered Mr. Richard Whitehead standing in the cotton patch, near the lane fence; we called him over into the lane, and Will, the executioner, was near at hand, with his fatal axe, to send him to an untimely grave. As we pushed on to the house, I discovered some one run round the garden, and thinking it was some

of the white family, I pursued them, but finding it was a servant girl belonging to the house, I returned to commence the work of death, but they whom I left, had not been idle; all the family were already murdered, but Mrs. Whitehead and her daughter Margaret. As I came round to the door I saw Will pulling Mrs. Whitehead out of the house, and at the step he nearly severed her head from her body, with his broad axe. Miss Margaret, when I discovered her, had concealed herself in the corner, formed by the projection of cellar cap from the house; on my approach she fled, but was soon overtaken, and after repeated blows with a sword, I killed her by a blow on the head, with a fence rail. By this time, the six who had gone by Mr. Bryant's, rejoined us, and informed me they had done the work of death assigned them. We again divided, part going to Mr. Richard Porter's, and from thence to Nathaniel Francis', the others to Mr. Howell Harris', and Mr. T. Doyles. On my reaching Mr. Porter's, he had escaped with his family. I understood there, that the alarm had already spread, and I immediately returned to bring up those sent to Mr. Doyles, and Mr. Howell Harris'; the party I left going on to Mr. Francis', having told them I would join them in that neighborhood. I met these sent to Mr. Doyles' and Mr. Harris' returning, having met Mr. Doyle on the road and killed him; and learning from some who joined them, that Mr. Harris was from home, I immediately pursued the course taken by the party gone on before; but knowing they would complete the work of death and pillage, at Mr. Francis' before I could get there, I went to Mr. Peter Edwards', expecting to find them there, but they had been here also. I then went to Mr. John T. Barrow's, they had been here and murdered him. I pursued on their track to Capt. Newit Harris', where I found the greater part mounted, and ready to start; the men now amounting to about forty, shouted and hurraed as I rode up, some were in the yard, loading their guns, others drinking.

They said Captain Harris and his family had escaped, the property in the house they destroyed, robbing him of money and other valuables. I ordered them to mount and march instantly, this was about nine or ten o'clock, Monday morning. I proceeded to Mr. Levi Waller's, two or three miles distant. I took my station in the rear, and as it was my object to carry terror and devastation wherever we went, I placed fifteen or twenty of the best armed and most relied on, in front, who generally approached the houses as fast as their horses could run; this was for two purposes, to prevent escape and strike terror to the inhabitants —on this account I never got to the houses, after leaving Mrs. Whitehead's, until the murders were committed, except in one case. I sometimes got in sight in time to see the work of death completed, viewed the mangled bodies as they lay, in silent satisfaction, and immediately started in quest of other victims—Having murdered Mrs. Waller and ten children, we started for Mr. William Williams'—having killed him and two little boys that were there; while engaged in this, Mrs. Williams fled and got some distance from the house, but she was pursued, overtaken, and compelled to get up behind one of the company, who brought her back, and after showing her the mangled body of her lifeless husband, she was told to get down and lay by his side, where she was shot dead. I then started for Mr. Jacob Williams, where the family were murdered—Here he found a young man named Drury, who had come on business with Mr. Williams—he was pursued, overtaken and shot. Mrs. Vaughan was the next place we visited—and after murdering the family here, I determined on starting for Jerusalem—Our number amounted now to fifty or sixty, all mounted and armed with guns, axes, swords and clubs—On reaching Mr. James W. Parker's gate, immediately on the road leading to Jerusalem, and about three miles distant, it was proposed to me to call there, but I objected, as I knew he was gone to

Jerusalem, and my object was to reach there as soon as possible; but some of the men having relations at Mr. Parker's it was agreed that they might call and get his people. I remained at the gate on the road, with seven or eight; the others going across the field to the house, about half a mile off. After waiting some time for them, I became impatient, and started to the house for them, and on our return we were met by a party of white men, who had pursued our blood-stained track, and who had fired on those at the gate, and dispersed them, which I knew nothing of, not having been at that time rejoined by any of them—Immediately on discovering the whites, I ordered my men to halt and form, as they appeared to be alarmed—The white men, eighteen in number, approached us in about one hundred yards, when one of them fired, (this was against the positive orders of Captain Alexander P. Peete, who commanded, and who had directed the men to reserve their fire until within thirty paces)—And I discovered about half of them retreating, I then ordered my men to fire and rush on them; the few remaining stood their ground until we approached within fifty yards, when they fired and retreated. We pursued and overtook some of them who we thought we left dead; (they were not killed) after pursuing them about two hundred yards, and rising a little hill, I discovered they were met by another party, and had halted, and were reloading their guns, (this was a small party from Jerusalem who knew the negroes were in the field, and had just tied their horses to await their return to the road, knowing that Mr. Parker and family were in Jerusalem, but knew nothing of the party that had gone in with Captain Peete; on hearing the firing they immediately rushed to the spot and arrived just in time to arrest the progress of these barbarous villains, and save the lives of their friends and fellow citizens). Thinking that those who retreated first, and the party who fired on us at fifty or sixty yards distant, had all fallen back to meet others

with ammunition. As I saw them reloading their guns, and more coming up than I saw at first, and several of my bravest men being wounded, the others became panick struck and squandered over the field; the white men pursued and fired on us several times. Hark had his horse shot under him, and I caught another for him as it was running by me; five or six of my men were wounded, but none left on the field; finding myself defeated here I instantly determined to go through a private way, and cross the Nottoway river at the Cypress Bridge, three miles below Jerusalem, and attack that place in the rear, as I expected they would look for me on the other road, and I had a great desire to get there to procure arms and ammunition. After going a short distance in this private way, accompanied by about twenty men, I overtook two or three who told me the others were dispersed in every direction. After trying in vain to collect a sufficient force to proceed to Jerusalem, I determined to return, as I was sure they would make back to their old neighborhood, where they would rejoin me, make new recruits, and come down again. On my way back, I called at Mrs. Thomas's, Mrs. Spencer's, and several other places, the white families having fled, we found no more victims to gratify our thirst for blood, we stopped at Maj. Ridley's quarter for the night, and being joined by four of his men, with the recruits made since my defeat, we mustered now about forty strong. After placing out sentinels, I laid down to sleep, but was quickly roused by a great racket; starting up, I found some mounted, and others in great confusion; one of the sentinels having given the alarm that we were about to be attacked, I ordered some to ride round and reconnoitre, and on their return the others being more alarmed, not knowing who they were, fled in different ways, so that I was reduced to about twenty again; with this I determined to attempt to recruit, and proceed on to rally in the neighborhood, I had left. Dr. Blunt's was the nearest house,

which we reached just before day; on riding up the yard, Hark fired a gun. We expected Dr. Blunt and his family were at Maj. Ridley's, as I knew there was a company of men there; the gun was fired to ascertain if any of the family were at home; we were immediately fired upon and retreated, leaving several of my men. I do not know what became of them, as I never saw them afterwards. Pursuing our course back and coming in sight of Captain Harris', where we had been the day before, we discovered a party of white men at the house, on which all deserted me but two, (Jacob and Nat), we concealed ourselves in the woods until near night, when I sent them in search of Henry, Sam, Nelson, and Hark, and directed them to rally all they could, at the place we had had our dinner the Sunday before, where they would find me, and I accordingly returned there as soon as it was dark and remained until Wednesday evening, when discovering white men riding around the place as though they were looking for some one, and none of my men joining me, I concluded Jacob and Nat had been taken, and compelled to betray me. On this I gave up all hope for the present; and on Thursday night after having supplied myself with provisions from Mr. Travis's, I scratched a hole under a pile of fence rails in a field, where I concealed myself for six weeks, never leaving my hiding place but for a few minutes in the dead of night to get water which was very near; thinking by this time I could venture out, I began to go about in the night and eaves drop the houses in the neighborhood; pursuing this course for about a fortnight and gathering little or no intelligence, afraid of speaking to any human being, and returning every morning to my cave before the dawn of day. I know not how long I might have led this life, if accident had not betrayed me, a dog in the neighborhood passing by my hiding place one night while I was out, was attracted by some meat I had in my cave, and crawled in and stole it, and was coming out just as I returned. A few nights after, two negroes having started to go hunting with the same dog, and passed that way, the dog came again to the place, and having just gone out to walk about, discovered me and barked, on which thinking myself discovered, I spoke to them to beg concealment. On making myself known they fled from me. Knowing then they would betray me, I immediately left my hiding place, and was pursued almost incessantly until I was taken a fortnight afterwards by Mr. Benjamin Phipps, in a little hole I had dug out with my sword, for the purpose of concealment, under the top of a fallen tree. On Mr. Phipps' discovering the place of my concealment, he cocked his gun and aimed at me. I requested him not to shoot and I would give up, upon which he demanded my sword. I delivered it to him, and he brought me to prison. During the time I was pursued, I had many hair breadth escapes, which your time will not permit you to relate. I am here loaded with chains, and willing to suffer the fate that awaits me.

27

The Militant South

John Hope Franklin

The Turner uprising sent spasms of hysteria over the South, especially in those areas where slaves outnumbered white people. How many more rebellions would follow? Who among one's own slaves could be trusted in so grim and treacherous a time? And was it not true what some Southern papers were saying—that William Lloyd Garrison and the Abolitionists and free Negroes were behind the Turner insurrection? For Southerners, threatened it seemed from all directions, had to blame somebody for Nat Turner besides themselves. And Negroes and Northern Abolitionists were convenient scapegoats. From then on, as Freehling suggested, Northern Abolitionism and slave revolution were inextricably linked in the Southern mind.

What followed was the Great Reaction, during which the South became a closed, martial society determined to preserve its slave-based civilization at all costs.

———————

Despite the fact that the plantation sought to be self-sufficient and that it succeeded in many respects, the maintenance of a stable institution of slavery was so important that owners early sought the cooperation of the entire community. This cooperation took the form of the patrol, which became an established institution in most areas of the South at an early date. There were many variations in its size and organization. The South Carolina law of 1690 provided that each patrol detachment should be composed of ten men under the captain of a militia company. The number was reduced to five in 1721. All white men were eligible for patrol service when the system was established. Between 1737 and 1819, however, patrol service was limited to men of some affluence, presumably slaveholders. In the latter year all white males over eighteen were made liable for patrol duty; non-slaveholders, however, were excused from duty after reaching the age of forty-five. In Alabama the law of 1819 required not less than three nor more than five owners of slaves for each patrol detachment, while the Mississippi law called for four men, slaveholders or non-slaveholders, for each detachment.

The duties of the patrols were similar in all places. The detachment was to ride its "beat" at night for the purpose of apprehending any and all Negroes who were not in their proper places. Alabama empowered its patrols to enter, in a peaceable manner, upon any plantation; "to enter by force, if necessary, all Negro cabins or quarters, kitchens and outhouses, and to apprehend all slaves who may there be found, not belonging to the plantation or household, without a pass from their owner or overseer; or strolling from place to place, without authority." There were variations in the disposition of offenders taken up by patrols. If the violators were free Negroes or runaways, they were to be taken before a justice of the

Reprinted by permission of the publishers from pp. 70–73, 76–90 of John Hope Franklin, *The Militant South, 1800–1861*. Cambridge, Mass.: The Belknap Press of Harvard University Press, Copyright, 1956, by the President and Fellows of Harvard College.

peace. If they were slaves, temporarily away from their master's plantation, they were to be summarily punished by a whipping, not to exceed thirty-nine lashes. There were, of course, abuses. On occasion, for example, members of the patrol whipped slaves who were legally away from their masters' premises or who were even "peaceably at home."

The patrol system tended to strengthen the position of the military in the Southern community. In most instances there was a substantial connection between the patrol and the militia, either through the control of one by the other or through identity of personnel. In South Carolina the patrol system was early merged into the militia, "making it a part of the military system, and devolving upon the military authority its arrangement and maintenance." There the "Beat Company" was composed of a captain and four others of the regular militia, all of whom were to be excused from any other military service. Sydnor has observed that in Mississippi the structure of the patrol was "but an adaptation of the militia to the control of slaves." In Alabama the infantry captains of the state militia completely dominated the selection of personnel for patrol duty and designated the officers. Under such circumstances the patrol system was simply an arm of the military.

.   .   .

The South's greatest nightmare was the fear of slave uprisings; and one of the most vigorous agitations of her martial spirit was evidenced whenever this fear was activated by even the slightest rumor of revolt. Fear easily and frequently mounted to uncontrollable alarm in which the conduct of some citizens could hardly be described as sober or responsible. "We regard our Negroes as JACOBINS" of the country, Edwin Clifford Holland declared. The whites should always be on their guard against them, and although there was no

reason to fear any permanent effects from insurrectionary activities, the Negroes "should be watched with an eye of steady and unremitted observation . . . Let it never be forgotten, that our Negroes are freely the JACOBINS of the country; that they are the ANARCHISTS and the DOMESTIC ENEMY: the COMMON ENEMY OF CIVILIZED SOCIETY, and the BARBARIANS WHO WOULD, IF THEY COULD, BECOME THE DESTROYERS OF OUR RACE."

A farmer's account of how the fear of revolts completely terrified some Alabama whites suggested to Olmsted both the extent of fear and the impact of fear upon the mind. The farmer said that when he was a boy "folks was dreadful frightened about the niggers. I remember they built pens in the woods," he continued, "where they could hide, and Christmas time they went and got into the pens, 'fraid the niggers was risin' . . . I remember the same thing where we was in South Carolina . . . we had all our things put up in bags, so we could tote 'em, if we heerd they was comin' our way."

This was hardly the usual reaction to threats of slave insurrections. To be sure, such grave eventualities threw them into a veritable paroxysm of fear; but they moved swiftly to put up a defense against the foe. Committees of safety sprang into existence with little prior notice, and all available military resources were mobilized for immediate action. These were not the times to entrust the lives of the citizens to the ordinary protective agencies of civil government. If a community or a state had any effective military force, this was the time for its deployment. Military patrols and guards were alerted, and volunteer troops and the regular militia were called into service. It was a tense martial air that these groups created. For all practical purposes, moreover, even the civil law of the community tended to break down in the face of the emergency. Something akin to martial law, with its arbitrary searches and seizures

and its summary trials and executions, prevailed until the danger had passed.

Instances when fears of uprisings were not followed by immediate militarization of a wide area of the Southern countryside are practically non-existent. When Gabriel attempted the revolt in Richmond in 1800, the Light Infantry Blues were called into immediate service, the public guard was organized and drilled to help avert the calamity, and Governor Monroe instructed every militia commander in the state to be ready to answer the call to duty. In 1822, when Charleston was thrown into a panic by rumors of Vesey's plot, all kinds of military groups were called into service. A person unfamiliar with the problem doubtless would have thought that such extensive mobilization was for the purpose of meeting some powerful foreign foe. The Neck Rangers, the Charleston Riflemen, the Light Infantry, and the Corps of Hussars were some of the established military organizations called up. A special city guard of one hundred and fifty troops was provided for Charleston. The cry for reinforcement by federal troops was answered before the danger had completely subsided. The attempted revolt of Nat Turner in 1831 brought military assistance, not only from the governor of the state, "acting with his characteristic energy," but from neighboring North Carolina counties, and from the federal government. Indeed, more troops reached Southampton County than were needed or could be accommodated. With artillery companies and a field piece from Fort Monroe, detachments of men from two warships, and hundreds of volunteers and militia men converging on the place, there was every suggestion of a large-scale impending battle.

There was a strong show of military force not only when large-scale plots like those of Gabriel, Vesey, and Turner were uncovered, but also whenever there was any intimation of insurrection, however slight. Even a cursory glance at the accounts of insurrections and

threats or rumors of insurrections reveals the role of the military. The rumor of revolt in Louisiana in January 1811, caused Governor Claiborne to call out the militia: a contingent of four hundred militiamen and sixty federal troops left Baton Rouge for the reported scene of action. Two years later the Virginia militia was ordered out to quell a suspected revolt in Lancaster. In 1816 the South Carolina militia took summary action against a group of Negroes suspected of subversive activities. The militia of Onslow County, North Carolina, was so tense during a "Negro hunt" in 1821 that its two detachments mistook each other for the Negro incendiaries and their exchange of fire caused several casualties. Alabama pressed its militia into service in 1841 to search for slave outlaws and to put down rumored uprisings.

Few ante-bellum years were completely free of at least rumors of slave revolts. Agitation for stronger defenses against slave depredations was almost constant, with some leaders advocating a state of continuous preparation for the dreaded day of insurrection. Governor Robert Hayne of South Carolina told the state legislature, "A state of military preparation must always be with us a state of perfect domestic security. A period of profound peace and consequent apathy may expose us to the danger of domestic insurrection." A New Orleans editor called for armed vigilance, adding that "The times are at least urgent for the exercise of the most watchful vigilance over the conduct of slaves and free colored persons."

A Southerner seeking military activity did not have to wait for war with Britain, Mexico, or the North. He could find it in the almost continuous campaign against the subversion of slavery. He could go with General Youngblood to annihilate a group of suspected slave rebels in South Carolina, or with Brigadier General Wade Hampton in 1811 in the march from Baton Rouge to an infected plantation in St. John the Baptist Parish. The citadels, sentries,

"Grapeshotted cannon," and alerted minute men became familiar and integral parts of the Southern scene and were regarded by many as indispensable for the preservation of the "cornerstone" of Southern civilization.

Slavery strengthened the military tradition in the South because owners found it desirable, even necessary, to build up a fighting force to keep the slaves under control. They also felt compelled to oppose outside attacks with a militant defense. They regarded the abolitionist attack as a war on their institutions. Calhoun called it "a war of religious and political fanaticism, mingled, on the part of the leaders, with ambition and the love of notoriety." The object being "to humble and debase us in our own estimation, and that of the world in general; to blast our reputation, while they overthrow our domestic institutions." As they read antislavery literature, observed the establishment of organizations dedicated to the destruction of slavery, and felt the sting of "subversive" activities like the Underground Railroad, Southerners reasoned that they were the targets of an all-out offensive war.

In the early thirties the scope of the abolitionist offensive was felt. These years saw the establishment of numerous militant antislavery societies. This decade saw the appearance of Garrison's uncompromising *Liberator* and the revolt of the Negro Nat Turner in Virginia. Petitions against slavery began to pour into Congress, and abolitionist literature flowed in an ever-swelling stream. Calhoun admonished, "if we do not defend ourselves none will defend us; if we yield we will be more and more pressed as we recede; and if we submit we will be trampled underfoot . . ."

These were more than rhetorical flourishes. As Garrison and his fellows forced the North to consider the danger of the ever increasing slave power, the Southern leaders asserted themselves. From dozens of pens came ardent defenses of a social structure by which they would live or die. In these "bloodless conquests of the pen" they hoped to surpass "in grandeur and extent the triumphs of war." They evolved a defense of slavery that was as full of fight as a state militia called out to quell a slave uprising. Chancellor Harper, Professor Dew, Governor Hammond, Fitzhugh, and others seemed aware of the fact that, however sound or logical their proslavery arguments might be, they must infuse in them a fighting spirit. The successful defense of slavery, whether by argument or by force, depended on the development of a powerful justification based on race superiority that would bring to its support all—or almost all—white elements in the South. Thus they redefined the "facts" of history, the "teachings" of the Bible, the "principles" of economics. Convinced that thought could not be free, they believed that there should be some positive modifications of the democratic principles enunciated by the founding fathers. They rejected the equalitarian teachings of Jefferson and asserted that the inequality of man was fundamental to all social organization. There were no rights that were natural or inalienable, they insisted. In his *Disquisition on Government*, Calhoun asserted that liberty was not the right of every man equally. Instead of being born free and equal, men "are born subject not only to parental authority, but to laws and institutions of the country where born, and under whose protection they draw their first breath." Fiery Thomas Cooper stopped working on the South Carolina statutes long enough to observe wryly, "we talk a great deal of nonsense about the rights of man. We say that man is born free, and equal to every other man. Nothing can be more untrue: no human being ever was, now is, or ever will be born free."

In the rejection of the principles of liberty and equality, political democracy was also rejected. "An unmixed democracy," said one

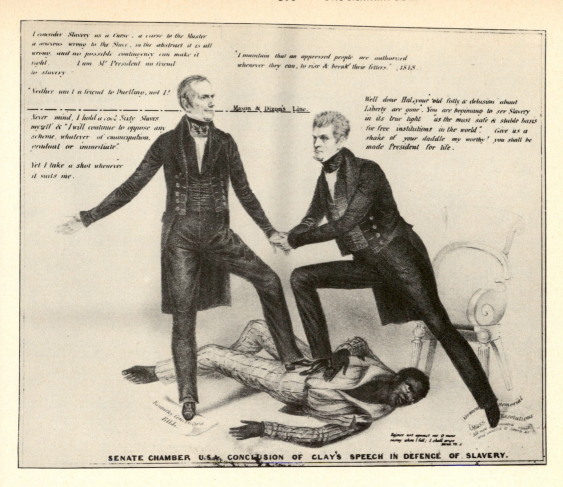

SENATE CHAMBER U.S.A. CONCLUSION OF CLAY'S SPEECH IN DEFENCE OF SLAVERY.

1839 cartoon showing John C. Calhoun (right) and Henry Clay (left) standing on a Negro. In antebellum America, most whites in North and South alike believed that Negroes were inferior. In the South itself, as Franklin states, the belief "was organized into a body of systematic thought . . . out of which emerged a doctrine of racial superiority to justify any kind of control maintained over the slave." (Courtesy of The Historical Society of Pennsylvania.)

Mississippian, "is capricious and unstable, and unless arrested by the hand of despotism, leads to anarchy . . ." There was too much talk about democracy and too little about the aristocratic tradition. "Too much liberty and equality beget a dissolute licentiousness and a contempt for law and order." Virginians and South Carolinians led the demand for a recognition of Southern honor because they were true to their ancient sentiments and "with constant pride they guard their unstained escutcheons." Life, liberty, and the pursuit of happiness were not inalienable rights. Every government, South Carolina's Chancellor William Harper explained, deprives men of life and liberty for offenses against society, while "all the laws of

society are intended for nothing else but to restrain men from the pursuit of happiness . . ." It followed, accordingly, that if the possession of a black skin was dangerous to society, then that society had the right to "protect itself by disfranchising the possessor of civil privileges and to continue the disability to his posterity . . ."

It was left to George Fitzhugh, that shrewd professional Southerner, to crystallize and summarize Southern thinking on social organization. Free society was an abject failure, he said; and its frantic, but serious consideration of radical movements like socialism, communism, and anarchism was a clear admission of its failure. If slavery was more widely accepted, man would not need to resort to the "unnatural remedies of woman's rights, limited marriages, voluntary divorces, and free love, as proposed by the abolitionists." Only in a slave society were there proper safeguards against unemployment and all the evils that follow as a country becomes densely settled and the supply of labor exceeds its demand. Fitzhugh, with a sneer at the North, observed that the "invention and use of the word Sociology in a free society and the science of which it treats, and the absence of such word and science in slave society shows that the former is afflicted with disease, the latter healthy." It was bad enough that free communities were failures, but it was intolerable that they should try to impose their impossible practices on the South. "For thirty years," he argued, "the South has been a field on which abolitionists, foreign and domestic, have carried on offensive warfare. Let us now, in turn, act on the offensive, transfer the seat of war, and invade the enemy's territory."

The South's society was to rest on the inequality of men in law and economics. Social efficiency and economic success demanded organization; and organization inevitably meant the enslavement of the ignorant and unfortunate. *Slavery was a positive good.* It was re-garded by James H. Hammond as "the greatest of all the great blessings which a kind providence has bestowed." It made possible the transformation of the South from a wilderness into a garden, and gave the owners the leisure in which to cultivate their minds and create a civilization rich in culture and gentility. More than that, it gave to the white man the only basis on which he could do something for a group of "hopelessly and permanently inferior" human beings.

The idea of the inferiority of the Negro enjoyed wide acceptance among Southerners of all classes and was an important ingredient in the theory of society promulgated by Southern leaders. It was organized into a body of systematic thought by the scientists and social scientists of the South, out of which emerged a doctrine of racial superiority to justify any kind of control maintained over the slave. In 1826, Dr. Thomas Cooper had said that he had not the slightest doubt that Negroes were of an "inferior variety of the human species; and not capable of the same improvement as the whites"; but, while a mere chemist was apparently unable to elaborate the theory, the leading physicians of the South were. Dr. S. C. Cartwright of the University of Louisiana was only one of a number of physicians who set themselves up as authorities on the ethnological inferiority of the Negro. In his view, the capacities of the Negro adult for learning were equal to those of a white infant; and the Negro could properly perform certain physiological functions only when under the control of white men. For example, Negroes "under the compulsive power of the white man . . . are made to labor or exercise, which makes the lungs perform the duty of vitalizing the blood more perfectly than is done when they are left free to indulge in idleness. It is the red, vital blood sent to the brain that liberates their mind when under the white man's control; and it is the want of a sufficiency of red, vital blood that chains their mind to ignorance and barbarism

when in freedom." Because of his inferiority, liberty and republican institutions were not only unsuited to the Negro, but actually poisonous to his happiness. Variations on this theme were still being played by many Southern "men of science" when Sumter was bombarded. Like racists in other parts of the world, Southerners sought support for their militant racist ideology by developing a common bond with the less privileged. The obvious basis was race, and outside the white race there was to be found no favor from God, no honor or respect from man. Indeed, those beyond the pale were the objects of scorn from the multitudes of the elect. By the time that Europeans were reading Gobineau's *Inequality of Races*, Southerners were reading Cartwright's *Slavery in the Light of Ethnology*. In both cases the authors conceded "good race" to some, and withheld it from others. In admitting all whites into the pseudo-nobility of race, Cartwright won their enthusiastic support in the struggle to preserve the integrity and honor of *the* race.

While uniting the various economically divergent groups of whites, the concept of race also strengthened the ardor of most Southerners to fight for the preservation of slavery. All slaves belonged to a degraded, "inferior" race; and, by the same token, all whites, however wretched some of them might be, were superior. In a race-conscious society whites at the lowest rung could identify themselves with the most privileged and affluent of the community. Thomas R. Dew, Professor of Political Law at the College of William and Mary, made this point clear when he said that in the South "no white man feels such inferiority of rank as to be unworthy of association with those around him. Color alone is here the badge of distinction, the true mark of aristocracy, and all who are white are equal in spite of the variety of occupation." De Bow asserted this even more vigorously in a widely circulated pamphlet published in 1860. At one point, he said that the non-slaveholding class was more deeply inter-

ested than any other in the maintenance of Southern institutions. He said that non-slaveholders were made up of two groups: those who desired slaves but were unable to purchase them; and those who were able but preferred to hire cheap white labor. He insisted that there was no group of whites in the South opposed to slavery. One of his principal arguments was that the non-slaveholder preserves the status of the white man "and is not regarded as an inferior or a dependent . . . No white man at the South serves another as a body servant, to clean his boots, wait on his table, and perform the menial services of his household. His blood revolts against this, and his necessities never drive him to it. He is a companion and an equal."

Southern planters paid considerable attention to the non-slaveholding element whenever its support was needed in the intersectional struggle. Their common origins, at times involving actual kinship of planters and yeomen, gave them a basis for working together in a common cause. The opportunities for social mobility, however rare, provided the dreams of yeomen. These dreams strengthened their attachment to the planter class; while the fear of competition with a large group of freedmen was a nightmare. But *race*—the common membership in a superior order of beings of both planters and poorer whites—was apparently the strongest point in the argument that the enslavement of the Negro was as good for small farmers as it was for large planters. The passion of the Southern planter and politician for oratory found ample release in the program to persuade Southern whites that theirs was a glorious civilization to be defended at all costs. In the absence of active and bitter class antagonisms, it was possible for the various white groups to cooperate especially against outside attacks and in behalf of slavery.

Most Southerners were not satisfied merely to have their leaders restate the theory of Southern society and argue with abolitionists in

Congress and other respectable places; they wanted to give effective and tangible support to their cause. Chancellor Harper had told them that, in the South as in Athens, "every citizen should be a soldier, and qualified to discharge efficiently the duties of a soldier." In *De Bow's Review* "A Virginian" advised his fellows that *"without ceasing to be free citizens, they must cultivate the virtues, the sentiments, nay, the habits and manners of soldiers."* They should be ready for vigorous, militant action to protect and defend the South's institutions. James Buckingham believed that they were determined to do exactly that. In 1839, he remarked, "Here in Georgia . . . as everywhere throughout the South, slavery is a topic upon which no man, and, above all, a foreigner, can open his lips without imminent personal danger, unless it is to defend and uphold the system." He stated further that the violence of the measures taken against the few who ventured to speak in favor of abolition was such as to strike terror in others.

There was no strong antislavery sentiment in the Southern states after 1830. Moreover, Northern antislavery organizations were doing little to incite the slaves to revolt or, except for sporadic underground railroad activities, to engage in other subversive activities. It was enough, however, for Southerners to believe either that abolitionists were active or that there was a possibility of their becoming active. This belief, running very strong at times, placed under suspicion everything Northern, including persons and ideas. "Upon a mere vague report, or bare suspicion," Harriet Martineau observed, "persons travelling through the South have been arrested, imprisoned, and, in some cases, flogged or otherwise tortured, on pretence that such persons desired to cause insurrection among the slaves. More than one innocent person has been hanged. . . ." She reported with horror that, after William Ellery Channing published his attack on slavery, several South Carolinians vowed that, should he

visit their state with a bodyguard of 20,000 men, he would not come out alive.

After 1830, the South increased its vigilance over outside subversion, and pursued the elusive, at times wholly imaginary, abolitionist with an ardor born of desperation. When they could not lay hands on him they seized the incendiary publications that were the products of his "fiendish" mind. In the summer of 1835, overpowering the city guard, they stormed the post office in Charleston and burned a bag of abolitionist literature. According to the postmaster, this act was not perpetrated by any "ignorant or infuriated rabble." In the same year, citizens of Fairfax County, Virginia, formed local vigilance committees in each militia district "to detect and bring to speedy punishment all persons circulating abolitionist literature." A correspondence committee of twenty was to keep in touch with developments in other parts of the South.

It was in 1835 that Sergeant S. Prentiss, rising to prominence in Mississippi, wrote his mother who had remained at their Maine home, that fifteen Negroes and six whites had been hanged in connection with an insurrection plot that never materialized. He added, "It certainly ought to serve as a warning to the abolitionists, not only of their own danger but of the great injury they are doing the slaves themselves by meddling with them." The hunt was on. In the last decade before the Civil War, mobs and vigilance committees arrested Northern "peddlers, book agents, traveling salesmen, and . . . school teachers." William Lloyd Garrison, indeed no impartial reporter of events, gathered enough information on the violent treatment of Northerners in the South to publish two tracts on the subject. He reported that in one Alabama town the militia was called out to eject an agent who was selling Fleetwood's *Life of Christ.* In Virginia "a company of brave and chivalrous militia was assembled, with muskets and bayonets in hand," to escort out of the community a Shaker who was peddling

garden seeds. He also reported that twenty-five vigilance committees had been set up in four Virginia counties to keep a strict eye on all suspicious persons "whose business is not known to be harmless or . . . who may express sentiments of sympathy . . . with abolitionists."

These incidents were, of course, excellent grist for Garrison's mill; and allowance should be made for any exaggeration that might have come from his zeal in reporting such incidents. They bear a striking resemblance, however, to those reported by more disinterested sources. When John C. Underwood of Clark County, Virginia, went to the Republican National Convention in 1856, his neighbors were outraged. In a mass meeting they passed resolutions condemning him of moral treason and threatening him with violence if he ever returned to Virginia. He moved out of the state and remained away until 1864.

·   ·   ·

All over the South mob action began to replace orderly judicial procedure, as the feeling against abolitionists mounted and as Southern views on race became crystallized. Even in North Carolina, where one citizen felt that there should be some distinction between that "civilized state and Mississippi and some other Western states," the fear of abolitionists caused many of its citizens to resort to drastic measures. In 1850, two missionaries, Adam Crooks and Jesse McBride, came into the state from Ohio, ostensibly to preach to those North Carolina Methodists who had not joined the newly organized Methodist Episcopal Church, South. Soon they were suspected of abolitionist activities, and McBride was convicted of distributing incendiary publications. According to one source they were "mobed and drove out of Gulford." Ten years later a vigilance committee threatened to deal violently with one John Stafford whose crime had been to give food and shelter to Crooks and McBride during their sojourn in the state. This was the kind of activity that Professor Benjamin S. Hedrick, dismissed from the University of North Carolina for his free-soil views, deprecated. Safe in New York City he asked Thomas Ruffin, Chief Justice of the North Carolina Supreme Court, to use his influence "to arrest the terrorism and fanaticism" that was rampant in the South. "If the same spirit of terror, mobs, arrests and violence continue," he declared, "it will not be long before civil war will rage at the South."

VIII   The Storm Gathers

28

"We Must Act Now and Decisively"

Avery Craven

The slavery controversy reached a crisis in 1849 when California asked to join the Union as a free state. Southern leaders emphatically opposed the move, contending that another free state would upset the balance of fifteen free and fifteen slave states in the Union. Soon, Southerners argued, the free states would dominate the federal government and would eventually attempt to abolish slavery, as Southerners had feared might happen since the 1820s. While this was simply not the case, since most Northerners were content to leave slavery alone where it already existed, Southerners nevertheless believed what they wanted to believe. Their most articulate spokesman, John C. Calhoun, warned ominously that the South would secede unless California's bid for statehood were rejected and Southerners were given extraordinary means to protect themselves and their peculiar institution (he suggested that they be given their own president). While Congress held stormy debates over the California problem and over the very nature of the Union, Southerners laid plans for a convention to meet at Nashville, Tennessee, to move for secession should California enter the Union as a free state. For a time, it looked as though the nation might disintegrate during that fateful winter of 1849–1850. But suddenly the political winds changed. President Zachary Taylor, who had opposed a Congressional compromise over California and championed his own plans, died of a heat stroke and a violent stomach disorder. The new president, Millard Fillmore of New York, supported a Congressional compromise. John C. Calhoun also died, thereby clearing the way for Southern acceptance of various compromise measures which Stephen A. Douglas of Illinois and Henry Clay of Kentucky were guiding through a badly divided Congress. The Compromise of 1850, as it finally emerged, brought California into the Union as a free state, organized the territories of Arizona and New Mexico on the basis of popular sovereignty (citizens there would vote on whether to legalize slavery or not), settled the disputed Texas-New Mexico boundary, abolished the slave trade—but not slavery itself—in Washington, D.C., and provided for a stringent new fugitive slave law, to be rigorously enforced by the federal government. Most Southern politicians approved the Compromise; pro-Union candidates won crucial state and local elections in the South itself; and the secession crisis passed.

Southerners, though, got more out of the Compromise than a new fugitive slave law. While California was a "free" state, inasmuch as her constitution outlawed slavery, her United States Senators turned out to be pro-Southern. Moreover, while Southerners were a distinct minority of the nation's population, they continued to control the crucial branches of the federal government— the presidency, the Senate, and the Supreme Court —and used these agencies to preserve and perpetuate slavery in the laws and legal decisions of the United States. Throughout the 1850s, most Southerners were obstinate nationalists, demanding that Northerners acquiesce in the fugitive slave law and show some respect for the property rights clause of the Fifth Amendment. They used secession only as a threat to consolidate their power in Washington.

But not all Southerners accepted the compromise of 1850 or wanted to remain in the Union on any terms. A handful of activists in the South—the "fire-eaters"—set about trying to convince Southerners that only through secession and an independent confederacy could they protect their slave-based society. Avery Craven recounts their

activities in the 1850s, as they tried to prepare the Southern mind for Southern independence.

"As was to have been expected," observed the Columbus, Georgia, *Sentinel* in January, 1851, "the storm which has just passed . . . has been succeeded by a calm. It is the calm of preparation, and not of peace; a cessation, not an end of the controversy. . . . The elements of that controversy are yet alive and they are destined to outlive the government. There is a feud between North and South which may be smothered, but never overcome."

Not everyone in the South took this gloomy view. Some regarded "the late compromise measures as the recognition of those great constitutional principles for which the South [had] always contended. In the repudiation of the Wilmot Proviso, and the enforcement of the Constitutional obligation to deliver up fugitive slaves, the North [had] given practical evidence of their intention to stand, in good faith, by the Constitutional Union of their fathers— recognizing and enforcing all the rights guaranteed by that solemn compact to their brethren of the South." The Union, they thought, deserved further trial.

Events were soon to show that the *Sentinel* was right and the compromisers entirely mistaken. The sectional conflict was not over. The radicals of neither section had changed their attitudes or their purposes in the slightest degree. They had not lost ground. In spite of the collapse of secession threats, sectional fears and resentments had been heightened. Each section had become more self-conscious and more certain that it differed in fundamental

From *The Coming of the Civil War*, Second Edition, by Avery Craven, published by University of Chicago Press. Copyright 1966 by Avery Craven. Reprinted by permission.

values from its rival. The crisis had been passed only because issues were still largely political rather than moral, and because sectional symbols and stereotypes were not completed. The term "Slave-power" did not, in 1850, conjure up before Northern minds the image of a single, great brutal force bent on destruction and evil doing. Until "Black Republicanism" made its appearance, Southern common folk could not wholeheartedly believe that the North wanted to reduce their section to dependence and social ruin. Until Uncle Tom, Bleeding Kansas, "Bully" Brooks, Dred Scott, and John Brown had done their work, the emotional force necessary to complete the distortions was not present. The next crisis would have a different outcome.

Southern radicals, soon to be known as "fire-eaters," early understood the reasons for their failure to secure united and positive action in 1850, and set about to remedy conditions. The Southern people, they were convinced, had not been thoroughly aroused to the danger. The masses had not realized that their section was hopelessly different from the North in values and interests, that its purposes could never be realized in the present Union. The Southern people had not seen the North in its true light as the determined enemy of Southern life and labor—selfish, grasping, and unscrupulous. They must be made to realize that the abolition of slavery and the economic plunder of their section were imminent. The South must achieve economic, social, and intellectual independence. That was a necessary preliminary step toward the inevitable break-up of the Union. The time was ripe for beginning.

The movement toward Southern self-sufficiency was not entirely new. The extreme Southern nationalist was already a familiar figure. For the past five or six years a few bold spirits in most of the Southern States had been openly advocating secession and boasting of the supremacy of Southern culture. Some of them were already working closely with a more

conservative and practical group who were attempting to improve agriculture, develop and extend commerce, improve Southern education, and develop a sectional literature.

The crisis of 1850 strengthened their hands. Under the text, "It is an ill wind that blows nobody good," the Mobile *Daily Register* noted that the Pandora box of slavery agitation had set the South to seeking economic independence. "We scarcely open one of our Southern exchanges," it said,

> without seeing an account of some new manufactory of cotton, iron, or wood, springing up in our midst. . . . But this is not all. Since the North has become expert at kidnapping our negroes, our people have learned to stay at home. Not one in ten of those among us, who spent their summers at the North ten years ago, now show their faces there. Mineral waters in many localities have been discovered. Bathing and other places of recreation, have sprung up among us, where, with the luxuries of life in profusion, our people of leisure and of means spend their summers, secure from the insolent sneers of fanatics. . . . The deep-seated determination of the South to become independent cannot be arrested.

The leaders of the movement were men of pronounced opinions and strong emotions. Conservatives were inclined to view them as extremists until the drift of events brought war near and turned them into prophets. Northern writers treated them as villains, and history has rewarded them with undeserved neglect. Their part in dividing a nation, however, was an important one, and Rhett, Yancey, Ruffin, and their fellow workers cannot be ignored in any attempt to understand how civil strife came to the United States.

Robert Barnwell Rhett, born Smith, came of New England forebears who had settled in the southernmost corner of South Carolina. He was one of fifteen children, and, for that reason, was early placed in the care of a grandmother who undertook his education. His father was an accomplished scholar—barrister from Middle Temple Bar in London—whose failures as a planter shunted him back and forth between the two Carolinas and kept him poor. His mother was a distant relative of John Quincy Adams!

We know little of Rhett's youth except that he was high-strung and without vices great or small. He studied law and, at the age of twenty-six, entered public life as the representative of his parish in the state legislature. Two years later [1828], in the tariff struggle, he revealed the temper and qualities which were to characterize his entire public life. While others hesitated, he spoke sharply for open resistance and rejoiced at the glorious inalienable right of a people to throw off an oppressive government. He praised revolution as "the dearest and holiest word to the brave and the free." The spirit of '76, he declared, was not dead in Carolina. By the late 'thirties, he was asking: "If a Confederacy of the Southern States could now be obtained, should we not deem it a happy termination?" He then offered a series of resolutions to the effect that the Constitution had proved inadequate to protect the Southern States in the peaceful enjoyment of their rights and property and should be amended "or the Union of the States dissolved."

As an editor of the Charleston *Mercury* and then as a representative in Congress, Rhett loyally supported Calhoun in his efforts to create a Southern bloc and to reach the presidency. Only once did he falter. When the great Carolinian acquiesced in the tariff of 1842, Rhett drew back and, at Bluffton, sounded the cry for a state convention and separate state action. But Calhoun kept developments in hand, and Rhett, eager to see his old chief secure the Democratic nomination in 1844, al-

lowed his movement to become only another episode which enemies might cite as evidence of South Carolina's disloyalty.

While hope for Calhoun's success remained, Rhett curbed his feelings; but after 1848 he prayed that the North would go the whole distance in abolishing slavery in the territories and the District of Columbia, so that the final contest would come and the South be set free. "You have tamely acquiesced," he chided his people, "until to hate and persecute the South has become a high passport to honor and power in the Union." He was convinced that North and South constituted two different peoples. Climate, crops, and slavery set the South apart. She must rule herself or perish.

After the Nashville Convention, he cast all restraint aside and openly and without reservation proclaimed himself a disunionist.

> Let it be, that I am a Traitor. The word has no terrors for me. . . . I have been born of Traitors, but thank God, they have been Traitors in the great cause of liberty, fighting against tyranny and oppression. Such treason will ever be mine whilst true to my lineage. . . . No, no, my friends! Smaller States before us struggled successfully, for their independence and freedom against far greater odds; and if it must be, we can make one brave, long, last, desperate struggle, for our rights and honor, ere the black pall of tyranny is stretched over the bier of our dead liberties. To meet death a little sooner or a little later, can be of consequence to very few of us. . . .

Other South Carolinians of the day, however, held life a trifle dearer than Rhett and viewed treason with more concern. They sent Rhett to the Senate in 1851, but they almost immediately thereafter gave the cooperationists control of the state. Sensing this reaction at home and hostility among his fellows in the Senate, Rhett resigned before the end of the session. He was convinced that his place was in the South; his task, that of stirring the whole section to a realization of its danger. While James L. Orr and other conservatives took charge in South Carolina, Rhett joined with Yancey in "preparation of the Southern mind." Throughout the 'fifties, he labored to reopen the slave trade, to organize committees of safety, and to devise a program on which the South could unite for independence. Year in and year out, he talked of Southern rights and Northern hostility. Well does he deserve the title, Father of Secession.

William Lowndes Yancey contributed even more than Rhett to the Southern movement. He was less forceful with his pen, but he excelled as an orator. Few Americans, even in a period which produced most of our great public speakers, were as effective in swaying audiences. Whenever Yancey spoke, and he was in constant demand throughout the 'fifties, great crowds gathered and stood at rapt attention for hours. History has designated him: The Orator of Secession.

Yancey's father, a lawyer friend of John C. Calhoun in Abbeville, South Carolina, died when his son was but three years of age [1817]. His mother remarried soon afterward [1822] and the new head of the family, Nathan Beman, called to the pastorate of the First Presbyterian Church of Troy, New York, carried the Yanceys northward. There, in a region of rapid economic change and intense social-intellectual ferment, young Yancey grew to manhood, obtained his early education, and prepared for Williams College. Troy was interesting training ground for a high-spirited youth. The Erie Canal was just being completed; factories, here and there, were opening their doors; the first of several agricultural revolutions, forced by Western competition, was under way. Near by, the Mormons had established anew direct contact with God, and the Locofocos were attempting to give the democratic dogmas a real social-

economic significance. To Beman's church, in 1826, came Charles Grandison Finney to preach the great revival. Weld and Tappan and Leavitt were friends of the family and Beman himself soon accepted the abolition doctrine. The region between Albany and Buffalo was just entering the era of isms, revivals, and reforms which was to make it the most vigorous and lively spot on the American continent during the next two decades.

For twelve impressionable years, three of them at Williams College, Yancey lived in this aggressively Northern environment. Then he returned to South Carolina and took up the study of law in the office of Benjamin F. Perry in Greenville. Two years later he married the daughter of a wealthy planter and moved to Dallas County, Alabama, then something of a frontier, and began the career of planter, editor, lawyer, and politician. At first he combined planting with the editing of a Wetumpka newspaper but, when his slaves were accidentally poisoned, he turned to the law and politics. From 1841 to 1846, he served his district first in the state legislature and then in Congress, resigning the latter office because of the "foul spell of party which binds and divides and distracts the South."

Yancey's return to private life, as a lawyer, launched him on his true public career. His magic gift of oratory turned his every appearance at court into an occasion and brought calls from far and wide to speak before political, agricultural, and sectional gatherings. Few peoples have ever matched those of the antebellum South in their devotion to oratory; Yancey, in the opinion of these seasoned critics, stood out like Saul of old above all who spoke.

After the introduction of the Wilmot Proviso, the invariable theme of all Yancey's orations became Southern wrongs and Southern rights. As he later put it:

All my aims and objects are to cast before the people of the South as great a mass of wrongs committed on them, injuries and insults that have been done, as I possibly can. One thing will catch our eye here and determine our hearts; another thing elsewhere; all united may yet produce spirit enough to lead us forward, to call forth a Lexington, to fight a Bunker's Hill, to drive the foe from the city of our rights.

His first move was to persuade the Alabama State Democratic Convention of 1848 to adopt a series of resolutions asserting the duty of the federal government to protect slave property in the territories and pledging the Alabama delegates to the National Convention to vote for no presidential or vice-presidential candidate who favored restrictions on slavery. Armed with his platform and the answers to a questionnaire he had addressed to all prospective candidates, he set out for Baltimore to attempt to shape the national party platform and candidates to its demands. Failing in this, he and one companion bolted the convention.

From that hour until the fateful day at Charleston in 1860 when he led the delegates of the Lower South out of the Democratic Convention and into civil war, Yancey labored for Southern unity and independence. Something about his zeal recalls the statement once made to a friend: "Twelve years of my life spent among New England farmers were not thrown away. Come see what a Yankee I am around my cattle sheds." With Edmund Ruffin, he organized *Southern Rights Associations* and then the *Leagues of United Southerners* in the hope that the dissemination of truth migh' help "true hearted son[s] of the South" to "know each other" and to "know too [their] foes." At home and throughout the South, his eloquence intensified the fears and deepened the hatreds of things Northern.

The third of this triumvirate was Edmund Ruffin of Virginia. Slight and frail, shy and hesitant, he lacked the personality and oratorical ability essential to political success in his

section. Yet pride and ambition and certainty of intellectual superiority had pushed him early into public life and consequent failure. That failure made him seek compensations and develop an alertness against suspected foes. He turned his talents to agriculture and worked out a theory of soil fertility which, in practice, transformed the face of his native state and brought increased prosperity and improved methods to much of the South. His agricultural periodical, *The Farmers' Register*, judged from any angle, was superior to any other publication of the kind in the United States. His *Essay on Calcareous Manures* has been called by a recent government expert "the most thorough piece of work on a special agricultural subject ever published in the English language." He taught and practised deeper and horizontal plowing, the growing of legumes, the rotation of crops, underground drainage, and the use of all kinds of fertilizers from calcareous matter to dried blood and ground bone. He doubled and quadrupled yields of wheat and corn and lifted real-estate values in Virginia by the millions of dollars. The agricultural renaissance which he inaugurated is, even today, a matter for astonishment.

But Ruffin was more than a progressive farmer in a frontier-wrecked agricultural world. He early became an intense Southern nationalist. His purpose in restoring soils was thereafter to check emigration and to create a prosperity which would enable the South to hold her own in population and representation, or to achieve her independence.

Ruffin's whole life, up to this time, had been a bitter fight against ill health, economic disasters, an indifferent public and cunning politicians. He now found in the Yankee a substitute for all foes and thwartings. His adversary was the enemy of farmers, enemy of slaveholders, enemy of gentlemen, enemy of a superior way of life, enemy of the South! All the force of bitter, pent-up emotions found outlet. Calm and satisfaction came to a troubled soul.

Edmund Ruffin, Virginia secessionist, called on the South to strengthen its economy through scientific agriculture. A champion of Southern independence, he blew his brains out when the Confederacy collapsed. (U.S. Signal Corps Photo No. 111-BA-1226 [Brady Collection] in the National Archives.)

The Wilmot Proviso deeply stirred him. In it he thought he saw complete proof of Northern determination to destroy slavery and the civilization builded upon it. He was convinced that the time had come for "separation from and independence of, the present Union." Another Haiti was preparing. The "degradation and final prostration" of his section were near at hand. The South must be aroused.

Ruffin's pen, so prolific in the production of agricultural advice, now turned to the service of slavery and sectional rights. Soon he gave up farming that he might better serve. Pamphlets, books, newspaper articles, and personal letters, in astonishing quantity and quality, carried his message. He travelled widely throughout the South, consulting with Rhett and Yancey and Hammond, attending meetings and conventions like a veritable Peter the Hermit, organizing Associations and Leagues, and always preaching the gospel of secession. When John Brown went to Harpers Ferry, Ruffin hurried there to gather up the pikes, "designed to slaughter sleeping Southern men and their awakened wives and children," and scattered them about the South where they would best teach their lesson. When the guns turned on Sumter, Ruffin was permitted to pull the first lanyard.

What Ruffin was to Southern agricultural improvement and independence, the more calm and conservative William Gregg was to manufactures. He was not, strictly speaking, a fire-eater, but no story of the efforts at Southern self-sufficiency would be complete without mention of his contribution. He was born in Virginia, but spent the greater part of his mature life in South Carolina. At Columbia and later at Charleston, he carried on the business of jeweler and silversmith. Then in the mid-'forties, he suddenly became an industrial enthusiast. With utter disregard for contemporary Southern opinion, he published a series of newspaper articles in praise of manufacturing and of Northern energy in its development. "It would indeed be well for us," he wrote, "if we were not so refined in politics—if the talent, which has been, for years past, and is now engaged in embittering our indolent people against their industrious neighbors of the North, had been with the same zeal engaged in promoting domestic industry and the encouragement of the mechanical arts." He urged his fellow Southerners to invite capital to come

to the South, put the "poor, ignorant, degraded white people" to work and scatter a few Lowells and Lawrences about the Southern countryside.

Example followed precept. In 1845, he organized the Graniteville (S. C.) Manufacturing Company and developed what was undoubtedly the most successful concern of the kind in the section. It became a model widely discussed and frequently copied. Gregg viewed it as a demonstration of Southern opportunities. Though he denounced the movement toward political independence, he labored as ardently as Ruffin himself for economic liberation. Without condemning the North, whose activity and enterprise he warmly admired, he sought the well-being of the lesser Southern whites and the wide prosperity of the section of his birth. In the end, he too became a Southern nationalist.

Rhett, Yancey, Ruffin, and Gregg were the great leaders, who during the stirring 'fifties were preparing the South for her attempt at independence. They were not, however, working alone. In every state they had able allies. James H. Hammond, son of a New England schoolteacher lodged in South Carolina, provided much of skill and industry toward economic diversification and especially the improvement of agriculture. By 1850, he had lost all faith in "any Constitutional Compact with the North" and declared that: "If we do not act now, we deliberately consign our children, not our posterity, but *our children* to the flames." "We must act *now,* and *decisively,*" he said. James D. B. DeBow, whose father had come from New Jersey to South Carolina, made the commercial and industrial development of the South his special concern. In the 'fifties, his *Review,* published at New Orleans, was the outstanding medium for the expression of extreme Southern opinion. It attained a circulation greater than that of any other magazine published in the section. DeBow's constant cry was, "action, Action, ACTION!!!—not in the

rhetoric of Congress, but in the busy hum of mechanism, and in the thrifty operations of the hammer and the anvil." "Light up the torches [of industry]" he urged, "on every hill top, by the side of every stream, from the shores of the Delaware to the farthest extremes of the Rio Grande—from the Ohio to the capes of Florida. Before heaven! we have work before us now." Roger Pryor of Virginia, William C. Dawson and Henry L. Benning of Georgia, and the editors of such newspapers as the Richmond *Enquirer*, the Raleigh *Standard*, the Mississippi *Free Trader*, the New Orleans *Daily Crescent*, and the *Southern Literary Messenger* —the list could be indefinitely extended— preached economic or political preparedness through the development of complete self-sufficiency. Slowly into Southern consciousness they wove the idea of an irrepressible conflict and the necessity for Southern strength with which to meet it.

. . .

The general call to action and renewed action along these lines was sounded in DeBow's *Review*, January, 1851.

. . . There are two things upon which the whole South seems now agreed, *as one man*, whatever minor points may separate us:— and these are, *that grievous wrongs have been done, as well as gratuitous insults offered us, by the free States of the North, and the Congress of the Union, and that the cup of forebearance or endurance is so full that a single drop shall make it overflow.* . . . The cup of endurance is full! Are we in earnest, men of the South, in this declaration, and do we realize in all its force how much is involved in it? *Is this the Southern platform?* Thank God, if we had such a platform to stand upon and unite together upon, we could then be respectable, could be feared, could present an unbroken phalanx to the invader, and bid him move and die. . . .

Then followed a program aimed to check future dangers and to prepare the South to meet them in case "the remaining drop . . . be poured out to swell over the already brimming cup." It proposed:

(1) A Southern Convention, not like that at Nashville, but one elected by all the people of the South, which was to demand "like the Barons of Runnymead, the *great Charter* of their liberties."

(2) A Southern Mercantile Convention to consider means by which the people might own their own ships and conduct their own trade with foreign nations.

(3) A Southern Manufacturing Convention where the people should agree "to manufacture at home every bale of cotton that we eventually consume and pay no more tribute to northern looms."

(4) The diversification of industry to the point where nothing would be purchased outside which could be made at home. The building of railroads and plank roads.

(5) The ending of annual vacation migrations to the North and the squandering of millions; the developing of Southern watering places; the education of children at home in the South; and the encouragement of a Southern literature.

Over and over again in the next few years these proposals were echoed throughout the South with local variations and shifting emphasis. In 1855, the Richmond *Enquirer* demanded "the declaration of our independence of the North in commercial, literary and other matters of equal importance." It rejoiced at the absence of Southern beaux and belles from Saratoga, Newport and other fashionable summer resorts at the North. It proclaimed the superiority of Southern schools and colleges, especially the University of Virginia and the Virginia Medical College, and denounced the sending of Southern youth to Northern schools where their minds were "poisoned by the incendiary teachings of fanatical professors . . . ,—im-

placable enemies of the South and of its patri-archal institutions." It wanted the South to build its own ships, carry its own trade, and manufacture for itself. But its goal was only self-sufficiency; it had no desire that men of the South should become "hucksters and cob-blers, shop-keepers and common carriers for mankind." For, it added: "It is reputable, hon-orable and desirable to build our own ships, carry our own trade, and manufacture for our-selves; but not for other people."

Three years later the *Southern Dial* (We-tumpka, Ala.) commented on the stupidity of quarelling "with the North for political offices and bounties, and then spend[ing] . . . precious energies in legislating ourselves, in our State halls, free and independent States, while we feed our minds on her literature, and our bodies on her luxuries, and clothe them in her manu-factured goods, make her vessels the carriers of our foreign trade, and her merchants our financial agents."

The *Dial* editor urged that the South stop "the drain of millions" paid to "northern schools and presses; stop the cost of travel among them; end all . . . trade there, and com-mercial and financial agencies." He advocated the building up of direct trade with Europe, Africa and China and South America. He wanted New Orleans, Mobile, Pensacola, Brunswick, Savannah, Charleston, Norfolk, Petersburg, Richmond and Baltimore to develop themselves into great thriving commercial and industrial centers, where a million new voters would dwell. Then indeed would Cotton be King and "educational independence" and "commercial independence . . . bring the North into political dependence upon the South."

Practical programs and steps toward the real-ization of these suggestions did not always fol-low impassioned utterance. Rural worlds are not much given to innovations and quick changes. Southern values had long been fixed by a widespread belief in the superiority of the agricultural way of life. The spell of cotton was still great. The capital necessary for new enter-prise was already tied up in land and labor, the directing ability already employed in planting and politics. The first problem was, therefore, to create an interest in, and a sentiment in favor of, new types of economic endeavor and new methods in the old ones. A program of education had to precede a program of action.

Talk and action, therefore, must both be considered in discussing developments in this period. And each movement must, moreover, be seen both as part of a series of changes nor-mally due in the section and as part of a new drive toward sectional independence.

Agricultural reform came first. It was already widespread and successful before the sectional flavor was added. John Taylor had led the way in Virginia back in the 1820's, when plows and plowing were poor, when the rotation of crops was difficult because of the failure of clover and other legumes, and when exhausted lands were being abandoned by the thousands who trekked westward. Edmund Ruffin had carried the work forward with his theory of soil acid-ity and the benefits to be derived by the appli-cation of calcareous materials. A new era had dawned. Agricultural societies had reorganized and agricultural periodicals had been estab-lished. New tools and new methods and new crops had appeared, and Virginians, who had earlier migrated from poverty-stricken fields, returned to find luxuriant corn in place of scanty hen's-grass. "Mother Earth has changed her face," one of them wrote. "Verdant fields," "luxuriant clover" and "abundant harvests have taken the place of broomstraw and pov-erty grass." The truck gardens around Norfolk sent great quantities of peas, strawberries, to-matoes, potatoes, cabbages, to Baltimore, Phila-delphia, New York, and Boston. By 1860, prof-its in the Virginia-Maryland gardens passed the million-dollar mark. Dairy farmers, tobacco farmers, stock raisers, and general diversified farmers could match in their prosperity the cotton growers of the Deep South.

From Virginia the move spread southward. Ruffin went to South Carolina on Hammond's invitation to conduct an agricultural survey, and together, Hammond and Ruffin preached the restoration of soils, the diversification of crops, and even the introduction of manufacturing in the interest of improved markets. Soon J. D. Legaré and G. R. Carroll were publishing the *Southern Agriculturalist* in Charleston, and just across the border in Augusta, their friends, J. W. Jones, James Camak, Daniel Lee, and D. Redmond were issuing the far more important *Southern Cultivator*. Even cotton planters on fresher lands, rice planters along the river swamps, and sugar planters in Louisiana were talking of better tools and better methods of raising their crops. Each group had its own agricultural paper and its recognized leaders. The South understood that its early years of careless, carefree exploitive agriculture were ended, and it was ready for a more scientific era. The accepted notion that Southern agriculture was a more tumble-down affair than was agriculture in other parts of the America of that day is the worst of myths. Only differing physical conditions made its problems greater and its appearance, in some places, more ragged.

How much did the new self-conscious drive toward Southern independence accelerate and intensify the agricultural efforts already under way? No final answer can be given to that question. Most of the leaders in agricultural reform became ardent Southern nationalists and increased their zeal and scope of action as they adopted this purpose for their endeavor. Ruffin travelled more widely and presented his agricultural program as a means of increasing the strength of the South "against the plundering and oppression of tariffs to protect Northern interest, compromises (so-called) to swell Northern power, pensions and bounty laws for the same purpose." He drew stirring pictures of an independent South, freed from paying tribute to Northern manufactories, carrying

its own produce, buying and selling in markets of its own choosing, and keeping for itself the wealth which in the past had gone to build New York and Boston. He was certain that a revived agriculture would either right political balances or prepare the way for a new nation.

DeBow was particularly eager to make the Southern planter independent of all outside supplies. "Let the farmer . . . make his bread, his meat, raise a few colts and hay to feed them," he wrote. "Let him increase the quantity of corn and forage until he can spare a little; . . . let him remember the old saying, 'a master's footsteps are manure to his land.'" J. H. Hammond in South Carolina, M. W. Philips in Mississippi, and N. B. Cloud in Alabama preached and practised the same doctrine. They were not able to entirely remake Southern agriculture before 1860, but they did bring improvement and enough of agricultural independence so that the food problem of the Confederate States in war days was reduced to a minimum. What was most important, they created confidence. "Let it be understood," said the *American Farmer* in 1859, "that there is no such thing as worn-out land; that expression conveys a falsehood. . . ." "A new era has dawned. . . . The noblest victory of modern times has been achieved," echoed a plain farmer.

The drive for sectional economic independence also included the stimulation of Southern manufactures. DeBow led off, saying:

> Let the South but adopt a system of manufactures and internal improvements to the extent which her interests require, her danger demands, and her ability is able to accomplish, and in a few years northern fanaticism and abolitionism may rave, gnash their teeth, and howl in vain.

A South Carolina editor urged "the necessity of bringing up the rising generation to MECHANICAL BUSINESS." In thoroughly unSouthern fashion, he spoke of the mechanic

arts as the arm of civilization and urged the people to do away with the foolish pride or objection to such measures. "If we educate one generation in the useful arts," he added, "we will soon free ourselves from our Northern foes. . . . The mechanic arts are the bone and sinew of the country and we can never be a *free* people unless we recognize them."

Like sentiments began to appear in newspapers throughout the South. All Southern editors regretted the slavish dependence upon the North. A few dared to denounce the "lack of enterprise and skill of our people" and even dared to assert that the tariff was not at all responsible for Southern ills. Here and there some editor contrasted the sleepy character of the Southern white and the wide-awake and busy temper of the Yankee. "There is nothing like the clattering of the busy looms, the scream of the steam horse, the incessant tink, tink, tink of the Tinker's hammer, and the ring of old Vulcan's anvil, to put springs into the heels of the multitude," said the Augusta *Chronicle and Sentinel*. "Let us build then," it continued, "our Woolen and Cotton mills, and beside the cotton mill erect the paper mill . . . and the lately invented rope machine. . . . Besides our Tanneries let us have boot and shoe factories, and . . . saw-mills, and . . . our own sash and blind and furniture manufactories. . . ."

The New Orleans *Daily Crescent* emphasized the fact that the "superlatively pious, Christian, philanthropic, generous and charitable commonwealth [of Massachusetts], the people of which [had] recently voted for a free-soil-abolition candidate for the Presidency to spite and insult the South, [made] . . . more money by the manufacture of the products of slave labor than [did] . . . any slave state from the growth of the raw material." This paper advocated true and complete independence by the manufacture of all clothing, by the raising of all foodstuffs, and the rearing of flocks and herds. "It is to our deficiencies in these re-

spects," it concluded, "that most of the outrages perpetrated upon us by the fanatics of the North are to be attributed. Were we practically independent we could afford to laugh to scorn their ravings and their threats. But we are not. . . ." In the same vein, the *Southern Literary Messenger* remarked that "men curse the Yankees as a pack of rogues, when they are clothed from head to foot in fabrics made on Yankee land. . . ."

Again it is impossible to say how much the sectional impulse added to the practical steps already being taken toward industrial development. Better cotton prices throughout the 1850's unquestionably strengthened the normal tendency to plant. Some leaders felt that the South owed its superior position to the great staple crops and to the agricultural virtues of the people. They did not take kindly to talk of imitating the Yankee world and of giving up King Cotton. But here and there we find planters who had resolved to buy "no Northern Cloth for . . . Negro's clothing, no Northern shoes, if others can be obtained, no Northern soap, candles, flour, or (Ohio) bacon, no Northern potatoes, cabbage, fish, or hay, no Northern butter, cheese or preserved fish, and no Northern refined sugar!" Items appear quite regularly in widely scattered newspapers, reporting the purchase by local planters of shoes in Petersburg, Virginia, or Mobile, Alabama, "in place of New York, Boston, or Philadelphia as heretofore"; of cloth at Graniteville, South Carolina, Prattville, Alabama, or Athens or Columbus, Georgia, instead of at Lowell or Lawrence.

Sectional patriotism, moreover, clearly weakened the old prejudice against industry in many centers and helped to account for its rapid growth in the period from 1850 to 1860 when the value of Southern manufactures increased 96.5 per cent; the capital invested, 73.6 per cent; and the labor employed, 25.3 per cent. That this growth indicated a desire to end dependence on the North is shown by the fact

that the largest increases were in industries competing with the North. Woolen manufactures increased 143.55 per cent; men's clothing, 65.76 per cent; and boots and shoes, 89.9 per cent. The production of paper and coal, meanwhile, trebled; flour, lumber, and tobacco more than doubled; and the value of bar, sheet, and railroad iron increased by more than half (63 per cent). Georgia took the lead but Tennessee and Alabama also made rapid gains, and Richmond and Petersburg in Virginia were rightly designated as industrial towns. Graniteville, where Gregg labored, and Prattville, where Daniel Pratt invested his capital and genius, were typical mill villages. The iron works at Richmond and the shipyards in Norfolk grew on Southern patronage and soon found staunch supporters in their own neighborhoods. The change being wrought was both material and mental.

29

Black Pawn on a Field of Peril

Bruce Catton

Though many Northerners viewed the South as a monolithic "Slave Power" out to dominate national life, it would be a mistake to think that Northern society at large was sympathetic to Abolitionism. On the contrary, the vast majority of Northerners in the 1850s continued to regard slavery as a local problem, which Southerners ought to solve by themselves; and they had a profound respect for Southern property rights as well. Maybe most Northerners thought slavery was unjust in the abstract. Yet they would never have dreamed of forcing emancipation on the South. In fact, many Northerners grimaced at the possibility that abolition might result in thousands of Southern blacks stampeding into the free states where they would take over white jobs and try to marry white daughters. Most whites in Ohio, Indiana, and Illinois, as V. Jacque Voegeli has demonstrated in *Free But Not Equal,* were Negrophobes to the core and made it emphatically clear that they did not want slaves or free blacks living next door to them.

If most Northerners were willing to leave slavery alone in the South itself, they wanted passionately to keep slavery out of the territories, which they hoped to save for "free white labor." That is why more and more Northerners in the 1850s became converted to freesoil or anti-extensionist doctrine (anti-extensionists are not to be confused with the Abolitionists—those who sought to eliminate slavery entirely, in the South as well as the territories, and who remained a small minority in the United States throughout the 1850s). What did more than any previous event to win Northerners to anti-extensionist doctrine was the passage of the Kansas-Nebraska Act in 1854. As the following narrative states, this highly controversial measure eradicated the long-standing Missouri Compromise line and decreed that from now on the citizens of each territory would vote on whether to have slavery or not. In theory, this meant that Southerners could take their slaves into Kansas and most other territories from Canada to Mexico. In the eyes of freesoilers and Abolitionists alike, it meant that the vast West was now open to a "Slave Power" invasion, and they exhorted Northerners to go out and save the West for free white men. With armed partisans from North and South pouring into Kansas, civil war soon exploded on the prairies there. In all the furor the old Whig party disintegrated; in its place a freesoil coalition of Northern Whigs, "Anti-Nebraska" Democrats, and political Abolitionists created a new political party—the Republicans—whose platform demanded emphatically that the national government exclude slavery from all federal territories.

With Southerners insisting that slavery must be protected in the territories, the Supreme Court moved to settle the issue once and for all. In 1857 the court handed down the Dred Scott decision, one of the most explosive in judicial history. Bruce Catton, who has a consummate ability to make the past come alive, recounts the story of Dred Scott and the case that bore his name, narrating the events against the backdrop of escalating sectional hostilities.

From Bruce Catton "The Dred Scott Case" (originally appeared in *American Heritage* under the title "Black Pawn on a Field of Peril") in *Quarrels That Have Shaped the Constitution,* edited by John A. Garraty. Copyright © 1963 by Harper & Row, Publishers, Inc. Reprinted by permission of the publisher.

Dred Scott was nobody in particular. A slave born of slave parents, unable to read or write, physically frail, he was a man without energy, who for a full decade drifted about in St. Louis as an errand boy and general odd-jobs factotum, an unremarkable bondsman on whom the burden of servitude rested rather lightly. Nobody directly concerned with him wanted him as a slave. As a chattel he was a liability rather than an asset, and in any case his various owners seem to have been antislavery people. Yet his unsuccessful legal battle to become free left an enduring shadow on the history of the United States and was an important factor in the coming of the Civil War.

He is remembered because in March, 1857, the Supreme Court of the United States handed down its decision in the case of *Dred Scott v. Sandford.* (That last name, by the way, was misspelled and should be Sanford: one minor mistake in a case clouded by larger errors.) The Chief Justice asserted that Scott and all men like him neither were nor ever could be citizens. This opinion was upset a few years later by marching armies, at the cost of much bloodshed, but the reversal came too late to be of any help to Dred Scott because he died before the Civil War began.

It is hard to feel that Scott was the prime mover in this momentous case that shook the entire nation. He unquestionably wanted very much to be free, and as his struggle progressed he appears to have enjoyed the backhanded sort of fame which it brought to him, but his part was chiefly that of a pawn. He was a counter played in a tense and ominous game, and the fact that this particular counter was played just when and as it was played was one of the reasons why the game at last broke up in a furious fight. Yet the whole of it touched Scott himself only indirectly.

Dred Scott was born in Southampton County, Virginia, somewhere around 1795, the property of a man named Peter Blow. In 1827, Blow moved to St. Louis, taking his family and his chattels with him. Four years later Peter Blow died, and Scott became the property of Blow's daughter Elizabeth, who in 1833 sold him to Dr. John Emerson, an army surgeon. In 1834 Dr. Emerson was transferred to duty at Rock Island, Illinois, and some time after he was transferred again to Fort Snelling, which lay farther up the Mississippi River in what was then Wisconsin Territory. Dr. Emerson took Scott with him as a body servant during all of this time, so that for approximately five years Scott lived on free soil. At the end of 1838 Dr. Emerson returned to St. Louis, taking Scott along, and soon after this Dr. Emerson died, leaving Scott to his widow, Mrs. Irene Sanford Emerson.

For some time Mrs. Emerson did what many slaveowners did in those days—hired her chattel out to various families who needed servants. Then, in the mid-1840's, she moved to New York, and she did not take Dred Scott with her. Instead she left him in St. Louis in the charge of the two sons of Scott's original owner, Henry and Taylor Blow. It was at about this time that the seeds of what was to become one of America's most famous court cases were planted.

Henry Blow was then in his thirties, a lawyer and businessman of some wealth and prominence. He was head of a railroad, active in developing lead-mining properties in southwestern Missouri; active also in the Whig party, beginning to be known as an opponent of the extension of slavery. (A few years later Henry Blow helped organize the Free Soil movement in Missouri, and eventually he became a Republican.) As an antislavery man, Blow wanted Scott freed, and in 1846 he helped finance a suit in the Missouri courts to have Scott declared free. Scott himself appears to have been a little hazy as to what this was all about, but he willingly signed his mark to the necessary papers, and the lawsuit was on.

At this point it becomes obvious that the real point to this proceeding was not so much to win freedom for Scott personally as to win a legal

Dred Scott, who thought his case a "heap of trouble," was amazed at all "de fuss" made over him in Washington. (Courtesy of the Missouri Historical Society.)

point in the broad fight against slavery as an institution. Mrs. Emerson obviously did not want to retain Scott as her slave, and she apparently was no believer in slavery—a few years later she became the wife of Calvin Clifford Chaffee, a radical antislavery congressman from Massachusetts. When she moved to New York she could easily have executed papers of manumission to give Scott his freedom. She did not do that; instead, she left him with the Blows, and when his lawsuit began she was technically the defendant—the case was listed formally as "Scott, a Man of Color, v. Emerson." The case is just a little mysterious, but it seems clear that

what everyone wanted was a definite ruling about the status of a slave whose master took him into free territory.

This was beginning to be an important point. The western country was opening up for settlement, and the law said that north of the Missouri Compromise line of 36 degrees, 30 minutes, the new territory was free soil. Exactly what would happen if a slaveowner took his slaves with him when he moved into such territory?

Lawyers for Dred Scott argued that his five-year sojourn on free soil had ended his bondage and that on his return to Missouri the state court should make formal declaration of his freedom. The lower court ruled in Scott's favor, but an appeal was taken—what everybody wanted, obviously, was a high-level finding that would stand as some sort of landmark—and the state supreme court eventually reversed the lower court, holding that Missouri law still applied and that Scott, as a resident of Missouri, must remain a slave.

The law's delays were as notorious then as they are now, and the case dragged on for six years; the ruling of the state supreme court was not handed down until 1852. During this time Scott remained under the nominal control of the county sheriff, who hired him out here and there for five dollars a month. Scott was in limbo, everybody's slave and nobody's slave; if he had any thoughts about this interminable process of determining his future, they were never recorded.

Meanwhile, things had been happening—not to Scott, but to the country that countenanced the institution that held him in slavery. The Mexican War had been fought and won, and the United States came into possession of a vast new area running all the way to the golden shores of California, one of the immediate results being that the whole slavery controversy became a dominant issue in national politics. Until now there had been a slight unstable equilibrium, with the Missouri Compromise decreeing that new territories created from Louisi-

ana Purchase lands lying north of the line that marked the southern boundary of Missouri should be free soil. This equilibrium vanished when the immense acquisitions of the Mexican War made it obvious that sooner or later many new states would be created, and the issue was pointed up when Congressman David Wilmot of Pennsylvania unsuccessfully tried to get Congress to pass a law providing that slavery be excluded from all the land that had been taken from Mexico. The question of slavery in the territories, by the early 1850's, had become the great, engrossing question in American politics.

It became important because the way this issue was settled would determine whether the institution of slavery could continue to expand or must be limited to the areas where it already existed. On the surface, it might seem to make very little difference to a planter in Alabama or a farmer in Ohio whether slaves could or could not be held in some such faraway place as New Mexico; actually, the future of slavery itself was at stake, and everybody knew it.

The Compromise of 1850 brought a temporary easing of the tension. Under this arrangement, California came in as a free state, a stronger fugitive slave law was enacted, and it was agreed that when new territories were organized out of the empty lands that had been taken from Mexico the inhabitants of those territories would themselves decide whether slavery was to be permitted or prohibited. This was the famous principle of popular sovereignty; it looked like a fair, democratic way to settle things, and for a short time the nation relaxed.

It did not relax very long. Senator Stephen A. Douglas of Illinois in 1854 brought in his Kansas-Nebraska Act, a measure to organize the new territories of Kansas and Nebraska. This area had been acquired through the Louisiana Purchase, and it lay north of the Missouri Compromise line of 36 degrees, 30 minutes, and hence these territories must be free soil. But Douglas was a Democrat, in a Democratic Congress, and the Democratic party was largely dominated by southerners, who were most unlikely to consent to the creation of two new free territories which would presently become free states. So Douglas, a firm believer in the principle of popular sovereignty, decided to extend that principle to Kansas and Nebraska. His act, which passed Congress after most heated debate, wiped out the Missouri Compromise line and provided that the settlers of Kansas and Nebraska could say whether slavery might exist there. Meanwhile, slaveowners and their chattels were free to move in.

When he introduced this bill Douglas commented that it would "raise [a] hell of a storm." He was entirely right. It did; and the slavery controversy returned to the center of the stage, never to leave it until the papers were signed at Appomattox Courthouse.

Of all of this Dred Scott knew nothing. He continued to shift back and forth on the little jobs for which he was now and then farmed out, totally unaware of the new currents that were swirling about him. But he suddenly became an important person because of that old lawsuit. Missouri slaveowners were moving into Kansas, taking their slaves with them; antislavery people from the North were also moving in, taking their antislavery convictions with them; and there were bitter clashes, with bloodshed and gunfire to focus national attention on the situation. The old question about the status of a slave whose owner took him into an area which the old Missouri Compromise called free soil had become a matter of vast consequence.

It was time, in other words, to get a ruling from the Supreme Court of the United States. The original lawsuit was revived. Mrs. Emerson transferred title to Scott to her brother, John F. A. Sanford of New York, and in 1854 the case, now known as *Dred Scott v. Sandford*, got on the docket in the federal circuit court for Missouri.

It was a bit complicated. If Scott was to sue Sanford in a federal court he had to show that he

was a citizen of Missouri—that is, a federal case had to involve an action between citizens of different states. Sanford's lawyers argued that as a Negro slave Scott was not a citizen of Missouri and that the federal court therefore lacked jurisdiction. The circuit court eventually ruled that way, and Scott's lawyers took the case to the Supreme Court on a writ of error. In 1856 the Supreme Court heard the arguments.

Bear in mind, again, that what happened to Scott in all of this was of no especial importance to anybody except Scott himself. What everybody wanted was a final ruling from the highest court in the land—a finding which (it was innocently hoped) would settle once and for all the disturbing question of slavery in the territories.

Three issues were involved. Was Scott actually a citizen of Missouri and so entitled to sue in a federal court? Did his residence on free soil give him a title to freedom which Missouri was bound to respect? Finally, was the Missouri Compromise itself, which had made Wisconsin Territory free soil, constitutional? (That is, did Congress actually have the power to prohibit slavery in a territory?) A final ruling on all of these points might have much to do with the question of slavery in Kansas.

So the Supreme Court had been given a very hot potato to handle, and the rising tumult in Kansas made it all the hotter. So did the presidential election of 1856, in which the new Republican party—a sectional northern party, dedicated chiefly to the theory that slavery must not be allowed to expand—showed enormous growth and came respectably close to electing John C. Frémont President of the United States. The whole argument over slavery, which was fast becoming too explosive for American political machinery to handle, had come to center on this question of slavery in the territories, and the Dred Scott case brought the question into sharp relief.

The Supreme Court could have avoided most of the thorns in this case simply by declaring that it lacked jurisdiction. A somewhat similar case had been handled so in 1850, and in the beginning most of the justices seem to have been disposed to follow that precedent. Justice Samuel Nelson prepared such an opinion: Missouri law controlled Scott's status, Missouri law said that he was still a slave, and as a slave he could not sue in the federal courts. Yet the pressures were too great for such an easy solution. The justices at last concluded to handle all of the issues. A brief glance at the make-up of the Court is in order.

Of the nine justices, five came from slave states: Chief Justice Roger B. Taney of Maryland, and Justices James M. Wayne of Georgia, John Catron of Tennessee, Peter V. Daniel of Virginia, and John A. Campbell of Alabama. Seven of the nine were Democrats—these five plus two northerners, Justices Samuel Nelson of New York and Robert C. Grier of Pennsylvania. Justice John McLean of Ohio was a Republican, and Justice Benjamin R. Curtis of Massachusetts was a Whig. All nine were men of integrity and repute, but everything considered, it might be hard for them to be completely objective about the issues that were presented to them.

It might be hard; and indeed it proved quite impossible for these men to limit themselves to the basic question about Scott's actual status. They had to say something, not just about one slave, but about all slaves.

To begin with, it soon became apparent that Justices McLean and Curtis were prepared to write dissenting opinions setting forth their views about the Missouri Compromise and the power of Congress to legislate about slavery in the territories. (They held that Scott had properly been made free by his sojourn on free soil, and that Congress had a constitutional right to outlaw slavery in the territories.) If these two dissenters were going to air their views on this latter point, those who disagreed with them would obviously do the same. In addition, many of the justices honestly believed that it was necessary to hand down a broad, definitive rul-

ing that would stand as a landmark, settling the territorial problem once and for all. Finally, Mr. James Buchanan exerted a little pressure of his own.

James Buchanan was elected President in the fall of 1856, and during the following winter—after the arguments had been heard, but before the Court had handed down its opinion—he was composing the address which he would deliver when he took the oath of office on March 4. He was bound to say something about popular sovereignty, and the issue was a tough one for a brand-new President to discuss, especially a President who owed his nomination and election largely to the fact that he had never been directly involved in the furious arguments over the territorial question. It occurred to him that it would be excellent if, in his inaugural, he could say that the question of Congress' constitutional power to legislate on slavery in the territories would very shortly be decided by the Supreme Court and that all good citizens might well stop agitating the issue and prepare to abide by the Court's ruling.

In February the President-elect wrote a letter to Justice Catron, setting forth his desire to say that the Supreme Court would presently settle this question. A bit later he wrote to Justice Grier in the same vein. Mr. Buchanan, clearly, was skirting the edge of outright impropriety; he was not exactly telling the justices what he wanted the Court to say, but he was making it clear that he wanted the Court to say *something*, and Justice Catron finally assured him that the Court would handle the matter and that Buchanan could safely say that the country ought to wait for its decision.

This Mr. Buchanan proceeded to do. In his inaugural address he remarked that the whole question of legalizing or prohibiting slavery in the territories was "a judicial question, which legitimately belongs to the Supreme Court of the United States, before whom it is now pending and will, it is understood, be speedily and finally settled. To their decision, in common

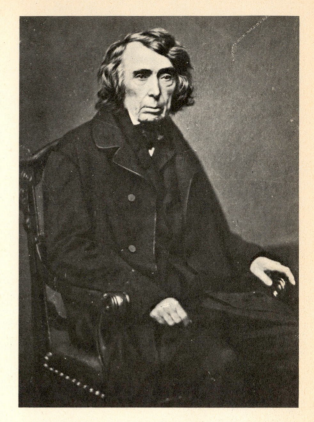

Chief Justice Roger B. Taney, whose decision rocked the freesoil North. "He walks with inverted and hesitant steps," fumed the New York Tribune. *"His forehead is contracted, his eyes sunken and his visage has a sinister expression." (Courtesy of The Library of Congress.)*

with all good citizens, I shall cheerfully submit, whatever this may be."

This set the stage. Two days later—on March 6, 1857—the Court handed down its decision, the gist of which was that Dred Scott was a slave and not a citizen, and hence could not sue in federal court, and that the Missouri Compromise was unconstitutional because Congress had no power to prohibit slavery in the territories. To

these basic findings there were just two dissents, those of Justices McLean and Curtis.

Thus the Supreme Court had (to use a police-court colloquialism) thrown the book at Dred Scott. But the case was most complicated. Each of the nine justices wrote an opinion; and although the majority agreed on the basic findings, they gave different reasons for their beliefs, and some of them remained silent on points which others considered highly important. In effect, the Court went beyond both Scott and the authority of Congress and discussed the whole rationale of slavery and the status of the Negro, and in all of this the sectional and political backgrounds of the justices were sharply emphasized. As Allan Nevins sums it up in his book, *The Emergence of Lincoln*:

> Three Southern judges declared that no Negro of slave ancestry could be entitled to citizenship; five Southern judges, with Nelson of New York, decided that Dred's status depended upon the laws of Missouri; five Southern judges, with Grier of Pennsylvania, maintained that any law excluding slavery from a territory was unconstitutional; and two Northern judges, McLean and Curtis, held that Dred was a citizen, that Missouri law did not control his status, and that Congress had a constitutional right to pass laws debarring slavery from any Territory.

It was Taney's opinion that went across the land like a thunderclap. Not only was Taney the Chief Justice; he was a man of immense prestige and learning, a veteran of Andrew Jackson's famous fight with the Bank of the United States, named Chief Justice by Jackson in 1835 as successor to John Marshall, one of the most impressive figures in American life. Taney was eighty now, shrunken, wispy, with a heavy shock of iron-gray hair framing a deeply lined face. Fires burned in him, but he was physically frail, and as he read his momentous opinion his voice was so low that many of the people in the courtroom could not catch his

words. Nevertheless, what he said was heard all across the country.

The Chief Justice addressed himself to the question of the constitutional power of Congress over the territories. It had been argued, he noted, that federal authority over the territories came from a clause permitting Congress to make rules and regulations for the government of the territories; but this, he held, was a mere emergency provision applying only to the lands ceded to the Confederation by the original states and did not apply to lands acquired after 1789. Properly, Congress had only those powers associated with the right to acquire territory and prepare it for statehood; it had no internal police authority, and while it might organize local territorial government it could not "infringe upon local rights of person or rights of property."

The right to hold slaves was a property right; since Congress could not interfere with a man's property rights, it could not prohibit slavery in the territories: "And no word can be found in the Constitution which gives Congress a greater power over slave property, or which entitles property of that kind to less protection, than property of any other description." To exclude slavery would violate the due process clause of the Fifth Amendment. Congress had nothing more than the power—"coupled with the duty" —to protect the owner in his property rights. Thus all territorial restrictions on slavery were dead.

Therefore the Missouri Compromise was unconstitutional. Its provision prohibiting slavery north of the 36 degree, 30 minute line was "not warranted by the Constitution" and was void. It was idle to argue that Dred Scott's residence on free soil had made him a free man, because slavery had not lawfully been excluded from Wisconsin Territory in the first place.

But that was not all. As a Negro of slave origins (said Taney) Scott could not be a citizen of the United States anyway. He and all people like him were simply ineligible. The Founding

Fathers who wrote the Declaration of Independence and framed the Constitution had been thinking only of white men. At the time the Constitution was adopted, and for a long time before that, there was general agreement that Negroes were "beings of an inferior order, and altogether unfit to associate with the white race, either in social or political relations; and so far inferior that they had no rights which the white man was bound to respect."

It is clear enough now that in making this remark the Chief Justice was in no sense laying down a rule of law for his own day; he was simply expressing what he believed was the prevailing opinion of Americans in the latter part of the eighteenth century. But his use of these words, embedded in an opinion which antislavery people were going to object to in any case, was in the highest degree unfortunate. To many people in the North it seemed that the Chief Justice had officially declared that the colored man had no rights which the white man was bound to respect. President Buchanan's pious hope that all good citizens would willingly accept the Court's finding in the Dred Scott case was bound to run onto this reef if on no other.

Only two other justices, Wayne and Daniel, joined with Taney in the opinion that no Negro could be a citizen. Justices Curtis and McLean dissented vigorously, and the remainder kept silent on this particular question. This made very little difference. The Missouri Compromise was unconstitutional—the first act of Congress to be declared unconstitutional since the famous *Marbury v. Madison* case in 1803—and Dred Scott was still a slave; the net effect of the decision was to give an immense impetus to the furious arguments over slavery and to help materially to make this issue so acute and so emotion-laden that it was too explosive for political settlement.

To the rising Republican party the ruling was simply a challenge to renewed struggle. This party was dedicated to the conviction that slavery must not be allowed to expand; now the High Court was formally saying that there was no legal way by which it could be excluded from the territories. Congress could not do it; a territorial legislature, as a creature of Congress, could not do it either. Only when the people of a territory drafted a constitution and prepared to enter the Union as a state could they adopt an effective antislavery law. To many northerners it seemed that, logically, the next step would be for the Court to declare that no state could outlaw slavery and that the institution must be legalized all across the country.

Free-soil adherents in the North promptly accepted the challenge which they found implicit in the decision. They expressed profound contempt for the Court itself, asserting that it was wholly biased in favor of the southern sectional interest and that its decision in the Dred Scott case had no moral substance and could not be permanently binding. For the moment, to be sure, the ruling was legally valid, but in effect the antislavery people of the North defied the Court. Seeking to take the territorial issue out of politics, the Court had instead put itself squarely and disastrously into politics. Never before had there been such a profound and widespread revulsion against a finding of the nation's highest judicial tribunal.

To the northern wing of the Democratic party —the wing that followed Senator Douglas— the ruling was equally disturbing, because it knocked the props out from under the doctrine of popular sovereignty. Douglas, to be sure, defended the Court against Republican criticism, declaring that "whoever resists the final decision of the highest judicial tribunal aims a deadly blow at our whole republican system of government," and expressed the conviction that the decision must not be made a political issue. But he was breaking with the Buchanan administration on the Kansas issue—the administration was accepting a rigged election which would give Kansas a constitution permitting slavery even though a majority of the voters obviously were antislavery. Douglas was fighting hard for

popular sovereignty, and the Dred Scott decision simply accentuated this issue by splitting the northern and southern wings of the Democratic party farther and farther apart.

For while the Douglas Democrats in the North continued to rely on popular sovereignty as the answer to the territorial problem, the southern Democrats were led by this decision to press forward in complete opposition to popular sovereignty. Now they demanded positive protection of the slaveowner's right to take his chattels with him when he moved into a territory. The decision said that nobody could outlaw slavery in a territory: the southerners felt it was only logical that the federal government act to protect slavery there by formal legislation. The northern and southern wings of the party could never agree on any such formula. In substance, the Court's decision was a weighty factor in determining that no Democrat who had any chance to carry the North could also carry the South, which meant that the presidential election of 1860 would be won by the Republicans, after which the discordant sections would find themselves at the parting of the ways. The irreconcilable sectionalism which would bring the country to civil war was accentuated by this ruling of the High Court.

Perhaps the real trouble with the decision was that the general trend of events was moving in the other direction. The New York *Herald*, on March 9, 1857, summed it up:

> The Washington politicians who believe that it [the Dred Scott decision] settles anything must be afflicted with very severe ophthalmia indeed. For while these venerable judges are discoursing on theoretical expansions of slavery to North and West, free labor is marching with a very tangible step into the heart of the strongest slaveholds of slavery. Chief Justice Taney lays out on paper an infinitude of new slave states and territories; he makes all the states in a measure slave states; but while the old gentleman is thus diverting his slippered leisure, free carpenters and blacksmiths and farmers with hoe, spade and plough are invading Missouri, Kentucky, Delaware, Maryland and Virginia, and quietly elbowing the slaves further South. It will take a good many Supreme Court decisions to reverse a law of nature such as we here see in operation.

All in all, the Dred Scott decision did the Court profound and lasting harm. Many years later Chief Justice Charles Evans Hughes remarked that it was a case in which the Court suffered from a self-inflicted wound, and characterized the ruling as a "public calamity." More than a century after the decision was handed down, a historian of the Court wrote of it as a "monumental indiscretion." The Court's prestige suffered immensely, and Justice Felix Frankfurter once remarked that after the Civil War, justices of the Supreme Court never mentioned the Dred Scott case, any more than a family in which a son had been hanged mentioned ropes and scaffolds.

In the end, the profound majority of people in the North, who, regardless of party labels, believed that slavery's expansion into the territories must be checked, agreed that while the Court's finding was binding it must eventually be reversed. A new administration would give the Court new justices and a new background, and in the course of time it would be shown that a nation whose majority did not want slavery to expand would be able to make its wish good. There was just one point on which Republicans, northern Democrats, and southern Democrats all agreed: the finding in respect to Dred Scott as a person remained good. He was still a slave.

Their legal efforts to have him declared free having failed, Dred Scott's owners manumitted him a few weeks later. On September 17, 1858, he died, in St. Louis, of tuberculosis. Henry Blow paid his funeral expenses.

30

To Purge This Land with Blood

Stephen B. Oates

John Brown was one American who decided that slavery was too entrenched in American society ever to be removed by peaceful means. In 1857, the year of the Dred Scott decision, he conceived a plan to overthrow slavery by invading Virginia with a guerrilla army; and in the ensuing two years he gathered a handful of supporters and solicited guns and money to carry out his projected invasion, to begin at Harpers Ferry in northern Virginia. The following narrative traces the genesis, execution, and explosive consequences of the Harpers Ferry attack.

"God sees it," John Brown said with tears in his fierce gray eyes. His son Jason nodded in solemn agreement. They were standing on the bank of the Marais des Cygnes, watching the free-state settlement of Osawatomie smoke and blaze against the Kansas sky. Yes, God saw it, the old man said: the homes of his friends going up in flames; the body of his son Frederick lying in the road near the Adairs' place; and

the Missouri raiders riding up and down the smoke-filled streets looting buildings and stampeding cattle with shouts and gunfire. It was August 30, 1856, and the Missourians were sacking Osawatomie in retaliation for Brown's own violent work some three months before, when he and his antislavery band, seeking revenge for numerous proslavery atrocities and hoping to create "a restraining fear," had taken five proslavery men from their homes along Pottawatomie Creek and hacked them to death with broadswords. An eye for an eye and a tooth for a tooth—that was the war cry of both sides in Bleeding Kansas—and now Osawatomie lay in flames, Brown himself had narrowly escaped capture, and one of his own sons lay in the Kansas dirt with a proslavery bullet in his heart. The old man trembled with grief and rage. "I have only a short time to live—only one death to die," he told Jason, "and I will die fighting for this cause. There will be no more peace in this land until slavery is done for. I will give them something else to do than to extend slave territory. I will carry the war into Africa."

On September 7, Brown rode into Lawrence with his gun across his saddle and his eyes burning more fiercely than ever. The old man was well known in this free-state settlement, and as he moved down the street men cheered "as loudly as if the President had come to town, but John Brown seemed not to hear it and paid not the slightest attention." For many days he came and went, his mind busy with plots. He was hiding out somewhere in or near Lawrence when Governor John W. Geary, head of the peace party in Kansas, led a force of cavalry out to end the "fratricidal strife" in the Law-

From Stephen B. Oates, "John Brown's Bloody Pilgrimage," *Southwest Review*, vol. LIII (Winter 1968), 1–22; and from Stephen B. Oates, *To Purge This Land With Blood: A Biography of John Brown* (Harper & Row, 1970).

rence vicinity and drive the Missourians out of the territory. In early October, with rumors about that Geary would arrest him, Brown and three of his sons—Jason, Owen, and John Jr.— rode out of Kansas and headed east. For already the old man was obsessed with visions of "God-fearing men, men who respect themselves," fighting in mountain passes and ravines for the liberation of the slaves. Already he believed that God was calling him to a greater destiny than the skirmishes he had been waging against slavery in Kansas. What was it the Prophet had said? "That it might be fulfilled which was spoken of the Lord by the prophet saying, Out of Egypt have I called my son." And John Brown of Osawatomie was ready now, after all these years of trial, to answer the call of his all-wise, just, and all-powerful God.

At fifty-six, Brown was an austere, polygonal man. If he was extremely religious, he could also be cruel and self-righteous, with an imperial egotism that made him intolerant and unappreciative of others, especially his own sons. He could become obsessed with a single idea—now slavery, now land speculation, now a wool crusade in Massachusetts, now a Negro community in upstate New York—and pursue that idea with single-minded determination. As a businessman, he could be conspicuously inept, with a talent for overstatement and exaggeration, especially when he was excited. But he could also be scrupulously honest. And he could be kind and gentle—extremely gentle. He could rock a baby lamb in his arms. He could stay up several nights caring for a sick child, or his ailing father, or his afflicted first wife. He could hold children on both knees and sing them the sad, melancholy refrains of Isaac Watts' old hymn, "Blow ye the trumpet, blow." He could stand at the graves of four of his children who had died of dysentery, weeping and praising God in an ecstasy of despair. He could

teach his children to fear God and keep the Commandments—and exhibit the most excruciating anxiety when they began questioning the value of religion. He could treat Negroes as fellow human beings, allowing them to eat at his table with his family and addressing his black workers as "Mr."—a significant trait in view of the anti-Negro prejudice that prevailed among a majority of Northerners and almost all Southerners in his time. He could offer to take a Negro child into his home and educate him. He could dream for years of establishing a Negro school, hide runaway slaves, and deplore racial discrimination in Northern churches. And he could feel an almost paralyzing bitterness toward slavery itself—that "sum of villainies," that "sin against God"—and toward all the people in the United States who sought to preserve and perpetuate it.

He was born in 1800 (the same year Nat Turner was born) in a stark, shutterless farmhouse in West Torrington, Connecticut. His father, a cobbler and tanner, who soon moved the family to Ohio's Western Reserve, taught the boy to fear an austere Calvinist God who demanded the most exacting obedience from the frail, wretched sinners He placed in this world. Brown's father also instructed him from early childhood to oppose slavery as an egregious sin against God. Brown's mother died when he was eight, a tragedy that left him devastated with grief. When his father remarried, Brown refused to accept his stepmother emotionally, and "pined after his own mother for years." He grew into an arrogant and contentious young man, who ordered others about, a brother remarked, like "A king against whom there is no rising up." Around girls, however, Brown was painfully shy, a quality which deprived him of "a suitable connecting link" between the sexes—and which, as he admitted himself, "might under some circumstances have proved my ruin." Although he dropped out of school at an early age, he read the Bible meticulously and committed its entire contents to

memory, taking pleasure in correcting anybody who quoted wrongly from it. In 1816, having been admitted to membership in the Congregational Church of Hudson, Ohio, he aspired to become a minister and traveled east to study. But he had to abandon his plans when he developed an inflammation of the eyes and ran short of funds. Failure was a leitmotif that was to run throughout his life.

Returning to Hudson, he built his own tannery and overcame his fears enough to marry Dianthe Lusk, who was pious and "remarkably plain." Dianthe bore seven children, whom Brown rigorously disciplined with a rod in one hand and a Bible in the other. In western Pennsylvania, where they resided for ten years, he organized an Independent Congregational Society and frequently preached, drawing his sermons from the works of Jonathan Edwards, whose mystical Calvinism greatly influenced Brown's own beliefs. In the late 1820s, though, there were signs that he was entering another season of trial. Dianthe showed symptoms of deep-rooted emotional troubles, and then she and two of their children died. He soon married again, this time to a large, reticent girl named Mary Ann Day. Mary gave him thirteen children, seven of whom died in childhood. There were tragedies in his worldly concerns too: he was wiped out in the Panic of 1837, declared bankrupt in 1842. But like other frontier businessmen, Brown had a reckless, go-ahead spirit. Recouping his fortunes, he plunged into another business venture, and another. Everything ended in failure.

As he grew older, Brown became more self-righteous and fixed in his convictions than ever. He lectured his children about Providential interpositions and their trial on earth, beseeching them to suffer the word of exhortation. He became increasingly disturbed by all the pro-slavery wickedness that prevailed in the United States. He worked on the Underground Railroad in Ohio, publicly opposed the state's "black laws," attempted to integrate a Congre-

John Brown around 1857. By that time Brown had left Bleeding Kansas and gone east to solicit guns and money for a secret "military" operation he had conceived against the South. (Courtesy of the Kansas State Historical Society.)

gational church he attended there and was expelled for his effort. After that, he grew more violent in his denunciations of slavery. He would gladly lay down his life for the destruction of that institution, because "death for a good cause," he told a friend, was "glorious." While living in Springfield, Massachusetts, he not only chided Negroes for passively submitting to white oppression but worked out a secret scheme to run slaves out of the South through a "Subterranean Pass Way." He told Frederick Douglass, whom he befriended, that he would like to arm the slaves he liberated, because using guns gave black men "a sense of

their manhood." In 1851 Brown exhorted Negroes to kill any Southerner or federal officer who tried to enforce the fugitive slave law and enlisted forty-four Springfield blacks into a mutual-defense organization called the "Branch of the United States League of Gileadites," based on the story of Gideon in the Book of Judges.

After a monumental debacle in the wool business, Brown returned to Ohio and tried to make ends meet as a wool grower and farmer. Still, he remained deeply troubled about the slavery sickness that infected his country; he openly castigated those "malignant spirits"—those "fiends clothed in human form"—who used the churches, the courts, and the national government to protect such an abomination, and advocated an immediate end to the corruption of "our truly republican and democratic institutions." But his words did no good: on May 30, 1854, President Pierce signed the Kansas-Nebraska Bill into law, an act which eradicated the old Missouri Compromise line and decreed that henceforth the citizens of each territory would vote on whether to have slavery or not. Unless they voted it down, Southerners could now take their slaves all over the West. At once, antislavery Northerners decried the act as a Southern conspiracy to seize the territories, and maybe the North as well. The first step in the plot was to occupy Kansas. Salmon P. Chase of Ohio saw it; so did William H. Seward of New York. "Come on, then, gentlemen of the slave States," Seward cried; "since there is no escaping your challenge, I accept it in behalf of the cause of freedom. We will engage in competition for the virgin soil of Kansas, and God give the victory to the side that is stronger in numbers as it is in right."

In response, hundreds of pioneers, mostly from the northwestern states, started for Kansas to make new lives for themselves on a "free-soil frontier." That fall five of Brown's sons emigrated as well. But not long after they arrived border Missourians invaded Kansas, voted illegally in elections there, and vowed to exterminate "every God-damned abolitionist in the Territory." Brown's sons wrote him about the Missourians' threats and beseeched him to join them with plenty of guns and swords, because "the storm every day thickens," John Jr. warned, and predicted that a "great struggle in arms, of Freedom and Despotism in America," was about to break out on the Kansas prairies.

Brown had already decided to migrate to Kansas for purposes of business and settlement. But when he received his sons' letters he gathered an arsenal of guns and broadswords and headed for Kansas to help save it from "Satan's legions." Violence broke out several months after he arrived there, as more columns of Missourians rode across the border to kill free-state men and terrorize free-state settlements. Brown flung himself into the struggle with uninhibited fury, riding to meet the Philistine slaveholders as Gideon had gone after the Midianites. The result was the shocking Pottawatomie murders, then open civil war, the sacking of Osawatomie, and the killing of Frederick. The Kansas civil war—"Bleeding Kansas," men called it—must have made it all very clear to him. God was at last calling him to his special destiny ("in all thy ways acknowledge Him & He shall direct thy paths") and had chosen this terrible war, including the death of his own son, to show Brown what must be done. For was it not so? that the Lord thy God was a wrathful God? And that He was calling Brown now to avenge the crimes of this guilty land, by striking a blow that would uproot slavery forever?

But before he could strike such a blow he needed money and guns, he must raise an army, he must have the support of powerful men. Leaving his sons in Ohio and New York State, he launched a fund-raising campaign that had all the fervor of a religious revival. He spoke at Philadelphia, New York, Syracuse, and Boston, but the talk he gave at the Town House in

Concord, on a chill winter night early in 1857, was perhaps his most impressive. With Ralph Waldo Emerson, Henry David Thoreau, Frank Sanborn (a school teacher and secretary of the Massachusetts State Kansas Committee) and other eminent reformers sitting in the audience, Brown recounted the Kansas civil war blow by blow, telling how the Border Ruffians had murdered innocent God-fearing people—people like those in his audience—and had shot his own son to death. He declared that proslavery killers like them "had a right to be hung"—a statement that pleased Emerson and Thoreau, who exchanged appreciative nods, and that brought murmurs of approval from the others. Brown did not, of course, mention the murders which he had instigated at Pottawatomie—and which he had long since rationalized in his own mind, insisting that they had been "decreed by Almighty God, ordained from eternity." (But it is significant that Brown had denied having any connection with the slayings when Sanborn had brought them up earlier that day.) When the murmurs died away, Brown assailed Geary's peace party with stabbing gestures, contending that what Kansas needed was men who would fight—and it needed money, too, a great deal of money. He went on, "without ever giving the least vent to his pent-up fire," Thoreau observed, to speak of his family sufferings: how his wife and daughters were living in near destitution in North Elba while he and his sons were fighting God's war against an institution of the Devil and the forces of evil that sought to spread it. His vow that he and his remaining sons would never stop fighting until the war was won brought enthusiastic applause from the townspeople, who then filed out into the cold night convinced that Brown was "the rarest of heroes," as Emerson put it, "a true idealist, with no by-ends of his own."

But Brown's talk of continuing the fight in Kansas was a blind for something far larger, and Emerson especially should have detected it. For in one of their conversations in Emerson's home, Brown made a telling remark: he said that he believed in two things—the Bible and the Declaration of Independence—and that it was "better that a whole generation of men, women and children should pass away by a violent death than that a word of either should be violated in this country." Emerson stared at him for a moment, then nodded his approval: he thought the old man was speaking symbolically, as Emerson liked to do himself. But Brown was dead serious. He had never been more serious in his life.

A few days later Brown talked to a forge-master in Collinsville, Connecticut, and gave him an order for a thousand pikes "for our freestate settlers in Kansas," making a down payment of $500 with a promise of an additional $500 on delivery. The forge-master was more than happy to have Brown's business. But he was puzzled. Brown had implied during their conversation that Kansas was full of revolvers and "Beecher's Bibles." What did he want with a thousand pikes? Also, why should he want a Connecticut forge-master to make them when a blacksmith in Kansas could do it just as well?

Back in Kansas again, at a camp site on the prairie near Topeka. Cold November winds howled out of the night as Brown piled wood on a smoking campfire. Four men sat near, listening intently to what Brown was saying. These initial recruits for his guerrilla company were all veterans of the Kansas civil war and all were in their twenties, although John E. Cook, a one-time law clerk from Connecticut who sat nearest Brown, looked and talked like a perpetually excited sixteen-year-old. Behind Cook sat Charles W. Moffet, a drifter from Iowa, and Aaron D. Stevens, a powerful six-footer with "black, brooding eyes" and a native of Connecticut. At sixteen he had run away from home to fight in the Mexican War, had slugged an officer in a drunken brawl at Taos,

and had been thrown in Fort Leavenworth on a commuted death sentence, only to escape and join the Free-State forces in Kansas. The fourth man was John Henry Kagi, a twenty-two-year-old schoolteacher from Ohio whose abolitionism was as deeply principled as it was intractable.

The four men spoke to Brown with deep respect, for they regarded him as a brave and high-minded warrior who would lay down his life to liberate the black man, and they were willing now to put their lives, and their destinies, in his hands. But they wanted to know what specific plans he had made. They all knew he had other recruits. Where was it he wanted them to serve?

But Brown would only say that they were going back east to drill, since things were quiet in Kansas now and it was too cold to do much campaigning out here. His sons and several other volunteers—Charles Tidd, William Leeman, and a couple of others they knew—would go along. Then he gave Cook a draft for $82.68 and said, "Get that cashed in Lawrence tomorrow. We'll meet again at Tabor in Iowa. Then I'll tell you what we are going to do. If you want hard fighting you'll get plenty of it."

At Tabor, Brown gathered nine recruits around him. "Our ultimate destination," he said with a look of grim determination, "is Virginia."

It was too late to settle the slave question through politics, Brown argued. Only violence and bloodshed could settle it now. It was February, 1858. Brown was standing in an upper room in Gerrit Smith's mansion in Peterboro, New York, and Smith himself, a wealthy reformer who once had demanded all-out war against slavery in Kansas, even if that meant fighting the United States government, was glancing at Frank Sanborn, who had just arrived from Boston and who was frowning intensely. There was no recourse left to the black

man, Brown went on, but in God and a massive uprising in which the blood of slaveholders would be spilled. This was a terrible thing, he admitted, but slavery was a terrible wrong, and the unrepentant southerners deserved violent punishment for it. It was God's will, Brown continued, that *he* should incite this insurrection—by a forced march on Virginia, the queen of the slave states, with an army of liberation which he was already raising. And even if the insurrection failed—although he was confident that it would not—it would nevertheless congeal northern hatred for slavery and provoke a crisis, perhaps a war, in which slavery would die. But he needed financial support if "my mission," as he called it, was to succeed. Would Smith and Sanborn help? Smith seemed willing, but Sanborn shook his head. The whole thing was so utterly fantastic . . . Sanborn did not see how it could possibly work. But Brown was intractable, swore he would carry on without their support if they had no faith in him. "We cannot give him up to die alone," Smith said; "we must support him." Sanborn was so impressed with Brown's courage, and with the fiery obstinacy that burned in his eyes, that at last the young abolitionist came around. On February 24, after Sanborn had left for Boston, Brown thanked him by letter for making this "common cause with me." In a life of nearly sixty years, "I have only had *this one* opportunity" for "such mighty & soul satisfying rewards." While "I felt for a number of years *in earlier life:* a steady, strong, desire; *to die,*" now "I have not only felt quite willing to live: but have enjoyed life much; & am now rather anxious to live for a *few* years more." But the struggle would not be easy. Brown "would *flatter no man*" about that. "I *expect nothing* but to endure *hardship:* but I expect to effect a mighty conquest even though it be like the last victory of Samson."

In March, Brown traveled to Boston, where he revealed his plan to Theodore Parker and Thomas Wentworth Higginson, two eminent

Unitarian ministers; George Luther Stearns, a prominent businessman; and Samuel Gridley Howe, a dashing physician and reformer. None of them knew precisely where Brown intended to strike his blow (though he undoubtedly brought up Virginia in their conversations), but they formed a secret committee of six, including Smith and young Sanborn, and raised a considerable sum of money for him. They all thought the attempted insurrection might fail, but even so (as Brown had repeatedly argued) it might ignite a powder keg that would explode into civil war in which slavery would be destroyed.

For Brown and the Secret Six, violence— either insurrection or civil war—seemed to them the only alternative left in their troubled times. They had been reading their newspapers, studying Southern speeches, poring over Abolitionist tracts and pamphlets. The South was not going to repent and free the slaves, thereby removing an institution which they and all other Abolitionists regarded as an abominable violation of America's most cherished ideals of liberty and justice for all. On the contrary, Southerners adamantly defended slavery as a positive good, claiming that it was justified by history, condoned by the Bible, and ordained by God from the beginning of time. They argued that "niggers" were subhuman anyway and belonged in chains as naturally as cattle in pens. Such inferior brutes were not fit for liberty and equality; these were rights reserved only for white men (for Anglo-Saxon white men). In fact, Southerners were doing "niggers" a huge Christian favor by enslaving them.

Neither Brown nor his fellow conspirators, of course, understood what whorls of rationalization, what torment and terror, lay beneath the South's ringing "positive good" defense of slavery. All they knew was that the South not only was justifying the institution in the name of God and civilization, but was attempting to force slavery out into Kansas and the rest of the predominantly free-soil West, through

what seemed to them a program of invasion, atrocity, fraud, and subterfuge. In fact, at the very time the conspiracy was formed behind Brown in Boston, the proslavery Buchanan administration and the proslavery Senate were attempting to stamp slavery on the soil of Kansas (the first stage in a great Slave Power conspiracy?), despite overwhelming evidence that most settlers there wanted it to be a free state. On February 2, 1858, President Buchanan had called on Congress to admit Kansas into the Union as the sixteenth slave state; and many Southern leaders threatened violence if Congress did not respond. At the same time, Southern leaders demanded that the gag rule against Abolitionist petitions be resurrected, that sedition laws be passed prohibiting criticism of slavery, that even more stringent fugitive slave laws be enacted, that the Dred Scott decision be rigorously enforced, and that the U.S. Constitution always be construed as guaranteeing the right to own Negroes. Thus, from an Abolitionist view, the slaveholding South seemed more determined than ever to preserve slavery and to dominate the Union, at the expense of civil liberties and even democratic government itself.

This is not to say that all Abolitionists (a small minority of the Northern population anyway) were prepared to attack the South in order to block the alleged Slave Power conspiracy and preserve free government. On the contrary, a majority of them still searched desperately for some solution to the Southern problem short of violence. But Brown and the Secret Six— whether right or wrong—believed that all peaceful alternatives had failed and that only revolution or civil war was left in this "slave-cursed land." For them, the time had come when only war upon the South itself could destroy the Slave Power conspiracy, eradicate slavery, and restore their nation to God and the ideals of Jefferson's Declaration.

With the support of the Six, Brown now felt free to work with both hands. In May, he

turned up in Chatham, Canada, where he held a secret meeting in a Negro schoolhouse with eleven whites and thirty-four blacks. He told them that Negroes all over the South were ready for revolt. All they needed was a leader who would break their chains and lead them to freedom. And John Brown of Osawatomie was that leader. He explained that he would invade Virginia, in the region of the Blue Ridge Mountains, and march into Tennessee and northern Alabama. As he moved, thousands of slaves would rise up and rally to his standard. They would then wage war upon the plantations on the plains west and east of the mountains, which would serve as the base of operations.

"But what if troops are brought against you?" someone asked.

Brown waved aside all doubts. A small force trained in guerrilla warfare could easily defend those Thermopylae ravines against Southern militia or the United States Army. He believed that "all the free negroes in the Northern states" would also rally to his cause once the invasion began. Brown went on to read a constitution he had drawn up that would create a new state once the slaves were freed, with Brown as commander-in-chief and John Kagi (who stood at his side) as Secretary of War. The preamble of this remarkable document was actually a declaration of war, not only against the institution of slavery ("a most barbarous, unprovoked, and unjustifiable War" of one portion of American citizens against another), but also against all defenders of slavery who violated "those eternal and self-evident truths set forth in our Declaration of Independence."

The Negroes wholeheartedly approved of the ideals of Brown's constitution, but they were not so sure about joining his army of liberation. The thought of going back to the South terrified them. And the plan of invasion itself sounded fantastic—almost mad. They did not know. They had risked their lives, had suffered much hardship, to get to Canada and free-

dom. Were they willing to abandon that now? Were they willing to follow Brown and some boys back to that Gibraltar of slavery and possibly a horrible death in a carnage of racial violence? Furthermore, was Brown really an instrument of God to free the slaves? Or was he just a poor self-deluded old man?

There was an irritating delay when a drillmaster whom Brown had enlisted in his company defected and told what he knew to a United States senator and other politicians. Higginson, when he found out about it, wanted to push ahead anyway, but Brown's other backers were panic-stricken (would there be investigations? arrests?) and voted to send the old man back to Kansas until things cooled off. Brown was not happy about their decision, remarking that all of them except Higginson *"were not men of action."* But when they promised him an additional $2,000 if he would leave at once, he grudgingly rode back to the Territory. That December he executed a bold and bloody slave-running expedition into Missouri, one that almost started another civil war along the smoldering western border. When told that President Buchanan himself had denounced the raid and put a price on his head, Brown retorted that he would put a price of $2.50 on the head of the President.

But it was all a diversion to keep him associated with Kansas in the public mind. In the spring of 1859, even though he was suffering from an old case of malaria and "a terrible gathering" in his head, Brown nevertheless made his way back to Boston, promising himself there would be no postponements this time. On May 10, with "a little touch of insanity" in his "glittering gray blue eyes," Brown met with his secret backers in Boston. Two members, though, were conspicuously absent. Parker had become gravely ill with consumption and had left for Europe for health reasons. For Higginson, the plot "had all begun to seem to me

rather chimerical," and he remained at home in Worcester. But he did promise to send Brown something once the invasion was truly under way. Howe, Sanborn, and Stearns, however, thought the Kansas diversion had worked and gave Brown $2,000 to "raise the mill" somewhere in Virginia, bringing the committee's total contributions to the old man to just over $4,000. Stuffing the money in his pocket, Brown left, hardly aware of their handshakes and well-wishings. Shortly after that he went to Connecticut to expedite the shipment of pikes, and then set out to gather a hidden cache of guns in Ohio. "He means to be on the ground as soon as he can—perhaps so as to begin on the 4th of July," Sanborn wrote Higginson. "Now is the time to help in the movement, if ever, for within the next two months the experiment will be made."

Brown planned to launch his "experiment" at a town called Harpers Ferry, which stood on a narrow neck of land at the confluence of the Shenandoah and Potomac rivers in the Blue Ridge Mountains of northern Virginia. His prime military objective at Harpers Ferry was a federal arsenal and armory works whose store of guns he desperately needed. He had already sent John E. Cook to the village as an advance agent; and Cook had ingratiated himself with the townsfolk and taken a job on a canal across the Potomac by the time Brown arrived on July 3. With him were two of his sons—Oliver and Owen—and a twenty-six-year-old Kansan named Jeremiah Anderson, who personally vowed "to make this land of liberty and equality shake to the centre."

Leaving Cook in town with orders to keep his garrulous mouth shut and his eyes open, Brown rented a dilapidated two-story farmhouse about seven miles away on the Maryland side of the Potomac, giving his name as "Smith" and telling neighbors that he was a cattlebuyer from New York. While the commander-in-chief cultivated a beard and studied books on guerrilla warfare, a handful of young volunteers (all of them except two were under thirty) trickled in. Watson Brown, who had left his young wife and newborn child in North Elba, arrived on August 6. The Thompson brothers—William and Dauphin—were already there. Tidd, Stevens, Leeman, the Coppoc boys —Barclay and Edwin—and Albert Hazlett all reached the farm within a few weeks of one another. By early fall there were twenty recruits in all—fifteen whites and five Negroes. One of the Negroes was a freed mulatto named Dangerfield Newby, who, at forty-eight, was the oldest of the volunteers and who hoped to liberate his wife and seven children from a plantation near Brentville. John H. Kagi, Brown's noble-minded secretary of war, was in Chambersburg in Pennsylvania, the secret rendezvous for the pikes and a cache of rifles which John Brown, Jr., was to ship from Ohio.

As the band of men increased, great pains had to be taken to conceal them from the neighbors. Two Brown girls—seventeen-year-old Martha, Owen's wife, and fifteen-year-old Anne, one of Brown's daughters—arrived in July to keep house and divert suspicion. They cooked meals, washed and hung out clothes, and worked in the garden outside, talking cheerfully with neighbors who dropped by— usually around mealtime—to ask about Mr. Smith's work and to steal glances at the farmhouse (where the men were hiding in the attic scarcely daring to breathe). One barefoot old woman who lived down the road was especially bothersome; she and her flock of children came around "at all hours of the day" to pester the girls and poke around the house while they exchanged worried looks. "I used to give her everything she wanted or asked for to keep her on good terms," Anne recalled, "but we were in constant fear that she was either a spy or would betray us. It was like standing on a powder magazine, after a slow match had been lighted."

While the girls kept a constant vigil at the kitchen window, Brown gathered his men up-

stairs and finally disclosed his plans in full. Up to this point most of them thought they were going on a large slave-running expedition, but now the old man was saying things that made their mouths hang open. They were going to capture the arsenal first, he said, and then hold the town until the slaves from the surrounding area joined them; it might even be well to send agents out among the plantations to spread the word. But Brown got no further. First Tidd and then most of the others strenuously objected: for twenty-one men to try to capture and then hold an entire town against militia and possibly federal troops . . . it was suicidal. Cook, however, was enthusiastically in favor of the plan; Kagi also approved. The others, though, were as immovable as their fierce-eyed chief. Tempers flared; at one point there was a threat of mutiny. Tidd himself got so outraged that he left the farm and went to Cook's house "to cool off." In a show of anger, Brown then re-signed as commander-in-chief—a calculated move that warded off mutiny and brought them all back to his side, although a few were convinced that they were going to their deaths.

In the seemingly endless, nerve-racking days that followed, the men tried to keep themselves occupied: they read yellowed copies of the Baltimore *Sun* and Paine's *Age of Reason;* they studied warfare under Stevens, polished their rifles, played checkers, wrote letters to their families, and argued. When there was a thunderstorm, they jumped around, ran up and down the stairs, and shouted to let off steam. But in time the cramped quarters and constant worry made them all like caged animals. Hazlett and Leeman took to stealing out of the house at night and roaming through the woods and even going down to Harpers Ferry to see Cook. The old man, of course, gave them a tongue-lashing for this. But he knew what the trouble was. If he did not attack soon, they might all break under the strain. Where were the guns and pikes anyway? And all the volunteers he had expected from Pennsylvania and

Kansas? He had sent urgent pleas to his friends there as well as to his Negro allies in Canada. Where were the Negroes? They had more of a stake in this than any of the white volunteers. And there was the money problem. The $2,000 from the secret committee had melted away; Sanborn, Howe, and Smith had sent an additional $200, but that was not nearly enough. There were so many obstacles and delays. . . . Could it be that his plans were wrong, that God intended some other way? But the old man had put too much into this enterprise to believe that now. He held morning prayer meetings. He spent the nights, when he was not on the road to Chambersburg, reading his Bible by lamplight in the kitchen, while the girls did their best to cheer his restless men.

But late in September there was a propitious sign. Fifteen boxes of "tools"—198 Sharps rifles and 950 pikes—came in Chambersburg. In a few days he sent the girls home, then scratched off a note to John, Jr.: "If you were here, I could fully *explain* all but cannot do so now. From Harrisburg by Rail Road remember." The last obstacle to the attack—and any lingering doubt Brown may have had about his destiny—was removed when a late recruit, F. J. Meriam, arrived from Boston with $600 in gold. For Brown, that gold was an unmistakable sign that God wanted him to move. On October 10 Brown ordered Kagi to the farm. Just before dawn on the sixteenth he assembled his men in the living room for a final worship service. "And almost all things are by the law purged with blood; and without the shedding of blood there is no remission."

At eight o'clock that evening, leaving a rear guard at the farm, Brown climbed into a wagon loaded with pikes and tools, and led his men two-by-two into the damp moonless night.

When the town lights came into view, Tidd and Cook fell out of line and disappeared in the moving shadows of the woods. The others,

strung out like ghosts behind the creaking wagon, walked on stiffly, their stomachs tightening as they approached the Potomac. In a moment, Brown turned in the wagon seat and motioned; crouching low, the men crept across the railroad and wagon bridge, captured the night watchman, threatening to shoot him dead if he made a sound, and then deployed noiselessly across the Shenandoah bridge. There was not a sign of life in town: the streets were empty, the railroad station on Potomac Street was well lit, but no one was visible inside. While Newby, Will Thompson, and Oliver Brown remained at the bridges, the rest of the force stole up Potomac Street and took the watchman at the factory-looking arsenal by surprise, pinning him against the gate and securing both the arsenal and the armory across the street. "I came here from Kansas," Brown told the terrified watchman, "and this is a slave State; I want to free all the negroes in this State; I have possession now of the United States armory, and if the citizens interfere with me I must only burn the town and have blood." Then Kagi and two of the Negroes—Lewis Leary and John Copeland, a former Oberlin College student—manned Hall's Rifle Works a half mile above the armory on Shenandoah Street.

So far everything was going like clockwork. By now Owen Brown, one of the rear guard, should have moved to the schoolhouse near the farm where slaves from Maryland (Cook had assured his chief they would swarm in like bees) were to report. Around midnight a detachment of raiders brought three hostages into the armory yard—Colonel Lewis W. Washington, a wealthy planter and a great-grandnephew of the first President, and another farmer and his son—along with their slaves and their household weapons, including a magnificent sword of Washington's which Frederick the Great had allegedly given his illustrious relative. In the glare of torches, Brown told his frightened prisoners why he was here, then

armed their slaves with pikes and ordered them to stand guard. He was admiring the sword—a fine symbol for the revolution that had begun this night—when Tidd reported that telegraphs both east and west of town had been cut. Brown nodded. Now, as soon as Owen came with the slaves, he could garrison the village, take more hostages, and move on.

At 1:25 in the morning, while Brown's sentinels lay behind a barricade across the railroad bridge, an express train from Wheeling came chugging into Harpers Ferry—only to grind to a halt when the engineer learned of the obstruction. In a moment two men came walking down the track, but the raiders opened fire, driving them back on the run. Then the train itself backed up out of rifle range and stopped again, while the engineer shouted the alarm and anxious faces pressed against the windows of the passenger coaches. At that moment a free Negro named Hayward Shepherd, who worked at the station as baggagemaster, came down the trestlework looking for the night watchman. "Halt!" one of the raiders cried, but Shepherd kept coming. There was a crack of gunfire. The Negro staggered back along the trestlework and then fell mortally wounded with a bullet through his heart. The first blood in Brown's war against slavery had been spilled.

By now the gunfire and the unusual commotion around the arsenal had aroused the townspeople; they gathered in the streets with knives, axes, flintlocks, with any weapon they could pick up. What was it? What was happening? A slave insurrection, somebody said: thousands of them with some bloodthirsty whites murdering and looting around the armory. One of their own, the colored baggagemaster, had interfered and been shot dead; and somebody else reported that Thomas Boerley, the Irishman, had also been shot, and was lying in the street in a pool of blood. Panic-stricken, the townsmen fled with their families to Bolivar Heights in back of town. But in all the confusion they seemed not to notice the very slaves

they dreaded cowering in their midst, as terrified as any of the whites.

Down in town the bell on the Lutheran Church was tolling the alarm, calling to farmers all over the countryside: *insurrection, insurrection:* tolling on into the mist-swept morning. By that time the alarm was also spreading to other towns, as two villagers galloped madly along separate roads yelling at the top of their lungs: Insurrection at Harpers Ferry! Slaves raping and butchering in the streets! The thing all southerners had dreaded since Nat Turner's terrible uprising in 1831 was now upon them like a black plague. Soon church bells were tolling in Charlestown, in Shepherdstown and Martinsburg. At the same time Brown had thoughtlessly allowed the express train to push on; and it was now carrying the news to Monocacy and Frederick. From there the alarm would click over the telegraphs to Richmond and Washington, D.C., and would soon be blazing in headlines throughout the East, "Negro Insurrection at Harpers Ferry!" While all over the Blue Ridge Mountains of northern Virginia, in every town and village within a thirty-mile radius of the stricken hamlet, men were running about like angry ants, forming militia companies and setting out after the insurrectionists with shouts like lynch mobs.

By eleven o'clock that morning a general battle was raging at Harpers Ferry, as armed farmers and militiamen surrounded the town and laid down a blistering fire on both the rifle works and the armory where Brown and a dozen of his men were gathered. The speed with which the countryside had mobilized had taken Brown completely by surprise; flustered, he did not know what to do. Where was Owen with the slaves? Where were the recruits he still expected to pour in from Pennsylvania? As he peered out over the bullet-spattered armory yard, militiamen overran the bridges, driving the sentinels off with muskets blazing. Oliver Brown and Will Thompson made it back to the armory, but Dangerfield Newby fell with two bullets in him, the first of the raiders to die and the last hope of his wife whose letter he carried in his pocket: "Oh dear Dangerfield, come this fall without fail, money or no money I want to see you so much: that is one bright hope I have before me." Newby lay there in the street until somebody—an inflamed villager, a half-drunk militiaman—dragged him into the gutter and sliced his ears off as souvenirs.

As the townsmen, encouraged by the belligerence of the militia, swarmed off Bolivar Heights and joined in the fighting about the armory, Brown grudgingly admitted that he was trapped, that he could not wait for Owen to bring the slaves. The only thing he could do, cut off as he was from Kagi at the rifle works, and from Hazlett and Osborn P. Anderson who were holding the arsenal, was to negotiate for a cease fire, offering to release the hostages (including a number of armory employees captured that morning) if the town would let him and his men go free. He sent Will Thompson out under a flag of truce, but the excited crowd grabbed Thompson and took him off to the Galt House at gun point. Would they shoot him like a dog? Would they hang him? Brown grew desperate. Gathering the remnants of his force and the hostages in the fire-engine house at the front of the armory, he sent his son Watson and Aaron Stevens out under another white flag, but the mob gunned them both down. Watson crawled back to the engine house and doubled up in agony at the feet of his father. Stevens, though, lay bleeding in the gutter and might have died there had not one of the prisoners, a man named Joseph Brua, escaped from the watch-room of the engine house and gone to his aid. Thanks to this brave and humane man, Stevens was carried to the railroad station and given medical attention. Then, incredibly enough, Brua returned to the watch-room of the engine house and took his place there among the other prisoners.

But if there were acts of mercy on this dark, fog-ridden day, there were shocking indignities

and uninhibited hatred: the outrage committed on Newby's body, the shooting of Watson and Stevens under a flag of truce. It was no wonder that some of the raiders lost their courage and began to cry. It was no wonder that twenty-year-old William Leeman, the youngest of them, couldn't take it any longer, ran out the back door of the armory, leaped over the gate and fled for his life toward the river. But some militiamen saw him and gave chase, firing at him on the run. They finally overtook him on a small islet, where he lay with one shoulder smashed by their bullets and the other arm up, pleading with them to take him prisoner. They stuck their guns in his face and blew his brains out. His body lay there for hours, a target for a dozen marksmen that hate-filled afternoon, until at last, somehow, it slid into the water and floated in slow silent eddies toward the bridge.

Newby, Watson Brown, Stevens, and Leeman. The killing—and the vengeance—continued. Above the armory a large party of militiamen stormed the rifle works on Shenandoah Street, driving Kagi and two Negroes back toward the river where they were caught in a cross-fire. Knowing better than to surrender, they turned and ran as Leeman had done, but Kagi "fell and died in the water" with a bullet in his back. Leary was also mortally wounded and Copeland taken prisoner. A Negro with a gun. The white men went crazy. "Lynch him!" "Lynch him!" They were tying their handkerchiefs together in a makeshift noose when a doctor rode up, saw what was about to happen, and shielded the trembling Negro with his horse until some other militia arrived and took Copeland away to a safe place.

But the "now half-drunken and uncontrolled crowd" that thronged Potomac and Shenandoah streets were crying for blood. Hearing their shouts from behind the trestlework below the armory, kindly old Fontaine Beckham, the mayor of Harpers Ferry, was afraid a general carnage was near. Visibly upset, he went hur-

rying across the trestlework between some freight cars and a water tank, perhaps with the idea of trying to negotiate with the raiders and ending the bloodshed. But Edwin Coppoc, a Quaker boy from Springdale, Iowa, drew a bead on Beckham from the armory doorway: fired, missed, fired again, "and the dark wings again brushed the little town" as Mayor Beckham—the best friend the Negroes had in the county—slumped to the timbers. For in his Will Book the mayor had provided for the liberation upon his death of a Negro named Isaac Gilbert, his slave wife and three children. The Quaker's shot had freed them all.

At that moment it began to rain, compelling the villagers and militiamen to take cover. During the downpour word spread that the mayor had been killed, touching off one explosion of rage after another. The drunks in the saloon banged on the bars, fired their revolvers out the windows, and clamored for revenge. When the rain stopped the people spilled angrily into the streets, the saloonkeeper and a militiaman from Charlestown, both of them crazy with liquor, went over to the Wage-House where Will Thompson had been taken, grabbed him by the arms, and dragged him screaming and kicking down to the Potomac, where they shot him in the head with revolvers and flung his body into the water. According to one writer, Thompson "could be seen for a day or two after, lying at the bottom of the river, with his ghastly face still exhibiting his fearful death agony."

By now the mob of men around the armory, reinforced by six additional companies of militia, was prepared to take the raiders by storm. A skirmish line formed and snaked about the arsenal, only to find it deserted (for Hazlett and Osborn Anderson had escaped during the downpour, paddled across the Potomac in a stolen boat, and were now running through the Maryland woods toward the farmhouse). When the raiders in the engine house saw the skirmish line, they fired savagely and drove it

back. Militia officers then ordered Brown to surrender, but he refused. Sporadic firing broke out again, only to die away as night closed over Harpers Ferry.

Inside the engine house that night, painfully cold and pitch dark, Brown, four uninjured raiders, and eleven prisoners watched the hours drag by. One raider lay dead; Watson and Oliver Brown, who had also been wounded that afternoon, lay side by side on the floor, both of them choking and crying in intense pain. The exhausted, distraught old man paced back and forth muttering to himself and fingering Washington's sword. He paused, listening to the clank of arms outside, then started pacing again. Oliver, one of the prisoners remembered later, begged his father "again and again to be shot, in the agony of his wound." But Brown turned on him. "If you must die, die like a man." Then he turned to the prisoners in despair. "Gentlemen, if you knew of my past history you would not blame me for being here. I went to Kansas a peaceable man, and the pro-slavery people hunted me down like a wolf. I lost one of my sons there." He stood there trembling for a moment, then called to Oliver. There was no answer. "I guess he is dead," the old man said, and started pacing again.

When the first cold gray light of morning spread through the high windows of the engine house, Brown and the remaining raiders— Edwin Coppoc, Jeremiah Anderson, Dauphin Thompson, and Shields Green—took their places at the gun holes they had dug out of the walls, and winced at what they saw in the street outside: a company of United States horse marines under Colonel Robert E. Lee, dispatched from Washington by President Buchanan himself, had arrived during the night, and was now deployed in front of the engine house with bayonets and sledgehammers, while two thousand spectators looked on from sidewalks and buildings as far as the raiders could see. Brown had the doors barricaded and loopholed, but he knew they would

not hold against sledgehammers, he knew that his invasion had failed and that this was the end for him and the young men who stood by his side. Yet his face wore an expression of awakened resolution. Brown "was the coolest and firmest man I ever saw," Colonel Washington said. "With one son dead by his side, and another shot through, he felt the pulse of his dying son with one hand and held his rifle with the other, and commanded his men with the utmost composure, encouraging them to sell their lives as dearly as they could."

But the marines did not attack. Instead a tall, bearded trooper named Jeb Stuart approached under a flag of truce. Brown cracked the door, and with his rifle aimed at Stuart's head took a note from his outstretched hand. The note summoned Brown to surrender unconditionally, with assurances that he would be protected from harm and handed over to the proper authorities. Brown handed the note back with his fierce eyes on Stuart's. He would surrender, he said, only on terms that would allow him and his men to escape. At that one of the raiders begged Brown to give up, while the fearful prisoners wanted Lee himself to come and reason with the old man. But while they were arguing Stuart suddenly jumped away from the door and waved his cap; and the marines, with the spectators cheering wildly, rushed the engine house and started battering at the doors. The raiders fired back desperately, powder smoke wreathing out of the gun holes and cracks in the building, but nothing could stop the marines now: they tore down one of the doors with a heavy ladder and stormed inside; two of them fell, but the others swarmed on, pinning Jeremiah Anderson to the wall with a bayonet and running Dauphin Thompson through as he crawled whimpering under one of the fire engines. Colonel Washington then pointed to Brown, who was kneeling with his rifle cocked, and said, "This is Osawatomie." Lieutenant Israel Green struck Brown with his light dress sword

before the old man could fire, and then tried to run him through with such a savage thrust it almost lifted him off the floor, but the blade miraculously struck his belt buckle and bent double. As Brown fell, Green beat him on the head with the hilt of his weapon, and kept on beating him until the old man was unconscious. When Green at last got control of himself, he had Brown and the other dead and wounded raiders carried outside and laid on the grass. Colonel Lee inspected them himself, and when Brown regained consciousness, the colonel had a doctor tend his wounds.

Thus the war for slave liberation, thirty-six hours after it began, had ended in dismal failure. No uprisings had taken place anywhere in Virginia and Maryland, because the slaves there, lacking organization and leadership, having little if any knowledge of what was going on, and being afraid of Southern reprisals, had been both unable and unwilling to join him. The raid had cost a total of seventeen lives. Two slaves, three townsmen, a slaveholder, and one marine had been killed, and nine men had been wounded. Ten of Brown's own recruits, including two of his sons, had been killed or fatally injured, five raiders had been captured, and the rest had escaped, some for a few days, some for good. Brown himself, "cut and thrust and bleeding and in bonds," was lodged in the paymaster's office of the armory, where he displayed a "cool, collected, and indomitable" spirit even as a lynch mob formed in the street outside and cried for his head. That afternoon, while he lay on a pile of old bedding, he was interrogated for a full three hours by Henry A. Wise, governor of Virginia, and a retinue of officers, United States congressmen, and newspaper reporters. Brown refused to implicate anybody else in his war against slavery, blamed only himself for its failure. How could he possibly justify his acts? asked one of the interrogators. "I pity the poor in bondage that have none to help them," he said, with one eye on the martyrdom that was

nearly his now; "that is why I am here; not to gratify any personal animosity, revenge or vindictive spirit. It is my sympathy with the oppressed and the wronged, that are as good as you and as precious in the sight of God." Then he addressed the entire gathering. "I wish to say, furthermore, that you had better—all you people of the South—prepare yourselves for a settlement of that question that must come up for settlement sooner than you are prepared for it. . . . You may dispose of me very easily; I am nearly disposed of now; but this question is still to be settled—this negro question I mean —the end of that is not yet."

While a fierce debate over Brown's raid was taking shape between the South and antislavery Northerners, the militant old Calvinist "who was the stone God threw into the black pool of slavery" came to trial in a crowded courtroom in Charlestown, eight miles southwest of Harpers Ferry. On November 2, Brown was sentenced to die on the gallows for murder, treason against the state of Virginia, and conspiring with slaves to rebel. His lawyers, hoping to save his life, attempted to enter a plea of insanity based on affidavits from relatives and friends, who also wanted to save his life. But Brown would have none of it, angrily insisting that he was as sane as anybody. Governor Wise agreed and refused to stay his execution. "Let them hang me," Brown rejoiced. "I am worth inconceivably more to hang than for any other purpose." He wrote his sisters on November 27: "Oh my dear friends can you believe *it possible* that the Scaffold has *no terrors* for your *own* poor, old, unworthy brother? I *thank God* through Jesus Christ *my Lord: it is even so* I am now shedding tears: but they are no longer tears of *grief or sorrow.* I trust I have nearly DONE with those. I am weeping for *joy: & gratitude* that I can *in no other way* express."

Just before his execution he wrote his fam-

ily: "I have now no doubt but that our seeming *disaster:* will ultimately result in the most *glorious success.* So my dear *shattered: & broken* family; be of good cheer; & believe & trust in God. . . . Do not feel ashamed on my account; nor *for one moment* despair of the cause; or grow *weary* of *well doing.* I bless God; I never felt stronger confidence in the certain & near approach of a *bright Morning;* & a *glorious day.* . . ."

On the morning of December 2, 1859, he said goodbye to the other captive raiders, who were also sentenced to hang, and then he gave one of his guards a last prophetic message he had written to his countrymen: "I John Brown am now quite *certain* that the crimes of this *guilty, land: will* never be purged *away;* but with Blood. I had *as I now think:* vainly flattered myself that without *very much* bloodshed; it might be done."

An hour later John Brown "was hanging between heaven and earth" on a scaffold in an open field on the outskirts of Charlestown, with fifteen hundred soldiers and scores of spectators looking on in silence. Then the voice of Colonel J. T. L. Preston of the Virginia Military Institute rang out on the wind: "So perish all such enemies of Virginia! All such enemies of the Union! All such foes of the human race!"

Brown had hoped that, even if his attack should fail, it would still provoke a crisis over the slavery issue, and that was exactly what was happening. Democrats both North and South branded the raid as a Republican plot, and the Democratic Senate set up an investigating committee headed by James M. Mason of Virginia, with Jefferson Davis of Mississippi as chief inquisitor, to bring in Republican suspects. In the meantime, the real conspirators (except for Higginson, who manfully stood his ground) denied having any connection with the raid. When they learned that a carpetbag con-

taining Brown's secret papers and correspondence had been captured, Sanborn, Howe, and Stearns fled to Canada; Gerrit Smith conveniently went "insane," and just as conveniently recovered after the committee reported no evidence of a general conspiracy.

The Republicans, of course, disparaged Brown's raid as the work of a solitary fanatic, pointing out that they neither advocated nor sanctioned attacks on the South. "John Brown was no Republican," declared Lincoln himself, "and you have failed to implicate a single Republican in his Harper's Ferry enterprise." But gradually many of them came to admire Brown's courage and ideals, if not his methods. What he had done was admittedly a crime, but there were extenuating circumstances because of his worthy motives: he wanted to rid America of slavery, the central paradox of her history.

Still, a great mass of Northern opinion condemned Brown as a criminal, his raid as an inexcusable and unpardonable outrage, and asserted that hanging him was just. In Union meetings at Boston, New York, and other cities in the North, Yankees who sympathized with the South not only repudiated Brown's "socalled noble ideals," but acclaimed the Union and asserted Virginia's right to enslave Negroes.

Northern Abolitionists, on the other hand, trumpeted Harpers Ferry as "the best news that America ever had" and proclaimed Brown himself "the bravest and humanest man in all the country." Why? Because maybe now America would wake up and face the slavery curse forthrightly. How could she fail to see what was happening to her? How could she refuse to understand that if she did not eliminate slavery then more and more John Browns were bound to appear? Would the American people not do something at last to destroy the thing that had driven Brown to Harpers Ferry? So on the day he was hanged Abolitionists gathered in their churches, tolling bells and

singing hymns in his honor. Emerson called him "that new saint, than whom none purer or more brave was ever led by love of men into conflict and death,—the new saint" who "will make the gallows glorious like the cross." For Thoreau, who had wanted Brown to die and become a symbol for a crusade, it seemed that the entire North—"I mean the *living* North"—was now recognizing the "eternal justice and glory" of Brown's vision. Theodore Parker, writing from Rome, Italy, where he had gone to die, predicted that the raid would detonate a war in which "The Fire of Vengeance" would run "from man to man, from town to town" across the South. Longfellow agreed. "This will be a great day in our history; the date of a new Revolution,—quite as needed as the old one. Even now as I write, they are leading old John Brown to execution in Virginia for attempting to rescue slaves! This is sowing the wind to reap the whirlwind, which will come soon."

For the South, hearing statements like that, the whirlwind was already here. Southerners were virtually united in damning Brown's raid as "an act of war" perpetrated by "murderers, *traitors,* robbers, insurrectionists," and "waonton, malicious, unprovoked felons." The General Assembly of Virginia, in an ecstasy of rage and insecurity, declared that not just the Republican party but the entire North was behind it: the work of "fanatics"—all Northerners were fanatics—who wanted to incite "slaves to rapine and murder." The charge that the raid was a Northern plot echoed across Southern capitals. Rumors flew of other slave conspiracies. Towns from Richmond to Jackson mobilized local defense companies and arrested suspicious-looking strangers. Plantation owners tightened the discipline in their slave quarters, threatening to whip or hang any Negro who even *looked* rebellious. As Allan Nevins put it, "The Raid of twenty-two men

on one Virginia town had sent a spasm of uneasiness, resentment, and precautionary zeal from the Potomac to the Gulf."

Thus, as other writers have pointed out, Brown's raid had created a "Great Fear" in the South comparable to that which prevailed in rural France in the summer of 1789, when the peasants lived in mortal terror that the king's brigands were coming to slaughter them all. In this state of anxiety, compromise between North and South was henceforth impossible. Nobody was more exultant about the effects of Harpers Ferry than Southern fire-eaters like Fitzhugh and De Bow, and they used Brown's raid to whip up Southerners into a frenzy of anti-Northern, anti-Republican hatred. The North "has sanctioned and applauded theft, murder, treason," cried *De Bow's Review.* Harpers Ferry was "the first act in the grand tragedy of emancipation, and the subjugation of the South in bloody treason. . . . The vanguard of the great army intended for our subjugation has crossed our borders on Southern soil and shed Southern blood." The only solution for the South—the only way to save "our wives and daughters"—was secession and an independent Southern confederacy.

Thus "The Harper's Ferry invasion," announced the Richmond *Enquirer,* "has advanced the cause of Disunion more than any other event that has happened since the formation of the Government." "All Virginia," exhorted a member of the Virginia General Assembly, "should stand forth as one man and say to fanaticism, in her own language, whenever you advance a hostile foot upon our soil, we will welcome you with bloody hands and hospitable graves."

"I have said of Mr. Seward and his followers," cried a state senator of Mississippi, "that they are our enemies and we are *theirs*. He has declared that there is an 'irrepressible conflict' between us. So there is! He and his followers have declared war upon us, and I am for fighting it out to the bitter end."

31

Crisis of Fear

Steven A. Channing

ship of slaves not only as a status symbol but as the cornerstone of their whole society listened intently to what the fire-eaters said. Had Lincoln not proclaimed that this nation could not endure half slave and half free? Was he not of the same party as William H. Seward, who had asserted that the North and South were locked in an irrepressible conflict? Did Southerners have any choice but to protect their homes and family—their whole society—through an independent confederacy? Southern Unionists pleaded frantically for moderation and begged Lincoln to clarify his position. But Lincoln refused to do so, maintaining that he had already made his position clear on the issue of slavery in the South. His advisors, moreover, told him that even if he did win the presidency, Southern Unionism was too widespread for secession to triumph. They were wrong. When he carried the election of 1860 without receiving a single popular vote in ten Southern states, South Carolina and six other states of the Deep South left the Union.

Steven A. Channing narrates the secession movement in South Carolina and offers some sobering reflections about the crisis of fear that prevailed across the Deep South in the secession winter of 1860–1861.

Although Lincoln repeatedly asserted that the Republican Party had no intention of touching slavery in the South, people there were never convinced that the Republicans had had nothing to do with Brown's invasion. Unable to believe that the mass of conservative Northern opinion (which had damned the raid) was typical of the region, Southerners remained convinced that the North was teeming with "mad John Browns" and "Black Republican fanatics." And so the Great Fear persisted and deepened in that fateful year of 1860, as rumors of further Republican aggression multiplied over the South and "delusions of persecution and impending disaster flourished." As summer wore on and the crucial election of 1860 approached, secessionist orators harangued crowds with terrifying prophecies: if Abraham Lincoln and the "Black Republicans" won control of the federal government, they would invade the South and incite the slaves to insurrection, rape, and murder. Secessionist newspapers castigated Lincoln under lurid, black headlines as "a human viper," who, like John Brown, had committed himself to the violent destruction of the South's "ancestral institution" and the whole Southern Way of Life. Southerners who viewed the owner-

On the day that Charleston learned of Lincoln's election Jane Pettigrew, niece of James Louis Petigru, warned her husband that "The negroes are all of opinion that Lincoln is to come here to free them," but she adamantly assured him that "they are perfectly quiet & *nothing* is apprehended from them." Yet Charleston was alive with anxious vigilance patrols, drilling militia, and ceaseless rumors and evidences of black unrest. Writing at the same time from his plantation north of the city, Henry William Ravenel described the great "alarm among the people of servile insurrection." Ravenel refused

From pp. 271–293 in *Crisis of Fear* by Steven A. Channing. Copyright © 1970 by Steven A. Channing. Reprinted by permission of Simon and Schuster, Inc.

to believe that there could be a general, con-
certed insurrection because of the lack of communication between plantations; and, of
course, "the attachment of slaves to their masters is too strong to permit a suspicion of such
a design." Nevertheless, "there should be much
vigilance & police regulations . . . to keep off all
suspicious & designing persons."

The same dynamic operated day after day:
reports of slave insurrections coming in from
North Carolina, St. Petersburg, Florida, everywhere and nowhere; communities panicking;
no one disputing that the Negroes of Charleston, or Camden, or every other town believed
"that this election decides their freedom"; letters from militia officers unable to organize the
men in their neighborhoods into companies for
the service of the governor, because "They
dread more danger at home than abroad and
will not on that account, leave their families."
These many apprehensions and alarms seemed
justified time and again by the revelation of
abolitionist (or more likely, restless slave) activity from Charleston to Pickens. South Carolinians were to spend many uneasy Christmas
eves in the next few years, and the celebration
in 1860 was no exception. Letters written by a
farmer's wife in Abbeville district described
how the holiday was spent there. "I am happy
to inform you that christmas has come and
gone and we are still on the troubled waves of
existence," she wrote. "The men have been
very vigilant indeed, parties of them have
patroled nearly the whole night every night
during the week." A suspected abolitionist was
captured early in the week, and soon after news
came of "an alarming plot" discovered in a
nearby village. "Five negroes are to be hung,
twenty white men implicated all *southern born*,
the poor white *trash* who have associated with
negroes and are jealous of the higher classes
and think insurection [*sic*] will place all on a
footing and they get some plunder in the bargain." Still, Caroline Gilman, wife of Unitarian
minister Samuel Gilman, calmly told her daughters that there was no alarm among slaveholders, that no one avoided returning to his
plantation, that the "customary Christmas
revels" would go on, and that slaves would
dance and sing as before. In his final annual
message President Buchanan alluded to "fire &
poison" being carried into the South by Northerners. "Without interference from them," Mrs.
Gilman assured her daughters, "there is no
apprehension, but if a planter knew that his
slaves were tampered with by incendiaries the
case would be altered." To be sure, not every
South Carolinian accepted this comforting
thesis. As the danger of insurrection seemed to
come closer, many frantic appeals for better
vigilance by "our District police" were accompanied by criticism of the "general confidence
in the integrity of our slave population. . . .
The experience of other sections demonstrates
that this confidence may easily be misplaced."
On the whole, however, South Carolinians continued to believe what they wanted to believe,
and trusted in the fidelity of their bondsmen in
accordance with their idealized vision of race
relations long after that faith proved to be a
dubious warrant of conduct.

The recurrence of apparently self-contradictory
lines of belief or behavior was nowhere more
obvious than in the coexistence of the mili-
tarism which pervaded the entire state, with
the widespread confidence that there would
be no coercion by the Federal Government following secession. The question of the interminable agreements, real and imagined, which were
struck within the Buchanan Administration, or
of whether the President was guilty of treason,
stupidity, or rather a wise masterly inactivity,
has been fully treated. What is indisputable is
that the overwhelming majority of South Carolinians believed in the imminence of a peaceable acquiescence by the North to the secession
of the state.

They had good reason to think so. The

correspondence of all the state's leaders was replete with letters from Northern conservatives giving assurances that there would be no attempt to restrain the secession movement by force if their erring sister states chose disunion. Immediately after the act of disunion was ratified these disclaimers continued to pour in, often, like Boston's Charles Eliot Norton, giving congratulations and approval, or, like Thomas Bell, an Illinois farmer, pledging their support in putting down "this ungodly howling of Mr. Lincoln's Nigar Equality." Similar disavowals of hostility before secession were daily repeated by such future copperhead newspapers as the New York *Herald*. And, of course, there was the famous, and since disputed, offer by Horace Greeley's antislavery New York *Tribune* to let the slave states "depart in peace"; however ambiguous the "offer," it was promptly seized upon by Carolina editors to demonstrate the probability of Northern acquiescence to secession.

There were more dependable guarantees than these. Northern Democrats, who had been fuming at the Presidential election defeat which could have been averted, began speaking many thoughtless words to the South at the approach of secession, assuring against any support for military repression. Ohio congressman Clement Vallandigham gained considerable notoriety by his opposition to the war for the Union, but even before the secession of South Carolina he was loud in his promise that he would never cast a vote to maintain a civil war; and Vallandigham was only the most vocal of a significant number of Northern Democrats who considered coercion a more heinous crime than secession.

Pledges of non-interference came from the very highest political circles as well. In early October James Hammond's son reported a conversation with Joseph Lane, in which the Oregon Senator and Vice-Presidential candidate expressed the remarkable opinion that "he would not be surprised, and wished to see a Minister Plenipotentiary" from an independent South

Carolina coming to Washington within a month. "[Lane] desired me confidentially to say to you: let South Carolina sustain her honor in this crisis, maintain firmly all her constitutional rights, and by prompt action secure the cooperation of an immense body of sympathizers at the North." Hammond's son, a cadet at West Point where Lane was paying a visit, was now convinced, as he had not been before, that the best time for secession was during the Buchanan Administration. The President will "take no action until the matters are fairly discussed in Congress," young Hammond accurately predicted, and "it leaves ample space for the Seceders to organize themselves and for all parties to come to a clear understanding." This kind of reasoning played an important part in the decision to strike before the end of the year.

Such critical assurances continued right up to the moment of secession. On December 19, Congressman Bonham reported from Washington that Andrew Johnson had just delivered a combative speech denouncing the secession movement and promising not simply to crush the rebellion, but to reconstruct any state which attempted secession. According to Bonham, Johnson had declared that South Carolina would be "forced back as a conquered province." But Joe Lane spoke for more of his party colleagues when he rebuked Johnson and swore that "he & other Northern democrats will be there to meet Johnson & the invaders with their bloody flags." More interesting than Lane's militance were the sincere and quiet efforts of those Democrats, North and South, who considered disunion inevitable, to help make the disruption nonviolent. Typical perhaps were men like Thomas Caute Reynolds, a Missouri politician who, on December 15, wrote this remarkable message to William Porcher Miles from Washington:

I think I told you yesterday that I had made endeavors to induce Senator Douglas to declare against coercion; in consequence

of reports that he would soon make a speech in favor of it, some of the Mo. delegation requested me to see him again, and accordingly Mr. Rust of Ark. & I had an interview of four hours with him today. Without going into any detail or stating what views may have been advanced by any party to the interview, I can only say that my hope of a peaceable acquiescence of the Government in the secession of S. C.—since I presume that event inevitable—has considerably increased. I therefore write this to urge you to advocate the propriety of so arranging the secession movement that there shall be no collision with the federal government, even in the slightest particular, until *ample* time has been given it to consider its situation and hear from the tobacco (or border slave) states. The Legislature of Mo. meets on the 31st inst, a week before that of Virginia; and while our State has still a strong desire to maintain the union, I feel confident that the voice of her Legislature will be decided for the maintenance of peace so long as possible.—The main danger to it at present, would arise from any hasty attempt of S. C. to resume her sovereignty over the U.S. property within her borders.

Whatever the final verdict history renders on the role played by Buchanan in the secession crisis, one thing cannot be doubted: the people of South Carolina, from those in the highest echelon of the state to the great body of citizens, believed that a mutual agreement had been reached between state and national authorities which would protect them from any military action to thwart secession. To be sure, South Carolina had contributed her own share of bluster in an effort to prevent coercion. On November 24, for example, Barnwell Rhett sent a letter to Buchanan asserting that the state would unquestionably leave the Union in the near future, and that it was in the hands of the President alone "to make the event peaceful or

bloody. *If you send any more troops into Charleston Bay,*" Rhett warned, "*it will be bloody.*" Having thus tried to intimidate the President, Rhett sweetly concluded that his intention was simply to "inform," not to "direct," his judgment.

A more reliable source of reassurance for Carolina politicians was the steady stream of messages from William Henry Trescot, the state's lone representative in Washington, virtually guaranteeing that Buchanan could not move against South Carolina without destroying his cabinet, and affirming in the most unequivocal terms the fact that the President pledged positively to avoid the use of force. On the latter point, Buchanan had already employed his annual message to the nation on December 3 to deny the power of the executive to resist a secession. Moreover, the complicity of members of the cabinet in the secession movement, supplying guns and moral support, was an open secret, and at least as early as November 12, Governor Gist was authorizing frankly secessionist militia companies to organize under the Federal militia law, with federally supplied weapons. But above all there was the formal agreement struck between Buchanan and a delegation of South Carolina congressmen in early December, by which (however the President thought he understood it) the leaders of the state confidently assumed that the Federal Government had acceded to the secession of South Carolina, at least until such time, as Buchanan himself noted, as "Commissioners had been appointed to meet with the Federal Government in relation to the public property & until the decision was known. I informed them," the President concluded in a memorandum of his conversation with the South Carolina delegation, "that if they (the forts) were assailed this would put them completely in the wrong & making [sic] them the authors of the Civil War." It is true that this course of action was consistent with Buchanan's delineation of his executive authority, by which

he was constitutionally impotent to arrest the secession of an errant state. According to the President, Congress alone had the authority to arbitrate the case. But one may speculate on the consequences of a less compromising stand before the declaration of secession. Civil war was delayed under the Buchanan interregnum. Yet secession was unquestionably hastened by what he said, and did not say.

In the end the controversial issue of peaceable acquiescence to secession, like the motivation behind disunion itself, can only be understood as it was perceived by South Carolinians. The question of coercion was a significant one for them. As late as the convening of the state legislature at the moment of Lincoln's election there remained opposition to disunion, and still more, a reluctance to have the state secede hastily and alone. If the people were being asked to endorse an act of revolution, it was important to know whether or not that act would bring down the powerful arm of the nation to end it. The "signals" emanating from the North, from public meetings of conservative appeasers, from newspapers, from private correspondence, and from communications with the highest levels of the national government persuaded the people of South Carolina that there would be no coercion so long as aggression by the state was avoided. "Civil War," as Mrs. Gilman wrote, "was *foreign to the original plan.*"

In any popular movement there are, of course, those who crave the thrilling release of violence. South Carolinians were hardly an exception to this. Many of her most rabid secessionists had been eager for the catharsis of bloodshed for decades. But most of the state's citizens, however enraged they were over the apparent threat to their physical and social security posed by the Republican party, sought not to destroy their Northern countrymen, but to get away from them, and to do so without unnecessary conflict. Some Carolina leaders

recognized the possibility that the North would ignore the state's rights logic of secession, and would forcibly resist it. Those who opposed disunion, or even separate state action, harped on the potential for war in their vain effort to divert the revolution. Other men seemed reconciled to conflict, believing a short war and the establishment of a Southern nation preferable to no war and no security.

Secessionists, however, could not permit the fear of civil war to take hold. The thought of war would trouble any sane group of men. For a slaveholding society it was truly frightening. The farm journal of David Harris gives an illustration of the meaning of war even in his upcountry district. Harris was a slaveholder who operated a modest farm in Spartanburg. He had welcomed the secession of his state and spurned any suggestion of coercion. Finally, by late February 1861, he began to see the "probability of war," and his reaction, though belated, was typical. "I fear that we will have a long Civil, Bloody war—and perhaps an inserections [sic] among the slaves—" he wrote, "The Lord save us from such a horrid war." Because such fears had currency in South Carolina as the time of secession approached, and could have broken down the essential appearance of unity, the question of coercion became part of the propaganda campaign. In 1863 Unionist William John Grayson bitterly recalled how this aspect of the radical persuasion had operated.

To induce the simple people to plunge into the volcanic fires of revolution and war, they were told that the act of dissolution would produce no opposition of a serious nature; that not a drop of blood would be spilled; that no man's flocks, or herds, or negroes, or houses, or lands would be plundered or destroyed; that unbroken prosperity would follow the ordinance of secession; that cotton would control all Europe, and secure

open ports and boundless commerce with the whole world for the Southern States.

The secession of South Carolina was an affair of passion. The revolution could not have succeeded, and it certainly would not have instilled the astounding degree of unanimity in all classes and all sections that it did, were this not so. The emotional momentum was a function of the intensity of the fear which drove the revolution forward. Divisions, doubts about the wisdom or efficacy of secession were met, or overturned. The ostensible leaders of the movement could not agree on whether they had created this tempest, or had themselves been picked up and carried along by it. Barnwell politician Alfred Aldrich described events in terms which Rhett and many others could appreciate.

I do not believe the common people understand it, in fact, I know that they do not understand it; but whoever waited for the common people when a great move was to be made. We must make the move & force them to follow. This is the way of all revolutions & all great achievements, & he who waits until the mind of every body is made up will wait forever & never do any thing.

But there were many of Aldrich's associates who strongly disagreed with this description. Poet William Gilmore Simms drew endless pictures of the "landsturm," his romantic image of the essentially popular nature of the movement for secession. Alfred Huger, with his accustomed anxiety, warned his friend Joseph Holt that "this revolution is beyond the reach of human power. . . . We have no leaders of any prominence," Huger lamented, "the masses are in the front-rank and cannot be restrained." Such a state of affairs did not frighten everyone. Augustus Baldwin Longstreet, then president of South Carolina College in Columbia, wrote to the editor of the Richmond *Enquirer* on December 6 to refute charges that the secession movement in Carolina had been "gotten up" by the politicians for their own selfish purposes.

Never was there a greater mistake. It is the result of one universal outburst of indignation on the part of the people at Lincoln's election—the unanimous and almost spontaneous resolve, from the mountains to the sea-board, that they never should come under Black Republican rule. . . . You might as well attempt to control a tornado as to attempt to stop them from secession. They drive politicians before them like sheep.

Where was the truth in the kaleidoscope of power? Which way did the lines of action-reaction go, and who ruled whom? Textbook truths usually lie "somewhere in the middle." The answer to this riddle of authority and response probably rested in a like balance. Much has been written to show the deep division of the Southern people, including South Carolinians, on the question of secession. It nearly failed, it is said. More to the point is the fact that it was at last consummated. Against the twin forces of Unionism and fear of secession the revolution carried the day. Analyzing political feeling in the state, all who supported the movement were, of course, prosecessionists, and many of those who opposed immediate action were disunionists as well. Of those who resisted separate secession many may certainly be described as either timid men, men who wanted security, saw it in Southern nationalism, but also feared the unknowable changes that a revolution might bring; men who wanted secession to come, but only as a cooperative venture by a sizable portion of the slave states; or men who believed disunion to be inevitable, if not desirable, but craved some "overt act" of aggression by Lincoln to cite for their consciences and the eye of history. That immediate

secession triumphed over these sentiments is the remarkable phenomenon, not the fact that there was still a voice of conservatism in the lower South. Secession has been castigated as a usurpation because a majority allegedly did not support it wholeheartedly; yet these same historians applaud the glories of the American Revolution when all agree that barely one-third favored independence.

The Secession Convention which came together in Columbia on December 17, and in Charleston three days later, signed the declaration creating the independent republic of South Carolina, was as representative as it was distinguished. The wealthy, the powerful, the famous were there, as were many unassuming figures from districts across the state. Some had been elected as the traditional leaders in their home districts and parishes. Others perhaps gained the vote of their neighbors at the election on December 6 because of their ardent work for the revolution; one of the representatives from Williamsburg District had gained fame in his association with the Kingstree *Star* during its campaign against abolitionist influences in the region. The people had indeed responded to Lincoln's election with a ferocious roar; but that in part had been planned and hoped for by men such as Aldrich. Still, once those potent fears of secession which so damaged the plans of disunionists elsewhere were mollified or quelled in South Carolina, the movement for secession *was* a popular revolution, Simms's "landsturm." Shortly after the consummation of secession, Isaac Hayne wrote Charles Cotesworth Pinckney, Jr., to tell him the good news. The feeling in favor of the step throughout the state was so strong, Hayne wrote, that no one, not even the old gadflies Perry and Orr, had "dared to oppose the onward current." When the signed ordinance of secession was held up in crowded Institute Hall a thunderous shout filled the large chamber, and Hayne, "who put but little faith in the shout of the mob, felt at last that in *this*, the people were in earnest." Affairs had been put into such shape by the leaders as to compel a decision for secession. The people did not hesitate to endorse the compulsion. Plebiscitory democracy triumphed in South Carolina.

Secession was the product of logical reasoning within a framework of irrational perception. The party of Abraham Lincoln was inextricably identified with the spirit represented by John Brown, William Lloyd Garrison, and the furtive incendiary conceived to be lurking even then in the midst of the slaves. The election of Lincoln was at once the expression of the will of the Northern people to destroy slavery, and the key to that destruction. The constitutional election of a president seemed to many, North and South, an unjustifiable basis for secession. But it was believed that that election had signalled an acceptance of the antislavery dogmas by a clear majority of Northerners, and their intention to create the means to abolish slavery in America. Lincoln was elected, according to South Carolinians, on the platform of an "irrepressible conflict." This, as James Hammond believed, was "no mere political or ethical conflict, but a social conflict in which there is to be a war of races, to be waged at midnight with the torch, the knife & poison." Submission to the rule of the Republicans would be more than a dishonor. It would be an invitation to self-destruction. Implementing the power of the Presidency, and in time the rest of the Federal machinery, slavery would be legally abolished in time. What would that bring? Baptist minister James Furman thought he knew.

Then every negro in South Carolina and every other Southern State will be his own master; nay, more than that, will be the equal of every one of you. If you are tame

enough to submit, Abolition preachers will be at hand to consummate the marriage of your daughters to black husbands.

South Carolinians were repeatedly called on to explain the reasons for secession to their uncomprehending Northern friends and relatives. The description these Northerners received of the dominant new party—and of themselves—must have shocked them. "Who are these Black Republicans?" Sue Keitt, wife of the congressman, wrote to a woman in Philadelphia. "A motley throng of Sans culottes and Dames des Halles, Infidels and freelovers, interspersed by Bloomer women, fugitive slaves, and," worst of all, "amalgamationists." The Republican party was the incarnation of all the strange and frightening social and philosophical doctrines which were flourishing in free Northern society, doctrines which were not only alien but potentially disruptive to the allegedly more harmonious and conservative culture of the slave South. It has been suggested that slavery was merely a handle seized upon by extremists in both sections to wage a battle founded in far deeper antagonism. The election of 1860 proclaimed to the South that it must accept a new order of consolidation, industrialization, and democratization. According to this interpretation, secession spelled the rejection of these terms for the preservation of the Union by the old ruling classes.

There is no doubt that those who dominated political life in South Carolina feared the nature of the new social order rising in the North, and feared the party that stood for this order. "The concentration of absolute power in the hands of the North," Lawrence Keitt predicted, "will develop the wildest democracy ever seen on this earth—unless it shall have been matched in Paris in 1789—What of conservatism?—What of order?—What of social security or financial prosperity?" Many Carolinians believed that two separate and distinct civilizations existed

CHARLESTON

MERCURY

EXTRA:

Passed unanimously at 1.15 o'clock, P. M., December 20th, 1860.

AN ORDINANCE

To dissolve the Union between the State of South Carolina and other States united with her under the compact entitled "The Constitution of the United States of America."

We, the People of the State of South Carolina, in Convention assembled, do declare and ordain, and it is hereby declared and ordained,

That the Ordinance adopted by us in Convention, on the twenty-third day of May, in the year of our Lord one thousand seven hundred and eighty-eight, whereby the Constitution of the United States of America was ratified, and also, all Acts and parts of Acts of the General Assembly of this State, ratifying amendments of the said Constitution, are hereby repealed; and that the union now subsisting between South Carolina and other States, under the name of "The United States of America," is hereby dissolved.

THE

UNION

IS

DISSOLVED!

Front-page headlines of the Charleston Mercury *announcing the secession of South Carolina, December 20, 1860. (Courtesy of Rare Book Division, New York Public Library, Astor, Lenox and Tilden Foundations.)*

in America in 1860, one marked by "the calculating coolness and narrow minded prejudices of the Puritans of New England in conflict with the high and generous impulses of the cavalier of Virginia and the Carolinas." By pecuniary choice and racial compulsion the South had "opted" for slavery and out of that decision had arisen a superstructure of social attitudes and institutions which marked the uniqueness of the slaveholding South.

Moreover, just as Northerners failed to comprehend the Southern view of the world, many Carolinians refused to admit that there was, or could be, any moral or idealistic quality in the antislavery pillar of the Republican party. Hammond affirmed that if the Republicans could have been defeated at the polls in 1860 and 1864, abolitionism would have been abandoned, for "no great party question can retain its vitality in this country that cannot make a President." A number of his fellow citizens declared that they too rejected the "mock humanity" of the Republicans. The issue was one of political power, they said, of controlling the national government, of party spoils. There was an almost pathetic element in this refusal to admit, and inability to see, the sincerity of the moral quality of abolitionism. Nevertheless, particularly in the private correspondence of unassuming soldiers and farmers, one can see frequent references to resistance to the threat of Northern despotism, to the need to protect certain vaguely understood "right and privileges," often guaranteed by the Constitution. "I care nothing for the 'Peculiar institution' " claimed one former Unionist, "but I cant stand the idea of being domineered over by a set of Hypocritical scoundrels such as Sumner, Seward, Wilson, Hale, etc. etc."

Still, the conclusion is inescapable that the multiplicity of fears revolving around the maintenance of race controls for the Negro was not simply the prime concern of the people of South Carolina in their revolution, but was so very vast and frightening that it literally consumed the mass of lesser "causes" of secession which have inspired historians. James Hammond recognized the question of economic exploitation, and the fact that Southerners believed in Northern financial and commercial domination is clear. Nonetheless, the issue went virtually unnoticed in private exchanges throughout the year. Some leaders denounced what they thought was the injustice of the colonial status of the economic South, but this did not touch the hearts of the people, great and low. Attempts to organize such devices as direct steamship trade with Europe, use of homespun cloth, and conventions to promote Southern economic self-sufficiency were, like the more transparent plans for commercial non-intercourse, aimed at wielding the economic power of the region to gain political ends, specifically an end to agitation of the slavery question.

The glorious potential of an independent Southern nation held great emotional appeal for many, but no one was prepared to enter into the perilous business of nation building without some more basic incentive. South Carolina's spokesmen revelled in the contemplation of the political, economic, and social power of the South. They were eager to prove to the North and to the entire world that the South could establish a great nation in her own right. Yet who could fail to see that this was in part a rationalization for the strong desire to escape the moral obloquy heaped upon slaveholders by the North for so many years past; in part an element in the pro-slavery argument, which held a civilization based upon the peculiar institution to be the highest possible culture; and in part a function of the secession persuasion designed to attract and calm adherents to the cause.

As for the "dry prattle" about the constitution, the rights of minorities, and the like, there never was any confusion in the minds of most contemporaries that such arguments were masks for more fundamental emotional issues.

Trescot welcomed the speeches of William Seward because they eschewed textual interpretations of the Constitution, and frankly posed the only true and relevant question: "Do the wants of this great Anglo Saxon race, the need of our glorious and progressing free white civilization require the abolition of negro slavery?" Charles Hutson, son of William F. Hutson, a Beaufort rice planter and a signer of the secession ordinance, phrased the matter more directly. Writing from an army camp near Mt. Vernon, Virginia, in September 1861, Hutson commented on a sermon which described the cause of secession as the defense of the noble right of self-government. "It is insulting to the English common sense of the race which governs here," the young soldier retorted, "to tell them they are battling for an abstract right common to all humanity. Every reflecting child will glance at the darkey who waits on him & laugh at the idea of such an abstract right." And when the family of planter John Berkeley Grimball was torn apart by the secession crisis, his son Louis bitterly denounced his sister for charging that South Carolina had willfully destroyed the Union. "What are you writing?" he gasped. "You speak as if we are the aggressors, and would dissolve the union in Blood shed upon a *mere abstract principle,* when the fact is we are oppressed and are contending for all that we hold most dear—our Property—our institutions—our Honor—Aye and our very lives!" To understand what the revolution was all about, he advised his sister to return home from the North, and become a slaveholder herself. So, writing on a broader canvas, Arthur Perroneau Hayne assured President Buchanan that his acquiescence in secession was a noble act of humanity to the white people of the South.

Slavery with us is no abstraction—but a *great* and *vital fact.* Without it our every comfort would be taken from us. Our wives, our children, made unhappy—education, the light of knowledge—all *all* lost and our *people ruined for ever. Nothing short of separation from the Union can save us.*

The people of 1860 were usually frank in their language and clear in their thinking about the reasons for disunion. After the war, for many reasons men came forward to clothe the traumatic failure of the movement in the misty garments of high constitutional rights and sacred honor. Nevertheless, there were two "abstract rights" which were integral to secession, state sovereignty and property rights. No historian could surpass the discussion of these questions by wartime governor Andrew Gordon Magrath. From the fastness of his imprisonment in Fort Pulaski in 1865 Magrath looked back upon the cause of secession with a detachment which had not yet been colored by the sterilization and obfuscation of the postwar remembrance. There were tangential reasons for the revolution, Magrath allowed, but the central "motive power" was the belief that the ascendancy of the Republican party threatened to disturb their "right of property in slaves." To his credit, Magrath did see the rich variety of implications enmeshed in this property right. For those who did not own a slave, Lincoln's election implied that they might never be able to purchase that essential key to social and economic elevation. In addition, the former jurist understood that the people of the antebellum South conceived slavery to be the basis of stability for their social order, the foundation of their economy, and the source of their moral and cultural superiority. State sovereignty was an issue only because the retreat to the inviolability of state's rights had always been a refuge for those fearful of a challenge to their property. Certainly, the "right of property in slaves" is closer to the heart of the problem than "fear of the antislavery movement," or similar propositions which raise more questions than they answer.

Mid-nineteenth century Americans lived in

an age of romanticism. Men had fought for lesser glories than independence and Southern nationalism; and once the terrible momentum was begun, who could say for certain what myths, compulsions, and desires drove men on into revolution and civil war. But somewhere in the intellectual hiatus of the war the clear and concrete understanding of the cause of it all, an understanding shared by those who joined to tear away from the Union, was lost. For the people of South Carolina perpetuation of the Union beyond 1860 meant the steady and irresistible destruction of slavery, which was the first and last principle of life in that society, the only conceivable pattern of essential race control. Perpetuation of the Union, according to Senator Hammond, meant servile insurrection, and ultimately abolition. "We dissolve the Union to prevent it," he told a Northerner in 1861, "and [we] believe, I believe it will do it." Secession was a revolution of passion, and the passion was fear.

Here we have in charge the solution of the greatest problem of the ages. We are here two races—white and black—now both equally American, holding each other in the closest embrace and utterly unable to extricate ourselves from it. A problem so difficult, so complicated, and so momentous never was placed in charge of any portion of Mankind. And on its solution rests our all.

The nation was led into war in 1861 by the secession of the lower South, not by the desire of the Northern people either to end slavery or bring equality to the Negro. Subsequent generations of Americans came to condemn the racist fears and logic which had motivated that secession, yet the experience of our own time painfully suggests that it was easy to censure racism, but more difficult to obliterate it. If the history of race relations in the United States is an accurate measure, we can assume that there will not and perhaps cannot be a genuine reconciliation between the races, that white and black will never achieve equality because of the fears of the one, and their oppression of the other. But human experience also indicates the possibility of transcending history, for history is neither a lawgiver nor an impenetrable obstacle. As Hammond could not foresee, the solution must and will go on.

IX "This Mighty Scourge
of War"

32

Journey to Emancipation

Stephen B. Oates

Throughout the first year and a half of the Civil War, Lincoln insisted that the North was fighting strictly to save the Union, not to free the slaves. But a combination of problems and pressures caused him to change his mind; and in September, 1862, he issued the Preliminary Emancipation Proclamation, to take effect on January 1, 1863, which liberated the slaves in the rebellious states. Ever since then, legends have flourished about Lincoln as the Great Emancipator—a man who dedicated his life to liberty and equality for all. On the other hand, counter-legends of Lincoln as a Great Racist eventually emerged in the South. Which view is the true one? Should Lincoln be applauded as a great humanitarian? Or was he just another white bigot, as one writer recently contended? Or, as some of his contemporaries charged, was he an unscrupulous opportunist who eradicated slavery merely for political and military expediency? The following essay, drawing on a cornucopia of modern scholarship about Lincoln's life and the times in which he lived, tries to answer the enduring questions about Lincoln as emancipator. It not only traces his changing views about slavery and race and discusses his evolving emancipation policy, but tries to present a realistic portrait of one of the most mythologized men in all American history.

He comes to us in the mists of legend as a kind of homespun Socrates, brimming with prairie wit and folk wisdom. He is as honest, upright, God-fearing, generous, and patriotic an American as the Almighty ever created. Impervious to material rewards and social station, the Lincoln of mythology is the Great Commoner, a saintly Rail Splitter who spoke in a deep, fatherly voice about the genius of the plain folk. He comes to us, too, as the Great Emancipator who led the North off to Civil War to free the slaves—and afterward offered the South a tender and forgiving hand.

There is a counter-legend of Lincoln—one shared ironically enough by many white Southerners and certain black Americans of our time. This is the legend of Lincoln as bigot, as a white racist who championed segregation, opposed civil and political rights for black people, wanted them all thrown out of the country. This Lincoln is the great ancestor of racist James K. Vardaman of Mississippi, of "Bull" Connor of Birmingham, of the white citizens' councils, of the Knights of the Ku Klux Klan.

Neither of these views, of course, reveals much about the man who really lived—legends and politicized interpretations seldom do. If one tears Lincoln and his words out of historical context, one can twist him into anything one likes: a racist, a saint, a reactionary, a revolutionary, a capitalist, a communist, a warmonger, a pacifist. For my part, I will not try to squeeze this complex human being into any arbitrary, artificial category. Instead, I want to focus on the man as he lived, on the flesh-and-blood Lincoln,

This essay is is based on research and information contained in Stephen B. Oates, *With Malice Toward None: The Life of Abraham Lincoln* (Harper & Row, 1977).

that flawed and fatalistic individual who struggled with himself and his countrymen over the haunting moral paradox of slavery in a nation based on the Declaration of Independence. Discussing him realistically in his own time, I want to go back over Lincoln's journey to emancipation—a journey filled with ironies, doubt and despair, and a few unexpected turns, that led him to the Emancipation Proclamation and the Thirteenth Amendment that made it permanent.

2

But first let me describe him as a man. The real Lincoln was almost entirely self-educated, with a talent for expression that in another time and place might have led him into a literary career. He wrote poetry and studied Shakespeare, Byron, and Oliver Wendell Holmes, attracted especially to writings with tragic and melancholy themes. He examined the way celebrated orators turned a phrase or employed a figure of speech, admiring great truths greatly told. Though never much at impromptu oratory, he could hold an audience of 15,000 spellbound when reading from a written speech, singing out in a shrill, high-pitched voice that became his trademark.

He was an intense, brooding man, plagued with chronic depression most of his life. "I am now the most miserable man living," he said on one occasion in 1841. "If what I feel were equally distributed to the whole human family, there would not be one cheerful face on the earth." He added: "To remain as I am is impossible; I must die or be better."

At the time he said this, Lincoln had fears of sexual inadequacy, doubting his ability to please or even care for a wife. In 1842 he confided in his closest friend Joshua Speed about his troubles, and both confessed that they had fears of "nervous debility" with women. Speed went ahead and married anyway and then wrote Lincoln that their anxieties were groundless. "I tell you, Speed, our forebodings, for which you and

I are rather peculiar, are all the worst sort of nonsense," Lincoln rejoiced. Encouraged by Speed's success, Lincoln finally married Mary Todd; and she obviously helped him overcome his doubts, for they developed a strong and lasting physical love for one another.

Still, Lincoln remained a moody, melancholy person, given to long introspections about things like death and mortality. In truth, death was a lifelong obsession with him. His poetry, speeches, and letters are studded with allusions to it. He spoke of the transitory nature of human life, spoke of how all people in this world are fated to die in the end—all are fated to die. He saw himself as only a passing moment in a rushing river of time.

Preoccupied with death, he was also afraid of insanity, afraid (as he phrased it) of "the pangs that kill the mind." In his late thirties, he wrote and rewrote a poem about a boyhood friend, one Matthew Gentry, who became deranged and was locked "in mental night," condemned to a living death, spinning out of control in some inner void. Lincoln retained a morbid fascination with Gentry's condition, writing about how Gentry was more an object of dread than death itself: "A human form with reason fled, while wretched life remains." Yes, Lincoln was fascinated with madness, troubled by it, afraid that what had happened to Matthew could also happen to him—his own reason destroyed, Lincoln spinning in mindless night without the power to know.

Lincoln was a teetotaler because liquor left him "flabby and undone," blurring his mind and threatening his self-control. And he dreaded and avoided anything which threatened that. In one memorable speech, he heralded some great and distant day when all passions would be subdued, when reason would triumph and "*mind*, all conquering *mind*" would rule the earth.

One side of Lincoln was always supremely logical and analytical. He was entranced by the clarity of mathematics, and as an attorney

The strain of war: at left, Abraham Lincoln in Springfield, Illinois on June 3, 1860. (Courtesy of The Chicago Historical Society.) At right, after four years of war, Lincoln posed for photographer Alexander Gardner in Washington, April 10, 1865. (Courtesy of The Library of Congress.)

he could command a mass of technical data. Yet he was also extremely superstitious, believed in signs and visions, contended that dreams were auguries of approaching triumph or calamity. He was skeptical of organized religion and never joined a church; yet he argued that all human destinies were controlled by an omnipotent God.

It is true that Lincoln told folksy anecdotes to illustrate a point. But humor was also tremendous therapy for his depressions—a device "to whistle down sadness," as a friend put it. Lincoln liked all kinds of jokes, from bawdy tales to pungent rib-ticklers like "Bass-Ackwards," a story he wrote down and handed a bailiff one day. Filled with hilarious spoonerisms, "Bass-Ackwards" is about a fellow who gets thrown from his horse and lands in "a great *tow-curd*," which gives him a *"sick of fitness."* About *"bray dake,"* he comes to and dashes home to find "the

door sick abed, and his *wife* standing open." "But thank goodness," the punch line goes, "she is getting right *hat* and *farty* again."

Contrary to legend, Lincoln was anything but a common man. In point of fact, he was one of the most ambitious human beings his friends had ever seen, with an aspiration for high station in life that burned in him like a furnace. Instead of reading with an accomplished attorney, as was customary in those days, he taught himself the law entirely on his own. He was literally a self-made lawyer. Moreover, he entered the Illinois legislature at the age of twenty-five and became a leader of the state Whig party, a tireless party campaigner, and a regular candidate for public office.

As a self-made man, Lincoln felt embarrassed about his log-cabin origins and never liked to talk about them. He would never discuss his

parents and became permanently estranged from his father, who was all but illiterate. Lincoln once remarked that his father "never did more in the way of writing than to bunglingly sign his own name." When his father died in Illinois in 1851, Lincoln did not attend his funeral.

By the 1850s, Lincoln was one of the most sought-after attorneys in Illinois, with a reputation as a lawyer's lawyer—a knowledgeable jurist who argued appeal cases for other attorneys. He did his most influential legal work in the supreme court of Illinois, where he participated in 243 cases and won most of them. He commanded the respect of his colleagues, all of whom called him "Mr. Lincoln" or just "Lincoln." Nobody called him Abe—at least not to his face —because he loathed the nickname. It did not befit a respected professional who had struggled hard to overcome the limitations of his frontier background. Frankly, Lincoln enjoyed his status as a lawyer and politician, and he liked money, too, and used it to measure his worth. By the mid-1850s, thanks to a combination of talent and sheer hard work, Lincoln was a man of substantial wealth. He had an annual income of around $5,000—the equivalent of many times that today—and large financial and real estate investments.

Although a man of status and influence, Lincoln was as honest in real life as in the legend. Even his enemies conceded that he was incorruptible. Moreover, he possessed broad humanitarian views, some of them in advance of his time. Even though he was a teetotaler, he was extremely tolerant of alcoholics, regarding them not as criminals—the way most temperance people did—but as unfortunates who deserved understanding, not vilification. He noted that some of the world's most gifted artists had succumbed to alcoholism because they were too sensitive to cope with their insights into the human condition. He believed that women, like men, should vote so long as they all paid taxes. And he had no ethnic prejudices. His law partner, William Herndon, who raved against the

Irish, reported that Lincoln was not at all prejudiced against "the foreign element, tolerating— as I never could—even the Irish."

Politically, Lincoln was always nationalist in his outlook, an outlook that began when he was an Indiana farm boy tilling his father's mundane wheat field. While the plow horse was getting its breath at the end of a furrow, Lincoln would study Parson Weems's eulogistic biography of George Washington, and he would daydream about the Revolution and the origins of the Republic, daydream about Washington and Jefferson as great national statesmen who shaped the course of history. By the time he became a politician, Lincoln idolized the Founding Fathers as apostles of liberty (never mind for now that many of these apostles were also Southern slaveowners). Young Lincoln extolled the founders for beginning an experiment in popular government on these shores, to show a doubting Europe that people could govern themselves without hereditary monarchs and aristocracies. And the foundation of the American experiment was the Declaration of Independence, which in Lincoln's view contained the highest political truths in history: that all men are created equal and are entitled to freedom and the pursuit of happiness. Which for Lincoln meant that men like him were not chained to the condition of their births, that they could better their station in life and harvest the fruits of their own talents and industry. Thus he had a deep, personal reverence for the Declaration and insisted that all his political sentiments flowed from that document.

3

Which brings me to the problem and paradox of slavery in America. Lincoln maintained that he had always hated human bondage, as much as any Abolitionist. His family had opposed the peculiar institution, and Lincoln had grown up and entered Illinois politics thinking it wrong. But before 1854 (and the significance of that

date will become clear) Lincoln generally kept his own counsel about slavery and abolition. After all, slavery was the most combustible issue of his generation, and Lincoln observed early on what violent passions Negro bondage —and the question of race that underlay it— could arouse in white Americans. In his day, slavery was always more than just a labor system; it was also a tried and tested means of race control in a white supremacist South brimming with black people. Moreover, the North was also a white supremacist section, where the vast majority of whites opposed emancipation lest it result in a flood of Southern blacks into the free states. And Illinois was no exception, as most whites there were against abolition and were anti-Negro to the core. Lincoln, who had elected to work within the system, was not going to ruin his career by espousing an extremely unpopular cause. To be branded as an Abolitionist in central Illinois, his constituency as a legislator and a United States congressman, would have been certain political suicide. At the same time, attorney Lincoln conceded that Southern slavery had become a thoroughly entrenched institution, that bondage where it already existed was protected by the Constitution and could not be molested by the national government.

Still, slavery gnawed him. He realized what a monstrous contradiction it was that slavery should exist at all in a self-proclaimed free and enlightened republic. He who cherished the Declaration of Independence understood only too well how bondage mocked and contradicted that noble document. Too, he thought slavery a blight on the American experiment in popular government. It was, he believed, the one retrograde institution that robbed the Republic of its just example to the world, robbed the United States of the hope it should hold out to oppressed people everywhere.

He opposed slavery, too, because he had witnessed some of its evils firsthand. In 1841, on a steamboat journey down the Ohio River, he saw a group of manacled slaves on their way to the cruel cotton plantations of the Deep South. Lincoln was appalled at the sight of those chained Negroes. Fourteen years later he wrote that the spectacle "was a continual torment to me" and that he saw something like it every time he touched a slave border. Slavery, he said, "had the power to make me miserable."

Again, while serving in Congress from 1847 to 1849, he passed slave auction blocks in Washington. In fact, from the windows of the Capitol, he could observe the infamous "Georgia pen"—"a sort of Negro livery stable," as he described it, "where droves of negroes were collected, temporarily kept, and finally taken to Southern markets, precisely like droves of horses." The spectacle offended him. He agreed with a Whig colleague that the buying and selling of human beings in the United States capital was a national disgrace. Accordingly Lincoln drafted a gradual abolition bill for the District of Columbia. But powerful Southern politicians howled in protest, and his own Whig support fell away. At that, Lincoln dropped his bill and sat in glum silence as Congress rocked with debates—with drunken fistfights and rumbles of disunion—over the status of slavery out in the territories. Shocked at the behavior of his colleagues, Lincoln confessed that slavery was the one issue that threatened the stability of the Union.

What could be done? Slavery as an institution could not be removed, and yet it should not remain either. Trapped in what seemed an impossible dilemma, Lincoln persuaded himself that if slavery were confined to the South and left alone there, time would somehow solve the problem and slavery would ultimately die out. And he told himself that the Founding Fathers had felt the same way, that they, too, had expected slavery to perish some day. In Lincoln's interpretation, they had tolerated slavery as a necessary evil, agreeing that it could not be eradicated where it already flourished without causing wide-scale wreckage. But in his view they had taken steps to restrict its growth (had

excluded slavery from the old Northwest territories, had outlawed the international slave trade) and so to place the institution on the road to extinction.

So went Lincoln's argument before 1854. The solution was to bide one's time, trust the future to get rid of slavery and square America with her own ideals. And he convinced himself that when slavery was no longer workable, Southern whites would gradually liberate the blacks on their own. They would do so voluntarily.

To solve the ensuing problem of racial adjustment, Lincoln insisted that the federal government should colonize all blacks in Africa, an idea he got from his political idol, Whig national leader Henry Clay. Said Lincoln in 1852: If the Republic could remove the danger of slavery and restore "a captive people to their long-lost father-land," and do both so gradually "that neither races nor individuals shall have suffered by the change," then "it will indeed be a glorious consummation."

4

Then came 1854 and the momentous Kansas-Nebraska Act. It was the brainchild of Lincoln's archrival, pugnacious Stephen A. Douglas, leading Northern Democrat and senator from Illinois. Douglas' act overturned the old Missouri Compromise line, which excluded slavery from the vast northern area of the Louisiana Purchase; the act then established a new formula for dealing with slavery in the national lands: Now Congress would stay out of the matter, and the people of each territory would decide whether to retain or outlaw the institution. Until such time as the citizens of a territory voted on the issue, Southerners could take slavery into nearly all federal territories, including the new ones of Kansas and Nebraska. These were carved out of the northern section of the Louisiana Purchase. Thanks to the Kansas-Nebraska

Act, an area once preserved for freedom now seemed open to a proslavery invasion.

At once a storm of freesoil protest broke across the North, and scores of political leaders branded the Kansas-Nebraska Act as part of a sinister Southern plot to extend slave territory and augment Southern political power in Washington. There followed a series of political earthquakes. A civil war broke out in Kansas, as proslavery and freesoil pioneers came into bloody collisions on the prairie there—proof that slavery was far too volatile an issue ever to be solved as a purely local matter. At the same time, the old Whig party disintegrated. In its place emerged a new all-Northern party—the Republicans—dedicated to blocking the extension of slavery and to saving the cherished frontier for free white labor. Then in 1857 came the infamous Dred Scott decision, handed down by Taney's pro–Southern Supreme Court, which ruled that neither Congress nor a territorial government could outlaw slavery because to do so would violate Southern property rights. As Lincoln and many others observed, the net effect of the decision was to legalize slavery in all federal territories from Canada to Mexico.

The train of ominous events from Kansas-Nebraska to Dred Scott shook Lincoln to his foundations. In his view, the Southern-controlled Democratic party—the party that dominated the Senate, the Supreme Court, and the presidency—had instituted a revolt against the Founding Fathers and the entire course of the Republic so far as slavery was concerned. Now human bondage was not going to die out. Now it was going to expand and grow and continue indefinitely, as Southerners dragged manacled Negroes across the West, adapting slave labor to whatever conditions they found there, putting the slaves to work in mines and on farms. Now Southerners would create new slave states in the West and make slavery powerful and permanent in America. Now the Republic would never remove the cancer that infected its political system, would never remove the one insti-

tution that marred its global image, would never remove a "cruel wrong" that made a mockery of the Declaration.

Lincoln waded into the very thick of the anti-extension fight. He campaigned for the national Senate. He joined the Republican party. He thundered against the evil designs of the "Slave Power." As he did so, he was no longer the old Whig campaigner of the 1830s and 1840s. Now he spoke with an urgent sense of mission that gave his speeches a searching eloquence—a mission to save the Republic's noblest ideals, turn back the tide of slavery expansion, restrict the peculiar institution once again to the South, and place it back on the road to extinction, as Lincoln believed the Founding Fathers had so placed it.

By 1858, Lincoln, like a lot of other Republicans, began to see a grim proslavery conspiracy at work in the United States. The first stage was to betray the founders and send slavery flooding all over the West. At the same time, proslavery theorists were out to undermine the Declaration of Independence, to discredit its equality doctrine as "a self evident lie" (as many Southern spokesmen were actually saying), and to replace the Declaration with the principles of inequality and human servitude.

The next step in the conspiracy would be to nationalize slavery: The Taney Court, Lincoln feared, would hand down another decision, one declaring that states could not prohibit slavery either. Then the institution would sweep into Illinois, sweep into Indiana and Ohio, sweep into Pennsylvania and New York, sweep into Massachusetts and New England, sweep all over the Northern states, until at last slavery would be nationalized and America would end up a slave house. At that, as George Fitzhugh of Virginia advocated, the conspirators would enslave all American workers—white as well as black. The Northern free-labor system would be expunged, the Declaration of Independence overthrown, self-government abolished, and the conspirators would restore despotism with

class rule and an entrenched aristocracy. All the work since the Revolution of 1776 would be obliterated. The world's best hope—America's experiment in popular government—would be destroyed, and mankind would spin backward into feudalism.

For Lincoln and his Republican colleagues, it was imperative that the conspiracy be blocked in its initial stage—the expansion of slavery into the West. In 1858 Lincoln set out after Douglas' Senate seat, inveighing against the Little Giant for his part in the proslavery plot and warning Illinois—and Northerners beyond —that only the Republicans could save their free-labor system and their free government. Now Lincoln openly and fiercely declaimed his antislavery sentiments. He hated the institution. He hated slavery because it degraded blacks and whites alike. Because it prevented the Negro from "eating the bread which his own hand earns." Because it not only contradicted the Declaration of Independence, but violated the principles of free labor, self-help, social mobility, and economic independence, all of which lay at the center of Republican ideology, of Lincoln's ideology. Yet, while branding slavery as an evil and doing all they could to contain slavery in the South, Republicans would not, could not, menace the institution in those states where it already existed.

Douglas, fighting for his political life in free-soil Illinois, lashed back at Lincoln with unadulterated race baiting. Throughout the Great Debates of 1858, Douglas smeared Lincoln and his party as Black Republicans, as a gang of radical Abolitionists out to liberate all Southern slaves and bring them stampeding into Illinois and the rest of the North, where they would take away white jobs and copulate with white daughters. Again and again, Douglas accused Lincoln of desiring intermarriage and racial mongrelization.

Lincoln protested emphatically that race was not the issue between him and Douglas. The issue was whether slavery would ultimately

triumph or ultimately perish in the United States. But Douglas knew that anti-Negro feelings still prevailed in Illinois, and he hoped to whip Lincoln by playing on white racial fears.

Forced to take a stand lest Douglas ruin him with his allegations, Lincoln conceded that he was not for Negro political and social equality. He was not for enfranchising Negroes, was not for intermarriage. There was, he said, "a physical difference" between blacks and whites that would "probably" always prevent them from living together in perfect equality. Having confessed his racial views, Lincoln then qualified them: If Negroes were not the equal of Lincoln and Douglas in moral and intellectual endowment, they *were* equal to Lincoln, Douglas, and "every living man" in their right to liberty, equality of opportunity, and the fruits of their own labor. (Later he insisted that it was bondage that had "clouded the slaves' intellects" and that Negroes were capable of thinking like whites.) Moreover, Lincoln rejected "the counterfeit argument" that just because he did not want a black woman for a slave, he necessarily wanted her for a wife. He could just let her alone. Exasperated with Douglas and white Negrophobia in general, Lincoln begged American whites "to discard all this quibbling about this man and the other man—this race and that race and the other race being inferior," begged them to unite as one people and defend the ideals of the Declaration and its promise of liberty and opportunity for all.

Lincoln lost the 1858 Senate contest to Douglas. But in 1860 he won the Republican nomination for president and stood before the American electorate on the freesoil, free-labor principles of the Republican party. As the Republican standard-bearer, Lincoln was uncompromising in his determination to prohibit slavery in the territories by national law and to save the Republic (as he put it) from returning "class, caste, and despotism." He exhorted his fellow Republicans to stand firm in their duty: to brand slavery as an evil, to contain it in the South, to

look to the future for slavery to die a gradual death, and to promise colonization to solve the question of race. If the Republican position precipitated a crisis, it would have to be. Some day the American house must be free of slavery. That was the Republican vision, the distant horizon Lincoln saw.

Yet, for the benefit of Southerners, he repeated that he and his party would not harm slavery in the Southern states. The federal government had no constitutional authority in peacetime to tamper with a state institution like slavery inside that state.

But Southerners by 1860 were in no mood to believe anything Lincoln or any other Republican said. In Dixie, orators and editors alike castigated Lincoln as a black-hearted radical, a "sooty and scoundrelly" Abolitionist who wanted to free the slaves at once and mix the races. By turns, Southerners branded Lincoln as another John Brown. A mobocrat. A Southern hater. A chimpanzee. A lunatic. The "biggest ass in the United States." The evil chief of the North's "Black Republican, free love, free Nigger" party, whose victory would ring the bells of doom for the white man's South. If Lincoln won the White House, Southern spokesmen warned, the next thing Southerners would know, Republican troops would be invading their farms and plantations and liberating some four million slaves at bayonet point. "I shudder to contemplate it!" cried an Alabama white man. "What social monstrosities, what desolated fields, what civil broils, what robberies, rapes, and murders of the poorer whites by the emancipated blacks would then disfigure the whole fair face of this prosperous, smiling, and happy Southern land."

Thus when Lincoln won the election of 1860, the seven states of the Deep South, with their heavy slave concentrations, seceded from the Union and established a Southern Confederacy dedicated to the perservation of racial slavery. As the editor of the *Montgomery Mail* explained: "In this struggle for maintaining the

ascendancy of our race in the South—our home —we see no chance for victory but in withdrawing from the Union. To remain in the Union is to lose all that white men hold dear in government. We vote to get out."

With the border slave states also threatening to secede, Lincoln pleaded with Southerners to understand the Republican position on slavery. In his inaugural address of 1861, he assured them once again that the federal government would not free the slaves in the South, that it had no legal right to do so. He even gave his blessings to the original Thirteenth Amendment, just passed by Congress, that would have guaranteed slavery in the Southern states for as long as whites there wanted it. Lincoln endorsed the amendment because he thought it consistent with Republican ideology. Ironically, Southern secession and the outbreak of war prevented that amendment from ever being ratified.

When the rebels opened fire on Fort Sumter, the nation plunged into civil war, a war that began as a ninety-day skirmish for both sides, but that swelled instead into a vast and terrible carnage with consequences beyond calculation for those swept up in its flames. Lincoln, falling into a deep depression that would plague him through his presidency, remarked that the war was the supreme irony of his life: that he who sickened at the sight of blood, who abhorred stridency and physical violence, was caught in a national holocaust, a tornado of blood and wreckage with Lincoln himself whirling in its center.

5

At the outset of the war, Lincoln strove to be consistent with all he and his party had said about slavery: His purpose in the struggle was strictly to save the Union; it was not to free the slaves. He would crush the rebellion with his armies and restore the national authority in the

South with slavery intact. Then Lincoln and his party would resume and implement their policy of slave containment.

There were other reasons for Lincoln's hands-off policy about slavery. Four slave states— Delaware, Maryland, Kentucky, and Missouri —remained in the Union. Should he try to free the slaves, Lincoln feared it would send the crucial border spiraling into the Confederacy, something that would be catastrophic for the Union. A Confederate Maryland would create an impossible situation for Washington, D.C. And a Confederate Missouri and Kentucky would give the rebels potential bases from which to invade Illinois, Indiana, and Ohio. So Lincoln rejected emancipation in part to appease the loyal border.

He was also waging a bipartisan war effort, with Northern Democrats and Republicans alike enlisting in his armies to save the Union. Lincoln encouraged this because he insisted that it would take a united North to win the war. An emancipation policy, he feared, would alienate Northern Democrats, ignite a racial powder keg, and possibly cause a civil war in the rear. Then the Union really would be lost.

But the pressures and problems of civil war caused Lincoln to change his mind, caused him to abandon his hands-off policy and hurl an executive fist at slavery in the rebel states, thus making emancipation a Union war objective. The pressures operating on Lincoln were complex and merit careful discussion.

First, from the summer of 1861 on, several liberal Republican senators—Charles Sumner of Massachusetts and Bluff Ben Wade of Ohio, among others—sequestered themselves with Lincoln and implored and badgered him to free the slaves. Sumner, as Lincoln's personal friend and chief foreign policy adviser, was especially persistent—and persuasive. Before secession, of course, the liberal senators had all adhered to the Republican position on slavery in the South. But civil war had now removed their consti-

tutional scruples about the peculiar institution. After all, they told Lincoln, the Southern people were in rebellion against the national government; they could not resist that government and yet enjoy the protection of its laws. Now the senators argued that either the president or Congress could eradicate slavery by the War Power, and they wanted Lincoln to do it. If he emancipated the slaves, it would maim and cripple the Confederacy and hasten an end to the rebellion.

Second, they pointed out that slavery had caused the war, was the reason why the Southern states had seceded, and was now the cornerstone of the Confederacy. It was absurd, the senators contended, to fight a war without removing the thing that had brought it about. Should the South return to the Union with slavery intact, as Lincoln desired, Southerners would just start another war over slavery whenever they though it threatened again, so that the present struggle would have accomplished nothing, nothing at all. If Lincoln really wanted to save the Union, he must tear slavery out root and branch and smash the South's planter class —that mischievous class the senators thought had masterminded secession and fomented war.

Sumner, in his role as foreign policy adviser, also linked emancipation to foreign policy. On several occasions in 1861 and 1862, Britain seemed on the verge of recognizing the Confederacy as an independent nation—something that would be calamitous for the Union. As a member of the family of nations, the Confederacy could form alliances and seek mediation and perhaps armed intervention in the American conflict. But, Sumner argued, if Lincoln made the obliteration of slavery a Union war objective, Britain would balk at recognition and intervention. Why so? Because she was proud of her antislavery tradition, Sumner contended, and would refrain from helping the South protect human bondage from Lincoln's armies. And whatever powerful Britain did, the rest of

Europe was sure to follow.

Also, as Sumner kept reminding everyone, emancipation would break the chains of several million oppressed human beings and right America at last with her own ideals. Lincoln could no longer wait for the future to remove slavery. He must do it. The war, monstrous and terrible though it was, had given Lincoln the opportunity to do it.

There was still another argument for emancipation, an argument advanced not just by Sumner and his colleagues, but by members of Lincoln's cabinet as well. In 1862, his armies suffered from manpower shortages on every front. Thanks to repeated Union military failures and to a growing war weariness across the North, volunteering had fallen off sharply, and Union generals bombarded Washington with shrill complaints, insisting that they faced an overwhelming Southern foe and that they must have reinforcements before they could win battles or even fight. While Union commanders often exaggerated rebel strength, Union forces *did* need reinforcements to carry out a successful offensive war. As Sumner reminded Lincoln, the slaves were an untapped reservoir of strength. "You need more men," Sumner said, "not only at the North, but at the South. You need the slaves." If Lincoln freed them, he could recruit black men into his armed forces, thus helping to solve his manpower woes.

Lincoln was sympathetic to the entire range of arguments Sumner and his associates rehearsed for him. Personally, Lincoln said, he hated slavery as much as they did, and many of their points had already occurred to him. In fact, as early as November and December, 1861, Lincoln began wavering in his hands-off policy about slavery, began searching about for some compromise—something short of a sweeping emancipation decree. Again he seemed caught in an impossible dilemma: how to remove the cause of the War, keep Britain out of the conflict, cripple the Confederacy and help suppress

the rebellion, and yet retain the allegiance of Northern Democrats and the critical border?

In March, 1862, he proposed a plan to Congress he thought might work: a gradual, compensated emancipation program to commence in the loyal border states. According to Lincoln's plan, the border states would gradually abolish slavery themselves over the next thirty years, and the federal government would compensate slaveowners for their loss. The whole program was to be voluntary; the states would adopt their own emancipation laws without federal coercion.

At the same time, the federal government would sponsor a colonization program, which was also to be entirely voluntary. Without colonization, Lincoln understood only too well, most Northern whites would never accept emancipation, even if it were carried out by the states. From now on, every time he contemplated some new antislavery move, he made a great fuss about colonization: He embarked on a colonization project in Central America and another in Haiti, and he held an interview about colonization with Washington's black leaders, an interview he published in the press. In part, the ritual of colonization was designed to calm white racial fears.

If his gradual, state-guided plan were adopted, Lincoln contended that a presidential decree—federally enforced emancipation—would never be necessary. Abolition would begin on the local level in the loyal border and then be extended into the rebel states as they were conquered. Thus by a slow and salubrious process would the cause of the rebellion be removed and the future of the Union guaranteed.

Lincoln's plan did not work. It did not work because the border states refused to act. Lincoln could not even persuade Delaware, with its small and relatively harmless slave population, to adopt his program. In desperation, Lincoln on three different occasions—in the spring and summer of 1862—pleaded with border-state congressmen to endorse his program. In his

third meeting with them, held in the White House on July 12, Lincoln warned the border representatives that it was impossible now to restore the Union with slavery preserved. Slavery, he said, was doomed. They could not be blind to the signs, could not be blind to the fact that his plan was the only alternative to a more drastic move against slavery, one that would cause tremendous wreckage in the South. Please, he said, commend my gradual plan to your people.

But most of the border men turned him down. They thought his plan would cost too much, would only fan the flames of rebellion, would sow dangerous discontent in their own states. Their intransigence was a sober lesson to Lincoln. It was proof indeed that slaveowners—even loyal slaveowners—were too tied up in the slave system ever to free their own Negroes and voluntarily transform their way of life. If abolition must come, it must begin in the rebel South and then be extended into the loyal border later on. Which meant that the president must eradicate slavery himself. He could no longer avoid the responsibility. By mid–July, 1862, the pressures of the war had forced him to abandon his hands-off policy and "lay a strong hand on the colored element."

On July 13, the day after his last talk with the border men, Lincoln took a carriage ride with a couple of his cabinet secretaries. His conversation, when recounted in full, reveals a tougher Lincoln than the lenient and compromising president of the legend-building biographies. Lincoln said he was convinced that the war could no longer be won through forbearance toward Southern rebels, that it was "a duty on our part to liberate the slaves." The time had come to take a bold new path and hurl Union armies at "the heart of the rebellion," using the military to destroy the very institution that caused and now sustained the insurrection. Southerners could not throw off the Constitution and at the same time invoke it to protect slavery. They had started the war and must now face its consequences.

He had given this a lot of grave and painful

thought, he said, and had concluded that presidential emancipation was the last alternative, that it was "a military necessity absolutely essential to the preservation of the Union." Because the slaves were a tremendous source of strength to the rebellion, Lincoln must invite them to desert and "come to us and uniting with us they must be made free from rebel authority and rebel masters." He said his interview with the border men yesterday had forced him slowly but he believed correctly to this conclusion.

On July 22, 1862, Lincoln summoned his cabinet members and read them a draft of a Preliminary Emancipation Proclamation. Come January 1, 1863, in his capacity as commander in chief of the armed forces in time of war, Lincoln would free all the slaves everywhere in the rebel states. He would thus make it a Union objective to annihilate slavery as an institution in the Confederate South.

Contrary to what many historians have said, Lincoln's projected proclamation went further than anything Congress had done. True, Congress had just enacted (and Lincoln had just signed) the Second Confiscation Act, which provided for the seizure and liberation of all slaves of people who supported or participated in the rebellion. But most slaves would be freed only after protracted case-by-case litigation in the federal courts. Another section of the act did liberate certain categories of slaves without court action, but the bill remained a complicated and piecemeal effort at emancipation. Lincoln's proclamation, on the other hand, was a sweeping blow against slavery as an institution in all rebel states: The president cut through judicial red tape, announced that the executive branch would handle emancipation and that it would use the military to vanquish the cornerstone of the Confederate South. Again, he justified this as a military necessity to save the Union.

But Seward and other cabinet secretaries dissuaded Lincoln from issuing his proclamation in July. Seward argued that the Union had won no clear military victories, particularly in the showcase eastern theater. As a consequence, Europe would misconstrue the proclamation as "our last shriek on the retreat," as a wild and reckless attempt to compensate for Union military ineptitude by provoking a slave insurrection behind rebel lines. If Lincoln must give an emancipation order, Seward warned, he must wait until the Union won a military victory.

Lincoln finally agreed to wait, but he was not happy about it: The way George B. McClellan and his other generals had been fighting in the eastern theater, Lincoln had no idea when he would ever have a victory.

One of the great ironies of the war was that McClellan presented Lincoln with the triumph he needed. A Democrat who sympathized with Southern slavery and opposed wartime emancipation with a passion, McClellan outfought Lee at Antietam Creek in September, 1862, and drove the rebel army from the battlefield. Thereupon Lincoln issued his Preliminary Proclamation, with its warning that if the rebellion did not cease by January 1, 1863, the executive branch, including the army and navy, would destroy slavery in the rebel states.

As it turned out, the Preliminary Proclamation ignited a powder box of racial discontent in much of the lower North, especially the Midwest, and led to a Republican disaster in the fall by-elections of 1862. Already Northern Democrats were upset with Lincoln's harsh war measures, especially his use of martial law and military arrests. But Negro emancipation was more than they could stand, and they stumped the Northern states that fall, beating the drums of Negrophobia, warning of massive influxes of Southern blacks into the North once emancipation came. Sullen, war weary, and racially aroused, Northern voters dealt the Republicans a smashing blow, as the North's five most populous states—all of which had gone for Lincoln in 1860—now returned Democratic majorities to Congress. While the Republicans narrowly retained control of Congress, the future looked bleak indeed for 1864.

Republican analysts—and Lincoln himself—conceded that the Preliminary Proclamation was a major factor in the Republican defeat. But Lincoln told a delegation from Kentucky that he would rather die than retract a single word in his proclamation.

As the new year approached, conservative Republicans begged Lincoln to abandon his "reckless" emancipation scheme lest he shatter their demoralized party and wreck what remained of their country. But Lincoln stood firm. On New Year's Day, 1863, he officially signed the final Emancipation Proclamation in the White House. His hand trembled badly, not because he was nervous, but because he had been shaking hands all morning in a White House reception. He assured everyone present that he was never more certain of what he was doing. "If my name ever goes into history," he said, "it will be for this act." Then slowly and deliberately he wrote out his full name.

In the final proclamation, Lincoln temporarily exempted occupied Tennessee and certain occupied places in Louisiana and Virginia (later, in reconstructing those states, he withdrew the exemptions and made emancipation a mandatory part of his reconstruction program). For now he also excluded the loyal slave states, mainly to keep them in the Union; he intended to deal with them later. With these exceptions, the final proclamation declared that as of this day, all slaves in the rebellious states were "forever free." The document also asserted that black men—Southern and Northern alike—would now be enlisted in Union military forces.

Out the proclamation went to an anxious and dissident nation. Later in the day an interracial crowd gathered on the White House lawn, and Lincoln greeted the people from an open window. The blacks cheered and sang *Glory, Jubilee Has Come,* and told Lincoln that if he would "come out of that palace, they would hug him to death." A black preacher named Henry M. Turner exclaimed that "it is indeed a time of times," that "nothing like it will ever be seen again in this life."

6

Lincoln's proclamation was the most revolutionary measure ever to come from an American president up to that time. As Union armies punched into rebel territory, they would rip out slavery as an institution, automatically freeing all slaves in the areas and states they conquered. In this respect (as Lincoln said), the war brought on changes vaster, more fundamental and profound, than either side had expected when the struggle began. Now slavery would perish as the Confederacy perished, would die by degrees with every Union advance, every Union victory.

Moreover, word of the proclamation hummed across the slave grapevine in the Confederacy, and as Union armies drew near, more slaves than ever abandoned rebel farms and plantations and (as one said) "demonstrated with their feet" their desire for freedom.

The proclamation also opened the army to black volunteers, and Northern free Negroes and Southern ex-slaves now enlisted as Union soldiers. As Lincoln said, "the colored population is the great *available* and yet *unavailed* of, force for restoring the Union." And he now availed himself of that force. In all, some 180,000 Negro fighting men—most of them emancipated slaves—served in Union forces on every major battlefront, helping to liberate their brothers and sisters in bondage and to save the Union. As Lincoln observed, the blacks added enormous and indispensable strength to the Union war machine.

Unhappily, the blacks fought in segregated units under white officers and until late in the war received less pay than whites did. In 1864 Lincoln told Frederick Douglas that he disliked the practice of unequal pay, but that the government had to make some concessions to white prejudices, noting that a great many Northern whites opposed the use of black soldiers altogether. But he promised that they would eventually get equal pay—and they did. Moreover, Lincoln was proud of the performance of his black soldiers: He publicly praised them for

fighting "with clenched teeth, and steady eye, and well poised bayonet" to save the Union, while certain whites strove "with malignant heart" to hinder it.

After the proclamation, Lincoln had to confront the problem of race adjustment, of what to do with all the blacks liberated in the South. By the spring of 1863, he had pretty well written off colonization as unworkable. His colonization schemes all floundered, in part because the white promoters were dishonest or incompetent. But the main reason colonization failed was because most blacks adamantly refused to participate in Lincoln's voluntary program. Across the North, free Negroes denounced Lincoln's colonization efforts—this was their country too! they cried—and they petitioned him to deport slaveholders instead.

As a consequence, Lincoln had just about concluded that whites and liberated blacks must somehow learn how to live together in this country. Still, he needed some device for now, some program that would pacify white Northerners and convince them that Southern freedmen would not flock into their communities but would remain in the South instead. What Lincoln worked out was a refugee system, installed by his adjutant general in the occupied Mississippi Valley, which mobilized Southern blacks in the South, utilizing them in military and civilian pursuits there. According to the system, the adjutant general enrolled all able-bodied freedmen in the army, employed other ex-slaves as military laborers, and hired still others to work on farms and plantations for wages set by the government. While there were many faults with the system, it was based on sound Republican dogma: It kept Southern Negroes out of the North, and it got them jobs as wage earners, thus helping them to help themselves and preparing them for life in a free society.

Even so, emancipation remained the most explosive and unpopular act of Lincoln's presidency. By mid–1863, thousands of Democrats were in open revolt against his administration, denouncing Lincoln as an Abolitionist dictator who had surrendered to radicalism. In the Midwest, dissident Democrats launched a peace movement to throw "the shrieking abolitionist faction" out of office and negotiate a peace with the Confederacy that would somehow restore the Union with slavery intact. There were large antiwar rallies against Lincoln's war for slave liberation. Race and draft riots flared in several Northern cities.

With all the public unrest behind the lines, conservative Republicans again beseeched Lincoln to abandon emancipation and rescue his country "from the brink of ruin." But Lincoln seemed intractable. He had made up his mind to smash the slave society of the rebel South, made up his mind to eliminate "the cruel wrong" of Negro bondage, and no amount of public discontent, he indicated, was going to change his mind. "To use a coarse, but an expressive figure," he wrote one aggravated Democrat, "broken eggs cannot be mended. I have issued the Proclamation, and I cannot retract it." Senator Wade applauded Lincoln's stand. Though the president moved too slowly, Wade said, "when he puts his foot down, he is there."

He wavered once—in August, 1864, a time of unrelenting gloom for Lincoln when his popularity had sunk to an all-time low and it seemed he could not be re-elected. He confessed to Frederick Douglass that maybe the country would no longer sustain a war for slave emancipation, that maybe he should not pull the nation down a road it did not want to travel. On August 24 he even decided to offer Jefferson Davis peace terms that excluded emancipation as a condition, vaguely suggesting that slavery would be adjusted later "by peaceful means." But the next day Lincoln changed his mind. With awakened resolution, he vowed to fight the war through to unconditional surrender and to stick by emancipation come what may. He had made his promise of freedom to the slaves, and he meant to keep it so long as he was in office.

When he won the election of 1864, Lincoln interpreted it as a popular mandate for him and his emancipation policy. (It was not really: As

Sumner said, the election was "a vote *against* McClellan rather than *for* Lincoln.") Nevertheless, Lincoln used his re-election to push for a constitutional amendment that would guarantee the freedom of all slaves, those in the border states as well as those in the rebel South. Since issuing his proclamation, Lincoln had worried that it might be nullified in the courts or thrown out by a later Congress or a subsequent administration. Consequently he wanted a constitutional amendment that would safeguard his proclamation and prevent emancipation from ever being overturned.

As it happened, the Senate in May of 1864 had already passed an emancipation amendment, the present Thirteenth Amendment, but the House had voted it down. After that Lincoln had insisted that the Republican platform endorse the measure. And now, over the winter of 1864 and 1865, he put tremendous pressure on the House to approve the amendment, using all his powers of persuasion and patronage to get it through. He buttonholed conservative Republicans and opposition Democrats and exhorted them to support the amendment. He singled out "sinners" among the Democrats who were "on praying ground," and informed them that they had a lot better chance for the federal jobs they desired if they voted for the measure. Soon two Democrats swung over in favor of it. With the outcome still "very doubtful," Lincoln participated in certain negotiations never made public to bring conservative Republicans and opposition Democrats into line. On January 31, 1865, the House passed the present Thirteenth Amendment by just three votes more than the required two-thirds majority. William Lloyd Garrison gave Lincoln the credit for getting the amendment adopted.

Lincoln pronounced it "a great moral victory." When ratified by the states, the amendment would end slavery everywhere in America. He pointed across the Potomac. "If the people over the river had behaved themselves, I could not have done what I have."

7

Lincoln conceded, though, that he had not controlled the events of the war, but that events had controlled him instead, that God had controlled him. He spent a great many hours, especially at night when he could not sleep, trying to understand the meaning of the war, to understand why it had begun and grown into such a massive revolutionary struggle, consuming hundreds of thousands of lives (the final casualties would come to 618,000 on both sides). By his second inauguration, he had reached an apocalyptic conclusion about the nature of the war —had come to see it as divine punishment for the "great offense" of slavery, as a terrible retribution God had visited on a guilty people, in North as well as South. Lincoln's vision was close to that of Old John Brown, who had prophesied on the day he was hanged, on that balmy December day back in 1859, that the crime of slavery could not be purged away from this guilty land except by blood. Now, in his second inaugural address, Lincoln too contended that God perhaps had willed this "mighty scourge of War" on the United States, "until all the wealth piled by the bondman's two hundred and fifty years of unrequited toil shall be sunk, and until every drop of blood drawn with the lash, shall be paid by another drawn from the sword."

In the last paragraph of his address, Lincoln said he would bind the nation's wounds "with malice toward none" and "charity for all." Yet that did not mean he would be so gentle and forgiving in reconstruction as most biographers have contended. He would be magnanimous in the sense that he would not resort to mass executions or even mass imprisonment of Southern "traitors," as he repeatedly called them. He did not even want the leaders tried and jailed, though he would like to "frighten them out of the country." Nevertheless, still preoccupied with the war as a grim purgation which would cleanse and regenerate his country, Lincoln en-

dorsed a fairly tough policy toward the conquered South. After Lee surrendered in April, 1865, Lincoln publicly endorsed limited suffrage for Southern blacks, announcing that the intelligent ex-slaves and especially those who had served in Union military forces should have the vote. This put him in advance of most white people in the North. It put him ahead of most Republicans as well—including many of the so-called Radicals—who in April, 1865, shrank from Negro suffrage out of fear of their own white constituents. True, Sumner, Salmon Chase, and a few of their colleagues now demanded that all Southern black men be enfranchised in order to protect their freedom. But Lincoln was not far from their position. In a line in his last political speech, April 11, 1865, he granted that the Southern black man deserved the vote, though Lincoln was not quite ready to make that mandatory. But it seems clear in what direction he was heading.

Moreover, in cabinet meeting on Good Friday, 1865, Lincoln and all his secretaries endorsed the military approach to reconstruction and conceded that an army of occupation might be necessary to control the rebellious white majority in the conquered South. During the war, Lincoln had always thought the military indispensable in restoring civilian rule in the South. Without the army, he feared that the rebellious Southern majority would overwhelm the small Unionist minority in Dixie and maybe even re-enslave the blacks. And he was not about to let the latter happen. The army had liberated the blacks in the war, and the army might well have to safeguard their freedom in reconstruction.

8

He had come a long distance from the young Lincoln who had entered politics, quiet on slavery lest he be branded an Abolitionist, opposed to Negro political rights lest his political career be jeopardized, convinced that only the future could remove slavery in America. He had come a long way indeed. Frederick Douglass, who interviewed Lincoln in the White House in 1864, said he was "the first great man that I talked with in the United States freely who in no single instance reminded me of the difference between himself and myself, of the difference of color." Douglass, reflecting back on Lincoln's presidency, recalled how in the first year and a half of the war, Lincoln "was ready and willing" to sacrifice black people for the benefit and welfare of whites. But since the Preliminary Emancipation Proclamation, Douglass said, American blacks had taken Lincoln's measure and had come to admire and come to love this enigmatic man. Though Lincoln had taxed Negroes to the limit, they had decided, in the roll and tumble of events, that "the how and the man of our redemption had somehow met in the person of Abraham Lincoln."

But perhaps it was Lincoln himself who best summed up his journey to emancipation—his own as well as that of the slaves. In December, 1862, after the calamitous by-elections of that year, in the midst of rising racial protest against his emancipation policy, Lincoln asked Congress —and Northern whites beyond—for their support. "The dogmas of the quiet past," he reminded them, "are inadequate to the stormy present. The occasion is piled high with difficulty, and we must rise with the occasion. As our case is new, so we must think anew. We must disenthrall our selves, and then we shall save our country. Fellow-citizens, *we* cannot escape history. . . . The fiery trial through which we pass, will light us down, in honor or dishonor, to the latest generation. . . . In *giving* freedom to the slave, we *assure* freedom to the free—honorable alike in what we give, and what we preserve. We shall nobly save, or meanly lose, the last, best hope of earth."

33

Shadow
of Defeat

Charles P. Roland

From the outset, the Confederacy was beset with
internal problems: she lacked sound money, guns,
factories, food, railroads, and harmonious political
leadership. Her politicians fought like alley cats;
many of her state officials, more parochial than
they were patriotic, repeatedly interfered with the
national war effort. It can be argued that the Confederacy never became a nation at all, unable in
so short a time, with so many pressures and with a
constitution that guaranteed "state rights," to
create truly viable national institutions. Charles P.
Roland examines "the latent discord within the
Confederacy," suggesting that internal strife and
inherent structural weaknesses contributed
immeasurably to ultimate Confederate collapse.

Victory beguiled the Southern mind during the
summer of 1862 and veiled the latent discord
within the Confederacy. Addressing the Congress in August, shortly after the repulse of
McClellan's army at Richmond and on the eve
of the great Confederate victory at Second
Manassas, Davis said with sincerity:

Our Army has not faltered in any of the
various trials to which it has been subjected,
and the great body of the people has continued to manifest a zeal and unanimity
which not only cheer the battle-stained
soldier, but give assurance to the friends of
constitutional liberty of our final triumph in
the pending struggle against despotic usurpation.

The nationalized war effort appeared to have
brought independence within reach.

But the forces of dissent had not been destroyed; they were merely held in check. Indeed, they had continued to vex the Davis
administration even during its most auspicious
season, though with reduced vehemence. A
favorite subject of censure was the secrecy of
the government. This criticism was justified;
the President often failed to take Congress and
the people into his confidence, and Congress
frequently debated and enacted important legislation behind closed doors. Long after Davis
had sent agents to Europe for the purchase of
military supplies he was attacked in the
Charleston *Mercury* for failing to do so. It had
not occurred to him to inform the country of
such measures. A keen analyst of Davis' character has written that a "fireside chat" by him
would have been inconceivable.

. . . . .

Other measures considered by the President
and Congress essential to the defense of the
land aroused resentment and distrust among
many Southerners. One of the chief of these
was the suspension of the privilege of the writ
of habeas corpus, an action made necessary by
the turmoil arising in areas invaded or threatened by the Federal army. In February, 1862,

From pp. 74–99 in *The Confederacy* by Charles P.
Roland. © 1960 by The University of Chicago. Re-
printed by permission of The University of Chicago
Press.

immediately after the loss of Fort Donelson, Congress authorized the President to suspend the privilege of the writ and declare martial law in towns and districts menaced by the enemy. Suspension of the writ was a common practice in war, one often resorted to by the Lincoln government, but it keenly affronted the Southern sense of individual and local rights. It was looked upon by many as a dangerous encroachment of the central government upon the authority of the states. Davis discerned this anxiety, and exercised with profound caution the power granted him in the act.

Though used sparingly, the habeas corpus act soon was an abomination to the people. On the eve of Federal invasion, Davis suspended the writ in New Orleans to enable General Mansfield Lovell to preserve the city from chaos. Governor Thomas O. Moore of Louisiana promptly launched a bitter protest. Richmond was placed under martial law and purged of spies, traitors, and gamblers by the military governor, General John H. Winder. Winder's methods were insolent and despotic; they vastly intensified the loathing of the Southern people for martial law. Alarmed at the popular revulsion, Congress curtailed the President's power to withhold the writ. Davis subsequently invoked the act temporarily in portions of North and South Carolina, but forbore to do so in other areas where it was needed.

More disturbing than the presidential use of martial law was the proclamation of it by certain commanders in the field. To curb the civil disorder and defection that came in the wake of Federal invasion, Confederate generals in the summer of 1862 placed large portions of Arkansas, Louisiana, and Mississippi under martial law. General Braxton Bragg did the same for Atlanta. Powerful voices of reprobation were immediately raised throughout the South, including those of many former friends of the administration. To the enemies of the government, the imposition of martial law was but another step in the direction of tyranny.

The most vehement of critics were the Georgia triumvirate of Davis' opponents. Vice President Stephens denounced Braggs's action in Atlanta as being unconstitutional; Governor Joseph E. Brown declared it a subversion of the government and sovereignty of the state; and fractious Brigadier General Robert Toombs wrote: "Davis and his Jannissaries—the regular army —conspire for the destruction of all who will not bend to them, and avail themselves of the public danger to aid them in their selfish and infamous schemes." Led by Foote, the hostile wing of Congress heaped coals of wrath upon the President and his generals for their application of the act.

Opposition came to a head in the spring of 1863 when Representative Ethelbert Barksdale of Mississippi offered a bill empowering the President to suspend the writ at his discretion in any part of the Confederacy. Though the real purpose of this bill was known to be the enforcement of the conscription act and the curbing of Unionist activities, it was bitterly assailed as a menace to the constitutional liberty of all Southerners. Thus the foes of conscription cleverly drew support from many advocates of conscription in opposing the most effective act for enforcing it. Foote and others told lurid tales of the oppression of humble citizens by heartless military commanders, and the Barksdale bill was defeated. The Charleston *Mercury* expressed its satisfaction over the result, but solemnly warned readers to guard against renewed attempts to erect a military despotism.

But the most ominous controversy of all was that over the relationship between the Confederacy and her constituent parts—state rights as opposed to national authority. For as the conflict grew in intensity, so did the pressure of the Confederate government upon the several states for centralized control of the full resources of the South. This effort affronted the deep state-rights consciousness of many Southern leaders, who feared Confederate nation-

alism as much as they had that of the United States, and resistance to centralization rose in proportion to the pressure exerted in its behalf.

Early in the war every Southern state government had formed its own army for local defense, with the result that scores of thousands of men and vast quantities of arms and equipment were held out of Confederate service. The strength of these local military forces by spring 1862 varied from five to ten thousand men each. Southern military strategy was crippled by the insistence of state governors on the scattering of Confederate troops around the entire perimeter of the South, thus impairing the ability of the administration to concentrate its forces at critical points for decisive strokes against the enemy. General Albert Sidney Johnston strove futilely in the winter 1861/62 to accomplish such a concentration for the defense of the Mississippi Valley. Only at the last desperate hour, after the loss of Forts Henry and Donelson, was General Braxton Bragg with his well-trained force of ten thousand men ordered from Mobile and Pensacola to the support of Johnston's depleted army at Corinth, Mississippi. This junction made possible the Confederate counteroffensive at Shiloh, in which the Union army barely escaped destruction. A few thousand additional Confederate soldiers would have made victory certain; it has been estimated that at this time more than 100,000 troops were standing idle in state military formations throughout the Confederacy.

The conscription act of April, 1862, was in part designed to bring into the Confederate service these large numbers of state troops, and it would have done so if it had been fully supported by the state governments. But from the beginning it was not supported. Hardly a governor gave unqualified cooperation in the enforcement of the act. Instead, they began at once to find ways of evading it in order to maintain their own military forces and civil services. Sections of the act providing for the exemption of necessary state officials were seized upon as a means of nullifying it or reducing its effectiveness to the minimum. Governor Brown of Georgia was the arch obstructionist; with unsurpassed cunning he sought to render it meaningless in his state. Brown declared exempt all sheriffs, deputies, clerks, magistrates, notaries public, tax collectors, and state militia officers and was thus able to hold thousands of able-bodied men of military age out of the Confederate army. Most of the other Southern governors, though less outspoken in their resistance to the administration, followed a course of action quite like that of Brown. In spite of the vigorous application of the conscription act during the summer of 1862 by Secretary of War Randolph, it fell lamentably short of mustering the full strength of the South into the service of the Confederacy.

Had the prospect of early triumph remained undimmed, Davis probably could have curbed the centrifugal forces that were dissipating the energies of the South. Southern national consciousness and esprit de corps rose during the summer of 1862 with every success in the field. But the wine of victory was soon spent. An overture of liberation from Lee to the people of Maryland fell upon deaf ears, and on September 17 the Union army under McClellan attacked the Confederates at Sharpsburg with fury and superior numbers. McClellan moved with assurance, for he had been providentially warned of Lee's plans by the capture of a copy of his orders. The assault was beaten off through Lee's sterling leadership and the courage of his troops. Nevertheless, the campaign and the strategic initiative were lost; Lee was forced to withdraw into Virginia and await the renewal of the Federal offensive.

.   .   .

The winter 1862/63 and the following spring brought the Confederacy her greatest victories. Twice the Union army pressed south toward

the Southern capital. Twice it was severely beaten, first at Fredericksburg (December 13) and then at Chancellorsville (May 1-4). Lee and Jackson had confirmed their genius, and the Army of Northern Virginia its fortitude. But "Mighty Stonewall" fell at Chancellorsville and the South was filled with sorrow even as her hopes were rekindled by success. Chastened by grief and exalted by victory, the Southern people braced to a still greater effort and sacrifice.

Smiting of the Federal offensive at Chancellorsville in early May gave respite to the South, and again for a moment her leaders held the strategic initiative in the east. Seddon was still primarily concerned with the faltering armies beyond the Appalachians. On December 31 the forces of Bragg and Rosecrans had met in the battle of Murfreesboro, thirty miles southeast of Nashville. After two days of costly and indecisive combat Bragg had withdrawn. Now he was falling back upon Chattanooga, with Rosecrans pressing after him; the important Tennessee rail center was in grave danger of capture. Meantime, on the Mississippi River, Grant was closing the trap around Vicksburg, a position that could not now be reinforced from beyond the Mississippi, since the only Southern army capable of doing so had been smashed in December, 1862, in the battle of Prairie Grove, Arkansas. The double dissection of the Confederacy was well under way. Seddon planned a bold move to redress the balance in the west; Lee would hold in check the defeated and passive Union army facing him, at the same time sending a portion of his troops to join those of the lower Mississippi Valley in a decisive stroke against Grant. Lee objected, proposing instead to relieve pressure on the west by carrying the war to the enemy. Davis upheld Lee, and Seddon was dissuaded from his plan; the west remained the thinly manned and vulnerable rampart of the Confederacy.

On June 15 Lee's tattered veterans began marching north, crossing the Potomac. A great Southern victory on enemy soil might yet draw off the Union forces pressing upon Chattanooga and Vicksburg and induce the nations of Europe to give succor to the beleaguered Confederacy. This hope was short-lived. On July 1-3 the hosts of Lee and Meade met on the deadly field of Gettysburg; Lee's assaults were broken and the gray army recoiled, defeated and crippled, into Virginia. It would not again venture beyond the borders of this state. The day after Gettysburg brought still another disaster to Southern arms in the surrender of Vicksburg and its defenders. The tide of the Confederacy was in the ebb.

Victory and defeat between autumn 1862 and the following summer taxed the resources of the South beyond all previous exigency and spurred the Confederate government to draw into its service a fuller measure of the men and materials of the land. Ten days after the battle of Sharpsburg, Congress passed the second conscription act, authorizing the President to call out men up to forty-five years of age.

This act intensified the old friction between Confederate and state authorities over the control of Southern manpower. Anticipating state hostility, Davis besought the various governors to support the more sweeping policy of conscription and to aid in arresting those who attempted to evade it. He went in person to Mississippi where he appealed to the legislature for its indorsement of the act. Friends of the administration in Congress did the same before the lawmaking bodies of their respective states. Nor did support come from friends alone; some of the bitterest critics of Davis joined in the effort to make the act acceptable. Senator William L. Yancey, addressing the Alabama legislature in favor of the measure, delivered a powerful discourse on the need for centralized control of all the South's military resources; and the Charleston *Mercury* and Richmond *Examiner* supported the new law with their influence.

The opposition was just as determined to

render the act powerless. Notwithstanding that the Supreme Court of Georgia had ruled the first conscription act legal, Governor Brown now declared that the second measure should not be enforced in his state until it had been sanctioned by the legislature. Vice President Stephens again denounced the principle of conscription. Senator Benjamin H. Hill, unswerving supporter of the administration, pled with the Georgia lawmakers to approve the law, and to the bitter disappointment of Brown and Stephens they did so. Brown then resumed his customary tactics of obstruction in order to cripple conscription in Georgia.

Late in 1862 Brown gained a powerful ally in the election of Zebulon Vance as Governor of North Carolina. Vance, like Brown, was sprung from the Southern yeomanry and considered himself a champion of the common folk. A conservative and Unionist before the war, he had supported Bell and Everett in the presidential campaign of 1860. But Vance shared the belief of most Southern Unionists in the abstract legality of secession, and Lincoln's call for troops converted Vance into an active separatist. He pledged himself in the race for the governorship to a full prosecution of the war, and though he received the votes of the North Carolina Unionists because of his earlier record of conservatism, he was faithful to the campaign promise. He was profoundly devoted to the cause of Southern independence but just as sincerely dedicated to the principle of state rights; and he believed that the war could be more effectively waged through state than through Confederate control of the resources of the South. Vance soon took his place beside Brown as an implacable opponent of conscription and the centralized war effort.

The second conscription act contained a provision that excused from involuntary service the owners or overseers of plantations with as many as twenty Negro slaves. This measure was passed in the belief that it was needed in order to assure decorum among the Negroes and maximum production on the plantations. But it wreaked great mischief upon Southern morale and provided an easy target for those who opposed the principle of conscription. The law was vehemently denounced by the small farmers of the hill and piney woods areas of the South as discriminatory class legislation. It was grist for the mills of Brown and Vance.

Desertion thinned the Confederate ranks during the fall and winter of 1862 in the wake of reverses in the field and resentment over the new conscription law. The mountains of eastern Tennessee and western North Carolina and the hill country of Georgia, Alabama, and Mississippi teemed with shirkers and deserters formed into shotgun squads that boldly defied and sometimes killed the conscription officers. Davis traversed the South in December, urging a renewed faith in ultimate victory and explaining the necessity of exempting slaveowners or overseers from military service. He denied any intention of favoring the rich and declared that they bore their share of the burden of war; and he pointed to countless affluent planters and their sons in uniform and to others who wore souvenirs of combat in the form of empty sleeves, lamed figures, or marred features. Many of his hearers were convinced by these arguments, but many were not. To those who doubted, the "twenty nigger" law had converted the struggle for independence into a "rich man's war and a poor man's fight."

The victories of Fredericksburg and Chancellorsville stiffened the flagging spirit of the Southern people and a majority of them accepted Davis' explanations regarding the exemption of slaveowners. But a more insidious and dispiriting influence was abroad in the land; one that the government was incapable of curbing. Inflation was sapping the morale of the South. The quickening of military activities in the winter of 1862 and spring of 1863 bore heavily upon an empty treasury, and Memminger resigned himself to an endless issue of

treasury notes. Congress in March authorized an additional $50,000,000 a month of this dangerous medium to meet the rising costs of war. In an effort to prevent the inflation that must normally follow an increase in paper currency, a second provision was adopted for funding outstanding notes.

Financial distress drove Memminger to an unprecedented step, a resort to the tax in kind. Congress forebodingly complied with his request and in April, 1863, enacted a law requiring of planters and farmers one-tenth of all produce of the current year. At the same time an ad valorem tax of 8 per cent was laid on farm produce held from the 1862 season; a tax of 10 per cent was placed on profits made during 1862 from the purchase and resale of almost all kinds of goods; occupational licenses were adopted, ranging from $50 to $500; and a graduated income tax was established, with rates from 1 per cent on salaries over $1,000 to 15 per cent on incomes of more than $10,000 from sources other than salary. These were heroic measures; the Charleston *Mercury* gave the tax in kind its benediction. But this tax would ultimately become as offensive to the Southern farmers as conscription.

Memminger and the Congress strove in vain against inflation. The funding act brought in only a negligible fraction of the outstanding notes, and by September more than $600,000,000 in paper was in circulation. Government and private citizens alike were caught in the morass of unsound finance.

The swift-rising spiral of prices brought hoarding and speculation among producers, merchants, and men with capital; it brought deprivation and bitterness among consumers and those without the means to profit from it. By late 1862 it was impossible to know one day what the price of food and clothing would be next. Temptations of profiteering were too strong for the flesh to bear; innumerable Southerners ignored the strictures of press and public, the exhortations of the government,

and the pangs of conscience and yielded themselves to the seduction of easy gain. Entrepreneurs bought up and hoarded all available sugar, corn, salt, meat, molasses, whiskey, and other commodities, and manufacturers and farmers refused to sell their wares in the expectation of better prices tomorrow. Resentment among the less-favored classes waxed ominously, with groups of women in some instances staging "bread riots" in protest against runaway prices. Davis personally helped in April, 1863, to disperse a mob of angry women who were looting the stores of Richmond. To the victims of uncontrolled inflation the war was becoming an instrument for enriching the rich and impoverishing the poor.

Inflation brought other problems in its wake. Confederate commissary officers found it increasingly difficult to purchase food as government-fixed prices dropped far below those in the open market. Agents then resorted to impressment, seizing what they needed and giving certificates of indebtedness instead of money. This was often done with insolence and sometimes with brutality; it unfailingly provoked bitterness in the hearts of the victims. The evil was compounded by the contentiousness of Commissary General Lucius B. Northrop, who soon became one of the most despised men in the Confederacy. The newspapers and the people demanded relief from impressment, and Representative Foote denounced the system on the floor of Congress. In March, 1863, the Congress responded with a law requiring that price schedules be regularly published and arbitration boards set up to decide the just price of goods to be impressed. The remedy proved inadequate, and impressment took its place along with conscription and the tax in kind as a major depressant upon the spirit of the South.

If in her hour of triumph the South was sorely vexed, in the hour of defeat she was desolate. Simultaneous disasters at Gettysburg and Vicksburg cast an ominous shadow across

the land, filling the steadfast with foreboding and the timid with panic. Southerners of all classes and conditions sensed the portent of these reverses. Soldiers and their families exchanged letters admitting that the war was lost. A plantation girl who knew of Vicksburg but not of Gettysburg wrote in despair, "How has the mighty fallen. . . . Our only hope is in Lee the Invincible." A Louisiana sugar planter solemnly predicted: "The end of the Confederacy is in sight." Dispirited laborers on the streets of Richmond said that they had had enough of a hopeless conflict. Robert G. H. Kean, head of the Confederate Bureau of War, wrote in his diary that the South was almost exhausted; and again, as if in prayer, "Oh, for a man at the helm like William of Orange, a man of . . . heroic character and genius, . . . a man fertile in resources, equal to emergencies."

The man at the helm, Jefferson Davis, in fact possessed many elements of heroic character, and some of genius. American history records no more unshakable devotion to a cause than that of Davis to the Confederacy. His accomplishments with inferior resources and in the face of unparalleled adversity were worthy of esteem. The British statesman William Ewarts Gladstone said in the fall of 1862 that Davis had created a nation; Northern editors admitted grudgingly that he had wrought prodigies out of the material at hand, though to an evil purpose. Few men have shown more steadfast personal courage and dignity than did Davis in the hour of catastrophe. Nevertheless, he made costly mistakes. It is questionable that the Confederacy would have triumphed had these errors been avoided; failure to avoid them made defeat certain.

Ironically, one of Davis' most grievous mistakes was in the field of his deepest vanity—military affairs. He failed to give the Confederacy a unified command or a national strategy worthy of the national army which he fashioned with foresight and resourcefulness. Only through the timely concentration of a

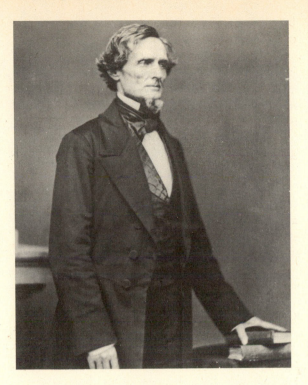

Jefferson Davis, President of the Confederacy. Aloof, dogmatic, and convinced of his own military genius, Davis would not tolerate criticism or disagreement; and he carried on destructive personal feuds with military and political leaders alike. (U.S. Signal Corps Photo No. 111-B-4146 [Brady Collection] in the National Archives.)

preponderance of her troops against exposed fractions of the enemy could the Confederacy hope to win. This principle was never fully applied. After Chancellorsville, Lee ought to have been appointed Confederate general in chief. Instead, Davis continued to perform this function. The nearest thing the Confederacy ever had to a unified command was three separate commands: Virginia under Lee; the Western Department under Joseph E. Johnston; and, after the fall of Vicksburg, the virtually autonomous Trans-Mississippi Department under Kirby Smith. There was deplorably little co-ordination or blending of

forces among these divisions; the right hand knew not what the left hand was about.

Whether Lee would have produced a comprehensive strategy for the South if given the opportunity is open to speculation. He commanded the Army of Northern Virginia superbly and kindled unbounded confidence in his prowess among the Southern people. One may reasonably believe that he would have risen to a broader responsibility, as did Grant in the Union cause, and would have given to the entire Confederacy the rare strategic insight and inspiring leadership that were lavished upon the more restricted theater of operations in Virginia. Such was not to be; Lee remained a mere army commander until disaster was unavoidable.

Davis' personality was ill-suited to the role he was called upon to play. Completely dedicated to the mission of defeating the enemy and establishing Southern independence, he tended to regard as a personal affront any criticism or disagreement with his methods. In this respect he resembled Woodrow Wilson of a later era; Davis found it impossible to compromise a principle, and he increasingly came to identify his own opinion with principle.

Davis is entitled to a generous measure of charity for this shortcoming; few men have ever been more severely provoked to indulge it. Beset by a powerful and relentless foe from without and fettered by the practitioners of state rights from within, he would have been more than mortal had he kept an enduring serenity. Instead, he became brittle and captious, jealously guarding the most minute prerogatives of his position and at times quarreling capriciously with subordinates and fellow citizens over points of military strategy, foreign and domestic policy, and official protocol. These clashes of personality have been explained as reflections of the very nature of Southern society. Planters fancied themselves as feudal lords holding absolute sway over manors and minions. This experience is said to have bred an exaggerated individualism that expressed itself in protest, first against the leaders of the United States, and after secession against the authorities of the Confederacy. The "bitter pride" of slavery had sown seeds of discord among the statesmen and soldiers of the South. Whatever the explanation, this vendetta of egos within the councils of the Southern republic unquestionably reduced her military potency and contributed to her destruction.

Early in the war Davis quarreled with some of the most outstanding generals of the Confederacy. This is not surprising, in view of Davis' temperament and background and the high estimate he placed on his own military insight. His keenest ambition was to lead armies in battle. Once when the Federal columns pressed close upon the South and Davis was in deep anxiety he said, "If I could take one wing and Lee the other, I think we could together wrest a victory from those people." Years after the war when asked by his daughter what he would most like to be if he could live his life over again, he replied, "I would be a cavalry officer and break squares." If without comparable experience or ambition, Lincoln often meddled for better or for worse in the plans of his generals, it is understandable that Davis should do so. But Davis dealt with men whose background and temperament were dangerously similar to his own. They were fully as jealous of their prerogatives and fully as capable of the tedious dialectics and caustic retorts to defend them. Verbal fire between the Chief Executive and his captains often waxed as hot as musketry in the field.

The most notorious of these feuds was between Davis and Joseph E. Johnston. Johnston was an aristocratic Virginian, sensitive of status, and not disposed to defer to the President's counsel on matters of strategy. Ill will first arose between them over the question of Johnston's rank in the Confederate army. He

felt entitled to the top rank since he had held a higher position in the United States army than any other Confederate. Upon learning that he had been placed fourth in the order of Southern generals he sent an indignant and intemperately worded letter of protest to Davis. It accomplished nothing. Davis replied stonily, "[Your] language is, as you say, unusual; [your] arguments and statements utterly one-sided, and [your] insinuations as unfounded as they are unbecoming." Johnston remained fourth in rank and never forgot the rebuff.

Davis was displeased with Johnston's conduct of the defense of Richmond and curt phrases were exchanged. When Johnston was wounded in the battle of Seven Pines, he was replaced by Lee and never reinstated to the command of the Virginia army. Seddon persuaded Davis to assign Johnston to the Western Department, where his behavior only increased the President's disfavor. Davis and Johnston each insisted that the other misunderstood the nature and difficulties of the command. Davis held Johnston responsible and reprimanded him severely for the loss of Vicksburg; Johnston defended himself testily and demanded a court of inquiry, which was never convened. The bitterness of the long controversy between the President and the General radiated to surrounding circles of friends and supporters inside and outside the government. Senator Wigfall was an admirer of Johnston and the leader of a group of congressmen who sought to keep him in high command and clear him of all imputations of weakness or misjudgment. Richmond society was caught up in the quarrel. Mrs. Johnston and Mrs. Wigfall drew apart from Mrs. Davis; and Mary Boykin Chesnut spoke of this hostility as the "woman's war at the Spotswood [Hotel]. . . ."

.   .   .

If the President's disfavor for certain of his generals withered Southern morale, so did his dogged loyalty for others. This trait first appeared in his refusal to bow to public demand and remove Albert Sidney Johnston after the loss of Forts Henry and Donelson. In Johnston's case Davis' judgment was later vindicated; in others it was not. This unpopular constancy is best observed in his support of Commissary General Lucius Northrop and General Braxton Bragg.

Northrop was a favorite mark for Confederate censure. A more difficult and thankless task than feeding the Southern army with the available supplies, money, and transportation would be hard to imagine; Northrop may have done as well as possible under the circumstances, though he unquestionably was an indiscreet and contentious man. The people of the South thought him also incompetent. One would be pressed to find a single favorable comment about Northrop, except in the writings of Davis and the President's staunchest supporter among Confederate scribes, Mary Boykin Chesnut. Mrs. Chesnut wrote disdainfully in 1861: "If I were to pick out the best-abused man in Richmond . . . I should say Mr. Commissary General Northrop was the most cursed and vilified. He is held accountable for everything that goes wrong in the army." Confederate commanders were unanimously critical of the Commissary General; the patient Lee once lectured Northrop sternly on the responsibilities of his department. Joseph E. Johnston and Beauregard considered him unfit. The press railed against Northrop, and Representative Foote once assaulted him bodily in a committee meeting. Davis was unmoved. He and Northrop had been friends before the war, and the President defended the unpopular officer and kept him at his post almost to the end, contrary to the wishes of the entire Confederacy.

Bragg was the most controversial of Southern generals, and the most discredited. History has been severe to Bragg. He was a man of sterling devotion to the Confederate cause and

an officer of extraordinary talent in certain aspects of his calling. As an organizer, instructor, and disciplinarian of troops he was without peer; and the Confederate army had sore need of these skills. Bragg's were the best-drilled soldiers at Shiloh, where, as Albert Sidney Johnston's chief of staff, he did yeoman service in readying the entire Southern force for its first great trial by fire. Assigned later to command the western army, Bragg showed by his campaign into Kentucky in the fall 1862 that he was capable of bold and imaginative strategy.

Yet Bragg's shortcomings outweighed his assets as an independent commander. He was obstinate and fault-finding with subordinates. A sense of discipline perhaps suitable for regular troops was too demanding for volunteers and conscripts; Bragg was said once to have had a man executed for killing a chicken while on the march. Above all, Bragg lacked the spark of leadership to kindle full confidence among his soldiers and the stern volition to drive home a victory. Opposition to Bragg first became serious as a result of the faltering and unsuccessful Kentucky campaign; a storm of protest broke against him after the battle of Murfreesboro. His corps commanders said explicitly that they preferred another chief, and the newspapers of the South were unremitting in their censure. Davis confirmed his faith in Bragg, but directed the commander of the Western Department, Joseph E. Johnston, to investigate and relieve Bragg if he felt it advisable. Johnston made the investigation, but shrank from grasping the baton. Bragg was left in command, a source of increasing contention between Davis and Congress and between Davis and the South.

Defeat in the field and distress around the hearthstones of the South sharpened the as-perity between Davis and the congressional opposition. Wigfall in the Senate and Foote in the House remorselessly scored every measure of the administration for the prosecution of the war. The views of these men were irreconcilable, except for a common hatred of Davis and his cabinet and supporters. Wigfall approved the major policies of the government, such as conscription, impressment, and the tax in kind, but claimed that the war was being lost through the incompetent administration of them. This belief was shared by Senator William L. Yancey. Wigfall was a man of massive frame and tigerish eyes who voiced his disdain of Davis in baleful flashes of invective. Foote opposed the policies themselves, and, if possible, hated Davis even more intensely than did Wigfall. Foote was small and bald and of "colicky delivery," but an implacable antagonist. Together, Wigfall and Foote incalculably weakened the Southern cause.

During the first two years of the war the administration was generally supported by a majority in Congress and was able to carry most of its measures in spite of determined opposition. But Gettysburg and Vicksburg took their toll among Davis' supporters when congressional elections were held in the fall of 1863. The President was too preoccupied with military affairs to lend assistance to his adherents, and the popular mood was such as to have rendered it futile if he had. Many cooperative congressmen were defeated at the polls, and numerous others who had upheld the Davis government earlier in the war now joined the opposition. By 1864 every representative from the state of South Carolina was hostile to Davis; and thus it went throughout the South. The Confederacy entered her greatest trial with Congress and the Chief Executive hopelessly split.

34

Sherman—
Modern Warrior

B. H. Liddell Hart

Thanks to "a welter of conflicting pressure groups and political factions," a Civil War specialist recently observed, it was extremely difficult for the Union to apply "its enormous material and numerical superiority" against Confederate armies. This, along with incompetent Union generalship and a deadlock on the battlefronts during the first two years, explains why the North took so long to defeat a divided and troubled South. It was not until July, 1863, with simultaneous Union victories at Gettysburg and Vicksburg, that the North at last seemed able to utilize its superior strength. The Vicksburg campaign, moreover, made Union leaders aware of a new style of fighting that might break the military deadlock on the battlefields. During the Vicksburg operations, General Ulysses S. Grant threw military theory to the winds, broke off from his supply base, and campaigned south of the rebel river garrison, subsisting entirely off the country and thus maximizing his freedom of movement. William Tecumseh Sherman, one of Grant's corps commanders, especially grasped the significance of Grant's style of fighting. But even more than Grant, Sherman realized that modern wars were won not simply by fighting enemy armies, but by destroying the very ability of the enemy to wage war—that is, by wrecking railroads, burning fields, and destroying other economic resources. As a consequence, says British critic B. H. Liddell Hart, Sherman more than any other Civil War general understood the requirements and possibilities of war in the modern age.

The American Civil War produced nobody quite like William Tecumseh Sherman, the world's first modern "man of war." Not only was he a great commander; he also evolved fresh strategic techniques, and concepts developed from study of his operations had a far-reaching influence in the Second World War.

Sherman showed both the qualities and characteristics of genius. He was tall, lean, angular, loose-jointed, careless and unkempt in dress, with a restlessness of manner emphasized by his endless chain-smoking of cigars, and an insatiable curiosity, a raciness of language, and a fondness for picturesque phrases. But he was a blend of contrasting qualities. His dynamic energy went along with philosophical reflectiveness. He had faith in his own vision but a doubt of his own abilities that could only be dispelled gradually by actual achievement. He combined democratic tastes and manners with a deep and sardonic distrust of democracy. His rebelliousness was accompanied by a profound respect for law and order. His logical ruthlessness was coupled with compassion.

In generalship, he was brilliant, yet what made him outstanding was the way he came to see and exploit the changing conditions of warfare produced by mechanical and scientific developments.

The Civil War started with old-fashioned military concepts and weapons, but also with

---

some very new instruments whose influence had not yet been realized. Until the middle of the nineteenth century, the means of movement had been unchanged throughout the ages. Armies marched on foot or horseback, and their supplies were carried in vehicles drawn by horses or oxen. At sea, they moved on sailing ships dependent on the wind. Even in the Napoleonic era the smoothbore musket and cannon were little more effective than the medieval bow and the ancient catapult. Means of communication were limited to messengers on horseback.

But by the time of the Civil War, new *mechanical* means of movement and communication had become available. This was the first war in which the railroad, the steamship, and the electric telegraph played an important part. Weapons had not changed so much, but the war speeded their development. The muzzle-loaded smoothbore musket was gradually replaced by a muzzle-loaded rifle, which was much more accurate. Breech-loading rifles came into use before the end of the war, and the increasing range and effect of fire made attack more difficult and costly. Troops were forced to take shelter in trenches or behind breastworks. *Tactical* movement, on the battlefield, easily became stagnant.

Meanwhile the large-scale transportation facilities offered by the railroads led commanders and governments to mass at the railheads larger forces than could be fed if the enemy cut the lines. These forces tended to become too massive to be maneuverable. Thus *strategic* movement was also inclined to become stagnant.

The combination produced a state of deadlock—even in the West, where space was wide and appeared to offer ample scope for maneuver. In 1862 and again in 1863, successive efforts by the Union forces to push southward were blocked or paralyzed by Confederate cavalry raids on the rail lines of supply.

A better way of tackling the problem was initiated by Grant's indirect approach to Vicksburg in the spring of 1863. Grant cut off this key point on the Mississippi by a wide circuit eastward and then northward, during which he momentarily cut loose from his line of supply. Sherman, then his principal executive, learned most from the bold experiment, becoming the first commander to show a clear grasp of the new conditions of warfare. At the start of the war he was still conventional in military outlook, but his civilian experience during the immediate prewar years, his unconventional character, and the experience of this Vicksburg campaign helped him to shake off the shackles of orthodoxy.

He could also see the significance of another important change—the growth of population and industrialization. This brought increased dependence on supplies, on manufactured weapons, and on means of communication—among which were newspapers, as well as transport and telegraph. This increased both the economic target and the moral target, and made both more vulnerable. This in turn increased the incentive to strike at the sources of the opponent's armed power instead of striking at its shield—the armed forces.

Sherman's grasp of this is very clearly shown in his letters and in his plans. Viewed in retrospect, it is evident that he was startlingly ahead of his time. Nearly half a century before the development of aircraft, his operations in the last year of the Civil War foreshadowed the aim and course pursued by the bomber offensive of World War II.

The dual influences of heredity and environment can be clearly traced in the molding of Sherman's character and outlook. He came from a Puritan family which had left England about 1634 to seek freedom of conscience and wider opportunity in the New World. The family moved first to Connecticut, and then to Ohio, where Charles Robert Sherman became a judge. Developing a deep admiration for the Indian chief Tecumseh, he had his third son, born on

February 8, 1820, christened William Tecumseh Sherman.

The boy was left fatherless at the age of nine, but he was taken into the home of a friend, Senator Thomas Ewing, who helped him get an appointment to West Point when Sherman became sixteen. The four years there were purgatory, and it is evident that Sherman shared the feelings of Ulysses Grant, who wrote that the years "seemed about five times as long as Ohio years." Looking back, Sherman caustically remarked: "At the Academy I was not considered a good soldier, for at no time was I selected for any office. . . . Then, as now, neatness in dress and form, with a strict conformity, were the qualifications for office . . ." In studies Sherman ranked among the best, but he got so many demerits for nonconformity that he was in sixth place in the final class list.

Upon graduation, Sherman became an officer in the 3rd Artillery, in Florida, and he soon saw active service against the Seminole Indians. His letters to Ellen Ewing, the childhood playmate whom he subsequently married, show how much he enjoyed the excitement of the chase, but they also reveal his underlying sympathy with the chased, as well as his love of reading and of painting, his gift for writing, and his insatiable thirst for knowledge. They must sometimes have wearied a young girl thirsting for a more sentimental kind of communication.

Sherman missed the main action of the Mexican War, to his keen disappointment, through a posting to California, which he felt was a military backwater. But this widened his experience and eventually led to his being asked to return there, in 1853, as a working partner in a San Francisco banking house. He had married Ellen Ewing, and he was anxious to improve his family's prospects, so he quitted the Army at the age of thirty-three.

The boom was already subsiding, however, and many banks soon collapsed. In 1857 the parent bank in St. Louis was driven to suspend payment. That ended Sherman's banking career.

William Tecumseh Sherman, apostle of total war. "We are not only fighting hostile armies, but a hostile people," Sherman argued in 1864, "and must make old and young, rich and poor, feel the hard hand of war." (Courtesy of The Library of Congress.)

He then joined a law firm at Leavenworth, Kansas, where his flair for topography made him valuable in surveying new areas and roads. But legal disputes were not to his taste, and in 1859 he jumped at a chance to become head of a new "Seminary and Military Academy" in Louisiana.

The new post provided ample scope for his energy and organizing power. He gained an impressive ascendancy over the hot-blooded southern cadets and also over the diverse elements among the board of supervisors. His personal popularity was the more remarkable because his brother John, who had been elected

to Congress some years before, was regarded throughout the South as a "black Republican" and "awful abolitionist." Among his most staunch supporters were two of his future opponents on the battlefield, Braxton Bragg and P. G. T. Beauregard, who—by an irony of history—helped to dissuade him from accepting a tempting offer to go to England to represent a Cincinnati banking house in London, which would have removed the prospect of his playing a decisive part in the Civil War.

Sherman's letters in the summer of 1860 forecast that however "reasonable and moderate" Abraham Lincoln might be, in the South his name was like a red rag to a bull, so that his election to the Presidency would make civil war likely—"reason has very little influence in this world; prejudice governs." As Sherman saw it, the basic objection to secession was the danger to the economy of the North that would arise from southern free trade and hostile control of the Mississippi.

On January 10, 1861, the United States Arsenal at Baton Rouge was surrounded—and surrendered—although Louisiana had not yet seceded. Sherman promptly resigned his office, but on returning to the North he was shocked by the complacency that prevailed. Disgusted with the politicians on both sides, Sherman felt inclined to stand aside and leave them to get out of the mess they had produced. He turned down an offer to make him Assistant Secretary of War, and when Lincoln called for 75,000 volunteers to serve for three months, Sherman's comment was: "You might as well attempt to put out the flames of a burning house with a squirt-gun." He wrote: "I think it is to be a long war —very long—much longer than any politician thinks." At the same time, he urged to his brother that "the questions of the national integrity and slavery should be kept distinct, for otherwise it will gradually become a war of extermination—a war without end."

It was only when Lincoln decided to increase the Regular Army and called on men to volunteer for three years of duty that Sherman offered his services. He was given command of a brigade in the hastily improvised force of 30,000 men that marched out from Washington in July to tackle the Confederates at the First Bull Run. When this battle ended in a Union defeat, Sherman distinguished himself in covering the disorderly retreat and checking the pursuers. But as the retreat continued, even his regiments dissolved into the general stream of fugitives, and he bitterly reported that the whole army "has degenerated into an armed mob."

When the President drove round the camps, Sherman pointedly asked him to discourage all cheering, and told him that "what we needed were cool, thoughtful, hard-fighting soldiers— no more hurrahing, no more humbug." Lincoln took the rebuke in good part. When one of the officers complained that Sherman had threatened to shoot him for defiance of orders, Lincoln replied with a twinkle: "Well, if I were you and he threatened to shoot, I wouldn't trust him, for I believe he would do it."

As soon as it became clear that no immediate Confederate advance on Washington was likely, Sherman was sent westward to help in organizing Union forces in Kentucky. He considered that this area was of crucial importance defensively, and that offensively "the Mississippi River will be a grand theater of war . . . I think it of more importance than Richmond"; but he soon found that raising troops in Kentucky was an even harder job than rallying them near Washington. The next few months proved the most exasperating period of his life. His immediate superior collapsed under the strain, leaving Sherman, who took over from him reluctantly, to deal with both the military and the political difficulties.

His outbursts of temper in trying to inject some discipline into the motley collection of volunteers had already led them to nickname him "Old Pills," and he now came into bitter conflict with the local politicians and press. He also had a clash with Secretary of War Simon

Cameron, who came to Louisville on a short visit. Sherman, pointing out that he had only 20,000 men to cover a frontage of 300 miles, argued that at least 60,000 were needed for the immediate purpose, and 200,000 for an effective offensive down the Mississippi—a moderate estimate compared with the strength eventually expended. But the Secretary of War described it as an "insane" demand, and this careless phrase was exploited by Sherman's political and press critics, who now depicted him as a lunatic.

Such a blaring press campaign made his position impossible, so he suggested that it might be better if he were relieved of his command. His suggestion was promptly accepted, and he was transferred to a subordinate place under General Henry W. Halleck in the Department of the Missouri. But the stories about his insanity had preceded him, and he was looked at askance in many quarters, so that his own depression became acute. Relief came with the launching of the Union offensive in the West, which diverted the attention of the press to a fresh topic.

The offensive opened on January 19, 1862, when George H. Thomas broke the right end of the Confederate line by his victory at Mill Springs, Kentucky. It took on full momentum a few weeks later with the capture, by a spearhead force under Ulysses S. Grant, of Fort Henry on the Tennessee River and Fort Donelson on the Cumberland. In the next stage of the advance up the Tennessee, Sherman commanded a division under Grant, and his performance in the confused and seesaw Battle of Shiloh drew a special tribute from Grant to his "great judgment and skill on the management of his men." Halleck reported that Sherman had saved the situation and recommended that he be promoted to the rank of major general, which was done.

The Union offensive subsequently fizzled out as a result of diverging efforts, sluggish movements, and Confederate raids on its railroad lines of supply. But the comradeship which linked Sherman and Grant from Shiloh on, and the intuitive teamwork they developed, bore good fruit in the 1863 campaign—after the too-cautious Halleck had been shifted to Washington as general in chief and Grant had taken his place in the West. Sherman, now given command of a corps, was Grant's right hand in the bold strategic maneuver that, after a series of failures, brought about the fall of Vicksburg on July 4, 1863, and thereby gained complete control of the Mississippi. The Confederacy was thus deprived permanently of reinforcements and supplies from the trans-Mississippi states—with effects more far-reaching than the repulse of Lee at Gettysburg, which took place at the same moment.

Grant's approach to Vicksburg had started in mid-April when Union gunboats and transports, loaded with supplies, ran the gantlet of the Confederate batteries under cover of night to establish a new base some thirty miles south of the fortress. Grant then filtered two of his three corps down there by a newly made road on the west bank of the Mississippi, and crossed to the east bank with little opposition, helped by a distraction which Sherman created above Vicksburg. When Sherman's corps rejoined him, bringing a large wagon train with fresh supplies, Grant cut loose from his new base and marched northeastward on May 7 to place his army astride Vicksburg's line of supply and reinforcement from the east and drive Confederate General John C. Pemberton and his army back into Vicksburg. Although the Confederate garrison of Vicksburg beat off his assaults, its isolation and growing starvation produced its surrender six weeks later.

There was no immediate strategic exploitation of the Vicksburg victory, and the next move was delayed by prolonged arguments in Washington as to where and how Grant's army should be employed. The arguments were settled fortuitously, and in the end fortunately, by

the misfortune that General William S. Rose-crans' Army of the Cumberland suffered in Tennessee. Its southward advance in September met a heavy defeat at Chickamauga, and it became bottled up at Chattanooga. In this emergency Grant was given over-all command in the West, and Sherman succeeded to the command of his army. Grant moved to the rescue of Rosecrans and after a tough fight drove back the investing army. This victory opened the gateway into Georgia, the granary of the Confederacy, and thence into the eastern states as a whole. But in the following year, 1864, the Union came near to forfeiting the ultimate victory that appeared to be strategically assured. For the people of the North were growing weary under the prolonged strain of the struggle, and the peace party was gaining strength. The presidential election was due in November, and Lincoln was in danger of being ousted in favor of a President pledged to seek a compromise peace. He urgently needed to provide the people with clear evidence that there was good hope of early victory, and to this end he sent for Grant to take over the supreme command. Sherman was then appointed chief commander in the West; the "lunatic" now had 219,907 men, of whom about 100,000 were available for offensive operations in northern Georgia. For the coming campaign in the East, the main theater, Grant chose the old direct overland approach southward from the Rappahannock River toward Richmond, counting on his greatly superior weight of numbers to smash Lee's army, or at least to wear it down by a "continuous hammering."

His own "will to conquer," however, did not bring success. He failed to smash Lee's army, while the strength of his own had withered in the fierce battles of the Wilderness and Cold Harbor. The only strategic advantage gained— that of having worked close to the rear of Richmond—looked like a stalemate. The northern people were discouraged, and at the end of the summer Lincoln doubted that he could be re-elected. Yet when the outlook seemed darkest, it suddenly lightened, and in the November elections Lincoln was returned to power. Sherman's capture of Atlanta in September was the saving factor.

There was deep mutual understanding between Grant and Sherman, but there was also a significant contrast in outlook. Grant's success as a commander had been largely due to the way he applied "horse sense" unfettered by the harness of military doctrine and custom, but he had no marked originality of concept. Sherman was a man of vision, but started the war with the handicap of being too well versed in prevailing military theory and tactical manuals, and it was only when war experience helped to break this crust that his capacity for original thought had full play.

By 1864 the difference between the two men became apparent. While Grant's primary objective was the enemy's army, Sherman's was the seizure of strategic points. Atlanta, the base of the Confederate army opposing him in Georgia, was not only the junction of four important railways but also the source of vital supplies. As Sherman pointed out, it was "full of foundries, arsenals, and machine shops," as well as being of great importance psychologically as a symbol, and he held that "its capture would be the death knell of the Confederacy."

In the advance to Atlanta, Sherman's skill in maneuver was all the more notable because, by contrast to Grant in Virginia, he was tied to one railway line for his supplies. Moreover his starting point at Chattanooga was about 150 miles from his Nashville base and 330 miles from Louisville, the main source of supplies. That long line of supplies, lengthening as he advanced, was under threat everywhere from the raids of enemy cavalry and guerrillas. Yet, rather than commit his troops to a direct attack on an opponent well placed to block him, Sherman cut loose temporarily even from this supply line.

His ability to maneuver had been aided by the

drastic way in which he cut down transport before starting. Each division and brigade was allotted only enough wagons to carry food and ammunition, and every man brought five days' rations on his person or horse. Apart from these supply trains, only one wagon and one ambulance was allowed to each regiment, with a pack mule for the mess kit and baggage of the officers of each company. Tents were forbidden, except for the sick and wounded and one for each headquarters as an office. Clerical work in the field was reduced to a minimum by the use of permanent offices in the rear for the transaction and transmission of all routine correspondence. This made possible a severe restriction of the size of the various headquarters staffs.

Sherman's own habit of living "rough" made his troops more ready to follow his example, while his lack of regard for outward appearance and the trappings of dignity strongly appealed to such pioneer types. So did his air of restless energy and constant alertness. At night he would often be seen prowling around the camp with his feet in old slippers, his legs covered only by a pair of red flannel drawers, his tall, spare body wrapped in a travel-worn dressing gown, with sometimes a short blue cape or cloak over all as a concession to convention. He was the lightest sleeper in his army, and by four o'clock in the morning liked to be up and about, thinking or listening—for that, he said, was "the best time to hear any movement at a distance." While his eccentricities endeared him to the troops, his alertness inspired their confidence, and "There's Uncle Billy. All's right," became a common saying.

More forgiving than most commanders where tactical errors occurred, knowing that the enemy's resistance and counteraction is the most incalculable factor in war, Sherman would rarely tolerate excuses for delays in the movement of supplies, believing that, by due foresight, preparation, and initiative, material obstacles could always be overcome. Those who obstructed or clung to the letter of regulations

suffered sharply from his tongue. One officer who made difficulties was spurred to overcome them by the vehement retort, "If you don't have my army supplied, and keep it supplied, we'll eat your mules up, sir—eat your mules up." Later in the advance, when there was urgent need to replace a burnt railroad bridge and the chief engineer estimated that he would require four days for the task, Sherman is credited with the reply, "Sir, I give you forty-eight hours or a position in the front ranks."

When he had taken Atlanta, Sherman took a much bolder course, which carried greater strategic risks but diminished tactical risks. He felt sure that if he could march through Georgia and wreck its railway system, and then continue in the same way through South and North Carolina, the psychological impact of this strategic thrust into the heart of the South, coupled with the material effect of stopping the northward flow of supplies to Richmond and Lee's army, would produce the collapse of the Confederacy's resistance. So, ignoring Hood's army, which he had forced to evacuate Atlanta, he abandoned his own line of supply and set out on his famous "march to the sea" through Georgia—moving with the minimum of transport and living on the country while destroying its railways. Starting from Atlanta in mid-November, he reached the outskirts of Savannah within four weeks and there reopened his communications, this time by sea. A discerning Confederate commander and historian, General E. P. Alexander, wrote that "the moral effect of this march . . . was greater than would have been the most decided victory."

At the beginning of February, 1865, Sherman moved northward through the Carolinas toward Lee's rear. By mid-March, after reaching North Carolina, he heard from Grant that Lee's army "is now demoralized and deserting very fast, both to us and to their homes." Yet Grant's own army was still immobilized in the trench lines round Petersburg and Richmond, where it had been brought to a halt the previous summer. It

was not until the beginning of April that Grant resumed his advance. This now had a quick and dramatic success—retreating from Richmond, Lee's army was headed off and forced to surrender within a week.

Sherman's conduct of operations during the campaigns of 1864 and 1865 showed that the North had found a strategist who had diagnosed the causes of the prevalent paralysis and developed a remedy for it.

The increased facility of supply that came with the development of railroads had led commanders to build up increased numbers of troops at the railhead, without pausing to consider the hampering effect on their own power of maneuver. Thus the first result of the new means of strategic movement was, paradoxically, to reduce strategic mobility. The railroad fostered the expansion of armies—it could forward and feed many more than could operate effectively. It also tended to inflate their wants and demands, so that they became more closely tied to the railhead.

A further result was that their own strategic vulnerability increased because their sustenance and progress "hung on a thread"—the long stretch of rail line behind them, which could be all too easily cut by a small force maneuvering in such wide spaces. The Northern armies, accustomed to more plentiful rations, were more susceptible to paralysis than their opponents. That became increasingly evident in 1864, when, with growing strength, they pushed deeper into hostile territory. In the western theater the precarious situation of such rail-fed masses was exploited by the mobile raids of such brilliant Confederate cavalry leaders as Nathan Bedford Forrest and John Hunt Morgan.

Sherman grasped the problem and produced a solution—the only one then technically possible. The enemy had struck him through his rail communications; he would strike at theirs, while immunizing himself. He saw that to re-

gain and secure mobility he must free himself from dependence on a fixed line of supply. So he organized a force that was self-contained as to supplies, carrying the necessary minimum along with it and supplementing this by foraging from the countryside through which it passed. He then cut loose from his own railway.

Having shown in the march through Georgia how light an army could travel, Sherman now proved that it could move lighter still. Before starting northward through the Carolinas, he sought to convert his army "into a mobile machine willing and able to start at a moment's notice and to subsist on the scantiest of food." Although it was winter, officers as well as men were now made to bivouac in pairs under a strip of canvas stretched over sticks or boughs; all tents and camp furniture were discarded. Once again, as in his march on Atlanta, Sherman took a deceptive line between alternative objectives so that, time after time, his opponents could not concentrate their forces effectively to stop him.

Sherman's flexible organization of his army contributed almost as much as his variability of direction to his continuous progress. Moving on a wide and irregular front—with four, five, or six columns, each covered by a cloud of foragers —if one was blocked, others would be pushing on. The opposing forces became so jumpy that they repeatedly gave way to the psychological pressure and fell back before they felt any serious physical pressure. The mere shout, "We're Bill Sherman's raiders, you'd better git," sometimes sufficed to make opposing detachments retreat.

Sherman's strategy, and grand strategy, foreshadowed the aim that was pursued in the Allies' strategic bombing campaign of the Second World War. But that bombing offensive was too gradual in development to produce a quickly decisive effect, while it offered no such good opportunity for the opposing troops and people to escape from their leaders' grip by desertion and surrender—for it is not possible to surrender to

an attacker who stays aloft in the sky. A closer parallel to, and fulfillment of, Sherman's strategy is to be found in the paralyzing and demoralizing shock effect, on the opposing armies and peoples simultaneously, of the blitzkriegs of 1939–41 carried out by the Germans, who combined deep thrusting armored forces with air attack.

Since General Heinz Guderian, the creator and leader of the panzer forces, has stated that he derived this new technique from my writings, it may be of historical interest to mention that the concept developed in my mind partly in studying the course and effect of Sherman's operations.

This was the first war between modern democracies, and Sherman saw clearly that the resisting power of a democracy depends even more on the strength of the people's will than on the strength of its armies. His unchecked march through the heart of the South, destroying its resources, was the most effective way to create and spread a sense of helplessness that would undermine the will to continue the war. . . .

[Still] Sherman . . . bore in mind the need of moderation in making peace. That was shown in the generous terms of the agreement he drafted for the surrender of Johnston's army— an offer for which he was violently denounced by the government in Washington. Moreover, he persistently pressed the importance, for the future of the forcibly reunited nation, of reconciling the conquered section by good treatment and help toward its recovery. His vision extended beyond the horizon of war to the peace that would follow.

35

Assassin

Carl Sandburg

For a time in the summer and early fall of 1864, Lincoln was certain that he would not be re-elected. Administration critics were railing against the seemingly useless slaughter of Northern boys in the Wilderness and around Petersburg. Others were still castigating Lincoln for the Emancipation Proclamation, portraying him as a wild-eyed Abolitionist who would lure Southern Negroes into the North and bring about intermarriage and mongrelization of the white race. And there were dissident Republicans, too, who refused to support Lincoln's candidacy and planned to endorse John Charles Frémont as an independent. Convinced that he would be defeated, Lincoln wrote George B. McClellan, former commander of the Army of the Potomac and now Democratic candidate for president, and promised to help the general all he could when McClellan took office. But Lincoln never sent the letter. A sequence of portentous events now swung the election to his favor: a "peace plank" in the Democratic platform seemed to hurt McClellan; Sherman captured Atlanta, thus clearing the way for a march to the sea and restoring the public's faith in Lincoln's war policies; the Republicans won key elections in Maine and Vermont; and dissident Republicans finally announced their support of Lincoln. So the president won a second

term, declaring in his second inaugural address that this terrible war soon would end and that he would be lenient toward the vanquished South. Slowly, the war drew to a close: Sherman reached the Georgia Gulf and then fought his way north through the Carolinas. Sheridan's cavalry corps, after burning the Shenandoah Valley, joined Grant around Petersburg. Overwhelmingly outnumbered, Lee took his skeleton army out of Petersburg and headed west, hoping to unite with J. E. Johnston out in North Carolina. But Grant's columns surrounded him and on April 9, 1865, at Appomattox Court House, Lee surrendered. Later, Union officials captured Jefferson Davis and a retinue of Confederate officials, all fleeing into the Deep South.

Meanwhile, Lincoln visited occupied Richmond, with its shell-torn buildings and fire-scarred chimneys. He inspected the Confederate state house; and to the despair of his body guards, he walked through the streets without fear of assassination, as scores of Negroes crowded after him. Back in Washington, he received the news of Lee's surrender with a burst of cheer. At last, "this mighty scourge of war," as he had phrased it, was over. Still, his friends and closest advisors continued to worry about his life; and Lincoln too had strange forebodings. He recalled a vision he had had back in 1860—he lay down on a lounge in his home in Springfield, Illinois, and saw a double image of himself in a looking glass: one face was cheerful and redolent with life; the other was ghostly white. Mrs. Lincoln interpreted this to mean that her husband would live through his first term as president, but would die in his second. Now, as the war drew to a close, Lincoln had a haunting dream in which he awoke in the White House, hearing muffled voices and occasional sobbing. With mournful sounds following him, he went down to the East Room, where a crowd of people were gazing sadly at a corpse. "Who is dead in the White House?" Lincoln asked a soldier. "The president," the soldier answered; "He was killed by an assassin!"

Despite such troubling dreams, Lincoln made no special effort to protect himself. On April 11, two days after Appomattox, he gave an eloquent speech from the White House balcony, asserting that with malice toward none he would try to bind up the nation's wounds. On Good Friday, April 14, he and Mary Todd went to Ford's Theater to see *Our*

American Cousin, a highly acclaimed comedy starring the English actress Laura Keene. At about 10:30, John Wilkes Booth slipped into the president's box, shot Lincoln in the head with a derringer pistol, attacked Major Henry Rathbone with a dagger, and leaped dramatically from the box, only to catch his spur on the Union flag and sprawl to the stage, breaking his left shin bone just above the instep. Crying "sic semper tyrannis" (thus be it ever to tyrants), he dragged himself outside and galloped away into the night. Inside, the theater was pandemonium: screams, a tattoo of footsteps, a medley of voices. In the president's box, doctors resuscitated Lincoln with mouth-to-mouth respiration. They had him carried across the street to a tailor's house, where he lay unconscious. All night the doctors struggled to save him, with congressmen and cabinet members thronging the room and Mary Todd sobbing nearby. Word came that an assassin had tried to murder Secretary of State William H. Seward, that Washington was in a reign of terror. Was it an organized conspiracy? Who else would be killed? Secretary of War Stanton declared martial law, ordered a manhunt to commence at once, and came and went, signing orders with grim determination. At last, at 7:22 a.m. on April 15, Lincoln died—the first American president to be assassinated, himself a casualty of the war, another statistic added to the 360,000 Northerners and 258,000 Southerners who had perished in that conflict. Although he had been an enormously unpopular president, stridently criticized from all directions, now in death he became a national hero.

But what of the assassin? Who was this Booth, this man who emerged to write his name in blood across the pages of history? Carl Sandburg goes back into Booth's past and traces the anguished, tortuous path he took to Ford's Theater on that unforgettable night.

The tolling of the bells began in Washington. Likewise in New York, Boston, Chicago, Springfield, Peoria, metropolitan centers and crossroads villages, the day had tolling bells hour on hour, flags at half-mast, the gay bunting, red, white and blue festoons brought down and crape or any fold of black put out and hung up for sign of sorrow.

Out on the Illinois prairie of Coles County they went to a farmhouse and told the news to an old woman who answered: "I knowed when he went away he'd never come back alive." This was Sally Bush Lincoln, prepared for her sorrow which came that day.

Edwin Booth, the world's foremost Shakespearian actor, lay abed in Boston the morning of April 15 when a servant came in and told him that his brother, John Wilkes Booth, had shot and killed the President. And as Edwin Booth related it to Joseph Jefferson, his mind "accepted the fact at once," for he thought to himself that his brother "was capable of just such a wild and foolish action." Edwin Booth added: "It was just as if I was struck on the forehead by a hammer." To General Grant's secretary, his old friend Adam Badeau, Edwin Booth on Sunday, April 16, wrote, "Abraham Lincoln was my President for, in pure admiration of his noble career and his Christian principles, I did what I never did before—I voted and for him!"

The man hunters and the fugitive John Wilkes Booth were second in national interest only to the death of Lincoln. Who was this Booth? Out of a mediocre fame he had now wrapped the letters of his name with a weird infamy. His own Southern heroes almost universally repudiated him as a madman, one who fought foul. And he was that—a lunatic—a diabolically cunning athlete, swordsman, dead shot, horseman, actor. Now his face and name were published with a War Department promise of $50,000 for his capture dead or alive.

From pp. 717–727 in Abraham Lincoln: The Prairie Years and the War Years, One-Volume Edition, by Carl Sandburg, copyright, 1923, by Harcourt Brace Jovanovich, Inc.; copyright, 1954, by Carl Sandburg. Reprinted by permission of the publishers.

Lincoln's assassination caused spasms of fear and contrition everywhere in the North. Anxious to apprehend the killer and restore order, the War Department organized a full-scale manhunt and widely circulated the reward poster shown above. (Courtesy of The Library of Congress.)

John Wilkes Booth was one of ten children born to Mr. and Mrs. Junius Brutus Booth on a big wooded farm 25 miles from Baltimore. Junius Brutus Booth seemed to be a man filled with a compassion that often shook his controls and ran over into the pathetic, the ridiculous, even the comic. When he died in 1852 his feet had wandered before all shrines and altars and paid homage. He was brought up an Episcopalian; he made it a custom to keep some of the sacred days of the Koran; Catholic priests claimed him for one of their own because of his familiarity with their faith; and in synagogues he had been taken for a Jew when he joined fluently in their worship in their own tongue; Masons buried him in a Baptist vault. He was widely accepted as a figure in American cultural life, the supreme Shakespeare player.

He drank hard and often, and in moods and periods was definitely insane. In time Junius Brutus Booth came to sense the oncoming seizures of insanity and would make for home, where a rare and faithful wife nursed him through dark tortures. The daughter Asia wrote of these attacks being looked on in their home "with awe and reverence."

The son, John Wilkes Booth, had room to play, a 200-acre wooded farm, an oak-floored bedroom facing the east and the sunrise, on the walls deer antlers, swords, pistols, daggers, a bookcase holding Bulwer, Marryat, Byron, Shakespeare. Over the father's dark spells and grand whims, over Edwin's impenetrable melancholy, over the failings of others of the family, the mother and loyal Asia had no such brooding near to anguish as they gave the boy and youth Wilkes. They knew it was said "women spoiled him," that he did what he pleased and took what he wanted and kept his secrets. They saw vanity grow in him—vague, dark personal motives beyond reading and to be feared, projects and purposes vast with sick desire, dizzy with ego.

To the hanging of John Brown went J. Wilkes Booth as a lieutenant in the Richmond Grays. Though he hated John Brown's cause, he was fascinated and spellbound by the dramatic, lone-handed audacity of Old Ossawatomie.

His first stage successes came in Southern cities. As the Southern States moved into secession he moved North as a player. William Winter saw the young star's acting as "raw, crude and much given to boisterous declamation." He delighted in leaps and bounds while acting. The Baltimore *Sun* critic ticketed Wilkes Booth "the Gymnastic actor." There were fellow actors, such as E. L. Tilton, knocked into an orchestra pit while fencing with Wilkes Booth; some had been cut by his sword in mimic duels.

Over a piece of scenery more than five feet high, wrote W. J. Ferguson, he saw Wilkes Booth jump "with little effort." These unexpected feats were accepted as part of a "dashing buoyancy" natural to him. "I saw him, after a rehearsal," wrote Ferguson of Booth the swordsman, "take on two men at once with the foils and disarm them both within a few seconds." In a billiard-hall quarrel Ferguson saw Booth, swiftly and without anyone but Ferguson seeing him, throw a heavy book that hit a man in the back. The man turned, accused an innocent party, and started a free-for-all fight. The lights went out and Booth made his getaway, having had one more of his practical jokes.

In April '61, when Booth played with a stock company in Albany, the leading lady, Miss Henrietta Irving, rushed into his room at Stanwix Hall and with a dirk tried to stab him, landing only a light cut on his face. Then she retired to her own room and stabbed herself, though not seriously. A trifle short for heroic roles, noted Charles Wyndham, "he made up for the lack by his extraordinary presence and magnetism . . . He was the idol of women. They would rave of him, his voice, his hair, his eyes."

From '61 continuously as he traveled the North he spoke as openly as was convenient

for the Confederate cause. In Albany the theater treasurer found him at breakfast one morning and explained that he would ruin his engagement there and put himself in personal danger if he went on talking secession. "Is not this a democratic city?" asked Booth. The reply: "Democratic? yes—but disunion, no!" After which Booth quieted in his talk, though sullen and sour about being gagged.

In '64 when he was filling fewer engagements because of a failing voice, Booth seemed to have a deepening sense of guilt over keeping himself in safety and comfort while the war raged and the Southern cause sank lower. His broodings took two directions. He would perform a deed saving the Southern cause while at the same time giving the world a breathtaking dramatic performance. In August '64 he won two recruits to "the enterprise," as they termed it. Samuel Arnold and Michael O'Laughlin, two former schoolmates of Booth at St. Timothy's Hall, after two years in the Confederate Army, considered themselves "engaged" with Booth as leader. The "enterprise," worked out in their talks, designed the "capture" or "abduction" of the President. Having gotten their prisoner out of Washington down to Richmond, they would exchange him for enough Confederate prisoners to win the war.

Most of the time until April 14, 1865, Booth lived in Washington, checking in and out of his National Hotel quarters, taking many trips on errands whose purpose he kept secret. He studied Lincoln's ways and habits, particularly as a theatergoer. At both Grover's Theatre and Ford's, Booth was at home, receiving his mail at Ford's. The entries and exits of these theaters knew him, every door, corner, hall, lobby, passageway, familiar to him. To the stock actors, stagehands, front-office employees, he was a distinguished figure whose nod they valued.

In November he rode a horse over Maryland and Virginia south of Washington, studied the roads, paths and hiding places by day or night.

To Asia, in whom he had every trust, he gave an envelope later found to contain some bonds and oil stock certificates—and a letter. This gave the key to his scrambled brain, his vanity and self-importance, his desire to show the South that he was a Confederate hero even though they no longer loved him or cared about him. He referred in passing to his plan for making "a prisoner of this man, to whom she [the South] owes so much of her misery."

The letter indicated a "master mind," of a sort, holding sway over a little band of schemers and hopers meeting in a boardinghouse on H Street between Sixth and Seventh in Washington. They included a drugstore clerk, 20 years old, David E. Herold, out of work and seeking a job when Booth found him. Another was a hump-shouldered, scragglybearded fellow, dark, sly, fierce of looks though a coward in a pinch; he was of German descent, a carriage-maker at Port Tobacco, Virginia. Booth's promises of gold brought him in— George A. Atzerodt. Then there was a tall, broad-shouldered 20-year-old athlete joining ox and tiger in his frame, a veteran of Antietam and Chancellorsville, wounded at Gettysburg. In January '65 this youth after nearly four years of hard fighting at bloody salients had despaired of the Confederacy and deserted, happening in Baltimore when he was homeless, penniless, in rags, without money to buy food, to meet Booth, finding sympathy, praise, new clothes and money. This was the man known as Lewis Paine (Lewis Thornton Powell), whose entry into the Seward home had resulted in five persons stabbed and the Secretary of State narrowly missing a death wound. The keeper of the boardinghouse where the plotters met was the widow of a Confederate informer and dispatch-carrier, Mary E. Surratt.

Daily Mrs. Surratt saw her boarders acquainting themselves with weapons, holding vague whispered conversations, telling her nothing definite, intimating they would save the sinking Southern cause. The air had a touch

of terror. Daily she crossed herself and more often hurried to church to pray. Mrs. Surratt's son John H., Jr., at first opposed and then gave way to Booth's eloquence. Just old enough to vote, six feet tall, slender but powerful, blond, with eyes sunken under a bulging forehead, he knew his footing more surely than the others. He quit his job as an Adams Express Company clerk to join Booth. With him came one Louis J. Weichmann, a wavering, suspicious and careful young man who had been Surratt's chum for two years at college when Surratt studied for the priesthood. Weichmann had been a schoolteacher in Washington, later getting a clerkship in the office of the commissary general of prisoners.

Of the two former Maryland schoolmates of Booth, Samuel Arnold was a farm hand who hated farm work, rather lazy, a student of books with an unmanageable vocabulary; Michael O'Laughlin was a Baltimore livery-stable worker, fairly good at handling horses and better yet at carrying liquor. The crew filled the seven bedrooms of Mrs. Surratt's boardinghouse. Some of them subsisted on money furnished by Booth, and all except Weichmann were led and lighted by Booth's stratagems and wildfire eloquence over the glory awaiting them all for their service to the Confederacy.

On at least one day Booth prowled the White House grounds with Paine. And if later statements of Paine to Major Thomas T. Eckert were correct, Booth directly suggested to the powerful young panther from Florida that he should go into the White House, send in his card, enter Lincoln's office like any one of many petitioners—and then and there shoot the President. Booth seemed to have taunted Paine with lacking nerve in this. Yet on Booth's suggestion Paine lurked among bushes in front of the White House conservatory. After a light rain had come a freeze with a crust of ice crackling under footsteps. Lincoln walked by in company with Eckert, and Paine heard Lincoln

say, "Major, spread out, spread out, or we shall break through the ice." Paine in the bushes heard Lincoln telling Eckert of Illinois days once when neighbors returning from mill with their meal bags were crossing the frozen Sangamon River and as the ice cracked when they were part way over someone called the warning, "Spread out, spread out, or we shall break through the ice."

April 8 Washington is ablaze with flags and the North howling joy over the surrender of Lee's army. Paine, Atzerodt and Herold are left to Booth, awaiting his wish and whim. The evening of April 11 Booth is with Paine on the White House lawn near the window where the President speaks. He is shaken with rage at the President's saying the elective franchise, the ballot, should be given to the colored man, "the very intelligent, and . . . those who serve our cause as soldiers." He urges Paine to shoot the speaker, Paine protesting the risk is too great. The two walk away, Booth muttering, "That is the last speech he will ever make."

Events had swept away all doubts for Booth as to his course. He would be the whirlwind dark angel of retribution and justice—this was the fond wish. Never for a moment in the piled and ramified materials of evidence was there an indication that he examined his own heart and studied himself on the question of what was driving him on and whether he was first of all an actor. Until this week, believed his sister Asia, who perhaps understood him through a deeper love than he had ever had to search himself with, he was sane. "If Wilkes Booth was mad," she wrote, "his mind lost its balance between the fall of Richmond, and the terrific end."

In an inside coat pocket he carried the photographs of four actresses, beautiful women as the pictures rendered their faces, Fay Brown, Effie Germon, Alice Gray, Helen Western—and a fifth woman, half-smiling, later identified merely as "a Washington society woman." Whether any of them had intimacy of word

and mind with him so as to know the seething concentrated purpose that swept aside all other passions—the later record revealed nothing.

John Deery, who kept a bar in front of Grover's Theatre, during this April week saw Booth often. Said Deery, "He sometimes drank at my bar as much as a quart of brandy in the space of less than two hours of an evening." Later Deery was to judge of this, "Booth was crazy, but he didn't show it." His theory was that any natural and inherited insanity dominating Booth this week was heightened and accentuated by liquor.

On April 12 Booth writes to a woman in New York who signs herself "Etta." She answers April 13, "Yes, Dear, I can heartily sympathize with you, for I too, have had the blues ever since the fall of Richmond, and like you, feel like doing something desperate." He has enlisted her in some phase of his projects and she lets him know: "I have not yet had a favorable opportunity to do what *you* wished, and I so solemnly promised, and what, in my own heart, I feel ought to be done. I *remember* what happiness is in store for us if we succeed in our present undertakings." She informs him that "the means you gave me when we parted" is gone. She quotes, "Money makes the mare go" and assures him, "I do as you desired and keep as secluded as a nun, which is not agreeable to me as you have found."

On April 14 Booth writes to his mother a letter dated "2 A.M." of that day. "Dearest Mother:" he begins. "I know you hardly expect a letter from me. Excuse brevity; am in haste. With best love to you all I am your affectionate son ever. John." That was all. To his mother, to his brother Edwin, to such friends as John T. Ford and John Deery, no inklings of a deed and a motive for which he is willing to pay with his life. The word "assassin," several commentators were to note, took root from the word "hashish" or "hasheesh," an East Indian drug

that inflates the self-importance of the one eating it.

Between 11 and 12 o'clock of Good Friday morning, April 14, Booth comes to Ford's Theatre for his mail, hears that a messenger from the White House has engaged a box for the President that evening. He goes into action, hires a bay mare for himself to be ready at four o'clock in the afternoon. He calls on Mrs. Surratt just as she with Weichmann is leaving for Surrattsville, handing her a package holding a field glass to be delivered at a tavern there. To the empty Ford's Theatre he goes, seeing the two boxes thrown into one, the rocking chair brought for the President's corner of the box. He inspects locks, bores a hole through the box door, digs a niche in the plastered brick wall.

At seven in the evening Booth leaves his room at the National Hotel. In passing he asks the hotel clerk if he is going to Ford's Theatre this evening. The clerk hadn't thought about it. "There will be some fine acting there tonight," says Booth; he hurries to the Herndon House and sees Paine. They arrange their timing: at the same hour and minute of the clock that night Paine is to kill the Secretary of State and Booth is to kill the President. Atzerodt, run the further plans, is to kill Vice-President Johnson. Herold is to guide Paine to the Seward home and then hurry to the support of Atzerodt. On the street Booth talks with Atzerodt, who has heard of the fighting nerve of Andy Johnson and now tells Booth he enlisted for abduction but not killing. Atzerodt begs and whimpers. Booth storms at him and curses him.

Atzerodt, armed with a revolver he knows he can never use, drifts away, never to see Booth again. Early in the morning on foot headed toward his boyhood home 22 miles west of Washington, in Georgetown pawning his revolver for $10, was a muddled wanderer, one of the only three men in the world who could have told the police beforehand to the hour of Booth's intentions that night.

At a stable near Ford's and close to ten o'clock Booth, Paine and Herold get on their horses and part, Booth to go to Ford's, Herold to guide Paine to the Seward house. At the back door of Ford's Booth calls for the theater carpenter Spangler to hold his horse, enters and goes down under the stage, out of a private door into an alley and therefrom to the street in front of the theater. Spangler meantime calls the door boy John Peanuts to hold Booth's horse. Peanuts says he has to tend his door, Spangler saying if anything goes wrong to lay the blame on him. Out front on the street Booth sees the President's carriage at the curb, a crowd of curiosity seekers on the sidewalk, some of them waiting to have a look at the presidential party when it leaves the theater. The play is more than half over and a stir of voices and laughter drifts out from the windows to the lighted and cheerful street.

Booth walks past the doorkeeper Buckingham and with a pleasant smile and "You'll not want a ticket from *me?*" asks the time, and is pointed to the clock in the lobby. He requests a chew of tobacco from Buckingham, who draws a plug from which Booth takes a bite, as customary a proceeding as gentlemen of a previous generation exchanging snuff. On the street an actor who is to sing a new patriotic song asks the time and the theater costumer steps into the lobby and, looking at a large clock on the wall, calls out, "Ten minutes past ten." Booth opens a door from the lobby into the parquet, takes note of the presidential box, whether there are any visitors. He has seen *Our American Cousin* played and has calculated to fine points the strategic moment for his deed. Soon only one actor will be out front on the stage, only a woman and a boy in the wings. A laugh from the audience usually follows the exit of two ladies, a loud enough laugh perhaps to smother any unusual noises in a box.

Booth goes up the stairs leading to the dress circle, picks his way among chairs behind an outer row of seats, reaches the door of the passageway leading to the presidential box. He leans against the wall, takes a cool survey of the house. On the stage is only one actor. Booth knows him well, Harry Hawk, playing the character of Asa Trenchard, a supposedly salty American character. Mrs. Mountchessington has just left Asa alone with a rebuke that he was not "used to the manners of good society." Asa meditates alone over this: "Well, I guess I know enough to turn you inside out, old gal—you sockdologizing old mantrap."

Booth opens the door into the narrow hallway leading to the box, steps in, closes the door, fixes the bar in the mortised niche and against the door panel. On soft tiger feet he moves toward the box door, puts an eye to the hole bored through the door, sees his victim is precisely where he wishes and as he had planned. Softly he swings the door back and with his brass derringer pistol in the right hand and a long dagger in the other, he steps into the box.

Up till that instant any one of a million ordinary conceivable circumstances of fate could have intervened and made the next moment impossible. Yet not one of those potential circumstances arrived. What happened that next moment became world history —not because of him who did what was done, but because of the name, life and works of the victim of the deed.

"Think no more of him as your brother," wrote Edwin Booth to Asia; "he is dead to us now, as soon he must be to all the world, but imagine the boy you loved to be in that better part of his spirit, in another world." And referring to a weeping nameless betrothed one, Edwin added, "I have had a heart-broken letter from the poor little girl to whom he had promised so much happiness."

And the one man whose sworn duty it was to have intercepted the assassin—John F. Parker? There were charges brought against him by Superintendent A. C. Richards of the Metropolitan Police Force, "that Said Parker

was detailed to attend and protect the President Mr. Lincoln, that while the President was at Ford's Theatre on the night of the 14th of April last, Said Parker allowed a man to enter the President's private Box and Shoot the President." But there was no trial on these charges, and it was not till three years later that Parker was to be dishonorably dismissed from the police force for sleeping on his beat.

Neither Stanton nor La Fayette C. Baker nor any member of Congress nor any newspaper metropolitan or rural, nor any accustomed guardian of public welfare, took any but momentary interest in the one guard sworn to a sacred duty who distinguished himself as a marvelous cipher, a more curious derelict than any during the war shot by a firing squad for desertion, cowardice in the face of the enemy, or sleeping at the post of duty. The watchguards of public welfare all had other fish to fry, and it was to be many years before the dereliction of John F. Parker, a nonentity and as such a curiously odd number, was to be duly assessed.

How did Parker take the news of Lincoln's assassination? It woke some lethargy in his bones. Probably all night long he wandered half-dazed over the streets of Washington, stopping in saloons, gathering the news, wondering, bothering his head about what explanations he could make. At six in the morning, according to the police blotter, he brought to headquarters a woman of the streets he had arrested, her name Lizzie Williams. Parker had decided he would make it a matter of record that he was on the job as a police officer, that early in the morning he was on the job. So he brings in a forlorn, bedraggled streetwalker—against whom he proved no case, and Lizzie Williams was promptly discharged. This was his offering: instead of intercepting the killer of the President shortly after 10 P.M. he brings in to headquarters a battered and worn prostitute at 6 A.M. in a cold gray rain and the sky a noncommittal monotone.

The guard Crook awoke in his home the morning after Good Friday to hear the news, and his first thought was, "If I had been on duty at the theater, I would be dead now." His next thought was to wonder whether his fellow guard Parker was dead. Years later he was to wonder why the negligence of the guard on duty had "never been divulged," writing: "So far as I know, it was not even investigated by the police department. Yet, had he [Parker] done his duty, President Lincoln would not have been murdered by Booth." Crook reasoned that a single guard at the box entrance could have made a struggle and an outcry that would have resulted in the disarming of Booth. "It makes me feel rather bitter," wrote Crook, "when I remember that the President had said, just a few hours before, that he knew he could trust all his guards."

In company with Senator Ben Wade went Congressman Henry Laurens Dawes to greet in the Kirkwood House the newly sworn-in President Andrew Johnson. And Wade's greeting, as Congressman Dawes told it to his daughter Anna, ran: "Mr. Johnson, I thank God that you are here. Lincoln had too much of the milk of human kindness to deal with these damned rebels. Now they will be dealt with according to their deserts." This feeling ran through a caucus of the Republican party radicals meeting that day to consider, as Congressman George Julian phrased it, "a line of policy less conciliatory than that of Mr. Lincoln."

Of the new President little was known, and from the Judge Advocate's office, at headquarters of the Department of the South, Hilton Head, South Carolina, John C. Gray, Jr., wrote to John C. Ropes: "He may turn out more of a man than we hope. Henry Ward Beecher told an officer on the dock [at Charleston] a few hours after the news was announced of Lincoln's death, that Johnson's little finger was

stronger than Lincoln's loins, and though I have heard nothing so bad myself, I can see that a good many think that Mr. Lincoln would have been too lenient with the rebels."

The single event of an assassination swept away a thousand foundations carefully laid and protected by the living Lincoln. A long series of delicate roots of human relationships the living Lincoln had nursed and guarded were torn up in a night.

One question was held pertinent: What from year to year during the war did Wilkes Booth meet that might generate a motive and play on it and shake it with finality? He saw and heard hundreds of men of the educated and privileged classes indulging in an almost unrestricted freedom of speech. Did they tell him anything else of import than that this one man had by his own whim and determination carried the war on through four devastating, howling, bitter years of agony? On the head of this one man Lincoln had been heaped a thousand infamies any one of which could easily inflame the mind of a vain and cunning fool. What was one more killing of a man in a land already strewn with corpses and cripples and famished skeletons in prisons?

The New York *Herald* on Easter Sunday, April 16, editorialized on the press as no factor of enlightenment, no sobering influence at all. It said directly that newspaper editors shared in the guilt of leading an assassin toward his bloody work. "It is as clear as day that the real origin of that dreadful act is to be found in the fiendish and malignant spirit developed and fostered by the rebel press North and South. That press has, in the most devilish manner, urged men to the commission of this very deed."

Party spirit and its mouthpieces, the press, the politicians and orators, came in for blame from *Harper's Weekly*. Directly and indirectly, openly and cunningly, the passions of men were set on fire by "the assertion that Mr. Lincoln was responsible for the war, that he

had opened all the yawning graves and tumbled the victims in . . . Is it surprising that somebody should have believed all this, that somebody should have said, if there is a tyranny it can not be very criminal to slay the tyrant?"

Mrs. Chesnut saw a tide rolling toward her people, writing in her diary: "Lincoln, old Abe Lincoln, has been killed . . . Why? By whom? It is simply maddening . . . I know this foul murder will bring upon us worse miseries."

Sherman on his way to a conference with the Confederate General Joseph E. Johnston had a decoded telegram handed him from Stanton: "President Lincoln was murdered about 10 o'clock last night." Sherman pledged the operator to say nothing to anyone of the telegram. When Sherman and Johnston sat alone in a small farmhouse, Sherman handed over the telegram. Johnston read. On his forehead slowly came sweat "in large drops," as Sherman watched him, Sherman remembering so clearly and for so long a time afterward how one of the greatest of Confederate captains said that "Mr. Lincoln was the best friend they had" and the assassination was "the greatest possible calamity to the South." In the surrender terms they were to sign, Sherman's motive, according to his keenest interpreter, probably ranged around a thought: "Lincoln is dead. I will make his kind of a peace." When later the dread news was given to Sherman's army, many were ready to burn the city of Raleigh to the ground. Logan made speeches against it, other officers intervened, and discipline prevailed.

Now Laura Keene and Harry Hawk and the cast of *Our American Cousin* were in jail, detained for inquiry. Now the gentle sister Asia Booth was taken from her Philadelphia home to a Washington prison. Now the brother Edwin announced he would play no more drama for the American public—not for years, if ever again. Now the pursuit of the fugitive Jefferson Davis was urged more furiously by Stanton. Now a colonel had come to Charles A. Dana's

house early of a morning to say, "Mr. Lincoln is dead and Mr. Stanton directs you to arrest Jacob Thompson." Lincoln had said No to this but now Stanton and a host of officials had no hesitations about drastic policies of punishment.

The fugitive Jefferson Davis wrote later of his dominant feeling: "The news [of the assassination] was to me very sad, for I felt that Mr. Johnson was a malignant man, and without the power or generosity which I believed Mr. Lincoln possessed." *Harper's Weekly* reported: "Roger A. Pryor stated in Petersburg that he believed Mr. Lincoln indispensable to the restoration of peace, and regretted his death more than any military mishap of the South. General Lee at first refused to hear the details of the murder . . . He said that when he dispossessed himself of the command of the rebel forces he kept in mind President Lincoln's benignity, and surrendered as much to the latter's goodness as to Grant's artillery. The General said that he regretted Mr. Lincoln's death as much as any man in the North."

Yet Booth had not entirely miscalculated. A small extremist minority element North and South exulted over his deed. In front of the New York post office April 15 a man saluted someone, "Did you hear of Abe's last joke?" In a few minutes he was encircled by raging men beating his head and crying "Hang him!" "Kill him!" "Hang the bastard up!" Police rescuers took a volley of bricks and stones. A young Englishman, Peter Britton, having had a few drinks, chronicled the New York *Herald*, walked Vandewater Street snarling oaths at Lincoln, saying, "I came a good ways to see the --- -- ----- buried." Rescued by police from an excited crowd and taken before Justice Dowling, Britton was sentenced to six months in prison at hard labor. Police Sergeant Walsh of the 6th precinct, at the corner of Chatham and Pearl Streets threw a knockout blow to the mouth of one George Wells on hearing from that mouth: "Old Abe, the son of a bitch, is

dead, and he ought to have been killed long ago." Justice Dowling sent Wells to prison for six months.

New York, the major draft-riot city, saw more of this tumult than other places. From coast to coast, however, there was a Copperhead minority to whom Booth was a hero. At Swampscott, Massachusetts, dispatches recited that one George Stone "said in public it was the best news we had received for four years, and gave three cheers." Citizens and soldiers tarred and feathered Stone. In most of these cases the offender spoke his first personal reaction to the news, without stopping to think of his community's reaction. The Lincoln-haters at first had no notion of how crushed with grief, how exquisitely sensitive, were an overwhelming number of Lincoln loyalists.

In Chicago on Madison Street and on Canal Street men and boys sent rocks crashing through the big glass windows of several places where a Copperhead saloonkeeper had hung in the front window a large portrait of J. Wilkes Booth.

The North was in grief. Everywhere the eye might turn hung the sign of this grief. The sermons, editorials, talk in streets, houses, saloons, railroad cars and streetcars, the black bunting and the crape—these were attempts to say something that could not be said. Men tried to talk about it and the words failed and they came back to silence. To say nothing was best. Lincoln was dead. Was there anything more to say? A great Friend of Man had suddenly vanished. Nothing could be done about it. Silence, grief and quiet resolves, these only were left for those who admired and loved and felt themselves close to a living presence that was one of them.

On April 21, a nine-car funeral train pulled out of Washington with bells clanging and bore Lincoln's body on a 1700-mile pilgrimage back home to Illinois. Five days later, on April 26, federal soldiers and detectives cornered and killed John Wilkes Booth at a tobacco farm near Port Royal, Virginia.

X To Bind the
Nation's Wounds

36

Black and White Reconstruction

W. E. B. Du Bois

Until the 1930s, historical writers viewed Reconstruction as "a tragic era" when fanatical Radicals like Old Thad Stevens and Charles Sumner attempted to create a Congressional dictatorship in Washington, to "put the colored people on top" in the South, and to turn that maligned region over to hordes of beady-eyed Carpetbaggers and roguish Scalawags who "stole the South blind." According to this view, still popular among many Americans today, Reconstruction was a "blackout of honest government," a time when the "Southern people were literally put to the torch," a period so rife with "political rancor, and social violence and disorder," that nothing good came out of it. Possibly the only good that happened was the triumph of white supremacy, when Southern ex-Confederates took their states away from "the niggers and Carpetbaggers" and put an end to the corruption. From about 1900 to the 1930s, a whole procession of books appeared which advanced this view of Reconstruction, but it found its most popular expression in D. W. Griffith's epochal motion picture, *Birth of a Nation*, a blatantly racist film which eulogized the Ku Klux Klan. Produced in 1915, *Birth of a Nation* played to millions of white Americans over the ensuing decades.

The underlying assumption of the old view of Reconstruction was that Negroes were inherently inferior—they were "lazy, dishonest, and extravagant"—and so any attempt to grant them equal political rights with white people was misguided. But in the 1930s some historical writers began to question the conventional wisdom about Reconstruction, including the anti-Negro prejudice that underlay it. Among these was a bold and eloquent black intellectual named W. E. B. Du Bois, who had been educated at Fisk, Harvard, and the University of Berlin, had participated in the Niagara Movement for Negro rights, had helped found the N.A.A.C.P., and had organized the first Pan-African Congress. In *Black Reconstruction*, published in 1935, Du Bois elaborated on ideas he had already set forth in *The Souls of Black Folk* (1903) and in his memorable address to the American Historical Association in 1909. While Du Bois' new work was marred by a Marxian emphasis on economic developments and class struggle, he nevertheless called for whites to throw out the old racial stereotypes and to approach the period with a more open mind. In his own efforts to do that, he became one of the pioneers of modern "revisionist" thinking about the Reconstruction era. Once science and psychology had dispelled the myth that Negroes were inferior to whites, most historical writers abandoned the old interpretation with its racist tendencies and tried to approach Reconstruction with more critical detachment and more insight into the complexities of that troubled period. Since then, at least two parallel reinterpretations have been under way. One has sought to reevaluate the role of Andrew Johnson in the rise of Congressional or "Radical" Reconstruction. Another has offered a more benign view of Radical Reconstruction itself, contending that it was neither harsh nor even very radical. The writings of David Donald and Kenneth M. Stampp, which follow Du Bois' selection, embody these parallel "revisionist" evaluations of the Reconstruction story.

Here Du Bois himself summarizes American attitudes toward Reconstruction up to the mid-1930s and examines some of the older views and stereotypes of that controversial and highly significant era.

The Propaganda of History

How the facts of American history have in the last half century been falsified because the nation was ashamed. The South was ashamed because it fought to perpetuate human slavery. The North was ashamed because it had to call in the black men to save the Union, abolish slavery and establish democracy.

What are American children taught today about Reconstruction? Helen Boardman has made a study of current textbooks and notes these three dominant theses:

1. *All Negroes were ignorant.*

"All were ignorant of public business." (Woodburn and Moran, "Elementary American History and Government," p. 397.)

"Although the Negroes were now free, they were also ignorant and unfit to govern themselves." (Everett Barnes, "American History for Grammar Grades," p. 334.)

"The Negroes got control of these states. They had been slaves all their lives, and were so ignorant they did not even know the letters of the alphabet. Yet they now sat in the state legislatures and made the laws." (D. H. Montgomery, "The Leading Facts of American History," p. 332.)

"In the South, the Negroes who had so suddenly gained their freedom did not know what to do with it." (Hubert Cornish and Thomas Hughes, "History of the United States for Schools," p. 345.)

"In the legislatures, the Negroes were so ignorant that they could only watch their white leaders—carpetbaggers, and vote aye or no as they were told." (S. E. Forman, "Advanced American History," Revised Edition, p. 452.)

"Some legislatures were made up of a few

From W. E. B. Du Bois, *Black Reconstruction in America, 1860–1880*, [1935] New York: Russell & Russell, 1956, pp. 711–719, 721–723.

dishonest white men and several Negroes, many too ignorant to know anything about law-making." (Hubert Cornish and Thomas Hughes, "History of the United States for Schools," p. 349.)

2. *All Negroes were lazy, dishonest and extravagant.*

"These men knew not only nothing about the government, but also cared for nothing except what they could gain for themselves." (Helen F. Giles, "How the United States Became a World Power," p. 7.)

"Legislatures were often at the mercy of Negroes, childishly ignorant, who sold their votes openly, and whose 'loyalty' was gained by allowing them to eat, drink and clothe themselves at the state's expense." (William J. Long, "America—A History of Our Country," p. 392.)

"Some Negroes spent their money foolishly, and were worse off than they had been before." (Carl Russell Fish, "History of America," p. 385.)

"This assistance led many freed men to believe that they need no longer work. They also ignorantly believed that the lands of their former masters were to be turned over by Congress to them, and that every Negro was to have as his allotment 'forty acres and a mule.'" (W. F. Gordy, "History of the United States," Part II, p. 336.)

"Thinking that slavery meant toil and that freedom meant only idleness, the slave after he was set free was disposed to try out his freedom by refusing to work." (S. E. Forman, "Advanced American History," Revised Edition.)

"They began to wander about, stealing and plundering. In one week, in a Georgia town, 150 Negroes were arrested for thieving." (Helen F. Giles, "How the United States Became a World Power," p. 6.)

3. *Negroes were responsible for bad government during Reconstruction:*

"Foolish laws were passed by the black law-

makers, the public money was wasted terribly and thousands of dollars were stolen straight. Self-respecting Southerners chafed under the horrible régime." (Emerson David Fite, "These United States," p. 37.)

"In the exhausted states already amply 'punished' by the desolation of war, the rule of the Negro and his unscrupulous carpetbagger and scalawag patrons, was an orgy of extravagance, fraud and disgusting incompetency." (David Saville Muzzey, "History of the American People," p. 408.)

"The picture of Reconstruction which the average pupil in these sixteen States receives is limited to the South. The South found it necessary to pass Black Codes for the control of the shiftless and sometimes vicious freedmen. The Freedmen's Bureau caused the Negroes to look to the North rather than to the South for support and by giving them a false sense of equality did more harm than good. With the scalawags, the ignorant and non-propertyholding Negroes under the leadership of the carpetbaggers, engaged in a wild orgy of spending in the legislatures. The humiliation and distress of the Southern whites was in part relieved by the Ku Klux Klan, a secret organization which frightened the superstitious blacks."

Grounded in such elementary and high school teaching, an American youth attending college today would learn from current textbooks of history that the Constitution recognized slavery; that the chance of getting rid of slavery by peaceful methods was ruined by the Abolitionists; that after the period of Andrew Jackson, the two sections of the United States "had become fully conscious of their conflicting interests. Two irreconcilable forms of civilization . . . in the North, the democratic . . . in the South, a more stationary and aristocratic civilization." He would read that Harriet Beecher Stowe brought on the Civil War; that the assault on Charles Sumner was due to his "coarse invective" against a South Carolina Senator; and that Negroes were the only people to achieve emancipation with no effort on their part. That Reconstruction was a disgraceful attempt to subject white people to ignorant Negro rule; and that, according to a Harvard professor of history (the italics are ours), "Legislative expenses were grotesquely extravagant; the *colored members in some states engaging in a saturnalia of corrupt expenditure*" (Encyclopaedia Britannica, 14th Edition, Volume 22, p. 815, by Frederick Jackson Turner).

In other words, he would in all probability complete his education without any idea of the part which the black race has played in America; of the tremendous moral problem of abolition; of the cause and meaning of the Civil War and the relation which Reconstruction had to democratic government and the labor movement today.

Herein lies more than mere omission and difference of emphasis. The treatment of the period of Reconstruction reflects small credit upon American historians as scientists. We have too often a deliberate attempt so to change the facts of history that the story will make pleasant reading for Americans. The editors of the fourteenth edition of the Encyclopaedia Britannica asked me for an article on the history of the American Negro. From my manuscript they cut out all my references to Reconstruction. I insisted on including the following statement:

"White historians have ascribed the faults and failures of Reconstruction to Negro ignorance and corruption. But the Negro insists that it was Negro loyalty and the Negro vote alone that restored the South to the Union; established the new democracy, both for white and black, and instituted the public schools."

This the editor refused to print, although he said that the article otherwise was "in my judgment, and in the judgment of others in the office, an excellent one, and one with which it seems to me we may all be well satisfied." I was not satisfied and refused to allow the article to appear.

War and especially civil strife leave terrible wounds. It is the duty of humanity to heal them. It was therefore soon conceived as neither wise nor patriotic to speak of all the causes of strife and the terrible results to which sectional differences in the United States had led. And so, first of all, we minimized the slavery controversy which convulsed the nation from the Missouri Compromise down to the Civil War. On top of that, we passed by Reconstruction with a phrase of regret or disgust.

But are these reasons of courtesy and philanthropy sufficient for denying Truth? If history is going to be scientific, if the record of human action is going to be set down with that accuracy and faithfulness of detail which will allow its use as a measuring rod and guidepost for the future of nations, there must be set some standards of ethics in research and interpretation.

If, on the other hand, we are going to use history for our pleasure and amusement, for inflating our national ego, and giving us a false but pleasurable sense of accomplishment, then we must give up the idea of history either as a science or as an art using the results of science, and admit frankly that we are using a version of historic fact in order to influence and educate the new generation along the way we wish.

It is propaganda like this that has led men in the past to insist that history is "lies agreed upon"; and to point out the danger in such misinformation. It is indeed extremely doubtful if any permanent benefit comes to the world through such action. Nations reel and stagger on their way; they make hideous mistakes; they commit frightful wrongs; they do great and beautiful things. And shall we not best guide humanity by telling the truth about all this, so far as the truth is ascertainable?

Here in the United States we have a clear example. It was morally wrong and economically retrogressive to build human slavery in the United States in the eighteenth century. We know that now, perfectly well; and there were many Americans North and South who knew this and said it in the eighteenth century. Today, in the face of new slavery established elsewhere in the world under other names and guises, we ought to emphasize this lesson of the past. Moreover, it is not well to be reticent in describing that past. Our histories tend to discuss American slavery so impartially, that in the end nobody seems to have done wrong and everybody was right. Slavery appears to have been thrust upon unwilling helpless America, while the South was blameless in becoming its center. The difference of development, North and South, is explained as a sort of working out of cosmic social and economic law.

One reads, for instance, Charles and Mary Beard's "Rise of American Civilization," with a comfortable feeling that nothing right or wrong is involved. Manufacturing and industry develop in the North; agrarian feudalism develops in the South. They clash, as winds and waters strive, and the stronger forces develop the tremendous industrial machine that governs us so magnificently and selfishly today.

Yet in this sweeping mechanistic interpretation, there is no room for the real plot of the story, for the clear mistake and guilt of rebuilding a new slavery of the working class in the midst of a fateful experiment in democracy; for the triumph of sheer moral courage and sacrifice in the abolition crusade; and for the hurt and struggle of degraded black millions in their fight for freedom and their attempt to enter democracy. Can all this be omitted or half suppressed in a treatise that calls itself scientific?

Or, to come nearer the center and climax of this fascinating history: What was slavery in the United States? Just what did it mean to the owner and the owned? Shall we accept the conventional story of the old slave plantation and its owner's fine, aristocratic life of cultured leisure? Or shall we note slave biographies, like those of Charles Ball, Sojourner Truth, Harriet Tubman and Frederick Douglass; the

careful observations of Olmsted and the indictment of Hinton Helper?

No one can read that first thin autobiography of Frederick Douglass and have left many illusions about slavery. And if truth is our object, no amount of flowery romance and the personal reminiscences of its protected beneficiaries can keep the world from knowing that slavery was a cruel, dirty, costly and inexcusable anachronism, which nearly ruined the world's greatest experiment in democracy. No serious and unbiased student can be deceived by the fairy tale of a beautiful Southern slave civilization. If those who really had opportunity to know the South before the war wrote the truth, it was a center of widespread ignorance, undeveloped resources, suppressed humanity and unrestrained passions, with whatever veneer of manners and culture that could lie above these depths.

Coming now to the Civil War, how for a moment can anyone who reads the *Congressional Globe* from 1850 to 1860, the lives of contemporary statesmen and public characters, North and South, the discourses in the newspapers and accounts of meetings and speeches, doubt that Negro slavery was the cause of the Civil War? What do we gain by evading this clear fact, and talking in vague ways about "Union" and "State Rights" and differences in civilization as the cause of that catastrophe?

Of all historic facts there can be none clearer than that for four long and fearful years the South fought to perpetuate human slavery; and that the nation which "rose so bright and fair and died so pure of stain" was one that had a perfect right to be ashamed of its birth and glad of its death. Yet one monument in North Carolina achieves the impossible by recording of Confederate soldiers: "They died fighting for liberty!"

On the other hand, consider the North and the Civil War. Why should we be deliberately false, like Woodward, in "Meet General Grant," and represent the North as magnanimously freeing the slave without any effort on his part?

"The American Negroes are the only people in the history of the world, so far as I know, that ever became free without any effort of their own. . . .

"They had not started the war nor ended it. They twanged banjos around the railroad stations, sang melodious spirituals, and believed that some Yankee would soon come along and give each of them forty acres of land and a mule."

The North went to war without the slightest idea of freeing the slave. The great majority of Northerners from Lincoln down pledged themselves to protect slavery, and they hated and harried Abolitionists. But on the other hand, the thesis which Beale tends to support that the whole North during and after the war was chiefly interested in making money, is only half true; it was abolition and belief in democracy that gained for a time the upper hand after the war and led the North in Reconstruction; business followed abolition in order to maintain the tariff, pay the bonds and defend the banks. To call this business program "the program of the North" and ignore abolition is unhistorical. In growing ascendancy for a calculable time was a great moral movement which turned the North from its economic defense of slavery and led it to Emancipation. Abolitionists attacked slavery because it was wrong and their moral battle cannot be truthfully minimized or forgotten. Nor does this fact deny that the majority of Northerners before the war were not abolitionists, that they attacked slavery only in order to win the war and enfranchised the Negro to secure this result.

One has but to read the debates in Congress and state papers from Abraham Lincoln down to know that the decisive action which ended the Civil War was the emancipation and arming of the black slave; that, as Lincoln said: "Without the military help of black freedmen, the war against the South could not have been

won." The freedmen, far from being the inert recipients of freedom at the hands of philanthropists, furnished 200,000 soldiers in the Civil War who took part in nearly 200 battles and skirmishes, and in addition perhaps 300,000 others as effective laborers and helpers. In proportion to population, more Negroes than whites fought in the Civil War. These people, withdrawn from the support of the Confederacy, with threat of the withdrawal of millions more, made the opposition of the slaveholder useless, unless they themselves freed and armed their own slaves. This was exactly what they started to do; they were only restrained by realizing that such action removed the very cause for which they began fighting. Yet one would search current American histories almost in vain to find a clear statement or even faint recognition of these perfectly well-authenticated facts.

All this is but preliminary to the kernel of the historic problem with which this book deals, and that is Reconstruction. The chorus of agreement concerning the attempt to reconstruct and organize the South after the Civil War and emancipation is overwhelming. There is scarce a child in the street that cannot tell you that the whole effort was a hideous mistake and an unfortunate incident, based on ignorance, revenge and the perverse determination to attempt the impossible; that the history of the United States from 1866 to 1876 is something of which the nation ought to be ashamed and which did more to retard and set back the American Negro than anything that has happened to him; while at the same time it grievously and wantonly wounded again a part of the nation already hurt to death.

True it is that the Northern historians writing just after the war had scant sympathy for the South, and wrote ruthlessly of "rebels" and "slave-drivers." They had at least the excuse of a war psychosis.

As a young labor leader, Will Herberg, writes: "The great traditions of this period and especially of Reconstruction are shamelessly repudiated by the official heirs of Stevens and Sumner. In the last quarter of a century hardly a single book had appeared consistently championing or sympathetically interpreting the great ideals of the crusade against slavery, whereas scores and hundreds have dropped from the presses in ignoble 'extenuation' of the North, in open apology for the Confederacy, in measureless abuse of the Radical figures of Reconstruction. The Reconstruction period as the logical culmination of decades of previous development, has borne the brunt of the reaction."

First of all, we have James Ford Rhodes' history of the United States. Rhodes was trained not as an historian but as an Ohio business man. He had no broad formal education. When he had accumulated a fortune, he surrounded himself with a retinue of clerks and proceeded to manufacture a history of the United States by mass production. His method was simple. He gathered a vast number of authorities; he selected from these authorities those whose testimony supported his thesis, and he discarded the others. The majority report of the great Ku Klux investigation, for instance, he laid aside in favor of the minority report, simply because the latter supported his sincere belief. In the report and testimony of the Reconstruction Committee of Fifteen, he did practically the same thing.

Above all, he begins his inquiry convinced, without admitting any necessity of investigation, the Negroes are an inferior race:

"No large policy in our country has ever been so conspicuous a failure as that of forcing universal Negro suffrage upon the South. The Negroes who simply acted out their nature, were not to blame. How indeed could they acquire political honesty? What idea could barbarism thrust into slavery obtain of the rights of property? . . .

"From the Republican policy came no real good to the Negroes. Most of them developed

As Du Bois points out, "The freedmen, far from being the inert recipients of freedom at the hands of philanthropists, furnished 200,000 soldiers in the Civil War who took part in nearly 200 battles and skirmishes." The men above belonged to the 107th U.S. "Colored" Infantry, stationed at Fort Corcoran near Washington, D.C. (Courtesy of The Library of Congress.)

no political capacity, and the few who raised themselves above the mass, did not reach a high order of intelligence."

Rhodes was primarily the historian of property; of economic history and the labor movement, he knew nothing; of democratic government, he was contemptuous. He was trained to make profits. He used his profits to write history. He speaks again and again of the rulership of "intelligence and property" and he makes a plea that intelligent use of the ballot for the benefit of property is the only real foundation of democracy.

The real frontal attack on Reconstruction, as interpreted by the leaders of national thought in 1870 and for some time thereafter, came from the universities and particularly from Columbia and Johns Hopkins.

The movement began with Columbia University and with the advent of John W. Burgess of Tennessee and William A. Dunning of New Jersey as professors of political science and history.

Burgess was an ex-Confederate soldier who started to a little Southern college with a box of books, a box of tallow candles and a Negro boy; and his attitude toward the Negro race in after years was subtly colored by this early conception of Negroes as essentially property like books and candles. Dunning was a kindly and impressive professor who was deeply influenced by a growing group of young Southern students and began with them to re-write the history of the nation from 1860 to 1880, in more or less conscious opposition to the classic interpretations of New England.

Burgess was frank and determined in his anti-Negro thought. He expounded his theory of Nordic supremacy which colored all his political theories:

"The claim that there is nothing in the color of the skin from the point of view of political ethics is a great sophism. A black skin means membership in a race of men which has never of itself succeeded in subjecting passion to reason, has never, therefore, created any civilization of any kind. To put such a race of men in possession of a 'state' government in a system of federal government is to trust them with the development of political and legal civilization upon the most important subjects of human life, and to do this in communities with a large white population is simply to establish barbarism in power over civilization."

Burgess is a Tory and open apostle of reaction. He tells us that the nation now believes "that it is the white man's mission, his duty and his right, to hold the reins of political power in his own hands for the civilization of the world and the welfare of mankind."

For this reason America is following "the European idea of the duty of civilized races to impose their political sovereignty upon civilized, or half civilized, or not fully civilized, races anywhere and everywhere in the world."

He complacently believes that "There is something natural in the subordination of an inferior race to a superior race, even to the point of the enslavement of the inferior race, but there is nothing natural in the opposite." He therefore denominates Reconstruction as the rule "of the uncivilized Negroes over the whites of the South." This has been the teaching of one of our greatest universities for nearly fifty years.

Dunning was less dogmatic as a writer, and his own statements are often judicious. But even Dunning can declare that "all the forces [in the South] that made for civilization were dominated by a mass of barbarous freedmen"; and that "the antithesis and antipathy of race and color were crucial and ineradicable." The work of most of the students whom he taught and encouraged has been one-sided and partisan to the last degree. Johns Hopkins University has issued a series of studies similar to Columbia's; Southern teachers have been welcomed to many Northern universities, where often Negro students have been systematically discouraged, and thus a nation-wide university

attitude has arisen by which propaganda against the Negro has been carried on unquestioned.

The Columbia school of historians and social investigators have issued between 1895 and the present time sixteen studies of Reconstruction in the Southern States, all based on the same thesis and all done according to the same method: first, endless sympathy with the white South; second, ridicule, contempt or silence for the Negro; third, a judicial attitude towards the North, which concludes that the North under great misapprehension did a grievous wrong, but eventually saw its mistake and retreated. . . .

.   .   .

The chief witness in Reconstruction, the emancipated slave himself, has been almost barred from court. His written Reconstruction record has been largely destroyed and nearly always neglected. Only three or four states have preserved the debates in the Reconstruction conventions; there are few biographies of black leaders. The Negro is refused a hearing because he was poor and ignorant. It is therefore assumed that all Negroes in Reconstruction were ignorant and silly and that therefore a history of Reconstruction in any state can quite ignore him. The result is that most unfair caricatures of Negroes have been carefully preserved; but serious speeches, successful administration and upright character are almost universally ignored and forgotten. Wherever a black head rises to historic view, it is promptly slain by an adjective—"shrewd," "notorious," "cunning"—or pilloried by a sneer; or put out of view by some quite unproven charge of bad moral character. In other words, every effort has been made to treat the Negro's part in Reconstruction with silence and contempt.

When recently a student tried to write on education in Florida, he found that the official records of the excellent administration of the colored Superintendent of Education, Gibbs, who virtually established the Florida public school, had been destroyed. Alabama has tried to obliterate all printed records of Reconstruction.

Especially noticeable is the fact that little attempt has been made to trace carefully the rise and economic development of the poor whites and their relation to the planters and to Negro labor after the war. There were five million or more non-slaveholding whites in the South in 1860 and less than two million in the families of all slaveholders. Yet one might almost gather from contemporary history that the five million left no history and had no descendants. The extraordinary history of the rise and triumph of the poor whites has been largely neglected, even by Southern white students.

The whole development of Reconstruction was primarily an economic development, but no economic history or proper material for it has been written. It has been regarded as a purely political matter, and of politics most naturally divorced from industry.

All this is reflected in the textbooks of the day and in the encyclopedias, until we have got to the place where we cannot use our experiences during and after the Civil War for the uplift and enlightenment of mankind. We have spoiled and misconceived the position of the historian. If we are going, in the future, not simply with regard to this one question, but with regard to all social problems, to be able to use human experience for the guidance of mankind, we have got clearly to distinguish between fact and desire.

In the first place, somebody in each era must make clear the facts with utter disregard to his own wish and desire and belief. What we have got to know, so far as possible, are the things that actually happened in the world. Then with that much clear and open to every reader, the philosopher and prophet has a chance to interpret these facts; but the historian has no

right, posing as scientist, to conceal or distort facts; and until we distinguish between these two functions of the chronicler of human action, we are going to render it easy for a muddled world out of sheer ignorance to make the same mistake ten times over.

One is astonished in the study of history at the recurrence of the idea that evil must be forgotten, distorted, skimmed over. We must not remember that Daniel Webster got drunk but only remember that he was a splendid constitutional lawyer. We must forget that George Washington was a slave owner, or that Thomas Jefferson had mulatto children, or that Alexander Hamilton had Negro blood, and simply remember the things we regard as creditable and inspiring. The difficulty, of course, with this philosophy is that history loses its value as an incentive and example; it paints perfect men and noble nations, but it does not tell the truth.

No one reading the history of the United States during 1850–1860 can have the slightest doubt left in his mind that Negro slavery was the cause of the Civil War, and yet during and since we learn that a great nation murdered thousands and destroyed millions on account of abstract doctrines concerning the nature of the Federal Union. Since the attitude of the nation concerning state rights has been revolutionized by the development of the central government since the war, the whole argument becomes an astonishing *reductio ad absurdum,* leaving us apparently with no cause for the Civil War except the recent reiteration of statements which make the great public men on one side narrow, hypocritical fanatics and liars, while the leaders on the other side were extraordinary and unexampled for their beauty, unselfishness and fairness.

Not a single great leader of the nation during the Civil War and Reconstruction has escaped attack and libel. The magnificent figures of Charles Sumner and Thaddeus Stevens have been besmirched almost beyond recognition. We have been cajoling and flattering the South and slurring the North, because the South is determined to re-write the history of slavery and the North is not interested in history but in wealth.

This, then, is the book basis upon which today we judge Reconstruction. In order to paint the South as a martyr to inescapable fate, to make the North the magnanimous emancipator, and to ridicule the Negro as the impossible joke in the whole development, we have in fifty years, by libel, innuendo and silence, so completely misstated and obliterated the history of the Negro in America and his relation to its work and government that today it is almost unknown. This may be fine romance, but it is not science. It may be inspiring, but it is certainly not the truth. And beyond this it is dangerous. It is not only part foundation of our present lawlessness and loss of democratic ideals; it has, more than that, led the world to embrace and worship the color bar as social salvation and it is helping to range mankind in ranks of mutual hatred and contempt, at the summons of a cheap and false myth.

37

Why They Impeached Andrew Johnson

David Donald

A native Mississippian, David Donald has written extensively on the Civil War and Reconstruction period. He, too, views Reconstruction as a tragic era, not because "fiendish" Radicals like Sumner tried to put "knavish" blacks on top, but because America "failed to adopt Sumner's principles and failed to reconstruct our whole society on the basis of equal rights for all."

In the following essay, which reflects the "revisionist" reassessment of Andrew Johnson in the Reconstruction story, Donald examines how Congressional Reconstruction emerged from the political struggles of 1865–1867. He concludes that Johnson invited much of that program—and the impeachment proceedings which followed—because of his own intransigence.

Reconstruction after the Civil War posed some of the most discouraging problems ever faced by American statesmen. The South was prostrate. Its defeated armies straggled homeward through a countryside desolated by war. Southern soil was untilled and exhausted; southern factories and railroads were worn out. The four billion dollars of southern capital invested in Negro slaves was wiped out by advancing Union armies, "the most stupendous act of sequestration in the history of Anglo-American jurisprudence." The white inhabitants of eleven states had somehow to be reclaimed from rebellion and restored to a firm loyalty to the United States. Their four million former slaves had simultaneously to be guided into a proper use of their new-found freedom.

For the victorious Union government there was no time for reflection. Immediate decisions had to be made. Thousands of destitute whites and Negroes had to be fed before long-range plans of rebuilding the southern economy could be drafted. Some kind of government had to be established in these former Confederate states, to preserve order and to direct the work of restoration.

A score of intricate questions must be answered: Should the defeated southerners be punished or pardoned? How should genuinely loyal southern Unionists be rewarded? What was to be the social, economic, and political status of the now free Negroes? What civil rights did they have? Ought they to have the ballot? Should they be given a freehold of property? Was Reconstruction to be controlled by the national government, or should the southern states work out their own salvation? If the federal government supervised the process, should the President or the Congress be in control?

Intricate as were the problems, in early April, 1865, they did not seem insuperable. President Abraham Lincoln was winning the peace as he had already won the war. He was

From "Why They Impeached Andrew Johnson" by David Donald. Copyright © 1956 by American Heritage Publishing Co., Inc. Reprinted by permission from *American Heritage*, December 1956, pp. 21–25, 102–103.

careful to keep every detail of Reconstruction in his own hands; unwilling to be committed to any "exclusive, and inflexible plan," he was working out a pragmatic program of restoration not, perhaps, entirely satisfactory to any group, but reasonably acceptable to all sections. With his enormous prestige as commander of the victorious North and as victor in the 1864 election, he was able to promise freedom to the Negro, charity to the southern white, security to the North.

The blighting of these auspicious beginnings is one of the saddest stories in American history. The reconciliation of the sections, which seemed so imminent in 1865, was delayed for more than ten years. Northern magnanimity toward a fallen foe curdled into bitter distrust. Southern whites rejected moderate leaders, and inveterate racists spoke for the new South. The Negro, after serving as a political pawn for a decade, was relegated to a second-class citizenship, from which he is yet struggling to emerge. Rarely has democratic government so completely failed as during the Reconstruction decade.

The responsibility for this collapse of American statesmanship is, of course, complex. History is not a tale of deep-dyed villains or pure-as-snow heroes. Part of the blame must fall upon ex-Confederates who refused to recognize that the war was over; part upon freedmen who confused liberty with license and the ballot box with the lunch pail; part upon northern anti-slavery extremists who identified patriotism with loyalty to the Republican party; part upon the land speculators, treasury grafters, and railroad promoters who were unwilling to have a genuine peace lest it end their looting of the public till.

Yet these divisive forces were not bound to triumph. Their success was due to the failure of constructive statesmanship that could channel the magnanimous feelings shared by most Americans into a positive program of reconstruction. President Andrew Johnson was called upon for positive leadership, and he did not meet the challenge.

Andrew Johnson's greatest weakness was his insensitivity to public opinion. In contrast to Lincoln, who said, "Public opinion in this country is everything," Johnson made a career of battling the popular will. A poor white, a runaway tailor's apprentice, a self-educated Tennessee politician, Johnson was a living defiance to the dominant southern belief that leadership belonged to the plantation aristocracy.

As senator from Tennessee, he defied the sentiment of his section in 1861 and refused to join the secessionist movement. When Lincoln later appointed him military governor of occupied Tennessee, Johnson found Nashville "a furnace of treason," but he braved social ostracism and threats of assassination and discharged his duties with boldness and efficiency.

Such a man was temperamentally unable to understand the northern mood in 1865, much less to yield to it. For four years the northern people had been whipped into wartime frenzy by propaganda tales of Confederate atrocities. The assassination of Lincoln by a southern sympathizer confirmed their belief in southern brutality and heartlessness. Few northerners felt vindictive toward the South, but most felt that the rebellion they had crushed must never rise again. Johnson ignored this postwar psychosis gripping the North and plunged ahead with his program of rapidly restoring the southern states to the Union. In May, 1865, without any previous preparation of public opinion, he issued a proclamation of amnesty, granting forgiveness to nearly all the millions of former rebels and welcoming them back into peaceful fraternity. Some few Confederate leaders were excluded from his general amnesty, but even they could secure pardon by special petition. For weeks the White House corridors were thronged with ex-Confederate

statesmen and former southern generals who daily received presidential forgiveness.

Ignoring public opinion by pardoning the former Confederates, Johnson actually entrusted the formation of new governments in the South to them. The provisional governments established by the President proceeded, with a good deal of reluctance, to rescind their secession ordinances, to abolish slavery, and to repudiate the Confederate debt. Then, with far more enthusiasm, they turned to electing governors, representatives, and senators. By December, 1865, the southern states had their delegations in Washington waiting for admission by Congress. Alexander H. Stephens, once vice president of the Confederacy, was chosen senator from Georgia; not one of the North Carolina delegation could take a loyalty oath; and all of South Carolina's congressmen had "either held office under the Confederate States, or been in the army, or countenanced in some way the Rebellion."

Johnson himself was appalled. "There seems in many of the elections something like defiance, which is all out of place at this time," he protested. Yet on December 5 he strongly urged the Congress to seat these southern representatives "and thereby complete the work of reconstruction." But the southern states were omitted from the roll call.

Such open defiance of northern opinion was dangerous under the best of circumstances, but in Johnson's case it was little more than suicidal. The President seemed not to realize the weakness of his position. He was the representative of no major interest and had no genuine political following. He had been considered for the vice presidency in 1864 because, as a southerner and a former slaveholder, he could lend plausibility to the Republican pretension that the old parties were dead and that Lincoln was the nominee of a new, nonsectional National Union party.

A political accident, the new Vice President did little to endear himself to his countrymen. At Lincoln's second inauguration Johnson appeared before the Senate in an obviously inebriated state and made a long, intemperate harangue about his plebeian origins and his hard-won success. President, Cabinet, and senators were humiliated by the shameful display, and Charles Sumner felt that "the Senate should call upon him to resign." Historians now know that Andrew Johnson was not a heavy drinker. At the time of his inaugural display, he was just recovering from a severe attack of typhoid fever. Feeling ill just before he entered the Senate chamber, he asked for some liquor to steady his nerves, and either his weakened condition or abnormal sensitivity to alcohol betrayed him.

Lincoln reassured Republicans who were worried over the affair: "I have known Andy for many years; he made a bad slip the other day, but you need not be scared. Andy ain't a drunkard." Never again was Andrew Johnson seen under the influence of alcohol, but his reformation came too late. His performance on March 4, 1865, seriously undermined his political usefulness and permitted his opponents to discredit him as a pothouse politician. Johnson was catapulted into the presidency by John Wilkes Booth's bullet. From the outset his position was weak, but it was not necessarily untenable. The President's chronic lack of discretion made it so. Where common sense dictated that a chief executive in so disadvantageous a position should act with great caution, Johnson proceeded to imitate Old Hickory, Andrew Jackson, his political idol. If Congress crossed his will, he did not hesitate to defy it. Was he not "the Tribune of the People"?

Sure of his rectitude, Johnson was indifferent to prudence. He never learned that the President of the United States cannot afford to be a quarreler. Apprenticed in the rough-and-tumble politics of frontier Tennessee, where orators exchanged violent personalities, crude humor, and bitter denunciations, Johnson continued to make stump speeches from the White House. All too often he spoke extemporaneously, and he permitted hecklers in his audience

to draw from him angry charges against his critics.

On Washington's birthday in 1866, against the advice of his more sober advisers, the President made an impromptu address to justify his Reconstruction policy. "I fought traitors and treason in the South," he told the crowd; "now when I turn around, and at the other end of the line find men—I care not by what name you call them—who will stand opposed to the restoration of the Union of these States, I am free to say to you that I am still in the field."

During the "great applause" which followed, a nameless voice shouted, "Give us the names at the other end. . . . Who are they?"

"You ask me who they are," Johnson retorted. "I say Thaddeus Stevens of Pennsylvania is one; I say Mr. Sumner is another; and Wendell Phillips is another." Increasing applause urged him to continue. "Are those who want to destroy our institutions . . . not satisfied with the blood that has been shed? . . . Does not the blood of Lincoln appease the vengeance and wrath of the opponents of this government?"

The President's remarks were as untrue as they were impolitic. Not only was it manifestly false to assert that the leading Republican in the House and the most conspicuous Republican in the Senate were opposed to "the fundamental principles of this government" or that they had been responsible for Lincoln's assassination; it was incredible political folly to impute such actions to men with whom the President had to work daily. But Andrew Johnson never learned that the President of the United States must function as a party leader.

There was a temperamental coldness about this plain-featured, grave man that kept him from easy, intimate relations with even his political supporters. His massive head, dark, luxuriant hair, deep-set and piercing eyes, and cleft square chin seemed to Charles Dickens to indicate "courage, watchfulness, and certainly strength of purpose," but his was a grim face,

with "no genial sunlight in it." The coldness and reserve that marked Johnson's public associations doubtless stemmed from a deep-seated feeling of insecurity; this self-educated tailor whose wife had taught him how to write could never expose himself by letting down his guard and relaxing.

Johnson knew none of the arts of managing men, and he seemed unaware that face-saving is important for a politician. When he became President, Johnson was besieged by advisers of all political complexions. To each he listened gravely and non-committally, raising no questions and by his silence seeming to give consent. With Radical Senator Sumner, already intent upon giving the freedmen both homesteads and the ballot, he had repeated interviews during the first month of his presidency. "His manner has been excellent, & even sympathetic," Sumner reported triumphantly. With Chief Justice Salmon P. Chase, Sumner urged Johnson to support immediate Negro suffrage and found the President was "well-disposed, & sees the rights & necessities of the case." In the middle of May, 1865, Sumner reassured a Republican caucus that the President was a true Radical; he had listened repeatedly to the Senator and had told him "there is no difference between us." Before the end of the month the rug was pulled from under Sumner's feet. Johnson issued his proclamation for the reconstruction of North Carolina, making no provisions for Negro suffrage. Sumner first learned about it through the newspapers.

While he was making up his mind, Johnson appeared silently receptive to all ideas; when he had made a decision, his mind was immovably closed, and he defended his course with all the obstinacy of a weak man. In December, alarmed by Johnson's Reconstruction proclamations, Sumner again sought an interview with the President. "No longer sympathetic, or even kindly," Sumner found, "he was harsh, petulant, and unreasonable." The Senator was depressed by Johnson's "prejudice, ignorance, and perversity" on the Negro suf-

frage issue. Far from listening amiably to Sumner's argument that the South was still torn by violence and not yet ready for readmission, Johnson attacked him with cheap analogies. "Are there no murders in Massachusetts?" the President asked.

"Unhappily yes," Sumner replied, "sometimes."

"Are there no assaults in Boston? Do not men there sometimes knock each other down, so that the police is obliged to interfere?"

"Unhappily yes."

"Would you consent that Massachusetts, on this account, should be excluded from Congress?" Johnson triumphantly queried. In the excitement of the argument, the President unconsciously used Sumner's hat, which the Senator had placed on the floor beside his chair, as a spittoon!

Had Johnson been as resolute in action as he was in argument, he might conceivably have carried much of his party with him on his Reconstruction program. Promptness, publicity, and persuasion could have created a presidential following. Instead Johnson boggled. Though he talked boastfully of "kicking out" officers who failed to support his plan, he was slow to act. His own Cabinet, from the very beginning, contained members who disagreed with him, and his secretary of war, Edwin M. Stanton, was openly in league with the Republican elements most hostile to the President. For more than two years he impotently hoped that Stanton would resign; then in 1867, after Congress had passed the Tenure of Office Act, he tried to oust the Secretary. This belated firmness, against the letter of the law, led directly to Johnson's impeachment trial.

Instead of working with his party leaders and building up political support among Republicans, Johnson in 1866 undertook to organize his friends into a new party. In August a convention of white southerners, northern Democrats, moderate Republicans, and presidential appointees assembled in Philadelphia to endorse Johnson's policy. Union General Darius Couch of Massachusetts marched arm in arm down the convention aisle with Governor James L. Orr of South Carolina, to symbolize the states reunited under Johnson's rule. The convention produced fervid oratory, a dignified statement of principles—but not much else. Like most third-party reformist movements it lacked local support and grass-roots organization.

Johnson himself was unable to breathe life into his stillborn third party. Deciding to take his case to the people, he accepted an invitation to speak at a great Chicago memorial honoring Stephen A. Douglas. When his special train left Washington on August 28 for a "swing around the circle," the President was accompanied by a few Cabinet members who shared his views and by the war heroes Grant and Farragut.

At first all went well. There were some calculated political snubs to the President, but he managed at Philadelphia, New York, and Albany to present his ideas soberly and cogently to the people. But Johnson's friends were worried lest his tongue again get out of control. "In all frankness," a senator wrote him, do not "allow the excitement of the moment to draw from you any *extemporaneous speeches*."

At St. Louis, when a Radical voice shouted that Johnson was a "Judas," the President flamed up in rage. "There was a Judas and he was one of the twelve apostles," he retorted. ". . . . The twelve apostles had a Christ. . . . If I have played the Judas, who has been my Christ that I have played the Judas with? Was it Thad Stevens? Was it Wendell Phillips? Was it Charles Sumner?" Over mingled hisses and applause, he shouted, "These are the men that stop and compare themselves with the Saviour; and everybody that differs with them . . . is to be denounced as a Judas."

Johnson had played into his enemies' hands. His Radical foes denounced him as a "trick-

Republican congressmen who managed the impeachment of Andrew Johnson in 1868. Back row (left to right): James F. Wilson, George S. Boutwell, and John A. Logan. Front row (left to right): Benjamin F. Butler, Thaddeus Stevens, Thomas Williams, and John A. Bingham. Photograph by Matthew Brady. (U.S. Signal Corps Photo No. 111-B-4371 [Brady Collection] in the National Archives.)

ster," a "culprit," a man "touched with insanity, corrupted with lust, stimulated with drink." More serious in consequence was the reaction of northern moderates, such as James Russell Lowell, who wrote, "What an anti-Johnson lecturer we have in Johnson! Sumner has been right about the *cuss* from the first. . . ." The fall elections were an over-whelming repudiation of the President and his Reconstruction policy.

Johnson's want of political sagacity strengthened the very elements in the Republican party which he most feared. In 1865 the Republicans had no clearly defined attitude toward Reconstruction. Moderates like Gideon Welles and Orville Browning wanted to see the southern

states restored with a minimum of restrictions; Radicals like Sumner and Stevens demanded that the entire southern social system be revolutionized. Some Republicans were passionately concerned with the plight of the freedmen; others were more interested in maintaining the high tariff and land grant legislation enacted during the war. Many thought mostly of keeping themselves in office, and many genuinely believed, with Sumner, that "the Republican party, in its objects, is identical with country and with mankind." These diverse elements came slowly to adopt the idea of harsh Reconstruction, but Johnson's stubborn persistency in his policy left them no alternative. Every step the President took seemed to provide "a new encouragement to (1) the rebels at the South, (2) the Democrats at the North and (3) the discontented elements everywhere." Not many Republicans would agree with Sumner that Johnson's program was "a defiance to God and Truth," but there was genuine concern that the victory won by the war was being frittered away.

The provisional governments established by the President in the South seemed to be dubiously loyal. They were reluctant to rescind their secession ordinances and to repudiate the Confederate debt, and they chose high-ranking ex-Confederates to represent them in Congress. Northerners were even more alarmed when these southern governments began to legislate upon the Negro's civil rights. Some laws were necessary—in order to give former slaves the right to marry, to hold property, to sue and be sued, and the like—but the Johnson legislatures went far beyond these immediate needs. South Carolina, for example, enacted that no Negro could pursue the trade "of an artisan, mechanic, or shopkeeper, or any other trade or employment besides that of husbandry" without a special license. Alabama provided that "any stubborn or refractory servants" or "servants who loiter away their time" should be fined $50 and, if they could not pay, be hired out for six months' labor. Mississippi ordered that every Negro under eighteen years of age who was an orphan or not supported by his parents must be apprenticed to some white person, preferably the former owner of the slave. Such southern laws indicated a determination to keep the Negro in a state of peonage.

It was impossible to expect a newly emancipated race to be content with such a limping freedom. The thousands of Negroes who had served in the Union armies and had helped conquer their former Confederate masters were not willing to abandon their new-found liberty. In rural areas southern whites kept these Negroes under control through the Ku Klux Klan. But in southern cities white hegemony was less secure, and racial friction erupted in mob violence. In May, 1866, a quarrel between a Memphis Negro and a white teamster led to a riot in which the city police and the poor whites raided the Negro quarters and burned and killed promiscuously. Far more serious was the disturbance in New Orleans two months later. The Republican party in Louisiana was split into pro-Johnson conservatives and Negro suffrage advocates. The latter group determined to hold a constitutional convention, of dubious legality, in New Orleans, in order to secure the ballot for the free men and the offices for themselves. Through imbecility in the War Department, the Federal troops occupying the city were left without orders, and the mayor of New Orleans, strongly opposed to Negro equality, had the responsibility for preserving order. There were acts of provocation on both sides, and finally, on July 30, a procession of Negroes marching toward the convention hall was attacked.

"A shot was fired . . . by a policeman, or some colored man in the procession," General Philip Sheridan reported. "This led to other shots, and a rush after the procession. On arrival at the front of the Institute [where the convention met], there was some throwing of brick-bats by both sides. The police . . . were vigorously marched to the scene of disorder. The procession entered the Institute with the

flag, about six or eight remaining outside. A row occurred between a policeman and one of these colored men, and a shot was again fired by one of the parties, which led to an indiscriminate firing on the building, through the windows, by the policemen.

"This had been going on for a short time, when a white flag was displayed from the windows of the Institute, whereupon the firing ceased and the police rushed into the building. . . . The policemen opened an indiscriminate fire upon the audience until they had emptied their revolvers, when they retired, and those inside barricaded the doors. The door was broken in, and the firing again commenced when many of the colored and white people either escaped out of the door, or were passed out by the policemen inside, but as they came out, the policemen who formed the circle nearest the building fired upon them, and they were again fired upon by the citizens that formed the outer circle."

Thirty-seven Negroes and three of their white friends were killed; 119 Negroes and seventeen of their white sympathizers were wounded. Of their assailants, ten were wounded and but one killed. President Johnson was, of course, horrified by these outbreaks, but the Memphis and New Orleans riots, together with the Black Codes, afforded a devastating illustration of how the President's policy actually operated. The southern states, it was clear, were not going to protect the Negroes' basic rights. They were only grudgingly going to accept the results of the war. Yet, with Johnson's blessing, these same states were expecting a stronger voice in Congress than ever. Before 1860, southern representation in Congress had been based upon the white population plus three fifths of the slaves; now the Negroes, though not permitted to vote, were to be counted like all other citizens, and southern states would be entitled to at least nine additional congressmen. Joining with the northern Copperheads, the southerners could easily regain at the next presidential election

all that had been lost on the Civil War battlefield.

It was this political exigency, not misguided sentimentality nor vindictiveness, which united Republicans in opposition to the President.

Johnson's defenders have pictured Radical Reconstruction as the work of a fanatical minority, led by Sumner and Stevens, who drove their reluctant colleagues into adopting coercive measures against the South. In fact, every major piece of Radical legislation was adopted by the nearly unanimous vote of the entire Republican membership of Congress. Andrew Johnson had left them no other choice. Because he insisted upon rushing Confederate-dominated states back into the Union, Republicans moved to disqualify Confederate leaders under the Fourteenth Amendment. When, through Johnson's urging, the southern states rejected that amendment, the Republicans in Congress unwillingly came to see Negro suffrage as the only counterweight against Democratic majorities in the South. With the Reconstruction Acts of 1867 the way was open for a true Radical program toward the South, harsh and thorough.

Andrew Johnson became a cipher in the White House, futilely disapproving bills which were promptly passed over his veto. Through his failure to reckon with public opinion, his unwillingness to recognize his weak position, his inability to function as a party leader, he had sacrificed all influence with the party which had elected him and had turned over its control to Radicals vindictively opposed to his policies. In March, 1868, Andrew Johnson was summoned before the Senate of the United States to be tried on eleven accusations of high crimes and misdemeanors. By a narrow margin the Senate failed to convict him, and historians have dismissed the charges as flimsy and false. Yet perhaps before the bar of history itself Andrew Johnson must be impeached with an even graver charge—that through political ineptitude he threw away a magnificent opportunity.

38

Radical
Rule in the South

Kenneth M. Stampp

In *The Era of Reconstruction*, Kenneth Stampp
offers a thoroughgoing "revisionist" critique of
the entire Reconstruction period. He agrees with
David Donald that Johnson's intransigence—
along with the black codes adopted by Southern
ex-confederates—helped bring on Radical Reconstruction. But Stampp goes on to argue that the
so-called Radical Republicans were not really
vindictive (given the nature of the Civil War)
and that their program was neither harsh nor
very thorough. In his chapter on Republican rule
in the South, excerpted here, Stampp eschews the
black-and-white stereotypes of the old interpretation and attempts to portray what the much-
maligned carpetbaggers, scalawags, and Negro
politicians were really like. And he asks—and
tries to answer as fairly as he can—some crucial
questions: Was corruption in the South widespread
or isolated during Radical rule? Did the Republican regimes do anything constructive? How
vindictive were they toward the ex-Confederates?
And what, finally, is the legacy of Radical Reconstruction for our own time?

When Lord Bryce, in the 1880's, wrote *The
American Commonwealth*, he commented at
length on the southern state governments created under the radical plan of reconstruction.
What he had to say about them was not remarkable for its originality, but a few passages
are worth quoting to give the flavor of the approaching historical consensus. "Such a Saturnalia of robbery and jobbery has seldom been
seen in any civilized country. . . . The position
of these [radical] adventurers was like that of a
Roman provincial governor in the latter days of
the Republic. . . . [All] voting power lay with
those who were wholly unfit for citizenship,
and had no interest as taxpayers, in good government. . . . [Since] the legislatures were reckless and corrupt, the judges for the most part
subservient, the Federal military officers bound
to support what purported to be the constitutional authorities of the State, Congress distant
and little inclined to listen to the complaints of
those whom it distrusted as rebels, greed was
unchecked and roguery unabashed."[1] In drawing this unpleasant picture Lord Bryce anticipated the generalizations of the Dunningites,
as did many others.

Each of the eleven states of the former Confederacy, during all or part of the decade between 1867 and 1877, fell under the control of
the radical Republicans. Tennessee was the first
to be captured by them—indeed, it never had
a Johnson government—but it was also the
first to be lost. Tennessee was "redeemed," as
southern white Democrats liked to call their
return to power, as early as 1869. The last
three states to be redeemed were South Carolina, Florida, and Louisiana, where the radical
regimes lasted until the spring of 1877.

What, according to the conservatives, were

From pp. 155–185 in *The Era of Reconstruction* by
Kenneth M. Stampp. Copyright © 1965 by Kenneth M.
Stampp. Reprinted by permission of Alfred A. Knopf.

[1] James Bryce: *The American Commonwealth*, 3 vols.
(New York, 1888), Vol. II, pp. 476–8.

the sins of the radical governments? The new governments, they said, expelled from power the South's experienced statesmen and natural leaders and replaced them with untrained men who were almost uniformly incompetent and corrupt. Among the radical leaders, the Yankee carpetbaggers, crafty adventurers who invaded the postwar South for political and economic plunder, were the most notorious. The scalawags, who assisted the carpetbaggers, were mostly degraded and depraved poor whites, betrayers of their race and section who sought a share of the radical spoils. The Negroes, ignorant and illiterate, played an essentially passive political role, casting their votes as radical agents of the Union League and Freedmen's Bureau told them to. Since the members of the radical coalition owned little or no property themselves, they increased state and local taxes until they came near to ruining the whole class of white property holders. Their extravagant appropriations, their waste, fraud, and corruption, caused shocking increases in southern state debts and brought some states to the edge of bankruptcy. Finally, said the conservatives, the radical governments threatened to destroy the white civilization of the South and to reduce it to African barbarism.

We must first consider the charge that the radicals expelled from power the South's natural leaders. One of the characters in Margaret Mitchell's popular novel, *Gone With the Wind*, complains that everybody who was anybody in the good old days was nobody in the radical regimes. A conservative Tennesseean reported that the radicals in his state were "the party paying no taxes, riding poor horses, wearing dirty shirts, and having no use for soap." According to a Nashville newspaper, most of the so-called loyal men of the South were "the merest trash that could be collected in a civilized community, of no personal credit or social responsibility." Thus, concludes a historian of reconstruction in Tennessee, "the power, wealth, culture, and natural leadership" of the

state had been evicted from political control.[2] An upper-class Virginian sent Thad Stevens a bitter protest against being subjected to "our former slaves and the mean white surfs [*sic*] of the earth. . . . We are the children of the Lees, Clays, Henrys, Jeffersons and Jacksons. Tell me if we are to be ruled by these people." This would seem to suggest that to some extent and in some places southern class divisions were sharpened during the era of reconstruction. But southern conservatives exaggerated the degree to which the division between them and the radicals was along class lines.

In any case, those who have referred to the South's antebellum political rulers as its natural leaders are seldom explicit about what they mean. Remembering what had happened to the South under the guidance of her prewar politicians, it would be hard to argue that they had won the right to lead because they had governed so wisely or so well. If it is valid to judge statesmen by their understanding of the problems of their age, and by their efforts to find constructive solutions, the old southern leaders would have to be pronounced failures on both counts; and many of them were, moreover, singularly irresponsible. Their strength was rooted in their economic power derived from large property holdings, and in their experience in the techniques of political manipulation. The conservatives' repeated complaint that the radicals paid no taxes and owned little property is highly suggestive, for their whole conception of natural political leadership ultimately boils down to this. When the radicals won control in the South, they did not displace a responsible political élite which had traditionally taken a large view of things; nor did they discharge a trained body of civil servants. This being the case, the change in leadership was far less disastrous than it has often been made to appear.

But the customary charges against the new southern leadership are extremely severe and

[2] E. Merton Coulter: *William G. Brownlow* (Chapel Hill, 1937), pp. 282–3, 337.

need to be weighed carefully. It is essential, therefore, to examine in some detail each of the three elements in the radical coalition—the carpetbaggers, scalawags, and Negroes—to test the validity of the generalizations conservatives used to characterize them. The term "carpetbagger" was applied to recent northern settlers in the South who actively supported the radical Republicans.[3] Since the term has an invidious connotation, it is used here only for lack of another that is equally familiar but morally neutral. The so-called carpetbaggers were not all poor men who carried their meager possessions with them in carpetbags; they were not all ignorant; they were not all corrupt. Rather, they were a heterogeneous lot who moved to the South for a variety of reasons.

Among the carpetbaggers were some who fitted the stereotype: disreputable opportunists and corruptionists who went south in search of political plunder or public office. Because these carpetbaggers were so conspicuous and gained such notoriety, conservative southern Democrats succeeded in portraying them as typical, though actually they constituted a small minority.

Few of the carpetbaggers came to the South originally for the purpose of entering politics; many of them arrived before 1867 when political careers were not even open to them. They migrated to the South in the same manner and for the same reasons that other Americans migrated to the West. They hoped to buy cotton lands or to enter legitimate business enterprises: to develop natural resources, build factories, promote railroads, represent insurance companies, or engage in trade. A large proportion of the carpetbaggers were veterans of the Union Army who were pleased with the southern climate and believed that they had discovered a land of opportunity. Others came as teachers, clergymen, officers of the Freedmen's Bureau, or agents of the various northern benevolent societies organized to give aid to the Negroes. These people went south to set up schools for Negroes and poor whites, to establish churches, and to distribute clothing and medical supplies. They were of all types—some well trained for their jobs, others not. Seldom, however, can they be dismissed as meddlesome fools, or can the genuineness of their humanitarian impulses be doubted. But whether honest or dishonest, northern settlers who became active in radical politics incurred the wrath of most white southern conservatives. For their supreme offense was not corruption but attempting to organize the Negroes for political action.

A scalawag is by definition a scamp, and white Southerners who collaborated with the radicals were thus stigmatized by the pejorative term that identified them. In southern society, according to one critic, scalawags constituted the "tory and deserter element, with a few from the obstructionists of the war time and malcontents of the present who wanted office."[4] But here, as in the case of the carpetbaggers, the facts were more complex than this. All scalawags were not degraded poor whites, depraved corruptionists, or cynical opportunists who betrayed the South for the spoils of office.

The cases of three distinguished scalawags will illustrate the inadequacy of any simple generalization about the character or origin of this class of radicals. The first is that of Lieutenant General James A. Longstreet of the Confederate Army, a graduate of West Point and one of Lee's ablest corps commanders. After the war Longstreet moved to New Orleans and became a partner in a cotton factorage business

---

[3] "From contemporary usage . . . we derive the following as a non-valuational definition: the men called carpetbaggers were *white Northerners who went south after the beginning of the Civil War and, sooner or later, became active in politics as Republicans.*" Richard N. Current: "Carpetbaggers Reconsidered," in *A Festschrift for Frederick B. Artz* (Durham, 1964), p. 144.

[4] Walter L. Fleming: *Civil War and Reconstruction in Alabama* (New York, 1905), p. 402.

and head of an insurance firm. In 1867, arguing that the vanquished must accept the terms of the victors, he joined the Republican party and endorsed radical reconstruction. In 1868 he supported Grant for President, and in subsequent years Republican administrations gave him a variety of offices in the federal civil service. The second case is that of James L. Orr of South Carolina, a secessionist who had sat in the Confederate Senate. After serving as the Johnsonian governor of his state, Orr switched to the radicals and in 1868 was rewarded with a circuit judgeship. In a private letter he explained why he now supported the Republicans: It is "important for our prominent men to identify themselves with the radicals for the purpose of controlling their action and preventing mischief to the state." The third case is that of R. W. Flournoy, a large slaveholder in ante-bellum Mississippi. Flournoy joined the radicals not for personal gain but because of a humanitarian interest in the welfare of the freedmen. In a letter to Stevens he once explained that he supported the Republicans as the party to whom the Negro "can alone look . . . for protection." Flournoy's support of racial equality made him one of the most hated scalawags in the state. None of these men fitted the scalawag stereotype.

Others unfortunately did. Among those who gave the scalawags their reputation for corruption was Franklin J. Moses, Jr., of South Carolina. The son of a distinguished father, Moses entered politics before the war and was known as an ardent secessionist. In 1867, after a brief period as a Johnsonian, he joined the radicals. Both as a legislator and, from 1872 to 1874, as governor he looted the public treasury and repeatedly accepted bribes for using his influence to secure the passage of legislation. Other scalawags appeared to be pure opportunists who simply joined the winning side. Joseph E. Brown, Georgia's Civil War governor, provides a classic example. After the war, claiming that he had sense enough to know

when he was defeated, Brown quit the Democrats and urged Southerners to accept the radicals' terms. During the years of reconstruction, in addition to his political activities, he found the time (and the opportunity) to become a wealthy capitalist: president of a railroad, a steamship company, a coal company, and an iron company. When the radicals were overthrown in Georgia, Brown, as always, landed on his feet and returned to the Democratic party. Now he helped to organize a powerful Democratic machine that dominated the state for many years and eventually sent him to the United States Senate.

Always a minority of the southern white population, more numerous in some states than in others,[5] the scalawags usually belonged to one or more of four distinct groups. The first and largest of these groups was the Unionists. Having been exposed to severe persecution from their Confederate neighbors during the war, southern Unionists were often the most vindictive of the radicals; they were quite willing to support those who would now retaliate against the secessionists, and they hoped that congressional reconstruction would give them political control in their states. Early in 1866 a North Carolinian wrote Stevens that Union men were disillusioned with Johnson but still hoped "that traitors will be punished for the treatment that union men received at their hands."

However, a very large proportion of this Unionist-scalawag element had little enthusiasm for one aspect of the radical program: the granting of equal civil and political rights to the Negroes. They favored the disenfranchisement of the Confederates to enable them to dominate

[5] In the presidential election of 1872, according to a recent estimate, approximately 150,000 white Southerners voted Republican; they constituted about 20 per cent of the white voters. These scalawags were most numerous in Tennessee, North Carolina, Arkansas, Texas, and Virginia. Allen W. Trelease: "Who Were the Scalawags?" *Journal of Southern History*, XXIX (1963), p. 458.

the new state governments, but they were reluctant to accept Negro suffrage. "There is some small amount of squirming about the privileges extended to the recent slaves," a Virginia Unionist informed Stevens, "but time will overcome all this as there is no union man who does not infinitely more fear and dread the domination of the recent Rebels than that of the recent slaves." In 1866, General Clinton B. Fisk, an officer of the Freedmen's Bureau, told the congressional Committee on Reconstruction that in Tennessee "among the bitterest opponents of the negro . . . are the intensely radical loyalists of the [eastern] mountain districts. . . . The great opposition to the measure in the Tennessee legislature, giving the negro the right to testify and an equality before the law, has come from that section, chiefly. In Middle Tennessee and in West Tennessee the largest and the wealthiest planters . . . have more cordially cooperated with me in my duties than the people of East Tennessee." The planters believed that they could control the Negro vote, and the scalawags feared that they would.

Insofar as there was any relationship between scalawags and the class structure of the South, it resulted from the fact that a minority of the poor whites and yeoman farmers were attracted to the radical cause.[6] There had always been, as we have seen, an undercurrent of tension between them and the planter class, and some of them deserted President Johnson when it appeared that his program would return the planters to power. Lower-class whites who joined the radicals sometimes hoped for a seizure of the planters' lands. In South Carolina, according to a Union officer, the idea of confiscation "was received with more favor by this caste than by the Negroes." He recalled numerous occasions when "dirty, ragged, stupid creatures slyly inquired of me, 'When is our folks a-gwine to git the lan'?'" But it was never easy for the yeomen or poor whites

to become scalawags, for support of the radicals meant collaboration with Negroes, or at least acquiescence in Negro suffrage. As a result, this class of scalawags was most numerous in areas with a small Negro population. Elsewhere a few lower-class whites managed to submerge their race prejudice, but the great majority preferred the old conservative leadership to a party that seemed to preach equality of the races.

A third source of scalawag strength came from Southerners engaged in business enterprise and from those living in regions, such as East Tennessee, western Virginia and North Carolina, and northern Alabama, which were rich in natural resources and had an industrial potential. Among such men there was considerable support for the economic policies of the Republican party—for the national banking system, the protective tariff, and federal appropriations for internal improvements. In general, the radical governments invited northern capitalists to invest in the South, granted loans or subsidies to the railroads, and gave charters and franchises to new corporations. Some of the scalawags were thus identified with the concept of a New South whose economy would be more diversified than that of the Old.

Finally, the radicals drew a little of their scalawag support and some of their leaders from upper-class Southerners who had been affiliated with the Whig party before the Civil War. The Whig party had been particularly attractive to the more affluent and socially secure members of southern society, and after the war many Whigs were reluctant to join their old foes, the Democrats. A few of them now looked upon the Republican party as the heir to the Whig tradition and wondered whether it might be possible not only to join but also to control its organization in the South. Upper-class Whig scalawags found it relatively easy to accept equal civil and political rights for Negroes, first, because among them race hatred was less often the prime motivating force of political action and, second, because they were

[6] Most of the lower-class whites who became scalawags had been Unionists, but some had supported the Confederacy.

optimistic about their chances of controlling the Negro vote. In Mississippi, for example, James L. Alcorn, elected governor on the Republican ticket in 1869, had been a prominent Whig planter before the war, as had been numerous other leading scalawags. Thus it would appear that the scalawags were in part an absurd coalition of class-conscious poor whites and yeoman farmers who hated the planters, and class-conscious Whig planters and businessmen who disliked the egalitarian Democrats. But politics has a logic of its own, and the history of American political parties is full of contradictions such as this.

Joining the carpetbaggers and scalawags in the radical coalition was the mass of southern Negroes, most of them illiterate, many easily intimidated. Because of their political inexperience and economic helplessness, they were sometimes misled and victimized not only by Republicans but also by southern white Democrats. But it would be far from the truth to say that their political behavior during reconstruction was altogether passive or irresponsible. This was untrue, if for no other reason, because the issues of reconstruction, so far as the Negroes were concerned, were relatively simple and clear-cut. Given their condition and the limited political choices open to them, most Negroes responded to the appeals of rival politicians in a manner that had an obvious logic to it.

To begin with, suffrage was not something thrust upon an indifferent mass of Negroes. Their leaders had demanded it from the start; and when the Johnson governments limited the ballot to the whites, many meetings of southern Negroes sent protests to Congress. In Tennessee, for example, Negroes first petitioned the legislature for the ballot, then asked Congress not to seat Tennesseeans until their petition was granted. On May 7, 1866, a meeting of freedmen in New Bern, North Carolina, resolved "That so long as the Federal Government refuses to grant us the right to protect ourselves by means of the ballot . . . we will

hold it responsible before God for our protection."

Moreover, most Negroes fully appreciated the importance of achieving literacy, and they took advantage of the limited educational opportunities offered them with almost pathetic eagerness. They also understood that in the rural South land was the key to economic independence and that they needed government aid to get it. In 1865 they heard rumors that Congress would provide each of them with forty acres and a mule at Christmas time; the next year they heard the same rumors again; once more in 1867 they hoped to get land when the radicals formulated their reconstruction program. But each time the Negroes were disappointed, and by 1868 they knew that the Republicans in Congress were not going to assist them.

Nevertheless, an overwhelming majority of Negro voters continued to support the Republican party, and in 1868 they helped to elevate General Grant to the presidency. In the political campaigns of the reconstruction era, Democratic candidates occasionally tried to bid for the Negro vote, but the record of the Johnson governments and the commitment of the Democratic party to white supremacy caused the mass of Negroes to remain loyal Republicans. "The blacks know that many conservatives hope to reduce them again to some form of peonage," a Tennessee carpetbagger wrote Stevens. "Under the impulse of this fear they will roll up their whole strength . . . and will go entirely for the Republican candidate whoever he may be." As long as southern Democrats opposed Negro suffrage and insisted that white supremacy was the central political issue, this condition could hardly have changed. It was this that made it easy for the agents of the Republican Union League to mobilize and "control" the Negro vote. Yet white Democrats often cited this solid Negro support of the Republicans to illustrate the political irresponsibility of the freedmen. It was a curious argument, however, for the practical choice offered

the Negro voters was between a party that gave them civil and political rights and a party whose stock-in-trade was racist demagoguery.

Perhaps the most important generalizations to be made about the role of the Negroes in reconstruction are the following. First, while they had influence in all of the southern radical governments—more in some than in others—they did not control any of them. They served in all of the state legislatures, but only in South Carolina, one of the two southern states in which they outnumbered the whites, were they in the majority.[7] In Mississippi, the other state in which the Negroes had a numerical majority, the carpetbaggers controlled politics; while in Tennessee, where the scalawags dominated the radical government, there were practically no Negro officeholders at all. Few Negroes were elected to higher offices; none became the governor of a state. At various times South Carolina had a Negro lieutenant governor, secretary of state, treasurer, speaker of the house, and associate justice of the state supreme court; Mississippi had a Negro lieutenant governor, secretary of state, superintendent of education, and speaker of the house; Louisiana had a Negro lieutenant governor, secretary of state, treasurer, and superintendent of public education; Florida had a Negro secretary of state, and superintendent of public instruction. Nearly all of them were men of ability and integrity. Fourteen Negroes were elected to the United States House of Representatives, six of them from South Carolina. Two Mississippi Negroes served in the United States Senate; Hiram R. Revels for a one-year unexpired term, and Blanche K. Bruce for a full term. (Revels and Bruce, incidentally, are the only Negroes who have ever been elected to the Senate from any state, North or South.)* In general, however, white men dominated the higher offices of the southern radical governments. The Negroes, though filling many city and county offices, ordinarily were unable to advance beyond the state legislatures.

Second, the Negroes soon developed their own leadership and were not always the mere tools of white Republicans. In 1868 a Florida carpetbagger reported to Stevens that white radicals were having trouble getting the Negroes to support ratification of the new state constitution. "The colored preachers," he wrote, "are *the great power* in controlling and uniting the colored vote, and they are looked to, as political leaders, with more confidence . . . than to any other source of instruction and control." Some of the Negro leaders were corruptible, some incorruptible; some had great ability, some little. Most of them were conservatives on all issues except civil and political rights.

Finally, the Negroes were seldom vindictive in their use of political power or in their attitude toward native whites. To be sure, there were plenty of cases of friction between Negroes and whites, and Negro militiamen were sometimes inordinately aggressive. But in no southern state did any responsible Negro leader, or any substantial Negro group, attempt to get complete political control into the hands of the freedmen.[8] All they asked for was equal political rights and equality before the law. Thus, in 1866, a group of North Carolina Negroes in thanking Congress for the Civil Rights Act promised that "whenever the Elective Franchise is also guaranteed to us we will ask no further special protection from the Federal Government, for then united with our white friends in the South we will be able to secure for ourselves every desired or desirable means of prosperity." Negroes did not desire to have political parties divided along racial

[7] South Carolina's first radical legislature contained 87 Negroes and 69 whites. The Negroes, however, had a majority only in the lower house. The upper house contained twice as many whites as Negroes.

* In 1966, after this was written, Edward Brooke was elected U.S. Senator in Massachusetts—ed.

[8] However, Negro leaders did protest when they thought that white radicals were trying to monopolize the offices.

South Carolina legislature during Radical Reconstruction. Of the
146 members of that legislature, 90 were blacks. Like the Negroes
in other Republican legislatures in the South, "nearly all of them
were men of ability and integrity." While the South Carolina
legislature was hardly a model of efficiency or honesty, as Stampp
points out, it did try to restore the state's war-ravaged economy
and to establish a good public school system. It also passed a law
which made it a crime to call a man "yankee" or "nigger." (Courtesy of The Library of Congress.)

lines; rather, unlike most white Democrats, they were eager to drop the race issue and work with the whites within the existing party framework.

Many Negroes at this time were even willing to postpone action on social segregation, especially in the schools, preferring to avoid conflict over this issue while they concentrated on civil and political rights. A South Carolina Negro legislator declared: "I venture to say to my white fellow-citizens that we, the colored people, are not in quest of social equality. I for one do not ask to be introduced in your family circle if you are not disposed to receive me there." And yet a northern white conservative affirmed that in South Carolina radical reconstruction "is barbarism overwhelming civilization by physical force. It is the slave rioting in the halls of his master, and putting that master under his feet." Such a description should be taken for what it was: the hyperbole of partisan politics.

The first step in the organization of new southern state governments, as required by the reconstruction acts, was the election of delegates to conventions to frame new state constitutions. Since these conventions were controlled by the radicals, since they were the first political bodies in the South to contain Negroes,[9] white conservatives subjected them to violent denunciation. They contemptuously called them "black and tan conventions"; they described the delegates as "baboons, monkeys, mules," or "ragamuffins and jailbirds." The South Caro-

lina convention, according to a local newspaper, was the "maddest, most infamous revolution in history."

Yet, the invectives notwithstanding, there was nothing mad and little revolutionary about the work of these conventions.[10] In fact, one of the most significant observations to be made about them is that the delegates showed little interest in experimentation. For the most part the radicals wrote orthodox state constitutions, borrowing heavily from the previous constitutions and from those of other states. To find fault with the way these southern constitutions were drawn is to find fault with the way most new state constitutions have been drawn; to criticize their basic political structure is to criticize the basic political structure of all the states. They were neither original nor unique. There was no inclination to test, say, the unicameral legislature, or novel executive or judicial systems.

Nor did the conventions attempt radical experiments in the field of social or economic policy. Since land reform had been defeated in Congress, a few delegates tried to achieve it through state action. The South Carolina convention provided for the creation of a commission to purchase land for sale to Negroes. In Louisiana, some Negro delegates proposed that when planters sold their estates purchases of more than 150 acres be prohibited. One white scalawag suggested a double tax on uncultivated land. A few delegates in other states advocated various policies designed to force the breakup of large estates. But these and all other attacks upon landed property were easily defeated.

As for the freedmen, the new constitutions proclaimed the equality of all men by quoting or paraphrasing the Declaration of Independ-

[9] The number of Negroes and whites in the various conventions was as follows:

	Negro	White
Alabama	18	90
Arkansas	8	58
Florida	18	27
Georgia	33	137
Louisiana	49	49
Mississippi	16	84
North Carolina	15	118
South Carolina	76	48
Virginia	25	80
Texas	9	81

[10] The Democrats accused the Republican delegates of wasting time and of extravagance. The printing bills of some of these conventions were unnecessarily high, but in general these accusations have relatively little evidence to support them.

ence. Negroes were given the same civil and political rights as white men. "The equality of all persons before the law," proclaimed the Arkansas constitution, "is recognized and shall ever remain inviolate; nor shall any citizen ever be deprived of any right, privilege, or immunity, nor exempted from any burden or duty, on account of race, color, or previous condition." But on the subject of the social relations of Negroes and whites, most of the radical constitutions were evasive. South Carolina provided that its public schools were to be open to all "without regard to race or color," but only the state university actually made an attempt at integration. The Louisiana constitution declared: "There shall be no separate schools or institutions of learning established exclusively for any race by the State of Louisiana." In New Orleans from 1871 to 1877 about one third of the public schools were integrated, and white resistance was remarkably mild; but elsewhere in Louisiana segregation was the rule. Outside of South Carolina and Louisiana the radicals made no explicit constitutional provision for social integration. The Mississippi convention first defeated a proposal that segregated schools be required, then defeated a proposal that they be prohibited; the result was that the new constitution ignored the issue altogether. The only reference to segregation in it was a vague statement that "the rights of all citizens to travel upon public conveyances shall not be infringed upon, nor in any manner abridged in this state." But whether or not this clause prohibited segregation in public transportation is far from clear.

Yet, though the new constitutions were essentially conservative documents, they did accomplish some modest reforms, most of which were long overdue. In general, they eliminated certain undemocratic features of the old constitutions, for example, the inequitable systems of legislative apportionment that had discriminated against the interior regions of Virginia, North Carolina, and South Carolina.

In the states of the Southeast, many offices that had previously been appointive were now made elective, and county government was taken out of the hands of local oligarchies. The rights of women were enlarged, tax systems were made more equitable, penal codes were reformed, and the number of crimes punishable by death was reduced. Most of the constitutions provided for substantial improvements in the state systems of public education and in the facilities for the care of the physically and mentally handicapped and of the poor.[11]

In South Carolina, according to the historians of reconstruction in that state, the radical convention was an orderly body which accomplished its work with reasonable dispatch. It produced a constitution "as good as any other constitution that state has ever had"—good enough to remain in force for nearly two decades after the white Democrats regained control. This was, in fact, the state's first really democratic constitution; for, in addition to removing distinctions based on race, it provided for manhood suffrage, abolished property qualifications for officeholding, gave the voters the power for the first time to select the governor and other state officers, and transferred the election of presidential electors from the legislature to the voters. Another important provision related to public education: unlike the previous constitution, "the fundamental law of the state carried the obligation of universal education" and aimed at "the creation of a school system like that of Northern states." Other reforms included an extension of women's rights, adoption of the state's first divorce law, strengthening of the state's fiscal power, revision of the tax system, and modern-

---

[11] Attempts to accomplish a sweeping disenfranchisement of Confederate sympathizers were defeated either in the conventions or, as in Virginia and Mississippi, by popular vote. The disenfranchisement accomplished by these constitutions seldom went beyond those disqualified for holding office by the Fourteenth Amendment, and all made provision for the eventual restoration of the franchise even to them.

ization of the judiciary and of county government.[12]

The responsible behavior of South Carolina's radical constitutional convention was in striking contrast to the angry and irresponsible criticism of the Democrats. Chiefly because of its provisions for racial equality, they ridiculed the new constitution as "the work of sixty-odd negroes, many of them ignorant and depraved, together with fifty white men, outcasts of Northern society, and Southern renegades, betrayers of their race and country." Specifically, the Democrats charged that manhood suffrage was designed to further the ambitions of "mean whites"; that Negro suffrage would bring ruin to the state; that the judicial reforms were "repugnant to our customs and habits of thought"; and that the public school requirements were "a fruitful source of peculant corruption." In spite of this fanciful criticism by a party whose chief appeal was to racial bigotry, the work of the radical convention was ratified by a majority of nearly three to one.

At the time that the new constitutions were ratified, elections were held for state officers and legislators. After the elections, when Congress approved of the constitutions, political power was transferred from the military to the new civil governments. Thus began the era of radical government in the South—an era which, according to tradition, produced some of the worst state administrations in American history. Some of the southern radical regimes earned their evil reputations, others did not; but viewed collectively, there was much in the record they made to justify severe criticism. To say that they were not always models of efficiency and integrity would be something of an understatement. "The great impediment of the Republican party in this state," wrote a Tennessee radical, "is the incompetence of its leaders. . . . After the war the loyal people in

many counties had no competent men to be judges, lawyers or political leaders." Indeed, all of the radical governments suffered more or less from the incompetence of some, the dishonesty of a few, and above all the inexperience of most of the officeholders. Unquestionably the poorest records were made in South Carolina during the administrations of the carpetbagger Robert K. Scott and the scalawag Franklin J. Moses, Jr., and in Louisiana during the administrations of the carpetbaggers Henry C. Warmoth and William P. Kellogg.

The sins of various radical governments included fraudulent bond issues; graft in land sales or purchases and in the letting of contracts for public works; and waste and extravagance in the use of state funds. Governor Warmoth was reputed to have pocketed $100,000 during his first year in office, though his salary was $8,000; another governor was accused of stealing and selling the supplies of the Freedmen's Bureau. A scalawag governor admitted taking bribes of more than $40,000; another fraudulently endorsed state bonds over to a group of railroad promoters. In Louisiana under both Warmoth and Kellogg there was corruption in the granting of charters and franchises, in the negotiation of construction contracts, in the use of school funds, in the collection of state taxes, and in the awarding of printing contracts. Some of the radical legislators, especially in South Carolina, apparently made bribery an integral part of the process of transacting legislative business. One South Carolina legislature issued bonds valued at $1,590,000 to redeem bank notes valued at $500,000; it voted a bonus of $1,000 to the speaker when he lost that amount in a bet on a horse race. For a time the legislators of this state enjoyed the services of a free restaurant and bar established for their private use; they billed the state for such "legislative supplies" as hams, ladies' bonnets, perfumes, champagne, and (for one unfortunate member) a coffin. The cost of state printing in South Caro-

---

[12] Francis B. Simkins and Robert H. Woody: *South Carolina during Reconstruction* (Chapel Hill, 1932), pp. 90–111.

lina between 1868 and 1876 was greater than the cost had been from 1789 to 1868. On one occasion, as the legislature was about to adjourn, a Democratic newspaper in Charleston wrote the following epitaph: "In life it has been unlovely, and in death it has not belied its record. As it lived, it has died—an uncouth, malformed and abortive monstrosity, its birth a blunder, its life a crime, and its death a blessing."

Meanwhile, the credit of some of the southern states was impaired as public debts mounted. In Florida the state debt increased from $524,000 in 1868 to $5,621,000 in 1874. In South Carolina a legislative committee reported that between 1868 and 1871 the state debt had increased from $5,403,000 to $15,768,000, but another committee insisted that it had increased to $29,159,000. By 1872 the debts of the eleven states of the former Confederacy had increased by approximately $132,000,000. The burden on taxpayers grew apace. Between 1860 and 1870 South Carolina's tax rate more than doubled, while property values declined by more than fifty per cent. In Tennessee a radical reported that during the first three years after the war taxes had increased sevenfold, though property had declined in value by one third. Throughout the South the tax burden was four times as great in 1870 as it had been in 1860. Such rates, complained many southern landholders, were confiscatory; and, indeed, taxes and other adversities of the postwar years forced some of them to sell all or part of their lands. Sympathy for South Carolina's planter aristocracy caused a northern conservative to ask: "When before did mankind behold the spectacle of a rich, high-spirited, cultivated, self-governed people suddenly cast down, bereft of their possessions, and put under the feet of the slaves they had held in bondage for centuries?"

High taxes, mounting debts, corruption, extravagance, and waste, however, do not constitute the complete record of the radical regimes.

Moreover, to stop with a mere description of their misdeeds would be to leave all the crucial questions unanswered—to distort the picture and to view it without perspective. For example, if some of these governments contained an uncommonly large number of inexperienced or incompetent officeholders, if much of their support came from an untutored electorate, there was an obvious reason for this. Howard K. Beale, in a critique of various reconstruction legends, observed that the political rulers of the ante-bellum South "had fastened ignorance or inexperience on millions of whites as well as Negroes and that it was this ignorance and inexperience that caused trouble when Radicals were in power. . . . Wealthy Southerners . . . seldom recognized the need for general education of even the *white* masses."[13] Even in 1865 the men who won control of the Johnson governments showed little disposition to adopt the needed reforms. In South Carolina the Johnsonians did almost nothing to establish a system of public education, and at the time that the radicals came to power only one eighth of the white children of school age were attending school. The Negroes, of course, had been ignored entirely. It was probably no coincidence that the radicals made their poorest record in South Carolina, the state which had done the least for education and whose prewar government had been the least democratic.

As for the corruption of the radical governments, this phenomenon can be understood only when it is related to the times and to conditions throughout the country. One must remember that the administrations of President Grant set the moral tone for American government at all levels, national, state, and local. The best-remembered episodes of the Grant era are its numerous scandals—the Crédit Mobilier and the Whiskey Ring being the most spectacular of them—involving members of

[13] Howard K. Beale: "On Rewriting Reconstruction History," *American Historical Review*, XLV (1940), pp. 807–27.

Congress as well as men in high administration circles. There were, moreover, singularly corrupt Republican machines in control of various northern states, including Massachusetts, New York, and Pennsylvania. But corruption was not a phenomenon peculiar to Republicans of the Gilded Age, as the incredible operations of the so-called Tweed Ring in New York City will testify. Indeed, the thefts of public funds by this organization of white Tammany Democrats surpassed the total thefts in all the southern states combined.

Clearly the presence of carpetbaggers, scalawags, and Negroes in the radical governments was not in itself a sufficient explanation for the appearance of corruption. The South was being affected by the same forces that were affecting the rest of the country. No doubt the most important of these forces were, first, the social disorganization that accompanied the Civil War and hit the defeated and demoralized South with particular severity; and, second, the frantic economic expansion of the postwar period, when the American economy was dominated by a group of extraordinarily talented but irresponsible and undisciplined business leaders. These entrepreneurs' rather flexible standards of public morality provided an unfortunate model for the politicians.

Whether southern Democrats would have been able to resist the corrupting forces of the postwar decade had they remained in power is by no means certain. Perhaps the old ruling class would have been somewhat less vulnerable to the temptations of the Gilded Age, but the record of the Johnson governments was spotty at best. In Louisiana the conservative government created by Lincoln and Johnson wasted a great deal of public money. In Mississippi the state treasurer of the Johnson government embezzled $62,000. (This, by the way, far surpassed the record of the only thief in the radical government, who embezzled $7,000.) E. Merton Coulter discovered that during the era of reconstruction some Democratic office-

holders "partook of the same financial characteristics as Radicals" and "took advantage of openings" when they found them. He quotes a Georgia editor who claimed that the extravagance and corruption "benefitted about as many Democrats as Republicans"; and he notes that a Democratic administration in Alabama "in lack of honesty differed little from the administrations of the Radicals between whom it was sandwiched."[14]

In the 1870's, when the South's so-called "natural leaders" returned to power, that troubled section did not always find itself governed by politicians distinguished for their selfless devotion to public service. In Mississippi the treasurer of the Democratic regime that overthrew the radicals in 1875 immediately embezzled $316,000, which broke all previous records! Elsewhere in the next decade eight other state treasurers were guilty of defalcations or embezzlements, including one in Louisiana who defrauded the state of more than a million dollars. Georgia was now ruled by a Democratic machine that was both ruthless and corrupt, a machine whose record was so offensive that by the end of the 1880's the white masses—some even willing to accept Negro support—rose in political rebellion against it. Reports about the Mississippi Democratic regime of the late nineteenth century are particularly colorful. One white editor charged that an "infamous ring" of "corrupt office-seekers . . . [had] debauched the ballot boxes . . . incurred useless and extravagant expenditures, raised the taxes, [and] plunged the State into debt." At the Mississippi constitutional convention of 1890, a white Democratic delegate gave the following description of politics in his state during the previous fifteen years: "Sir, it is no secret that there has not been a full vote and a fair count in Mississippi since 1875. . . . In other words we have been stuffing ballot boxes, committing perjury, and here and

[14] Coulter, *The South during Reconstruction*, pp. 152–3.

there in the state carrying the elections by fraud and violence. . . . No man can be in favor of perpetuating the election methods which have prevailed in Mississippi since 1875 who is not a moral idiot." Twelve years later an editor claimed that it would tax "the range and scope of the most fertile and versatile imagination to picture a condition of greater political rottenness" than existed in Mississippi at that time.

In the final analysis the crucial question about the extravagance and peculations of the radical governments is who the chief beneficiaries were. Only a few of the Negro and white radical leaders profited personally. The funds they stole, the money that prodigal legislators used for their own benefit, accounted for only a small fraction of the increased debts of the southern states. Nor did the total sums involved in bribery rise to a very impressive figure. And why was the tar brush applied exclusively to those who accepted the bribes and not to those who offered them? Under these circumstances is it really more blessed to give than to receive? For when the bribe-givers are identified we have located those who profited most from radical misdeeds. These men were the construction contractors, business speculators, and railroad promoters, or their agents, who hoped to persuade legislators to give them contracts, franchises, charters, subsidies, financial grants, or guarantees. They were the men who were also corrupting Congressmen and northern legislatures.

In Virginia much of the history of reconstruction concerns the rivalry of the Baltimore and Ohio Railroad and the Southside line for control of the Virginia and Tennessee Railroad. Both lines fought to control elections and legislators and backed whichever party promised to serve them, until, in 1870, the legislature ended the dispute by approving the consolidation plans of the Southside. Louisiana's reconstruction politics was enlivened by the attempt of a railroad and steamship corporation, headed by Charles Morgan of New York, to prevent the state from subsidizing a rival line between New Orleans and Houston, until Morgan forced the new line to take him in. In Alabama the North and South Railroad and the Alabama and Chattanooga Railroad battled for access to the ore deposits around Birmingham. In the process the competing groups corrupted both Johnson and radical legislatures, and in the latter both Republicans and Democrats.

Most of the debt increases in the southern states resulted not from the thefts and extravagance of radical legislators but from the grants and guarantees they gave to railroad promoters, among whom were always some native white Democrats. In Florida more than sixty per cent of the debt incurred by the radical regime was in the form of railroad guarantee bonds. In North Carolina the radical government, prodded by the carpetbagger Milton S. Littlefield, a skilled lobbyist, issued millions of dollars of railroad bonds. Among those who benefited were many of the state's "best citizens," including George W. Swepson, a local business promoter and Democrat. Most of Alabama's reconstruction debt—$18,000,000 out of $20,500,000—was in the form of state bonds issued to subsidize railroad construction, for which the state obtained liens upon railroad property. When one measure for state aid was before the Alabama legislature, many Democrats were among the lobbyists working for its passage. Yet, complained a radical, the Democrats who expect to profit from the bill "will use the argument that the Republican party had a majority in the Legislature, and will falsely, but hopefully, charge it upon Republicans as a partisan crime against the state."

Indeed, all of the southern states, except Mississippi, used state credit to finance the rebuilding and expansion of their railroads, for private sources of credit were inadequate. This policy had been developed before the war; it was continued under the Johnsonians; and in some cases when the Democrats overthrew the

radicals there was no decline in the state's generosity to the railroads. While the radicals controlled the southern legislatures, not only they but many members of the Democratic minority as well voted for railroad bond issues. According to an historian of reconstruction in Louisiana, "Such measures were supported by members of both parties, often introduced by Democrats, in every case supported by a large majority of Democrats in both houses."[15] The subservience of many postwar southern legislatures to the demands of railroad and other business promoters is in some respects less shocking than pathetic. For it expressed a kind of blind faith shared by many Southerners of both parties that railroad building and industrialization would swiftly solve all of their section's problems. No price seemed too high for such a miracle.

In several states, for obviously partisan reasons, the actual increase in the size of the public debt was grossly exaggerated. In Mississippi, for example, there was a durable legend among white Democrats that the radicals had added $20,000,000 to the state debt, when, in fact, they added only $500,000. Mississippi radicals had guarded against extravagance by inserting a clause in the constitution of 1868 prohibiting the pledging of state funds to aid private corporations—a clause which the conservatives, incidentally, had opposed. In Alabama, apart from railroad bonds secured by railroad property, the radicals added only $2,500,000 to the state debt. They did not leave a debt of $30,000,000 as conservatives claimed. In most other states, when loans to the railroads are subtracted, the increases in state debts for which the radicals were responsible appear far less staggering.

As for taxes, one of the positive achievements of many of the radical governments was the adoption of more equitable tax systems which put a heavier burden upon the planters.

[15] Ella Lonn: *Reconstruction in Louisiana after 1868* (New York, 1918), pp. 36–7.

Before the war the southern state governments had performed few public services and the tax burden on the landed class had been negligible; hence the vehement protests of the landholders were sometimes as much against radical tax policies as against the alleged waste of taxpayers' money. The restoration governments often brought with them a return to the old inequitable fiscal systems. In Mississippi the subsequent claim of the conservatives that they had reduced the tax burden the radicals had placed upon property holders was quite misleading. The conservatives did lower the state property tax, but, as a consequence, they found it necessary to shift various services and administrative burdens from the state to the counties. This led to an increase in the cost of county government, an increase in the rate of county taxes, and a net increase in total taxes, state and county, that Mississippi property holders had to pay.

As a matter of fact, taxes, government expenditures, and public debts were bound to increase in the southern states during the postwar years no matter who controlled them. For there was no way to escape the staggering job of physical reconstruction—the repair of public buildings, bridges, and roads—and costs had started to go up under the Johnson governments before the radicals came to power. So far from the expenditures of the reconstruction era being totally lost in waste and fraud, much of this physical reconstruction was accomplished while the radicals were in office. They expanded the state railroad systems, increased public services, and provided public school systems—in some states for the first time. Since schools and other public services were now provided for Negroes as well as for whites, a considerable increase in the cost of state government could hardly have been avoided. In Florida between 1869 and 1873 the number of children enrolled in the public schools trebled; in South Carolina between 1868 and 1876 the number increased from 30,000 to 123,000. The

economies achieved by some of the restoration governments came at the expense of the schools and various state institutions such as hospitals for the insane. The southern propertied classes had always been reluctant to tax themselves to support education or state hospitals, and in many cases the budget-cutting of the conservatives simply strangled them.

Thus radical rule, in spite of its shortcomings, was by no means synonymous with incompetence and corruption; far too many carpetbagger, scalawag, and Negro politicians made creditable records to warrant such a generalization. Moreover, conditions were improving in the final years of reconstruction. In South Carolina the last radical administration, that of the carpetbagger Governor Daniel H. Chamberlain, was dedicated to reform; in Florida "the financial steadiness of the state government increased toward the end of Republican rule."[16] In Mississippi the radicals made a remarkably good record. The first radical governor, James L. Alcorn, a scalawag, was a man of complete integrity; the second, Adelbert Ames, a carpetbagger, was honest, able, and sincerely devoted to protecting the rights of the Negroes. Mississippi radicals, according to Vernon L. Wharton, established a system of public education far better than any the state had known before; reorganized the state judiciary and adopted a new code of laws; renovated public buildings and constructed new ones, including state hospitals at Natchez and Vicksburg; and provided better state asylums for the blind, deaf, and dumb. The radicals, Wharton concludes, gave Mississippi "a government of greatly expanded functions at a cost that was low in comparison with that of almost any other state."[17] No major political scandal occurred in Mississippi during the years of radical rule—indeed, it was the best governed state in the postwar South. Yet white conservatives attacked the radical regime in Mississippi as violently as they did in South Carolina, which suggests that their basic grievance was not corruption but race policy.

Finally, granting all their mistakes, the radical governments were by far the most democratic the South had ever known. They were the only governments in southern history to extend to Negroes complete civil and political equality, and to try to protect them in the enjoyment of the rights they were granted. The overthrow of these governments was hardly a victory of political democracy, for the conservatives who "redeemed" the South tried to relegate poor men, Negro and white, once more to political obscurity. Near the end of the nineteenth century another battle for political democracy would have to be waged; but this time it would be, for the most part, a more limited version—for whites only. As for the Negroes, they would have to struggle for another century to regain what they had won—and then lost—in the years of radical reconstruction.

[16] William W. Davis: *The Civil War and Reconstruction in Florida* (New York, 1913), pp. 672–3.

[17] Wharton, *The Negro in Mississippi*, pp. 179–80.